I0021378

INC 2002
University of Plymouth, UK
16-18 July 2002

Proceedings of the
3rd International Network Conference

Editors

Dr Steven M Furnell
Mr Paul S Dowland

Network Research Group,
University of Plymouth

ISBN 1-84102-105-9

Preface

This book presents the proceedings of the Third International Network Conference (INC 2002), hosted by the Network Research Group at the University of Plymouth, UK, from 16th to 18th July 2002.

Since its inception, an important aim of the INC series has been to provide an opportunity for those involved in the design, development and use of network systems and applications to meet, share their ideas and exchange opinions. The 2002 event again succeeds in this aim by bringing together leading figures from academia and industry, and enabling the presentation and discussion of the latest advances in the research and commercial domains.

INC 2002 has attracted authors from 23 countries and these proceedings contain a total of 72 papers, organised into eight thematic chapters. The papers cover many aspects of modern networking, including web technologies and applications, network management, multimedia integration, security and privacy, distributed technologies, mobile networking, and the applications and impacts of network technology. As such, it is hoped that all readers will find material that suits their areas of interest, and I would like to thank the authors for their hard work, and their willingness to share their ideas and results with the wider community.

Each paper was subjected to a careful review by members of the International Programme Committee, in order to ensure their quality and relevance to the themes of the conference. The papers were subsequently revised and developed where appropriate, taking into account the comments of the reviewers. At this point, I would like to express sincere thanks to the members of the committee, as their work has ultimately resulted in an excellent and varied conference programme.

The conference team is also most grateful to Jeremy Ward (Symantec Security Services) and Dieter Gollmann (Microsoft Research) for accepting our invitation to share their expertise in the keynote lectures.

Finally, on behalf of the INC 2002 organising committee, I would like to extend our thanks to the Institution of Electrical Engineers, the British Computer Society, Emerald, the international journal Internet Research, and Orange Personal Communications Services for their continued support as sponsors of the conference.

I hope that all of our delegates enjoy the conference, and that other readers of these proceedings will be able to join us on the next occasion.

Dr Steven Furnell
Conference Chairman, INC 2002

Plymouth, July 2002

About the Network Research Group

The INC series of conferences is organised by the Network Research Group at the University of Plymouth, UK.

The Network Research Group (NRG) is a specialised information technology and networking research facility at the University of Plymouth. Originally established in 1985, the NRG conducts research in the areas of IT Security, Internet and WWW technologies, Network Management, and Mobility. The group has a proven pedigree, including projects conducted for, and in collaboration with, commercial companies, as well as participation in European research initiatives. Over the years, our research activities have led to numerous successful projects, along with associated publications and patents.

At the time of writing, the NRG has nine affiliated full-time academic staff, and thirteen active research degree projects (at PhD and MPhil levels). The group also supports the MSc Network Systems Engineering course, and hosts a significant number of research-related projects from this programme.

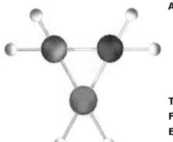

Address	Network Research Group
	University of Plymouth
	Drake Circus
	Plymouth
	PL4 8AA
	United Kingdom
Telephone	+44 (0) 1752 233521
Fax	+44 (0) 1752 233520
Email	info@network-research-group.com
URL	www.network-research-group.com

INC 2002 Committees

International Programme Committee

Darren Ballard	Cisco Systems	UK
Udo Bleimann	University of Applied Sciences, Darmstadt	Germany
Gerrit Bleumer	Francotyp-Postalia	Germany
David Finkel	Worcester Polytechnic Institute	USA
Kevin Fitzgerald	KPMG	Australia
Steven Furnell (chair)	University of Plymouth	UK
Bogdan Ghita	University of Plymouth	UK
Carsten Griwodz	University of Oslo	Norway
Holger Hofmann	ABB Corporate Research Center	Germany
Elizabeth Joyce	Symnatec	UK
Sokratis Katsikas	University of the Aegean	Greece
Dominique Le Foll	Acterna	UK
John Lindsay	Kingston University	UK
Benn Lines	University of Plymouth	UK
Les Lloyd	Rollins College	USA
Joseph Morrissey	Cap Gemini Ernst & Young	UK
Georg Müeller	mFormation Technologies Inc	UK
Sead Muftic	Stockholm University	Sweden
Andrew Phippen	University of Plymouth	UK
Karl Posch	Graz University of Technology	Austria
Seppo Puuronen	University of Jyvaskyla	Finland
Kimmo Raatikainen	University of Helsinki	Finland
Paul Reynolds	Orange Personal Communication Services Limited	UK
Peter Sanders	University of Plymouth	UK
David Schwartz	Bar-Ilan University	Israel
Simon Shepherd	Universtiy of Bradford	UK
Jeanne Stynes	Cork Institute of Technology	Ireland
Roussow von Solms	Port Elizabeth Technikon	South Africa
Matthew Warren	Deakin University	Australia

Local Organising Committee

Nathan Clarke
Paul Dowland (chair)
Steven Furnell
Jayne Garcia
Bogdan Ghita
Denise Horne
Benn Lines
Maria Papadaki

Keynote Speakers and Session Chairs

Introductory Addresses

Dr Steven Furnell, University of Plymouth
   Introduction and welcome to INC 2002

Keynote Lectures

Dr Jeremy Ward, Symantec Security Services
   Get protected - or get regulated

Professor Dieter Gollmann, Microsoft Research
   Why trust is bad for security

Session Chairs

Mr Ian Barlow, University of Plymouth (Plymouth, UK)

Mr Gerrit Bleumer, Francotyp-Postalia (Birkenwerder, Germany)

Professor Udo Bleimann, University of Applied Sciences (Darmstadt, Germany)

Professor David Finkel, Worcester Polytechnic Institute Worcester, USA)

Dr Steven Furnell, University of Plymouth (Plymouth, UK)

Dr Carsten Griwodz, University of Oslo (Oslo, Norway)

Dr Holger D. Hofmann, ABB Corporate Research Center (Heidelberg, Germany)

Professor William Hutchinson, (Mt Lawley, Australia)

Mr Dominique Le Foll, Acterna (Plymouth, UK)

Dr Benn Lines, University of Plymouth (Plymouth, UK)

Dr Andrew Phippen, University of Plymouth (Plymouth, UK)

Professor Paul Reynolds, Orange Personal Communications Services (Bristol, UK)

Professor Peter Sanders, University of Plymouth (Plymouth, UK)

Dr Jeanne Stynes, Cork Institute of Technology (Cork, Ireland)

Dr Matthew Warren, Deakin University (Geelong, Australia)

Contents

CHAPTER 3 Multimedia over IP

CHAPTER 4 Quality of Service

CHAPTER 5 Security and Privacy

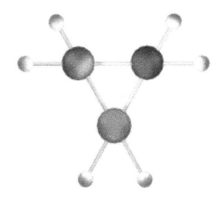

Chapter 1

Web Technologies and Applications

Web Portal for Multicast Communication Management

H. Mannaert[1,2], B. De Gruyter[2], and P. Adriaenssens[2]

[1]Management Information Systems, University of Antwerp, Belgium
[2]Research & Development Department, Cast4All, Belgium
email: herwig.mannaert@ua.ac.be

Abstract

For broadband applications like content distribution and e-learning, people start turning to IP multicast, sending the content only to a selected user list. Though a wide range of application software for multicast applications has been developed, it is usually monolithic, and requires dedicated client software and separate hardware provisioning. In this paper, a web portal is presented for multicast communication management, providing fully automatic service management with integrated provisioning of hardware equipment. The portal is based on an open and configurable object-oriented framework, that allows self-provisioning by the user and the seamless integration with all types of multicast application software. As its topological structure is ideally suited for multicasting, and it allows the accurate control of the transmission bandwidth, the portal focuses currently on satellite as a delivery medium. The software architecture and the implementation of the operational web portal for multicast communications are described.

Keywords

Web Portal, Multicast, Service Management, Satellite Communications.

1. Introduction

Broadband network technologies for the distribution of digital information and real-time multimedia create a wide range of possibilities for applications like collaborative teamwork, content distribution, digital cinema, e-learning, etc. While traditional media like television broadcast content to all users and digital IP networks operate mainly based on a point-to-point paradigm, people start turning to IP multicast, sending the content to only those users that have been chosen to receive it. People trying to put multicast technologies to work however, still encounter many problems at the network and application level.

In this paper we describe a web portal for the management of multicast communications, enabling everyone with an Internet connection and a web browser to serve as a multicast content provider. The portal provides fully integrated provisioning and service management, and is completely open and configurable, allowing the seamless integration of different types of hardware equipment and application software. Due to its ideal topological structure for multicast communications, and the possibility for accurate control of the communication bandwidth, the portal focuses at present on satellite as a delivery medium.

2. Purpose and Scope

2.1 DVB-S IP Multicasting

As clearly explained in (Parnes *et al*, 2000), the traditional usage of unicast to distribute broadband content leads to redundant data crossing the network when the path between sender and receiver shares common network links. Though the usage of terrestrial multicast communications saves valuable network resources and allows for a more efficient distribution of content, it faces a number of complicated routing problems and requires router support. Since its conception in 1988 (Deering, 1988), multicast routing has evolved greatly and has also become a lot harder to manage due to the different needs between the usage with small groups of subscribers and large groups of subscribers. Although there are now terrestrial solutions available (Boivie *et al*, 2000) for small group multicast, service providers do still not routinely enable IP multicast in routers, and multicast routing protocols cannot yet scale globally (Parnes *et al*, 2000). It is important to realize that terrestrial multicast distribution of data is a fundamentally complicated topological problem. Routing algorithms need to compute and decide where the data is needed in the network. And even when the data is only sent where it is needed, a large number of network links and resources still need to process and send the multicast data.

Satellite-based multicast communications provide an interesting alternative, given the inherent simple topology and multicast nature of DVB-S (Digital Video Broadcasting - Satellite) communications. As illustrated in the global architecture for multicast distribution in figure 1, the IP multicast data is encapsulated in a DVB-S stream by a so-called DVB-S/IP gateway, uplinked to the satellite transponder, and through the satellite downlink available on every station equipped with a DVB-S receiving board in a region usually as large as an entire continent. The main issue using satellite as a delivery medium is that the DVB-S/IP gateways, encapsulating the IP data packets in a stream, do not provide standard support for multicast routing protocols, and every multicast route needs to be explicitly provisioned. Moreover, the control mechanisms of these gateways are usually dependent on the equipment vendor. The web portal proposes an engine framework that creates and deletes IP multicast routes with a specified bandwidth as an integrated part of the communication management, and defines interfaces that can be implemented for multiple DVB-S/IP gateways. This approach moves all complexity in the network architecture to the network edges, in accordance with (Metz, 2000), and can therefore be managed at those edges.

2.2 Open Technology Platform

A wide range of application software for (satellite-based) multicast communications has already been developed by research institutes and companies like Kencast[TM], Skystream[TM], Talarian[TM], Fantastic[TM], Deuromedia[TM], and others. Though the available software solutions provide many features for multicast services and network management, most products are monolithic, proprietary and tied to specific hardware equipment or coding algorithms, making flexible integration and collaboration virtually impossible. Moreover, most existing software

---

[TM] All product names referenced herein are trademarks of their respective companies.

solutions do not provide integrated creation and deletion of IP multicast routes on DVB-S/IP gateways, requiring manual interaction. We therefore feel that there is a strong need for an open and flexible provisioning framework, that:

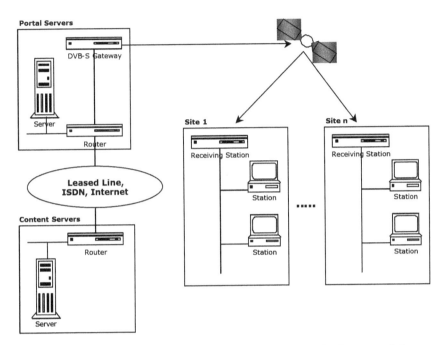

Figure 1: Global architecture of the satellite-based communication network for multicast data transmission, with content servers and receiving stations.

- supports route provisioning for hardware equipment like DVB-S/IP gateways from multiple vendors, and leaves at the same time the other modules independent from the satellite delivery medium.
- provides a generic engine for order entry, support, content retrieval, (multicast) route provisioning, data coding and transmission, network management and maintenance, billing and invoicing.
- provides unified web-based access to all (satellite-based) communication services, including unicast TCP connectivity with a terrestrial return channel as described in [5].
- allows to use various implementations for the different application components, like file pushing servers, streaming servers, forward error correction algorithms, etc.
- enables multicast application developers to implement easily new types of applications, environments, and tool suites, for instance in the area of collaborative applications and frameworks as described in (Parnes *et al*, 2000) and (McCanne, 1999).

We propose a web portal for multicast communication management based on an open and configurable object-oriented framework, that exhibits all of these characteristics. In many ways the framework is in accordance with the generic programmable architecture for the provisioning of hybrid services proposed in (Gbaguidi *et al*, 1999). Based on Java and the *Java 2 Enterprise Edition (J2EE)* platform, it can be accessed as a web portal by human users, and as a web service by applications. In this way, the portal framework puts multicast services under the customer's control, often referred to as self-provisioning. It also incorporates an engineering process that enables the creation and control of service logics, whereas other programmability projects, as for instance the *Telecommunications Information Networking Architecture (TINA)* and more recently the *Java Advanced Intelligent Network solution (JAIN)*, focus on communication topology and network-centric modelling.

3. Software Architecture

3.1 System Model

We designed the portal as an asynchronous system, where communication orders are securely stored in a central database upon acceptance, and a provisioning engine is responsible for sequencing and executing the various service tasks. This decoupling between order entry and provisioning ensures that users are not trapped online during slow or failing provisioning activities. The conceptual entities of the multicast communication management platform - like receiving stations and groups, portal users and profiles, and service orders and accounts - are represented as *entity Enterprise Java Beans (EJBs)*. The different actions of the multicast management platform, like data retrieval, coding, pushing, and route creation, correspond to *session Enterprise Java Beans*. These beans have a simple service interface, exporting a process method taking a ServiceOrder object or a service order XML string:

```
process(ServiceOrder aServiceOrder)
process(String aServiceOrderXMLString)
```

For every service session bean, a method allows to select the specific implementation for that task. For instance in the case of the forward error coding, the method

```
setFileCoder(String aFileCoderImplementation)
```

allows at the moment to specify the usage of the Kencast[TM] or Swarmcast software for forward error correction[3], located in different implementations of the FileCoder interface. The same mechanism that allows for the selection of multiple implementations is used for the different communication services like file fetching and file pushing, and for the control of network elements as well. In order to create routes on a DVB-S/IP gateway for instance, the interface DvbGwRouter needs to be implemented. At present, only an implementation for the Skystream SMR[TM] DVB-S/IP gateway is provided.

[TM] All product names referenced herein are trademarks of their respective companies.

[3] Forward error correction is an error coding mechanism that allows the loss of significant parts of a data transmission that is used for (satellite-based) multicast transmissions.

3.2 Role-Based Access

The web interface of the multicast management system is based on the widely accepted paradigm of role-based portals. Currently, three user roles or profiles with corresponding access rights are defined:

- *Master user*, having the overview and control of the entire portal and network.
- *Account administrator*, with an overview and control of a customer account and the corresponding subnetwork. He can for instance create and modify receiving stations, receiver groups, and other standard users for that subnetwork.
- *Account user*, able to view the subnetwork of his account and to schedule communication services, like file deliveries or live multicast streaming to selected user groups.

For all requested tasks, the underlying service engine will make the necessary complex configurations of the edge network elements, like provisioning the DVB-S/IP gateway, and configuring the receiving stations at the edge of the network that are responsible for distributing the received multicast satellite data using standard IGMP. The user profile also allows an account administrator to provide some standard settings for the account, like the default ftp server for content retrieval, the default error coding mechanism to be used, etc.

As represented in figure 2, the portal application for human interaction with the multicast communication management platform is designed as a multi-tier web application, fully based on open standards like XML and J2EE. Requests are dispatched to Java portal code in the webtier, coordinated by a servlet container that provides session integrity to users. The presentation services in the webtier use an XML publishing framework, ensuring a structural decoupling between content creation, processing logic, and rendering and formatting. The presentation code accesses the application logic in the EJB tier, providing transactional integrity, and ensuring that only complete and validated communication orders are entered in the database and confirmed to the user. It is also possible to access the EJB application logic using an XML interface and EJB-client code.

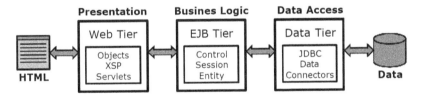

Figure 2: The multi-tier architecture of the web portal is based on a presentation or webtier with an XML publishing framework, an EJB tier with application logic, and a database tier.

3.3 Service Engine

The sequencing and execution of all communication and service management tasks is coordinated by a service engine. This includes:

- *Actual provisioning:* to fetch remote content, to define routes in DVB-S/IP gateways and routers, to start and stop file pushing and streaming servers, to create and modify user groups in gateways and multicast application software.
- *Network management:* to acknowledge and validate file deliveries on receiving stations, to monitor and maintain those receiving stations, and to perform client software updates.
- *Billing and invoicing:* to perform automated billing and invoicing to users based on communication time, volume, or permanent bandwidth.

The service engine is implemented as a state machine that triggers the appropriate action at the appropriate time, based on the continuous monitoring of all communication order states. For the distribution of a file to a specified receiving group for instance, the following actions are performed by the service engine:

- Retrieving the specified file on the appropriate server.
- Performing forward error correction on the file.
- Creating the IP multicast route for the specified receiver group with the specified bandwidth just before the specified transmission time.
- Transmitting the file over the created route with the specified bandwidth at the specified transmission time.
- Checking after the transmission the arrival and validation of the file at the different receiving stations.
- Deleting the IP multicast route after the validated delivery.

The service engine spawns a separate thread for every action that needs to be executed. Upon successful completion of the task, the state of the communication order is updated in a single transaction. For the single task of creating an IP multicast route in the DVB-S/IP gateway, represented in figure 3, the following steps are performed:

- Selecting a service order that requires the creation of a route at this time.
- Spawning a new service thread.
- Setting the status of the service order to a transient state.
- Performing the creation of the route using the appropriate implementation object.
- Setting the status of the service order to the next state.

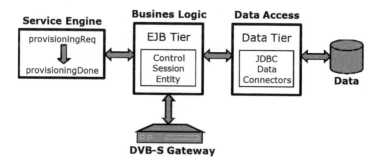

Figure 3: Executing the task of route creation. The service engine activates the application logic in the EJB tier to perform the various steps of the task.

4. Acknowledgements

This work is supported by the European Space Agency's Artes IV Program under the ESTEC Contract 15462/01/NL/US.

5. References

Boivie, R., Feldman, N. and Metz, C. (2000), "Small Group Multicast: A New Solution for Multicasting on the Internet", *IEEE Internet Computing*, vol. 4, no. 3.

Deering, D. (1988), "Multicast routing in Internetworks and Extended LANs", *Proc. SigComm 88*, ACM Press.

Gbaguidi, C., Hubaux, J-P., Hamdi, M. and Tantawi, A.N. (1999), "A Programmable Architecture for the Provision of Hyrid Services", *IEEE Commun. Magazine*, vol.37, no. 7.

McCanne, S. (1999), "Scalable Multimedia Communication Using IP Multicast and Lightweight Sessions", *IEEE Internet Computing*, pp. 33-39, vol. 3, no. 2.

Metz, C. (2000), "IP over 2000: Where Have We Been and Where Are We Going?" *IEEE Internet Computing*, vol. 4, no. 1.

Metz, C. (2000), "IP-over-Satellite: Internet Connectivity Blasts off", *IEEE Internet Computing*, pp. 84-89, vol. 4, no. 4.

Parnes, P., Synnes, K. and Schefström, D. (2000), "mSTAR : Enabling Collaborative Applications on the Internet", *IEEE Internet Computing*, pp. 32-39, vol. 4, no. 5.

WebRUM: A Model for Measuring Web-Wide Resource Usage

M.P. Evans[†] and S.M. Furnell[‡]

[†] School Of Mathematics, Kingston University, Kingston, Surrey, UK
[‡]Network Research Group, Department of Communication and Electronic Engineering, University of Plymouth, Plymouth, UK.
e-mail: M.Evans@computer.org

Abstract

Web resource usage statistics enable server owners to monitor how their users use their web sites, and for advertisers to monitor how often their advertisements are viewed. However, there is currently no way to measure how web resources are used across the whole web. The problems of capturing the required information and providing acceptable system performance present significant hurdles to the development of such a system. Overcoming these hurdles, though, would lead to a web service that could reveal the changing interests of society, and provide deep insights into the changing nature of the web, not to mention the value it would have as a marketing tool. As such, we have developed a model, called WebRUM, which can overcome these hurdles by extending a resource migration mechanism that we have previously designed. The paper describes the mechanism, and shows how it can be extended to measure web-wide resource usage. The information stored by the model is defined, and the performance of a prototype mechanism is presented to demonstrate the effectiveness of the design.

Keywords

Web, server usage log, access log, web metrics, Request Router, distributed database, access patterns

1. Introduction

Web site owners require detailed statistics on the web resources (HTML documents, images, Java applets, etc.) that their users download. Usually, this information is recorded into a web server access log, which provides a history of the resources served by the server, and so helps the server owner keep track of the usage of a web site. However, of far more interest to historians, sociologists, and others interested in the changing interests of the online society, would be a system capable of measuring the resource usage of the web as a whole. Such a system would provide dynamic insights into the changing nature of web usage, as well as accurate marketing information for the web site owner, and more effective navigation for the user.

This paper presents a model for such a system. Although the model is only described, its core architecture is based on a fully tested prototype, and is capable of scaling to many times the size of today's web (Google currently indexes 2,073,418,204 HTML documents (Google, 2002a)). The paper is presented as follows: Section 2 provides a brief overview of current techniques for recording resource usage, and their limitations. Section 3 presents our model for recording resource usage across the web. Section 4 discusses the advantages of measuring web-wide resource usage by providing examples of new applications that can use the usage information. Finally, section 5 discusses issues and further work, before the paper provides its conclusion.

2. Current Techniques for Measuring Resource Usage

Measuring resource usage is important for web site owners and advertisers alike, especially as the dominant revenue stream for web site owners has traditionally been advertising. However, as the following list shows, existing techniques are unsuitable for measuring usage across the web:

- *Web Server Access Logs*
  The most common technique for recording resource usage is to analyse a web server access log, which records details about the user's request, the server's response, and the resource that was requested (see section 3.2.3). However, the information contained in a web server log is specific to that server only, and is accessible only to the server owner. Capturing web-wide information is therefore impossible.

- *Web Bugs*
  A web bug is a client-based solution that subverts the HTML *IMG* element to record usage patterns of advertisements (Krishnamurthy and Rexford, 20001). A web bug is usually a one-pixel image that is transparent, and so invisible to the end user. However, the web bug is served by an advertiser's server, rather than the server of the web page in which it is embedded, and so both servers effectively record the usage of the web page. This technique works well, as the advertiser's server can capture web-wide information. However, it has raised a number of serious privacy concerns, as a web bug can effectively track an *individual user* across the web (Bugnosis, 2000). Although the companies do this to target advertisements at users more accurately based on their browsing behaviour, it is disconcerting at best to know that your movements are being recorded without your consent or even knowledge, and that a profile of your browsing behaviour that you cannot access is being kept without your permission. In addition, the information captured is not comprehensive enough to measure web-wide usage, as web bugs can only record information on the web pages that contain them, and cannot record usage of non-HTML resources.

- *Browser modification*
  A user's browser can be modified to report the user's navigation behaviour directly to a server whenever the user navigates to a new page. Google adopts this approach with its *GoogleBar* technology (Google, 2002b), but uses it to increase and continuously update its database of indexed web pages and hyperlinks. However, such an approach requires the user to explicitly install the browser update. Furthermore, it requires a large user base for it to work, and so can only be implemented by large companies such as search engines or portals, who, understandably, would be reluctant to provide open access to such information.

- *Proxy or caching proxy server*
  An intervening proxy server can record the requests that pass through it, capturing usage information from those clients connected to it. However, this approach requires

many users to explicitly connect to the proxy server, which is unlikely, and would put a large strain on the architecture of the proxy server.

3. A Model for Measuring Web-Wide Resource Usage

In order to accurately measure resource usage across the web, a new approach is called for that can record the web's resource usage comprehensively, efficiently, anonymously, and openly. The new approach that we envisage involves a new web-specific name resolution service that is distinct from the Internet's Domain Name System (DNS). In previous papers (Evans and Furnell (2001), Evans and Furnell (2002)), we have proposed that the DNS is becoming increasingly unsuitable for use as the web's principle name resolution service. Specifically:

- the DNS is designed to map a hostname onto an IP address, whereas the web needs a system to map a resource name onto a location;
- the DNS deliberately constrains its namespace as it only has to deal with the names of servers, whereas the web needs an unconstrained namespace to cater for all different types of resources and the needs of their owners;
- neither the DNS nor the web's main resource identifier (the URL) has any way of storing and referencing a resource's time of creation.

Our solution to these problems was the design of a new name resolution service called the *Resource Locator Service* (RLS), which was designed principally to provide an unconstrained namespace; to enable resource migration; and to locate a resource according to its position in time as well as space. Of particular use to measuring web-wide resource usage, however, is that a client must query the RLS for the location of every *resource*, in order for the RLS to support resource migration (see Evans and Furnell (2001)). The DNS, in contrast, is only queried for the IP address of every web server. As such, the RLS implicitly captures the usage of every resource requested by the clients that use it. In addition, the RLS has been designed to be scalable, and can support a system many times the size of the web. The RLS therefore provides an ideal platform for the design of a system to measure web-wide resource usage.

3.1   An Overview of the Resource Locator Service

The RLS has already been described in detail in Evans and Furnell (2001), and Evans and Furnell (2002). However, this section provides a brief overview.

3.1.1   Architectural Overview

The RLS is designed to locate a resource when given its name, and can do so transparently to either the client, or the server. It is backwards compatible with all web entities, ensuring it can be used wherever it is required. Its architecture comprises a distributed database, deployed across a network of nodes called *Locators* that form the RLS's *Locator Network*. A Locator performs a similar role to the DNS, but with granularity at the resource level.

Figure 1 shows a high level view of the RLS. The Locator Network provides the RLS's resolution service, mapping a resource's name onto its location, and redirecting the client to the resource's correct location using the HTTP redirect mechanism (Fielding et al, 1999). Although this is not the most efficient approach, it facilitates backwards compatibility, enabling all web entities to use the RLS.

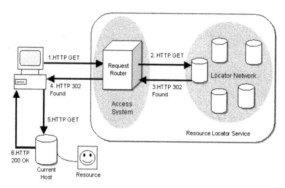

Figure 1 - Architecture of the Resource Locator Service

In order for the client to find the Locator that holds the required name/location mapping, some form of mediation is required between the client and the Locator Network that can transparently route the client's request without requiring any modifications to the client or server. The RLS achieves this through the use of a Request Router, which routes HTTP requests to an appropriate Locator.

3.1.2 The Request Router

The Request Router (RR) is the key to the system. It is a scalable component that can route a request deterministically to any of over 4 billion Locators, while adding only a single HTTP request and response as network overhead. In addition, it is extremely flexible, and can be used wherever it is required, whether it be the client, server, or elsewhere in the network. It provides transparent, scalable mediation between the web and the RLS through the use of a hash routing algorithm (based on the Cache Array Routing Protocol (CARP) (Valloppillil and Ross, 1998)), which takes a resource's name and maps it onto a hash space. The hash space is partitioned such that the name is mapped onto one and only one Locator (see Ross (1997), Thaler and Ravishankar (1997)). By requiring the Locators to be named according to a predetermined URL pattern that contains a zero-based linear numbering component (e.g. *www.locator0.net*, *www.locator1.net*, *www.locator2.net*, etc.), the name of the resource and the number of Locators in the system is all that is required to identify the appropriate Locator. In addition, the load across the nodes is equally balanced, yet there is no inter-node communication, virtually eliminating network overhead (see Evans and Furnell (2001) for more details).

3.1.3 Scalability

A prototype of the RLS has been developed and presented in Evans and Furnell (2001). The prototype showed that the Request Router took only 0.718 seconds to find the appropriate

Locator in a system of 100,000 Locators, each of which can potentially hold the name/location information of millions of resources (see Figure 2). Total added latency was just 1.582 seconds, but a more optimal design should significantly reduce this figure.

Number of Locators	Download time for www.lycos.co.uk (time without RLS = 7.608 sec)	Overhead
1	8.477 seconds	0.869 secs
1,000	8.483 seconds	0.875 secs
10,000	8.546 seconds	0.938 secs
100,000	9.190 seconds	1.582 secs
1,000,000	15.985 seconds	8.377 secs

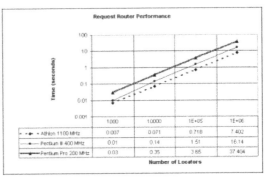

Figure 2 - Performance of the Resource Locator Service

3.1.4 Flexibility

The RR acts as an index into the distributed nodes of the Locator Network. Because it is decoupled from the RLS, it can be deployed virtually anywhere on the web. For example, it can be:

- embedded into an HTML document as a Java applet, ActiveX control or even script;
- built into a browser;
- designed as a browser plug-in;
- built into a server, or added as a server module;
- embedded within a proxy server or a reverse proxy server;

In this way, the RR can be integrated into the web at whichever part of the web's architecture it is required.

3.2 Extending the Resource Locator Service to Measure Web Resource Usage

As has been shown, the RLS provides an efficient and scalable platform upon which to build a system for measuring web-wide resource usage. In this section, we show how the RLS can be extended to capture web-wide usage information by recording details of the location queries made to it. In order to maintain efficiency, a separate system, called the Web Resource Usage Monitor (WebRUM), has been designed to store and manage this information.

3.2.1 Architectural Overview of WebRUM

WebRUM comprises a distributed database whose nodes are accessed using a Request Router specific to the system (specifically, the URL pattern *http://www.nodeX.WebRUM.net* should

15

be used). Each time a client queries the RLS, information about the query (such as the resource requested, a user-session identifier, etc.) is passed onto the appropriate WebRUM node using a WebRUM RR. In this way, WebRUM captures comprehensive usage information on resources from across the web (see Figure 3).

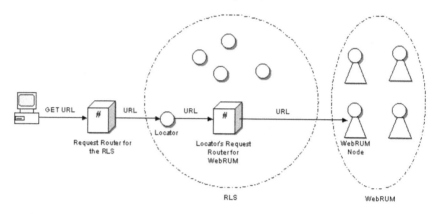

Figure 3 - How WebRUM integrates with the RLS

Because it uses a Request Router, all information for a specific resource is contained on one WebRUM node, significantly reducing the network overhead, and balancing the load across the entire WebRUM system. Note that the information passed to WebRUM is derived primarily from the client's header fields made in its initial request to the RLS. WebRUM can derive no information from the response of the server, as both it and the RLS are independent from the server's operation. As such, queries for resources that are not registered with the RLS (i.e. those that would cause the RLS to return an *Error 404* message) must not be passed onto WebRUM. In this way, WebRUM does not measure the usage of resources that cannot be located.

3.2.2 Addressing Privacy Concerns

For WebRUM to be adopted, it must enable individual users to retain their anonymity, yet still enable individual user sessions to be recorded. The RLS enforces this by making the user's IP address or hostname persistent yet anonymous (e.g. by using a hash function), and passing this onto WebRUM. In this way, the same identifier used across different HTTP requests from the same user session can be persisted, but WebRUM cannot use it to identify the specific user.

3.2.3 Defining the Information Stored by WebRUM

The information captured by WebRUM is a combination of that contained within existing web server log files, and the client's HTTP request header. Tables 1 and 2 show the information stored by log files that are compliant with the two most common log file formats, the Common Log Format (CLF, defined in Luotonen (1995)) and the Extended Common Log Format (ECLF, defined in Hallam-Baker and Behlendorf (1996)). As can be seen, some of this information, such as Request Processing Time, is server-specific, and so of no use to WebRUM, while other items of information, such as Response Code, is returned by the server, and so is not accessible. As such, WebRUM must use what it can from these log files, plus some items of information extracted from the HTTP request. Table 3 shows the minimum set of information that WebRUM must store. This set can be increased by storing resource attributes in the RLS (e.g. byte size).

Field	Description
Remote host	Remote hostname or IP address of client
Remote logname	The remote logname of the user (i.e. the logname the user uses to log onto their current client. In practice, this information is rarely present).
Authenticated username	User's username (note that this will only be present if the associated resource requires that the user authenticate herself before the resource can be transferred).
Date	Date and time of the request
Request line	The request line of the request header (i.e. Method, URI, and protocol version)
Response code	The HTTP status code returned to the client
Bytes	The content length of the resource returned to the client

Table 1 - Fields contained within the Common Log Format (Luotonen, 1995)

Field	Description
Referer	The URI of the web page from where the resource was requested
Request Processing Time	The length of time taken from when the request was received to when the response was sent
User Agent	The name and other details of the application that sent the request. Information can include such details as operating system and hardware platform upon which the application was running.

Table 2 – Additional Commonly Supported Fields used in ECLF Log Files (Krishnamurthy and Rexford, 2001)

Field	Description
Remote host	Anonymised hostname of client
Referer	The URI of the web page from where the resource was requested.
User Agent	The name and other details of the application that sent the request. Information can include such details as operating system and hardware platform upon which the application was running.
Date	Date and time of the request (recorded by the WebRUM node at the time it receives the information from the Locator (GMT), formatted according to RFC 1123 (Braden, 1989).
Request line	The request line of the request header (i.e. Method, URI, and protocol version)
Language	The language that the client requires the resource to be in, as specified by the Accept-Language header of the initial request

Table 3 - Information Stored by WebRUM

3.2.4 Accessing WebRUM's Information

Accessing the information from the correct WebRUM node is very simple. To retrieve information about a specific resource, a client application needs the name of the resource (usually its URL), and a WebRUM RR. The resource name acts as an index into WebRUM, identifying the WebRUM node that stores the usage information for that resource. Once the appropriate node is found, retrieving the required information from it will depend upon the type of query the user wishes to make. To facilitate this, we intend to use the newly defined XQuery query language (Boag et al, 2002), enabling the user to send an SQL-like query formatted in XML to the appropriate WebRUM node via HTTP. At present, however, this feature is undefined.

4. Applications of WebRUM

Supposing that WebRUM was embraced by the web community and widely supported, what are the types of queries that will be asked of it? Some examples include:

- What are the most/least popular resources/images/web pages etc. on the web?
- How have the most/least popular resources changed over time?
- How have the most/least popular resources changed during significant events (e.g. The Queen's Golden Jubilee, September 11th, etc.)
- Which languages are the most popular on the web?
- Which countries use the web the most/least?
- How many bytes of information are transferred in a given period of time?
- How many resources/images/web pages/etc. are there on the web?

Such statistics provide an insight into the changing nature of the online society, and of society in general. However, WebRUM can also act as a platform for the provision of other services that cannot currently be provided, as the following sub-sections describe.

4.1   Enhanced Navigation

WebRUM can enhance the user's ability to navigate the web by dynamically providing information about a hyperlink *before* the user clicks on it. In this way, the user can make a more informed judgement on whether or not to see the resource referenced by the hyperlink before 'rewarding' it with a hit.

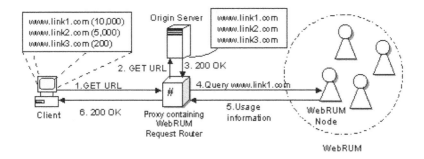

Figure 4 - Using WebRUM to Enhance Navigation

Figure 4 shows how this can be achieved. Here, a proxy server intercepts the client's request for a web page, and queries WebRUM to determine the number of times the hyperlinks within the web page have been clicked. The proxy then dynamically inserts the usage information into the web page, enabling the user to see at a glance the popularity of each hyperlink.

This is a trivial example of how WebRUM's information can be used to enhance user navigation. Other studies have found strong regularities in users' browsing behaviour (e.g., Hochheiser and Schneiderman, 1999, Huberman et al., 1998), indicating that more complex heuristics can be applied to WebRUM's information to further enhance navigation.

4.2   Charting the Web's Traffic Patterns

Many experiments have been conducted that attempt to display the structure of the web (see Dodge and Kitchin (2001) for many examples). However, WebRUM will be able to provide far more detail, providing dynamic charts that provide the web site owner with information such as:

- Which hyperlinks linking to the owner's resource provide the most/least traffic?
- How many people visit the web pages that link to the owner's resource?
- How much traffic does a web page direct to the owner's resource compared with the traffic that the page directs to other resources?
- Which hyperlinks on the web would provide the most/least traffic?

5. Issues and Further Work

WebRUM could change the nature of the web fundamentally, providing a unique tool for exploring the changing interests of society. However, there are a number of issues that must be overcome if it is to be deployed successfully:

- *WebRUM relies upon wide adoption of the RLS.*
  The RLS is still in prototype form, and so WebRUM cannot be developed in the near future. However, the two systems can be separated, enabling WebRUM to be self-supporting if necessary.

- *Performance*
  WebRUM can scale to support over 4 billion individual nodes. However, the processing and network demands on each node may be huge, depending upon the nature and volume of queries sent to it. In addition, collating information from across WebRUM nodes would increase the load and network overheads of the system. Further work must examine the use of caching techniques and distinct caching servers that simply return results to common queries in order to manage the load.

- *Security*
  WebRUM nodes may be at risk from Denial of Service attacks (Krishnamurthy and Rexford, 2001). In addition, care should be taken to ensure only genuine RLS Locators provide the usage information.

6. Conclusion

We have a presented a model for measuring web-wide resource usage that has the potential to reveal insights into society, including its hopes, fears, interests and concerns. In addition, the model can provide a powerful tool for web site owners and advertisers, providing an independent source of quality marketing information. Although there is much work still to be done, we believe the concept of measuring web-wide resource usage has the potential to transform the web.

7. References

Boag, S., Chamberlin, D., Fernandez, M., Florescu, D., Robie, J., Simeon, J., and Stefanescu, M. (2002), "XQuery 1.0: An XML Query Language", W3C Working Draft, 30th April 2002, http://www.w3.org/TR/xquery.

Braden, R. (1989), "Requirements for Internet Hosts - Communication layers, STD 3", RFC 1123, October 1989.

Bugnosis (2000), "Web Bug FAQ", http://www.bugnosis.org/faq.html

Dodge, M., and Kitchin, R., (2001), "Atlas of Cyberspace", Addison Wesley, 2001.

Evans, M.P., and Furnell, S.M. (2001), "The Resource Locator Service: Fixing a Flaw in the Web", Computer Networks, Vol. 37 (3-4) (2001) pp. 307–330, November 2001.

Evans, M.P., and Furnell, S.M. (2002), "A Web-Based Resource Migration Protocol Using WebDAV", in: Proceedings of the Eleventh International World Wide Web Conference, Honolulu, Hawaii, May 7th-11th 2002, http://www2002.org/CDROM/refereed/359/index.html

Fielding, R, Gettys, J., Mogul, J.C., Nielsen, H.F., Masinter, L., Leach, P., and Berners-Lee, T. (1999), "HyperText Transfer Protocol – HTTP/1.1", RFC 2616, June 1999, http://www.ietf.org/rfc/rfc2616.txt

Google (2002a), Google Search Engine web site, http://www.google.com

Google (2002b), Google Toolbar page, http://toolbar.google.com/

Hallam-Baker, P.M., and Behlendorf, B. (1996), Extended Log File Format, http://www.w3.org/TR/WD-logfile.html, March 1996

Hochheiser, H., and Schneiderman, B. (1999), "Understanding Patterns of User Visits to Web Sites: Interactive Starfield Visualizations of WWW Log Data", In: Proceedings of ASIS '99, 1999.

Huberman, B.A., Pirolli, P.L.T., Pitkow, J.E., and Lukse, R.M. (1998), "Strong Regularities in World Wide Surfing", Science, Vol.280, 3rd April 1998

Krishnamurthy, B., and Rexford, J (2001), "Web Protocols and Practice: HTTP 1.1, Networking Protocols, Caching, and Traffic Measurement", Addison Wesley, 2001.

Luotonen, A., (1995), "The Common Logfile Format", July 1995, http://www.w3.org/Daemon/User/Config/Logging.html.

Ross, K.W. (1997) "Hash Routing for Collections of Shared Web Caches", IEEE Network, November/December 1997, pp. 37–44.

Thaler, D.G. and Ravishankar, C.V. (1998), "Using Name Based Mappings to Increase Hit Rates", IEEE/ACM Transactions on Networking, 6(1), Feb. 1998.

Valloppillil, V., and Ross, K.W. (1998), "Cache Array Routing Protocol v1.0", Internet Draft, draft-vinod-carp-v1-02.txt, February 26, 1998, http://www.cs-ipv6.lancs.ac.uk/ipv6/documents/standards/general-comms/internet-drafts/draft-vinod-carp-v1-03.txt

Impact of Partial Reliability on
Web Image Transport Performance

Johan Garcia and Anna Brunstrom

Dept. of Computer Science, Karlstad University, Karlstad, Sweden
Email: {Johan.Garcia, Anna.Brunstrom}@kau.se

Abstract

This paper reports on experiments with a web-browsing application using PRTP, a new TCP-based protocol. PRTP makes it possible for an application to specify, and receive, a more flexible transport service than with TCP or UDP. A web application using PRTP is presented, and experiments examining the performance implications of using PRTP instead of TCP are discussed. The experiments used actual implementations of TCP and PRTP to conduct web page transfers over a network capable of emulating different network characteristics. The JPEG part of the web pages were recoded using a robust JPEG coding and transmitted using the partially reliable transport service made possible by PRTP. A novelty in these experiments was that the packet loss could be controlled in detail, allowing specific packets in a stream to be lost as opposed to losing packets with a certain probability. The experiments were carried out for five different network characteristics, each at six different loss ratios, using three different web pages. The results show that using a partially reliable transport service in conjunction with the application presented provides throughput gains in the majority of cases, at the expense of slightly degraded image quality. The gains relative to TCP are up to 41% with a mean of 7.2%.

Keywords

WWW, partial reliability, TCP, JPEG, network emulation

1 Introduction

There are two major Internet transport layer protocols, TCP (Postel, 1981) and UDP (Postel, 1980). They both provide a data transport service to the application layer above, but with different characteristics. TCP provides a reliable, ordered, congestion and flow-controlled transport service while UDP provides a simpler unreliable service. Currently, an application can basically choose between using one of the two transport layer protocols and has no finer control of what service the transport layer provides. If the requirements of the application on the transport service is in some sense lower than what TCP provides, TCP can in this case be said to provide an overly ambitious service. A more flexible transport protocol may more closely tailor its service to what the application actually requires. If the application for example can accept a small, limited number of losses and still work satisfactorily, this lower reliability demand may lead to better throughput or lower jitter for the application. A number of trade-offs clearly exist between the different demands put on the transport layer. A lower demand in one end is likely to lead to a positive effect in another end. This paper explores one of the possible trade-offs, that between reliability and application related throughput.

To make a trade-off, the transport layer must have mechanisms to support the trade-off. TCP and UDP have basically no provisions for applications to make trade-offs in the service delivered to them. One approach to making trade-offs possible is to use UDP and enhance it with functions such as reordering and reliability at the application layer and to make the trade-offs there. This however entails a considerable amount of work and would be heavily tied to the specific application. In this paper we discuss another approach to enabling trade-offs. By implementing a simple receiver-side modification of TCP, a new and more flexible transport protocol named PRTP is created (Asplund et al., 2000). The ability to perform partially reliable transport of data (Amer et al., 1994) is the new extension provied by PRTP (Partially Reliable Transport Protocol), in addition to the functionality of the TCP base. The PRTP application interface lets the application inform the transport layer of its reliability requirements. This provides the application the possibility to specify its reliability requirements more finely than simply using TCP's reliable or UDP's unreliable service.

Application experiments were done to quantify the benefits of the new trade-off. The application used in the experiments encompasses the delivery of web pages to a standard browser. Web pages typically consist of HTML text, GIF images and JPEG images. In the experiments, JPEG images were transferred using PRTP and the performance relative to regular TCP was evaluated. In order to adapt the JPEG image data for partial reliability, recoding was done by a pair of proxies. The experimental results show that increased throughput is indeed achieved at the web page level, but this comes at the expense of slightly degraded JPEG image quality. The results also highlight the potential of using deterministic packet loss generation as opposed to stochastic packet loss generation when carrying out protocol experiments.

The remainder of this paper is structured as follows. The next section provides background information and presents related work. Section 3 describes the experimental setup and Section 4 gives the results. Section 5 gives the conclusions drawn from this work.

2   Background

Our test system for the use of partial reliability includes three major components: a partially reliable transport protocol, a robust JPEG coder (ITU-T, 1992) and a proxy solution to provide easy, application-level integration of partial reliability. The use of proxies is discussed in for example (Bharadvaj et al., 1998; Fox et al., 1996; Han et al., 1998). The rest of this section focuses on the first two components.

2.1   PRTP

The Partially Reliable Transport Protocol (PRTP) is based on TCP but with modifications so that it also provides a partially reliable service. An application can specify a required reliability level (RRL) between 0 and 100 percent. PRTP then ensures that this reliability level will be maintained until a new reliability level is specified or until the connection terminates. When losses occur in the network, PRTP will not retransmit lost data as long as the RRL can be upheld without retransmissions. It is the reduction in the number of retransmissions required that allows reliability to be traded for improved throughput and/or jitter.

In order to ensure the RRL requested by the application, PRTP maintains a measure of the service provided so far, called the current reliability level (CRL). In addition to the RRL, the application also specifies an aging factor. The aging factor is used in computing the CRL and controls the aging of previously transmitted data. The aging controls the response of PRTP to burst losses and is introduced to avoid the phenomenon of losing large chunks of data in the later parts of long connections. For further details see (Asplund et al., 2000; Brunstrom et al., 2000).

From the above description it should be clear that PRTP essentially acknowledges lost data as long as the losses result in a connection reliability above the RRL. One problem with this approach is that it interferes with the congestion avoidance mechanisms of TCP. This is addressed by a newly developed refinement of the protocol called PRTP-ECN, which is described in (Grinnemo and Brunstrom, 2001b). An analytical study of the behavior of PRTP-ECN is available in (Grinnemo and Brunstrom, 2001a). We used PRTP for the experiments presented in this paper, but the altered congestion avoidance behavior was less of an issue since we only considered data transfers of small sizes.

A novel feature of PRTP is that it is fully receiver-based. It requires only limited changes to the TCP receiver, and thus the sender can use a standard TCP stack. In relation to previous work, PRTP therefore incorporates the concept of partial reliability into the TCP/IP stack in a more seamless fashion. Partially ordered/partially reliable transport protocols and their potential performance gains have been studied extensively at LAAS-CNRS (Chassot et al., 1996; Diaz et al., 1994; Rojas et al., 1999) and at the University of Delaware (Amer et al., 1994; Marasli et al., 1996). This work in particular resulted in POC (Amer et al., 1994; Diaz et al., 1994), a partially ordered and partially reliable transport protocol specifically targeting multimedia applications[1]. Early work in this area has also been done by Dempsey (Dempsey, 1994).

Recent work in the Internet Engineering Task Force (IETF) has led to the Stream Control Transfer Protocol (SCTP) (Stewart, 2000), which provides transport layer flexibility by allowing relaxed ordering constraints. An unreliable data mode extension is also considered for SCTP (Xie et al., 2001). This extension would provide more flexible reliability for a stream by allowing only a limited number of retransmissions to be performed.

2.2 Robust JPEG

As previously discussed, PRTP does provide added flexibility to an application. For PRTP to be worthwhile, there must exist applications that can benefit from the added flexibility. Since the concept of partial reliability has not been widespread, few applications make explicit use of it. Applications tend either to demand full reliability or try to do the best possible with whatever data received. The transfer of JPEG images is an example of the first, since they normally will become heavily corrupted after a single loss. To evaluate the effectiveness of partial reliability for a web-browsing type of application, we developed a more robust variant of the JPEG coding. The main components of this robust coding are the use of extended resynchronization markers, interleaving and error concealment. The use of extended resynchronization makers allows the receiver to confine the losses more tightly than regular JPEG markers, leading to less wasted data for each loss. The interleaving spreads out the image data so that a lost packet does not blank out a portion of the image, but rather the loss is spread over the whole image. This spreading also helps the error concealment as it tries to extrapolate lost data from the remaining data in the image. These mechanisms combined lead to a coding that is well equipped to handle packet losses and that degrades gracefully. Further details on the coding are available in (Garcia and Brunstrom, 2000). Together with PRTP, this coding can provide a lower bound on the image quality, coupled with an increase in throughput achieved by not retransmitting all lost data.

The required recoding of JPEG images into robust JPEG may be done either statically as the images are stored on the webserver or dynamically at a proxy in the network. The proxy is placed somewhere on the "server" side of the problematic link; for example, the proxy could be placed at the interconnection between the Internet and a wireless access network.

---

[1]It should be mentioned in this context that an early version of POC was suggested as an extension to TCP (Connolly et al., 1994). However, the extension required major modifications to TCP and the protocol was redesigned as a stand-alone protocol prior to implementation.

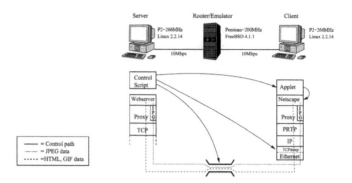

Figure 1: Experimental setup

Other proposals for transferring image data include FLIIT (Danskin et al., 1995), in which a wavelet based coding scheme is coupled to a transport protocol using rate-based congestion control. Another approach that explores the effects of partial order at the transport level in conjunction with suitable coding is presented in (Iren, 1999), with a focus on progressive display quality rather than total throughput. The principle of using the data received immediately and then adding retransmissions later is proposed in (Han and Messerschmitt, 1999), which reports on a progressively reliable transport protocol for multimedia applications. ITP (Raman et al., 2000) is a recent UDP-based partially reliable protocol for image transfer.

3 Experimental Setup

The setup used for the experiments is shown in Figure 1. A Netscape browser on the client machine was used to download data from the server. The client and server were connected via a router/emulator. The server also ran the master control script that controlled the experiments. The script controlled the link emulation parameters used in the router/emulator and sent new page requests to the Netscape browser via an applet. Netscape was configured to use a client proxy, and the proxy used PRTP connections with an RRL of 85% for all JPEG image requests. For HTML, GIF and other requests the proxy used PRTP connections with an RRL of 100%. An RRL setting of 100% results in PRTP having exactly the same behavior as TCP. The connections were routed through the router/emulator, which introduced losses and applied bandwidth restrictions and delay as appropriate for the test case. On the server side, the data was provided by a webserver. In the experiments the serverside proxy was placed in the same machine as the webserver, but in a real-life scenario it can just as well be placed somewhere else. During the experiments all traffic was recorded by a tcpdump process running at the client for later analysis.

3.1 Experiment Parameters

Experiments were carried out for five different test cases modeled after real environments. The details of the test cases are given in Table 1. For each test case, five different loss ratios were used in addition to a lossless run. The losses were constructed by losing 1, 2, 3, 5 and 10 packets in a repeating window of 64 packets, which corresponds to loss ratios of roughly 2%,

Testcase	Downlink bw	Uplink bw	Delay
GSM	7680 bps	7680 bps	310 ms
Modem	48 Kbps	33,6Kbps	35 ms
Inet 400	400 Kbps	400 Kbps	12 ms
Inet 150	150 Kbps	150 Kbps	30 ms
Inet 60	60 Kbps	60 Kbps	180 ms

Table 1: Test case parameters

Webpage number	HTML size (kb)	GIF size (kb)	JPEG size (kb)
1	1	-	61
2	6		15,6,37,21
3	15	1,4,6,9	8,12,12,21,37

Table 2: Web page data sizes

3%, 5%, 8% and 16%. For each of the five loss ratios, five different loss patterns were used where each loss pattern corresponds to one specific sequence of lost packets. The 25 different loss patterns were obtained by using a random number generator. For each loss pattern, eight measurement runs were conducted with the RRL for JPEG transfer set to 85%. Using the same loss pattern, eight new runs were conducted with the RRL set to 100%. This made it possible to compute the impact of using partial reliability versus baseline TCP, which is what a setting of RRL to 100% equates to. The deterministic loss generation used in the experiments should be noted. It is common in the literature to use losses that are introduced randomly, or stochastically, according to some probability, such as 2%, 3% etc. Due to the randomness, the actual amount of lost packets, as well as their positions, will vary between runs of the experiments. Before performing the experiments we implemented support for deterministic losses in the FreeBSD kernel code responsible for the Dummynet (Rizzo, 1997) network emulation functionality. The modification means that all runs with the same loss pattern will lose exactly the same amount of packets at exactly the same position, as specified by the pattern. The absolute and relative position of losses can have a great impact on the measured result and, if deterministic losses had not been used, these effects would have contributed to the experimental error. Five different loss patterns were used for each loss ratio to capture the position-dependent variations and to lessen the risk of biasing the results by an atypical effect occurring for a single pattern.

The measurements were conducted for three different loads, web pages 1-3, with the characteristics shown in Table 2. It should be noted that only the JPEG data was transferred using RRL=85%. Hence, it was only the transfer of JPEG data that contributed to the throughput difference between TCP and PRTP, which was the metric used for evaluation.

3.2 Data Collection

The time required to complete the transfer of one web page was extracted from the traces collected by tcpdump at the client side. The time calculated was the time from the first SYN packet to the last packet of the last connection containing any data. The total number of measurements made were 5 test cases x 5 loss ratios x 5 loss patterns x 2 protocols x 8 replications x 3 web pages = 6000 measurements, which became 6240 when the lossless runs were included. The measurements contained some spurious outliers. It is believed that these outliers stem from variability originally introduced by the java-based proxy, which at times caused a slight change in the relative order of two parallel TCP connections. The small change in the relative order was then accentuated when losses occurred, resulting in a considerable impact on the measured value. However, the effects of outliers were negated by using the median of the eight replicated measurements as the point estimate for the throughput. The PRTP throughput estimate was then divided by the TCP throughput estimate to get a gain value. The arithmetic mean was used to perform further aggregation of the gain values.

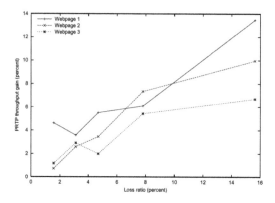

Figure 2: Throughput increase versus loss

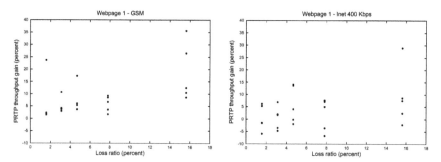

Figure 3: GSM test case   **Figure 4: Inet 400 Kbps test case**

4   Results

The main objective of the experiments was to evaluate the application performance gains made possible by allowing a more flexible transport of media data that can tolerate a limited amount of loss. At the highest level of aggregation, the results for PRTP as compared to regular TCP are shown in Figure 2. The results indicate that there is a gain, and that the gain increases as the loss ratio increases. Since the experiments were conducted with PRTP at a fixed reliability level of 85%, a higher loss ratio should translate to a greater gain for loss ratios below 15%. All three web pages show better performance. Web page 1, which had the largest ratio of JPEG data, shows the greatest improvement.

A more detailed presentation of a subset of the data is provided in Figures 3 and 4. For two of the test cases, the figures shows the web page 1 results for each of the five different loss patterns used at each loss ratio. The spread between different loss patterns at the same loss ratio is clearly evident. If stochastic loss generation had been used this spread would have been included in the experimental error. As indicated mainly in Figure 4, some measurements show a negative effect of using PRTP. One reason for this is the fact that the relative position of the

PRTP losses for a given loss pattern shifted relative to the TCP losses, since PRTP did not have to perform as many retransmissions. For some loss patterns, these shifts affected PRTP so that PRTP had to recover from later losses by a time-consuming timeout, whereas TCP could use the fast retransmit mechanism. Of the 390 gain values, 298 show a gain for PRTP with a maximum gain of 41.0% and a mean gain of 7.2%. Negative gain is evident in 82 values with a minimum of -15.5% and a mean of -3.2%. For ten values, the gain rounds off to 0%.

Although not included in this paper due to size constraints, it should be noted that the use of deterministic loss generation makes it possible to perform more detailed analysis of individual TCP-PRTP pairs. We have performed such analysis for some pairs, and one interesting finding is TCPs weakness in handling losses that occur late in a connection when the retransmission timeout has been inflated by buffering.

5 Conclusions

The transport service provided by the current Internet is realized by TCP or UDP. These two protocols offer limited flexibility for applications to make the various trade-offs that are possible, given the underlying network technology. New protocols such as SCTP (Stewart, 2000) provide more flexibility, but the potential gains of this flexibility have not been sufficiently explored. We implemented the experimental PRTP protocol to provide the opportunity to explore the application effects of the trade-off that exists between relaxed reliability on the one side and improved throughput and jitter on the other. To be able to perform application level experiments, we developed supporting software such as java-based recoding proxies and a robust JPEG coder. In addition we also implemented and used deterministic packet losses for network emulation, a concept which may have an impact on future protocol testing. We intend to do a more thorough evaluation of the impact of using deterministic versus stochastic packet losses in the near future.

One of the major goals of this paper is to present experimental results that highlight the benefits of allowing flexible trade-offs at the transport layer. The results of the experiments show that a gain in application throughput is indeed possible as a result of the more flexible reliability provided by PRTP. This does not come completely for free, however, but is achieved at the cost of a slight degradation in image quality. The possible gain, and the usefulness of this gain, are obviously application-dependent. In future work we intend to study SCTP and evaluate the impact of the increased flexibility relative to TCP on both protocol and application performance.

References

Amer, P. D., C.Chassot, Connolly, T., Diaz, M., and Conrad, P. (1994). Partial order transport service for multimedia and other applications. *IEEE/ACM Transactions on Networking*, 2(5).

Asplund, K., Garcia, J., Brunstrom, A., and Schneyer, S. (2000). Decreasing Transfer Delay Through Partial Reliability. *Proceedings of PROMS 2000*.

Bharadvaj, H., Joshi, A., and Auephanwiriyakul, S. (1998). An active transcoding proxy to support mobile web access. *Proceedings of the 17th IEEE Symposium on Reliable Distributed Systems*.

Brunstrom, A., Asplund, K., and Garcia, J. (2000). Enhancing TCP performance by allowing controlled loss. *Proceedings SSGRR 2000 Computer & eBusiness Conference, L'Aquila, Italy*.

Chassot, C., Diaz, M., and Lozes, A. (1996). From the partial order connection concept to partial order multimedia transport connections. *Journal for High Speed Networks*, 5(2):181–191.

Connolly, T., Amer, P., and Conrad, P. (1994). RFC 1693: An extension to TCP: Partial order service.

Danskin, J. M., Davis, G. M., and Song, X. (1995). Fast lossy internet image transmission. In *Proceedings of ACM Multimedia*.

Dempsey, B. J. (1994). Retransmission-based error control for continuous media. *PhD thesis, University of Virginia*.

Diaz, M., Lopez, A., Chassot, C., and Amer, P. (1994). Partial order connections: a new concept for high speed and multimedia services and protocols. *Annales des telecoms*, 49(5-6).

Fox, A., Gribble, S. D., Brewer, E. A., and Amir, E. (1996). Adapting to network and client variability via on-demand dynamic distillation. *Proc. Seventh Intl. Conf. on Arch. Support for Prog. Lang. and Oper. Sys. (ASPLOS-VII), Cambridge, MA*.

Garcia, J. and Brunstrom, A. (2000). A robust JPEG coder for a partially reliable transport service. In *Proceedings 7th Int. Workshop on Interactive Distributed Multimedia Systems and Telecommunication Services (IDMS 2000)*, Enschede, The Netherlands. Springer.

Grinnemo, K.-J. and Brunstrom, A. (2001a). Enhancing TCP for applications with soft real-time constraints. *Proceedings of SPIE (Multimedia Systems and Applications IV)*, 4518.

Grinnemo, K.-J. and Brunstrom, A. (2001b). Evaluation of the QoS offered by PRTP-ECN - a TCP-compliant partially reliable protocol. *Proceedings of IWQoS 2001, Karlsruhe, Germany*, pages 217–231.

Han, R., Bhagwat, P., LaMaire, R., Mummert, T., Perret, V., and Rubas, J. (1998). Dynamic adaptation in an image transcoding proxy for mobile www browsing. *IEEE Personal Communication*, 5(6):8–17.

Han, R. and Messerschmitt, D. (1999). A progressively reliable transport protocol for interactive wireless multimedia. *Multimedia Systems, Springer-Verlag*, 7(2):141–156.

Iren, S. (1999). *Network-conscious Image Compression*. PhD thesis, University of Delaware.

ITU-T (1992). Recommendation T.81 - digital compression and coding of continuous-tone still images. *Geneva, Switzerland*.

Marasli, R., Amer, P. D., and Conrad, P. T. (1996). Retransmission-based partially reliable transport service: An analytic model. *Proceedings of INFOCOM '96*.

Postel, J. (1980). RFC 768: User datagram protocol.

Postel, J. (1981). RFC 793: Transmission control protocol.

Raman, S., Balakrishnan, H., and Srinivasan, M. (2000). ITP: An image transport protocol for the internet. *Proc. Intl. Conference on Network Protocols, Japan*.

Rizzo, L. (1997). Dummynet: a simple approach to the evaluation of network protocols. *ACM Computer Communication Review*, 27(1):31–41.

Rojas, L., Chaput, E., Dairaine, L., Senac, P., and Diaz, M. (1999). Transport of video over partial order connections. *Computer Networks*, 31(7):709–725.

Stewart, R. (2000). RFC 2960: Stream Control Transmission Protocol.

Xie, Q., Stewart, R. R., Sharp, C., and Rytina, I. (2001). SCTP unreliable data mode extension. *Internet draft draft-ietf-tsvwg-usctp-00.txt, Work in progress*.

Agent-based Sophisticated and Scalable Scheduling Method

YunHee Shin, Sook-Heon Lee, HyunKi Baik, Gyeong-Hun Kim, Myong-soon Park

Dept. of Computer Science and Engineering, Korea University, Seoul, Korea
e-mail: {goodday, tonaido, gibson, kgh, myongsp}@ilab.korea.ac.kr

Abstract

Linux Virtual Server (LVS) is highly scalable and available server built on a cluster of real servers. For offering the successful service, there are many scheduling methods in LVS. But traditional scheduling methods are not offered sophisticated load balancing because it is regardless of the real load information of real servers. Agent-based scheduling method is considered the real load information of real servers such as the presenting in 'Bit Project No.61'. But load balancer has a lot of additional communication overhead .

We propose ABSS: Agent-based Sophisticated and Scalable Scheduling Method which can be considered the real load information for sophisticated load balancing and be reduced the additional communication overhead of load balancer by using the itinerant load information packet.

Keywords

web server cluster, agent, scheduling, load balancing

1. Introduction

With the explosive growth of the Internet and its increasingly important role on our lives, the traffic on the Internet is increasing dramatically, which has been growing at over 100% annual rate. The load on popular Internet sites is growing rapidly, example the popular WWW sites such as the Lycos and AltaVista receive three to ten million accesses a day. Thus the need of scalable and high available server is more increasing.

The single server solution, which is to upgrade the server to a higher performance server, has its shortcomings to meet the requirements. The upgrading process is complex, and the original machine may be wasted. When requests increase, it will be overloaded soon so that we have to upgrade again. The server is a single point of failure. The higher end the server is upgraded to, the higher cost we have to pay.

Clusters of servers, connected by a fast network, are emerging as a viable architecture for building a high- performance and highly available server. This type of loose-coupled architecture is more scalable, more cost- effective and more reliable than a single processor system or a tightly coupled multiprocessor system. That is cluster for web server is satisfies the requirements that is scalability, availability, cost-effective.

Linux Virtual Server(LVS) is highly scalable and highly available server built on a cluster of real servers. But the architecture of LVS cluster is centralized. The front-end of the real server is a load balancer, which schedules requests to the different servers. So how to schedule is important influence on performance of the LVS cluster.

The typical scheduling methods for LVS are Round- Robin Scheduling, Least-Connection Scheduling. Such scheduling methods aren't based on the real load information of the real servers. So it is able to cause load imbalance for the real servers. The unbalancing of load brings about the failure of real server because of heavy load, and then needs more real servers.

Therefore sophisticated scheduling method is required for supporting the successful service that is the original goal of the web server cluster.

Agent-based scheduling that is a sophisticated scheduling method is presented in 'Bit Project No.61'. It's method is as following. Agent program is installed in real servers and load balancer. Through the agent, the load balancer gains the load information of the real servers by every time. It achieve the sophisticated load balancing but have the heavily communication overhead during the load balancer and real servers.

In this paper, we propose the Agent-based Sophisticated and Scalable (ABSS) scheduling method that is a sophisticated load balancing technique and reduce the additional communication overhead of the load balancer.

The rest of the paper is organized as follows: Section 2 describes a related work for scheduling techniques. Section 3 presents our main idea, Agent-based Sophisticated and Scalable(ABSS) scheduling method. Section 4 evaluates the performance of the ABSS. Section 5 concludes this paper and presents some future work.

2. Related Works

In this section we describe the scheduling methods in the LVS.

2.1 Scheduling method that don't consider the real load information

2.1.1 Round-Robin Scheduling Method

Round-robin scheduling algorithm, in its word meaning, directs the network connections to the different server in a round-robin manner. It treats all real servers as equals regardless of number of connections or response time.

It does not consider any state information of real servers and all requests are treated same load. So it cause load imbalance between real servers..

2.1.2 Least Connection Scheduling Method

The least-connection scheduling algorithm directs network connections to the server with the least number of established connections. The increment and decrement of live connections can be counted by detecting SYN(initializing a session) and FIN(terminating a session) flags in the TCP packets sent from client side respectively.

This is one of dynamic scheduling algorithms; because it needs to count live connections for each server dynamically.

However it does not taken into account the size of each request and character of each request. Some request are needed lightly load, the others need heavily load. Also some request need intensive I/O load, the others need internsive CPU load.

So it can't do sophisticated scheduling.

2.2 Scheduling method that consider the real load information

2.2.1 Agent-based Scheduling method

Agent-based scheduling method is one of the Least Loaded Scheduling methods and it is presented in 'Bit Project No.61'. Agent program is installed in real servers and load balancer. Through the agent, the load balancer gains the load information of the real servers by every time and save own load table. Thus, when the request is received, load balancer selects the real server that has the least load for offering service. So it is able to achieve the sophisticated load balancing. But load balancer have the a lot of communication overhead because load balancer send the real servers the packets that have request load information and receive the response packets from real servers. As the real servers are more increasing, the communication overheads of the load balancer are more increasing. It is add the single-point-of-bottleneck of the load balancer. So is able to cause low scalability.

3. ABSS Scheduling Method

We propose a scheduling method that offer the sophisticated load balancing and reduce the additional communication overhead of the load balancer for LVS.
Load balancer and real servers have agent program for processing load information packet. Load balancer send it to the first real server and then the first Real Server add own load information to it and then send it to the next server.
Finally the load information packet is sent to the load balancer. And the load balancer is determined the scheduling by the real load information of real servers.
It is described the architecture of ABSS scheduling method in section 3.1 and mechanism in section 3.2 and algorithm in section 3.3 and internal implementation in section 3.3 and additional advantages of in section 3.4.

3.1 Architecture

The basic architecture of ABSS scheduling method is the same as that of LVS. But Agent program is running in load balancer and real servers so load information packet is able to itinerate real servers and is able to gain load information of real servers. The architecture of ABSS scheduling method illustrates in Figure 1 including.

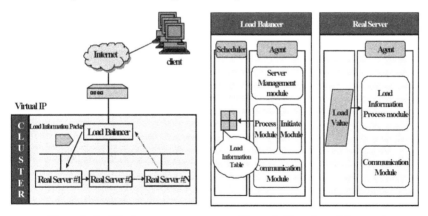

Figure 1. Architecture   **Figure 2. Overview of the agent**

<The agent of the load balancer>
The agent of load balancer is operate as daemon and is composed of load information packet creation module, load information packet communication module, load information packet process module, and real server management module.
1)creating module : create a new load information packet and call the communication module.
2)communication module : send a load information packet to the first real server and got a load information from the last real server and call the process module.
3)process module : copy the load information packet to its own load information table and call the creation module.
4)Real server management module : determine the order of real servers. It operates when new real server is discovered or is removed.

<The agent of the real server>
The agent of real server is operate as daemon and is composed of load information packet communication module and load information packet process module.
1)communication module : got a load information packet or send it to the next real server
2)process module : bring its own system load information(e.g. CPU, Memory amount) and add that load information to load information packet.

3.2 Mechanism

The agent of load balancer sends the order of real servers to real servers whenever new real server is discovered or fault is sensed. So real server is able to know previous server address and next server address.
The agent of load balancer send a packet that is responsible for gaining load information of real servers to the first real server. (I call the packet load information packet) and the first real server receive it and add own system load information to it and then send it to the next real server and that process is repeated until that it reach the last real server. And then the load information packet is returned to load balancer.
Load balancer save the content of the load information packet in own load information table. And load balancer creates new load information packet and sends it to the first real server so procedure is repeated. Load balancer determines the schedule with the real load information in load information table.

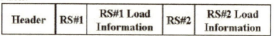

Header	RS#1	RS#1 Load Information	RS#2	RS#2 Load Information

Figure 3. Structure of the load information packet

3.3 Algorithm

Algorithm for offering the service used ABSS Scheduling method is as following.
The request of the clients are sent to the load balancer through multicasting method. Load balancer is scheduling with the client's request packet in order to the determining the real server for the services as following.
The request of client is divided several packets. The first packet means the start of request and it tis called SIN packet. And the last packet means the end of request and it is called FIN packet. And the rest is general packet.
Figure 4 describes algorithm of each packet.

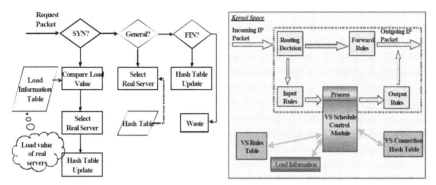

Figure 4. Algorithm   Figure 5. Internal Implementation

If request packet is SYN packet, load balancer select a real server that has the least load referred to load information table and sent the request packet to the selected real server. Then load balancer stores the scheduling result at the hash table. If request packet is general packet, load balancer finds real server that offered the service previously through the hash table. If request packet is FIN packet, load balancer removes the content from the hash table.
Finally load balancer is sophisticated scheduling with real load information.

3.4 Internal Implementation

First of all, agent program is installed in load balancer and real servers. Load information table have to be added in load balancer and scheduling algorithm have to be changed. The internal architecture of load balancer is illustrated in Figure 5 include:

3.5 Additional Advantage

In this section we describe additional advantage of ABSS scheduling method.

-Fault Management
ABSS scheduling method is able to be used to perform the fault management for the real servers without additional communication.
Real servers is able to sense the failure of the next real server when a real server request for sending the load information packet to the next real server. At this time a real server inform the load balancer about the failure of the next real server. Thus fault management of real servers is able to be performed easily.

4. Simulation

In this section, we evaluate the performance of the proposed approach.
The first goal of proposed approach is to offer sophisticated load balancing. And the second goal is to reduce the additional communication overhead of the load balancer.
In order to verify the first goal, we evaluate the load value of the real servers as each scheduling method through the simulation.

And we also estimate the additional communication overhead of the load balancer.

4.1 Simulation Environment

We developed a simulator using linux c language. We use the log file of the Turbo Linux web site. It contatins about 4700 requests for a total period of 10 minutes and we give the request packet with different weight value that indicate required load value(cpu utilization). It consists of a load balancer and four real servers. We assume that a real server process 100 load per second and that transmission of the load information packet between two servers is 0.3ms.

For making the model simplify, we assume that the load is the cpu utilization that is the most influential factor.

4.2 Simulation Result & Analysis

4.2.1 Sophisticated Scheduling

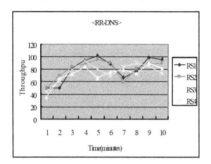
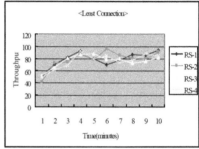

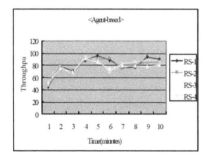
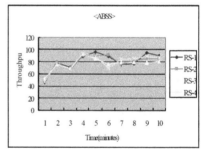

The above figures depict the throughput of the real servers. As it can be seen, the load difference of the real servers is the most in Round-robin scheduling method. And the load difference is the least in Agent-based scheduling method and ABSS scheduling method.

The following table 1 shows the standard deviation between the real servers for each scheduling methods. It means that Agent-based scheduling method and ABSS scheduling method are more sophisticated scheduling method than Round-robin scheduling method and Least-connection scheduling method.

Round-robin	8.5
Least-connection	6.9
Agent-based	4.1
ABSS	4.1

Table 1. Standard deviation

Therefore proposed approach is able to achieve the whole load balance.

4.2.2 Additional communication overhead of load balancer
We compare additional communication overhead as calculate communication number between load balancer and real servers for gaining the load information.
Agent-based scheduling method has $N*2$ additional communication overhead. ABSS scheduling method have 2 additional communication overhead. (N is number of real servers)
Therefore proposed approach is able to reduce the additional communication overhead of the load balancer as compared with the Agent-based scheduling method.

5. Conclusion

This paper describes the motivation, design goal, activation mechanism and evaluate the performance of ABSS(Agent-based Sophisticated and Scalable) scheduling method. The goal of the proposed approach is to provide the sophisticated scheduling with less additional communication overhead of the load balancer. So proposed approach gain the real load information of the real servers from itinerate load information packet and determine to schedule with the real load information. We evaluate proposed approach is more sophisticated than previous scheduling methods that aren't consider the real load information through the simulation and can reduce more the additional communication overhead than Agent-based scheduling method through the calculation of the communication number between load balancer and real servers.
Therefore ABSS scheduling method will make a successful service as do sophistication with less additional communication overhead.

6. References

A. Dahlin, M. Froberg, J. Walerud and P. Winroth, (1998), "EDDIE:A Robust and Scalable Internet Server", http://www.eddieware.org/, May, 1998

A. Iyengar, A. MacNair and E. Nguyen, (1997), "An Analysis of Web Server Performance", IEEE GLOBECOM'97, Volume: 3, pp. 1973-1947, 1977

C. R. Attanasio and S. E. Smith, (1992), A virtual Multiprocessor implemented by an encapsulated cluster of loosely coupled computers, IBM Research Report RC18442, 1992

D. Andresen, T. Yang, V. Holmedahl, O. H. Ibarra, (1996), "SWEB: Towards a Scalable World Wide Web Server on Multicomputer", IEEE Proceedings of IPPS' 96

D. Dias, W. Kish, R. Mukherjee, and R. Tewari, (1996), A scalable and highly available web server, IEEE International Conference on Data Engineering, New Orleans, February, 1996

E. Levy-Abegnoli, A. Iyengar, J. Song, and D. Dias, (1999), "Design and Performance of a Web Server Accelerator", INFOCOM, Network, March, 1999

G Hunt, G Goldszmidt, R. King, and R. Mukherjee, (1998), Network Dispatcher: a connection router for scalable Internet service, Computer Networks and ISDN Systems, Vol. 30, pp. 347~357, 1998

H. Bryhni, E. Klovning and O. Kure, (2000), "A Comparison of Load Balancing Techniques for Scalable Web Server", pp58-63, IEEE Network, July/August 2000.

High Available Cluster System, Bit Project No.61, 2001

Linux Virtual Server open project sites, http://www.linuxvirtualserver.org/

P. Srisuresh and D. Gan, (1998), Load Sharing Using Network Address Translation(LSNAT), The Internet Society, RFC2391, August, 1998

S.H. Lee, H. S. Shin, M. S. Park, (2001), IA-LVS:Design of the Improving Availability for Linux Virtual Server, Proceeding of the 2nd International Conference on SNPD' 01, 2001-12-04

V. Cardellini, M. Colajanni and P. S. Yu, (1999), "Dynamic Load Balancing on Web-Server Systems", IEEE Internet Computing, pp. 28-39. May-June, 1999

V. S. Pai, M. Aron, G. B. M. Svendsen, P. Druschel, (1998), Locality-aware request distribution in cluster-based network servers, ASPLOS-VIII, San Jose, CA, Oct, 1998

W. Zhang, (2000),"Linux Virtual Servers for Scalable Network Services" Ottawa Linux Symposium, July 19~20, 2000

W. Zhang, S. Jin, and Q. Wu, (1999) "Creating Linux Virtual Servers", the 5th Annual Linux expo May 20~22, 1999. Raleigh, North Carolina

Y. M. Teo, R. Ayani, (2001), "Comparison of Load Balancing Strategies on Cluster-based Web Servers", Transactions of the Society for Modeling and Simulation, 2001

Supporting Persistent Connection in Layer-7 Web Switch

Mon-Yen Luo and Chu-Sing Yang

Department of Computer Science and Engineering
National Sun Yat-Sen University
Kaohsiung, Taiwan, R.O.C

Abstract

Content-aware routing, routing packets based on information at layer 7 of OSI protocol stack, has drawn a large amount of attention recently, both in the academic and commercial communities. However, the Web standards protocol emphasizes use of persistent connections to convey several HTTP requests to the server on a single TCP connection. This creates significant challenges for the layer-7 web switches, and may constrain the policies they can support. This paper discusses the performance problem of persistent connection in the context of layer-7 web switch. We also describe the design, implementation, and performance of an efficient approach to address this issue.

Keywords

Web Switch, Layer-7 routing, Server Cluster

1. Introduction

It seems clear that the future network devices will need to handle at least some traffic based on application layer information. The most common example is the need of content-based routing in the server cluster system that has become widespread, as the explosive growth of the Web is straining the architecture of many Internet sites. Given a clustered server, a network device or front-end node (generally termed Web switch or server load balancer in the industry parlance) is needed to route the incoming request to the server best suited to respond. Over the past few years, several approaches or mechanisms have been proposed to enable such a request routing. Examples include DNS aliasing, TCP connection routing (Layer-4 routing), and HTTP redirection. However, as Web services and contents become more and more sophisticated, such simple routing schemes are no longer sufficient (Yang and Luo, 1999). For example, the need of running business on the Internet introduces the necessity of providing guarantee that mission-critical applications will receive priority service. Therefore, we can clearly observe an evolution of such Web switch from its initial role of stateless load Web switchs into intelligent devices that have finer-grained and intelligent control over the system resource allocated to specific content, users and applications.

Consequently, the idea of layer-7 routing (or so-called URL-aware routing, content-aware routing), routing incoming request based on its requested content, has drawn a large amount of attention recently, both in the academic and commercial communities (Examples include Alteon, Cisco, F5 Lab, Foundry, Notel, etc.). The content-aware routing mechanism can offer many potential benefits (Yang and Luo, 1999), such as sophisticated load balancing, QoS support, guarantee of session integrity, flexibility in content deployment, etc. However, the layer-7 Web switching is problematic in the presence of persistent connection that becomes a default with HTTP/1.1 and gets increasingly deployed. Persistent connection allows several HTTP requests to be sent over a single TCP connection, thereby reducing client latency and server overhead (Mogul 1995a). The problem with persistent connections is that layer-7 switches operate at the granularity of HTTP requests, and thereby requests in a single connection may have to be assigned to different back-end servers to satisfy some kind of distribution policies. This paper describes efficient mechanisms to support persistent connections in the web switch with layer-7 routing mechanism. This is a follow-up paper of our previous work (Yang and Luo, 1999). In previous paper we did not explain the mechanisms designed for supporting persistent connections due to space limitation. We report experimental results from a prototype cluster implementation. The results show that persistent connections can be supported efficiently on cluster-based Web servers with content-based request distribution.

2. Background

This section first provides background information on content-aware request routing and the related works. We then state the performance problems caused by the persistent connection in more detail.

2.1 Content-aware Request Routing

The main idea of the content-aware routing is to look deeper into incoming packets for retrieving some application-level information (e.g., URL, cookie, or host field), so that it can perform intelligent request routing based on such information. The major challenge in designing the content-aware mechanism is the connection-oriented semantics of TCP protocol that the Web service is based on. Whenever a client tries to issue a request to the Web server, it must first establish a TCP connection to the server. As a result, the routing mechanism has to establish a TCP connection with the client so that it can examine the subsequent HTTP requests to perform content-aware routing. When the routing decision has been made, relaying the HTTP request (or migrating the established connection) from the Web switch to the selected server becomes a challenging problem.

Numerous approaches have been proposed to address the above problem. The proposed approaches includes delayed-binding (Resonate), TCP handoff (Pai et al, 1998), TCP binding (Yang and Luo, 1999), TCP splicing (Apostolopoulos, 2000). The content-aware routing mechanism can support more sophisticated request-distribution policies and many promising benefits. Some sophisticated load-balancing algorithms have been designed based on the concept of content-aware routing such as LARD (Pai et al, 1998). It can also enable flexible content placement, so that it allows content partition on different server nodes for different file types to improve responses (Yang and Luo, 2000). Furthermore, we have implemented a low-overhead fault-resilience mechanism (Luo and Yang, 2001) based on the content-aware routing mechanism.

2.2 The Performance Problem With Persistent Connection

Persistent connections allow HTTP clients to submit multiple requests to a given server using a single TCP connection, thereby reducing client latency and server overhead. Unfortunately, persistent connections pose performance problems for clusters that use content-aware request distribution, while requests in a single connection may have to be assigned to different back-end nodes to satisfy some kind of distribution policies. For example, as in the scenario illustrated in the Figure 1, SRV1 and SRV 2 are two of the back-end servers in a server cluster and FE is their front-end Web switch. Here, we assume that that the content is partitioned among the back-end servers, in which SRV1 has the object A, B, E and SRV2 has object C, D.

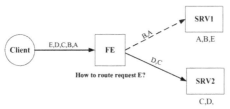

Figure 1. Problem with Persistent Connection

Suppose that a client sends requests for objects A, B, C, D, E on a single persistent connection consequently. The FE will first create a persistent connection to SRV1 to relay the request A and B to SRV1. However, to route request C, the FE needs to create another TCP connection to SRV2, which requires a certain amount processing overhead. In general, it needs to terminate the previous connection with SRV1 otherwise the idle unused connection will cause resource consumption. This includes allocated port number, buffer, PCB data structure (Mogul 1995b), and more importantly, a HTTP server process may be tied up with this persistent connection even though the request has been served. However, even if we terminate the unused connection immediately, the associated resources may be held for a while because the TCP specification (RFC 793) requires that the host remember the information of the closed connection for a while (i.e. in TIME_WAIT state). This will result in an accumulation of unused connections in this "TIME_WAIT" state in the server, which can severely reduce its performance and throughput (Mogul 1995b). In addition, the connection termination will sacrifice the benefit of persistent connection, since it cannot fully utilize the available network bandwidth for the first round-trips of the newly connection. This is because current TCP implementations use a technique called *slow-start* (Wright and Stevens, 1994) to probe the network and adapt its congestion control parameters to the current condition of the network.

Chase also noticed that many content-aware routing schemes in use today are incompatible with persistent connections (Chase 2001). In addition, some routing mechanisms used in Web switches now on the market support persistent connections by routing all requests on each connection to the server selected to handle the first request arriving on the connection. However, this will sacrifice the benefits of content-aware routing (e.g., route requests to improve server cache performance such as LARD algorithm). Aron et al noticed this problem in the context of their locality-aware request distribution policy (Aron et al 2000). They proposed an approach termed back-end forwarding to address this problem. In back-end forwarding, the FE can route the request C to the SRV1 with extra information that this request would best be served by SRV2. Then, the SRV1 will request the content from SRV2 and then forward the response to the client. The disadvantages of this approach are the increased user-perceived latency and the risk of rendering the back-end network a potential bottleneck.

3. Our Content-aware Routing Mechanism

This section will present the design of the content-aware routing mechanism (termed distributor for short) of our Web switch, and how to address the problem caused by the persistent connection. To explain the operation of our mechanism, we look at the sequence of events when a client requests a Web page from a Web server, and then show how our approach operations fit into the packet exchange (see Figure 2 for explanation).

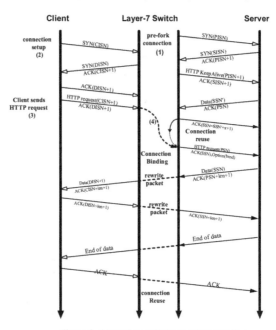

Figure 2. Operation of Content-aware Routing

3.1 Connection setup

When a client tries to initiate an HTTP request, the client-side browser first sends a SYN packet containing the client's initial sequence number (CISN) to initiate a TCP connection. After receiving the SYN packet, the distributor creates an entry in an internal table termed mapping table for this connection. The mapping table is composed of three parts: host table, port table, and server table. The distributor first creates an entry in the host table using the source IP address to be the search key. That is, each entry in the host table represents a host that is communicating with the server to access services. The distributor also allocates a port table linked to each client host when the entry of host table is created. The port table is indexed by the source port number of client's packet, consequently, each entry in the port table represents a current TCP connection connected to the server. The distributor records the TCP's state information selected by the client (e.g., initial sequence number) in the entry of port table. The distributor then handshakes with the client to complete the TCP connection establishment. We term this connection as client-side connection in the following sections.

Generally, once a client starts to access a Web server, a burst of subsequent connections will be issued from the same client. For example, if a client has retrieved an HTML file, it may generate requests for all the embedded images and send them along several TCP connections in parallel. Consequently, the special design of our mapping table is intended to aggregate consecutive and concurrent connections from the same client host. In the following sections, we will demonstrate that aggregating connection at the host level will yield several substantial benefits. The size of the port table allocated to each client will depend on whether the client endpoints are personal computers, shared workstations, or proxy servers. Such a classification is based on the number of concurrent TCP connections. The single host such as personal computer generally has few concurrent connections connected to a site. However, if the client endpoint is a shared workstation or even proxy server, there will be a huge number of concurrent TCP connections. Consequently, the allocation of port table is always started from a small table. A larger table will be allocated if the concurrent TCP connections form the endpoint is beyond a threshold.

3.2 Transmitting the HTTP Request

After the client-side TCP connection setup is completed, the client sends packets conveying the HTTP request, which contains the URL and other HTTP client header information. Based on the requested content, the distributor consults an internal data structure termed *URL table* to assign the incoming request to one of the web servers. The URL table holds information (e.g., location of the document, document sizes, type, priority, etc.) that helps the Web switch to make routing decisions. The readers are referred to our paper (Luo and Yang, 2002) for further details about the URL table.

When the distributor selects a server that is best suited to this request, it then chooses an idle already-open connection (we term it server-side connection) from the available connection list (i.e. server table) of the target server. The idle already-open connections may come from reused connection or pre-forked connection. In the previous example in Figure 1, after serving request A, B, the connection connected to SRV1 will be an idle connection that can be kept and reused later.

We had designed and implemented a connection-management mechanism (Yang and Luo, 1999) in our Web switch to strike a good balance between the benefits and costs of maintaining open connections. The connection-management module uses two parameters to control the number of established persistent connections of each back-end server: maximum number of connections (MAX for short) and minimum number of connections (MIN for short). MAX defines the threshold between system trashing and maximum optimization of system resources. The distributor periodically queries each server node for its current load to determine the value of MAX. The connection management mechanism keeps a fixed limit (MIN) on the number of available persistent connections. If the number of already-open connections is below the MIN, the distributor starts to pre-fork a number of persistent connections. When the total connections (used and unused) reach MAX, it stops pre-forking connections.

Of course, we cannot arbitrary select an idle connection to bind with a given client-side connection. We will discuss the selection policy in section 3.3. After the connection binding is determined, the distributor stores the pointer of the selected connection in the entry of the port table, binding the client-side connection to the server-side connection. Then the distributor will change the packet's IP and TCP headers to relay the packet from the client-side connection to the server-side connection.

3.3 Server Response and Subsequent Requests

When the designated server receives the request, it parses the URL to determine the content requested. It then fulfills the request and transmits the response to the client. The server response also needs the reverse packet modification so that the client can transparently receive and recognize these packets. In some implementation, these response packets have to be directed to the frond-end Web switch to perform the reverse packet-rewriting. However, such a design will render the Web switch a performance bottleneck.

To efficiently forward the response packets, we also implemented a loadable module that can be loaded into the kernel of the backend servers. The distributor will send the binding information to it, and then the backend module can change the outgoing packets so that they can go directly to the client without going through the Web switch (please notice that this is different from the standard approach in Figure 2). As a result, the processing burden of the Web switch can be greatly reduced, since the amount of data sent from the server to the client is significantly larger than the amount of data sent from the client to the server.

In a typical Web session, the client will first retrieve a HTML file, and then the browser will open multiple persistent connections in parallel to retrieve the embedded images or other objects. Most browsers also limit the number of parallel connections (a user-configurable limit, defaulting to four). As a result, some subsequent requests are conveyed in the way of reusing already-open connection. The distributor handles the newly created connection in the same way described above. To the subsequent request, the distributor will select a suitable already-established server-side connection to handle the request. The key idea of our approach is to select a server-side connection with the congestion window size that is best matched the network state (i.e., available bandwidth) of client-side connection. The TCP protocol stack uses congestion window size to track the available bandwidth in the network and govern the amount of data that can be transmitted at any given time. The distributor can meter the available bandwidth (i.e., the congestion window size of client-side connection) by observing the ACK sent by the client. It will select an idle server-side connection with the congestion windows size that is best close to (but not over) the available bandwidth. With such a design, we can seamlessly relay a request to a reused connection and avoid the slow-start restart problem, thereby reducing the client perceived latency.

3.4 Connection Reuse or Termination

If the response of a request has been successfully received by the client, its server-side connection can be used by other requests by the same or even other clients. However, to the front-end Web switch, it will be difficult to determining when a transfer has completed and the new request can be started. Generally, the EOF (End of File) in the HTTP response can be the mark to identify that the data transfer has been completed. However, such a sign cannot be received by the distributor because the response packets do not go through the Web switch. Therefore, we use the following approach to address this problem.

If the loadable module at back-end server discovers the response has been completed, it will inform the distributor this event by sending a control message to it. The control message also conveys the current congestion windows size of this connection. When receiving such a control message, the distributor will record the congestion window size in the entry of connection table and mark this connection "available". The record of congestion windows size will be used in selection policy described in section 3.3.

Although reusing the pre-forked or already-open connections can reduce server overhead and latency of establishing a new connection, however, a surfeit of idle open TCP connection incurs a waste of system resource. Therefore, we use a timeout mechanism in the connection management module described in section 3.3 to close the surfeit of idle connections. To date we use a trivial fixed length timeout policy for closing idle connections. An adaptive timeout mechanism may be more appropriate in some cases. This is an area of further research and beyond the scope of this paper.

4. Performance Result

We currently maintain an Internet server cluster composed of the following machines: four Pentium Pro machines (200 MHz CPU with 64MB memory), ten Pentium-2 machines (300 MHz CPU with 128 MB memory), and sixteen Pentium-4 machines (1400 MHz CPU with 512 MB memory). We currently use a Pentium-2 machine (350 MHz CPU with 128 MB memory) running Linux to execute the request routing mechanism and approaches proposed in this paper. For the purpose of performance analysis, we had collected the packet level traces of the web traffic to and from our server system for about four months. The packets trace consists of over 300 million HTTP requests.

To evaluate the performance benefits of our mechanisms that support persistent connection in the server cluster with content-aware routing, we place a client running a modified WebStone benchmark on a remote location to retrieve a Web page (with 21 embedded images) stored at our server cluster over the WAN. The average latency of downloading the whole page is 2.8 second. We also extracted each user sessions from the packet-level trace. We then replayed the packets of the above user session on another server cluster that have the same configuration but be equipped with conventional content-aware routing mechanism. We term this environment as baseline system in the following sections. The average latency of downloading the whole page in the baseline system is 6.5 second. Compared with the performance data of the two configurations, we can clearly see the performance benefits of our proposed mechanisms. Such a performance gain was consistent when we performed the same test several times. The Figure 3 demonstrates the network dynamic of one of these tests.

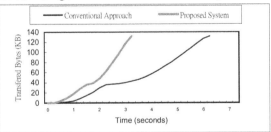

Figure 3. Packets exchange of the HTTP sessions

The performance gain is because our design can effectively reuse the server-side connections, thereby avoiding the slow-start restart problem and reducing the server overhead. To verify the reduction of the server overhead, we instrumented the Linux kernel of one of the back-end servers. We measured the network resource of this node on a busy period (for one hour) of our Web site. We then replayed the packet trace on the baseline system again. The comparison result is presented in Table 1.

	Proposed System	Baseline System
Throughput (requests/sec)	2487	1763
Active TCP Connections (connections/sec)	873	1367
Connections in TIME-WAIT (Connections/sec)	3125	26789
CPU Utilization	57%	76%

Table 1. Performance comparison

We can clearly see that our approach can increase the throughput and reduce the system overhead. This performance gain is because our approach can effectively reuse a smaller number of persistent server-side connections to convey the clients' requests, keeping each backend server to handle fewer connections and operate more efficiently via decreasing connections in TIME_WAIT state.

5. Conclusion

This paper indicates an important performance problem caused by persistent connection in layer-7 Web switch. We showed that the persistent connection defined in Web standard is problematic with the naïve content-aware routing mechanism. We also provide solutions to address these issues. The implemented mechanisms have proven that our approach is effective.

Reference

G. Apostolopoulos, D. Aubespin, V. Peris, P. Pradhan, D. Saha (2000), "Design, implementation and performance of a content-based switch," Proceedings of the Infocom 2000.

Alteon WebSystems, Alteon 180 Web Switch http://www.alteon.com/

M. Aron, D. Sanders, P. Druschel, and W. Zwaenepoel (2000), "Scalable content-aware request distribution in cluster-based network servers," Proceedings of the 2000 USENIX Annual Technical Conference.

J. Chase (2001), "Server switching: yesterday and tomorrow," Proceedings of the Second IEEE Workshop on Internet Applications.

Cisco Systems, Cisco Content Networking Devices. http://www.cisco.com/

F5 Networks. BigIP. http://www.f5labs.com/

Foundry ServerIron, http://www.foundrynet.com/products/webswitches/.

M. Y. Luo and C. S. Yang (2002), "Content management on server farm with layer-7 routing," Proceedings of 17th ACM Symposium on Applied Computing.

J. C. Mogul (1995), "The case for persistent-connection HTTP," Proceedings of the SIGCOMM'95.

J. C. Mogul (1995), "Network behavior of a busy Web server and its clients," Technical Report 95/5, Digital Western Research Lab.

Nortel Networks. ACE switch 180e. http://www.nortelnetworks.com/

V. Pai, M. Aron, M. Svendsen, G. Banga, P. Druschel, W. Zwaenepoel, and E. Nahum (1998), "Locality-aware request distribution in cluster-based network servers," Proceedings of the 8th ASPLOS.

Jon B. Postel. *Transmission Control Protocol*. RFC 793, Network Information Center, September 1981.

Resonate, http://www.resonate.com/.

G. Wright and W. R. Stevens (1994), *TCP/IP Illustrated, Volume1*, Addison-Wesley, Reading.

C. S. Yang and M. Y. Luo (1999), "Efficient support for content-based routing in web server clusters," Proceedings of the 2nd USENIX Symposium on Internet Technologies and Systems.

C. S. Yang and M. Y. Luo (2000), "Efficient content placement and management on cluster-based Web servers," Proceedings of the Seventh IEEE/IFIP Network Operations and Management Symposium.

C. S. Yang and M. Y. Luo (2000), "Realizing fault resilience in Web-server cluster," Proceedings of the 13th ACM/IEEE Conference on High Performance Networking and Computing.

Adaptive Content Delivery for Scalable Web Servers

Rahul Pradhan and Mark Claypool

Department of Computer Science
Worcester Polytechnic Institute
Worcester, MA 01609, USA
claypool@cs.wpi.edu

Abstract

The phenomenal growth in the use of the World Wide Web often places a heavy load on networks and servers, threatening to increase Web server response time and raising scalability issues for both the network and the server. Rather than large response times or connection failures that occur with typical loaded Web servers, clients are often willing to receive a degraded, less resource intensive version of the requested content. We propose and evaluate a server system that is capable of quantifying the load on a Web server and scaling the Web content delivered to a lower quality upon detecting high load, thus satisfying more clients and reducing response times. We experimentally evaluate our adaptive server system and compare it with a non-adaptive server. We find that our adaptive content delivery server system can support as much as 25% more static requests, 15% more dynamic requests and twice as many multimedia requests as a non-adaptive server.

1 Introduction

The number of people on the World Wide Web is expected to reach 320 million by 2002 (*The Internet, Technology, Analysis and Forecast* 1999) with the top 100 most frequently accessed Web sites (*Hot 100 Sites* n.d.) getting more than a million requests per day. When the request rate on a Web server increases beyond server capacity, the server becomes unresponsive and starts rejecting connections. Web servers that do not respond quickly under heavy loads can slow down a network connection, deny service to clients and cause network failures. The inability of Web servers to degrade gracefully under load results in connections being denied, which translates to a loss in revenue for today's Internet economies (*Scaling the Internet Web Servers* n.d.) and loss of interest from customers (Bhatti, Bouch and Kuchinsky 2000).

To reduce server load, (Andersen and McCune 1998, Colajanni, Yu, Cardellini, Papazoglou, Takiazawa, Kramer and Chanson 1998, Colajanni, Yu and Cardellini 1997) propose distributing load across geographically separated servers. (Mourad and Liu 1997) proposes redirection servers to transparently redistribute users' requests. Numerous networking companies (*Nortel Networks* n.d., *Cisco Systems* n.d., *Quickweb: Intel Corporation* n.d.) have commercial products to load balance a server. However, even a load-balanced site can still suffer from a single server being overloaded. And over-provisioning a Web server with twice the normal capacity cannot always prevent overload conditions (Schechter, Krishnan and M.Smith 1998) since Web loads tends to be bursty.

Another approach to reducing server load is to serve reduced Web content. Reducing the number of embedded objects per page can also result in significant additional resource savings (Abdelzaher and Bhatti 1999). Reducing the number of local links, followed manually by administrators of large sites such as CNN (upon overload due to breaking news (Vahdat, Eastham, Yoshokawa, Belani, Anderson, Culler and Dahlin 1998)) can also reduce load. "Thumbnails" of images can further reduce load by only serving large images when a user specifically requests them. While effective, most of these techniques are not automated to respond to server load dynamically.

Server load may be automatically reduced through the use of adaptive content delivery. Current adaptive content delivery techniques primarily consider network bandwidth as a measure of the load on the server (Abdelzaher and Bhatti 1999). However, server overload may also occur due to the saturation of the CPU or the disk on the server. Streaming multimedia applications are often directly affected by CPU and disk utilization. Dynamic Web page generation techniques, too, are also resource intensive, as they often require some processing.

We propose an approach that detects when a server is overloaded and adapts content to serve more clients and reduce response times. Building upon work in (Abdelzaher and Bhatti 1999), we use request rate and network bandwidth as criteria for switching content, and in addition consider CPU and disk utilization when determining server load. We develop a measure of server load based on the CPU utilization, disk utilization, the outgoing network bandwidth and the observed request rate that is effective for both multimedia and dynamic pages.

Our server adapts content *apriori* and stores two copies of content that differ in quality and processing requirements. Building upon (Ma, Bedner, Chang, Kuchinsky and Zhang 2000), we adapt static Web pages by number of embedded images, dynamic Web pages by processing time, and images and video by picture quality. Switching the quality of the content is done transparently; the client always retrieves the original URL, but the actual content is linked in with soft links (or short-cuts) for either high quality or low quality, as appropriate.

We build a system which dynamically adapts the content delivered to the client according to the server load. Our system is designed for a graceful degradation of server performance under heavy load rather than cope with sustained server overload. If the server is lightly loaded then high quality is served, otherwise the low quality, less resource intensive version is served.

We experimentally measure the effect of our load monitoring process and the benefits of our adaptive server under conditions of high load. Our analysis shows that our adaptive server can support about 25% more static requests, 15% more dynamic requests and double the number of multimedia requests as a non-adaptive server.

The rest of this paper is organized as follows: Section 2 shows the effect of system load on server performance, providing thresholds for content adaptation; Section 3 shows the results of experiments measuring performance for both the adaptive and non-adaptive server for static, dynamic and multimedia workloads; and Section 4 concludes and presents some possible future work.

2   Web Server Load Monitoring

This section describes our techniques to measure the server load. Our measurement of server load is to determine when the system is loaded such that response times start to degrade. Although our current implementation is specific to the Linux operating system, the techniques we propose are general enough to apply to any Web server system.

Linux provides a virtual file system known as the **proc** file system that acts as an interface to the internal data structures in the kernel. The **proc** file system contains information on every process, the processor utilization, the internal workings of the kernel, the number of bytes read and written from disk, and the number and sizes of packets sent and received over the network interfaces.

To measure CPU utilization we made use of the *top* system command, which obtains statistics from **proc** files. *Top* reports the percentage of CPU time in user mode, system mode, running niced tasks, and idle. We measure the processor utilization as the sum of the user and system processes.

To measure network utilization, we use the **/proc/dev** file which contains statistics such as the number of packets sent or received. We calculate the network utilization as the number of bytes sent or received over the theoretical maximum (10 Mbps on our server).

To measure disk utilization, we use the **/proc/stat** file which contains statistics about the number of blocks read and written. We calculate the disk utilization as the number of bytes read or written over the theoretical maximum (24 Mbps on our server).

To obtain average utilization values rather than bursty instantaneous values we use exponential averaging. We use a weighting of 0.40 as it seemed to be effective in pilot studies for providing an appropriately responsive server. We also use 40 seconds as our timing interval utilization measurements, as it best captured the variation in the utilization values during our pilot studies.

For each measure of load, we use load thresholds at which we determine the server is at high or low load and switch content to high or low quality, as appropriate. We set

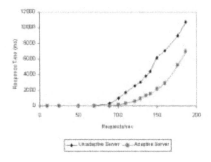 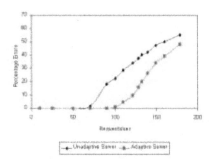

Figure 1: Response Time vs. Request Rate   Figure 2: Error Rate vs. Request Rate

two threshold values for each utilization parameter, a high threshold value and a low threshold value, to prevent the system from oscillating from high quality to low quality too frequently. We set the load thresholds based on baseline experiments, but do not present the results here due to space constraints. More details on our load measurement techniques can be found in (Pradhan and Claypool 2001).

Based on the results from (Pradhan and Claypool 2001), we selected the following threshold values: for CPU utilization, we chose 75% and 60% as the high and low thresholds; for network utilization, we use 55% and 35% as the high and low thresholds; and for disk utilization we used 75% and 60% as the high and low thresholds.

3   Adaptive Web Server Performance

To evaluate our Web server system, we use three client machines simulating multiple Web clients issuing uniform sized HTTP GET requests via *httperf*. The clients were connected to the network with a standard 10 Mbps Ethernet link. The hardware platform that we used for our experiments was an Intel Pentium III, 500 MHz with a SCSI disk, 128 MB of main memory, and a standard 10 Mbps Ethernet card. The Linux version was 2.2.14. The Web server software used was Apache (*The Apache Web Server Project* n.d.) version 1.3.12.

We evaluate the performance for our system based on the throughput, response time, error rates and the number of concurrent multimedia and dynamic clients the Web server supports. Throughput is the responses rate (responses/sec) from the server. Response time is the time it takes from the sending of a request until the arrival of the last byte of the response at the client. Error rate is the rate at which a failure occurs in the client in an interaction with the server, typically from an overflow in the connection queue of a busy server.

For the adaptive server system and the non-adaptive server, we compare the perfor-

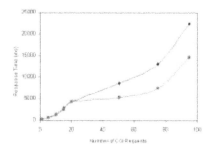 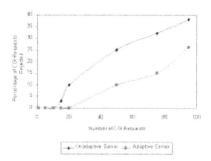

Figure 3: Response Time vs. Number of   Figure 4: Failure Rate vs. Number of CGI
CGI Clients   Clients

mance for a static HTTP workload, a continuous media workload and a dynamic workload
and analyze the overhead incurred by our system.

Figure 1 shows the average response time for each request. The response time starts
out at a minimum of 4.8 ms and then increases slowly as more requests are received
until it reaches the maximum server capacity after which it increases exponentially. The
response time graph for the adaptive server is shifted to the left indicating that acceptable
response times are obtained for more requests per second.

Figure 2 shows a graph of the error rates as the percentage of requests that failed.
As the request rate increases, the server gets saturated and the number of requests that
are rejected increases. The adaptive server has a lower error rate than the non-adaptive
server under heavy loads.

Figure 3 shows a graph for dynamic requests. The horizontal axis represents the
number of concurrent CGI requests while the vertical axis represents the response time
in milliseconds. As shown in the graph, the response time increases almost linearly in
both cases until about 20 concurrent CGI requests. After 20 requests, the non-adaptive
server performance degrades considerably, while the adaptive server performance remains
almost constant, since the server is now serving smaller, less resource intensive files.

Figure 4 shows a graph of the failure rate. The horizontal axis represents the number of
concurrent CGI requests while the vertical axis represents the percentage of CGI requests
rejected. The adaptive server rejects fewer requests as compared to the non-adaptive
server which reaches saturation earlier due to its resource intensive content.

This section evaluates the benefits of the adaptive content delivery system for continuous media requests. We built a streaming MPEG server to serve MPEG-1 files with
quality various content for adaptation. We built a MPEG client which connected to our
streaming server. We varied the number of clients and noted the corresponding frames
per second sent by the server.

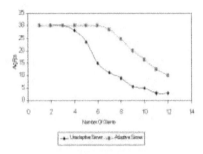 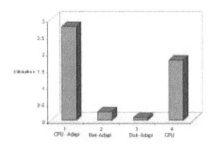

Figure 5: Frame Rate vs. Number of Mul-   Figure 6: Overhead for the Adaptive Con-
timedia Clients   tent Delivery System

Figure 5 shows the frames per second sent to the client versus the number of clients requesting the file. As observed from the graph, as the number of clients increases the processing load on the server increases and it cannot maintain a 30 frames per second rate. For the non-adaptive server, the frames per second sent falls below 30 after the 3rd client and it falls below 15 frames per second after 5 concurrent clients. On the other hand, the adaptive server can handle 6 concurrent multimedia clients and it falls below 15 frames per second only after 10 concurrent clients. The adaptation leads to the server sending a smaller video frames which significantly reduces the load on the server resulting in a better frame rate.

Lastly, we examine how much load our adaptive system itself induces on the server. Figure 6 shows the overhead for the content adaptation system. The utilization values shown are the average values for 1000 seconds run on an idle system. The graph shows the CPU utilization for both the adaptive and non-adaptive server, and the network and disk utilization values for the adaptive server.

The values for the CPU utilization for a non-adaptive server show the minimal overhead for our system. We could not measure network and disk utilization without our load monitoring module in place, but these numbers with our system itself are already extremely low.

4   Conclusions

The phenomenal growth in the Internet traffic has placed a heavy load on Web servers. Heavy bursts of traffic overload servers leading to sluggish response times or rejection of requests. Current content adaptation techniques are not particularly well suited to multimedia traffic and dynamic Web pages. Both multimedia and dynamic Web pages have stringent processing, storage and delivery requirements. Hence, serving a variety of requests in a timely manner albeit at a lower quality is of primary concern.

In this paper, we propose an adaptive content delivery system that is light-weight, stand-alone and capable of quantifying the load on the server and transparently adapting the delivered content depending upon the server load. Our system measures the load on the server in terms of its CPU, disk and network utilization to determine the utilization values beyond which to switch content. The content switching is done transparently to both the client and the server.

We evaluated the performance of our system for static, dynamic and multimedia workloads, including a streaming MPEG server and client that can react to the server load by scaling the quality of frames transmitted. We compared the performance of the adaptive content delivery system with a non-adaptive system under similar conditions. We find our adaptive system can serve as many as 25% more static clients. Our system also serves 15% more dynamic clients and almost twice the number of multimedia clients at acceptable frame rates than a non-adaptive server. The adaptive system also shows significant savings in response times for the client.

The main benefits of our approach include: measurement of server load based upon network and disk utilization, in addition to CPU utilization; alleviating server load by a graceful degradation of server performance; transparent content switching for content adaptation; and no requirement of modification to existing server software, browser or HTTP protocol.

For future work, our measure of response time could be used to predict service times. A function to predict service times could be the basis of an admission control technique used to admit only those clients which can be served within a pre-defined response time limit. This can be of great advantage to ISP's and video servers who have clients who require guaranteed response times.

Also, our content adaptation approach can be combined with client resource determination techniques to deliver the quality tailored to each client. Client browsers could explicitly request various quality levels from the server based on client side resources or personal preferences. Our transparent content switching technique can be used to serve different quality content to heterogeneous clients such as desktops, mobile phones or PDA's.

References

Abdelzaher, T. and Bhatti, N.: 1999, Adaptive Content Delivery For Web Server QoS, *International Workshop On Quality of Service*.

Andersen, D. and McCune, T.: 1998, Towards a Heirarchial Scheduling System for Distributed WWW Server Cluster, *Proceedings of The Seventh International Symposium on High Performance Distributed Computing*.

Bhatti, N., Bouch, A. and Kuchinsky, A.: 2000, Integrating User Perceived Quality Into Web Server Design, *Technical report*, HP Laboratories, Palo Alto.

Cisco Systems: n.d. Internet site
http://www.cisco.com.

Colajanni, M., Yu, P. and Cardellini, V.: 1997, Scheduling Algorithms For Distributed Web Server, *Proceedings of 17th International Conference on Distributed Computing Systems*.

Colajanni, M., Yu, P., Cardellini, V., Papazoglou, M., Takiazawa, M., Kramer, B. and Chanson, S.: 1998, Dynamic Load Balancing in Geographically Distributed Heterogeneous Servers, *Proceedings of The 18th International Conference on Distributed Computing Systems*.

Hot 100 Sites: n.d. Internet site http://www.100hot.com.

Ma, W., Bedner, I., Chang, G., Kuchinsky, A. and Zhang, H.: 2000, A Framework for Adaptive Content Delivery in Heterogeneous Network Environments , *Hewlett Packard Labs*.

Mourad, A. and Liu, H.: 1997, Scalable Web Server Architectures, *Proceedings of The Second IEEE Symposium on Computer and Communications*.

Nortel Networks: n.d. Internet site http://www.nortelnetworks.com.

Pradhan, R. and Claypool, M.: 2001, Adaptive Multimedia Content Delivery for Scalable Web Server, *Technical Report WPI-CS-TR-01-21*, Worcester Polytechnic Institute.

Quickweb: Intel Corporation: n.d. Internet site http://www.intel.com/quickweb.

Scaling the Internet Web Servers: n.d. Internet site
http://www.cisco.com/warp/public/cc/pd/cxsr/400/tech/scale_wp.htm.

Schechter, S., Krishnan, M. and M.Smith: 1998, Using Path Profiles to Predict http Requests, *Proceedings of Seventh International World Wide Web Conference*.

The Apache Web Server Project: n.d. Internet site http://www.apache.org.

The Internet, Technology, Analysis and Forecast: 1999.

Vahdat, A., Eastham, P., Yoshokawa, C., Belani, E., Anderson, T., Culler, D. and Dahlin, M.: 1998, Web OS: Operating System Services for Wide Area Applications, *Proceedings of Seventh International Symposium on High Performance Distributed Computing*.

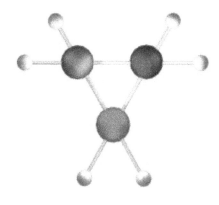

Chapter 2

Network Technologies

A Loss Detection Service for Active Reliable Multicast Protocols

M. Maimour and C. D. Pham

RESAM, Lyon1. ENS, 46 allee d'Italie
69364 Lyon Cedex 07 - France
email:{mmaimour,cpham}@ens-lyon.fr

Abstract

Reliable multicast protocols have gained popularity with active service contributions where routers implement additional functionalities. Reducing the delay of recovery is one of the desirable features of a reliable multicast protocol. In this paper we propose an active-based architecture with specialized routers. Using simulations we show how this architecture with the proposed services (mainly the loss recovery from the receivers and the loss detection at the routers), could improve the performances of a reliable multicast application in term of the recovery delay.

Keywords

Reliable Multicast, Active Networks.

1 Introduction

Multicast handles one-to-many communications with one sender transmitting the same data to more than one receiver. At the network level IP multicast provides an efficient one-to-many IP packets delivery but without any reliability guarantees. However data dissemination applications such as distributed computing or interactive simulations require a reliable transfer. In early ACK-based protocols, the sender is responsible for both the loss detection and the recovery (Strayer et al., 1992). These protocols do not scale well to a large number of receivers due to the ACK implosion problem. The use of NACKs instead of ACKs moves the loss detection responsibility to the receivers. The problem then turns into a NACK implosion problem when a large number of receivers have subscribed to the multicast session. The next step in improving scalability is the use of the local recoveries where the retransmission of a lost packet can be performed by some other nodes in the multicast tree (Floyd et al., 1997; Paul and Sabnani, 1997; Yavatkar et al., 1995; Papadopoulos et al., 1998; Speakman et al., 1998; Holbrook et al., 1995). Local recoveries can dramatically decrease the recovery latency. There are basically 2 possibilities for enabling local recoveries: (i) use some receivers or dedicated servers as repliers, or (ii) use network elements such as routers. For instance, the replier could be any receiver in the neighborhood (SRM (Floyd et al., 1997)), a designated receiver (RMTP (Paul and Sabnani, 1997), TMTP (Yavatkar et al., 1995), LMS (Papadopoulos et al., 1998), PGM (Speakman et al., 1998)) or a logging server (LBRM (Holbrook et al., 1995)) in a hierarchical structure.

Active networks (Tennehouse et al., 1997) open new perspectives in providing more efficient solutions for the problem of the feedback implosion. Active approaches benefit from the assistance of the routers which are able to perform customized computations on the messages flowing through them. ARM (Active Reliable Multicast) (Lehman et al., 1998) is one example of such approaches that was recently proposed in the research community. The main contribution of active services is a *best-effort* cache of data packets to allow the active router to retransmit the lost data packet instead of the source. A receiver experiencing a packet loss sends immediately a NACK to the source. Active services in routers then consist in the aggregation of the multiple NACKs. In practice, most of router's caching means are limited and the routers must support many sessions in parallel. Using a replier has the main advantage of requiring a memory usage as low as possible within network elements and is potentially more scalable. DyRAM (Dynamic Replier Active Reliable Multicast) (Maimour and Pham, 2002) is an other active approach that provides a solution to the problem of scalability at the routers by enabling local recovery from the receivers without any caching at the routers.

In (Maimour and Pham, 2001) we proposed and analyzed a new active service that consists in the loss detection by the routers themselves. In this case, routers are capable to detect packet losses and consequently generate corresponding NACKs to be sent to the source. In this paper, some results of this analytical study will be exploited to propose an active-based reliable multicast architecture more dedicated to our DyRAM protocol. The rest of the paper is organized as follows. Section 2 gives an overview of the DyRAM protocol. Section 3 presents the loss detection service. In section 4, our active-based architecture is presented. Section 5 shows how the loss detection service combined with the proposed architecture could improve the DyRAM protocol. Section 6 concludes the paper.

2 DyRAM: an overview

In this section, an overview of DyRAM is given. For a more detailed description, the reader is referred to (Maimour and Pham, 2002). DyRAM is based on a tree structure constructed on a per-packet basis with the assistance of the routers. The protocol uses a NACK-based scheme with a receiver-based local recovery where receivers are responsible for both the loss detection and in some cases the retransmission of repair packets. A receiver detects a loss by sequence gaps and upon the detection of a loss, a receiver immediately sends a NACK toward the source and sets a timer. Since NACKs and repairs may also be lost, a receiver will re-send a similar NACK when the requested repair has not been received within the timeout interval. In order to limit the processing overheads of duplicate NACKs and to avoid the corresponding retransmissions, the source, the active routers and the receivers ignore similar NACKs for a certain period of time. Routers maintain information about NACKs flowing through them. For each received NACK, the router creates or simply updates an existing NACK state (NS) structure. Such a structure contains during its life time the following information:

- seq: the sequence number of the requested packet,
- $time$: the time when the last valid NACK for this packet has been received and forwarded toward the source,

- *rank*: the rank of the last received NACK. The last valid NACK has rank 1; the next received one, which is not valid, has rank 2 and so forth . . . ,

- *subList*: a subcast list that contains the list of links (downstream or upstream) on which NACKs for this packet have arrived.

2.1 NACK suppression and subcast

On receipt of a NACK packet, a router would look for a corresponding NS structure. If such a structure exists, the router concludes that at least one similar NACK has already been processed otherwise a new NS structure will be created for this NACK. In the former case the router additionally checks if this NACK is valid (not a duplicate one), and if so, the router will forward it on the elected replier link. Otherwise this NACK will serve to properly update the NS structure (rank and subcast list) and is dropped afterward.

The subcast list in the NS structure contains the set of links (downstream or upstream) from which a NACK has been received. When a data packet arrives at an active router it will simply be forwarded on all the downstream links if it is an original transmission. If the data packet is a repair packet the router searches for a corresponding NS structure and will send the repair on all the links that appear in the subcast list.

2.2 Replier election

On reception of a valid NACK, the router initializes a timer noted DTD (Delay To Decide) in order to collect during this time window as much information as possible about the links affected by a loss (updates of the subcast list). On expiration of the DTD timer, the router is able to choose a replier link among those that are not in the subcast list. This link may end up to be the upstream one if all the downstream links appear to be in the subcast list. In an attempt to avoid for the overloading of a particular downstream link, the router always try to choose a different link from the previously elected one (if available) by respecting a ring order among them, thus realizing when possible a load balance.

In order to decrease the overhead (longer recovery latency) introduced by the DTD timer 2 optimizations are proposed. First, when a router receives NACK packets from all of the downstream links before the expiration of the DTD timer it will immediately forward the last NACK received toward the source and will cancel the replier election process. The second optimization consists in keeping track within a router of the received data packets in order to quickly detect packet losses occurring from upstream and affecting all its subtree. This can be done simply by maintaining a track list structure (TL) for each multicast session handled by the router. A TL has three components:

- *lastOrdered* is the sequence number of the last data packet received in order. All packets with a sequence number less or equal to *lastOrdered* have definitely been received by the router.

- $lastReceived$ is the sequence number of the last received data packet. All packets with a sequence number greater than $lastReceived$ have not been received by the router.

- $lostList$ contains the list of data packets not received by the router with sequence number greater than $lastOrdered$ and less than $lastReceived$. This list is empty when ($lastReceived < lastOrdered + 1$) and contains at least one element otherwise.

A router maintaining such a track list (TL) structure is able to decide in some cases to forward the NACK immediately toward the source instead of waiting for the expiration of the DTD timer. These cases include the case when the requested data packet sequence number is greater than $lastOrdered$ and contained in the $lostList$. The subcast list is updated so that the repair packet (from the source) would be forwarded on all downstream links.

3 The active loss detection service

Earlier reliable multicast protocols put the burden of both the loss detection and the recovery at the sender side. These protocols are TCP-like and use ACKs combined with timers to detect losses. These ACK-based schemes violate the IP-Multicast Model (Deering and Cheriton, 1990) where the source is not aware of the identity of the receivers. The use of NACKs instead of ACKs moves the loss detection responsibility to the receivers. A receiver detects a loss on receipt of an out-of-order data packet or on a timeout expiration. When a loss is detected, the receiver would send a NACK to the source requesting the lost data packet.

The repair latency can be reduced if the lost packet could be requested as soon as possible. This can be achieved by enabling routers to detect losses and therefore to generate NACKs to be sent to the source. An active router detects a loss when a gap occurs in the data packet sequence. On a loss detection, the router would generate immediately a NACK packet toward the source. If the router has already sent a similar NACK for a lost packet then it would not send a NACK for a given amount of time. This "*discard delay*" is set at least to the RTT between this router and the source. During this period, all NACK packets received for this data packet from the downstream links are ignored. The loss detection service can be implemented without adding any more soft state at the routers. The NS and the TL structures are sufficient to implement this service. With respect to the main algorithms of DyRAM, only the data packet service is modified to take into account the loss detection service. When an active router receives a data packet, it will execute the data packet service given below :

Update the TL $trackList$ of the session
if DP is a repair **then**
  Look for the corresponding NACK state structure NS
  if such a structure exists **then**
    send DP through links in $NS.subList$
    free NS
  else if the DP arrived from the upstream link **then**
    forward DP on all the downstream links
  else {the DP arrived from downstream, link i}
    forward the DP on all the downstream links except link i
  end if

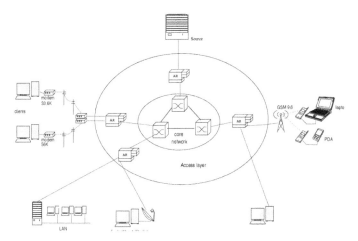

Figure 1: Active-based reliable multicast architecture

else
    Forward DP on all the downstream links
    for each DP_{lost} with $((DP_{lost}.seq > TL.lastOrdered + 1)$ and $(DP_{lost}.seq \in TL.lostList))$ **do**
    send a NACK($DP_{lost}.seq$) to the source
    Create or update the corresponding NS structure NS_{lost}:
    $NS_{lost}.seq \leftarrow DP_{lost}.seq$
    $NS_{lost}.time \leftarrow current\ time$
    $NS_{lost}.subList \leftarrow$ all the links downstream
    end for
end if

4   An active-based reliable multicast architecture

We consider the IP multicast model introduced by Deering (Deering and Cheriton, 1990). The source sends messages to a multicast address subscribed to by all the receivers. The sender need not know the receivers identities. A receiver can join or leave a multicast session as it wishes by simply sending a *join* or a *leave* message via IGMP (Internet Group Management Protocol). The routers has to make their best effort to deliver the traffic from the sender to each receiver. The packets will be duplicated in the network as needed thus reducing bandwidth consumption compared to the unicast approach. Our reliable protocol DyRAM works on top of UDP and will guarantee that all the sent packets are received by all the receivers of the multicast group.

Our architecture (see figure 1) is based on a virtual topology of active routers which are able to perform customized computations (services) on the messages (data packets and NACKs) flowing through them. We only consider active routers at the edge of the core network. This is due to the fact that the core network is reliable and a very high-speed network. Adding complex processing functions inside the core network will certainly slow down the packet forwarding functions.

For the realization of our active approach, we propose the *programmable switch approach* which maintains the existing packet format. Programs are injected separately from the processing of messages. Initially, and using a reliable channel, the source injects the required set of services by sending them to the multicast address. In our case this consists in two services, a data packet service and a NACK service. Afterwards, the source begins the multicast of the data packets. When an active router receives a packet, it first looks for the appropriate service deduced from the packet header. Consequently a data packet would be processed by a data packet service and a NACK would be processed by a NACK service.

To dynamically handle the multicast group topology changes, active routers have to be able to add or remove the required services. An active router that leaves the multicast session has simply to remove the associated services. However when an active router joins a multicast tree, it has to easily download the required services. This can be achieved by requesting the services from the closest active router which has already installed them. If there is no such active router then the services need to be sent from the source. The required services are always transmitted via a reliable channel. These operations are usually handled by the active execution environment.

All the active routers are assumed to perform at least two active services, the NACK suppression service and the subcast functionality. The active router which is located at the sender's side just before the core network is called the *source router*. As have been shown in (Maimour and Pham, 2001), the loss detection service is only beneficial if the loss detection capable-router is close enough to the source. Consequently the source router is the best candidate to perform the loss detection service in addition to the two previous services. The other active routers should only perform the replier election service as seen in the previous section.

5   Simulation results

A set of simulations are performed to show how a loss detection service could decrease the delay of recovery of an active reliable multicast protocol. To do so, four protocols noted A, D, $DyRAM$ and $DyRAM^+$ are simulated on a network model derived from the proposed architecture. In addition to the source active router A_S, we consider N active routers A_i, $i \in \{1 \ldots N\}$. Each active router A_i is responsible of B receivers forming a local group. All of the four protocols benefit from the NACK suppression and the subcast services. Whereas A only benefits from these two services, D benefits from the loss detection service at the source router. $DyRAM$ is similar to DyRAM where local recoveries from the receivers are possible. $DyRAM^+$ behaves like $DyRAM$ except that additionally the source router performs the loss detection service. In our loss model, we consider both the spatial and the temporal correlation of data packet losses. The spatial correlation is introduced by considering a per-link loss rate and the core network is considered reliable. The temporal correlation of losses is achieved by using the same model as in (Maimour and Pham, 2002). We also consider that there is l_b backbone links between the source router A_S and every active router A_i. The simulations are implemented using the PARSEC language developed at UCLA (Bagrodia et al., 1998).

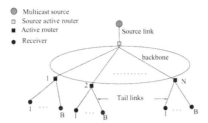

Figure 2: Network model

For all the simulations, we set $l_b = 55$. A NACK and a data packet are considered to be of 32 and 1024 bytes respectively. All simulation model values are normalized to the NACK transmission time (e.g. the time required to send or receive a NACK is set to 1, for a data packet this time is set to 32). For the processing overheads at the routers, we assume that both NACKs and data packets are processed in 32 time units. These values are derived from measures in (Lehman et al., 1998).

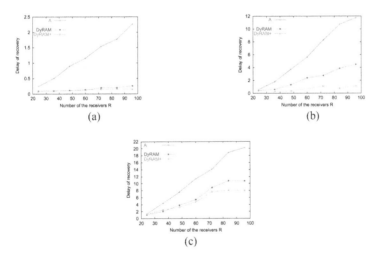

Figure 3: The recovery delay with (a) $p = 0.05$, **(b)** $p = 0.25$ **and (c)** $p = 0.50$

Figure 3 plots the recovery delay (normalized to the RTT) for the four protocols as a function of the number of the receivers for different loss rates. First of all, it is noticeable that protocols $DyRAM$ and $DyRAM^+$ with local recovery from the receivers always perform better. For instance, we can see in figure 3(a) that $DyRAM$ goes up to 10 times faster than A for a loss rate of 5%. Now, when the loss detection service is applied to A (giving protocol D) the recovery delay can be reduced. In fact as we can see for the different loss rates, D always performs better than A thanks to the loss detection service. When applying the loss detection service to $DyRAM$, the delay of recovery decreased mainly for high loss rates and a large number of receivers. For instance, the loss detection service allows DyRAM to go 4 times faster for 96 receivers and a loss rate of 25%. We can also notice in figures 3(a)(c) that $DyRAM$ slightly performs better than $DyRAM^+$ when the number of receivers is small. Therefore it is unjustified to perform the loss detection service for a few number of receivers since the local recovery is sufficient to reduce the recovery delay. This does not appear to be a limitation of the loss detection service since a multicast session has generally to support a large number of receivers.

6 Conclusions

In this paper, we proposed an active-based reliable multicast architecture with specialized routers more dedicated to our DyRAM protocol. Adding a loss detection service to the DyRAM protocol at the source router helps to reduce the delay of recovery without overwhelming the other active routers that perform the replier election service. Simulation results have shown that the DyRAM protocol performs better with the loss detection service especially for big loss rate when increasing the number of the receivers.

References

Bagrodia, R. et al. (1998). Parsec: A parallel simulation environment for complex systems. *Computer Magazine*.

Deering, S. E. and Cheriton, D. R. (1990). Multicast routing in datagrams internetworks and extended lans. In *ACM Transactions on Computer Systems*, pages 85–110.

Floyd, S., Jacobson, V., Liu, C.-G., McCanne, S., and Zhang, L. (1997). A reliable multicast framework for light-weight sessions and application level framing. *IEEE/ACM Transactions on Networking*, 5(6):784–803.

Holbrook, H. W., Singhal, S. K., and Cheriton, D. R. (1995). Log-based receiver-reliable multicast for distributed interactive simulation. In *SIGCOMM*, pages 328–341.

Lehman, L., Garland, S., and Tennehouse, D. (1998). Active reliable multicast. In *Proceeding of the IEEE INFOCOM, San Francisco, CA*.

Maimour, M. and Pham, C. (2002). Dynamic replier active reliable multicast (dyram). In *To appear in Proceedings of the Seventh IEEE Symposium on Computers and Communications (ISCC 2002)*.

Maimour, M. and Pham, C. D. (2001). An analysis of a router-based loss detection service for active reliable multicast protocols. Technical report, RESAM, http://www.ens-lyon.fr/~mmaimour/Paper/TR/TR03-2001.ps.gz.

Papadopoulos, C., Parulkar, G. M., and Varghese, G. (1998). An error control scheme for large-scale multicast applications. In *Proceeding of the IEEE INFOCOM*, pages 1188–1996.

Paul, S. and Sabnani, K. (1997). Reliable multicast transport protocol (RMTP). *IEEE journal of Selected Areas in Communication, Special Issue on Network Support for Multipoint Communications, Special ISSue on Network support for Multipoint Communication*, 15(3):407–421.

Speakman, T. et al. (1998). Pgm reliable transport protocol specification. internet draft.

Strayer, T. W., Dempsey, B. J., and Weaver, A. C. (1992). XTP – THE XPRESS TRANSFER PROTOCOL. *Addison-Wesley Publishing Company*, page 580 pages.

Tennehouse, D. L., Smith, J. M., Sincoskie, W. D., Wetherall, D. J., and Winden, G. J. (1997). A survey of active network research. *IEEE Communication Magazine*, pages 80–86.

Yavatkar, R., Griffoen, J., and Sudan, M. (1995). A reliable dissemination protocol for interactive collaborative applications. In *ACM Multimedia*, pages 333–344.

Configurable network management for small and medium networks distributed over a wide area

A. Vizcaíno, F. Alba, J. Poncela, J. T. Entrambasaguas

Dept. of Ingeniería de Comunicaciones, University of Málaga, Málaga (Spain)
e-mail: javier@ic.uma.es

Abstract

This paper describes a management system developed to control and monitor a network of programmable telephones. The network includes intermediary nodes that control, monitor and program the terminals with a proprietary interface. The nodes themselves are managed using SNMP. The resulting system provides central management of the whole network and remote access, via Web, for limited management of groups of terminals. Implementation has been done using an extensible SNMP agent and commercial management tools. The system is quite flexible and may be adapted to other networks with short development time.

Keywords

Network management, development management tools, SNMP, non-IP networks, extensible agent, intermediary equipment, Web management

1. Introduction

The increasing complexity of network architectures and devices makes network management an important aspect for network administration and maintenance. Nowadays, most network devices include standard management functionality. However, an important percentage of equipments lack this feature, usually because of economic reasons. For this group, the management solutions must necessarily be different.

At the same time, the concept of Customer Network Management (CNM) has grown in importance. Network users not only expect a reliable and efficient network access, but also they are willing to take control of their own devices connected to such network. Provision of these services can be seen as an added value in the network operator portfolio. To minimize costs bore by users of the service, Web access has proved to be an interesting option.

In this paper we present the implementation of a management system for a network of public terminals. The network is constituted by two levels of equipments: the public terminals themselves, and a group of nodes which control the formers. The number of these terminals will usually be high; in this situation, the management functionality may be decentralized, delegating part of it to the nodes, as proposed in (Goldszmidt et al, 1995). The approach used to develop the management system has involved the use of commercial and free-use tools, providing a balance between cost and development time.

In section 2, the network and the requirements of the management system are presented. In section 3, some implementation decisions are analyzed. The management system and its components are described in section 4. Some considerations about the adaptability of this system are discussed in section 5. Finally, some conclusions are drawn.

2. Management scenario. Requirements of the management system

The aim of this project is the development of a management system which matches certain requirements and adapts to special characteristics of the managed network. The network has two main components:

- Programmable telephone terminals.
- A certain number of network devices, Intermediary Equipments (IE), which are in charge of programming the terminals according to the information contained in them. Every IE is assigned the configuration of several telephone terminals. Basically, an IE is a Linux system equipped with a number of modems.

Telephones and IE are connected via modem through Public Switched Telephone Network (see Figure 1). Communication is always initiative of the terminal: it calls the IE (manually, under operator action, or automatically, using terminal's own programming), and if IE has a free modem to attend the call, the information interchange begins. Basically, terminal sends to the IE its characteristics and internal status, and IE sends to the terminal the new programming (if necessary) and the date and time of next automatic call (if the terminal has this capability).

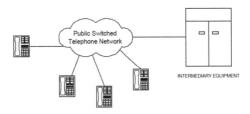

Figure 1: Managed network

It can be seen that IEs provide a kind of low-level management of the telephones. Indeed, an IE performs some programming on every terminal (following the information contained in the database controlled by the management system) and processes the result of this task to provide meaningful information to the manager. This strategy may be considered as a delegation of functions from manager to network nodes which allows a more convenient management of distributed networks (Goldszmidt et al, 1995).

The management system must monitor and control the information database contained in the IE. This information is relative to the terminals programming, as well as the IE itself. IE will program every telephone according to the data it has in its database, which is to be controlled remotely from the management system. Basic requirements for this management system are:

- IE network will be managed remotely through a heterogeneous IP network.
- Management for IEs and telephones must be independent.

- IE/terminal communications logs will be stored in the IE to be displayed in the management system.
- Special events on IEs shall be reported immediately to management system operators.
- The system must supply a graphical, easy to use operator interface.
- Management system will have two levels of operation: management of the terminals and administration of the system.
- Terminals may be grouped in clusters. Web consoles for independent management of each cluster will be provided.
- User access to management system must be secure.

3. Implementation decisions

There are several management schemes which provide different approaches, each of them basically characterized by the way the management intelligence is distributed over the network.

Simple Network Management Protocol (SNMP) is an application protocol which belongs to TCP/IP protocols suite. SNMP is the *de facto* industry standard for network management because of its simplicity and easy implementation (Stallings, 1997). Two later versions of this protocol have been developed: SNMPv2 and SNMPv3 (Zeltsermann, 1999). These versions implement means to provide extensibility and more efficient security mechanisms.

Figure 1 shows SNMP management scheme. It's a centralized structure, where a manager can control a large number of agents. Communication is, generally, an initiative of the manager, which polls an agent to retrieve or to change some information. In addition, an agent can send to the manager unsolicited information.

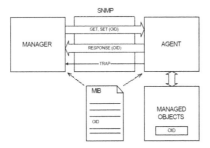

Figure 2: SNMP management scheme

From the requirements specified for our management system, SNMP covers the ones relative to basic management:

- SNMP runs over UDP/IP.
- IE and terminal management may be separated by using different MIBs.
- Logs and other structured data can be easily modelled.
- SNMP agents can monitor the IE and send specific traps when an event occurs.

Other requirements may be covered by using some of the various management tools which implement SNMP and provide user security and maintenance and/or Internet access in addition. The use of these tools, together with the simplicity of SNMP, allow a short development time, something not possible with more complex or proprietary (non standard) management schemes.

4. Description of management system

The management system has been developed to provide efficient and easy-to-use management of the network described in the previous section. Some concrete parts of the management system were created using a previously existing tool, conveniently adapted to provide the proper functionality for this system.

4.1 System structure

The management system consists of the following elements, which will be described in the next sections:

- A set of proprietary MIBs that model the management view of IEs and terminals.
- An agent located in every IE.
- A manager.
- System user interface.
- Customer user interface.

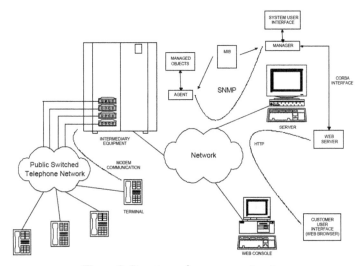

Figure 3: Structure of management system

The system user interface offers management of the whole system, including IEs and all terminals. Customer user interface provides limited management of groups of terminals. This second interface is implemented with remote Web consoles.

4.2 MIBs

Three MIBs have been defined to provide independent management for terminals, IEs, and modems installed on the IEs. They have been built following the rules and recommendations defined for SNMP MIBs in (Perkins and McGinnis, 1997). This management information models the database contained in a IE: the approach of defining MIBs oriented to databases is a characteristic of many enterprise management schemes, not only those based in SNMP, but also applications which make use of the database technology to provide management functionality (Haritsa et al, 1993).

The management information includes a list of installed terminals, software versions, status of modems, a log of terminal-IE connections, and parameters for terminal-IE connection establishment. This information has been organized grouping related single objects in MIB Groups (e. g. Connection Parameters group), and defining structured data in IE with SNMP tables (e. g. Subscriber Table, Modem Table, Historic Table).

4.3 Agent

The agent included in the *Net-SNMP* package (Net-SNMP, 2001) has been used. It's a free-use software, programmed in C language, which showed appropriate to system requirements, basically because of these particular features:

- It provides a full-operating agent.
- New functionality may be added using the included API.
- It supports the addition of proprietary management information.
- It's possible to relate traps to IE events, and report these traps to the manager.
- Net-SNMP may run on Linux: this allows to run the agent on the IE itself, which facilitates the implementation of the IE/agent interface.

Net-SNMP agent implements several standard and commonly used MIBs. To extend its functionality with our MIBs, new software modules must be implemented in order to provide access to the managed objects. These modules can be loaded into the agent even during runtime, and be unloaded when it's no more necessary.

The agent accesses the IE to retrieve the information contained in its database. IE receives messages containing information about the request: object identifier, number of row (in case of accessing a table), access mode (read or write), and data to be written when necessary. As response, IE sends the result of the previous command, which will be passed to the agent, and finally to the manager. Terminal data is checked and abnormal status is reported to the manager via trap messages.

Software modules are created in a two step process. First, a program template is generated for every proprietary MIB. These templates contain the list of attributes (OID, data type and access mode) of the managed objects, and the declaration of those functions required to access these objects. Afterwards, the algorithm needed for each function must be programmed. The resulting code is then compiled to build a dynamic library that can be loaded in the agent when needed.

4.4 Manager and system user interface

The manager acts as the central node of the management system, polling several agents to retrieve and/or set management information using SNMP. The manager contains models of the devices, to which the corresponding MIB is associated. In addition, it graphically shows this information to system operators, informs them of events occurred in a specific IE, and provides different access privileges depending on permissions.

The chosen tool to implement the manager was *Aprisma Spectrum Enterprise Manager* (Aprisma, 2001), which may run on Solaris and Windows NT operating systems. This is a general management platform which provides management capabilities adapted to various kinds of devices, networks and management protocols. The following tool features have been useful when implementing our manager:

- Implements SNMP protocol.
- Developers may load new MIBs.
- SNMP traps can be mapped to events and alarms, providing two-level severity reports.
- Offers a graphical editor to design the user interface of the management system.
- Several access levels to devices, networks and management screens may be defined.

The system user interface is structured to offer a clear and efficient access to management information. In different screens, the user can modify the status of a modem, modify the IE-terminal communication parameters, add new software versions and delete the obsolete ones, register and unregister terminals, and examine the connection logs. Additionally, using a navigation screen, which shows all the available screens organized in a tree structure, the user can easily access all information.

An IE model has been created, and the three MIBs have been associated to it. In the model, every managed object is represented as an attribute. Some problems have arisen when working with these models: reloading a MIB forces to remake the management screens, as the attribute identifiers are not updated; also, certain SNMP types are inappropriately mapped. These drawbacks must be overcome manually.

The management console includes alarm handling. When a trap is received, it generates the associated alarm. Operators can check the causes of the generation of the trap and act in consequence. IE and terminal reported events are assigned different priorities depending on their importance.

4.5 Customer user interface

Management can also be performed remotely, accessing the manager from Web browsers. Using this access, a limited management of clusters of terminals may be done. These clusters can be seen as virtual private networks, where the operators could get, at any time, updated information about the status of their terminals, without waiting for the periodic report from the system administrator.

Web management requires a properly configured Web browser, a Web server and a CORBA interface (see Figure 3). This interface maps the management information retrieved by the manager into forms which may be loaded in the Web browser. This way, the management may be done from many locations, extending the scope of utilization of the system (King and Hunt, 2000). A security mechanism restricts user access to specified devices and screens.

Management information is presented to the user with the same structure and organization as described in the previous section. The same functionality as in the local user interface is offered, excepting the access to table entries, which has to be individually implemented for every table entry. This fact is a big inconvenience if the number of rows of the table is undetermined. Management screens are designed as HTML forms; at runtime, management information is loaded into these forms when the user requests the page.

5. Adaptability of the system

The management system has been developed using two basic elements: a) A standard management protocol (SNMP): it's simple to implement and use, and meets the requirements; b) Commercial and free-use management tools which can be used to develop management systems.

This management scheme is highly flexible, and allows to develop efficient management systems with low consumption of resources (hardware, time and personnel). Once the basic knowledge has been acquired, development of other management systems is a question of days. For example, this system can be adapted to a network of IP phones in the term of one week with a two-people team; the tasks included the MIB definition, agent and manager adaption, and testing.

Apart from the process we have used, various approaches to develop management systems in a rapid way have been proposed, commonly based on both software development and concrete management considerations. In (Deri, 1997) several development tools are examined (HTML/VRML, Java/TCL, RAD), all of them leaning on a core software for network management called Liaison, which implements CMIP and SNMP. The solution proposed in this paper comprises most benefits of these other approaches: low development time, high desktop integration (provided by the intuitive graphical user interface), and platform independence (provided by the Web console).

Management tools like Spectrum use to include models to manage (via SNMP or other management protocols) generic devices (SNMP devices, UNIX systems...) with limited management functionality, and commercial network devices (routers, bridges...) with enhanced management functions, according to every device architecture. A network device intended to be managed with SNMP will contain management information from standard MIBs as well as enterprise MIBs. To access this additional information, commonly not present in the SNMP model of the management tool, some development is necessary.

These comments may be extended to any kind of non-IP device. As we have seen in the previous description, IEs are managed with SNMP, providing high-level management, while these IEs perform a low-level, proprietary management of a non-IP network. The information employed by the IEs to perform this low-level management may be modelled as a database and then managed at a higher level.

6. Conclusions

This paper has described a simple and configurable scheme to manage networks of terminals spread over a wide area. The employed architecture, with a high-level management of the IEs and the low-level management they perform on the telephones, presents a certain decentralization of the management functionality. Information about terminals is retrieved by the IEs, and then stored in their databases; this way, the management system can access this information without polling the terminals directly. For the purpose of our system, this approach of decentralizing the management is more efficient than implementing the solution proposed by SNMP architecture.

The combined use of commercial and free-use tools has helped to rapidly build the system. New functionality may be added by simply upgrading developer's own device models and designing new management screens. Due to its flexibility, this architecture and tools can be used to manage a wide range of networks and devices.

7. Acknowledgements

This work has been partially supported by Spanish Comisión Interministerial de Ciencia y Tecnología and European Commission under grant 1FD97-1829.

8. References

Aprisma Management Technologies (2001), *Spectrum 6.0.3 Documentation CD*, http://www.aprisma.com

Deri, L. (1997), "Rapid Network Management Application Development", *ECOOP '97 Workshop on OO Technology, Jyvaskyla, Finland, June 1997*.

Haritsa, J. R., Ball, M. O., Roussopoulos, N., Datta, A. and Baras, J. S. (1993), "MANDATE: MAnaging *IEEE Journal on Selected Areas in Communications*, Vol. 11, No. 9, pp1360-1372.

King, A. and Hunt, R. (2000), "Protocols and architecture for managing TCP/IP network infrastructures", *Computer Communications*, No. 23, pp1558–1572.

Metrix Systems (2000), *Metrix Web Console 2.1 Administrator's Guide*, http://www.metrixsystems.com

Goldszmidt, G., Meyer, K., Erlinger, M., Betser, J., Sunshine, C., and Yemini, Y. (1995), "Decentralizing Control and Intelligence in Network Management", *Proceedings of the 4th International Symposium on Integrated Network Management, Santa Barbara, CA, May 1995*.

Net-SNMP Project (2001), *The Net-SNMP Project Home Page*, http://net-snmp.sourceforge.net

Perkins, D. and McGinnis, E. (1997), *Understanding SNMP MIBs*, Prentice Hall, New Jersey.

Stallings, W. (1997), *SNMP, SNMPv2 and RMON: practical network management*, Addison-Wesley, Reading.

Zeltserman, D. (1999), *A practical guide to SNMPv3 and networks management*, Prentice Hall, New Jersey.

Smart Push Model in Distributed Network Monitoring

Chanki Jeong

Department of Electrical and Computer Engineering
Florida Institute of Technology, Melbourne, Florida 32901-6995
Email: cjeong@fit.edu

Abstract

Current network management systems (NMSs) based on SNMP are inherently designed with a centralized computing paradigm. It is now well known that this type of management systems embodies many structural problems such as a single point of failure, management communication bottleneck and overhead, and higher computing requirement of a single system. Especially, the polling-oriented mode (pull mode) of SNMP operation involves substantial data transmission between manager and agents that can add a considerable stress on the user data traffic of the network. Here, we introduce a new management concept called smart push model for distributed network monitoring. In this model, mobile management components are used to execute network monitoring tasks closer to or on the distributed network elements where network problems are monitored quickly or are reported automatically without the need of polling. Monitoring policies can be easily changed as administrative requirements change, by the administrator remotely controlling the delegated components, accessing their methods, and modifying their properties. In addition, the mobile components incorporate the extended concept of the meta-variable representing semantic or high-level compression of the MIB (Management Information Base) variables. It provides a natural filtering of the management data.

Keyword: Distributed Network Monitoring, Smart Push, SNMP, Flexible Server, Mobile Component

1. Introduction

Network management architectures like SNMP (Simple Network Management Protocol) and CMIP (Common Management Information Protocol) are defined in terms of manager and agent. The network manager accesses management data through the management agent that resides on the network elements. Network elements are any network connected equipments, network-connected computers, and also, network-based applications. The agent maintains MIBs composed of management variables describing the operation of network elements, providing the primitive management services (e.g., *(M)-get* and *(M)-set*) to the manager where the network administrator monitors and controls networks or network elements.

NMSs based on SNMP are inherently designed with a centralized computing paradigm. The polling-oriented mode (pull mode) of operation of SNMP has many drawbacks in respect to performance, scalability and inefficient use of network resources (Goldszmidt and Yemini, 1995). Most MIB variables are transitive, changing very quickly. The management data may be useless without retrieving them in time. The management capability is bounded by the rate at which managers can handle management data and network events. For example, NMSs try to keep their local information repository as recent as possible with lookup of MIB variables. The pull mode involves substantial data transmission between manager and agent that can add a considerable stress on the original network traffic. The protocol inefficiency of the SNMP makes the above situation worse. In the SNMP Protocol Data Unit (PDU) the amount of administrative data transferred is very large compared to the actual data, i.e., compare the Object Identifier (OID) (e.g., *1.3.6.1.2.1.2.1.0*) used only to name a MIB variable (*ifNumber*) with the actual value (e.g., 7).

Over last decade, network environment has been dramatically complicated in terms of the number of network elements and the size of MIBs to be monitored, which makes the management more and more difficult. Today a high-end network element (e.g., Cisco Router) can have as many as tens of thousand MIB variables or more. With the addition of many new standard MIBs, we have also seen a growing number of vendor-specific MIBs that represents diverse management features. This explosive semantic heterogeneity of MIB variables makes the development of management applications very difficult. In addition, due to the high-speed network or network elements, the time period over which the network behaviors need to be monitored is too short where the polled data may easily exceed the processing capacity of network management systems, quickly going beyond the limit of the bandwidth available. In particular, the current management paradigm is unsuitable to address manageability of this high-speed network or elements.

Martin-Flatin (Martin-Flatin, 1999) introduced the novel concept called push model, and showed the advantages of using HTTP rather than SNMP to transport management data from agents to managers without polling. In this model, management agents advertise MIB variables they support and distribute the management data subscribed by the administrator to the manager. We try to push this model in more advanced direction in terms of flexibility and efficiency. The management of large, complex, and high-speed networks may be dramatically improved by moving management intelligence closer to or on the network elements being managed, by tailoring management data on the elements to the current interests of the administrator, and by automating monitoring, reporting, and even control. This most radical concept came from Management by Delegation (MbD) (Goldszmidt and Yemini, 1998). One approach is SNMPscript (Levi and Schoenwaelder, 1998). However, SNMPscript has serious restrictions related to its expression as a programming language and to the limited area of its applicability (SNMP only). Mobile agents (Bieszczad *et al.*, 1998) (Puliafito and Tomarchio, 2000) which add the concept of mobility to MbD have been investigated since the late 90's. Due to the operation characteristics and scalability problem, the mobile agent paradigm may not be applied to a general network management model while it is well fitted to a few specific management problems (e.g., network flow monitoring).

Network administrators are looking to lower costs, increase flexibility, and reduce the complexity involved in managing their networks. We propose a new management concept called smart push model for distributed network monitoring. The model is implemented on the Chameleon framework that we have designed and is presented in Section 2. In this model, the mobile management components are used to execute network monitoring tasks closer to or on the distributed network elements where network problems are monitored quickly or are reported automatically without the need of polling. Monitoring policies can change easily as administrative requirements change, by the administrator remotely controlling the delegated components, accessing their methods, and modifying their properties. Compared with other delegation approaches, it is important to note that the delegates themselves export their methods and properties to managers, being easily customized according to the current monitoring interest of the administrator where great flexibility and efficiency is gained.

2. Chameleon: A New Architecture

Chameleon is a flexible[1], dynamically extensible architecture and framework for network-management software development. The Chameleon has been designed with the intent to simplify the implementation of flexibly distributed network management applications. The Chameleon is based upon established software-development paradigms: mobile-code paradigm and software-component paradigm. This approach will make distributed network management software easy to develop and use, overcoming typical problems that affect current network management systems. Chameleon is composed of three core elements: Flexible Server, Mobile Management Component (or mobile objects), and Management Adapter, being implemented in Java language. Figure 1 presents an outline of the Chameleon architecture.

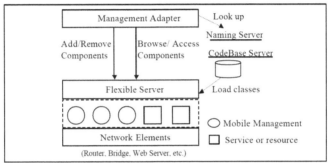

Figure 1: Chameleon Environment

2.1 Flexible Server

A Flexible Server is a remote object[2] that implements the *Chameleon* remote interface[3]. It incorporates a software backplane, which provides a mechanism that expedites dynamic composition of network management components. While the Flexible Server itself dose not reflect the management domain, management intelligence is realized in management components and services. Its core role is to keep a list of management components and provide them with references to other management components, services, and resources they can use to perform network management.

The extension of management capabilities of a Flexible Server is achieved by installing management services. Management services offer basic services (e.g., MIB access) that all management components need and use. Management services are any Class objects that define an interface protocol (a contract) between the factory object of management services and an arbitrary object associated with a mobile management component in a Flexible Server. Actual implementation of management services is realized in the factory object that acts like a service provider.

---

[1] It is not dependent on a specific platform. It is transparent to the location. It is open to dynamic management environments.

[2] Objects that have methods that can be called beyond networks or virtual machines are remote objects.

[3] A remote interface is an abstract class (a contract between clients and remote objects), which defines the methods that can be remotely called.

Management adapters add management components to Flexible Servers on demand when they are needed, where management adapters should also be able to browse the mobile management components embedded in a Flexible Server and remove the management components when no longer in use. While management components are moved and live in a Flexible Server, the Flexible Server should provide a component-based runtime environment that defines how management components interact with a Flexible Server, which allows management components to use management services or system resources and to communicate with other components. The runtime environment is characterized by an inversion of control: the control is passed to a management component through a reactive control-dispatching mechanism. When a management component is dropped into the runtime environment of the Flexible Server, an event is fired, where the Flexible Server provides the components with a reference to itself and the component can interrogate the environments in order to employ management services and to access other components for bigger and complete management solutions. The Flexible Server is a multithreaded environment within which independent management components act and interact.

2.2 Mobile Management Component

Mobile objects are objects that move between two Java Virtual Machines (processes) on the same host or the network. Both the state and code of the object can move from one application to the other application across the network (Nelson 1999). Mobile objects provide basis for the dynamically extensible capability of the Chameleon. With the help of Remote Method Invocation (RMI), a mobile object can be delegated as a normal remote invocation-style communication. An extension on the concept of mobile objects leads to the introduction of mobile components derived from the Java component model. Mobile components provide an extended component model that enables management components to move across a network. A mobile management component is a mobile object that extends JavaBean and has management intelligence. Any management component that follows the Bean component protocol can be a member of the Flexible Server, where it can exploit management services and communicate with other management components.

A mobile management component should be able to act without user intervention on the Flexible Server in order to complete its management task. An active management components that encapsulate its own thread of execution on its behalf is useful and indispensable in the Chameleon architecture. An active management component needs to implement the *Runnable* interface (i.e., run () method). Its active method employs the management intelligence.

2.3 Management Adapter

A management adapter uses the RMI call semantics in order to delegate the mobile management components to Flexible Servers; it locates Flexible Servers using a naming system and creates mobile management components, which it adds to Flexible Servers through remote method calls. It also receives condensed and semantic management information (high-level management information) by the response of its delegation or remote access. Management adapters can browse management components with a remote interface and remotely access fine-grained management functions of the components. When management components are delegated, a management adapter delegates the components to a Flexible Server (*delegate unicast*), a subset of Flexible Servers (*delegate multicast*) or all of

Flexible Servers (*delegate broadcast*) according to the delegation policy (IP addresses) defined by a network administrator.

3. Smart Push model

Our approach to network monitoring calls for the dynamic distribution of the monitoring tasks in the network. It enables shorter monitoring loops, removes long haul dissemination of redundant and unimportant management data, and hence reduces network overhand of management data and the CPU burden of centralized management system. Figure 2 shows our approach, which represents a smart push model based on the Chameleon paradigm for network monitoring. The Chameleon allows the dynamic distribution of active monitoring components programmed in a high-level programming language (Java), in the network, providing a SNMP interface used by the delegated monitoring components. Instead of being restricted to a limited set of hard-wired data collection primitive on a polling basis over a network link, the high-level programming interface allows to dynamically add, remove and update monitoring capability at the network elements directly. The SNMP interface is not specific to Flexible Manager of the Chameleon, so it should be possible to employ any other management architecture (e.g., CMIP). The interface built as a local service in the Flexible Server provides the dispatched monitoring components with access to the SNMP agent or SNMP MIBs. The monitoring components interact with the service through the Flexible Server, invoke SNMP get or set operations to retrieve management data, and push the result from high-level evaluation of the data to managers.

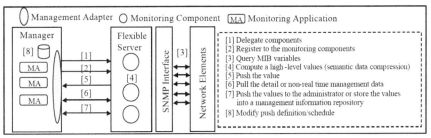

Figure 2: Smart Push Model

The deployment of the Chameleon may increase the resource consumption on network elements hosting the Flexible Server and monitoring components. In the Chameleon, activation mechanism can help to minimize the system resources that are used by the Flexible Server or components; the components are activated (i.e., instantiated and exported) on demand without running all the time. However, some network elements with limited computing power may not be able to incorporate the Chameleon. In order to manage such elements, we can deploy the Flexible Server of the Chameleon on a platform with sufficient resource closer to such network elements to be monitored. In this way, a network administrator is able to monitor any network elements.

The management adapter plays a key role in the design and development of a monitoring system based on the Chameleon. The management adapter integrates the network manager into the smart push components or system by providing a monitoring interface to network elements. The management user interface is designed with Web technology like HTML, applet, servlet, and etc. Web technology help to simplify and unify the management interface. Here, the Web browser becomes a monitoring console through which a network administrator watches the network. This mobilizes the access point of network monitoring, allowing network administrators or users to monitor the network at any time and anywhere.

The Web browser downloads an applet including fault or performance indicators (e.g., graphic icon and sound) where the indicators are continuously refreshed by monitoring applications evaluating the recent network information pushed from remote monitoring components. The other approach is to use a regular Java program to dynamically generate a HTML page including monitoring indicators. The HTML page is automatically pulled at regular interval. If an indicator (an icon) changes its color to red or yellow, it means that a network element or network entered some kind of critical state. In this situation, the network administrator clicks the icon and more detailed information (e.g., other icon group or tabular information) is provided. Through all this, the network administrators or users do not need to know that the monitoring system is based on the Chameleon, as the management adapter handles all the detail involved with delegating monitoring components or using them. The management adapter allows the network administrator or manager to access the methods or properties of the monitoring components where the push definition or push schedule is dynamically altered according to the current monitoring policy defined by the administrator. The push definition is to describe at which MIB variables the monitoring component wants to look and push schedule is to describe at what frequency the component retrieves and pushes MIB variables, or the high-level value computed from several MIB variables. In the other side, pull model can be also implemented without any modification of our approach. A method of the delegated monitoring component employs some management intelligence like a monitoring algorithm or a MIB table lookup procedure and is accessed by only remote method calls when needed. The pull model may complement the push model and both model are easily combined where the better monitoring algorithms can be evaluated.

Over the last decade, network environment has been dramatically complicated in terms of the number of network elements and the size of MIBs to be monitored, which makes the network monitoring more and more effortful. A network element (e.g., high-end router) may have tends of thousand of MIB variable to be monitored. These MIB variables are not information but simple data. Network administrators or manager must cope with these raw data: simple data is difficulty to interpret rather than information. In our approach, monitoring applications or monitoring components can be viewed as an information producer which collects MIB values, analyzes it, and produce high-level information (e.g., indicators) for administrators. An extension of a Meta-Variable (MV) concept (Wellens and Auerbach, 1996) is employed in the manager and monitoring components (see Figure 3 and Table 1).

An Extended Meta-Variable (EMV) is defined as a function of real MIB variables and meta-variables. The EMVs that are presented or visualized to the network administrator are called the indicators representing network fault, performance problem, and security problem. To evaluate these EMVs, the manager or delegated monitoring components would have to perform the EMV functions which may be a simple mathematical formula (or program logic) or an complex AI feature. For example, a smart monitoring function may be an expert system that has an inference engine to detect critical situations. The output of such complex system evaluating potentially hundreds of MIB variables is usually a decision as to whether or not an action should be taken.

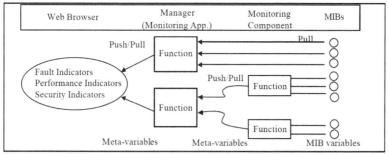

Figure 3: Overview of Extended Meta-Variables Concept

Meta-variables	Functions f(MIB variables)
If Forwarding Rates	$(\text{ifInOctets}_{y\text{-}x} - \text{ifOutOctets}_{y\text{-}x}) / (y\text{-}x)$
If Utilization	$(\text{ifInOctets}_{y\text{-}x} + \text{ifOutOctets}_{y\text{-}x}) / ((y\text{-}x)^*\text{ifSpeed})$
If Percent Input Errors	$\text{ifInErrors}_{y\text{-}x}/(\text{ifInUcastPkts}_{y\text{-}x}+\text{ifInNUcastPkts}_{y\text{-}x})$
If Percent Output Errors	$\text{ifOutErrors}_{y\text{-}x}/(\text{ifOutUcastPkts}_{y\text{-}x}+\text{ifOutNUcastPkts}_{y\text{-}x})$

If: interface x, y: MIB variable lookup time

Table 1: An Example of Simple Meta-Variables

In this case, the delegated components can do any corrective action on the network element and the network can be self-managed. In the EMV, a set of network elements (or a set of MIB values from different MIB groups (or MIBs)) is treated logically as a collection. Thus MVs can be defined which gives the state of health of such collections. Such information in nature leads to automatic root cause analysis by pinpointing the problem clusters and identifying the possible cause of problem. If used appropriately, the smart push model employing the EMVs can lead to more efficient distributed network monitoring.

4. Implementation

This section presents some initial results from building a prototype of smart push model to prove our concept. We installed the Chameleon system on 5 machines (PCs and a SUN, see Figure 4). The delegated components in the Flexible Server should speak SNMP to retrieve MIB variables. A SNMP stack was added as a local service to the Flexible Server. In order to develop the prototype quickly and be able to focus on high-level functionality, we used an on-line available SNMP stack (OutBack Resource Group). To demonstrate the Chameleon and smart push model, networked PCs with a SNMP agent were used.

We have implemented two basic types of mobile components: MibBrowser component and EmvEvaluator component. After being delegated, the MibBrowser component queries MIB variables (e.g., get or get-next) through the local SNMP interface, waits for the reply from the SNMP stack, saves the data obtained in an internal structure. Then if it has finished looking up the requested MIB variables, it pushes the information packed in a variable (e.g., vector) to the manager. The administrator or manager can continuously look up the MIB variables in either push (or pull) basis according to the current monitoring interest or schedule (see Figure 5). The EmvEvaluator monitor a few meta-variables (e.g., interface utilization) defined in the previous section, pushing the result values to manager based on the push schedule. In addition, if the value of the meta-variables hit the predefined threshold, an alarm is sent to the manager. After the manager or the monitoring applications receive the pushed information from the components, it dynamically generates and pushes HTML pages including the data (e.g., MIB values or indicators) to web browser, if necessary, storing the values as history data in a database (see Figure 6).

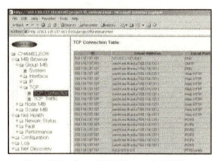

Figure 5: Lookup of TCP Connection Tables

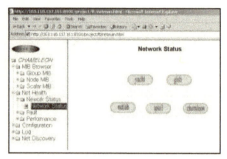

Figure 6: Network Status Monitoring (Interface Utilization)

5. Conclusion

This paper describes a new management concept called smart push model based on the Chameleon framework for dynamic and distributed network monitoring. The Chameleon is designed to simplify the implementation of flexible distributed network management. To prove our concept, two examples (MibBrowser and EmvEvaluator components) have been implemented and introduced in the Chameleon. The management of large, complex, and high-speed networks can be dramatically improved by delegating monitoring components, by tailoring the management data on the network elements to the current interest of the administrators, and by automating monitoring and reporting.

6. References

Bieszczad, A. and Pagurek, B. and White, T. (1998), "Mobile Agents for Network manager", *IEEE Communications Surveys*, Vol.1 No.1.

Goldszmidt, G. and Yemini, Y. (1995), "Distributed Management by Delegation", *15th International Conference on Distributed Computing Systems*.

Goldszmidtz, G. and Yemini, Y. (1998), "Delegated Agents for Network Management", *IEEE Communication Magazine*.

Levi, D. B. and Schoenwaelder, J. (1998), "Script MIB", *The Internet Draft*.

Martin-Flatin, J.P. (1999) "Push vs. Pull in Web-Based Network Management", *6th IEEE International Symposium on Integrated Network Management*, Boston, Maryland, USA.

Nelson, J. (1999), "Programming Mobile Objects with Java", *Wiley & Sons*.

OutBack Resource Group: "JSNMP v2", URL http://www.outbackinc.com

Puliafito, A. and Tomarchio, O. (2000), "Using Mobile Agents to implement flexible Network Management Strategies", *Computer Communication Journal*, 23(98).

Wellens, C. and Auerbach, K. (1996), "Toward Useful Management", *The Simple Time*.

On Lifetime Extension and Route Stabilization of Energy-Efficient Broadcast Routing over MANET

Intae Kang and Radha Poovendran

Department of Electrical Engineering
University of Washington, Seattle, WA. 98195-2500, U.S.A.
e-mail: {kangit, radha}@ee.washington.edu

Abstract

In this paper, we address the problem of energy efficient multicast routing in wireless Mobile Adhoc NETwork (MANET). It is a challenging environment because every node operates on limited battery resource and multi-hop routing paths are used over constantly changing network environments due to node mobility. We define the network lifetime as duration of time until first node failure due to battery energy exhaustion, and show that network lifetime for a multicast session can be significantly extended by additionally considering the residual battery energy as a parameter in cost metric functions for constructing a power efficient routing tree. Using simulation results, we show that the lifetime extension can lead to oscillatory behavior of routing path selection. We propose a solution to stabilize the oscillations by considering a statistical measure in our cost metric and present simulations that show the oscillation can be reduced greatly at a small cost of network lifetime.

Keywords

MANET, Adhoc Networks, Energy Efficient Routing, Multicasting Tree, BIP Algorithm

1. Introduction

The military mobile network consisting of soldiers on the move, emergency search and rescue, dynamic coalitions and ubiquitous computing are some of the applications that make use of wireless mobile adhoc networking that make extensive use of multicast/broadcast communications (Singh *et al*, 1998). A salient feature of many of these networks is the use of micro-processor embedded, energy constrained devices that have the capability to perform advanced computations. Due to the battery energy constraint of these devices, it is essential to develop computational/networking algorithms and protocols that are optimized for energy consumption under each clock cycle. The battery energy of a transmitting node can be depleted due to : (a) computational processing at the node, (b) transmission attenuation due to path loss, and (c) the need to maintain the transmission above a certain threshold due to signal interference.

Designing energy-efficient unicast algorithms and protocols has been an active area of research (Chang and Tassiulas, 2000), (Singh *et al*, 1998), and (Toh, 2001). A recent study (Lee *et al*, 2000) presents extensive comparison on the performance of different multicast routing protocols suitable for MANET and concludes that ODMRP which combines on-demand and mesh-based approach has the best performance when energy is not a constraint. Since the ODMRP uses a flooding scheme to set up the routes, the use of it in the case of energy constrained networks will lead to rapid battery exhaustion. Hence, new approaches that incorporate energy constraints and increase lifetime of the node battery are needed.

In a series of recent papers, (Wan *et al*, 2001) and (Wieselthier *et al*, 2000) presented an approach that tries to develop energy-efficient broadcast routing trees. They presented a tree construction algorithm that makes use of needed power expenditure by the nodes in developing an energy-efficient routing solution.

In this paper, we show that their solution can be improved to extend the overall lifetime of the network significantly. Such an extension also comes with the additional challenges of route path oscillations that need to be reduced/damped using statistical techniques.

In the next section, some preliminary background on BIP algorithm is outlined. In section 3, we discuss the problem of determining and exchanging transmission power level, which is essential for actually constructing a power efficient tree. In sections 4 and 5, we propose different metrics to increase network lifetime and reduce oscillations. Section 6 presents our simulation model and summarizes the main simulation results and section 7 concludes this paper with our future research.

2. Background

In this paper, the best effort to conserve energy at each instance of time and to extend the lifetime of the multicast session is made using a power efficient multicast tree and by updating this tree regularly in a strategic manner. We use a recently proposed power-efficient multicast tree construction algorithm as a building block and construct our cost functions. Based on these newly proposed cost functions, we derive solutions that lead to significant improvements in extending the network lifetime while reducing the oscillations in routing algorithms. We now review the broadcast advantage feature of the omni-directional antenna in wireless medium, also available in (Wieselthier *et al*, 2000).

Figure 1: (a) Geometric construct of a sender S and receivers M_1 and M_2 (b) Wireless broadcast advantage

2.1   Wireless Broadcast Advantage

Fig.1(a) shows a single sender S with receivers M_1 and M_2 at distances of d_1 and d_2, respectively, from the sender. We assume that $d_2 > d_1$ and the received power at a node varies as $d_i^{-\alpha}$ (i=1, 2) where α is the path loss factor satisfying ($2 \leq \alpha \leq 4$). Hence, the transmission power required to reach a node at a distance d_i is proportional to d_i^{α} assuming the proportionality constant is 1. Fig.1(b) shows the broadcast nature of the wireless medium for omni-directional antenna in which a unit of message sent to receiver A at the boundary of the circle reaches every node within the circle for "free." In order to transmit an identical message to nodes M_1 and M_2, S can use two unicast transmissions with individual power d_1^{α} and d_2^{α} with total expenditure of $(d_1^{\alpha} + d_2^{\alpha})$. However, it can be reduced to max($d_1^{\alpha}, d_2^{\alpha}$) by taking advantage of the fact that the wireless medium is naturally "broadcast." Under this assumption, the sender has to choose between the following two strategies: (a) if $d_2^{\alpha} > d_1^{\alpha} + d_{12}^{\alpha}$, transmit to M_1 and let M_1 transmit to M_2, (b) otherwise, transmit to M_2 (M_1 will automatically receive it due to wireless broadcast advantage since $d_2 > d_1$). Hence, joint consideration of transmission and routing leads to savings in battery energy.

For an arbitrary network topology, the construction of a routing tree with globally minimum total power expenditure does not have a known algorithm. However, there is a suboptimal solution (Wieselthier *et al*, 2000) called the *Broadcast Incremental Power* (BIP) algorithm that uses a greedy approach to construct a tree. We describe it below.

2.2 Description of the BIP Algorithm

Input: given an undirected weighted graph $G(N, A)$, where N: set of nodes, A: set of edges
Initialization: set $T := \{S\}$ where S is the source node of multicast session.
  Set $P(i) := 0$ for all $1 \leq i \leq |N|$ where $P(i)$ is the transmission power of node i.
Procedure: while $|T| \neq |N|$
  find an edge $(i, j) \in T \times (N-T)$ such that incremental power $\Delta P_{ij} = d_{ij}^{\alpha} - P(i)$ is minimum.
  add node j to T, i.e., $T := T \cup \{j\}$.
  set $P(i) := P(i) + \Delta P_{ij}$.

The BIP algorithm uses the broadcast advantage property while constructing a power efficient tree. As with other heuristic greedy algorithms, this algorithm is not globally optimal in producing a multicast tree with minimum total power expenditure. Currently, there is no known algorithm (except exhaustive search) that leads to a globally optimal solution and is also computationally efficient. Moreover, due to the distributed nature of adhoc networks, the source node may not have global knowledge of network topology in advance, without which tree construction is not possible. This point is not addressed in the original paper (Wieselthier et al, 2000). We present schemes to collect network topology information for three specific cases.

3. Transmitting Power Information for Power-Efficient Tree Construction

Since the senders (source/relaying nodes) do not know the appropriate transmission power level a priori to reach intended receivers, some strategies should be developed to decide the power level based on the feedback from the receivers. The mechanism of exchanging power information is important to maintain the network connectivity. We present solutions to this problem for three different cases depending on the availability of location information and/or the ability for a receiver to sense the power level. In presenting our solutions, we assume that a transmitter can adjust its power level dynamically.

3.1 Proposed solution when the location information is available

In this scenario, it is assumed that location information is provided by using global positioning system (GPS) and each mobile host is equipped with a GPS receiver. The idea of applying GPS to unicast routing was first reported in (Ko and Vaidya, 1998), but their use of GPS was to limit the search space in route discovery process to reduce control overhead, not to determine the transmission power level.

We assume that each node i knows (x_i, y_i) coordinates of itself at every instance of time. By including these coordinates into the header of each packet, and by collecting the positions of multicast member nodes, the sender can easily construct a multicast tree based on the BIP algorithm. Since the coordinate pair can be inserted directly into the IP header, a routing algorithm which resides in the network layer can easily utilize that information. Now the sender node i transmits its beacon or HELLO packet with maximum available power P_{max} where the node i inserts its coordinate. If a receiver node j is within the transmission range, it can record the coordinate of node i (the backward channel is established). As a response, node j also transmits with its maximum power by inserting its coordinates in the beacon packet (the forward channel is established). Hence, the amount of minimum transmit power to maintain the link can be easily calculated and the senders can switch to power efficient mode and transmit data packets with minimum required power to preserve battery resource. Because high reliability is usually required for control packets, they have higher priority than data packets, and thus flooding with maximum power P_{max} is assumed for the controls packets. If additional information such as velocity is given by GPS, we can constructively utilize this information to optimize several other criteria.

3.2 When receiver can measure the power level of the received signal

Let the sender and the receiver be denoted by indices i and j. If a receiver can sense the power level of the received signal denoted as P_j, it can record and transmit this value back to the sender i. The sender can make use of the knowledge about the attenuation factor α and the maximum power P_{max} to compute the required power to node j as $P_{ij} = P_{max}/P_j$. Note that since the power level keeps changing in a wireless environment depending on the node speed and surrounding environment due to multipath fading and shadowing, the recorded value should be a statistical average value over a short term interval.

3.3 Location information is unavailable and receiver cannot measure the power level

This is the most strict environment in the sense that no information is available which facilitates easy determination of relevant transmit power. One possible solution to determine the power level in this environment is to use an *expanding ring search*, which is a technique sometimes used in other network applications such as in IGMP. At the network layer, a series of packets are generated with specified power level, $P_1 < P_2 < \ldots < P_L \leq P_{max}$. Every bit in each control packet is transmitted with the same power level specified in the header. Note that once one of the packets with power P_i ($1 \leq i \leq L$) is captured by the receiver, it can extract the specified power level from the packet header and ignores all the subsequent packets with larger power levels $P_{i+1}, P_{i+2}, \ldots, P_L$. This can be achieved by utilizing a broadcast ID and the source address together. Notice that the same broadcast ID should be used for each packet because only one of them will be captured at the receiver and all the others are discarded, i.e., if the source address and the broadcast ID of the packets are the same, only the first captured one with minimum attainable power level is kept.

A guard time between the control packets is desirable to reduce the collision at the receiver and to give enough transition time for a RF transceiver to switch to relevant transmission power level. In this way, a receiver can determine the minimum amount of power level to establish a link from a sender to itself. Although there is a continuous range of assignable power levels, the number of levels should be quantized to a finite number to reduce delay. The choice of individual power level P_i and the number of levels will induce inherent performance degradation (accuracy of minimum power level) which is an inevitable result due to the unavailability of local information and direct power measurement.

4. Proposed Cost Metrics for Network Lifetime Extension

We define the *network lifetime* as duration of time until the first node in a network fails due to the battery exhaustion. If all the nodes have identical initial energy levels, the node which dies first will be the one which spends the battery energy at the highest rate. If we want to extend the lifetime of the network, it is critical to incorporate the residual battery energy into route updates. Although the BIP algorithm produces a power efficient multicast routing tree for a single transmission of a packet (which is efficient for a short term period), it does not deal with maximization of the lifetime (which is a long term concept) of a network. Moreover, in a more realistic scenario, the tree structure derived by BIP can not be maintained for a long period of time due to the host mobility, changing environment and dynamic membership change in multicast session, and eventually it has to be updated either periodically or when the network configuration changes. We reformulate the BIP as an optimization problem and propose a modified metric for lifetime extension.

4.1 Reformulation of the BIP algorithm

Finding a multicast routing tree T_{BIP} with BIP algorithm can be reformulated as a corresponding optimization problem as follows:

$$T_{BIP} \cong \arg\min_{T \subset G(N,A)} \sum_{(i,j) \in T} \Delta P_{ij} \qquad (1)$$

over all possible trees T that are subgraphs of $G(N,A)$ and all edges (i, j) contained in the tree T. Note that (1) is written as an approximation not an equality, because BIP algorithm is not guaranteed to produce a global solution. Similar formulation will be adopted throughout this section for notational simplicity. The exact meaning of it should be interpreted as an algorithmic description explained in section 2.2. The objective here is to minimize the total incremental transmission power defined as a sum of all non-zero incremental powers. The corresponding total transmit power assigned to the tree is:

$$P_{total}(T_{BIP}) = \sum_{(i,j) \in T_{BIP}} \Delta P_{ij} = \sum_{i \in N} P(i).$$

It was the main contribution of (Wieselthier *et al*, 2000) that the total power can be approximately minimized in wireless environment by solving the optimization problem (1).

4.2 Proposed cost metric for extending network lifetime using Weighted BIP (WBIP)

We noted that the original BIP algorithm in (1) does not incorporate the residual battery energy into route tree selection. In order to incorporate the residual battery energy into the cost function, we weigh the incremental power ΔP_{ij} while constructing the total weighted cost function C_{ij}. The weighting function denoted by W_i for node i is a time dependent function. The corresponding optimal tree is given by:

$$T_{WBIP} \cong \arg\min_{T \subset G(N,A)} \sum_{(i,j) \in T} W_i \Delta P_{ij} \text{ where } W_i = E_{total} / \left(E_{total} - \sum_{k=0}^{n} E_{ik} \right) \qquad (2)$$

and E_{total} is the initial battery energy of node i, and E_{ik} represents the amount of energy consumed at node i during the k-th update interval (Δt). Therefore, the denominator of W_i represents the remaining battery energy of node i at time $t = n \Delta t$. Notice here that the weighting factor W_i is initially set to unity (therefore, BIP) and as time progresses and as more energy is consumed, W_i is monotonically increasing (i.e., $W_i \geq 1$). The cost metric $C_{ij} \equiv W_i \Delta P_{ij}$ (WBIP) includes both *node-based* cost and *link-based* cost. The battery energy, which is a characteristic of a node, is represented in W_i. The more a node has remaining energy, the less W_i is and, therefore, there is a greater chance for this node with large battery capacity to be assigned with a larger transmit power. The reason for W_i being called node-based cost is that this value is equally weighted to all links to which this node is incident. On the other hand, ΔP_{ij} is a link-based cost because different values are assigned for each link (i, j). Although the new cost metric will lead to extension of lifetime of the network, it can often lead to an undesirable oscillatory behavior among paths of the route tree. We first illustrate this behavior and then propose a convex cost function that can reduce the oscillations among routes.

5. Routing Path Oscillations and Proposed Solution

In Fig.2, we present the WBIP based routing tree solution at different time instances for 15 nodes in 10×10 grid with $\alpha = 2$. The oscillations of the route paths for different time instances are visually clear if we consider the lower half of the network. The remaining battery level is represented with a shaded rectangle. It can be observed that the battery depletion is evenly distributed among the nodes with this metric. However, the oscillations can have an adverse

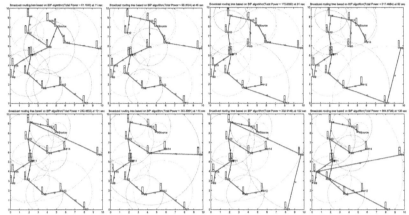

Figure 2: Routing tree oscillation problem for a sample network configuration with 15 nodes

effect on designing a routing protocol because it can result in out-of-order packet arrivals. We now present a modification to the cost metric function that will reduce the route oscillations.

5.1 Proposed cost metric for simultaneously extending lifetime and reducing route path oscillations (WBIPST): Oscillations in routing paths is not a new problem. Some counter measures for oscillation problem are provided in (Khanna and Zinky, 1989). In the case of energy-efficient broadcast, the oscillations arise since the WBIP is sensitive to any small change in remaining battery energy level of a node. Our approach uses a statistical measure to reduce oscillations by averaging the costs of links over a time period spanning more than one update intervals (minimizing variance of the link costs is another possible choice). The cost metric proposed for longer lifetime of the network with stability (WBIPST) is given as:

$$T_{WBIPST} \cong \arg\min_{T \subset G(N,A)} \sum_{(i,j) \in T} \overline{W}_i^t \Delta P_{ij} \quad \text{where } \overline{W}_i^t = \lambda_t W_i^t + (1-\lambda_t)\overline{W}_i^{t-1} \qquad (3)$$

and λ_t is a time dependent function satisfying $0 \le \lambda_t \le 1$ for all time. This is a modification to (2) with a convex combination of the weighted average of the previous average value and current cost metric value. This cost metric is also a time dependent function and less sensitive to residual battery energy. Note that trees found with these newly proposed metrics (2) and (3) are constructed in the same greedy fashion as BIP and also not guaranteed to be optimal but better than BIP in terms of lifetime extension.

6. Simulation Results

In this section simulations are performed with a simplified network model according to the different metrics BIP, WBIP and WBIPST presented in the previous section. Within a 10×10 square grid region, network configurations are randomly generated with uniform distribution of nodes and multicast trees are constructed from the source node. Path loss exponents of $\alpha =$ 2, 3 and 4 are separately considered in the simulation. To isolate the effect of each metric, all the generated nodes are assumed to be in the multicast group (broadcasting). Initial energy of the battery in each node is assumed to be 1000 units and the broadcast tree is updated at every specified update interval (Δt). Constant bit rate (CBR) traffic model is used. The simulation results are for the static network topology without node mobility and no restriction on the maximum available transmission power $P_{max} = \infty$ is imposed. At every update interval, the

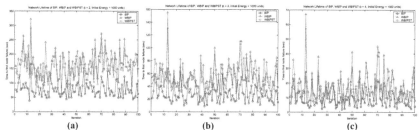

(a)   (b)   (c)

Figure 3: Network lifetime of BIP,WBIP and WBIPST for (a) α=2 (b) α=3 (c) α=4 (100 network instances)

Path	Mean/STD of Network Lifetime(sec)			Gain	Mean/STD of Oscillation		
Loss	BIP	WBIP	WBIPST	(%)	BIP	WBIP	WBIPST
α=2	78.1/24.8	170.8/43.5	147.4/40.5	118.7	0	2203.1/655.3	920.1/495.9
α=3	27.7/12.8	58.9/20.9	50.3/17.6	112.6	0	667.3/290.1	283.8/155.6
α=4	9.2/5.7	17.7/10.1	15.6/8.7	92.4	0	173.6/124.7	90.4/63.7

Table 1: Mean and standard deviation of network lifetime and oscillations for 100 network instances: 20 nodes, Δt = 1(sec) where gain ≡ (WBIP−BIP)/WBIP×100%

amount of energy consumed during the time period is subtracted from the corresponding remaining energy level. Also, the energy consumption by transmission power only is assumed because reception or idle period power is relatively small compared to transmission power.

In Fig.3, the network lifetime is compared for different values of α = 2, 3 and 4 and for Δt = 1 second with 20 nodes. We used the function λ_t = $1/t$ in (3), which is equivalent to recursive formulation of time average, but other functions are also under investigation. In each case, 100 different network topologies are generated and network lifetime was calculated. The same random seeds are used for each metric for valid comparison.

Table 1 summarizes the performance in terms of network lifetime and oscillation count, in which the mean value, standard deviation (STD) and gain (percentage increase in lifetime over BIP) are shown. The number of oscillations is counted as a total sum of the number of link changes from a previous tree to a current tree until the first node failure. As propagation constant α becomes larger, the lifetime of the network is shortened significantly because the power expenditure is much larger ($d_{ij}^4 >> d_{ij}^2$). However, standard deviation becomes smaller as α becomes larger. We can observe that, by using WBIP and WBIPST, network lifetime is roughly prolonged by a factor of two (~100%) compared to BIP when Δt = 1, which is a significant enhancement assuming the given fixed amount of initial battery energy. By using WBIPST, more than half (58%) reduction in oscillation from WBIP is achieved at the cost of around 14% decrease in network lifetime and this is the price paid to reduce route oscillation. We note that oscillation for BIP is identically zero for static network.

The dependence of percentage increase in mean network lifetime of WBIP on the update interval for 100 instances with 20 nodes is shown in Fig.4(a) for α = 2, 3 and 4. For an update interval of 1 second (Δt = 1), there is about 100% increase in lifetime which is consistent with the result in Table 1. It is evident from Fig.4(a) that if tree is updated more frequently, the lifetime is prolonged further. A higher update rate translates to greater control overhead. Therefore the control overhead should be further analyzed so that we can choose a proper update interval in protocol specification. The dependence of lifetime and oscillations on the node density (number of nodes per 10×10 region) with Δt = 1 second is presented in Fig.4(b and c). For α = 2, lifetime increases almost linearly to the node density whereas the increase is

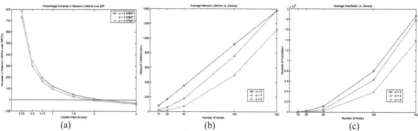

Figure 4: (a) Percentage increase in mean network lifetime vs. route update interval: 20 nodes (b) Network lifetime vs. node density: $\Delta t = 1$ sec (c) Routing path oscillation vs. node density: $\Delta t = 1$

more steep for $\alpha = 3$ and 4. In summary, our results show that there are essential trade-offs between network lifetime, oscillations, and update interval and therefore proper values should be chosen for protocol design.

7. Conclusions

Our contributions in this paper are, first, we looked at schemes that make the construction of a power-efficient tree possible for different scenarios, which will be used for protocol design. Second, we then presented modified cost function that enabled us to extend network lifetime significantly by a factor of two if the tree is updated every second. Finally, we introduced statistical measure in our proposed metric to damp route oscillations and showed that the oscillation can be cut down by half at a small cost of network lifetime.

Current trend of research in multicast routing protocols seems to be leaning toward mesh-based approach mainly because of superior performance of ODMRP. However, our results suggest that the tree-based protocols should also be further pursued because of their energy efficiency. Some of our planned future work involves finding a spanning tree with globally minimum total power, better metrics for lifetime extension and stability, and protocol design of this algorithm to conduct packet level simulation including node mobility.

8. References

Chang, J.H. and Tassiulas, L. (2000), "Energy conserving routing in wireless ad-hoc networks," *INFOCOM '2000.*

Khanna, A. and Zinky, J. (1989), "The revised ARPANET routing metric," *Proc of ACM SIGCOMM*, pp. 45-56.

Ko, Y.B. and Vaidya, N.H. (1998), "Location-aided routing (LAR) in mobile ad hoc networks," *Proc. MOBICOM*, pp. 66-75.

Lee, S.-J., Su, W., Hsu, J., Gerla, M. and Bagrodia, R. (2000), "A performance comparison study of ad hoc wireless multicast protocols," *INFOCOM 2000*, pp. 565-574.

Singh, S., Woo, M. and Raghavendra, C.S. (1998), "Power-aware routing in mobile ad hoc networks," *Proceedings of MOBICOM*, pp. 181-190.

Toh, C.-K. (2001), "Maximum battery life routing to support ubiquitous mobile computing in wireless ad hoc networks," *IEEE Communcations Magazine*, pp. 138-147.

Wan, P.-J., Calinescu, G., Li, X.-Y., and Frieder, O. (2001), "Minimum-Energy Broadcast Routing in Static Ad Hoc Wireless Networks." *Proc. IEEE INFOCOM 2001.*

Wieselthier, J.E., Nguyen, G.D. and Ephremides, A. (2000), "On the construction of energy-efficient broadcast and multicast trees in wireless networks," *Proc. IEEE INFOCOM 2000*, pp. 586--594.

Transition Strategies from IPv4 to IPv6: The case of GRNET

C. Bouras[1,2], P. Ganos[1], A. Karaliotas[1,2]

[1]Research Academic Computer Technology Institute, Patras, Greece
[2]Department of Computer Engineering and Informatics, University of Patras, Greece
e-mail: bouras@cti.gr

Abstract

In this paper we describe the results that came out from the project of employing the IPv6 protocol over the Greek Research & Technology Network (GRNET). In the way of this process one of the big issues that had to be considered was the transition strategy that would be deployed. The main goals of a transition strategy are to be smooth enough and therefore to put the less of configuration overhead to the end users and the network administrators.

Keywords

Networks, Protocols, IPv6, Transition mechanisms,

1. Introduction

The IP protocol and its current version, IP version 4, is the most widely used protocol in computer networks in our days. The big change that happened to the character of the Internet, from a rather academic network with low demands on resources to a commercial network with a variety of intensive applications running over it – considering also the integration of other communication services on it e.g. VoIP – showed the weakness of the fourth version to support the new networking applications. The reasons that led the Internet community to adopt the development of a new IP version are summarized in the following.

Lack of Addresses: The address space of IPv4 is 2^{32}. This space is decreasing because of the sub netting procedure and the dedicated areas in the IP space for several operations like private networks and multicasting. The IP space that has been left is running out. There are new demands for IPs, while new devices tend to connect to the IP networks, such as home devices and mobile phones.

Performance-Manageability: The lack of hierarchy levels in IP addresses results the existence of too many -hard to manage- routing entries to the routers. Also, several applications demand for Quality of Service (QoS) support from IPv4 and this shortcoming is overleaped by the use of protocols in higher levels with uncertain results.

Security: Considering the wide spread of Internet and its use for several transactions, like financial ones, the security is an issue that has to be supported by the IP protocol, which must be able to provide reliable and efficient security mechanisms.

Automatic Address Assignment: The configuration procedure in IPv4 hosts is complex and requires human interference. Users would prefer a procedure of type "plug and play". When a computer is plugged to the IP network, the connection parameters may be configured automatically without the human interference. This capability is suitable enough for mobile users.

The new version of IP protocol, IP version 6, seems to be a satisfactory solution of the above limitations (Deering and Hinden, 1998). It is foreseen that the deployment of IPv6 is probably inevitable and it is only a matter of time to see exactly when ipv6 will become the basic internetworking protocol. Since the number of network applications that currently IPv4 supports, is enormous and the porting procedure will cost much in terms of money and time, the only applicable solution that will lead to a global dominance of IPv6 is the coexistence of IPv4 and IPv6 for a quite large period of time. In a mixed situation, where both protocols co-exist communication between IPv4 hosts over an IPv6 network, IPv6 hosts over an IPv4 network and IPv6 host and an IPv4 host must be achievable.

2. Transition Mechanisms

The transition mechanisms are considered as a toolset to enable the smooth transition to the new version of the IP protocol. These mechanisms are divided into three (3) main categories depending on their operation and the way of their implementation: Dual Stack Mechanisms, Tunneling Mechanisms and Translation Mechanisms.

2.1. Dual Stack Mechanisms (DSM)

This mechanism is the deployment of a quite simple idea. Any host that desires to participate both in IPv4 and IPv6 networks has to maintain both stacks on its network interface(s). It enables a full IPv4 end-to-end communication between a dual stack host within an IPv6 only network and an IPv4 only host. The DST mechanism is based on tunneling mechanism using a dynamic tunnel interface combined with temporary IPv4 address assignment provided by a DHCPv6 server.

The Dual Stack Transition Mechanism (DSTM) is based on the usage of a DHCPv6 server, which assigns temporarily global IPv4 addresses to IPv6 hosts that wish to communicate with an IPv4 only host (Tsirtsis, 2000). The IPv4 packets are encapsulated into IPv6 packets through a DTI interface and are transferred within the IPv6 network to the Border Router, which interconnects the IPv6 network with the IPv4 network.

One critical issue for the implementation of the DST mechanism is the support of the Domain Name Service (DNS) and the impact of this service to the preference of a host to the IPv4 and/or the IPv6 protocol (Gilligan and Nordmark, 2000). In order a network host to be capable to communicate with other hosts by the use of both protocols, this host has to dispose the appropriate libraries and to ask the DNS for the address of IPv4, IPv6 and IPv4/IPv6 hosts. This means that the libraries have to be able to handle both A records (IPv4) and AAAA/A6 records (IPv6). It is concluded that the DNS support in DST mechanisms is a parameter that affects the network performance.

The operation of the DSTM is bi-directional, which means that the initialization of the communication may take place either from the IPv6 host side or the IPv4 host side. This is a major advantage of DTSM compared to other mechanisms, which allow the initialization of the communication only from the IPv6 host side. The DSTM requires the usage of a DHCP server and optionally the usage of a DNS server for the dynamic import of the temporary IPv4 address into the DNS database. Thus, the implementation of the DSTM matches more to small and medium network sizes that already use a DHCP server for the sharing of global IPv4 addresses. The main limitation for the implementation of DSTM focuses on the non-availability of a DHCPv6 server, because the standardization process has not been completed yet.

2.2. Tunneling Mechanisms

The tunnelling mechanisms may be used for the IPv6 communication over the existing IPv4 infrastructure and vice-versa. They are based on the encapsulation of IPv6 packets into IPv4 packets and the transmission over the IPv4 network. The two endpoints of the tunnel need to be dual stack routers or hosts.

The tunneling mechanisms are mainly divided into two main categories according to the way they are created: either by direct configuration on the endpoints of the tunnel or by coding of the address of the endpoint into the IPv6 address.

The first category supports the following two (2) mechanisms:

Configured Tunneling Mechanism: The term "Configured Tunnel" refers to the explicit definition in each endpoint of the tunnel of the IPv4 address of the opposite endpoint. According to this mechanism the IPv6 packets are encapsulated into IPv4 packets. The destination address of the IPv4 packets has been indicated in the creation of the tunneling interface on the router, while the source address is the IPv4 address of the interface. By this way routers build point-to-point links over the IPv4 infrastructure and these links are used for the transmission of the IPv6 packets. The implementation cost of the Configured Tunneling Mechanism is low because it allows the parallel development of the IPv6 infrastructure without the usage of separate physical links.

Tunnel Broker Mechanism: Tunnel Broker is a mechanism designed for users that want to participate to the IPv6 network but they are isolated from any native IPv6 network or for users who wish an early IPv6 adoption (Durant, Fasano et al, 2001). It provides quick connectivity to the IPv6 network in addition to the low administration cost. The tunnel broker assigns an IPv6 address to the Dual Stack host, which returns along with its DNS name and client configuration information. The main components of this mechanism are the tunnel broker entity and the tunnel broker server. The tunnel broker entity is used for the registration of the user and the tunnel activation for the connection to the IPv6 network. The tunnel broker server is an IPv4/IPv6 router connected to both networks.

The tunnel broker mechanism is targeted to the connectivity to the IPv6 network of remote users and small sites. However, it offers high scalability and can support a large number of remote users. This mechanism presents a limitation for the support of users who use private IPv4 addresses (NAT mechanism). Also, it is aimed more at short-term periods of native IPv6 connectivity rather than providing long term access.

The second category supports the following three (3) mechanisms:

Automatic Tunneling Mechanism: This mechanism utilizes the IPv4 compatible IPv6 addresses (Gilligan and Nordmark, 2000). For the application of this mechanism it is required only the installation of a software module to the hosts. This module is a pseudo-interface, which is responsible for the encapsulation of IPv6 packets into IPv4 packets and their forwarding over the IPv4 interface. This mechanism requires globally routable IPv4 addresses and excludes private addresses.

Usually, this mechanism is used in combination with a configured tunnel, in order to make able the IPv6 host to communicate with the total of IPv6 hosts (native IPv6 hosts and hosts using the 6to4 mechanism) and not only with hosts using automatic tunneling. As the automatic tunneling mechanism allows to remote hosts to have access to the IPv6 network and operates with a simple and flexible way, this mechanism can be combined with other mechanisms in order to achieve an end-to-end communication.

6to4 Transition Mechanism: The 6to4 mechanism enables IPv6 sites to connect to other IPv6 sites over the IPv4 network (Carpenter and Moore, 2001), (Tsirtsis, 2000). It does not employ any tunneling mechanism neither the host needs to have an IPv4 compatible IPv6 address. The only requirement is the IPv6 router to have a routable IPv4 address. This mechanism uses the IPv4 infrastructure for the interconnection of remote IPv6 hosts. It faces the IPv4 network as a unicast point-to-point link layer and implements the IPv6 network using encapsulation techniques. 6to4 mechanism has been assigned the IPv6 prefix 2002/16.

The main aim of this mechanism is to allow isolated IPv6 sites/hosts, which are attached to an IPv4 network with no IPv6 support to communicate with other IPv6 domains. Another advantage is that the 6to4 mechanism may be used in networks that have private IPv4 addresses and only one routable address, while it is not affected by the presence of firewalls and NAT boxes. The 6to4 mechanism supports the progressive migration from IPv4 to 6to4 and later to native IPv6.

6over4 Mechanism: The 6over4 mechanism allows isolated IPv6 hosts to act like fully functional IPv6 hosts even without direct contact with an IPv6 router (Carpenter and Jung, 1999). This mechanism utilizes the IPv4 multicast domain, that is considered as the link layer over which the IPv6 stack is built. In this case, the IPv4 domain has to support multicast operations. Also, if connections with external IPv6 sites have to be supported, then it is required a router that applies the same mechanism to the link connected to the multicast domain. The 6over4 mechanism does not use IPv4 compatible IPv6 addresses or configured tunnels. Also it is provides independence on the technology of the used links and the topology of the IPv6 network. Usually the 6over4 mechanism is called as a "virtual Ethernet".

2.3. Translation Mechanisms

The translation mechanisms aim to allow the communication between hosts that support different protocols. They may be applied in networks where only one protocol is used, while it is desirable the support of services of the other protocol, for example support of IPv4 services in IPv6 hosts. The most well known translation mechanisms are described briefly in the following.

Header Conversion: According to this mechanism the IPv4 headers are translated to IPv6 headers and vice-versa. It is similar to the NAT protocol (IPv4-to-IPv4 Header Conversion). Although this mechanism is fast enough, it appears some limitations to its application, for example it does not support translation in the application layer.

NAT-PT (Network Address Translation –Protocol Translation): The NAT-PT mechanism allows to native IPv6 hosts and applications to communicate with IPv4 hosts and applications respectively. The host that makes the translation lies on the borders between the IPv4 and IPv6 networks. Each host acting as an address translator keeps a pool of addresses that are assigned dynamically to IPv6 hosts and a session is generated between two hosts supporting different protocols. The NAT-PT mechanism supports both address and header translation. The implementation of the NAT-PT mechanism is simple and does not require any extra configuration to the hosts. However, this mechanism does not support the implementation of end-to-end security strategies and requires the usage of a large IPv4 space.

Mechanism type	Implication on application	IPv4 address requirements	Hosts/Site mechanism	Comments
Dual stack	None	Permanent or Pool of addresses allocated by a DHCP server.	Site/Host	Very simple to set up, available to every node supporting IPv6 stack.
DSTM	None	Pool of addresses required for AIIH server.	Site/Host	Allows hosts to run end-to-end IPv4 application within an IPv6 only network. Allows IPv4/IPv6 of IPv6-only host application to communicate with either IPv4 or IPv6 end point without need of specific ALG.
6to4	Applications need to be ported to interface with the IPv6 stack.	IPv4 address of border routers.	Site/Host	Allows to automatically joining IPv6 network separated by an IPv4 only network. Each IPv6 network needs to have a 6to4 border router.
Tunnel Broker	Applications need to be ported to interface with the IPv6 stack.	One for the dual stack host. At least one for the tunnel broker implementation.	Site/Host	Allows an isolated IPv4 host within an IPv6 only network, to reach an IPv6 wide network.
6over4	Applications need to be ported to interface with the IPv6 stack.	One per host	Host	Allows to automatically joining IPv6 network separated by an IPv4 only network. The IPv4 network needs to support multicast. Each IPv6 network needs to have a 6over4-border router.
NAT-PT	Applications including IP addresses in the packet payload need the availability of a dedicated ALG into the NAT-PT router.	Pool of IPv4 addresses needed.	Site	Needs specific ALG for DNS, FTP, IPSEC, … Mechanism located in a single point.
SOCKS64		The Socks Server must have an IPv4 address	Site	Allows IPv4 applications to communicate with IPv6-only hosts and vice-versa.

Table 1: Overview of Transition Mechanisms

Address Mapping: This technique refers to one-to-one correspondence between IPv6 destination addresses and IPv4 source addresses and vice-versa.

Socks: Socks is a gateway mechanism implemented by a "Socks Server", that acts as a relay mechanism in TCP or UDP sessions between two hosts supporting different protocols (one IPv4 host and the other IPv6 host) (Toutain and Afifi, 2000). Socks is considered is a unidirectional mechanism and may be used for the connection of an IPv4 network to an IPv6 network and vice-versa. Its main disadvantage is that the connections have to be initialized by the hosts lying behind the Sock Server. Table 1 summarizes the transition mechanisms (EuresCom Project P1009 results, 2001).

3. Transition Scenarios applied on the Greek Research & Technology Network (GRNET)

GRNET is the Greek Research & Technology Network, providing Internet services to the Greek Academic and Research community. It interconnects Universities and Research Centers in Greece, as well as other R&D Departments of industrial organizations through an advanced high-speed network. Like many other NRNs, GRNET maintains a pilot IPv6 network in order to enable its users to familiarize with the new protocol. The IPv6 network was built over the IPv4 infrastructure so that the core IPv6 links are not actually native IPv6 links but IPv6 over IPv4 tunnels that interconnect the IPv6 routers of the participating organizations and the core IPv6 router of GRNET. The topology implemented is a star one. The figure 1 shows the topology of the IPv6 network of GRNET.

Figure 1: IPv6 Network Topology of GRNET

3.1. Address assignment

GRNET is the administrative authority of a SLA, the 3FFE:2D00::/24 that has been assigned to it by the RIPE for the needs that will come up during the deployment of the IPv6 protocol at the east Mediterranean area. Following the guidelines of RFC 2450 an address plan was designed so as to distribute the allocated address space to the possible clients (Universities, Technology and Research Institutes etc) (Hinden, 1998). The decision was to allocate 3 bits for sharing between the Mediterranean countries, the next 5 bits for the big ISPs in each country, leaving the total of 96 bits to be consumed by the customers. This leads to 8 countries, 32 big ISPs in each country and each ISP can support up to ~65000 clients. Since the last 64 bits comprise the host part, each client disposes 16 bits for the internal sub netting.

3.2. Motivation

The IPv6 backbone of GRNET comprises of an IPv6 router that is connected through IPv6 over IPv4 tunnels to each client and with 6bone too. Initially in each Academic Institute there was a small IPv6 LAN that was connected to the local IPv6 router. This small IPv6 LAN was the test best where the new protocol had been tested on and a knowledge base obtained by technicians so they could support the expanding procedure to the end user. The last one was the challenge that had to been taken: How the IPv6 network could reach to the end user? The main goal was to use the IPv6 backbone in a manner similar to the use of the IPv4 backbone, meaning that all IPv6 traffic from every Institute should cross the local IPv6 router. The reasons that enforced this policy were mainly administrative in terms of traffic measurement and accounting. So we focused on transition techniques that could provide this characteristic.

Although it is common accepted that the IPv6 will be the internetworking protocol of the next years and the users have to get familiar with it, there were certain reasons that kept us from enabling the protocol to the entire network and make it a full dual stack network and thus providing end to end communication with both protocols.

In the following we describe the techniques that were proposed to the Network Operation Centers of the Academic Institutes in order to provide IPv6 services to the end users.

3.3. The Tunnel Broker solution for GRNET

In order to provide IPv6 services to the end users without investing many resources or making changes to the network, one of the apparent solutions is the deployment of the tunnel broker.

Our approach is described in figure 2. We setup a server that implements the user interface and also has the permissions to change the routers configuration in order to setup the tunnels. The tunnel broker software checks the IPv4 address of every user, determines in which Institute he belongs to and setups a tunnel between the user and his local IPv6 router. If the Institute does not maintain an IPv6 router then the tunnel is established between the user and the backbone IPv6 router.

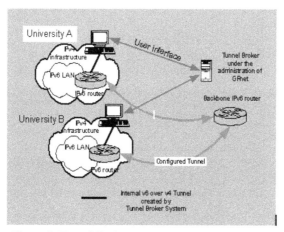

Figure 2: Tunnel Broker operation in GRNET

3.4. The configured tunnels solution for GRNET

The second solution in order to provide IPv6 connectivity to the end user was to deploy configured tunnels between specific routers and the local IPv6 router. Each University used the IPv6 space that had been assigned to it by GRNET. The topology that is implemented inside the campus networks is a mesh one meaning that there is a tunnel between each pair of routers participating to the IPv6 network. Each router with an IPv6 interface activated on it has been configured with a static route for all native IPv6 addresses pointing to the local IPv6 router, which is connected to the 6bone through the tunneling interface of the backbone IPv6 router.

4. Future work

Using the mechanisms described above GRNET could provide IPv6 connectivity to any end user at the participating institutes. However, the variation of network architectures, technologies and demands that exist in each academic institute enforces us to deploy a mixture of the described techniques. The main target is to select the appropriate technique for each institute in order to provide better IPv6 service and smoother transition procedure for the end user and the network administrators. Our future work includes the deployment of combination of 6to4, automatic tunneling and configured tunneling techniques inside campus networks and the use of translating techniques (e.g. NAT-PT) wherever IPv6-only clouds are created.

5. Conclusion

The transition to the next version of the IP protocol inside the GRNET is a long-term procedure that is considered to consume a lot of resources. The whole toolset of transition tools that have been defined and tested will provide the "middle step" in order to make the whole procedure smooth for the end users and the administrators. Currently, we are studying on more techniques in order to cover all the possible cases of implementation.

6. References

Carpenter, B. and Jung, C. (1999), *"Transmission of IPv6 over IPv4 Domains without Explicit Tunnels"*, RFC 2529.

Carpenter, B. and Moore, K. (2001), *"Connection of IPv6 Domains via IPv4 Clouds"*, RFC3056.

Crawford, M. and Huitema, C. (2000), *"DNS Extensions to Support IPv6 Address Aggregation and Renumbering"*, RFC 2874.

Deering, S. and Hinden, R, (1998), *"Internet Protocol Version 6 (IPv6) Specification"*, RFC 2460.

Durand, A. and Buclin, B. (1999), *"6Bone Backbone Routing Guidelines"*, RFC2546.

Durant, A. Fasano, P. Gardini, I. and Lento, D. (2001) *"IPv6 Tunnel Broker"*, RFC 3053.

EuresCom Project P1009 results (2001), *"Armstrong IPv6 deployment -A small step for IP but a giant leap for mankind"*.

EuresCom Project P1009 results, (2001), *"Transition Mechanisms Overview"*.

Gilligan, R. and Nordmark, E. (2000), *"Transition Mechanisms for IPv6 Hosts and Routers"*, RFC 2893.

Hinden, R. (1998), *"Proposed TLA and NLA Assignment Rules"* RFC 2450.

Kitamura, H. (2001), *"A SOCKS-based IPv6/IPv4 Gateway Mechanism"*, RFC 3089.

Toutain, L. and Afifi, H. (2000) *"Dynamic Tunnelling: A new method for the IPv4-IPv6 Transition"* draft-ietf-ngtrans-dti-00.txt.

Tsirtsis, G, and Srisuresh, P. (2000), *"Network Address Translation - Protocol Translation (NAT-PT)"*, RFC 2766.

Tsirtsis, G. (2000), *"Dual stack deployment using DSTM and 6to4"* draft-ietf-ngtrans-6to4-dstm-00.txt.

Stability on end-to-end path in the Internet

Jingping Bi, Qi Wu, Zhongcheng Li

Institute of Computing Technology, Chinese Academy of Sciences
Beijing 100080, P.R.China
{jpingbi, abewu, zcli}@ict.ac.cn

Abstract

In recent years, the research on end-to-end behavior in the Internet has made some improvements, but it is only lo-calized on the study about measurement metrics such as packet delay and packet loss to the study on packet behavior, while it is only a few about the study on to how to evaluate the performance of paths according to measurement metrics. We put forward an evaluating metric being based on end-to-end path: stability metric, which evaluates the stability of a path. It is a metric to evaluate network path stability. Then we introduce the characteristic of stability metric and its main influencing factor. In the end, we use posip to measure and analyze 43 paths in CERNET and CSTNET in China, then use the metric to evaluate the corresponding conclusions and acquire good effect.

Key Words

evaluating metric, end-to-end behavior, stability metric

1. Introduction

With the rapid development of the Internet and the increase of users relying on the network, the normal running of the Internet becomes more and more important. But with the enlargement of net-work scale, expanding of real-time operation and improving of users' demand on network speed and network performance, the problem becomes more and more serious. From the beginning of 90s, many research institutes such as IEPM (Paxson and Almes et al, 1998), NIMI (Paxson and Mahdavi et al, 1998) (Paxson 1997) (Paxson 1999), IPMA, Surveyor, RIPETT, WAND, NLANR, skitter and vBNS have made lots of measurements and researches to the Internet, and presented a series of measurement metrics.

At present, it has had many products in the presenting way of measurement metrics. For exam-ple, (Paxson and Almes et al, 1998) and (Cerf, 1991) present instructional proposal on how to present measurement metrics. But as a whole, measurement evaluation metrics in packet behavior of the Internet are poor. What have been standardized are: connectivity (Mahdavi and Paxson, 1999), one-way delay (Almes and Kalidindi et al, 1999-a), one-way packet loss (Almes and Kalidindi et al, 1999-b), round-trip time (Almes and Kalidindi et al, 1999-c).

The above metrics focus on measurement metrics such as packet delay and packet loss, there are no evaluation metrics related to end-to-end path. By measuring and analyzing CERNET (China Education and Research NETwork) and CSTNET (China Science and Technology NETwork) in our country, we present an evaluation metric based on end-to-end path characteristics: stability metric, which evaluate the stability of a path. Section 2 presents the computing method. Section 3 discusses its characteristics. Section 4 puts forward the main influencing factors. Section 5 introduces the experiment and section 6 concludes the paper.

(Notes: We use 5 min as a default computation unit to compute stability metric in the paper, paths in the figure are sorted by inherent delay from small to large).

2. Stability metric – metric evaluating end-to-end path stability

2.1 The meaning for presenting stability metric

Network stability is an important metric to assure the normal running of network, while path stability is one of the important component to evaluate network stability. Stability of end-to-end path not only relies on telecommunication exchange system of the bottom layer, but also relies on the upper layer software and hardware component aiming at Internet packet exchange transporting and routing structure. In the network, there are many upper layer applications such as video and audio that are sensitive to packet delay variation and packet loss. Once packet loss rate reaches a certain degree or delay variation is very large, it may lead to abnormal running of upper applications such as http, ftp and telnet. How to evaluate stability of end-to-end path objectively and reasonably, how is the path stability we use now, these are problems we care about and need to resolve.

We usually use many fundamental measurement metrics such as packet delay and packet loss, which indicate loss and delay status packet transmitting in network, but these measurement metrics can't give users a direct show on the paths stabilities. To solve this problem, we present an explicit evaluation parameter—stability metric, which is related to packet delay and packet loss. It describes stability status of paths by idiographic value. By using this parameter, we can have a deep understanding on stability of a network path, and a direct basis for further improvement of path stability.

Stability metric shows stability of the observed end-to-end paths in the appointed time scale, it is a variable changeable with time; The predictability of stability metric points out the degree that path is predictable, the expectation of stability metric points out the average stability state of each path and its variance indicates fluctuating range of stability metric in general case. The predictable value of stability metric and routing measured path passing by relate with network status where the path is and have no relation with time. To each path, average stability metric is relatively stable.

2.2 Way for computing stability metric

Firstly, we make the following hypothesis to the measurement of paths: Set the measurement start time be t, the end time be t+dt, and then the measurement persisting time is dt. Before presenting the evaluating method, we introduce the concepts of connectivity rate and stability rate firstly.

Connectivity rate (Cr):

Definition: In time interval dt, the ratio between the successful times and total times of measurement.

We suppose the total times of measurement in time scale dt is N_{total}, the successful times of measurement is N_{suc}, then we define the computing formula of connectivity rate in the following:

$$c_r = N_{suc} / N_{total} \qquad (1)$$

Stability rate (Sr):

In time interval dt, delay in each measurement is respectively di $(i=1, 2, ..., n)$, $n=N_{suc}$, then sample variance of delay is:

$$DX = \sqrt{\frac{1}{n-1}\sum_{i=1}^{n}(d_i - \frac{1}{n}\sum_{i=1}^{n}d_i)^2} \qquad (2)$$

Set

$$S_r' = DX / Min \qquad then \ S_r' \in [0, \infty) \qquad (3)$$

In the above formula (3), Min is the Inherent delay of the measured path.

We use the formula $y=x/(x+1)$ to normalize S_r' and get the increasing function which ranges from 0 to1.

$$S_r = S_r'/(S_r'+1) \quad then \quad S_r \in [0,1) \qquad (4)$$

STability metric (ST$_r$)

The computing method of stability metric is

$$ST_r = \frac{1}{\sqrt{2}} * \sqrt{C_r^2 + (1 - S_r)^2} \qquad (5)$$

Where ST_r ranges from 0 to 1. One can see, the smaller of packet loss rate and packet delay jitter of network, the larger ST_r; the larger stability metric, the better path stability.

● **Disposal of marginal measurement data**

We may encounter some special measurement data, and then process as follows:

(1) No measurement packets are received (namely N_{suc}=0). We have no way to compute standard variance. According to the principle that the smaller the stability metric is, the worse path stability status is, we let Sr(t,dt)=1. Then we can get STr(t,dt)=0.

(2) Only one measurement packet is received. According to formula (1), connectivity rate Cr $(t,dt) = 1/N_{total}$, we still can't compute standard variance at this time. According to the principle that the smaller the stability metric, the worse path stability status, we let $S_r(t,dt)=1$. Then we can get the following stability metric:

$$ST_r(t,dt) = \frac{1}{\sqrt{2}} * \sqrt{C_r^2(t,dt) + (1 - S_r(t,dt))^2}$$

$$= \frac{1}{\sqrt{2} * N_{total}} \qquad (6)$$

3. Characteristics of stability metric

Stability metric reflects end-to-end path stability, and which has the following characteristics:

3.1 Predictable value of path stability

Stability metric indicates path stability in some period of time. It is closely related with the measured moment. We analyze the expectation and variance of stability metric and present the concept of predictable value of path stability. Let's make the following supposition firstly:

Set the expectation of stability metric be $M(i)$, its variance be $\sigma(i)$, and i is the number of measured paths

$$M(i) = \frac{1}{n_i} \sum_{j=1}^{n_i} ST_{r(i,j)} \qquad (7)$$

$$\sigma(i) = \sqrt{\frac{1}{n_i - 1} \sum_{j=1}^{n_i} (ST_{r(i,j)} - \frac{1}{n_i} \sum_{j=1}^{n_i} ST_{r(i,j)})^2} \qquad (8)$$

We define $\quad \Pr e(i) = \sigma(i)/M(i) \qquad (9)$

Where $ST_{r(i,j)}$ is the stability metric measurement result of the ith path and the jth time scale.

Pre (i) is termed as the predictable value of the path stability, and it indicates the stability degree measured path that can be predicted. The smaller *Pre (i)*, the better the predictability of path stability. The following figure shows the predictable state of the measured path, where path numbers are sorted according to inherent delay of paths from small to large.

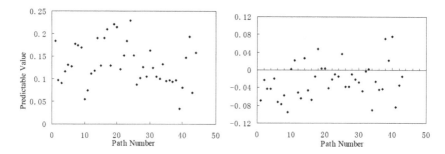

Figure 1 predictable value of path stability   Figure 2   Difference of stability metric between a day and an hour

X-axis in figure 1 represents path numbers, and Y-axis represents the corresponding predictable value of path stability. One can see that, path 39 (159.226.39.106-159.226.148.1) and path 10 (202.38.64.241-202.112.17.38) are the two most stable paths in the measured time interval, while path 19 (202.197.97.58-202.112.10.2) and path 17 (202.197.97.58- 202.112.17.38) are the two most unstable paths. This indicates that the stability of path 39 and 10 is predictable in a large degree, while the stability of path 19 and 17 can hardly predict.

3.2 Stability metric of an end-to-end path being in busy is usually smaller than in idle

Packet loss rate and delay jitter of an end-to-end path being in busy is usually larger than in idle, so the corresponding stability metric is smaller, we'll validate it in § 4.2.

3.3 Expectation and variance of stability metric

Expectation of stability metric reflects the average stability of a path, its variance reflects jitter state of path stability, and which indicates the predictability of stability status of the measured path. If variance of stability metric for the measured path is small, then it indicates that stability of the path is good, and path stability is predictable; Contrarily, if variance is large, then stability of the path is indicated to be bad, and path stability can't be predicted. Variance and expectation only relate with reasonability and quantity of sample data and don't relate with time scale of sampling. To better reflect general stability and its predictability of the measured paths, sample data should include different hours as many as possible (network state for different hours is distinct).

Variance of stability metric is a long-term statistical data, the difference between it and stability metric of a specific time interval is that it has no relation with time and is relatively stable. It is a characteristic closely related with the path and the actual network. It reflects stability characteristic of the path. Only when the path makes physical upgrading and physical topology or operation in network changes greatly, can the parameter change greatly.

3.4 Stability metric of a day is usually more stable and less jitter than of an hour

End-to-end path usually shows different network characteristics in distinct time interval of a day, and it often congests in some period of time and is in idle state in other periods. But flow characteristics of a path in a day are usually relatively stable. To validate if the stability metric of a day is more stable than that of an hour, we make statistics and analysis to measurement data, X-axis in figure 2 is path number and Y-axis is the standard variance difference between the stability of a day and of an hour. One can see that, 79% paths fit with the characteristics, which shows that stability metric jitter of an hour is indeed larger than that of a day.

4. Influencing factors of stability metric

One can see from the above formulae, the value of stability metric mainly related with packet loss rate and delay variance, but this is only external phenomenon. What essential factors affect stability metric? We think they contain path itself factor, network congestion and all kinds of routing abnormal status. The detailed analysis is made in the following.

4.1. Path factors

Stability metric closely relates with path characters, which reflects path stability in special period of time. End-to-end path usually consists of various links connected with routers or other intermediate devices. When packets transmit in the paths, they may traverse many sub-networks. Different paths consist of distinct transmitting media such as twisted-pair and fiber. The types of Intermediate devices are various such as Cisco router and Dlink switch. Types of sub-network are multifarious, such as Ethernet and ATM. After all, different physical mediae form distinct end-to-end paths, so even if the same network traffics transmit in different end-to-end paths, their path stabilities are different. Figure 3 shows that stability characteristics expressed by each path are different.

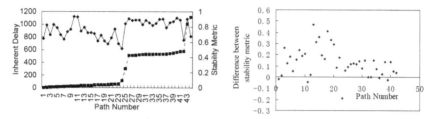

Figure 3 stability metric of each path

Figure 4   Contrast to stability of path
in busy and idle state

Figure 3 sorts all of the measured paths by inherent delay ascendingly, where the low line is inherent delay of paths, and the upper line is the corresponding stability metric expectation. In the general case, inherent delay of path using satellite channel is larger than using wire channel (Inherent delay of satellite channel is commonly about 500ms). At the same time, from the figure we can see that stability metric of paths are mostly higher using satellite channel than using wire channel. This indicates that the corresponding stability metric of each path is determined by its own characteristic.

4.2. Network congestion

Packet loss rate of network is usually small in idle state and packets rarely wait in queue in transmitting, the corresponding delay variance is not large. In this case, stability of the whole path is good. On the contrary, when network is very busy, network congestion and packet loss phenomena often happen, and waiting time of packets queuing in the router will consequently change and delay variance will increase, which will affect stability metric of paths.

To validate if stability metric will become worse in the state of network congestion and how is the change of stability metric compared with idle state. We choose two periods of time 0:00-1:00 (t1) and 10:00-11:00 (t2), paths in t2 are usually busier than in t1. Figure 4 reflects the comparative results of two periods of time in a day, where Y-axis represents the difference between t1 and t2. One can see, stability for 60% of the paths in t1 is much better than in t2 (difference of the value of stability metric is larger than 0.1), stability metric for over 90% of paths are better in t1 than in t2. We then conclude that stability of network in idle state is better than in congestion state.

4.3. Some kinds of abnormal routing phenomena

It usually has some abnormal routings when packet transmit in a path, such as routing jitter, routing loop, erroneous routing, routing change, routing outage and so on. We divide them into two kinds: routing change and routing unreachable. What effects will them have on stability metric?   In the following, we analyze several kinds of main routing states that may affect stability.

● Routing jitter

Jitter usually means rapidly changing routing. In the measurement of routing behavior, we often see `traceroute` goes through more than one routing when it passes by network. For example, more than two nodes response to probing packets sent by one hop in `traceroute`.

Routing jitter usually can be classified into the following two expressing forms in figure 5.

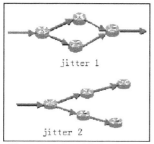

Figure 5   Two kinds of routing
jitter expression forms

Figure 6 Measurement paths covering
sketch-map

In form 1, jitter phenomenon only occurs in some hop of the probing results of `traceroute`, and the two routers including jitter are very close in IP address. In this case, it has no large effect on delay characteristic whichever router probing packet goes and has little effect on stability metric.

In form 2, jitter occurs in many hops of the probing results. In this case, it'll exist two or more paths that have large difference, and probability different paths having different hop numbers is larger than 75% (Paxson, 1997), so we can determine which routing goes according to different TTL values in ack packet, and then can get stability metric of different paths.

● **Routing loop**

Routing loop means the following: supposing routing table in router R1 indicates that to transmit a packet to host H, it should send this packet along a path which includes router R2. But due to inconsistency, routing table in R2 shows that it should transmit this packet to H using the path including R1, and then we think it exists routing loop in the network. In this case, packets will loop in R1 and R2 until its TTL overflow and lead to being unable to reach H or the loop being interrupted by routing updating. Routing loop often occurs in packet transmitting.

In the experiment, routing loop we observed mostly can persist several hours or longer, it greatly influences normal running of network and normal transmitting of packets. In this case, packets loss rate can reach 100%, smooth rate is 1, and stability metric is 0. That is to say, when routing loop occurs, routing is interrupted, packets are unable to transmit and stability metric reach minimum 0.

● **Routing unreachable**

Routing unreachable indicates that packet can't reach remote host. Routing is unreachable may due to routing being down or remote host being down in paths. In this instance, it will have the same consequence as persisting routing loop, stability metric reaches minimum 0.

● **Routing outage**

When a series of consecutive `traceroute` are interrupted, the most possible reason is the temporary loss of network connection, or serious congestion of consecutive 10s or more. Routing outage evidently influences the normal transmission of packets and leads to increase of packets loss rate, so it will lead to declining of stability metric value. If the persisting time of routing outage is long, then it will greatly debase stability of network and even it will have the possibility of making stability metric of a path reach minimum value in the state of persisting routing outage.

5. Experiment

To validate efficiency of stability metric, we make measurement and analysis in CERNET and CSTNET in China. In the experiment, ICT (Institute of Computer Technology) of CAS, Hunan University, Chinese science and technology University, ShanDong University, Inner Mongolia University and Chongqing University of Posts and Telecommunications are chosen as measurement nodes, and choose ICT of CAS to collect data at the same time. It covers 43 paths around the country, as shown in figure 6, where only WAN paths and no LAN and MAN paths are marked out.

In the experiment, Posip is used as measurement tool, and `traceroute` as assistant routing measurement tool. Posip which uses possion method to sample is a round-trip delay measurement tool we wrote based on current ping tool.

6. Conclusions

We make measurement and analysis to CERNET and CSTNET and provide path evaluation parameter: stability metric, which uses the value in $[0,1]$ to make visual evaluation about path stability. Then we analyze characteristics of stability metric, which includes: 1) The smaller the predictive value of path stability, the better predictability of path; 2) Stability of end-to-end path is smaller being busy than being idle; 3) Expectation of stability metric shows the average stability status of the measured paths in the observed period of time; Variance reflects the jitter status of the path stability; 4) Stability metric is more stable and less jitter in a day than in an hour. In the end, we present main the factors affecting path stability as follows: (1) path factor; (2) network congestion; (3) some kinds of abnormal routing phenomena.

References

Almes, G. and Kalidindi, S. and Zekauskas, M. (1999-a), "A One-way Delay Metric for IPPM", *Internet Engineering Task Force*, RFC 2679.

Almes, G. and Kalidindi, S. and Zekauskas, M. (1999-b), "A one-way Packet Loss Metric for IPPM", *Internet Engineering Task Force*, RFC 2680.

Almes, G. and Kalidindi, S. and Zekauskas, M. (1999-c), "A Round-trip Delay Metric for IPPM", *Internet Engineering Task Force*, RFC 2681.

Cerf, V. G. (1991), "Guidelines for Internet Measurement Activities", *Internet Engineering Task Force*, RFC 1262.

Mahdavi, J. and Paxson V. (1999), "IPPM Metrics for Measuring Connectivity", *Internet Engineering Task Force*, RFC 2498.

Paxson, V. (1997), "End-to-End Routing Behavior in the Internet", *IEEE/ACM Transactions on Networking*, Vol. 5, No. 5, pp601-615.

Paxson, V. (1999), "End-to-End Internet Packet Dynamics," *IEEE/ACM Transactions on Networking*, Vol. 7, No. 3, pp277-291.

Paxson, V. and Almes, G. and Mahdavi, J. and Mathis M. (1998), "Framework for IP Performance Metrics", *Internet Engineering Task Force*, RFC 2330.

Paxson, V. and Mahdavi J. and Adams A. and Mathis M. (1998), "An Architecture for Large-Scale Internet Measurement", *IEEE Communications*, Vol. 36, No. 8, pp48-54.

Two Special Register Addressing Modes for Internet Protocol Processing[*]

Yutai Ma, Axel Jantsch and Hannu Tenhunen

Department of Microelectronics and Information Technology

Royal Institute of Technology, Sweden

Abstract

One of the significant differences between internet protocol processing and scientific computations is data structure and related memory addressing. We propose two special addressing modes: tree addressing mode and base address plus small displacement addressing mode, which support TREE and STRUCT data structures. Case studies show that the two special register addressing modes can achieve 12% to 22% performance improvement. A load/store unit with 7 pipeline stages was designed and simulated on SYNOPSYS with 0.6 μm CMOS technology. It can work at 113 MHz. The two special addressing modes contribute 6.3% of hardware cost.

Keywords

Protocol Processor, Register Addressing Modes, Load/Store Unit.

1 Introduction

The quick shift from Megabit transmission rate to Gigabit transmission rate raises high speed processing requirement for network devices. Currently, many network processors have been used on the Internet backbones. These processors are all built by using general-purpose microprocessors or general-purpose embedded microprocessors.

Is it possible to develop high performance microprocessors for internet protocol processing, which can upgrade with the advance of semiconductor technology as well? Some research have shown that it is possible to enhance the performance of general-purpose microprocessors by incorporating specific functionalities which match internet protocol processing characteristics. These special programmable protocol processors can be used as accelerators. On the other hand, some techniques could be applied to general-purpose microprocessors just like some functionalities for multimedia applications have been added to general-purpose microprocessors.

There are many differences between internet protocol processing and scientific computations. For example, bit-string operations, high speed I/O operations, data structures and register addressing modes, etc. These features give us possibilities to

---

[*]This work was supported by INTELECT programme, the Foundation for Strategic Research, Sweden.

STRUCT	# Elements	Description
m_buf	7	Packet Buffer
ifnet	18	Network Interface
ifaddr	9	Interface Address
domain	10	protocol domain
protosw	14	Processing Entrance
ip	11	IP Packet
tcphdr	10	TCP Header
tcpcb	44	TCP Control Block
socket	21	Socket Structure
socketbuf	9	Send/Receive Buffer

Table 1: Typical STRUCT Data Structures

optimize general-purpose microprocessors and develop special programmable protocol processors for internet applications.

In this paper we investigate some typical data structure and register addressing features in internet protocol processing. Tree addressing mode and base address plus small displacement addressing mode are proposed. Hardware cost analysis and performance gain analysis are conducted. Case studies show that processing speed can be improved by 12% to 22% . A load/store unit with these two addressing modes are designed and synthesized on SYNOPSYS with 0.6 μm CMOS technology. The circuit can work at 113 MHz clock rate with 7 pipeline stages. The two special addressing circuit only gives 6.3% of hardware cost.

2 Motivation

TREE and STRUCT data structures are widely used in Internet protocol processing. For example, queue priority management relies on TREE data structure to perform priority insertion and deletion and packet management. For rate based packet scheduling algorithms, TREE is a good data structure to manage and sort incoming packets into output links. TREE data structure also can be used efficiently for memory allocation and de-allocation for incoming and outgoing packets. Some typical STRUCT data structures and the number of elements are listed in Table 1, these data structures are used in (Wright and Stevens, 1994). We see that they all have less than 64 elements. From these examples we see that memory addressing modes for TREE data structure and base address plus a small displacement for STRUCT data structure should be provided.

Typical operations on TREE data structure include traversing a parent node down to its child nodes and traversing a node to its parent node. For the former case it takes 2 to 3 instructions and for the latter case it takes 2 instructions. It is desirable to have TREE addressing capability for load/store instructions so that accessing a TREE node can be performed by using one instruction.

Addressing Mode	Time Delay
32-bit Frame Addr + 32-bit Base Addr + 32-bit Offset Addr	8.9 ns
32-bit Base Addr + 6-bit Offset	3.7 ns

Table 2: Time Delay Comparison of Addressing Modes (0.6 μm CMOS process, cla90000 library)

As we know, adder time delay is proportional to $2 \log_2 n$, where n is word length. Therefore, even if word length of one operand is shortened, the time delay still can be reduced due to reduced logic complexity. On the other hand, We have seen from Table 1 that small address offsets are used to access most of the STRUCT data structures. Thus base plus small displacement addressing mode can speed up address generation.

Simulation results on SYNOPSYS with 0.6 μm CMOS process are shown in Table 2. We choose 6 bits for small displacement in our current design due to word length limit. However, it covers most of the STRUCT data structures in Internet protocol processing. We believe that it is reasonable to choose one byte or two bytes as small displacement for 64 and 128-bit instruction words. Therefore, two sparate logic blocks should be provided, one for base address plus small displacement, another one for base address plus full displacement and the full displacement addition is pipelined in two clock cycles.

3 Load/Store Unit Design

3.1 Addressing Modes

As discussed in section 2, addressing modes for load and store instructions (with or without post update actions) are supported in the load/store unit, which are shown in Table 3. A global frame register for accessing global variables, a local frame register for accessing procedure local variables, and a zero frame register for STRUCT or array variable pointers are supported in the load/store unit.

Rd ← Mem([Rs] + small_offset)
Rd ← Mem([Rs] + [Rt])
Rd ← Mem([Rs] + [Rt]/2)
Rd ← Mem([Rs] + [Rt]*2)
Rd ← Mem([Rs] + [Rt]*2 + 1)
Rd ← Mem([Frame Reg] + [Rs] + [Rt])
Rd ← Mem([Frame Reg] + [Rs] + [Rt]/2)
Rd ← Mem([Frame Reg] + [Rs] + [Rt]*2)
Rd ← Mem([Frame Reg] + [Rs] + [Rt]*2 + 1)

Table 3: Load/Store Addressing Modes

3.2 Instruction Format

Load/store instruction format is shown in Figure 1. Applications of using the above addressing modes to access a variable, an array element, a STRUCT element, a node of TREE data structure are illustrated in Table 4. We see that TREE and STRUCT data structures (with less than 64 elements) can be accessed efficiently.

31	25 24	23	16 15	11 10 9	8	7	6 5	0
Opcode	I/R	DR	Base AR	FP	Update	Mode	Offset	

31	25 24	23	16 15	11 10 9	8	7	6 5	0
Opcode	I/R	DR	Base AR	FP	Update	Mode	Offset AR	

Opcode	Instruction Operation Code
I/R	Immediate Offset or Register Offset
DR	Source/Destination Data Register
Base AR	Base Address Register
FP	Frame register: Global/Local/Zero
Update	Post-Update Offset Address Register
Mode	Register Addressing Mode
Offset	Immediate Offset Number
Offset AR	Offset Address Register

Figure 1: Load/Store Instruction Format

Data Structure	Instruction
Scalar	load Rd, [Rs, #num]
Variable	load Rd, [Rs.fp, Rt]
Array	load Rd, [Rs, #num]
Element	load Rd, [Rs.fp, Rt]
STRUCT	load Rd, [Rs, #num]
Element	load Rd, [Rs.fp, Rt]
TREE Node	load Rd, [Rs.fp, Rt.tree_p]
	load Rd, [Rs.fp, Rt.tree_lc]
	load Rd, [Rs.fp, Rt.tree_lr]
	load Rd, [Rs.fp, Rt.tree_p]!
	load Rd, [Rs.fp, Rt.tree_lc]!
	load Rd, [Rs.fp, Rt.tree_lr]!

Table 4: Variable Access Examples

3.3 Load/Store Pipeline

The load/store unit executes load/store instructions on a 7 stage pipeline: instruction fetch (IF), instruction decode (ID), register read (RR), memory address calculation (EX1 and EX2), memory read/write (MR/MW), and register write (RW), as shown in Figure 2.

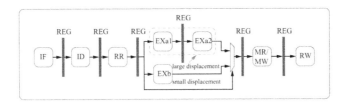

Figure 2: Load/Store Instruction Pipeline

Memory addressing with base address and small displacement is executed by one clock cycle for address generation, and for other modes it takes two clock cycles for address generation. Therefore, a load instruction takes 6 or 7 clock cycles to finish from instruction fetch to the point that data is read into a data register. For store instruction, it takes 5 or 6 clock cycles to finish.

4 Simulation Result

A load/store unit model has been built up and was simulated on SYNOPSYS with cla90000 library in 0.6 μm CMOS process. The simulation result is shown in Table 5. The load/store unit compries 7 pipeline stages as described in section 3.3

Clock Cycle	8.8 NS
Pipeline Stages	7
Combinational	2538 NAND2
Noncombinational	4860 NAND2
Total Area Cost	7398 NAND2
Power Consumption	50.2 mW

Table 5: Load/Store Unit Simulation

From the area cost analysis of Table 6 we see that around 77% of the area cost attributes to address and data input/output and pipeline control logic, while addressing with base address plus small displacement and tree addressing modes only contribute

Logic Block	Area	Percentage
Small Displacement	336	4.5%
Full Displacement	1240	16.8%
Tree Addressing Mode	133	1.8%
Other Combinational	829	11.2%
Registers	4860	65.7%

Table 6: Area Cost Analysis of The LSU

4.5% and 1.8% of the total area cost, respectively. This indicates that these two special addressing modes can be implemented efficiently and the hardware cost added to the load/store unit can be ignored.

From the simulation results we see that it is possible to integrate some particular addressing capabilities to improve the overall performance of internet protocol processing with very low hardware overhead.

5   Case Study

To verify effectiveness of the two special addressing modes, we choose two applications: queue priority management (Bhagwan and Lin, 2000) and Ethernet input packet processing (Wright and Stevens, 1994) to analyze the perofrmance in quantity.

(Bhagwan and Lin, 2000) proposed a TREE data structure for queue priority management. We use their algorithms as a case study to veriry effectiveness of the TREE addressing mode. Performance analysis is shown in Table 7.

Measure	Enqueue	Dequeue
# Instr.	24	22
# Load/Store Instr.	7	6
# Instr. Savings	3	5
Savings in Percentage	12.5%	22.75%

Table 7: Analysis of TREE Addressing Mode
for Queue Priority Management

The Ethernet input function (leread and ether_input) (Wright and Stevens, 1994) is transformed into assembly code on our protocol processor model. Many STRUCT data structures are used in this program. For example, le_softc, arpcom, ifnet, if_data, ifqueue, mbuf, ether_header, etc. This code is used to verify effectiveness of the addressing mode of base address plus small displacement. Analysis results are shown in Table 8.

Measure	leread	ether_input
# Instr.	66	64
# Load/Store Instr.	13	12
# Clock Cycle Savings	13	12
Savings in Percentage	19.7%	18.75%

Table 8: Analysis of Base Address Plus Small
Displacement for Ethernet Input Function

6   Summary

There are many differences between internet protocol processing and scientific and engineering computations. To achieve high processing speed of internet protocols, those differences must be taken into account in microprocessor design.

We proposed two special register addressing modes: tree and base address plus small displacement. These two addressing modes are targeted for TREE and STRUCT data structures. The case studies show that performance can be improved by 12% to 22%.

A load/store unit with the two special addressing modes has been designed and synthesized on SYNOPSYS with 0.6 μm CMOS process. It can work at 113 MHz. The simulation results show that the two special addressing modes only impose 6.3% hardware cost to the load/store unit. This indicates that they can be implemented efficiently.

References

Bhagwan, R. and Lin, B. (2000),"Fast and scalable priority queue architecture for high-speed network switches", *Proceedings of IEEE INFOCOM*, Tel Aviv, Israel.

Wright, G.R. and Stevens, W.R. (1994), "*TCP/IP Illustrated: The Implementation*", Vol.2, Addison-Wesley Publishing Company, Reading, Massachusetts.

Self-Similar Network Traffic Simulation

Diane T. Lark, Martha Evens, and William Lidinsky

Illinois Institute of Technology, Chicago, Illinois, USA
e-mail: diane_lark@hp.com

Abstract

It has been shown that much real world computer network traffic exhibits self-similar rather than Poisson behavior. This explains why network devices designed using simulation and analysis tools based upon Poisson models have led to results that differ considerably from those observed in the real world. Investigations including significant studies by Bellcore, the University of California at Berkeley, Boston University and others have conclusively demonstrated that much computer network traffic is self-similar in nature.

In order to be useful, future network simulations and analyses must have a self-similar basis. With respect to simulation, a needed component is a generator capable of inserting tailored self-similar traffic into a network. But ideally such a generator should be able to produce different degrees of self-similar traffic and be able to relate other traffic parameters such as file size, packet and segment size and client/server request/response distributions.

An experimental system called SURGE (Scalable URL Reference Generator) has the potential for filling this need. The developers produced evidence that it generated a higher degree of self-similarity under heavy loads that other load generators. Questions remained as to whether SURGE produces repeatable and precise results with comparable degrees of self-similarity to that observed in the real world given equivalent workloads. Our efforts have shown that SURGE produced repeatable and precise results that were representative of real world network traffic.

This paper reports on the sensitivity of self-similar properties observed in the simulated network traffic when accessing only a percentage of the distinct files during a SURGE simulation. Once this sensitivity is understood, SURGE can be a useful tool for simulating self-similar traffic and can be profitably used by network designers and analysts to predict network behavior.

Keywords

SURGE, Wavelet estimator, Hurst value, parameter estimation

1. Introduction

Leland et al. [Leland et al., 1995] showed that ethernet traffic exhibited self-similar statistical properties in the sense that self-similarity existed when two subsets of data were identical over multiple time scales. Long-range dependence, or the Joseph effect, was another important property. Here, correlations decay very slowly. A second team, Paxson and Floyd [Paxson and Floyd, 1995], established that the Poisson distribution was inappropriate for network modeling due to the long-range dependence observed in network traffic. Crovella and Bestavros [Crovella and Bestavros, 1997] discovered that HTTP traffic exhibited self-similar properties. Barford and Crovella [Barford and Crovella, 1998 and 1999] introduced SURGE and demonstrated that their workload generator was capable of simulating workloads that generated network traffic with statistical self-similarity properties. Their generator produced higher degrees of self-similarity under heavy loads. They attributed the inability of SPECWeb96 to generate comparable degrees of self-similarity to the fact that it utilizes a fixed-request generation rate. In effect, as the number of requests increased, the time between requests decreased. Traffic burstiness diminished with increased load.

SURGE (Scalable URL Reference Generator) has been shown to produce realistic loads that generate network traffic with self-similar properties. Our efforts have shown that, when used properly and carefully it can be used by those with the primary interest of generating network traffic with self-similar properties.

This paper reports on the sensitivities and impacts on the degree of self-similarity when used improperly. It first provides background information concerning the experimental apparatus, SURGE, and prior research results with respect to repeatability, precision and realism. It then describes the methodology employed to collect and analyze the data. Finally, the results are explained.

2. Background

This section gives a brief description of the experimental equipment and of SURGE itself. It then explains the results of our earlier work on the validation of SURGE.

2.1. Experimental Apparatus and Processes

The experimental apparatus consisted of five systems; one functioned as the Web server and four functioned as workload generators or clients. Three systems were 1GHz Pentium III HP Pavilion 7940 computers and two systems were 66MHz Pentium II ACP computers. The Web server was an HP Pavilion with 384MB RAM. The other two HP Pavilions had 128MB RAM each. The two ACP systems had 64MB RAM each. All systems ran Red Hat Linux. These five systems were connected to an 8-port Linksys switch to form an isolated LAN.

Software employed included Apache and SURGE. Apache was modified to increase the number of maximum threads from 150 to 1024. The Web server functioned as the network time server via NTP (Network Time Protocol). Our process for selecting the appropriate separation point between the distribution tail and the body was performed according to the process outlined by [Barford et al., 1999]. Separation of data between body and tail was determined, MLE (Maximum Likelihood Estimators) were applied to ensure that data were representative of the population, and α was determined using linear regression. Mathematica was used for these purposes. Tcpdump was used to collect network traces for analysis.

Determining the degree of self-similarity was accomplished by using Matlab routines developed by Veitch and Abry [Veitch and Abry, 1999] who used Discrete Wavelet Transforms to analyze self-similar and long-range dependent processes. The advantage these routines offered over other tools (i.e. Variance Time Plot, R/S Analysis, and Periodogram) was the inclusion of Confidence Intervals. Another tool, the Whittle estimator does provide confidence intervals but was complex to use. The Matlab routines analyzed the network traces and produced values representative of self-similarity, namely H (Hurst) and α. The following equation shows the relationship between H and α:

$$H = (1 + \alpha) / 2$$

where α refers to the Pareto distribution shape parameter. Hurst values between 0.5 and 1.0 indicate self-similarity. As it approaches 1.0, the degree of self-similarity increases.

2.2.   SURGE Workload Generator

SURGE was developed by [Barford and Crovella, 1998]. Their efforts showed that it produced high degrees of self-similarity in network traffic under heavy loads. Barford and Crovella [Barford and Crovella, 1998] defined six workload characterization influences based upon efforts by other researchers. These workload characteristics were 1) server file size, 2) request size, 3) relative file popularity, 4) embedded file references, 5) temporal locality of reference, and 6) idle periods of individual users. Distribution models were specified for each and employed by each UE (User-Equivalent). Each UE was a bursty process that exhibited long periods of activity followed by long periods of inactivity.

The concept of a UE was developed to capture the behavior of a real Web user [Barford and Crovella, 1998]. Each UE represented a separate ON/OFF process that generated requests and remained idle according to its distributional model. Forerunners of SURGE used a fixed rate source with a constant number of threads and a constant request rate. The OFF time was determined by dividing the target rate by the number of threads. Idle, or OFF, times were not preserved. As the workload intensified, the idle times of threads grew shorter and exhibited lower variability in demand. This method failed to produce the burstiness necessary to generate self-similar traffic. In contrast, the UE used a variable rate source to determine idle time. As the number of threads increased, the idle times were preserved because they followed the distributional model. Default workload characterization distributional models [Barford and Crovella, 1998] and the distribution parameter values appear in Table 1.

Char	Model	Probability Density Function	Parm
File Sizes – Body	Lognormal	$p(x) = \dfrac{1}{x\sigma\sqrt{2x}} e^{-(\ln x - \mu)^2 / 2\sigma^2}$	$\mu=9.36;$ $\sigma=1.32$
File Sizes – Tail	Pareto	$p(x) = \alpha k^{\alpha} x^{-(\alpha+1)}$	$\kappa=9300$ $\alpha=1.0$
Popularity	Zipf	$p = kr^{-1}$	
Temporal Locality	Lognormal	$p(x) = \dfrac{1}{x\sigma\sqrt{2x}} e^{-(\ln x - \mu)^2 / 2\sigma^2}$	$\mu=1.5;$ $\sigma=0.80$
Request Sizes	Lognormal	$p(x) = \dfrac{1}{x\sigma\sqrt{2x}} e^{-(\ln x - \mu)^2 / 2\sigma^2}$	$\mu=7.88;$ $\sigma=1.34$
Request Sizes	Pareto	$p(x) = \alpha k^{\alpha} x^{-(\alpha+1)}$	$\kappa=3558;$ $\alpha=1.177$
Active Off Times	Weibull	$p(x) = \dfrac{bx^{b-1}}{a^b} e^{-(x/a)^b}$	$a=1.46;$ $b=0.382$
Inactive Off Times	Pareto	$p(x) = \alpha k^{\alpha} x^{-(\alpha+1)}$	$\kappa=1;$ $\alpha=1.5$
Embedded References	Pareto	$p(x) = \alpha k^{\alpha} x^{-(\alpha+1)}$	$\kappa=1;$ $\alpha=2.43$

Table 1. SURGE Default Distribution Parameters

Combining the above distributional models into a single representative workload exhibiting those characteristics introduced two problems [Barford and Crovella, 1998]. The first was how to generate the appropriate number of requests for the desired file sizes. The second was how to generate a request stream that exhibited temporal locality.

The first problem was handled by [Barford and Crovella, 1998] through a method designed to match requests to files and to generate a representative output sequence. The matching problem involved the popularity, file size, and request size distributions. No matter how many clients were involved with issuing requests, the distribution models for popularity and file size needed to be generated according to the defined distribution model parameter values. Success was determined by the difference between the desired number of references to a file size and the actual number of references to that file size. Two methods were assessed by [Barford and Crovella, 1998]. Splitting the head of the distribution from the tail of the distribution produced optimal results when matching. Matching the distribution tail resulted in close fits. Large errors were not introduced in the body of the distribution.

The second problem was addressed by placing file names in a stack and defining a small window in which each file was assigned a weight with a value proportional to the outstanding requests for that file [Barford and Crovella, 1998]. The file at the top of the stack was based upon the probabilistic weight of the files within the window. The file sequence generation produced the appropriate file distribution, and the stack distance values followed the lognormal distribution. However, distributions would be less accurate when numerous clients were configured since clients could not share a common list without associated synchronization overhead. SURGE managed this situation by generating independent file name sequences and their associated stack distance properties. The lognormal distribution output values were scaled according to the number of clients. This produced the same stack distance distribution as the single client.

2.3. Earlier Research Results

Based on the analyses performed during our earlier research, we concluded that SURGE generated repeatable results with respect to total data transferred, number of connections, distinct files accessed, and long-range dependence. It also proved to be precise with respect to reproduction of the tail for the file size and request size distribution provided the distributions were stable. Stable Pareto distributions have $0 < \alpha < 2$ [Evans et al., 1993]. Results indicated that the simulation distribution for request size was more difficult to reproduce due to the combinatorial methods employed by the authors of the tool and the sensitivity to the number of distinct files accessed. Accessing the available files repeatedly produced distributions that differed from that input as well as produced self-similarity results not representative of the intended workload. During set up of the Web server, the tester selects the number of distinct files. Accessing all distinct files must be achievable within a reasonable time frame. This earlier work suggested the importance of determining the appropriate job duration in order to simulate the expected workload. Our data also showed that for duplicating real-world workloads, SURGE produced representative burstiness in traffic provided the distributions were stable. In addition, we discovered that it was unlikely to match the real-world values for both total bytes transferred and total files transferred. This can be attributed to the fact that the original file set was represented by a distribution that was used to generate a different file set used in the simulation. Overall, we concluded that SURGE was a reasonable tool for simulating repeatable, precise, and real-world workloads.

3. Testing and Analysis Cycle

A number of simulation and analysis cycles were necessary in order to better understand the relationship between the self-similarity in simulated network traffic and the number of distinct files accessed during the simulation. Our first goal was to illustrate the resulting file and request size distributions and to demonstrate that the intended workload is reproduced when 99-100% of the distinct files were accessed. The second goal was to evaluate the behavior of network traffic self-similarity during a simulation when the desired workload was achieved and when it was not achieved.

We collected and analyzed data that showed the variation in the expected workload versus the resultant workload. Next we assessed the Hurst parameter for several series where the load and job duration were held constant, where the job duration was held constant but the load was increased, and, last where the load was held constant but the job duration was increased. In all three scenarios, the number of distinct files accessed was noted.

4. Hurst Value Sensitivity Results

Determining the job duration of the simulation was crucial in producing the desired simulated workload. Since the base workload was characterized by the distributions of those parameters defined in Table 1, the resulting simulation values should match the input values as close as possible. Data collected during prior research efforts suggested that the point at which the resulting distributions most closely match the input value was when all distinct files were accessed. To demonstrate this, eight tests were executed for one hour each with the load ranging from 300 UEs to 1350 UEs. The file size distribution input value for α was 1.0 and the request size distribution input value for α was 1.177. Input values for file and request size are represented using dashed lines. 75% of the available 2,000 distinct files were accessed during the 300 UE test and 99% were accessed in the 1350 UE test. Figure 1 illustrates the results of these tests.

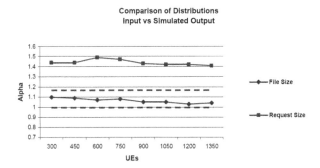

Figure 1. Comparison of Input vs. Simulated Output Distributions

In Figure 1, the upper tails of the file size distributions for the tests are 10% and 4% higher than the input values for the 300 and 1350 UE tests, respectively. The upper tails of the request size distributions are 22% and 20% higher than the input values for the 300 and 1350 UE tests, respectively. The simulation generated distributions that approached the input values as more of the distinct files were accessed.

Assessing the distributions for file and request size at the point where all the available files were accessed required additional tests. Two series, of five tests each, were conducted. The load was held constant at 1200 UEs for each test and the job duration was increased from one hour to five hours. The first series of five tests had 600 UEs and the second series had 900 UEs. There were 2000 distinct files available. The 600UE test accessed 1907 of them during the one hour test and all 2000 files during the five hour test. The 900 UE test accessed 1976 distinct files during the one hour test and all 2000 files during the four hour test.

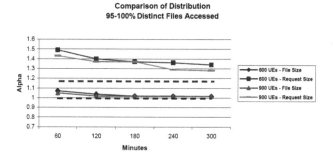

Comparison of Distribution
95-100% Distinct Files Accessed

Figure 2. Distribution results when all distinct files were accessed

The tail of the file size distribution for the 600 and 900 UE, one hour, tests were 7% and 5% higher, respectively, than the input value. 95% and 99% of the distinct files were accessed for these 600 and 900 UE tests, respectively. Both series were within 2% of the input distribution for the file size when all 2000 files were accessed. The tail of the request size distribution for the 600 and 900 UE, 60-minute tests were 27% and 21% higher, respectively, than the input value. During the 300-minute test, the 600 UE test accessed all distinct files and the resultant distribution was 14% higher than the input value. The 900 UE test accessed all 2000 distinct files during the 240-minute test and the resultant distribution was only 9% higher. The evidence shown in both Figures 1 and 2 suggest the importance of selecting a job duration that ensures all distinct files are accessed.

This raised questions concerning the impact on network traffic self-similarity using SURGE. One question was whether the degree of self-similarity was consistent given the same load and the same job duration. Another question was how does the job duration affect the burstiness in traffic. And finally, was this network traffic property sensitive to simulation executions that were too long, or not long enough. The next sections specifically address these questions.

Our data indicated that SURGE produced consistent results for the degree of self-similarity in simulated network traffic. This was demonstrated by executing three series of six tests each.

The series' job durations were selected according to the percentage of available distinct files accessed. The percentage accessed ranged between 97% and 100%. The Base series used the SURGE default distributions. Two series used distributions from real world examples, the first was extracted from [Crovella and Bestavros, 1997], and the second was developed from the Illinois Institute of Technology at Rice Campus Web site. Table 2 lists the defining characteristics for the Base series and both real world examples.

Series Name	User Load (UEs)	Job Duration (minutes)	# Distinct Files	% Distinct Files Accessed	Mean (Hurst)	Standard Deviation (Hurst)
Base	1200	40	2000	97%	0.74	0.014
IIT*	1100	5	344	100%	0.798	0.006
BC*	1200	210	4683	99%	0.818	0.01

Table 2. Series Characteristics
*Real-world Examples

Based upon the results of the above, the degree of self-similarity is relatively constant for the same load and the same job duration.

Next, we investigated the relationship between the percent of distinct files accessed and the degree of self-similarity. To accomplish this we executed three separate series of tests. The first of these three series examined the Hurst value given the same load over an increased time frame. This would, in effect, increase the number of distinct files accessed. Eight tests were executed with a 60-minute job duration and a simulated user load ranging from 300 UEs to 1350 UEs. The number of distinct files accessed ranged between 87% and 99%. Figure 3 illustrates the increase of the Hurst value as both the load is increased and the number of distinct files accessed hits 99%.

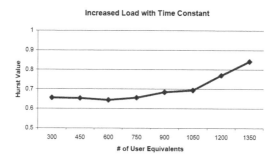

Figure 3. Increased Load with Time Constant

The other two series produced similar results from a different perspective. For both series, the load was held constant and the duration of the job increased. As the time increased, so would the number of files accessed. Each series consisted of five tests. The first series had a 600 UE load and the second had a 900 UE load. The test job durations ranged from 60 to 300 minutes. The 60-minute, 600 UE load test accessed 95% of the distinct files and the 900 UE load test accessed 99% of the distinct files. With the 600 UE load, all files were accessed during the 300-

minute test. The 900 UE load accessed all files during the 240 minute test. Figure 4 depicts the impact on the degree of self-similarity.

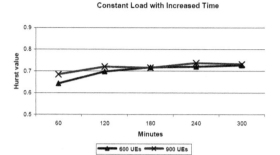

Figure 4. Constant Load with Increased Time

The Mean Hurst value for the 600 UE series was 0.7006 with a Standard Deviation of 0.034. The Mean Hurst value for the 900 UE series was 0.7174 with a Standard Deviation of 0.02. The 600 UE series appears relatively stable beginning at 180 minutes with a Mean Hurst value of 0.721 and a Standard Deviation of 0.005. The 900 UE series appears stable at 120 minutes with a Mean Hurst value of 0.726 and a Standard Deviation of 0.01. 99.85% of the distinct files were accessed at exactly this point for both series.

Based upon the results of the three series reflected in Figures 3 and 4, the job duration did in fact play a role in the degree of self-similarity and was dependent on all distinct files being accessed. It was clear from the above that it was important to select a job duration that would be long enough for all distinct files to be accessed. Therefore, the job duration could be too short to provide accurate Hurst value results. One question remained and that was whether the job duration could be too long. One last series was executed to investigate this. Empirical data indicated that 100% of the 344 distinct files for the IIT series were accessed in five minutes. Six tests comprised this series. The simulated user load was held constant at 1100 UEs and the job duration was increased from four minutes to 60 minutes. We chose to start the tests at the point prior to all distinct files being accessed and then to monitor the behavior of the Hurst parameter beyond that point. Figure 5 shows the results.

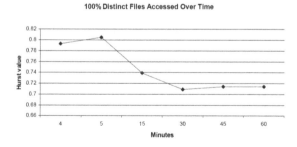

Figure 5. 100% Distinct Files Accessed Over Time

Figure 5 suggests that executing a simulation longer than necessary impacts the results of the Hurst value. We offer as an explanation that once SURGE proceeds through the entire list of distinct files and then begins to repeat the list, the resultant workload would be different than specified by the input. Therefore, we recommend that the total number of distinct files selected be accessible within a reasonable time period, and second, that the tester execute preliminary tests in order to converge on the appropriate job duration for the succeeding tests.

5. Conclusion

We have spent considerable effort understanding and validating SURGE. We believe that this tool offers a reasonable approach for those who wish to simulate realistic Web server workloads as well as those network designers who are searching for a tool that could be applied for general purposes such as simply generating network traffic with self-similar properties. Our work has shown that this tool produces repeatable, precise and realistic results. However, proper use is important. Care must be taken in selecting the appropriate job duration for the simulations. All the distinct files must be accessed during the simulation. Convergence on the simulation time frame should be done prior to the actual simulations. If this is not done, the Hurst value result will be skewed and will not reflect the burstiness associated with the intended workload.

Our efforts will continue by further researching the sensitivity between the degree of self-similarity and workload parameter distributions.

6. References

Barford, P. and Crovella, M. (1998), "Generating Representative Web Workloads for Network and Server Performance Evaluation", *1998 ACM Sigmetrics Conference Performance Review Proceedings*, pp. 151-160.

Barford, P. and Crovella, M. (1999), "Measuring Web Performance in the Wide Area", Boston University, *BU-CS-99-0004*.

Barford, P., Bestavros, A., Bradley, A., and Crovella, M. (1999), "Changes in Web Client Access Patterns Characteristics and Caching Implications", *World Wide Web, Special Issue on Characterization and Performance Evaluation*, Vol. 2, pp. 15-28.

Crovella, M.E. and Bestavros, A. (1997), "Self-similarity in World Wide Web Traffic: Evidence and Possible Causes", *IEEE/ACM Transactions on Networking*, Vol. 5, No. 6, pp. 835-846.

Evans, M., Hastings, N., and Peacock, B. (1993), *Statistical Distributions*, 2nd Edition, John Wiley & Sons, New York, NY.

Leland, W. E., Taqqu, M. S., Willinger, W., and Wilson, D. V. (1995), "On the Self-Similar Nature of Ethernet Traffic (extended version), *IEEE/ACM Transactions on Networking,* Vol. 2, No. 1, pp. 1-15.

Paxson, V., and Floyd, S. (1995), "Wide Area Traffic: The Failure of Poisson Modeling", *IEEE/ACM Transactions on Networking*, Vol. 3, No. 3, pp. 226-244.

Veitch, D., and Abry, P. (1999), "A Wavelet Based Joint Estimator of the Parameters of Long-Range Dependence", *IEEE Trans. Info. Th., special issue on Multiscale Statistical Signal Analysis and its Applications,* Vol. 45, No. 3, pp. 878-897.

Supporting Secure, Ad Hoc Joins for Tactical Targeting Network Technology

Joshua B. Datko, Margaret M. McMahon, and Donald M. Needham
Computer Science Department, United States Naval Academy, Annapolis, MD 21401 USA
e-mail: [m021530,mmmcmahn,needham]@usna.edu

Abstract

The Defense Advanced Research Project Agency's Tactical Targeting Network Technology (TTNT) initiative focuses on improving distributed command and control in tactical military environments. A goal of TTNT is to provide a low-latency, high bandwidth, and dynamically re-configurable network infrastructure that can disclose the full potential of the network to the warfighter. We examine existing joining algorithms to determine their compatibilities and abilities to meet the networking needs of TTNT from a security perspective. We identify and outline protocols needed to support such a TTNT Network, and present an algorithm that provides a foundation for secure, ad hoc joining within a distributed, mobile, wireless network.

Keywords

Mobile and Ad Hoc Networking, Mobile and Networked Applications, Network Security.

1.   Introduction

The emerging Tactical Targeting Network Technology (TTNT) (DARPA, 2000) is a realization of the Network-Centric Warfare (NCW) concept (Alberts, Garstka, and Stein, 1999). The NCW concept defines a networking system composed of a series of "grids" that, when combined, allow a heighten degree of battlespace awareness. A NCW system attains this increased awareness by distributing the command and control entities across the network. The focus of TTNT is to achieve the NCW warfare mission through the establishment of a distributed, dynamically reconfigurable network. Such a network is expected to aid every warfighting entity, but especially tactical aircraft due to the high-speed nature of tactical aviation environments. With TTNT, aircraft can spread target quality information through ad hoc connections, which hopes to improve reaction time to "pop-up" targets (Perkins, 2001).

Two key components of TTNT are *computational grids* and *net-centricity.* An electric power infrastructure provides clients with instantaneous and convenient access, enabling end-users to power a myriad of devices. Likewise, a computational grid attempts to provide the same access to its clients.   The grid forces operations away from the individual platform and towards the networked entities (Foster and Kesselman, 1999). Critical aspects of net-centricity include the ability of a networking infrastructure to provide services on-demand and the ability of the network to be self-administering. A large collaboration of platforms, like the Internet, is not inherently net-centric. Such a network merely allows computational entities to connect to each other. In a net-centric system, the network itself is the computational entity. A net-centric system can be expected to serve the user more efficiently through its ability to manage its own resources. To establish net-centricity, each of the NCW grids is composed of three specialized grids: the information grid, the sensor grid, and the engagement grid (Manola, 1999). The information grid is a networking-hardware construct that provides the mechanism for data communication. It also facilitates an interface for its users to access the information they need.

An area related to our work involves Mobile, Ad hoc, Networks (MANETs), which are inherently unstructured due to their dynamic topology (Corson, 2000). Since entities continuously join and exit the network, the state of the network is in perpetual flux. This uncertainty, especially in a TTNT environment, dramatically increases the problem of securing the network due to the difficulty in establishing and maintaining a trust relationship in a MANET. Various partial solutions exist in emerging MANETs, including the absence of security, simple "shared-secret" authentication, and full Public Key Infrastructures (PKI). Currently, standards like the IEEE 802.11 standard for wireless Local Area Networks implement a symmetric key approach, which reduces the management complexity and encourages faster connection establishment. However, as argued by Schneier (Schneier, 2001), symmetric key solutions do not provide strong security and are easily susceptible to eavesdropping.

Other related areas include enhanced authentication protocols such as Kerberos (Sirbu, 2001). However, Kerberos's network authentication support lacks an adaptive approach to network joining management and is therefore not currently suitable for the TTNT domain. Similarly, Bluetooth's challenge-response authentication scheme does not provide support for a grid-like infrastructure (Held, 2000), and is not scalable to accommodate TTNT due to its limited, proximity-based, nature.

The remainder of this paper is organized as follows. In Section 2 we present the requirements and specifications of our distributed, ad hoc, joining algorithm. In Section 3, we examine our experimental procedure for implementing our joining algorithm. Section 4 contains an analysis of the results of our experiments. Finally, in Section 5 we present our conclusions and discuss our ongoing and future work.

2 A Distributed, Ad Hoc Joining Algorithm

In this section, we discuss the aspects of PKI that are suitable for use in our joining algorithm, describe domain sets that provide classification sets within the TTNT domain, and examine our ad hoc PKI connection as applied to our authentication process.

2.1 PKI Assumption

Conventional PKI is cumbersome in dealing with unknown, ad hoc connecting entities because most protocols involve frequent, trusted, third party access. The nature of the TTNT environment requires secure and rapid connections between parties that may not be close enough (both in a physical and network sense) to access a trusted third party. We use a public-key distributed authentication scheme similar to those in Kerberos (Sirbu, 2001). A completely traditional PKI implementation is not suitable for TTNT because of the complications with the wireless and mobile aspects. However, a PKI can serve as a valuable framework due to the intrinsic structure embedded in TTNT's native military environment. A modified PKI approach must apply a distributed authentication technique and not require trusted third-party references at the time a join request occurs, since such a restriction will inhibit our desired ad hoc connectivity. We assume that trusted third parties exist in the TTNT network that are both cryptographically and physically secure. For the application of tactical aircraft, military air bases and aircraft carriers are prime candidates to act as trusted parties. These secure servers will act as the infrastructure's certification authorities (CA) and provide a reliable digital signature framework. While the network users are in its presence, the CA will perform certificate and key management to maintain a current network state. The PKI framework facilitates faster authentication methods because communicating entities will most likely be either local or inter-domain.

2.2 PKI Domain Sets

Fig. 2 shows a graphical representation of the TTNT domain classification. Network entities will form ad hoc connections most often with their local domain members, however, TTNT entities will also have membership to larger domain levels. Authentication outside a local domain is possible with a hierarchical certificate structure. The military environment, for which TTNT is designed, is well suited for such a PKI.

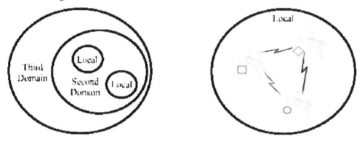

Fig. 1. TTNT Domain Classification

In the TTNT environment, aircraft need to communicate most frequently with other aircraft from their squadron; therefore they all share a local CA. Once the verification process extends from the local reference, authentication time and computation complexity will increase. The second and third domains in Fig. 2 represent broader unit classifications in the TTNT domain scope. For example, two entities from different local domains will have to utilize their shared second domain CA for authentication. The local domain level consists of platforms from the same squadron, ship, or aircraft carrier. As shown in Fig. 2, a sample local domain can contain tactical fighters that may exhibit different NCW characteristics. In keeping with the symbols used in NCW, the square, diamond and circle in Fig. 2 respectively represent a shooter, decision-maker, and sensor platform. A tactical fighter attempting to join a network that is composed of fighters from its own squadron is considered local to the network. Such aircraft would share the same immediate CA, in this case the air-craft carrier. Classifying TTNT entities by "same service" denotes the next domain. The same-service classification adds complexity to the joining process because the certificate chains increase in length. Likewise, the classifications further expand to include same-county, and coalition-forces domains.

2.3   Ad Hoc PKI Connection

After certificate initialization, entities are prepared to participate in the TTNT network. Fig. 3 depicts the scenario in which entity A is acting independently, and discovers a TTNT network via a multicast-discovery protocol. Entity A begins to authenticate with entity B, which is already a member of the network. To guarantee authentication, each member participates in a distributed, public-key protocol. In this case, both A and B share CA_1 in their certificate chain, demonstrating that both entities have an established relationship prior to attempting an ad hoc connection.

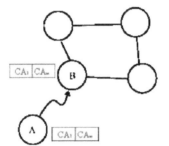

Fig. 2. Ad Hoc Certificate Validation

3   Joining Phase Experiments

We conducted our experimental implementation of the joining algorithm using Sun Microsystems' Jini Technology version 1.1 (Arnold, 2000). Our joining algorithm is divided into three phases: initialization, discovery, and authentication. As shown in Fig. 4, the initialization phase requires that the authentication service provider register itself with a decision maker entity. This allows the decision maker entity to provide a lookup service for subsequent services that may register with the

Fig. 3. Initialization Phase of the Joining Algorithm

decision maker. A joining entity searches for and locates a TTNT network during the discovery phase. To focus our discussion of operations during this phase, we make the assumptions that the network exists, and that the joining entity discovers the network. The actual discovery protocol is independent to the joining algorithm. A multicast protocol is preferable due to the wireless nature of TTNT, and we currently use Jini's multicast protocol for our implementation. However, we plan to validate the feasibility of other multicast protocols, specifically Macker's Multicast Dissemination Protocol (Macker and Adamson, 1999).

In order to authenticate, the joining entities participate in a four part procedure:
- **Obtain Proxy.** The first procedure in the authentication phase is for the lookup service provider (LSP) to provide a proxy to the joining entity (JE) so it may communicate directly with the authentication service provider (ASP).
- **Client Sends Certificate.** Once the client has obtained the service's proxy, it sends its public key and certificate chain directly to the authentication service. The authentication service then computes the validity of the certificate and decides whether or not to authenticate the entity.
- **Authentication Service Acknowledgement.** The authentication service responds directly back to the joining entity with an acknowledgement. The client sends pertinent routing information to the service when the client sends it its certificate, ensuring that the service may respond in this step.
- **Acceptance.** Assuming that the entity was positively authenticated, it may now participate on the TTNT network. Authentication allows the entity to communicate and interact with the other entities on the network. Furthermore, it may now serve a role in authenticating other entities as they appear.

Fig. 5 depicts the discovery phase and illustrates a joining entity attempting to locate a network. As shown in Fig. 5, the previous authentication procedure is applied to a possible TTNT scenario. A sensor on the aircraft is trying to join a pre-established network of similar aircraft. In this scenario, the sensor may be the aircraft's radar that has discovered a target and it is attempting to communicate to neighboring aircraft that a threat exists.

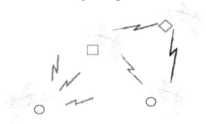

Figure 5 - TTNT Scenario Application

Once the network receives the joining aircraft's request, the network (via the lookup service provider) responds with the location of the authentication service provider, which as shown in Fig. 5, resides on the decision maker (diamond marked) aircraft. The joining aircraft then contacts the authentication service directly and sends its certificate. If the authentication is successful, the authentication service responds with a session key, thus granting access to the network. We assume that the two entities have a high level of trust due to their pre-established relationship. The joining algorithm scales up to handle similar scenarios when the common CA is outside the local group. Although the validation time to find the common CA increases as a result, the entities still have a pre-defined relationship that establishes an *a priori* trust classification.

4 Analysis of Results

The Jini implementation supported our algorithm's design goals of allowing distributed, ad hoc, and net-centric connections. The location and procedures of the authentication service appeared transparent to client, which was able to access the service through a simplified interface. The client connected, and used the service without knowledge of the service's location, and without knowledge that the service indeed existed. Jini supports the ability to facilitate the connectivity required for the joining algorithm's operation.

To establish the desired implementation, we modeled the authentication procedure as a Jini service. The authentication service is responsible for deciding whether or not a client can be allowed to access the network, therefore the client must call it before other services may be requested. Before a client can access the service, however, the service object must register with a lookup service. In response, the service object uploads its proxy to the lookup service so that clients may download it. When a sensory object requests authentication from the network, the lookup service responds with the downloadable proxy. Once the lookup server has responded, the sensor then contacts the authentication server directly to proceed. This portion of the joining algorithm is implemented in Jini by having the sensor object contact the authentication server via its published proxy.

4.1 Modeling the Authentication Protocol as a Jini Service

We modeled and tested the algorithm using Jini technology. Using Jini technology, the network provides the user with the desired service by first locating and then installing the necessary components. Jini offers automated synchronization of network resources, which is an important requirement of TTNT. There are two main factors that motivated the decision to model the authentication protocol as a Jini service. First, a Jini service is ubiquitous across the network to the client. This feature facilitates the net-centric component required for TTNT operation. Currently, we are using Jini's default lookup service mechanism to support the grid work for the authentication service. This service follows the traditional Jini model where the service will first publish itself with a lookup service. When a client requests the service, it probes for a lookup service and then downloads the requested service's proxy object. This proxy object is then used to communicate directly with the service. The second advantage of authentication protocol implementation as a Jini service is that the server on which the authentication service resides can maintain supervisory privileges of the algorithm operations.

4.2 Need for Trust Assigning Procedure

We conclude from our experimental results that ad hoc, distributed, net-centric joining can occur securely with a reference PKI. However, the network should be able to accommodate a joining entity that lies outside of the TTNT domain classifications. In a practical TTNT application, this would represent a tactical fighter entity attempting to join a network composed of aircraft from a different branch of military service. The challenging problem in this scenario is that the joining entity may need rapid access to network resources, for example information concerning a nearby target, but the access time is delayed due to a lack of, or complex, certificate chain configuration. To facilitate a join where an entity can produce characteristics necessary for proper PKI authentication, we are currently incorporating a trust assigning portion to our joining algorithm.

The trust assignment procedure will classify entities into different trust levels based on the security credentials they provide. For example, an entity that can produce a fully qualified certificate will be assigned to the most trusted level, whereas an entity with an expired certificate will be placed in one of the lowest levels. Included in the trust assignment process is the ability to accept recommendations from other entities. Therefore, entities already on the network may make trust assertions for a joining entity, which will reflect in the joining entity's trust classification. TTNT security policies will account for the addition of marginally trusted entities to maintain network security. The addition of trust classification into the TTNT joining algorithm will support rapidity of access without compromising security. This trust assigning algorithm adheres to the following assumptions:

-   That not all entities on the network are fully trusted.
-   An entity's trust rating may increase or decrease.
-   A federated network of entities can perform effective trust management.

The incorporation of trust assignment improves upon an oversight in the Jini and Bluetooth security models. Both Jini and Bluetooth hold to the assumption that once an entity is authenticated, it is a member of a static classification. Jini, through Java security implementations, supports access restrictions, however, these restrictions are pre-defined during development. Further work is in progress on Jini security modifications that support enhanced distributed and ad hoc connections (Eronen, 2001), however, work is still needed to allow adaptive joining policies at the time of joining. Bluetooth's security relies on a symmetric password protocol, which does not allow dynamic re-configurability in terms of security. A trust-assigning algorithm would be beneficial in furthering the net-centricity of a system by enabling the network to dynamically classify joining entities.

5 Conclusions and Future Work

In this paper we illustrated the shortcomings of the standard Jini and Bluetooth algorithms with respect to the Tactical Targeting Network Technology (TTNT) domain. Jini neither defines an authentication algorithm nor incorporates trust-based decisions. Bluetooth applies a questionable symmetric key algorithm that fails to provide a sufficient level of security for TTNT. We examined various utility protocols that support TTNT and described several multicast discovery protocols that could support the initial step in the joining algorithm. We also discussed the need for a distributed public key protocol to enable ad hoc connections in a dynamic environment.

We presented an algorithm that facilitates wireless ad hoc joining requests with the key assumption that an *a priori* public-key infrastructure is in place. Enhancing the algorithm to support trust classifiable ad hoc connections, with entities unknown to the public-key infrastructure is currently a work in progress. The updated algorithm will incorporate network trust models to allow "levels" of trust on the network. In order to enable rapid, purely ad hoc connections, the network protocol necessarily needs the joining algorithm to make the decision to allow an entity to join, and if so, to what degree the entity should be trusted.

We are currently conducting further empirical analysis on the growth in validation time for the joining algorithm. We plan to experiment with varying domain level complexities to determine an algorithmic running time. For our trust-based extension currently in development, we are planning to obtain general asymptotic analysis in the complexity of a multi-level trust authentication scheme.

In future work, we are considering whether a separate algorithm can be created to perform trust management and maintenance after the entity has joined the network. This algorithm's focus will be to promote an entity's trust rating based on its behavior, and would dynamically poll the network for updated trust ratings. Also, it would be interesting to compare our algorithm with a joining algorithm that does not assume that an implemented PKI exists. In the absence of a PKI, the network would be truly distributed and decentralized, changing many assumptions concerning security.

6 References

Alberts, D., Garstka J., and Stein, F. (1999), "Network Centric Warfare: Developing and Leveraging Information Superiority", *CCRP Vol 88*, Washington, D.C.

Arnold, K. (2000), *The Jini Specifications*, 2nd ed, Addison-Wesley.

Corson, S. (2000), *Mobile Ad Hoc Networking (MANET)*. Networking Working Group. www.isi.edu/in-notes/rfc2501.txt.

DARPA (2000), "Tactical Targeting Network Technology", *Defense Advanced Research Projects Agency*, Reference Number-TTNT-ID-00.

Eronen, P. (2001), "Security in the Jini Networking Technology: A Decentralized Trust Management Approach", Masters Thesis, Helsinki University of Technology, Department of Computer Science and Engineering.

Foster, I. and Kesselman C. (1999), *The Grid: Blueprint for a New Computing Infrastructure*. Morgan Kaufmann, California.

Held, G. (2000), *Data over Wireless Networks : Bluetooth, Wap, and Wireless LANs*, McGraw-Hill.

Macker, J. and Adamson, B. (1999), "The Multicast Dissemination Protocol (MDP)", Internet Engineering Task Force.

Manola, F. (1999), "Characterizing the Agent Grid", *Object Services and Consulting Inc.* www.objs.com/agility/tech-reports/990623-characterizing-the-agent-grid.html.

Perkins, C. (2001), *Ad Hoc Networking*, Addison-Wesley, New York.

Schneier, B. (2001), "802.11 Security." *Crypto-Gram Newsletter*, March 15, 2001.

Sirbu, M. (2001), "Distributed Authentication in Kerberos Using Public Key Cryptography", *Information Networking Institute's Net Bill*, Carnegie Mellon University.

A Scalable Path Restoration Scheme for MPLS Network

Daniel Won-Kyu Hong[1] and Choong Seon Hong[2]

[1] Access Network Lab., R&D Group, KT
463-1 Junmin-Dong Yusung-Gu, Daejeon 305-811 South Korea
Tel: +82 42 870 8254   Fax: +82 42 870 8019
E-mail: wkhong@kt.co.kr

[2] School of Electronics and Information, Hyung Hee University
1 Seocheon-Ri Kihung Yongin, Kyungki-Do 449-701 South Korea
Tel: +82 31 201 2532   Fax: +82 31 204 8115
E-mail: cshong@khu.ac.kr

Abstract

In this paper, we propose a scalable label switched path (LSP) restoration scheme using transient backup path for MPLS traffic engineering, which focuses on the maximization of network resource utilization better than the restoration speed. However, it does not prominently degrade the performance of restoration speed comparing with the existing backup path driven approaches [Huang 2000, Haskin 2000], which establishes the working and backup paths simultaneously for fast restoration and lacks resource utilization and backup path protection schemes. Our model may provide the moderated restoration speed comparing with the existing backup path approaches, maximize network resource utilization and protect backup path without requiring much longer restoration time. We define the transient backup path model that dynamically establishes a transient backup path taking into account the current network status and topology when node or link goes down and automatically releases it when node or links goes up. We will show the procedure how it restores the faulty working path without prominent performance degradation with maximization of network resource utilization comparing with the existing backup path driven restoration methods [Huang 2000, Haskin 2000]. Through simulation, the performance of proposed restoration scheme is measured and compared with the existing schemes in terms of packet loss, packet re-ordering and network resource utilization.

1. Introduction

Traffic engineering is the process of controlling how traffic flows through one's network so as to optimize resource utilization and network performance [Rosen 1999]. Traffic engineering is needed in the Internet mainly because current IGPs always use the shortest paths to forward traffic [Awduche and Malcolm 1999, Awduche 1999, Notel 1999, Andreson 1999, Sharma and Crane 2001]. Using shortest paths conserves network resources, but it may also cause the following problems: (1) the shortest paths from different sources overlap at some links, causing congestion on those links and (2) the traffic from a source to a destination exceeds the capacity of the shortest path, while a longer path between these two routers is under-utilized.

To avoid such problems, IETF has been standardizing Multi-Protocol Label Switching (MPLS) that is a new technology enabling the setup of Label Switched Paths (LSPs) through an IP network. Initially, the idea of IP label switching was to speed up the packet forwarding in routers via simple table lookups instead of longest-matching prefix algorithms. It computes routes that are subject to constraints such as bandwidth and administrative policy using Constraint-based Routing (CBR). Network traffic is hence distributed more evenly. In addition, it provides the capacity that can establish a Constraint-based Routed LSP (CR-LDP), which is Explicit-Routed Label Switched Path (ER-LSP) based on the QoS. Because CBR considers more than network topology in computing routes, it may find a longer but lightly loaded path better than the heavily loaded shortest path.

However, in the meantime rerouting method for traffic engineering in IP networks became the driving force behind MPLS. The ability to protect traffic around failure or congestion in a LSP can be important in mission critical MPLS network. In addition, network topologies are never stable over time. Under these environments, a MPLS traffic engineering system that expects to deliver service and remain optimized must respond to the time varying topological changes stems from node/link failure. Restoration is necessary for two different aspects. One is fast restoration and the other is optimized restoration. Fast restoration minimizes service disruptions for the flows affected by an outage using the backup path. Optimized restoration serves to alternative optimized traffic flow in line with a changed network topology. However, fast restoration cannot provide fast change of traffic flows any more when the backup and working paths go down simultaneously and cannot increase network resource utilization. On the other hand, optimized restoration requires longer restoration time.

In this paper, we propose a LSP restoration scheme using transient backup path for MPLS traffic engineering, which focuses on the maximization of network resource utilization better than the restoration speed. However, it does not prominently degrade the performance of restoration speed comparing with the existing backup path driven approaches [Huang 2000, Haskin 2000], which establishes the working and backup paths simultaneously for fast restoration and lacks resource utilization and backup path protection schemes. Our model may provide the moderated restoration speed comparing with the existing backup path approaches, maximize network resource utilization and protect backup path without requiring much longer restoration time. We define the transient backup path model that dynamically establishes a transient backup path taking into account the current network status and topology when node or link goes down and automatically releases it when node or links goes up. We propose a dynamic transient backup path calculation algorithm and show the procedure how it restores the faulty working path without prominent performance degradation with maximization of network resource utilization comparing with the existing backup path driven restoration methods [Huang 2000, Haskin 2000]. Through simulation, the performance of proposed restoration scheme is measured and compared with the existing schemes in terms of packet loss, concurrent failure of working and backup paths and network resource utilization.

The rest of this paper is organized as follows. Section 2 overviews and analysis the existing fast and optimized rerouting schemes. Section 3 illustrates our rerouting model. Section 4 describes performances measured and compared with the fast and optimized rerouting schemes following the concluding remarks in Section 5.

2. Related Works

There are two major restoration schemes [Huang 2000, Haskin 2000]. They use the pre-negotiated protection scheme that a backup path is established in line with the establishment of working path in order to reduce path switching time when there is abnormality at the working path. Figure 1 shows the two restoration schemes.

In the case of first restoration scheme using *1:1 restoration scheme* [Huang 2000], the working LSP between Protection Ingress LSR (PIL) and Protection Merging LSR (PML) is established and the backup LSP that does not utilize the links traversed by the working LSP is established. When LSR8 detects abnormalities such as fault or congestion, it sends an abnormality notification to PIL corresponding to LSR0 in Figure 1. On receiving the abnormality notification, PIL redirects the packet flow from the working LSP to the backup LSP traversing <LSR0-LSR1-LSR2-LSR3-LSR4-LSR9>.

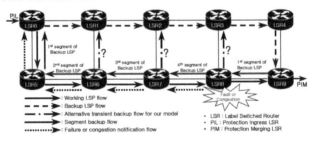

Figure 1. Fast and optimized rerouting schemes and other consideration point

In the case of second restoration scheme using *alternative label switched path scheme* [Haskin 2000], the working LSP between PIL and PML is established and the first segment of backup path between PML and PIL in the reverse direction of the work LSP is established that is corresponding to the double dashed arrow line in Figure 1. Subsequently, the second and final segments of backup LSP are established between PIL and PML along a transmission path that does not utilize the working LSP [Ahn 2001]. When LSR5 detects abnormalities such as fault or congestion, the packets flows is rerouted along the backup LSP, <LSR7-LSR6-LSR6-LSR0-LSR1-LSR2-LSR3-LSR4>.

In the second case restoration scheme, there is almost no packet loss during abnormalities and is some transit delay due to the longer hop of backup LSP. However, it needs not reordering the packet flow from backup LSP to working LSP when the abnormalities at LSR8 are solved [Ahn 2001]. In the first case restoration scheme, there is almost no overhead for reordering packet flow during abnormalities and is some packet loss because PIL does not redirects the packet flow from working LSP to backup LSP until it receives the abnormality notification message from LSR8 detecting the abnormalities.

3. Scalable Restoration Scheme Using Transient Backup Path

In the previous section, we discuss two major restoration schemes based on the pre-negotiated backup path driven approach. They show the following critical disadvantages: (1) lack of resource utilization, (2) lack of alternative mechanism for the concurrent faults of working and backup LSPs, and (3) high resource consumption for simultaneous establishment of working and backup LSPs. To solve these problems, we propose a scalable restoration mechanism using transient backup path concept.

Transient backup path is established when node or link goes down taking into account current network status and topology and is released when node or link goes up. It is an alternative path deserving the same traffic parameters as working path and detouring the fault portion of working path. However, the scope of alternative path is not fixed, it can be determined by the transit backup path routing algorithm. Our transit backup path routing algorithm finds the most reasonable path under the current network topology and status. We define the two routing metrics of *available bandwidth (AVA)* and *reachability (R = Normal/Degraded/Abnormal)* for each transmission link, for example *(AVA,R) = (40,N)*. The reachability represents the operational status of transmission link such as normal, degraded, and abnormal.

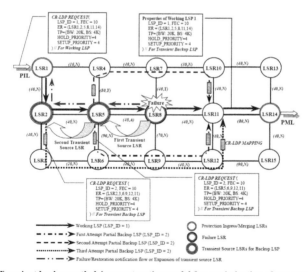

Figure 2. Transient backup path driven restoration model for maximization of resource utilization

Figure 2 shows our transient backup path driven restoration model for maximization of network resource utilization and Figure 3 shows the restoration algorithm using the transient backup path model. The restoration procedure using our transient backup path concept is as follows:

1. A working LSP between PIL and PML is established along LSR1-2-5-8-11-14 by issuing CRLDP-REQUEST message, as shown in Figure 2.
2. LSR8 detects abnormality such as congestion or fault and notifies it to adjacent LSR in reverse direction of working LSP.
3. LSR5 receiving failure notification can be the transient source LSR to find optimal transient backup route. On the other hand, LSR5 can easily find the list of LSRs along working LSP in *ER* of CR-LDP or *Path Vector* of LDP. LSR determines a transient destination LSRs that is the adjacent LSR of faulty LSR in forward direction, for example the transient destination LSR can be LSR11 in Figure 2.
4. The transient source LSR finds the most reasonable path to the transient destination LSR using the Bounded Flooding Routing Algorithm (BFRA) [Hong 2000] that can provide the optimal route taking into account multiple routing metrics such as bandwidth, delay, etc. For example, there are two shortest paths between LSR5 and LSR11: one is along LSR5-4-7-10-11 and the other is along LSR5-6-9-12-11. If their hop count is equal, we select the path having the largest residual bandwidth along the selected route.
5. After finding an optimal transient backup route, the transient source LSR establishes the explicit route using CRLDP-REQUEST message and the transient destination LSR issues the CRLDP-MAPPING message to redirect the packet flow to newly established transient backup path. Now, we restore the failed working path using transient backup path.
6. If LSR8 detects clearance of abnormality, we redirect the packet flow from transient backup LSP to existing working LSP and release the transient backup LSP using CRLDP-RELEASE message.

There is one more importance concept of restoration scope extension. If we failed to find an optimal route for transient backup path, we will extend the restoration scope by adjusting the transient source LSR. For example, the first transient source LSR5 filed to find an optimal route, it issues logical failure notification to its adjacent LSR2 in the backward direction of working LSP in Figure 2. However, the transient destination LSR is not changed. The LSR2 establish the extended transient backup path between LSR2 and LSR 11 by repeating above steps 2-6.

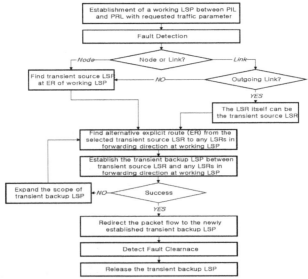

Figure 3. Restoration algorithm of transient backup path scheme

The restoration scope expansion can be done until the transient source LSR is corresponding to the PLR.
Our restoration scheme using transient backup path has the following advantages:

- It can maximize the network resource utilization because it finds the transient backup route with the most recent network status and topology at the abnormalities, which was impossible in existing restoration schemes.
- It can save network resource because it need not establish the backup path prior to the occurrence of abnormalities and it immediately releases the transient backup path just after clearance of abnormalities.
- It need not take into account the backup path protection scheme because it does not simultaneously maintain the backup path with working path. If any part of transient backup path is in faulty, we can find another transient backup path with the same scheme.

4. Simulation and Performance Analysis

In order to simulate the proposed restoration scheme, the 1:1 protection scheme [Huang 2000] and the alternative label switched path scheme [Haskin 2000], we used the QOS Routing Simulator (QRS) [Helsinki 2001] under such simulation environment as shown in Figure 4. Each LSR is connected with a duplex link with the 10Mbps bandwidth, 10ms delay and a CBQ queue. We use one pair of real-time traffic that is inserted into LSR0 corresponding to PIL and escaped from LSE10 corresponding PML. We use real-time traffic model for setting up LSPs with specific bandwidth requirements as the QoS traffic. For this, the traffic generator generates 256 byte long packets at 2Mpbs and at the constant bit rate. To detect any abnormalities of the working path, we monitor all LSRs at every 10ms.

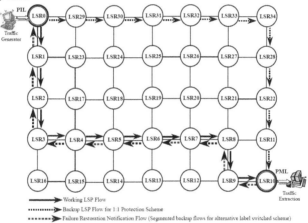

Figure 4. Simulated network topology for performance evaluation

There are various performance evaluation criterions in related with MPLS path restoration such as recovery time, full restoration time, setup vulnerability, backup capacity, additive latency, re-ordering, state overhead, loss, and coverage [9]. Because our algorithm focuses on the maximization of network resource utilization and moderation of path restoration speed, we evaluate loss, re-ordering and resource utilization of the proposed transient backup path protection scheme. Because we use QoS traffic for performance evaluation, a working LSP and a transient backup LSP for QoS traffic are established by using CR-LSP, which is guaranteed the bandwidth required but can not utilize the rest bandwidth of links.

Figure 5 shows the pack loss in the case of LSR failure along the working LSP. We measured the packet loss on the 1:1 protection scheme, alternative label switched protection scheme, and our transient backup path restoration scheme. Our restoration scheme shows much higher performance than the existing restoration schemes under the simulated network topology of Figure 4. The 1:1 protection scheme and the alternative label switched path scheme have some problem that the number of the dropped packets increases in proportion to the distance between PIL corresponding to LSR0 and LSR detecting the failure. Though our restoration scheme also has some problem of packet loss during the establishment of the transient backup path detouring the faulty LSR, it shows nearly constant packet loss of approximate 50 byte packets under the simulated network topology as shown in Figure 4.

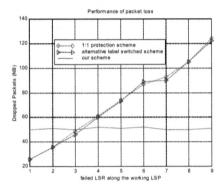

Figure 5. Packet loss in the case of LSR failure along the working LSP

Figure 6 shows the packet re-ordering performance by the location of failed LSR. In the case of alternative label switched path scheme, it has almost no problem in re-ordering of packets for changing traffic flow from working path to predetermined backup path. However, the 1:1 protection scheme has some problem that the number of re-ordered packets increases in proportion to the distance between PIL and the LSR detecting the failure. Unfortunately, our restoration scheme shows bad re-ordering performance than other schemes. It was mainly caused by the overhead for the dynamic establishment of transient backup path detouring the faulty LSR and the twice re-ordering at the source and sink of transient backup path.

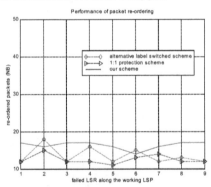

Figure 6. Re-ordering performance in the case of LSR8 failure along the working LSP

Figure 7 shows the performance of network resource utilization. In order to measure the network resource utilization, we define resource metrics as label, bandwidth, and buffer used for the working and backup paths. The proposed scheme shows the best performance than other schemes in terms of resource utilization. Because it finds the transient backup path detouring the faulty working path taking into account the global network resource status at the time of failure, it can maximize the network resource utilization. From the perspective of restoration speed, our scheme showed the moderated performance between 1:1 protection scheme and alternative label switched path scheme or the slightly degraded performance than the 1:1 protection scheme according to the fault location.

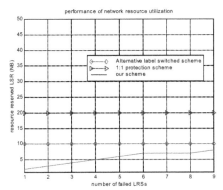

Figure 7. Resource utilization performance

5. Concluding Remarks

This paper proposed a LSP restoration scheme using transient backup path for MPLS traffic engineering, which focuses on the maximization of network resource utilization better than the restoration speed. It provided the moderated restoration speed comparing with the existing backup path approaches [Huang 2000, Haskin 2000], maximize network resource utilization and protect backup path without requiring much longer restoration time. We defined the transient backup path model that dynamically establishes a transient backup path taking into account the current network status and topology when node or link goes down and automatically releases it when node or links goes up. We showed the procedure how it restores the faulty working path without prominent performance degradation with maximization of network resource utilization comparing with the existing backup path driven restoration methods.

Through simulation and performance comparison with existing restoration schemes in terms of packet loss, re-ordering and resource utilization, it has been proved that our restoration scheme using transient backup path showed the most higher performance in terms of network resource utilization, good performance in terms of network resource utilization and packet loss than other schemes. In addition, it showed the moderated restoration speed in comparison with the existing schemes according to the fault location. Another important aspect of our restoration scheme is that it need not take into account the current failures of working and backup paths because it does not maintain any backup path prior to the failure. However, it showed poor re-ordering performance than the existing schemes. We need to further study the scheme to enhance the re-ordering performance of packet flow.

References

E. Rosen, A. Viswanathan and R. Callon (1999), "Multiprotocol Label Switching Architecture," *Internet Draft* <*draft-ietf-mpls-arch-06.txt*>.

D. Awduche, J. J. Malcolm, J. Agogbua, M. O'Dell and J. McNabus (1999), "Requirements for Traffic Engineering over MPLS," *RFC2702*.

D. Awduche et al. (1999), "Requirements for Traffic Engineering Over MPLS," *REC 2702*.

Changcheng Huang, Vishal Shrma, Srinivas Makam, Ken Owens (2000), "A Path Protection/Restoration Mechanism for MPLS Networks," *Internet Draft* <draft-chang-mpls-path-protection-02.txt>.

Dimietry Haskin, Ram Krishnan (2000), "A Method for Setting an Alternative Label Switched Paths to Handle

Fast Reroute," *Internet Draft*.<draft- haskin-mpls-fast-reroute-05.txt>.

Nortel Networks, Ennovate Networks, IBM Corp, Cisco Systems (1999), "LDP Specification," Internet Draft.

Loa Andersson, Brad Cain, Bilel Jamoussi (1999), "Requirement Framework for Fast Re-route with MPLS," *Internet Draft*.

Daniel W.K.Hong and D.S.Yun (2000), "Network Management with Bounded Flooding Routing Algorithm to Ensure IP QoS over ATM Virtual Path Network," *Proc. of IEEE International Conference on Network Management and Operation (NOMS)*.

Vishal Sharma, Ben-Mark Crane, Ken Owens, Changcheng Huang, Fiffi Hellstrand, Brad Cain, Seyhan Civanlar and Angela Chiu (2001), "Framework for MPLS-based Recovery," *Internet Draft <draft-ietf-mpls-recovery-frmwrk-03.txt>*.

Gaeil Ahn and Woojik Chun (2001), "MPLS Restoration Scheme using Least-Cost Based Dynamic Backup Path," *Proceedings of International Conference on Networking (ICN2001)*.

Helsinki University of Technology (2001), "QoS Routing Simulator (QRS) Version2.0," Available at *http://www.tct.hut.fi/~pgzhang/QRS/index.html*.

Impact of heavy traffic beyond communication range in multi-hops ad-hoc networks

Dominique Dhoutaut and Isabelle Guérin-Lassous

Equipe ARES - CITI Domaine Scientifique de la Doua

Bât. Léonard de Vinci 21, av. Jean Capelle

69621 Villeurbanne - FRANCE

Dominique.Dhoutaut@ens-lyon.fr Isabelle.Guerin-Lassous@ens-lyon.fr

Abstract

For commercial availability reasons, most actual multi-hops ad-hoc simulations and test-beds are based on 802.11 (1999) and its medium access method CSMA/CA. But this standard has not been designed for that kind of network and presents serious flaws in this context. In this paper, we shall try to highlight problems that can appear in the **non-direct** neighborhood of important data flows in ad-hoc networks. In some situations, the fairness of the medium access can indeed be very poor. Various techniques could be used to solve this problem. In this paper we present one solution, which only requires minor modifications to the standard.

Keywords

Ad-hoc networks, Radio interferences, Medium access, 802.11

1 Introduction

Ad-hoc technologies (according to the definition given by the manet working group at IETF - see Corson & Macker (1999), namely mobiles associated in a network, without fixed facilities), are going to be more and more used on laptops and equivalents (ease of deployment and use, fault tolerance, and many more other advantages).

Most of the actual work on ad-hoc networks concerns routing algorithms. All these works generally assume that a fair medium access method is provided by the underlying layer. Most of the measurements and simulations in this field are based on 802.11 standard or its variants.

The radio medium has obviously some specificities. For example, it suffers from interferences and signal attenuation problems which are unknown in wired networks. To solve some of these problems, RTS/CTS mechanism has been proposed and included in 802.11. Moreover, a large number of alternative access methods have been proposed in the literature (V. Bharghavan & Zhang (1994), Garcia-Luna-Aceves & Fullmer (1999), Wang & Bensaou (2001)); but they do not address all the problems that appear when the mobiles causing the interferences are not in the communication range of each other.

Measurements and simulation of 802.11 networks using base stations usually give good results, mainly for two reasons: - Spatial re-use of the medium can be finely tuned (by assignating in a concerted manner different frequencies to base stations). This means that the fast attenuation of radio signals is taken into account, and that a same frequency can thus be used by more than one base station, provided that they are not too close to each other. - The base stations may be used to coordinate the mobiles which depend on them, thus providing a good fairness in the cell.

But if 802.11 technologies are used to build a multi-hops ad-hoc network (and base stations removed), this ability to planify and control transmissions in a centralized manner is lost, and problems appear.

In particular, to maintain the connectivity through the complete network, all the mobiles need to work on the same frequency (in traditional wireless cell based networks, only mobiles around a same base station have to work on the same frequency). These mobiles in the non-direct neighborhood increase the contention, because of the interferences they produce.

At the physical layer, to understand messages, a mobile needs to receive them with a power above a fixed level. A "communication region" can thus be considered around each mobile; anybody in this region being able to correctly send messages to it. A mobile located out of this region could nevertheless jam the reception, even if its signal is too low for direct communication. The 802.11 standard defines a carrier sense threshold (lower than the communication threshold) which determines a "jamming region" and is used to determine if the medium is free or not.

We shall begin in Section 2 by stating the limitation of the simulator we used. In Section 3, we shall present simulations results showing equity problems with the medium access method in ad-hoc networks context. We shall pay a particular attention to what happens when communication needs exceed what can be provided. In Section 4, a technique improving equity in a significative manner will be presented, which only require very small modifications to 802.11 MAC layer to be implemented. This article will be concluded in Section 5, by considering possible ameliorations of our technique and the relevance of the "injection" of neighborhood topology and traffic informations, still with the intention of improving the equity without sacrifying the performances.

2 Constraints and limitations of our simulations

The following simulations have been realized with Network Simulator 2 Project (2001) and its wireless module (which originally was an extension proposed by the Monarch Project (2002)). We have used the default parameters for 802.11 under ns2. The simulated hardware was a 2MBit/s card, working at 914 MHz. One of the major flaws of ns concerning radio interferences, is that the simulator does not add the different noises existing at a given instant. Instead, it only compares those noise one by one with the communication and carrier sense thresholds. In real world, independently harmless noises can add up and jam our communications. This kind of case is unfortunately not simulated in a correct manner. Given the nature of the problem, we can consider that the results obtained are optimistic (the interferences problems should be even more important).

In some of our simulations, we have used constant bit rate UDP flows. In real world, this kind of flow will unlikely be used. But in simulations, they allow the highlighting of layers 1 and 2 problems which would otherwise have been hidden. Using TCP, a number of other parameters should have been taken into account (in particular, the TCP window size, and the presence of reception acknowledgments would

Figure 1: topology used in the "chain" experiment

have drastically influenced the results). Several works have been conducted on the impact of the medium access method on TCP flows (Xu & Saadawi (2001),K. Tang & Gerla (2001)). But these papers focused on the interactions between mobiles able to communicate with each other. Our present work deals with what happens when mobiles jam each other without being able to communicate.

3 Simulations

3 Experiment 1 : "chain" of static mobiles, of variable length

The first experiment implement a varying length chain of mobiles (Figure 1). Each mobile can communicate with its direct neighbors (the mobiles are placed all 200 meters, their communication range is about 250 meters and they do not move during all the simulated time). As we have used the defaults thresholds of 802.11 and the "two-ray ground" reflection model of ns2, the jamming region of a node is two time larger than the communication region (so about 500 meters). In this simulations, a node is therefore able to jam its one and two hops neighbors. We have put a 2 Mbit/s UDP Constant Bit Rate source (the theoretical maximum allowed by the medium) at one end of the chain, and a receiver for this flow at the other end. Figure 2 presents the simulation results for chain lengths contained between 2 and 8 mobiles. The routing protocol used was DSR (see Johnson, Maltz, Hu & Jetcheva (2001)).

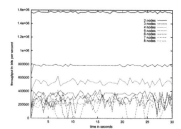 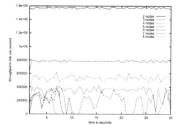

Figure 2: Throughput on the chain depending on the number of mobiles (DSR)

Figure 3: Throughput on the chain depending on the number of mobiles (AODV)

It clearly appears on Figure 2 that the bandwidth is shared between the mobiles, and that the throughput is subsequently reduced. One drawback of the intense contention at the medium access, is that the packets broadcasted by the routing protocol can be repeatedly blocked (no acknowledgment is indeed required for broadcasted packets). The transmitter will not known that these routing packets have been lost, and will not try to send them again (even if they are absolutely necessary for the routing).

As we used DSR in this simulation, as the "mobiles" did not moved and as the route as been established before the sending of the first data packet, the problem did not appeared (don't forget that DSR doesn't try to modify a route as long as it is up).

But when we use AODV (see Das, Perkins & Royer (2001)), then we can see (Figure 3) that when the chain length is increased (thus increasing the contention), the "hello" packets broadcasted for the route maintenance are lost. If too many are lost, the routes expire (curve 5,6,7 and 8 on Figure 3). In general however, any routing protocol which broadcast signaling packets may experiment this kind of problem. In our simulation, if the mobiles had moved, the route would have had to be rebuilt. In the case of DSR, this rebuilding would have been done by a flooding of Route Request packets. This problem may appear as well during the setting up of a route, when there is already a great activity in the network.

3 Experiment 2 : the three moving pairs

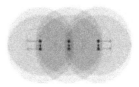

Figure 4: Initial positions of the pairs   Figure 5: Interferences in the experiment

This experiment highlights medium access unfairness. We used the configuration presented on Figure 4: Three pairs of mobiles are initially very close. Each pair is composed of one transmitter and one receiver. The transmitter tries to send a 2 Mbit/s UDP Constant Bit Rate flow. The mobiles of a pair stay very close to each other all the time. During the simulation, the central pair will stay at its initial position, while the others will move away from it in opposite directions at a speed of 25 meters per second (Figure 5). The Figure 6 show the throughputs measured for the three flows, depending on time. The phenomenon can be explained as follows:

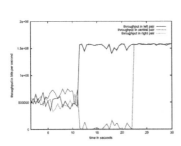

Figure 6: Throughput depending on time

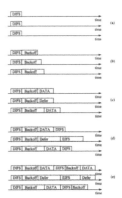

Figure 7: details of the medium access problem with EIFS

- from 0 to 5 seconds : the three pairs are in direct "contact" (in the same communication zone). Even when the network is saturated, as the throughputs requested are the same, the bandwidth is fairly

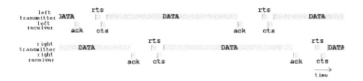

Figure 8: detail of the simulated transmissions during the 11 to 22 seconds period

shared (maximum physical throughput – around 1.6Mbit/s – divided by 3).

- from 5 to 11 seconds : the pairs can still jam each others, but direct communication are no possible anymore. Each time a mobile transmits a packet, the others know the channel is used, even if they may not understand what is said. For the same reasons of well-balanced requests, the medium access is quite fair.

- from 11 to 22 seconds : the central pair is in a different situation from the others. It is in the jamming region of the two others, while the laters are only jammed by the central pair. In this asymmetric context, the medium access mechanism presents flaws. As soon as the central pair loses the channel to a peripheral pair, it has no possibility to get the access back. What happens can be explained in this way : The central pair can only transmit when the others are silent. But as the others pairs do not jam each other, there is no reason for them to be synchronized. Therefore, there is no reason for their backoff periods to coincide. Moreover, the longer the payload, the smaller the chance of backoffs to occur at the same time (Figure 8). The phenomenon is amplified by another mechanism implemented in 802.11. The standard imposes that a mobile has to wait for an EIFS period when the channel becomes free again, after a message has not successfully been received.

The Figure 7 shows in a simplified way (for legibility reasons, the durations are not the real ones) what happens. Please note that even if unlike in this example, in reality all nodes begin at different times, the problem still appears after some time. First, the channel has to be free for a DIFS period before a node decides to transmit (Figure 7a). Then the nodes wait for a random backoff period (Figure 7b). As the transmitter of the first pair has finished its backoff and the channel is free, it begins transmitting, thus jamming the second pair (which enters a defer period until medium is free again). As the third pair has not been jammed, it has finished its backoff and has started to transmit too (Figure 7c). Because of the jamming coming from the third pair, the second has to defer for a longer time. And when the medium become free at last, it has to wait for a EIFS period (about 6 times longer than DIFS in our case). During this time, the two others have entered a new cycle (Figure 7d). And things start over ... (Figure 7e)

- beyond 22 seconds : the pairs are totally isolated and do not jam each other anymore. The observed throughput thus reaches the maximum value allowed by the medium.

3 Experiment 3 : the "static" chain and the roaming "troublemaker"

This experiment shows the impact of the phenomenon previously depicted in a more realistic situation. The topology of the experiment is shown on Figure 9. A UDP CBR flow goes through a "chain" of 6 mobiles (similar to those used in the first experiment, with a distance of 200 meters between each node).

One pair of mobiles (between which another UDP CBR flow exists) is initially located far away from the chain (outside interference region of the nodes of the chain). The mobiles of the pair are always very close to each other (1 meter) during all the simulation. The "mobiles" of the chain never move. During the simulation, the pair moves and progressively goes to the other side, crossing the chain.

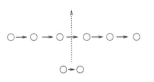

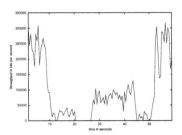

Figure 9: Topology used in the third experiment

Figure 10: mean throughput on the chain

Measures have been taken for various requested throughput for each flow (2000, 1333, 1000, 800, 400 and 200 kbit/s). Except when only 200 kbit/s are requested for each flow, the network capacity is saturated and not enough bandwidth can be provided. For legibility reasons, Figure 10 only presents the mean of measured throughputs. The symmetry is easily seen, as the two "holes" are corresponding to the phenomenon previously described (between 10 and 30 seconds, and between 45 and 50 seconds). This clearly show that the chain's flow is the most perturbated when the "troublemaker" flow is in its interference region.

4   A solution

The following solution has been elaborated in order to minimize the changes to the 802.11 MAC protocol, and if possible to remain compatible with mobiles running unmodified 802.11. We wanted a mechanism able to work even when communications between jamming/jammed mobiles are not possible at all. In this case, it may neither be possible to know which mobile is jamming us, nor if we are jamming someone else, techniques trying to compute exacts times to transmit for each node no longer work. The modifications we propose try to penalize mobiles which transmit too much, so that oppressed mobiles can still gain access to the medium.

The simplest way to impose such penalties is to act on the backoff period. So we have made the following changes to its computation:

At the beginning of each time period, all nodes are in the same situation. Next, each time a node gains access to the medium and sends a packet, a penalty is added to its backoff (thus the backoff for the next packet that will be sent by this mobile will be statistically greater). We furthermore precise that except for this penalty, the backoff is computed in the way indicated in 802.11 standard.

The penalty progression curve (Figure 11) is for now arbitrarily defined. It presents a lower "plateau" ("the first packets do not cost much"), then an abrupt ramp ("now it's time to let the others speak"), and finally a higher plateau (if we continue to increase penalty in an exponential manner, the throughput will be too reduced when a single flow is present in the network).At the beginning of each cycle, all the

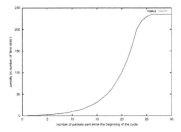

Figure 11: progression of the penalty depending on the number of packets already sent

penalties are set to zero. In this mechanism, the parameters we can adjust are essentially the length of the cycle and the shape of the penalty progression curve.

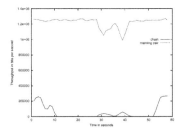

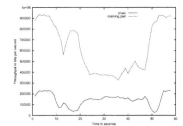

Figure 12: throughputs in the chain and trou-blemaker experiment (TCP, normal 802.11)

Figure 13: throughputs in the chain and trou-blemaker experiment (TCP, modified 802.11)

Even if this method is simple, it gives quite valuable results. In simulations, it appeared that the probability for a mobile to be completely run over by its non-direct neighbors is much smaller than with standard 802.11. And routing protocols benefit a lot of this (in particular proactive protocols). As probability for their packets to be lost in serie is lowered, the probability of needlessly dropping routes is greatly reduced.

We used again the "chain and troublemaker" example (Figure 9), but with TCP, and with a requested throughput of 2 Mbit/s. With standard 802.11, we got disastrous results (Figure 12). Keep in mind that the erratic behavior of the medium access mechanism for the chain prevents TCP acknowledgments to be sent in time, thus preventing ANY progress in the communication. The modified version looks quite better (Figure 13)

Of course, our method presents some drawbacks. We already talked about reduction of the maximum usable bandwidth for an unique node. As we statistically increment the backoff, the maximum number of packet per second is reduced. But this problem quickly becomes imperceptible when we increment the number of contending flows. The other important drawback is the bursty behavior of the communication, which can cause problems for some types of applications (multimedia in particular).

On the other hand, it has the advantage to remain compatible with mobiles using standard 802.11. Even if mobiles using the modified version are penalized (getting less bandwidth than others in case of contention), it will still works in an acceptable manner.

5   Conclusion

In this paper, using ns2 simulations, we have highlighted some flaws of 802.11 medium access method when used for ad-hoc networks. It appeared that as 802.11 has been primarily designed for base-stations based networks, it doesn't handle well the contention when direct communications are not possible. In particular, in case of heavy traffic between two nodes, other transmissions outside communication range but inside jamming region of the transmitter may be almost completely blocked. We have analyzed the problems and have proposed a simple, effective and compatible way to bypass them. However, our solution may be improved in various ways, in order to limit its drawbacks ("bursty" behavior, and in some case decrease of maximum bandwidth). One way would be to find better (dynamic ?) and more effective penalty progression shape. Another way would be to try to integrate to the penalty computation some information about the non-direct neighborhood. Those informations about activity in the vicinity could be, for example, obtained through packets exchanged by routing protocols (in particular by proactive routing protocols, but in general by all protocols making use of "hello" packets).

References

802.11, I. S. (1999), *IEEE Std 802.11, "Wireless Lan Media access control (MAC) and physical layer (PHY) specifications".*, IEEE Computer Society.

Corson, S. & Macker, J. (1999), *RFC2501 Mobile Ad hoc Networking (MANET): Routing Protocol Performance Issues and Evaluation Considerations*, IETF.

Das, S., Perkins, C. & Royer, E. (2001), 'Ad hoc on demand distance vector (aodv) routing'.

Garcia-Luna-Aceves, J. & Fullmer, C. (1999), 'Floor acquisition multiple access (fama) in single-channel wireless networks', *Mobile Networks and Applications, vol. 4, pp157-174*.

Johnson, D., Maltz, D., Hu, Y. & Jetcheva, J. (2001), 'The dynamic source routing protocol for mobile ad hoc networks'.

K. Tang, M. C. & Gerla, M. (2001), 'Effects of ad hoc mac layer medium access mechanisms under tcp'.

Project, T. M. (2002), 'The cmu monarch project's wireless and mobility extension to ns', http://www.monarch.cs.cmu.edu/.

Project, T. V. (2001), 'Network simulator 2', "http://www.isi.edu/nsnam/ns/".

V. Bharghavan, A. Demers, S. S. & Zhang, L. (1994), 'Macaw: A media access protocol for wireless lans"', *ACM SIGCOMM*.

Wang, Y. & Bensaou, B. (2001), Achieving fairness in ieee 802.11 dfwmac with variable packet lengths, *in* 'GLOBECOM 2001 proceedings'.

Xu, S. & Saadawi, T. (2001), 'Does the ieee 802.11 mac protocol work well in multihop wireless ad hoc networks?', *IEEE communications Magazine*.

A Simple ATM Backbone Network Reliability Model

Veena B. Mendiratta

Bell Labs, Lucent Technologies, Naperville, Illinois, USA
e-mail: veena@lucent.com

Abstract

This paper presents an ATM backbone network reliability model that illustrates how different levels of network reliability can be achieved given certain node and network characteristics using results on lower bounds for network reliability. We address network reliability with respect to *connectivity* and *performability* in a telecommunications network context. The connectivity aspect refers to the availability of a path from a source node to a destination node. The performability aspect refers to the ability of the network, in the presence of failures, to preserve existing connections and to initiate new connections. For the network connectivity analysis, node characteristics are specified in terms of the node system availability and the network characteristics are specified in terms of a constraint on the connectivity, that is, the network should not contain cutsets of smaller than a certain size. We calculate, for a given number of hops in the path, the following *all-terminal* reliability metrics in the presence of link and node failures: probability of setting up new calls successfully and the probability that an existing connection is lost. The first metric measures the availability of a network path between two nodes and the second metric measures the ability of the network to preserve existing connections in the presence of failures. We present model results for connectivity and performability for a range of values for the cutset size c and node availability, and analyze the impact of coverage for software failures on performability.

Keywords: ATM Network, Reliability Model, Telecommunications

1. Introduction

Network reliability refers to the reliability of the overall network to provide communication in the event of a failure of a component in the network, and it depends on the sustainability of both hardware and software. Traditionally, failures were primarily due to hardware malfunctions, and thus the emphasis was on element-level network availability and in turn, the determination of overall network availability. In current networks, most failures are due to fiber cable cuts, software causes and malicious attacks (Medhi, et al., 2000). Such failures can drop a significant number of existing connections. Thus the network should have the ability, with low latency, to detect and isolate a fault and reconnect the affected connections. In some cases, depending on the nature of the failure, the network may not have enough capacity to handle a major simultaneous *reconnect* phase (Medhi, 1999).

In this analysis we address network reliability with respect to connectivity and performability.

Connectivity: the availability of a path from a source node to a destination node.

Performability: the ability of the network, in the presence of failures, to preserve existing connections (no dropped calls) and to initiate new connections (no blocked calls).

The terms Switched Virtual Connection (SVC), connection and call are used interchangeably in this paper. Also, in this paper, the terms switch and node refer to an ATM switch.

This paper presents the ATM core network reliability analysis based on an assumed reference architecture and certain ATM switch characteristics. The purpose of this analysis is to illustrate some of the network reliability concepts and show the levels of network reliability that can be achieved given certain node and network characteristics. This analysis can be adapted to model specific network topologies to predict the ATM core network reliability for a given network. The paper is organized as follows: the reference network and associated network architecture assumptions are presented in Section 2; network reliability concepts are presented in Section 3; ATM switch reliability is characterized in Section 4; failure scenarios are presented in Section 5; Section 6 presents the network reliability model covering both connectivity (availability) and performability (lost calls); and the conclusions are presented in Section 7.

2. Reference Network

The reference network is shown in Figure 1 below where edge and core refer to ATM switches at the edge and core of the network respectively.

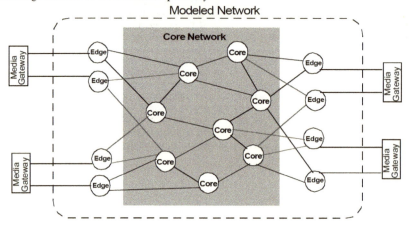

Figure 1. Reference Network

We make the following assumptions about the network architecture.

- Access to the core network is dual homed — each ATM edge switch is connected to at least 2 ATM switches in the core network and each Media Gateway is connected to at least 2 edge switches.

- Every switch in the core network is connected to at least 2 other switches in the core network, that is, all nodes are at least *2-connected*.

- All links are 1+1 APS, therefore, recovery from link failures occurs within 50 ms after detection (as per standards) without any impact on new or stable calls.

- In light of the previous assumption, in modeling network availability we only consider the impact of total node failures and in modeling lost calls we consider the impact of partial and total node failures.

- It is assumed that, at any given instance of time, only a single failure can occur in the modeled network and thus it is the detection and recovery from single faults in the network that is modeled.
- The network routing model stays sane.

3. Network Reliability Concepts and Metrics

Network connectivity: a pair of end points (O-D pair) is connected if there is a working path available between the end points. At any given time the connectivity C(t), may be estimated as

$$C(t) = \frac{\text{Number of connected O-D pairs}}{\text{Number of total O-D pairs}}$$

The network is considered operational if it is connected. There are various measures of connectivity (Colbourn, 1987).

- *Two-terminal* connectivity measures the ability of the network to satisfy the communication needs of a specific pair of nodes. *Two-terminal* reliability is defined as the probability that there exists at least one path in the network between the specified pair of nodes.
- *k-terminal* connectivity measures the ability of the network to satisfy the communication needs of a subset *k* of specified nodes. *k-terminal* reliability is defined as the probability that for the *k* specified target nodes there exists at least one path in the network between every pair of the *k* nodes.
- *All-terminal* connectivity measures the ability of the network to satisfy the communication needs of all nodes in the network. *All-terminal reliability* is defined as the probability that for every pair of nodes in the network there exists at least one path between the nodes; equivalently, it is the probability that the graph (network) contains at least a spanning tree.

The minimum over all *two-terminal values* can be interpreted as the reliability level guaranteed by the network to all users — guarantee a level of service. The *average* over all two-terminal values provides a measure of the resilience of the network — satisfactory service.
Our goal is to calculate, for a given number of hops in the path, the following *two-terminal* reliability metrics in the presence of link and node failures:
Probability[set up new calls successfully]
Probability[existing stable call or SVC is lost | with and without coverage for partial node failures due to software]
The first metric measures the availability of a network path between 2 nodes and the second metric measures the ability of the network to preserve existing calls in the presence of failures.

4. ATM Switch Reliability

We characterize the reliability of an ATM switch in terms of system failures and partial failures. System failures cause total loss of functionality of the switch and are the cause of system downtime or unavailability. A switch system failure will result in the loss of all the existing connections on the failed switch. Switch partial failures cause partial loss of switch functionality such as the loss of an Input/Output (I/O) module. If the cause of the failure is a hardware fault then this results in the loss of links terminating on the failed module for the duration of the repair interval. If the cause of the failure is a software fault then the duration of the partial outage is likely to be shorter — probably the time required to reboot the module. As stated above, most of the partial failures are likely to be due to software causes. In many ATM switches — for example, the Lucent GX 550 Multiservice Switch — most of the software for setting up and tearing down connections is in the I/O modules. This software is executed on a per call basis and a software execution time model may be used for predicting the software failure rate. In the event of an I/O module failure — hardware or software caused — the existing connections may or may not be dropped depending on the type of protection switching implemented for I/O module failures. Both cases will be modelled in predicting lost calls.

Based on the above, for purposes of ATM network reliability modeling, we characterize the switch reliability in terms of the following parameters

p = switch system availability

λ_t = failure events per year causing total switch failure

λ_s = software failures per connection setup for a core/edge switch

c = fault recovery coverage factor for recovery from software failures

C_s = maximum simultaneous connections per switch

C_y = maximum calls handled per switch per year

k = proportion of calls impacted per partial failure event

5. Failure Scenarios

The following elements can fail in an ATM network: the facility or link and the switch (total and partial failures). Protection switching will protect against all these failures. In some cases existing connections will be lost such as in total switch failures while for facility failures existing connections are generally preserved.

Facility failures. Facility failures are covered by link protection switching which, as per the standards, occurs within 50 ms of detection of a link failure and preserves existing connections; facility failures therefore, as stated in the assumptions, are not modeled explicitly in this analysis.

Switch partial failures. Partial failures such as Input/Output (I/O) module failures, depending on the implementation of protection features, may or may not cause the loss of existing connections. Both cases are modeled in the performability analysis.

Switch total failures. Core network ATM switch failures are protected by connecting every ATM switch to at least 2 other ATM switches, that is, all nodes are at least *2-connected*. ATM edge switch failures are protected by dual homing Media Gateways on 2 ATM edge switches. In the event of an ATM switch failure all stable calls are lost. ATM switch failures are modeled in this analysis.

6.   Network Reliability Model

6.1   Network Connectivity

The assumptions about dual homing and connectivity (c) of at least 2 for all nodes imply that there is no cutset of size 1 (c-1) or no single point of failure. A cutset is defined as a set of nodes $S \subseteq N$ for which $N-S$ is a failed state, that is, the network is not all-terminal connected in this state. For such a network, a lower bound on reliability may be computed as follows (Ball, et al., 1995). Assume every set of elements of size c is a cutset. For an m-element system the system reliability, R(p) is equivalent to the reliability of a K of N system with K=m-c+1 and N=m, and is given by

$$R(p) = \sum_{i = m - c + 1}^{m} \binom{m}{i} p^i (1 - p)^{m - i} \qquad \text{(EQ 1)}$$

where

p = reliability of a network node (ATM switch)

c = connectivity of a network node

Alternatively, if p is close to 1, the all-terminal reliability can also be approximated by

$$R(p) \approx 1 - C_c p^{m - c} (1 - p)^c \qquad \text{(EQ 2)}$$

where C_c is the number of cutsets of size c in the network. Using Eq 1, if c=2, p=0.9999 and m=8 then R(p) is 0.9999997, that is, the probability of all the end points in the system being connected is almost 1. Note that this is a lower bound and assumes that every pair of nodes constitutes a cutset — results in loss of connectivity — which obviously is pessimistic since only a subset of node pairs are cutsets. Using Eq 2, if c=2, p=0.9999, m=8 and C_c=4 then R(p) is 1, that is, the probability of all the end points in the system being connected is 1.

The connectivity is modeled for a range of parameter values: p = 0.999 to 0.99999, m = 4 to 24 and c = 2 to 3 using Eq 1; and the results are shown in Table 1.

Network Size, m	c = 2			c = 3		
	p=0.999	p=0.9999	p=0.99999	p=0.999	p=0.9999	p=0.99999
4	0.999994	1	1	1	1	1
8	0.999972	1	1	1	1	1
12	0.999934	0.999999	1	1	1	1
16	0.999881	0.999999	1	0.999999	1	1
20	0.999812	0.999998	1	0.999999	1	1
24	0.999728	0.999997	1	0.999998	1	1

Table 1: Expected Network Reliability

The results in Table 1 tell us the following: if all nodes in the network are at least 2-connected (c=2), then, even if the individual node availability is 0.9999 (p), the network reliability is better than 0.99999 for the range of network size modeled. Network reliability is defined as the probability that all the nodes in the network are connected.

6.2   Network Performability

The performability aspect that is modeled is the ability of the network, in the presence of failures, to preserve existing connections (no dropped calls) and to initiate new connections (no blocked calls). Other aspects of performability include the loss of capacity in the presence of node failures and performance characteristics such as delay in the presence of node failures; however, these aspects are not considered in this study. In the telecommunications network context, lost calls are measured in terms of calls lost per million calls. Usually this metric is calculated over a one year interval and is expressed in Defect Rate Per Million (DRM).

Calls may be lost due to the following failure events in the network: total switch failure and partial switch failure. Facility failures, as discussed in Section 5, are covered by link protection switching and, therefore, no calls are lost as a result of facility failures.

Loss of existing connections due to total switch failures in DRM, L_t is given by

$$L_t = \frac{\lambda_t \times C_s}{C_y} \times 10^6 \qquad \text{(EQ 3)}$$

Loss of existing connections due to partial switch failures in DRM, L_p is given by

$$L_p = \frac{\lambda_p \times C_y}{C_y} \times 10^6 \times (1 - c), \qquad \text{(EQ 4)}$$

where $c = 0$ for the case when there is no coverage for software faults.
Total lost calls in DRM, L is given by

$$L = L_t + L_p$$
$$= \frac{(\lambda_t \times C_s + \lambda_p \times C_y \times (1 - c))}{C_y} \times 10^6 \qquad \text{(EQ 5)}$$

Assuming the following values for the switch reliability parameters, the expected value of the predicted lost calls (in DRM) for edge and core switches is given in Table 2.

λ_t =   0.25 total failure events per year

λ_s = 1×10^{-9} software failures per connection setup for a core switch
       2×10^{-9} software failures per connection setup for an edge switch

c   =   0.99 coverage factor for recovery from software failures

C_s =   100,000 maximum simultaneous connections per switch

C_y = 7300×10^6 calls handled per switch per year

	L_t	L_p	L
Core switch - without coverage for SW faults - with coverage for SW faults	3.4	 1.0 0.01	 4.4 3.4
Edge switch - without coverage for SW faults - with coverage for SW faults	3.4	 2 0.02	 5.4 3.4

Table 2: Predicted Lost Calls per Switch in Defects Per Million (DRM)

Note from Table 2 that, for the assumed reliability characteristics, the calls lost due to total switch failures are significant contributors to the total DRM. For such a system reducing the total switch failure rate will provide greater improvement to the total DRM than reducing the software failure rate causing partial switch failures. The predicted DRM for the network based on the results in Table 2 with various numbers of hop nodes in the path is given in Table 3.

Network Path	DRM Without Coverage for Software Faults	DRM With Coverage for Software Faults
2 edge	10.8	6.8
2 edge + 1 core	15.2	10.2
2 edge + 2 core	19.6	13.6
2 edge + 3 core	24.0	18.0

Table 3: Predicted Defect Rate Per Million (DRM) for the ATM Network

We observe from Table 3, as expected, that the DRM increases with the number of hop nodes in the path. The DRM varies from about 11 for a network path with only edge nodes to 24 for a network path with edge nodes and 3 core nodes for a network of switches with no coverage for software faults; the comparable figures if the switches have coverage for software faults are 7 and 18 respectively. When the switches have coverage for software faults the primary contributor to DRM is calls lost due to total switch failures.

7. Conclusions

A simple ATM backbone network reliability model covering network connectivity and network performability was presented based on an assumed reference architecture in a telecommunications network context where the primary network activity is the setup and tear-down of SVCs. Network connectivity was defined as the probability that all the nodes in the network are connected. Based on the analysis presented we conclude that if all nodes in the core network are at least 2-connected (c=2), access to the network is dual-homed and the individual node availability is at least 0.9999, then, the network reliability is greater than 0.99999 for the range of network size modeled. The network performability aspect that was modeled is the ability of the network, in the presence of failures, to preserve existing connections and to initiate new connections. Based on assumed switch reliability characteristics the DRM is predicted as 18 to 24 for a connection involving 2 edge and 3 core switches.

This analysis has illustrated some of the network reliability concepts and shown the levels of network reliability that can be achieved given certain node and network characteristics. This type of modeling can be used in the early phases of network design and switch selection, in particular for comparing alternative solutions. In later phases of network design when the specific network topology is known this type of analysis can be combined with more detailed network reliability models and simulations.

8. References

Ball, M. O., Colbourn, C. J., and Provan, J. S. (1995), "Network Reliability", in *Network Models, Handbook of Operations Research and Management Science,* Vol. 7, Elsevier, Amsterdam, 673-762.

C. J. Colbourn (1987), *The Combinatorics of Network Reliability*, Oxford University Press, New York.

Medhi, D. (1999), "Network Reliability and Fault Tolerance", in *Wiley Encyclopedia of Electrical & Electronics Engineering.*

Medhi, D. and Tipper, D. (2000), "Multi-Layered Network Survivability — Models, Analysis, Architecture, Framework and Implementation: An Overview", in *Proceedings of the DARPA Information Survivability Conference and Exposition (DISCEX'2000)*, Hilton Head, South Carolina.

Journal of Network and Systems Management (1997), *Special Issue on Fault Management in Communication Networks*, Vol. 5, No. 2.

A Comparison of iSCSI and Fibre Channel for Storage Area Networks

S.Watts and I.Barlow

Network Research Group, University of Plymouth, Plymouth, UK

e-mail: steve.watts@quantum.com

Abstract

Storage Area Networks (SANs) are dedicated high-speed networks solely for the interconnection of storage devices; they provide a consolidation of data storage, high scalability and easier data management The Small Computer Systems Interface (SCSI) protocol is the industry standard for high-speed data transfer between computers and storage devices. Fibre Channel allows the SCSI protocol to be transported in a networked environment and is the incumbent technology used in Storage Area Networks. iSCSI is an emerging protocol that can transport SCSI using Transmission Control Protocol (TCP) over Internet Protocol (IP) and is designed to leverage existing IP networking technology and skills. This paper evaluates the suitability of iSCSI for Storage Area Networks. Using Fibre Channel as the benchmark, iSCSI is evaluated in terms of, protocol implementation and efficiency, transmission speeds and the suitability for use in different SAN environments.

Keywords

Storage Area Network, iSCSI, Fibre Channel

1. Introduction

Many organizations are experiencing a continual increase in their data storage requirements. To cope with this increasing demand for storage, several new technologies/architectures have evolved to allow easier storage scalability and management. Storage Area Networks (SANs) have addressed many issues by creating a network solely for the interconnection of storage devices. Whilst SANs are mainly used in local area environments, there is an increasing need for SANs to cover wider geographical distances to meet the needs of large organisations.

The SCSI protocol is the industry standard for high-speed, data transfer between computers and storage devices. SCSI supports a vast set of command codes to control devices such as Disk drives, CD-ROMs and Tape devices. Traditionally SCSI has used a parallel bus as the transport mechanism for directly attached storage devices. The distance limitations of parallel SCSI, a few metres and a maximum of 16 attached devices render it unsuitable for networked environments. The Fibre Channel Protocol (FCP) (Snively, 1995) and iSCSI (Satran, 2002) have been developed to allow SCSI commands and data to be transported in networked environments.

Fibre Channel is a mature, efficient protocol and it is the incumbent technology used for Storage Area Networks. However the high cost of FC products, distance limitations and specific skills required for installing and managing FC SANs has hampered their widespread deployment. iSCSI aims to leverage existing IP networking technology and skills to provide an alternative to Fibre Channel for Storage Area Networks. However, for iSCSI to compete with Fibre Channel it must be able to offer similar/improved features, performance and costs.

Section 2 provides a brief overview of Storage Area Networks. Section 3 and 4 provide a brief overview of Fibre Channel and iSCSI. Section 5 compares these two protocols. Section 6 discusses their suitability for SAN environments and Section 7 provides conclusions made from this research.

2. Storage Area Networks

Storage Area Networks (SANs) are dedicated high-speed networks solely for the interconnection of storage devices; they provide a consolidation of data storage, high scalability and easier data management. They relieve the core network of the burden of storage traffic, especially when performing back up operations, which is ideal for organisations that must have full network capacity at all times. Fibre channel has been the enabling technology for Storage Area Networks, allowing the SCSI protocol to be networked. By transporting the SCSI protocol over a network, multiple servers can share and access SAN attached storage devices as if they are directly attached storage.

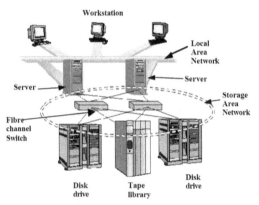

Figure 1 Storage Area Network (Auspex Inc)

3. Fibre Channel

The Fibre channel specification defines both the physical level, data link, network and transport layers to provide session control, transport, error handling and flow control for Upper Layer Protocols such as the Fibre Channel Protocol (FCP) for SCSI. Fibre Channel uses full-duplex links and can work in switched networks at transmission speeds of 2Gbits/sec.

Fibre channel uses frames, sequences and exchanges to describe data transfer. A frame (Figure 2) is the basic unit of data transfer. A sequence is a group of frames sent in one direction. An exchange consists of one or more sequences, exchanged in either direction. Each Frame begins and ends with a frame delimiter. The frame header is used to control link applications, device protocol transfers, and detect missing or out of order Frames. SCSI commands and data are encapsulated in a FCP 'Information Unit' in the frame data field. This Information Unit (IU) begins with a header describing the SCSI payload.

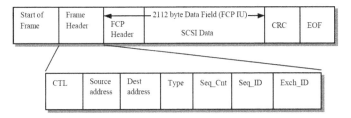

Figure 2 Fibre Channel frame format

Fibre Channel defines several classes of service to suit different applications. Principle classes are; Class 1: Connection orientated, Acknowledged delivery; Class 2: Connectionless, Acknowledged delivery; Class 3: Connectionless, Unacknowledged delivery (Datagram).

4. iSCSI

The iSCSI protocol encapsulates SCSI data and commands in iSCSI Protocol Data Units (PDU's). IP provides network addressing and TCP (Transmission Control Protocol) is used to provide a reliable end-to-end connection and flow control. The encapsulation of SCSI data and commands over IP allows data transfer to be made over any network topology. iSCSI provides login, session control and request/response primitives for the virtual SCSI connection. To achieve suitable data transfer speeds in LAN environments iSCSI uses Gigabit Ethernet (1Gbits/sec) as the transport medium. The near term arrival of 10-Gigabit Ethernet will offer very high potential data transfer rates for iSCSI.

iSCSI uses connections and sessions to describe data transfer. Communication between an initiator and target may occur over one or more TCP connections. One or more TCP connections linking an initiator and a target form a "session." A session is used to identify to a target all the connections with a given initiator. Figure 3 shows how the iSCSI PDU is encapsulated within an Ethernet Frame.

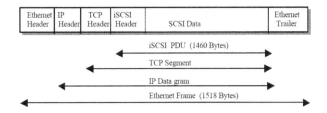

Figure 3   iSCSI Frame format

5. Protocol Comparison

5.1 Overview

Fibre Channel was designed from the outset to operate in local area environments over highly reliable, dedicated networks. The hardware based processing is all performed within the FC controller on the interface card and through its device driver presents a standard SCSI interface to the host operating system.

iSCSI relies upon TCP as the underlying transport protocol. TCP is optimised to run on unreliable networks and requires complex processing, needing to make several copies of data as it is passed through the protocol stack. The processing overhead for TCP algorithms consumes approximately one processor instruction per bit transferred (Farley, 2001). At gigabit speeds this would be unacceptable to perform on the host processor. Therefore an iSCSI Network Interface Card (NIC) will need to offload most of the TCP/IP handling onto dedicated hardware called TCP/IP offload engines (TOEs). For minimum host CPU overhead iSCSI could also be handled on the NIC. It would then become an integrated iSCSI NIC and present a standard SCSI interface to the host operating system, as with Fibre Channel.

5.2 Message acknowledgements

SCSI is a command-response protocol; therefore higher protocol acknowledgments are not necessary, because a response to a command or query is an acknowledgement in itself. Fibre Channel FCP generally uses class 3 (unacknowledged connectionless) service and relies on SCSI timeouts to retransmit unacknowledged commands or data. TCP however requires an acknowledgement for every segment sent to provide a reliable end-to-end connection. If a delivery acknowledgement is not received within a dynamically adjusted time-out period, that is dependent upon round-trip delay time, the segment is retransmitted. The use of full duplex connection in Gigabit Ethernet means that these acknowledgements do not affect the transmission bandwidth, however they do result in extra protocol processing overhead.

5.3 Flow control

Flow control attempts to maintain full link bandwidth whilst still preventing a destination port from being overrun with frames for which no memory has been allocated. The data transmission rate is adjusted to suit the receiver's ability to buffer and process incoming data. There could be many frames travelling across a link at any point in time, sending an individual frame and then waiting for an acknowledgement for that frame would be very inefficient. Therefore flow control mechanisms need to allow multiple frames to be sent before receiving individual acknowledgements. Fibre Channel uses a credit based flow control mechanism. Credit between two ports is established during login and is dependent upon the number of pre-allocated receive buffers. The sender decrements the credit count for each frame sent and may continue to send whilst this value remains positive. The credit count is incremented for each acknowledge received from the destination port. This type of flow control prevents congestion from occurring in FC networks.

TCP flow control requires the two end points to negotiate a window size based upon the amount of data buffering available. The window size is dynamically adjusted ('sliding window') to suit network conditions and represents the maximum number of segments that can be sent before acknowledgements are received. Although the window mechanism works well between end points, intermediate network components can still become congested. During periods of congestion, segments are dropped and delivery acknowledgement timeouts occur. TCP will then slow down the data transmission rate by reducing the window size ('slow start') and retransmit lost segments. It can then take some time before TCP will operate at full speed again.

5.4 Framing

Fibre Channel has a native framing mechanism, which aligns the FCP Information Unit (containing SCSI data) with the Fibre Channel frame. Upon receipt of a frame, the FC controller can therefore immediately locate the header and read the frame header fields. Then using the Exchange ID, Sequence ID and Sequence count information, the FCP Information Unit can be processed and the associated SCSI data copied directly into host application memory. If frames are lost or corrupted, subsequent frames that are already propagating across the link can still be processed and placed directly into their correct memory locations. When the lost frames are re-transmitted and received, they will be copied directly into their memory locations and the higher application may begin processing. This substantially reduces the buffer requirements on the FC controller and results in low host processor overhead.

The ability to directly place incoming data to application memory is very efficient, it avoids the need to make resource intensive intermediate data copies in the host kernel memory, this is known as 'Zero copy'. Offloading TCP to an iSCSI NIC will provide zero copy for the host but the copying necessary for TCP still has to be performed on the NIC.

TCP is a byte-stream based protocol and does not have a built-in mechanism for signalling message boundaries. TCP guarantees that data-bytes are delivered in the order in which they were transmitted and is not concerned with transmitting discrete frames of data. TCP will segment the data according to the lower level transport requirements (=1460 bytes for Ethernet). It is therefore possible for an iSCSI PDU and data to span several TCP segments. It is also possible for an iSCSI PDU header not to be aligned with the start of a TCP segment but occur anywhere within that segment. To enable the start of the next PDU to be found in the delivered stream of bytes, an iSCSI PDU header contains a PDU length field to point to the start of the next PDU in the byte stream, see figure 4.

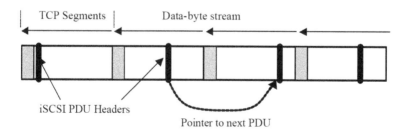

Figure 4   Non-alignment of iSCSI PDUs within TCP segments

Providing segments are received in order from the network, framing is not an issue; TCP processes the segments and sends the received byte-stream up to the iSCSI layer. Conditions may occur where segments are dropped due to congestion or segments are corrupted. TCP implementations store the subsequent TCP segments in temporary buffers until the missing TCP segments arrive, upon which the data must be reassembled. The reassembled byte-stream is then copied up to iSCSI. This process is transparent to iSCSI and it will carry on processing the received byte-stream as normal.

Reassembly buffers for TCP at gigabit speeds may need to be large. A 1Gbit/sec link transmits data-bytes at a rate of 100MB/sec (with 8B/10B encoding). If for example, the re-transmission timeout is 20ms and segments are being continually sent along the link. From the time the receiver detects a dropped segment to when the sender times out and re-transmits, the receiver must be able to buffer 2MB of data. On very long distance links, timeouts may need to be over a 100ms, resulting in buffering requirements of more than 100MB. These problems are even greater at links speeds of 10-Gbit/sec and higher. This will add significant cost to iSCSI implementations.

Furthermore, the reassembly memory must run at high speed; more than twice the link speed, to maintain full link bandwidth. This is due to the fact that once the re-transmitted segments are received all buffered data must reordered and then copied to application memory; at the same time new segments will be arriving over the link and this data must also be buffered and/or copied to application memory.

After a TCP segment loss it would be desirable to place iSCSI PDUs directly into application memory instead of buffering in a reassembly buffer. However, because iSCSI PDUs can occur anywhere within the byte-stream it would be difficult to find the next PDU header. Transport protocols are available that ensure the alignment of message boundaries to allow the iSCSI PDU header to be found directly, enabling the direct placement of data to application memory. Such protocols are User Datagram Protocol (UDP) and Stream Control Transmission Protocol (SCTP). However it is desirable to retain the use of TCP due to its maturity and ubiquitous use in IP networks.

Currently there are two main options to retain the use of TCP and reduce the size and latency of reassembly buffers. The current iSCSI draft (Satran, 2002) proposes the optional use of Fixed Interval Markers (FIM) placed in the byte-stream to point to the start of the next PDU. Instead of TCP temporarily storing segments subsequent to a segment drop, the byte-stream is examined to find the next FIM, after which the following PDUs can be located and directly copied to iSCSI, see figure 5. This scheme faces many potential problems such as requiring modifications to the TCP implementation, complexity and the probability of the marker byte pattern occurring naturally within the byte-stream.

The second option is to implement framing above TCP. A current IETF draft proposed by the Transport Area Working Group (Bailey, 2002) describes a TCP Upper Layer Framing protocol (TUF). TUF will act as a shim layer between TCP and iSCSI to provide direct memory placement semantics by aligning PDU headers with the start of TUF frames.

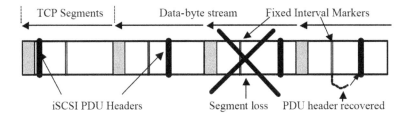

Figure 5   Fixed Interval Markers

5.5 Frame size

Most storage applications typically deal with 4K and 8K block sizes (due to memory page allocation). Therefore fragmentation and reassembly is required to map to the smaller Fibre Channel 2K and standard Ethernet 1.5K frame sizes. Gigabit Ethernet allows for Jumbo Frames (9K), these would reduce the fragmentation and assembly overhead. However Jumbo Frames can only be used in networks where all components support their use.

5.6 Error detection

Fibre Channel uses a 32-bit CRC to detect any errors in received frames and implements it in the FC interface. TCP uses a 16-bit checksum for error detection, but this is not considered to be robust enough for the type of data iSCSI is anticipated to carry. To improve error detection iSCSI can be optionally supplemented with a 32-bit CRC.

5.7 Security

Fibre Channel does not have a defined security mechanism as it is designed for use in dedicated LAN environments that are generally physically secure, and inaccessible by unauthorised people. The encryption and authentication mechanisms that can be used with IP such as IPsec (IP security) (Ababa, 2002) are fully available to iSCSI to provide secure data transfer over non-secure environments. The processing of encryption algorithms at gigabit speeds on large data blocks however will incur high processing overheads.

6. Discussion of Suitability for SAN Environments

Fibre Channel is optimised for use in local area SAN environments. The native framing mechanism, credit based flow control and datagram service class provide a highly efficient protocol under these conditions. Fibre Channel can transmit over distances of up to 10 km using non-standard single-mode fibre, but requires a dedicated link to be used. To connect FC devices over non-dedicated links, IP networks such as iSCSI need to be used, requiring a Gateway to provide protocol conversion.

In local area SAN environments the use of TCP's message acknowledgements and flow control mechanism; that can drop packets, add unnecessary overhead to the protocol processing. This makes iSCSI inefficient when compared to Fibre Channel in dedicated local area SANs. However, carrying iSCSI over existing networks or scaling an iSCSI based SAN to cover large distances does not present any problems in terms of protocol conversion because IP is the most widely used networking protocol. Therefore iSCSI can be used directly across any IP network or the Internet.

7. Conclusions

Fibre Channel SANs are currently expensive to set up and maintain. However, Fibre Channel is a mature protocol and has a large installed base in high-end SANs. It is very efficient and currently has a speed advantage of 2Gbit/sec compared to Gigabit Ethernet at 1Gbit/sec. The distance limitations of 10Km make it expensive to connect SANs over large distances, due to the Gateways required for protocol conversion.

The iSCSI protocol allows use of existing IP network technology and skills, but it is still in draft stage and therefore a very immature technology. TCP/IP offload onto the NIC reduces the host processors overhead. But without a suitable direct data placement mechanism such as framing, large amounts of memory may be required to buffer data, particularly over long links. The challenge is to provide efficient protocol handling whilst still keeping costs similar to or lower than for Fibre Channel. The arrival of 10-Gigabit Ethernet, due before Fibre Channel reaches this speed, leaves an opportunity for iSCSI to directly compete with Fibre Channel in the high-end SAN market. iSCSI could also be used to connect remote SANs over long distances using existing IP networks.

8. Acknowledgements

For support during this research we would like to thank David Cutler and Norman Gordon from M4 Data Ltd, Wells, Somerset, UK. Roland Burns of the TCS Centre, University of Plymouth, UK. Kitt Reeve, Dept of Communication and Electronic Engineering, University of Plymouth, UK and Steven Furnell, Network Research Group, University of Plymouth, UK.

9. References

Ababa, B. (2002), *"Securing Block Storage Protocols over IP"*, draft-ietf-ipssecurity-09.txt, www.ietf.org.

Bailey, S. (2002), *"TCP ULP Framing Protocol (TUF)"*, draft-ietf-tsvwg-tcp-ulp-frame-01, www.ietf.org.

Farley,M. (2001), *"Building Storage Networks"*, McGraw Hill, USA, p417.

Satran, J. (May 2002) *"Internet SCSI (iSCSI)"*, draft-ietf-ips-iSCSI-13.txt, www.ietf.org.

Snively, R. (1995), *"Information Technology –Fibre Channel Protocol for SCSI (SCSI-FCP)"*, ANSI Specification X2.269.

Design and Implementation of Large-scale Network Performance

Measurement and Analysis System

Jingping Bi, Qi Wu, Zhongcheng Li
Institute of Computing Technology, Chinese Academy of Sciences
Beijing 100080, P.R.China
{jpingbi, abewu, zcli}@ict.ac.cn

Abstract

This paper proposes the design and implementation methodology of a large-scale network performance measurement and analysis system – NIPMAS, which realizes performance measurement and fault locating of large-scale network based on active measurement techniques. The following implementation methodologies are analyzed in the paper: (1) measurement and analysis metrics ; (2) measurement and analysis methodologies and the crucial technology; (3) the design and implementation schemes. Measurement results of practical large-scale networks are shown to illustrate the effectiveness and efficiency of the system.

Keywords

Performance Measurement, Metric, Large-Scale Network

1. Introduction

With the rapid development of Internet and increase of users relying on the network, the normal running of network becomes more and more important, but Internet in China has not been fully measured all along. With the enlargement of Internet scale, expanding of real-time operation and improvement of the users' demand on network speed and network performance, the problem becomes more and more serious.

From the beginning of 90's, lots of measurements and studies of Internet have been done in many research institutes and a series of measurement metrics were presented. Vern Paxson made NPD (Network Probe Daemon) experiment and made large-scale Internet measurements in nine countries. His studies were focused on the end-to-end routing behavior and packet dynamics (Paxson and Mahdavi et al, 1998) (Paxson, 1997-a) (Paxson 1999) (Paxson, 1997-b). IEPM (Internet End-to-end Performance Measurement) focuses on the study of packet loss, RTT (Round-Trip Time), and reachability (Matthews and Cottrel, 2000) (Matthews and Cottrell et al, 2000). IPMA (Internet Performance Measurement and Analysis) investigates network performance and network protocols in LAN and WAN. Surveyor measures one-way delay, packet loss and routing information in Internet paths (Kalidindi and Zekauskas, 1999). Other projects such as RIPETT, WAND, TRIUMF, NLANR(McGregor and Braun et al, 2000), Skitter and vBNS also make measurements and studies to some aspects of Internet.

We implement a performance measurement and analysis system for large-scale networks – NIPMAS, which uses active measurement way and can reflect the network status from various

163

angles of network behavior, e.g. routing behavior, packet behavior. The system can also locate link faults. Compared with other systems, this system has general measurement contents, on-line analysis and fault location function.

The paper is organized as follows. Section 2 introduces the measurement metrics of the system. Section 3 discusses the architecture and implementation of the system. Section 4 shows measurement result of a practical large-scale network to illustrate the effectiveness and efficiency of the system. Section 5 concludes the paper.

2. Measurement and analyzing metrics

In NIPMAS, we consider three classes of measurement parameters, which reflect packet behavior, routing behavior and system behavior respectively.

2.1. Packet Behavior

Packet behavior characterizes the behavior of packets transmitting in the network, such as packet delay and packet loss rate. When packet delay or packet loss rate becomes too large, it is always thought that the network is in congested or abnormal case, such as some link or intermediate device being in trouble. NIPMAS can measure and analyze packet loss rates, packet delay, minimum delay, average delay, delay variance and stability of networks.

In the following, we introduce the concept the Stability metric:

Definition 1: STability metric (ST_r)

ST_r is a parameter we present for evaluating path stability, which describes stability case of a path by value between 0 and 1.

Supposing the beginning time of measurement is t and the end time is t+dt, then the measurement persisting time is dt. Before presenting the evaluation way, we introduce the concepts of connectivity rate and stability rate firstly.

Connectivity rate (Cr):

Definition: During time interval dt, the ratio between the successful times and total times of measurement.

We suppose the total times of measurement in time interval dt is N_{total}, the successful times of measurement is N_{suc}, then we define connectivity rate as follows:

$$C_r = N_{suc} / N_{total} \qquad (1)$$

Stability rate (Sr):

In time interval dt, delay in each measurement is respectively d_i $(i=1, 2, ..., N_{suc})$, DX is the variance of d_i, Min is the Inherent delay of the measured path, then the stability rate is:

$$S_r = DX / (Min + DX) \qquad (2)$$

STability metric (ST_r)

$$ST_r = \frac{1}{\sqrt{2}} * \sqrt{C_r^2 + (1 - S_r)^2} \qquad (3)$$

The range of STr is [0, 1]. In formula (3), the smaller of packet loss rate and packet delay jitter of network is, the larger of ST_r; the larger stability metric is, the better of the path stability.

Stability is an important metric of assuring the normal running of a network, and path stability is one of the important components of evaluating network stability. The parameter can provide direct base for the better improvement of path stability.

2.2. Routing Behavior

Routing behavior indicates the routing characteristics packets passing by during transmission. Because of the diversity of network topology and implementation among routing protocols such as RIP, BGP and OSPF, the routings packets passing by in the network are often very complicated and routing outage usually happens.

Definition 2: Routing Persisting Time

Supposing the routing from s to t at wire-time T_1 is P, it becomes P_2 at wire-time T_2, and it doesn't change between T_1 and T_2, then the persisting time of routing P from T_1 to T_2 is T_2-T_1.

The persisting time of routing P in (T, T+ Δ T) is the sum of time intervals in which the routing from s to t is P.

Definition 3: Routing Distribution and Prevalent Routing

We define the binary set $\mathscr{R}$ ={ $(P_1, p_1), (P_2, p_2), ..., (P_m, p_m)$ } as the routing distribution from node s to t in (T, T+ Δ T), if it satisfies:

(1) $P_1, ... , P_{m-1}$ and P_m are all routings from node s to t in (T, T+ Δ T);
If T_i is the persisting time of routing P_i, $T_i \in$ (T, T+ Δ T), then $p_i = T_i / \Delta T$.

Supposing $\mathscr{R}$ ={ $(P_1, p_1), (P_2, p_2), ..., (P_m, p_m)$ } is the routing distribution from s to t in (T, T+ Δ T), then we define the prevalent routing from node s to t in (T, T+ Δ T) is P_{ow} = {$P_i | p_i$ = max $(p_j, j=1, ..., m)$}.

The measurement of routing behavior contains two parts: measurement of single routing and measurement of multiple routings. For the former, the routing reachability and identify abnormal routing are analyzed, such as routing loop and routing unreachable. For the latter, routing distribution, routing jitter, prevalent routing, and routing persisting time are analyzed.

2.3. System behavior

System behavior is the characteristics of network in static and dynamic case such as bottleneck bandwidth and throughput.

Network often reduces the transmission speed for a bottleneck on some link in a path during transmission, while the bottleneck is often due to the too narrow bandwidth and the packets are congested in the place during transmission. The measurement of system behavior can determine the bottleneck of each path and throughput of many applications, such as FTP and UUCP.

Definition 4: Original bandwidth

The maximum data transmission rate of a link is called original bandwidth.

Definition 5: Bottleneck bandwidth

Supposing $P = (s, a_1, a_2, ..., a_n)$ is a reachable routing from node s to t at wire-time T, and the original bandwidth of link L_i connecting a_{i-1} and a_i is B_i, then the bottleneck bandwidth from s to t at wire-time T is $B_{bn}=Min\{b_i, i=1, ..., n\}$.

Bottleneck bandwidth will remain unchangeable in most of the networks as long as the routing remains unchangeable. Traffic in the network won't influence the bottleneck bandwidth.

Definition 6: server response time of type-P

Suppose the server receives the last bit of Type-P packet from the network at wire-time T_1, and it puts the first bit of the ack packet in the network at wire-time T_2, then Type-P server response time is defined as $T_p=T_2-T_1$. Type-P is the type of some kind of protocol in the application layer, such as Http and Telnet.

NIPMAS measures and analyzes bottleneck bandwidth of the paths, TCP throughput and the server response time of ftp, Http, Telnet and Pop3/Smtp.

3. System design and implementation

3.1. System structure

NIPMAS structure is shown in figure 1:

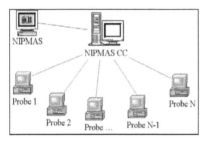 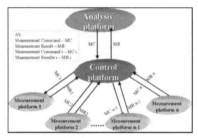

Figure 1 NIPMAS Structure　　　　　Figure 2　　Measurement control process

NIPMAS contains three components: analysis platform, control platform and measurement platform, where measurement/control platform is a distributed platform, control platform is installed in the central place of the measured network and responsible for issuing measurement commands to measurement platform, collecting measurement data, and sending data to analysis platform periodically; measurement platform is installed in some main places in the measured network and responsible for performing measurement commands. Analysis platform is installed in another computer which is in the same place as control platform and responsible for analyzing measurement data, and issuing the analysis results in web.

3.2. System modules

NIPMAS includes 7 main modules: measurement control, GIS, on-line statistical chart, network specialist, fault management, user/admission management and system self-monitoring.

(1) Measurement Control

Analysis platform issues periodic measurement commands to control platform, and which sends measurement commands to each measurement platform which will send the measurement data back to control platform after finishing measuring. Then analysis platform automatically collects the measurement data from control platform. The structure is displayed in figure 2.

During measurement, we use the following three classes of measurement tools:

- A tool `Posip` based on `Ping` is written to measure packet delay and packet loss rate. `Posip` uses poisson sampling way rather than periodic sampling method used in `Ping` to avoid the side effect that periodic measurement bring.

- The tool `traceroute` is used to measure various routing behaviors, which can help us find the routing factors affecting packet transmission speed.

- The tool `Pchar` and `treno` are used to measure bottleneck bandwidth and TCP throughput.

(2) GIS

GIS is a system integrating hardware, software and program, which solves the sophisticated plans, management and research problems by capturing, managing, disposing, analyzing, modeling and displaying space reference data. GIS can combine Information with geographical location conveniently and it is intuitionistic and visual, so it has been gradually used in many fields. So far, few network measurement and analysis systems have used the technology. NIPMAS displays all information in the system in detail by GIS.

Figure 3 is a sketch map using GIS to display network information. It displays information of many measured paths in main window and sub window simultaneously. By using GIS technology, we efficiently combine all information in the network with the actual geographical locations and visulizes network measurement and analysis.

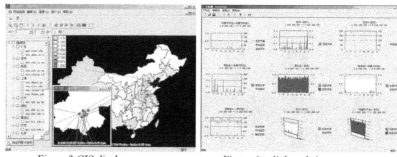

Figure 3 GIS display   Figure 4   link real-time measurement

(3) Real-time statistical chart

Statistical figure consists of two parts: automatic data view and historical data view. Automatic data view can automatically display the measured paths in which the newest measurement data arrived, as shown in figure 4; historical data view can see all statistical state at any time scale, path and time interval, as shown in figure 8.

Statistical figure view provides many kinds of displaying ways, such as histogram, line chart, area chart and scatterplot. It also can draw distribution figure of single variable and make distribution testing; statistical figure view can still make regression analysis about single variable and make correlation analysis between two variables, as shown in figure 6, 7 and 9.

(4) Network specialist

An important function of NIPMAS is to locate and display network fault. When problem occurs in a path of the network, the system can locate the network segment where problem occurs and point out the link in end-to-end path where problem occurs.

(1) Fault management

The faults in NIPMAS include two kinds: exterior network fault and interior system fault. This module realizes management of the two kinds of faults. Network faults include network disconnecting, network packet loss rate being too high, delay being too large, stability metric being too low, response time being too large and so on; system faults mainly include the connectivity problem occurring among measurement platforms, system software problem occurring in control platform and analysis platform. NIPMAS on the one hand uses sound and light to display network fault, on the other hand stores correlative information into database to upper analysis. When faults occurs, system contacts users in time as soon as possible.

(2) User /admission management

It indicates the management to users and their admission.

(3) System self-measurement

NIPMAS is a distributed system, so installation and running of the system need collaboration of many computers. Design of the module is to assure normal running of the whole distributed system and give an alarm or take measures at abnormal moment.

4. Application of the system

4.1. System installation

The installation platform is composed of the following two parts: analysis platform and measurement/control platform, analysis platform is installed in Windows 2000/NT, measurement/control platform is installed in FreeBSD for its stability.

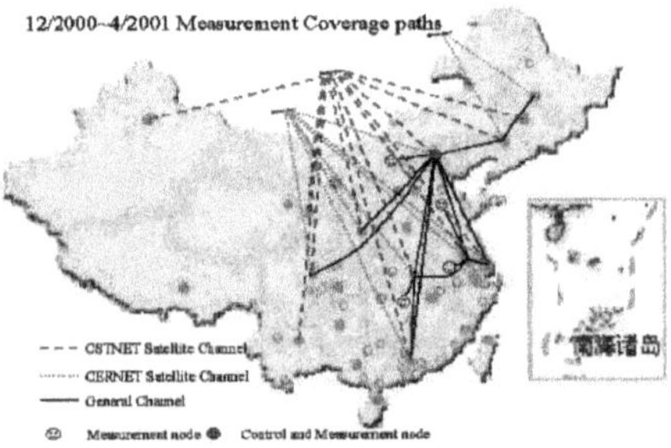

Figure 5 Measured paths

4.2. Application of the system

To validate usage effect of the system, we firstly make actual measurement and analysis in CERNET (China Education and Research NETwork) and CSTNET (China Science and Technology NETwork) of China.

In the measurement, we choose ICT (Institute of Computer Technology) of CAS in Beijing,

HuNan University in HuNan province, Chinese science and technology University in AnHui province, ShanDong University in ShanDong province, Inner Mongolia University in Inner Mongolia and Chongqing University of Posts and Telecommunications in Chongqing as measurement platforms, and install control platform and analysis platform in ICT of CAS at the same time. During measurement, we issue commands in Beijing to all of the measurement nodes, and measurement platforms perform commands and make measurements.

Figure 5 shows part of the measurement paths figure in experiment, and figure 6 gives the hop-by-hop link original bandwidth and delay from ICT to Shenyang Branch of CAS. From the figure, we can know that the link from 159.226.41.62 to 159.226.250.62 is the bandwidth bottleneck of the path, and this is also the place where congestion usually occurs.

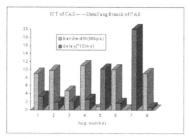

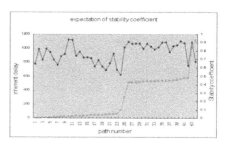

Figure 6 Network bottleneck analysis

Figure 7 Average stability metric and minimum delay of each path
(Path number sorted by minimum delay)

Figure 6 shows different parameters such as packet loss rate, packet delay, stability metric for part of the measured paths. Figure 7 gives the average stability metric and minimum delay of part of the measured paths. Figure 8 indicates packet loss rate, delay, delay variance and stability metric between 202.38.64.241 and 202.112.14.167 from 4/5/2001 16:11 to 4/6/2001 6:40. Figure 9 gives the delay distribution between 159.226.39.106 and 159.226.122.39 in 1/10/2001.

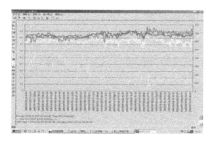

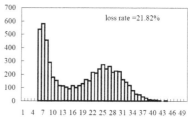

Figure 8 Packet behavior metrics in some time interval on the measured paths

Figure 9   packet loss rate distribution characteristic on the measured paths

5. Conclusions

To reflect Internet running status in China roundly, we design and realize a large-scale network performance measurement and analysis system based on active measurement - NIPMAS, and realize performance measurement and fault management of large-scale network. This system monitors and analyzes the end-to-end paths and reflects running state of network. In the course of implementation, we present measurement and analysis metrics, which roundly reflect network characteristics. in the following, design and implementation of the system are introduced. In the end, the system is validated in practical large-scale network in China and has a good effect. In the following work, we are ready to combine active measurement with passive measurement and strengthen fault management function. At the same time, we need to make further study on the predictability of network performance.

References

Kalidindi, S. and Zekauskas, M. J. (1999), "Surveyor: An Infrastructure for Internet Performance Measurements", June 1999, http://telesto.advanced.org/~kalidindi/papers/ INET/inet99.html.

Matthews, W. and Cottrel, L. (2000), "The PingER project: Active internet performance monitoring for the HENP community", *IEEE Communications*, Vol. 38, No. 5, pp130-136.

Matthews, W. and Cottrell, L. and Granieri, C. (2000), "International Network Connectivity and Performance, The Challenge from High Energy Physics", http://www.slac.stanford.edu/pubs/slacpubs/8000/slac-pub-8382.html.

McGregor, A. J. and Braun, H. W. and Brown, J. A. (2000), "The NLANR Network Analysis Infrastructure", *IEEE Communications Magazine,* Vol. 38, No. 5, pp. 122-128.

Paxson, V. (1997), "Measurements and Analysis of End-to-End Internet Dynamics", Ph.D. Thesis, University of California.

Paxson, V. (1997), "End-to-End Routing Behavior in the Internet", *IEEE/ACM Transactions on Networking*, Vol. 5, No. 5, pp601-615.

Paxson, V. (1999), "End-to-End Internet Packet Dynamics," *IEEE/ACM Transactions on Networking*, Vol. 7, No. 3, pp277-291.

Paxson, V. and Mahdavi J. and Adams A. and Mathis M. (1998), "An Architecture for Large-Scale Internet Measurement", *IEEE Communications*, Vol. 36, No. 8, pp48-54.

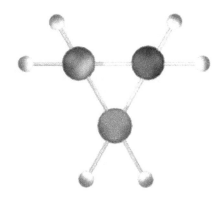

Chapter 3

Multimedia over IP

Improving the Start-Up Behaviour of TCP-friendly Media Transmissions

Jens Schmitt, Michael Zink, Steffen Theiss, Ralf Steinmetz

KOM, Darmstadt University of Technology, Merckstr. 25, D-64283 Darmstadt, Germany
email: {Jens.Schmitt, Michael.Zink, Steffen.Theiss, Ralf.Steinmetz}@kom.tu-darmstadt.de

Abstract

The Internet has built its success story to a large degree on the Transmission Control Protocol (TCP). Since TCP still represents the by far most important transport protocol in the current Internet traffic mix, new applications like media streaming need to take into account the social rules implied by TCP's congestion control algorithms, i.e., they need to behave *TCP-friendly*. One problem of this insight is that these new applications are not always well served by inheriting TCP's transmission scheme. In particular, TCP's initial start-up behaviour is a problem for streaming applications. In this paper, we try to address this problem by proposing a *reflective server design* which allows to do inter-session congestion control, i.e., to share network performance experiences between sessions to make informed congestion control decisions. Since our target application is media streaming, we show the design in the framework of a media server, which means in particular that we employ not TCP itself but a TCP-friendly transmissions scheme.

Keywords

TCP-friendliness, Slow-Start, Media Streaming

1 Introduction

TCP's congestion control involves two basic algorithms: slow start and congestion avoidance. During slow start (SS) a sender exponentially increases its sending window during each round trip time (RTT)[1] starting with a window size of 1 to trial the available bandwidth in the network. It thus makes no assumptions and tries to find out fast what could be its fair share of the available bandwidth. Once it encounters an error, either due to a retransmission time-out or due to 3 consecutive duplicate acknowledgments (fast retransmit), it halves its slow start threshold (sstresh) and does another SS. This repeats until slow start reaches sstresh without any losses, then the congestion avoidance (CA) phase is started. In CA the sender still probes the network for more capacity but now at a linear increase per RTT.

For new multimedia applications like media streaming TCP has several drawbacks:

- *retransmissions* are unnecessary since old (retransmitted) data is usually worthless for streaming applications,
- the *bandwidth* resulting from TCP's window-based congestion control algorithms tends to *oscillate* too much for streaming applications,
- the *initial slow start behaviour* is the exact opposite of what streaming applications would desire, namely an initially high rate that allows to fill the playback buffer such that later rate variations can be accommodated by the smoothing effects of the buffer.

This is why many of these applications employ UDP (User Datagram Protocol) as a transport protocol. However, UDP does not have a congestion control. That is why a number of TCP-friendly congestion control schemes have been devised for UDP transmissions. The definition of TCP-friendliness is phrased as "achieve fairness with concurrent TCP transmissions, i.e., achieve the same long-term average throughput as a TCP transmission".

---

1. For simplicity we neglect the dampening effect on the exponential increase due to ACK clocking.

If TCP-friendliness is accepted as a MUST in the Internet it needs to be observed that, while TCP-friendly transmission schemes can avoid the problems of retransmissions and unsteady bandwidth availability to some degree (we will discuss some proposals below), all TCP-friendly protocols inherit TCP's gross start-up behaviour resulting from slow start. Note that TCP's start-up behaviour has for some time been realized as a problem for transfers of short duration as typically seen for HTTP requests. Yet, also for long-term streaming applications in contrast to long-term file transfers the initial transmission performance is of high importance, since they need to present transmitted data (more or less) immediately to the user and it might be especially dissatisfying if the start of a media transmission is badly disturbed or heavily delayed due to a slow filling of the playback buffer (which might make the consumer switch away again). Besides, promising optimizations of media distribution systems like patching may involve short transfers, too (Hua et al. 1998).

On a higher level of abstraction one could argue that TCP is transiently unfair to new sessions which are still in their probing phase. Ideally, one would wish for a new session to start sending with its fair share and immediately go into a CA-like phase. The question now is how could we make a step towards this ideal behaviour. Since our target application is media streaming, we may assume that we have high-performance servers streaming the media towards a large number of clients. We are thus in a situation where TCP's zero knowledge assumption about the network state at the start of a new transmission towards a client is unnecessarily limiting since such a server could take advantage of the probing of past and concurrent transmissions to the same or "*similar*" clients. The server could thus improve its congestion control decisions by *reflecting* on past decisions / experience and could start the transmission at a higher rate avoiding the SS phase altogether. Of course, care must be taken to back-off from this rate immediately if the estimation of available bandwidth turns out to be erroneous.

2 Related Work & Own Contribution

2.1 TCP-Friendly Transmission Protocols

The design of TCP-friendly transmission protocols has recently experienced a lot of attention. A nice overview can be found in (Widmer et al. 2001). Their basic rationale is to avoid retransmissions and to improve TCP's oscillating bandwidth behaviour by smoothing the available bandwidth to a session. There is mainly two flavours:

- window-based schemes like (Bansal and Balakrishnan 2001, Jin et al. 2001),
- rate-based schemes like (Rejaie et al. 1999, Floyd et al. 2000, Rhee et al. 2000).

While window-based schemes inherit TCP's favourable self-clocking characteristic and can generally be assumed to react faster to dynamic changes in available bandwidth, rate-based schemes usually achieve a smoother transmission scheme which makes them more favourable for streaming applications. Furthermore, the rate-based TFRC (TCP-Friendly Rate Control) has been shown to react relatively fast to changes and has been extended to the multicast case (Widmer and Handley 2001). For these reasons we chose TFRC as the TCP-friendly transmission scheme which shall be integrated into our reflective server design.

2.2 Inter-Session Congestion Control

Directly related to our work is what we call inter-session congestion control. These proposals consider network performance experience from other concurrent or past sessions for their congestion control decisions. (Savage et al. 1999) introduces what they call inter-host congestion control and give some nice introductory motivation for the efficiency gains that may be achievable. Their sharing of congestion control information is solely based on what they call *network locality*, i.e., only destinations that have a common 24-bit subnet mask share information. Their proposal is restricted to TCP transmissions. Along the same lines yet more detailed is (Zhang et al. 2000), which proposes the use of a gateway. Again this work is only suited for Web-like traffic since only TCP is considered and they only share information between destinations with common 24-bit subnet masks (network locality).

In conclusion, while the above proposals are very interesting, they are specialized for TCP transmissions and may require substantial infrastructure changes due to the gateway approach. Furthermore, they employ a simple rule for sharing congestion control information, which, while it is empirically shown to be a good rule (Zhang et al. 2000), may be too restrictive for the case of a server-based inter-session congestion control for media streaming, which involves compared to a Web server a lesser number of sessions.

3 Reflective Media Server Design for Inter-Session Congestion Control

In this section, we give an overview of the high-level design of our reflective media server. The underlying principles of our reflective media server proposal is to gather past bandwidth availability data, process these data intelligently in order to make more *informed decisions* when starting a new TCP-friendly streaming session.

3.1 Overall Design

Two different, concurrently performed areas of operation can be distinguished for the reflective media server: the actual handling of media requests and the reflection on the corresponding transmission observations. The latter process of reflection is further on called *data management* because it involves the gathering and processing of statistical data for past sessions. The results from the data management operations are then exploited in serving the media requests, i.e., in the congestion-controlled *transmission* of the media objects. The following subtasks for the data management component can be identified:

- *data gathering*, i.e., record the data from sessions periodically for subsequent sessions,
- *data clustering*, i.e., explore the data on past and concurrent sessions for similarities in order to find maximum sharing rules between the recorded data,
- *data prediction*, i.e., forecast fair bandwidth share for a session based on the sharing rules constructed in the preceding step.

With respect to the transmission component: as discussed above we focus on the improvement of the start-up behaviour for media streams, i.e., we introduce an *informed start* which contrasts to slow start by assuming knowledge when choosing an initial transmission speed.

The overall scheme of our refective media server design is depicted in Figure 1.

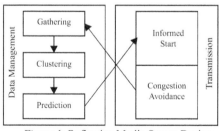

Figure 1: Reflective Media Server Design.

3.2 Data Management

Data Gathering: The major questions for data gathering are which data to gather and when. We decided to gather the available bandwidth values after they have reached a certain equilibrium state (i.e., the rate does not vary too much any more). The available bandwidth of each session (identified by the client's destination address) is tracked on two time-scales, one on the order of RTTs and one on the order of minutes. These serve different purposes. The longer time-scale values are used for identifying similar available bandwidth properties for different clients, i.e., they are input for the data clustering task. A time-scale on the order of minutes seems sufficient for that purpose based on the temporal stability observations reported in (Balakrishnan et al. 1997). The shorter time-scale values are used within the data prediction step and therefore need to be very recent.

Data Clustering: The data clustering subtask is a preparation step for the actual data prediction in order to make as much use as possible from the given data. In particular, we perform a cluster analysis along the available bandwidth samples of different sessions, which promises more comprehensive sharing rules than for a second-order criterion like network locality, since it allows to capture more similarities between clients / sessions, e.g., like the use of the same access technology which might always form a bottleneck or the situation when a transatlantic link is underdimensioned and a certain subset of clients is only reachable via this link. So, clients do neither need to share exactly the same bottleneck but only a structurally similar one, nor does the bottleneck need to be close to them. Furthermore, we cluster along available bandwidth trajectories, and not just single values, over relatively large time-scales (24 hours), which also allows to identify temporal similarities.

Since for individual clients the covering of a 24 hour interval by sampled available bandwidth values is likely to be insufficient, we first aggregate the samples of all clients of a network cloud defined by the common 24-bit subnet mask heuristic (network locality). The actual technique we then use for clustering the network clouds is so-called *agglomerative clustering* based on maximizing the inter-cluster distance while minimizing the intra-cluster distance where we use the euclidean distance norm for the bandwidth trajectories (Gordon 1999). The resulting clusters represent the sharing rules used for data prediction.

Data Prediction: The data prediction step takes as an input the short time-scale samples from the data gathering and uses the sharing rules resulting from the data clustering subtask to obtain a set of samples as large as possible to ensure an accurate prediction. The quantity to predict is the fair share of bandwidth available to a new media stream. Note that for different congestion control schemes this value may have to be transformed in the quantity that is relevant for the respective scheme, i.e., for a window-based scheme this has to be transformed into an initial window size (which would require to also sample the RTT, which for ease of discussion we have left out here since our focus is on rate-based schemes).

The actual prediction technique we use is an optimal linear predictor (Papoulis 1991), i.e., we make relatively little assumptions on the underlying stochastic process. This optimal linear predictor uses the existing realization of the stochastic process of the available bandwidth to set its linear coefficients such that the prediction error is minimized. This is only possible if the underlying process is ergodic, however, the results reported in (Balakrishnan et al. 1997) are encouraging with respect to this assumption. The number of linear coefficients that are employed depend on the number of samples that are available, the more samples are available the more linear coefficients are used resulting in a higher prediction accuracy. So, this is exactly the point where the maximization of the sharing rules is exploited.

3.3 TFRC Transmission Using *Informed Start*

Concurrently to the data management operations, the actual transmission of media streams takes place. As discussed above we chose TFRC as a (good) example of a TCP-friendly transmission protocol for media streams. Now, we describe how a TFRC-based media streaming can take advantage of the data gathered and evaluated by the data management component to improve a media stream's start-up behaviour by using what we call an *informed start* instead of the normal slow start algorithm. Therefore, we first discuss in a little bit more detail how TFRC works especially at start-up.

At the start-up of a session, TFRC mimics TCP's SS behaviour: it doubles its sending rate every RTT and even tries to emulate TCP's self-clocking characteristic by limiting the sending rate to two times the received bandwidth as reported by the receiver (which sends these reports every RTT). It does so until a loss event occurs. This enables then a receiver-based rough estimation of the loss rate as the corresponding loss rate for half of the current sending rate. This estimated loss rate is returned to the sender and used to compute the allowable sending rate using the TCP rate formula proposed in (Padhye et al. 1998). Furthermore, the sender then turns into a less aggressive CA-like behaviour which is again determined by the TCP rate formula: if the formula results in a higher value than the current sending rate then the sending rate is increased by one packet per RTT.

Assuming we have enough data to make a sensible fair share bandwidth prediction we can avoid the SS-like behaviour and start with the predicted bandwidth, i.e., perform an informed start (IS) and turn to the CA-like phase of TFRC directly. An IS requires, however, special care since the prediction might be wrong. In particular, IS works the following way:

- The transmission starts with the predicted rate. After 1.5 RTT the receiver calculates the corresponding loss rate from the inverse TCP rate formula and sends it towards the sender. It cannot invoke the TCP rate formula before because it requires an estimate of the RTT which is only determined after 1 RTT at the sender and then sent to the receiver (which takes another 0.5 RTT).
- Before the sender receives the first loss rate estimate the sender uses the minimum of predicted rate and received rate as reported by the receiver. This restriction minimizes the negative effect of a wrong prediction for the available fair share of the bandwidth.
- After it got the first loss rate estimation (after 2 RTT), the sender uses TFRC's normal CA-like behaviour further on.
- In case of packet loss two cases must be distinguished:
  (1) packet loss *before 2 RTT*: this indicates that the predicted available bandwidth was too optimistic and the sender should backoff immediately in order not to interfere with other TCP sessions. Of course, due to the packet loss we have a first estimate of the loss rate, however it is very likely to be too pessimistic since due to the overestimation of the allowed sending rate losses are probably excessive. Using that loss rate would consequently lead to an underestimation of the actual allowed sending rate. Fortunately, we also have the received rate as reported by the receiver as a further guide. While the received rate itself is obviously too high because we have been overly aggressive at the start-up, we can take a compromise between underestimating and overestimating the allowed sending rate by taking the mean of the fair bandwidth share as computed by the TCP rate formula and the received bandwidth. When the fair rate eventually becomes higher than the received rate we turn to CA-like TFRC behaviour.
  (2) packet loss *after 2 RTT*: here we just use normal TFRC behaviour, i.e., the loss rate is reported to the sender and the sender adapts its current sending rate.

A further question that comes up after this discussion is what happens if we underestimate the currently available bandwidth. Here, the problem is that since we do not use a SS-like trialling of the available bandwidth at the start of a new session we may remain in a state of underutilizing the fair share for that media stream. However, at least no other sessions suffer and probably for the case of media streaming we should actually reject the request for a new stream if the predicted available bandwidth is too low since we cannot expect our estimate to be too low and it is better not to start a session which can anyway not deliver the quality a user would expect.

4 Simulations

The aim of the following simulation experiments with the ns-2 simulator[2] is to show the basic improvements that can be achieved with an IS over the normal SS-like behaviour of TFRC. They are not about the analysis of the data management component of our reflective media server design, but make extreme assumptions on the outcome of the data management operations: the fair share bandwidth predictions are assumed to be either correct, far too high, or far too low. The simple simulation setup we used for these experiments is shown in Figure 2.

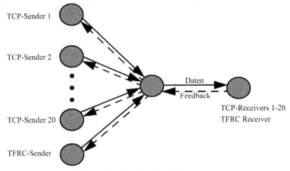

Figure 2: Simulation Setup.

The queue at the bottleneck link uses drop tail, all links are dimensioned at 10 Mb/s (or 1.25 MB/s) with a propagation delay of 10 ms. The TCP senders use TCP Reno (i.e., they employ fast retransmit) and all of them are all started at the beginning of the simulation runs (t=0s). At approximately t=4s they achieved an equilibrium state where they shared the available bandwidth at the bottleneck link fairly. Thus at t=4s we started our different versions of TFRC:

*   TFRC with usual SS,
*   TFRC with IS and correct prediction (CORR), i.e., the fair share bandwidth prediction is 1/ 21 of 1.25 MB/s ($\approx$ 60 KB/s)
*   TFRC with IS and far too high prediction (HIGH), in particular, the fair share bandwidth prediction is 3 times to high ($\approx$ 180 KB/s)
*   TFRC with IS and far too low prediction (LOW), in particular, the fair share bandwidth prediction is 3 times to low ($\approx$ 20 KB/s)

In Figure 3, the simulation outcomes for the different scenarios are given. Here, we have depicted the sending behaviour of one of the TCP senders (TCP-Sender 1[3]) vs. the respective TFRC sending behaviour in the relevant time-scale (from 3s to 15s).

---

2. http://www.isi.edu/nsmam/ns
3. The others showed the same behaviour, though with some phase shifts.

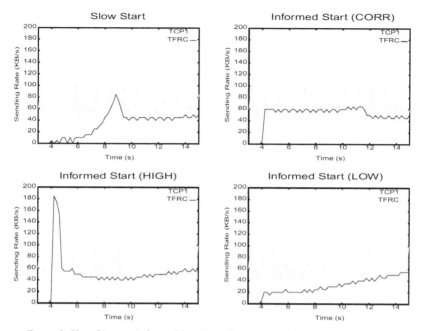

Figure 3: Slow Start vs. Informed Start TFRC with Differing Prediction Scenarios.

It is obvious that with a correct prediction we can substantially improve on TFRC's usual start-up behaviour resulting from SS: TFRC with SS took about 5s (from t = 4s to 9s) until it turns to a stable CA-like behaviour, whereas TFRC with IS(CORR) shows immediate stability from its start. Interestingly, also for a far too high prediction of the fair bandwidth share for the TFRC session, it takes only about 1s until a stable behaviour can be observed. So, we have achieved the goal of a fast reaction of the informed start on an overestimated bandwidth prediction. The case IS(LOW) shows that an underestimation requires a longer start-up phase until the fair bandwidth share is reached than the other cases (including the slow start case), yet it does so in a fairly smooth way which from the perspective of streaming applications should be desirable.

5 Conclusions

In this paper, we have investigated how TCP-friendly transmission schemes for media streaming could be enhanced to circumvent the inheritance of TCP's disadvantageous start-up behaviour by the use of inter-session congestion control. For that purpose we have introduced a reflective media server design and described its major functional components: data management and transmission. In contrast to previous work, we have focussed on the maximization of sharing rules between sessions by the use of cluster analysis techniques taking into account the specific requirements for media streaming servers. We have shown how TFRC, a special instance of a TCP-friendly transmission protocol can be extended to use an informed start based on the operations performed by the data management component of the reflective media server. By simulations we have shown the benefits of an informed start over the normal slow start-like behaviour of TFRC.

References

Balakrishnan, H., Stemm, M., Seshan, S., and Katz, R. H. (1997). Analyzing Stability in Wide-Area Network Performance. In *Proc. of the ACM SIGMETRICS, Seattle, WA*, pages 2–12.

Bansal, D. and Balakrishnan, H. (2001). TCP-friendly Congestion Control for Real-time Streaming Applications. In *Proceedings of the 20th Annual Joint Conference of the IEEE Computer and Communications Societies (INFOCOM'01)*. IEEE Computer Society Press, Anchorage, AK, USA.

Floyd, S., Handley, M., Padhye, J., and Widmer, J. (2000). Equation-Based Congestion Control for Unicast Applications. In *Proceedings of the ACM SIGCOMM '00 Conference on Applications, Technologies, Architectures, and Protocols for Computer Communication 2000, Stockholm, Sweden*, pages 43–56.

Gordon, A. (1999). *Classification*. Chapman-Hall.

Hua, K. A., Cai, Y., and Sheu, S. (1998). Patching: A Multicast Technique for True Video-on-Demand Services. In *Proceedings of the ACM Multimedia Conference 1998, Bristol, England*, pages 191–200.

Jin, S., Guo, L., Matta, I., and Bestavros, A. (2001). TCP-friendly SIMD Congestion Control and Its Convergence Behavior. In *Proceedings of ICNP'2001: The 9th IEEE International Conference on Network Protocols, Riverside, CA*.

Padhye, J., Firoiu, V., Towsley, D., and Kurose, J. (1998). Modeling TCP Throughput: A Simple Model and its Empirical Validation. In *ACM SIGCOMM '98 Conference on Applications, Technologies, Architectures, and Protocols for Computer Communication*, pages 303–314, Vancouver, CA.

Papoulis, A. (1991). *Probability, Random Variables, and Stochastic Processes*. McGraw-Hill.

Rejaie, R., Handley, M., and Estrin, D. (1999). RAP: An End-to-End Rate-based Congestion Control Mechanism for Realtime Streams in the Internet. In *Proceedings of the Eighteenth Annual Joint Conference of the IEEE Computer and Communications Societies 1999, New York, NY, USA*, pages 395–399.

Rhee, I., Ozdemir, V., and Yi, Y. (2000). TEAR: TCP emulation at receivers - flow control for multimedia streaming. Technical report, North Carolina State University.

Savage, S., Cardwell, N., and Anderson, T. (1999). The Case for Informed Transport Protocols. In *Proceedings of the Seventh Workshop on Hot Topics in Operating Systems, Rio Rico, AZ*.

Widmer, J., Denda, R., and Mauve, M. (2001). A Survey on TCP-Friendly Congestion Control. *Special Issue of the IEEE Network Magazine "Control of Best Effort Traffic"*, 15(3):28–37.

Widmer, J. and Handley, M. (2001). Extending Equation-Based Congestion Control to Multicast Applications . In *Proceedings of the ACM SIGCOMM '01 Conference on Applications, Technologies, Architectures, and Protocols for Computer Communication 2001, San Diego, CA*, pages 275–285.

Zhang, Y., Qiu, L., and Keshav, S. (2000). Speeding Up Short Data Transfers: Theory, Architecture Support, and Simulation Results. In *Proceedings of NOSSDAV 2000*.

Investigating Interaction of Audio and Video Quality as Perceived in Low-Cost Multimedia Conferencing Systems

L.Mued, B.Lines, S.Furnell and P.Reynolds

Network Research Group, Department of Communication and
Electronic Engineering, University of Plymouth, United Kingdom
E-mail: lmued@jack.see.plymouth.ac.uk

Abstract

This paper concentrates on investigating the interaction effect of the two media of audio and video. The study shows a comprehensive evaluation of achievable audio and video quality undertaken based upon different sets of impairments between audio and video, prior to transmission. Tests have been designed to investigate the impact of audio only, video only and combination of both audio and video on perceived multimedia quality. The tests have been conducted on two different task scenarios, i.e. passive communication (listening/viewing to 'talking head') and interactive communication (person to person). The research concentrates on quantifying the effects of network impairments (packet loss) on perceived audio and video quality, as well as finding the psychological effects or correlations between audio and video in multimedia applications. The results presented in this paper show the strong interaction dependency between audio and video. It was justified that video has a unique benefit on multimedia quality for its psychological effects. The findings also concluded that the sensory interactions, and the attention given to a particular aspect of performance, are clearly content-dependent.

1. Introduction

The aim of the paper is to investigate the interaction effect between the perceived audio and video quality in multimedia services. Previous research has claimed that a user's assessment of audio quality is influenced by the presence of video in multimedia applications (Watson and Sasse, 1996). For this reason, the experiments were based on investigating and quantifying the potential interaction effect between audio and video when transport mechanism carrying the two medias is subject to packet loss.

The importance of good quality audio in a conference cannot be overstated (Kawalek, 1995)(Kitawaki and Nagabuchi, 1998). Since true lip reading is impossible for most people, effective communication cannot be achieved without intelligible audio. Likewise, audio delay can make interactive communication difficult. Also, audio that is not synchronized with video can be distracting due to loss of lip synchronisation.

Current desktop videoconferencing systems transmit between 2 and 8 frames of video per second (Quarter Common Interchange Format, QCIF–176x144 pixels/ Common Interchange Format, CIF–352x288 pixels), with poor resolution and unsynchronized audio and video. The presence of video which enables interpersonal face-to-face communication is prevalent and much preferred over all human means of interactions (Tang and Issacs, 1993). Studies show that, in workplace settings, even when people are given a choice between different means of communication, such as email, phone and face-to-face, they still choose face-to-face meetings for planning and definitional tasks (Finholt et al, 1990). This is evidence that videoconfencing has unique benefits over audio only commmunication for most class of task.

Many studies have investigated the influence that video mediation has on the process of communication. Some research findings claim that the presence of a video channel does not directly improve the task performance in the context of desktop videoconferencing (DVC) (Wilson and Sasse, 2000a). However, it has been suggested that the main use of the video link in DVC is psychological (Hardman *et al*, 1998) such as to clarify meaning, to provide a means of common reference, to check whether anyone was speaking during an unusually long silence, to give psychological reassurance that the other participants were actually there by creating a sense of presence etc. Thus, it is stated that, in general, video is better than audio for interruptions, naturalness, interactivity, feedback and attention (Sellen, 1992).

In summary, whilst good quality video is beneficial to enhance many interactive tasks, sufficient audio quality is an essential for real-time interaction. The question is, what quality is good enough to meet end user's requirements?

To date, there is no standard consensus to clarify multimedia quality of service (QoS). In conjunction, effective evaluation methods are vital to determine the quality the users need to successfully perform tasks in videoconferences. However, it is stated that assessing the quality of audio and video over IP network offers a great challenge due to its constantly changing and unpredictable nature (Wilson and Sasse, 2000a). On the other hand, to determine multimedia conferencing quality has certain difficulties, as there is no recognized industry consensus of what really determines audio and video quality. At present, it is often questioned whether the quality of the audio and video in multimedia conferencing is adequate to carry its task performance (Wilson and Sasse, 2000b). Many researchers claim that different tasks performed by the end user will require different levels of audio and video quality. In some cases it may be necessary to prioritise video over audio, or vice versa, depending on the type of session. For example, language teaching in a distance learning application will require better audio, as opposed to a remote interview that demands a good quality of video as well. Therefore, it is essential to investigate what quality is necessary for each specific application. The aim of this research is to establish taxonomy of real-time multimedia task and applications, and to determine the maximum and minimum audio and video quality boundaries for the given tasks.

2. The Experiment Approaches: Rationale and Procedure

As previously stated, the experiments were based upon investigating a potential interaction effect between audio and video media in DVC systems in the presence of packet loss. The approach is to send the audio and video component with respect to the assigned quality for each media, in two different task performances (i.e. interactive and passive interactions). The proposed method will be to degrade the quality of audio and to upgrade the quality of video, or vice-versa, before sending it through a "connectionless" network. At the receiving end, the subjects will evaluate individual quality of audio, video and combined audiovisual of low bit rate videoconferencing. The method of assessment being used is the subjective test method, called Mean Opinion Score (MOS) which is the standard recommended by the International Telecommunications Union (ITU-T, 1984). The MOS is typically a 5-point rating scale, covering the options Excellent (5), Good (4), Fair (3), Poor (2) and Bad (1).

The perceived quality of audio and video over one conference is affected by different network factors (e.g. packet loss), hardware (e.g. headset), CPU power, CODEC, task performance, background noise and lighting, and loading on the individual's workstation (Mued *et al*,

2001). Therefore, in the experiment, maintaining the above variables constant (for both end users), except packet loss, is vital to ensure the validity of the results.

Current Internet-based solutions for multimedia conferencing involve the use of separate TCP/RTP sessions for the audio and video signals (Schulzrinne *et al*, 1996). In the experiments, a network emulation tool (NISTNet) is used to introduce different sets of impairments (packet loss) on each audio and video stream (for example, audio is degraded by 5% packet loss while video quality is unimpaired or vice versa).

Figure 1 below depicts the VoIP (Voice over IP) test bed configuration used for the experiments, and the various elements illustrated are described below.

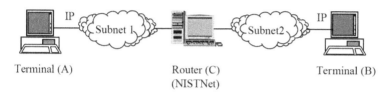

Terminal (A)   Router (C)   Terminal (B)
                            (NISTNet)

Figure 1: Test bed configuration

Terminal A & B: Two identical videoconferencing systems (hardware and software), running Microsoft NetMeeting, placed in two separate rooms, to be used by the subjects to rate Mean Opinion Scores of the perceived audio and video quality. CPUs: 200 MHz Pentium processors, 64 MB RAM, were used. The QCIF - 176x144 pixels frame size is used. The video setting was unchanged throughout the test, which was 'better quality' video. For the audio CODEC, a G723.1, 6400bit/sec was employed.

Router (NISTNet): A network emulation package (Carson, 2000) that runs on Linux. By operating at the IP (Internet Protocol) level, it allows a PC-based router to emulate numerous complex IP networks performance scenarios. In our experiment, it was used to introduce different sets of packet loss for audio and video streams.

Subnet 1& 2: IP networks

The test activity of the project is organised in a number of steps. First, tests are carried out under error free network environment. Second, different set of network impairments (packet loss) are introduced to the separate audio and video stream in order to evaluate their impact on the perceived quality. The conditions under considerations are:

video (v)/audio (a) (%)	v/a	v/a	v/a	v/a	v/a	v/a	v/a
v degraded/a (0% loss)	0/0	1/0	1.5/0	2/0	2.5/0	3/0	4/0
v (0% loss)/a degraded	0/0	0/9	0/10	0/15	0/25	0/30	0/35
v (%) degraded/a (%)	0/0	1/9	1/10	1.5/15	2/25	2.5/30	3/35
v poor (4%)/a degraded	0/0	4/9	4/10	4/15	4/25	4/30	
v degraded / a poor (35%)	0/0	1.5/35	2/35	2.5/35	3/35		

Table 2.1 Packet Loss of Video (v) and Audio (a) Under Test, in Percentage

The test was conducted on two different task scenarios i.e. (a) Interactive test and (b) Passive test

(a) Interactive test

There were 20 adult individuals involved in the test. The subjects were allowed to select their own issue for discussion, with which they were comfortable, so as to enable the interactions. It is stated that informal communication tends to be representative of individuals who are familiar with each other (Issacs and Tang, 1994). Hence, to maximise task motivation and to ensure subjects are fully at ease with each other, individuals (subjects) who were acquainted with one another were selected for the tests. This is vital so as to ensure the validity of the results.

For each new set of impairments of audio and video, after every discussion, the subjects were asked to rate the perceived quality of (a) audio, (b) video and (c) combined audiovideo. The discussions were limited two minutes. For control purposes, initially, tests were carried out under error- free condition, i.e. 0% packet loss.

(b) Passive test

A number of 20 adult individuals volunteered for the test. They were asked to view and to listen to a 'talking head', reading a short sentence to them. First, for control purposes, tests were carried out under conditions that used no packet loss and each medium (i.e. audio, video and combined audiovideo) were evaluated. Second, packet loss was introduced in order to evaluate its impact on the perceived quality. For each set of impairments, the subjects were asked to rate the perceived quality of (a) audio, (b) video and (c) combined audiovideo, which took approximately two minutes for each setting.

3. Results and Observations

All the figures below show the results obtained from the test and the observations made are described in this section.

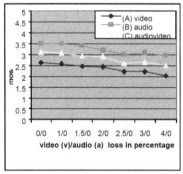

Figure 2: Interactive test – Video Degraded; Audio Constant

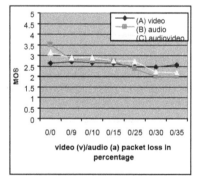

Figure 3: Interactive test – Video Constant; Audio Degraded

Figures 2 and 3 show MOS of packet loss impact on the perceived quality of (A) video, (B) audio and (C) combined audiovideo as obtained in interactive test. It can be seen that when video is degraded, audio scores also decreased by 0.5 (MOS), for video packet loss in the range of 1%-4%, even though the audio quality was kept constant. However, the MOS for video, while its quality being held at constant (i.e.0 % loss), is not affected by the change in audio quality. The rating for video stays at ± 2.6 (MOS) for audio loss raging from 9%-35%. However, the MOS for the perceived quality of combined audiovideo for both test scenarios is approximately the same, i.e. ± 0.1 (MOS) difference, when audio loss is below 30% loss. The score for combined audiovideo drops by 0.4 (MOS) upon reaching 30% audio loss and above. This implies that good audio is critical in interactive test.

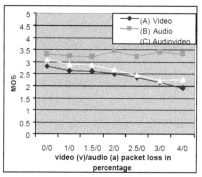

**Figure 4: Passive test – Video
Degraded; Audio Constant**

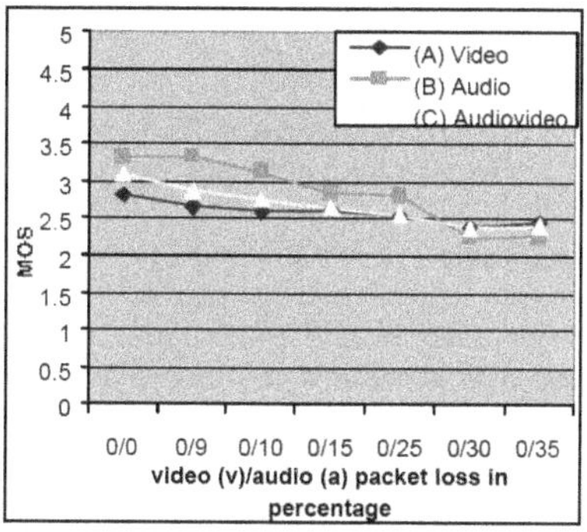

**Figure 5: Passive test – Video
Constant; Audio Degraded**

Figures 4 and 5 show MOS of packet loss impact on the perceived quality of (A) video, (B) audio and (C) combined audiovideo as obtained in passive test. Unlike the interactive test, the MOS for audio is not affected by the degradation in video (see figures 2 and 4). Also, by referring to Figure 5, there is slight drop in video score, i.e. 0.36 (MOS), when audio loss ranging from 0%-35%. The MOS for combined audiovideo is affected severely by the change in video loss as compared to audio loss.

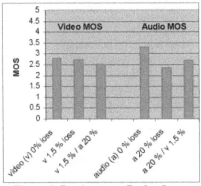
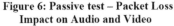
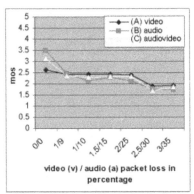

Figure 6: Passive test – Packet Loss Impact on Audio and Video

Figure 7: Interactive test – Audio and Video Degraded

Figure 6 above shows the MOS results of the perceived audio and video quality, indicating the impact of having audio only or video only and comparing these results that when audio and video are both present during the test. The result indicates the strong interaction dependency between audio and video. It is revealed that the perceived quality of audio increases with the presence of video. For example, for 20% audio loss (the 5th column in Figure 6), the MOS is 2.3 without the presence of video. However, with the presence of video, the same audio sample gives MOS rating of 2.7 (final column in Figure 6). This indicates that video information enhances speech only communication. On the other hand, perceived video quality degrades when poor quality of audio was present. Another example, Figure 2 shows how perceived audio quality (for a specific audio condition) changes as the video quality deteriorates. When the video quality is high (0% loss), the audio MOS is 3.5, and when the video quality is poor the audio MOS is 2.9, even though the actual audio quality used is unchanged. This shows that video is an important determinant to justify multimedia quality.

Figure 7 shows the effect of packet loss on the perceived multimedia quality as observed in the interactive test. By comparing this result with that in Figure 2 (video constant; audio degraded), it is evident that the audio score gives higher rating with good video (i.e. 0% loss), even though the audio was degraded by the same amount of loss through out the test.

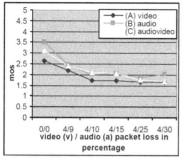

Figure 8: Interactive test – Video Poor (4% loss); Audio Degraded

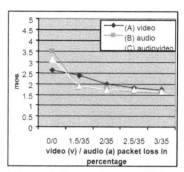

Figure 9: Interactive test – Video Degraded; Audio Poor (35% loss)

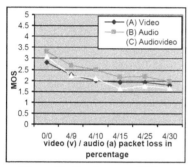

Figure 10: Passive test – Video Poor (4% loss); Audio Degraded

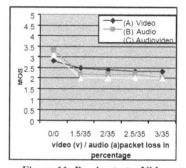

Figure 11: Passive test – Video Degraded; Audio Poor (35% loss)

Figures 8 to 11 show the MOS rating of the perceived quality of video, audio and combined audiovideo with respect to high video loss (4%) and high audio loss (35%), as observed in interactive test (Figure 8 and 9) and passive test (Figure 10 and 11). It can be seen that, when video is poor, i.e. 4%loss, the passive test (Figure 10) gives a higher MOS rating for the perceived quality of video and audio only as compared to that in interactive test (Figure 8). However, audiovideo rating for passive test shows lower scores as compared to that of interactive test. Figure 9 shows that, when audio is very poor, interactive test scores very low MOS for the perceived multimedia quality. Hence, interactive test severely depends on sufficient audio quality.

4. Research Problem

Task performance is dynamically varying, i.e. varying in subject's movements is difficult to maintain. This could lead to varying in frame rates that could result in inconsistent in image degradation. In future, implement the use of recorded audio and video clips as sample material.

187

Subjective quality evaluation in the prolonged field trial approach suffers from the problem of lack of control over a large variety of variables, such as different lighting levels, inconsistent task performance, the different of sensory and perceptual ability of subjects to identify errors in the perceived audio and video signal, and possibly the expected emotional state of a subject, etc.

5. Conclusions and Future Work

The results concluded that there is strong interaction independency between audio and video media. For example, it can be seen that the MOS of audio increases with the presence of video. It is also observed that, video adds value to a conference and enhances interactivity. Thus, it is evident that video is an important determinant to justify multimedia quality. As in the case of interactive test, video scores are not affected by the audio quality, whilst audio scores deteriorated as video is degraded. Therefore, it is justified that, the importance of video at the expense of audio cannot be underestimated, as video has a psychological effect on interactive communications, such as for interruptions, naturalness, interactivity, feedback and attention.

From the observation, the sensory interactions, and the attention given to a particular aspect of performance, are clearly content-dependent, i.e. if a person is reading text from a screen, the quality of the audio has little significance; likewise, if a person is casually chatting (interactive communication), the quality of the video is of less important of than that of the audio. This finding also confirmed with the previous research result which that states subjects are less susceptible to poor video in interactive communication, i.e. users did not report the difference between 12 and 25 frames per second (fps) when involved in an engaging task (Anderson *et al*, 2000).

The results also suggested that, increase in task difficulties have the effect of decreasing the subjective video and audio quality. For example, in passive test, where user are required to understand the read material, the overall scores for the combined audio and video quality in passive test are much lower than that in interactive test.

The continuing work in this area is to conduct similar test on varieties of task performances, such as, discussing and viewing still and moving objects (one-to-one person), one to many e.g. remote lecturing, cooperative task, and conflictive tasks. More comprehensive tests on audio video quality will be conducted, where the subject views a series of test audio/video clips, containing different types of audio and video content; at the end of each clip an evaluation of overall audio-video quality for the clip is made. Clips may be 20-30 seconds in duration.

The future approach is also to investigate how audio and video degradation can affect subjective evaluations of audio/video quality with respect to different duration, intensity and frequency of error occurred in a single event. As we already justified that the quality requirements for audio and video will be task dependent, work is also needed to specify more precisely the set of tasks for which video information is useful and vide-versa.

The final aim is to produce taxonomy of real-time multimedia task and applications, and to determine the maximum and minimum audio and video quality thresholds for a number of these tasks. A subsequent application developer could apply the defined taxonomy of audio and video quality to design a new DVC system with improved bandwidth usage and quality. In addition, the taxonomy could also be used by service provider to infer objective or subjective QoS requirements for particular services, and hence, to charge accordingly.

References

Anderson, A.H., Smallwood, L., MacDonald, R., Mullin, J., Fleming, A. and O'Malley, C. (2000) Video data and video links in mediated communication: what do users value? *International Journal of Human-Computer Studies*, 52(1), 165-187.

Carson, M. (2000), NIST Net Home Page, <URL: http://snad.ncsl.nist.gov/itg/nistnet/ >

Finholt, T., Sproull, L and Kiesler, S. (1990), "Communication and Performance in Ad Hoc Task Groups". In J. Galegher, R.E. Kraut, and C. Egido, editors, *Intellectual Teamwork*, pages 291--325, Hillsdale, NJ, Lawrence Erlbaum Associates, Inc.

Hardman, V., Sasse M. A. and Kouvelas, I. (1998), "Successful Multiparty Audio Communication over the Internet", *Communications of the ACM*, Vol. 41(5), pp 74-80.

Isaacs, E. and Tang, J. (1994), 'What Video Can and Cannot Do for Collaboration: A Case Study', *Multimedia Systems 2*, pp 6-73.

International Telecommunications Union (ITU) (1996), Methods for Subjective Determination of Transmission Quality, *Recommendation P.800*, ITU-T.

Kawalek, J (1995), "A User Perspective for QoS Management", *Proceeding of 3rd International Conference on Intelligence in Broadband Services and Network*, IS & N 1995, Crete, Greece.

Kitawaki, N. & Nagabuchi, H. (1998), "Quality Assessment of Speech Coding and Speech Synthesis Systems", *IEEE Communications Magazine*, October, 1998, pp.36-44.

Mued, L., Lines, B., Furnell, S. and Reynolds, P. (2001), "Performance Evaluation of Desktop Videoconferencing", *Proceedings of PG Net 2001* – 2nd Annual Postgraduate Symposium on the Convergence of Telecommunications, Networking and Broadcasting, Liverpool, UK pp13-17.

Schulzrinne, H., Casner, S., Frederick, R. and Jacobson, V. (1996), RFC 1889: RTP for Real Time Application, Audio-Video Transport Working Group.
Sellen, A. J (1992), "Speech Patterns in Video-mediated Conversations", *Conference proceedings on Human Factors in Computing Systems*, Monterey, California, US, pp 49-59.

Tang, J. C. & Isaacs, E. A. (1993), Why Do Users Like Video: Study of Multimedia Supported Collaboration", *Computer Supported Cooperative Work 1*, pp163-196.

Watson, A. and Sasse, M.A. (1996) " Evaluating Audio and Video quality in Low-Cost Multimedia Conferencing Systems," *Interacting with computers*, 8, pp. 255-275.

Wilson, G. and Sasse, M. A. (2000a), "Do Users Always Know What's Good For Them? Utilising Physiological Responses to Access Media Quality", In S. McDonald, Y. Waern & G. Cockton [Eds.]: People and Computers XIV - Usability or Else! *Proceedings of HCI 2000* (September 5th - 8th, Sunderland, UK), pp. 327-339. Springer.

Wilson, G. and Sasse, M.A. (2000b), "Investigating the Impact of Audio Degradations on Users: Subjective vs. Objective Assessment Methods". In C. Paris, N. Ozkan, S. Howard & S. Lu (eds.) Proceedings of OZCHI 2000: Interfacing Reality in the New Millennium, pp135-142, December 4th - 8th, Sydney, Australia. ISBN 0-643-06633-0.

Multiparty Conference Signalling using the Session Initiation Protocol (SIP)

I. Miladinovic[1,2] and J. Stadler[1,2]

[1]Institute of Communication Networks, Vienna University of Technology,
Favoritenstrasse 9/388, 1040 Vienna, Austria,
{igor.miladinovic, johannes.stadler}@tuwien.ac.at, http://www.ikn.tuwien.ac.at

[2]Forschungszentrum Telekomunikation Wien (ftw.),
Tech Gate Vienna, Donau City Strasse 1, 1220 Vienna, Austria

Abstract

This paper introduces an extension of the Session Initiation Protocol (SIP) for closed multiparty conferences. In a closed conference the identity of all conference participants is known by others and all participants have to be notified when a new user joins the conference. The extension expands SIP for the functionality for discovery of participant identities in a conference. Furthermore, it ensures that each conference participant is notified before a new participant joins. We also verify this extension by applying it to two SIP conference models – conference with the conference server and full-mesh conference. A comparison of these conference models completes this paper.

Keywords

Multiparty conferencing, signalling, SIP, full-mesh conferencing, conference server

1   Introduction

Multiparty conferences are becoming an important issue not only for Internet applications but also for mobile networks application. One of the reasons for that is the introduction of Universal Mobile Telecommunications System (UMTS), which offers considerably more bandwidth than Global System for Mobile Communication (GSM). This bandwidth is necessary especially for video conferencing.

Depending on the access to the conference, we can differentiate between open and closed conferences. In an open conference everyone can join the conference without notification of current conference participants. It is also not necessary that a participant knows the identity of other participants. Examples for open conferences are TV-channel distributions, open meetings, presentations and lectures, etc. These conferences are usually large and use multicast (Williamson, 2000, Goncalves and Niles, 1999) for data transmission.

In a closed conference the identity of each participant is known to the other participants. Furthermore, if a new participant wants to join the conference, this should be announced to all current conference participants before the new participant joins the conference. Closed conferences are usually small and therefore rarely use multicast for data transmission, but rather unicast or explicit multicast (Boivie et al., 2001).

For the conference establishment, maintaining and termination a signalling protocol is necessary. In a closed conference the signalling protocol should also manage participant identities and distribute them to all conference participants. Researching the Session Initiation Protocol (SIP) (Handley et al., 1999) of the Internet Engineering Task Force (IETF), which will be used as signalling protocol in UMTS (from release 5), we have seen that SIP does not support participant discovery. Therefore, we have developed a SIP extension that fulfils the needs of closed multiparty conferences as mentioned above. In this paper we describe this extension and apply it on two different conference models.

2 Related Protocols

This chapter briefly overviews SIP describing basic SIP components, messages and functionality. We also go into Real-Time Transport Protocol (RTP) and Real-Time Control Protocol (RTCP) in order to explain the conference participant discovery proposed in (Rosenberg and Schulzrinne, 2001).

2.1 SIP

Session Initiation Protocol (SIP) (Handley et al., 1999) is an application layer protocol used for signalling in IP networks developed by the Multiparty Multimedia Session Control (MMUSIC) working group of the IETF. Now a SIP working group has been formed that continues the development of this protocol.

SIP is a text-based Hypertext Transfer Protocol (HTTP) (Fielding et al., 1999) like protocol that is used for establishment, modification and termination of all types of sessions. There are two types of messages in SIP, requests and responses. The type of a request is specified by its method. The SIP standard defines six methods: INVITE, ACK, BYE, CANCEL, OPTIONS and REGISTER. Both, requests and responses contain headers that obtain additional information (e.g. "to", "from", "subject" etc.). A SIP message also carries a description of the session in its body. The session is usually described by the Session Description Protocol (SDP) (Handley and Jacobson, 1998). For transport of real-time media data (voice and video) in a session RTP (Schulzrinne et al., 1996) is used.

There are two types of entities in SIP, SIP User Agents (UA) and SIP network servers. A SIP UA could be seen as end device and acts either as user terminal or as automated connection endpoint, for instance a call answering machine. Network servers are used for call routing and they can be enabled to perform different kinds of applications. They are divided into proxy servers, redirect servers and registers.

SIP uses a three-way handshake for call-setup. Firstly, an INVITE request is sent, secondly this request is responded with an OK response and thirdly an ACK request is sent to confirm the call-setup. Instead of the OK response another response can be sent if the call-setup fails (e.g. DECLINE response if the callee declines the call). To terminate the call a BYE request is sent which is replied with an OK response.

Signalling of multiparty conferences is also supported by SIP, but there is neither a possibility for discovery of participant identities using SIP nor a mechanism to ensure that all participants are notified when a new user joins the conference. The discovery of participant identities is realized through RTCP and has the drawback that before a RTP connection is established the discovery is not possible. Moreover, the participant identity can be suppressed by a participant in "stealth mode".

SIP is also an extendable protocol (Rosenberg and Schulzrinne, 2002). There are different SIP extensions that extend SIP for new methods and/or headers (Roach, 2002, Rosenberg et al., 2001, Campbell et al., 2002). Especially interesting for this paper is the REFER method (Sparks, 2001), which can be used for signalling of conferences with the conference server.

2.2 RTP

In most cases, transmission of real-time based data takes place by using the User Datagram Protocol (UDP) (Postel, 1980). This is due to the fact that the connection-less UDP implies a much lower protocol overhead than the connection oriented Transmission Control Protocol (TCP) (Postel, 1981). Obviously, it is unfavourable to lose packets in real-time connections, but in comparison to non real-time data connections it is tolerable in small amounts.

Without a reliable connection on the transport layer, a lot of problems are passed up to the higher layers. The most important of these are packet loss, packet reordering, jitter compensation, inter-media synchronisation and intra-media synchronisation. The Real-time Transport Protocol (RTP) has been developed to overcome these effects. Since it became a RFC in 1996 it has evolved to the industrial standard in this area, not at least because it is referred to by both, IETF and ITU.

The functionality of RTP is simple. The data to send is divided into smaller parts, covered by a RTP header. The most important parts of this header are the sequence number and the timestamp. The former enables reordering of received packets and detection of packet loss, respectively. The latter provides the functionality of intra- and inter-media synchronisation. Moreover it is important to mention that there is a header field, identifying the type of the payload. An extendible list of predefined payload-types for RTP is given in (Schulzrinne, 1996). The last untreated shortcoming mentioned above is the jitter. RTP is not able to prevent jitter but it provides enough parameters to compensate its effects. In fact it is the Real-time Transport Control Protocol, also defined in (Schulzrinne et al., 1996) which enables the senders and receivers to adapt their sending rates and buffer sizes. RTCP has to be supported by RTP devices in any case. It is suggested that the proportional relation of RTCP in RTP traffic should not exceed 5 percent.

There are several types of messages specified for RTCP. Most important of these are the Sender Report (SR), the Reception Report (RR), the Session Description (SDES) and the Explicit Leave (BYE). The combination of SR and RR provides parameters of packet loss, round trip time and jitter estimation back to the sending device. The SDES provides information like the canonical end-point name, the user name, the e-mail addressor, the phone number of the sending user's host, respectively the sending user. This information is used in (Rosenberg and Schulzrinne, 2001) for discovery of conference participant identities.

3   SIP Extension for closed conferences

In this chapter we describe the SIP extension by means of applying it on two SIP conferencing models. We will show the initialisation of a three participant conference for both of these models in two cases - when the conferences is initiated as a three participant conference and when the conference originates by adding a participant to a two party SIP call. These conferences are called ad-hoc conferences.

The extension expands SIP for one new method and one new header. The method is called CONF and has the purpose to distribute identities of conference participants. This method must contain the new header called "participant", which contains a list of SIP addresses of all conference participants except the sender and the receiver of the message. Optionally, for each participant in the list a status parameter can be presented, which may take the following values: "active", "invited" or "joining". If this parameter is missing, the status "active" is assumed (default value).

The CONF method is only allowed within a call; otherwise it should be responded with a BAD REQUEST response. When a UA receives the CONF method, it must check the list given in the "participant" header with its own list of participants. If there is any difference an update of the own list must be made. This list also contains users that want to join the conference, which is indicated by the "status" parameter. In order to verify this SIP extension let us consider an initialisation scenario in two conference models suited for small conferences - conferences with the conference server and full-mesh conferences.

3.1   Conferences with the conference server

Conferences with the conference server in SIP are described in (Rosenberg and Schulzrinne, 2001). As mentioned before, RTCP is used for the discovery of participant identities and there is no possibility for participant discovery before staring the RTP stream. Therefore, a called user does not know who is in the conference before accepting the invitation. We have modified this conference scenario and added the participant discovery to SIP.

In this model a conference is identified by the request URI. This is a part of a SIP request that specifies the destination of the request. Conference participants must know the request URI to participate in the conference. Therefore, a mechanism is necessary to distribute it. For this purpose the method REFER and the headers "refer-to" and "referred-by" are used. The user who receives a REFER request does not know the identities of all conference participants, but only of the participant who sent this message. Using the "participant" header in a REFER request solves this problem.

Let us consider the initialisation of a three participant conference where user A wants to initiate a conference with users B and C. The first step is that A generates and distributes the conference request URL. This part is also called announcement of the conference. The distribution is carried out by sending the REFER request to B and C. This request contains a "participant" header that indicates the potential conference participants, for example B receives the REFER request that contains the address of C with status "invited" in the "participant" header and knows that C is a potential participant of this conference.

After the conference announcement each user sends an INVITE request to the conference server using the request URL generated by A. These messages are shown in figure 1.

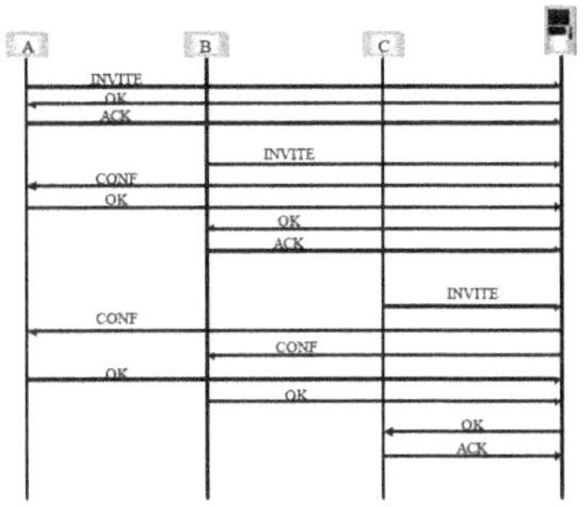

Figure 1: Initialisation of a conference with the conference server

Firstly, A sends the INVITE request to the conference server and creates a new conference. Secondly, B also sends the INVITE request (note that the order of users invitation is not important, i.e. B or C can also send first INVITE), but the conference server finds this conference and sends the CONF request to all participants of this conference (at this point the only participant of the conference is A) to let them know about the new participant B. By this way, all conference participants can learn about the new participant before the new participant joins the conference. The new participant also knows about the other participants because of the "participant" header in REFER. This header is also presented in the OK response from the conference server to the new participant (in this case B) in order to make sure that B's list of participants is up-to-date. Finally, C sends the INVITE request to the conference server, the conference server notifies A and B about the new participant using the CONF request and afterwards sends the OK response with the actual list of participants to C. The same mechanism is used when a participant leaves the conference.

The second case we want to treat here is when A and B are in a two party call and want to initiate a conference with C. The only way to do this is to terminate the existing call and to make a new one with the conference server. Like in the first case, A generates the conference request URI and sends it in the REFER request to B, but in this case A connects to the conference server before sending the REFER request to B. Using the conference request URI, B also connects to the conference server and A is notified about this by receiving the CONF method from the server. Afterwards, A ends the first call with B and sends the REFER request to C. The participation of C in the conference is carried out in exactly the same way as in the first case.

3.2   Full-mesh conferences

In a full-mesh conference a conference participant has a signalling connection with each other participant. Unlike conferences with the conference server, there is no additional network element necessary, which represents a single point of failure, and the state of the conference is maintained by each UA involved in the conference. Therefore, there is no need for a conference identifier that must be distributed to all conference participants.

Consider the same example as in 3.1, where A wants to initiate a conference with B and C. This example is pictured in the figure 2.

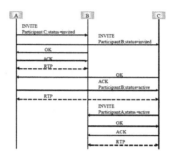

Figure 2: Initialisation of a full-mesh conference with three participants

In order to initiate the conference A sends INVITE requests to B and C with the "participant" header that contains the SIP address of C and B, respectively. In both cases the status parameter is set to "invited". This way users B and C are aware that it is an invitation to a conference and, furthermore, they also know the other potential participants. Let us say that user B wants to participate and responds with an OK response to A. Afterwards, A confirms the invitation by sending ACK and data transmission between A und B starts (indicated by "RTP" in figure 2). Suppose that C also wants to participate in the conference and sends an OK response to A. The ACK request from A contains the "participant" header with the SIP address of B with the "active" status. Therefore, C knows that B already participates and therefore sends an INVITE request to B. The "participant" header in this request specifies other participants (in this example it is only A). B answers this request with an OK response, because B already knows about C and C confirms this initialisation by sending an ACK request. Thereafter, the data transmission between all participants is established. When a participant leaves the conference it sends the BYE request to all other conference participants.

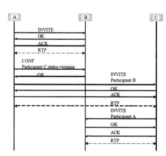

Figure 3: Ad-hoc conference scenario

An ad-hoc conference scenario where A and B are in a two party call at the beginning is shown in figure 3. During the call between A and B, which is indicated by the "RTP" in figure 3, A decides to invite C. Firstly, A has to notify B about this invitation by sending the

CONF request to B. The header "participant" in this request indicates that C is a potential participant. B replies this request with an OK response and afterwards A can send an INVITE request to C. Because of the "participant" header, C knows that it is a conference and can accept or decline this invitation. In this example C accepts the invitation from A and finally initialises the call with B as in the case of conference initialisation.

4   Signalling traffic

In this section we investigate signalling traffic in a conference produced by sending of CONF messages. For simplicity, the reliability mechanism in SIP, which is based on repeated messages, is not considered here. Provisional responses after an INVITE request are also not included in this analysis, because these responses are optional. Note that provisional responses increase SIP signalling without this extension and not the signalling caused by CONF method.

In order to obtain the number of messages that are sent in a conference, we implemented a prototype of a SIP UA and a SIP conference server. With this implementation we measured the number of messages that are sent in an ad-hoc conference in both modes, full-mesh and with a conference server. The number of conference participants varies from three to seven.

In a full-mesh conference (figure 4a) the number of messages caused by this extension (dashed line) is always less than the number of messages caused by SIP signalling (dotted line) and takes 25% and almost 33% of overall signalling messages for four and seven participants, respectively. Overall signalling traffic is quite big with 93 messages for seven participants.

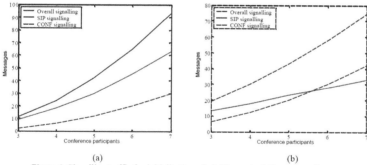

(a)   (b)

Figure 4: Signalling traffic for initialisation of a bridge and a full-mesh conference

In conferences with a conference server (figure 4b) there is only one connection with the conference server per participant. The SIP signalling traffic increases linear with the number of participants. Note that the traffic necessary for conference announcement is also included in this analysis. The number of messages generated by CONF requests and responses is slightly higher than for full-mesh conferences. For conferences with more than five participants, it is also higher than the number of SIP signalling messages. For four participants it amounts to 40% and for seven participants even to 56% of overall signalling traffic, which is considerably less with 75 messages for seven participants than for full-mesh conferences.

However, the overall traffic for conferences with three participants is bigger than for full-mesh conferences (19 vs. 11 messages) and it is also bigger for conferences with four and five participants.

5 Conclusion

SIP signalling of multiparty conferences does not include discovery of participant identities, which is necessary for closed conferences. In order to solve this problem, we have introduced a SIP extension that adds support for closed conferences to SIP. We described the functionality of this extension on the basis of two conference models.

The first conference model uses a conference server for managing the conference. Using the SIP extension, the identity of all participants in the conference is known by others. If a user is invited to join a conference, the extension ensures that this user gets a list of current conference participants. The drawback of this model is that an additional network element is necessary that arouses scaling problems and also represents the single point of failure. In the case when a conference call is formed from a normal SIP call, the normal SIP call has to be terminated and a new call with the conference server must be initiated and it could be also seen as a drawback of this model.

The full-mesh conference model does not require any additional network element because the conference is maintained by UAs of the conference participants. Each participant has a signalling connection to all other participants. There is no single point of failure since the state of the conference is distributed. One drawback of this model is that the logic of the UA is slightly more complex. Another drawback is the rapidly increasing signalling traffic with the number of conference participants.

References

Williamson, B. (2000), *Developing IP Multicast Networks, Volume 1*, Cisco Press, ISBN: 1-57870-077-9.

Goncalves, M. and Niles, K. (1999), *IP Multicasting, Concept and Applications*, McGraw-Hill, ISBN: 0-07-913791-1.

Boivie, R., Feldman, N., Imai, Y., Livens, W., Ooms, D. and Paridaens, O. (2001), *Explicit Multicast (Xcast) Basic Specification*, IETF Internet Draft, work in progress.

Handley, M., Schulzrinne, H., Schooler, E. and Rosenberg, J. (1999), *SIP: Session Initiation Protocol*, IETF RFC 2543.

Fielding, R., Gettys, J., Mogul, J., Frystyk, H., Masinter, L., Leach, P. and Berners-Lee, T. (1999), *Hypertext Transfer Protocol - HTTP/1.1*, IETF RFC 2616.

Rosenberg, J. and Schulzrinne, H. (2001), *Models for Multi Party Conferencing in SIP*, IETF Internet Draft, work in progress.

Handley, M. and Jacobson, V. (1998), *SDP: Session Description Protocol*, IETF RFC 2327.

Schulzrinne, H., Casner, S., Frederick, R. and Jacobson, V. (1996), *RTP: A Transport Protocol for Real-Time Applications*, IETF RFC 1889.

Rosenberg, J. and Schulzrinne H. (2002), *Guidelines for Authors of SIP Extensions*, IETF Internet Draft, work in progress.

Roach, A. (2002): *SIP-Specific Event Notification*, IETF Internet Draft, work in progress.

Rosenberg, J., et al. (2001), *SIP Extensions for Presence*, IETF Internet Draft, work in progress.

Campbell, B., et al. (2002), *SIP Extensions for Instant Messaging*, IETF Internet Draft, work in progress.

Sparks, R. (2001), *The Refer Method*, IETF Internet Draft, work in progress.

Postel, J. (1980), *User Datagram Protocol*, IETF RFC 768.

Postel, J. (1981), *Transmission Control Protocol*, IETF RFC 793.

Schulzrinne H. (1996), *RTP Profile for Audio and Video Conferences with Minimal Control*, IETF RFC 1890.

RCAP: A Rate Control Proactive Protocol

D-H. Hoang[*], D. Reschke, W. Horn

Technical University of Ilmenau, Germany
{Hoang, Reschke, Horn}@prakinf.tu-ilmenau.de

Abstract

Delivering multimedia applications over wireless networks remains a challenging problem due to the nature of wireless channels such as low bandwidth, high error bit rate, variable link bandwidth etc. Without a suitable control, the Quality of Service (QoS) of such applications is adversely affected and the connection quality may become unacceptable. In this paper, we propose a rate control proactive scheme consisting of a rate control proactive protocol and a QoS watchdog at the base station of the wireless network. The scheme is based on TCP-like rate control and a bandwidth/channel estimation method, contrasts to other solutions that use RTS/CTS (Gomez et.al,1999) or dummy packets (Tang et.al,2001). The QoS watchdog is responsible for wireless bandwidth estimation and channel estimation. Thus the wireless loss is distinguished from congestion loss and a TCP-friendly performance is improved.

Keywords

Wireless Multimedia communication, Quality of Service, Mobile wireless Internet.

1. Introduction

The future mobile wireless networks are expected to support most types of services including data and multimedia applications. The ultimate goal of such networks is the convergence of both growing trends: Internet and mobile wireless access.

The internetworking layer of the Internet–the IP layer–was designed to provide a transparent interface between networks and applications. This design enables a diversity of applications and a wide variety of sublayer technologies, i.e. layers below IP. The current Internet offers only best-effort service, i.e. no Quality of Service (QoS includes delays, jitters, losses), thus there have been considerable works in the research community in order to provide QoS in the Internet. All of these approaches have argued that the service model of Internet needs to be extended. Two major models, Integrated Services (Shenker et.al,1997) and Differentiated Services (Blake et.al,1998) have been proposed in recent years. In these models, the IP layer is modified for providing better QoS to various applications or classes of applications.

The main reason for the impairments of QoS in the Internet is congestion. Several works proposed to use resource management in combination with fair queueing disciplines, with traffic shaping methods and admission control mechanisms at different levels. Another approaches are adaptive (i.e. network-aware) applications at application level. On the other hand, many new protocols such as Loss-Delay Adjustment Algorithm LDA (Sisalem and Schulzrinne,1998), Rate Adaptation Protocol RAP (Rejaie,et.al,1999) and TCP Friendly Rate Control Protocol TFRC(Padhye,et.al,1998) have been developed for multimedia applications.

However, the architectures and mechanisms developed for wired networks can not be directly applicable to wireless networks without considerations. Discussions on how to provide QoS to multimedia services in a mobile wireless environment have recently emerged due to the up

---

[*] With a Fellowship of the Alexander von Humboldt Foundation

and coming widespread use of multimedia applications in mobile wireless networks. Multimedia applications have strict requirements on bandwidth, throughput, delay, jitter, etc. what are known as QoS. A number of works have focused on either modification of existing schemes at different layers or development of new schemes (see Chalmer and Sloman, 1999 and references herein). The nature of wireless networks such as high bit error, fading, low bandwidth, hidden terminal etc. makes the problem of QoS provision more complex and harder to resolve. Losses due to wireless channel error may adversely affect the QoS. They should be distinctively considered in contra to congestion losses which are usually considered in most existing schemes. Providing QoS in wireless networks and a heterogeneous environment of wired and wireless networks remains a challenge.

In this paper, we propose a proactive QoS scheme, including a Rate Control proActive Protocol (RCAP) and a QoS watchdog at the base station of a wireless network, which is suitable for delivery of multimedia applications in heterogeneous wired and wireless environment. RCAP is a TCP friendly end-to-end scheme based on AIMD principle (Jacobson, 1988) and wireless bandwidth estimation (Hoang and Reschke,2001). The QoS watchdog at the base station is responsible for the bandwidth estimation on the wireless link and moreover for the probe of the wireless channel state. Using this agent, the wireless loss can be distinguished from congestion losses. In this paradigm, the performance of TCP friendly protocol is improved. The paper is organised as follows. In section 2, we review some of the related works. We describe our QoS watchdog and various aspects of RCAP protocol in section 3. Section 4 shows our simulation results and in section 5 we summarise the paper.

2. Background and Related Works

Congestion control and the principle of additive increase/multiple decrease AIMD have been well studied in the past. In wired networks packet losses are mainly due to congestion, thus TCP schemes and other TCP-like schemes such as LDA (Sisalem and Schulzrinne,1998), RAP (Rejaie, et.al,1999), TFRC (Padhye, et.al,1998) are based on this principle in order to adjust the transmission rate of the sender. All these schemes use closed-loop control, i.e. the feedback signal (acknowledgement ACK) from the receiver. When a packet loss is detected by a gap in the packet sequence numbers or by timeout, all previous schemes decrease the transmission rate. If no congestion, i.e. no packet loss occurs, the transmission rate is increased after every round-trip time (RTT). In fact, these schemes function effectively in the context of wired networks such as in the Internet.

However, the wireless networks have different characteristics. Link bandwidth of wireless networks depends on several factors including environmental conditions, location of the mobile hosts, etc. Moreover, the wireless links are characterised not only by a high link error rate but also by a highly time-varying bandwidth. Beside the losses due to congestion, packet losses can occur due to bit errors within the wireless links. This problem is well studied in numerous works. A summary can be found e.g. in (Vandalore, et.al,1999). In (Balakrishnan, et.al,1997), a snoop protocol is developed to improve the performance of TCP flows over wireless links. The snoop agent located at the base station caches every packet, suppresses the duplicate acknowledgements (ACKs) and triggers the retransmission of packets accordingly. However, TCP is not suitable for delivery of multimedia as argued several works (e.g. Rejaie, et.al,1999). In (Tang, et.al,2001), a rate control scheme was proposed for TCP-friendly connections over high bit error networks such as satellite networks. This scheme uses dummy packets to probe the available network resources.

The previous schemes have not addressed the problems due severe channel impairments and the simultaneous occurrence of congestion and wireless losses. In addition, there is a doubt if congestion or link error interval is behind the range of the round-trip time (RTT). Dummy packets proposed by (Tang, *et.al*,2001) may be lost and bring also many overheads.

Other works proposed are compensation mechanisms and channel predictions at lower time scales (see e.g. Gomez *et.al*,1999 and other references herein). Channel prediction was proposed to allow the sender to probe the state of wireless channel before any packet transmission. As indicated in (Gomez,*et.al*,1999) and other schemes, a handshake mechanism using RTS/CTS (Request to send/clear to send) signal pair is applied which usually operates at the MAC layer of the base station and mobile hosts.

Our work differs from previous works, as we propose an agent called QoS watchdog at the networking layer of the base station, which takes into account the bandwidth estimation and the channel prediction. Our proactive scheme attempts to take the advantage of cross-layer information by combining this QoS watchdog with a rate control protocol.

3. RCAP: a Rate Control proActive Protocol

In this section, we present a TCP-like rate control scheme for real-time constrained traffic such as streaming multimedia. Our scheme consists of a QoS watchdog for QoS monitoring (therefore we call "*proactive*" scheme) at the base station and the protocol agents at source and destination as depicted in Figure 1.

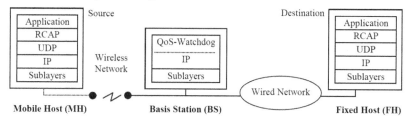

Figure 1. Network model of the proactive scheme

The RCAP agents operate in the application space, and run on top of UDP. No modification of the TCP/UDP/IP stack is needed at the endsystems.

One question may arise as to why the QoS watchdog component is needed. The reason is that the wireless link is more critical than the wired links and it should be especially considered. In our opinion, there is no other way for the sender at mobile host (MH) to quickly know the wireless losses, in order to make the relevant decision. Nevertheless, our QoS watchdog has additional function of bandwidth estimation. The watchdog agent is depicted above the IP layer (Figure1). However, this agent only carries out the support function to the QoS control and is in fact not an additional layer (such as transport layer) at the base station. In practice, the IP layer at the base station is to be modified to add this agent for QoS control (see also section 1). This modification does not disturb the end-to-end semantic of applications.

3.1. The QoS watchdog

We have to consider the transmission in both directions separately: transmission from the mobile host (MH) to a fixed host (FH) and transmission from the fixed host to a mobile host.

- Transmission from MH to FH:

The QoS watchdog has to estimate the wireless link bandwidth R_1. We take the bandwidth estimation method from our earlier works (Hoang and Reschke,2001) as follows:

$$R_{est} = \frac{L^k}{T}\left(1 - e^{-KT}\right) + R_{old}.e^{-KT} \qquad (1)$$

The estimated rate R_{est} is periodically updated by arriving of each packet based on an average rate $R_{old}*e^{-KT}$ and a variance, where L^k is the size of arriving packet k. K is a constant, and T is the arrival interval between two consecutive arriving packets. This term allows us to achieve the asymptotical established value for the bandwidth estimation.

Receiving packets from the sender, the QoS watchdog inserts the value R_1 in the packet headers, and forwards the packets onto the receiver. At the receiver, the bottleneck bandwidth of the connection along the path is estimated as R_2 (using Jacobson's Pathchar). Thus, the initial sending rate of the connection is calculated as $R_{init} = \mathbf{min}(R_1, R_2)$ which is then sent back to the sender using an ACK packet.

The RCAP source sends data packets with the sequence numbers. The QoS watchdog monitors the gap in the sequence of packets to detect losses due to wireless errors. Loss detection is also assumed if a timeout happens at the QoS watchdog. If a loss is detected, the QoS watchdog sends an explicit wireless loss indication to the RCAP source/destination to inform it about the situation. We emphasize here that the sending of loss indication is piggybacked (inband), no additional connection is needed. Also, the RCAP source starts a backoff period when a wireless error is detected during which it defers the transmission of further packets. It tries to communicate with the QoS watchdog to periodically probe the wireless channel. When the wireless channel becomes good again, a positive feedback is sent from the QoS watchdog to the sender.

The algorithm of QoS watchdog in this transmission direction is as follows:

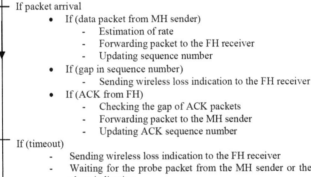

If packet arrival
- If (data packet from MH sender)
    - Estimation of rate
    - Forwarding packet to the FH receiver
    - Updating sequence number
- If (gap in sequence number)
    - Sending wireless loss indication to the FH receiver
- If (ACK from FH)
    - Checking the gap of ACK packets
    - Forwarding packet to the MH sender
    - Updating ACK sequence number

If (timeout)
    - Sending wireless loss indication to the FH receiver
    - Waiting for the probe packet from the MH sender or the connection close indication

- Transmission from FH to MH

In order to quickly know about the wireless channel state, we claim that the RCAP receiver sends back an ACK for any received packet. Nevertheless, the size of ACK packet is small in comparison to data packets, thus the overhead is kept small. The bandwidth estimation is done as in the transmission from MH to FH. The sender sets an initial sending rate accordingly.

By monitoring the sequence number of packets, the QoS watchdog detects the congestion loss in the path from the fixed host to the base station, if a gap in packet sequence is found. In this case, the QoS watchdog sends a congestion loss indication message to the sender at FH.

This indication is piggybacked in the ACK packet which will be sent from the MH to FH. After forwarding each packet to the MH, QoS watchdog waits for the ACK packet from the MH receiver. If a timeout or a gap in sequence number of ACK packets is detected, the wireless channel is assumed as bad. The QoS watchdog informs the FH about this and the RCAP sender at the FH side defers the transmission (within the deadline time of packets) by entering a backoff interval waiting for a positive acknowledgement from the QoS watchdog. The algorithm of QoS watchdog in the transmission from the fixed host FH to the mobile host MH is as follows:

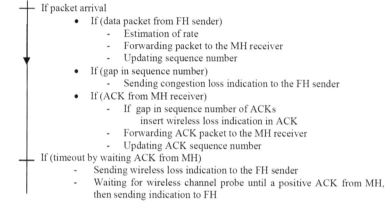

The function of the QoS watchdog can be enhanced by combining with the fair queueing scheme at the base station. No reservation is then needed. The weight of connection can be set by the estimated bandwidth, which is usually the rate according to the minimum quality requirement of the connection. Furthermore, the bad period (i.e. error interval) of a wireless channel can be credited and the connection can be compensated later when the channel becomes good again. In addition, the QoS watchdog may work together with the buffer management and a proxy at the higher level in the base station. One such high-level proxy is described in (Hoang and Reschke,2001). According to the estimation of wireless bandwidth, some low priority packets (for instance low priority video packets of layered coding scheme) can be discarded. A transcoding of data (e.g. different colors, picture sizes, resolutions etc.) is then useful, thus the wireless channel is not overloaded while maintaining an acceptable QoS to connections. However, this is the topic of further work.

3.2. RCAP protocol behaviour

As mentioned, a RCAP source sends data packets with sequence numbers and a RCAP destination acknowledges each packet with an ACK. Each ACK packet contains the sequence number of the transmitted packet. As shown in Figure 2, the RCAP protocol behavior is described using three states: Initial, steady and backoff state.

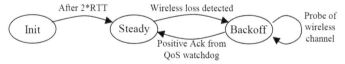

Figure 2. State model of the rate control proactive protocol

- Initial state

This state begins with the start of a new connection and will last for two RTTs. The quality of a multimedia connection is within a range of Q_{min} and Q_{max}. Q_{min} is the required quality and the service is not acceptable below this value. Q_{max} is the desired quality. The quality above this value is not necessary and there is then an undesired waste of resources. Hence, the rate of a connection should be in a range between R_{min} and R_{max}. Therefore, we should choose the initial rate R_{init} that is larger or equal to R_{min}.

The initial rate is calculated as follows at the receiver: $R_{init} = \min(R_1, R_2)$ where R_1 is the estimated rate of wireless link computed by the QoS watchdog. R_2 is the estimated rate at the receiver following the equation (1). R_1 and R_2 are estimated using back-by-back packets (such as packet pair technique). The RCAP receiver estimates the sending rate and sends this value back to the sender using ACK packets during two times of RTT.

- Steady state

In this state, RCAP at the receiver side estimates the link bandwidth along the path of connection based on the equation (1). In addition, RTT is calculated using the Jacobson's algorithm (Jacobson,1988) as follows: $RTT_{new} = (7/8)*RTT_{old} + (1/8)*RTT_{sample}$. This value will sent back to the RCAP sender by ACK packet.

If a gap in packet sequence number is detected, the RCAP receiver considers extra the information from the QoS watchdog attached in the packet header to see, whether the loss is due to congestion or due to wireless link error. A corresponding loss indication is set in the ACK packet, which is then sent back to the RCAP sender.

At the sender side, RCAP uses the information in ACK packets to achieve the estimated link bandwidth and information about network condition. RCAP sender calculates periodically RTT based on ACK packets and maintains the RTT value for its decision.

Based on the updated RTT value and the information in ACK packet, the RCAP sender makes the following decisions according to a TCP-friendly scheme (references to TCP-friendly schemes are given e.g. in Rejaie, *et.al*,1999 and Padhye,*et.al*,1998):

1) it increases the sending rate with:

$$R_{new} = \mathbf{min}(R_{old} + \Delta R, R_{max}) , \Delta R = 1/ SRTT \qquad (2)$$

after every time interval equal to SRTT (SRTT is the estimated round trip time) if no loss is detected.

2) it decreases the sending rate with:

$$R_{new} = \mathbf{max}(R_{old} / 2 , R_{min}) \qquad (3)$$

if a congestion loss is detected.

3) it begins the backoff state if a wireless loss is detected. Note that a timeout at the mobile host sender by waiting ACK also means wireless loss.

As we showed, RCAP uses an AIMD increase/decrease algorithm as suggested in (Jacobson,1988) in order to match the behavior of TCP connections. However, we suggest using R_{min} and R_{max} in equation (2) and (3) according to the acceptable range of the connection's QoS as we mentioned before.

Moreover, if the link bandwidth is estimated behind R_{min}, then the required QoS is not assured. This case may happen e.g. when the mobile host moves behind obstacles (hidden terminal effect) or a period of severe fading occurs during which the wireless link becomes more error-prone. In this situation, RCAP provides a feedback signal to the applications, claims it to reduce the rate (for instance change of coding, color depth, resolution etc. by adaptive or layering coding schemes) in order to maintain an acceptable QoS. Another possibility is to use a high level proxy as we mentioned before in section 3.1.

• Backoff state

The RCAP enters this state if a wireless loss is detected. The transmission is temporally deferred and a wireless channel probe is triggered (by this way, we can also save the scarce power of the mobile hosts). RCAP returns back to the steady state when a positive feedback (ACK) is received. The detection of this state and the probe of the wireless channel are done with the support of the QoS watchdog.

4. Simulation

This section is devoted to the simulation of the proposed scheme. We use one mobile host and one base station, which is connected to the fixed network consisting of two nodes. Following parameters are used in our simulation: the wireless link bandwidth is 1Mbps, packet size is 1000 Bytes and RTT is about 50ms. In the first scenario, we use various RCAP sources and in the second scenario, we compare the throughput of a TCP source and a RCAP source.

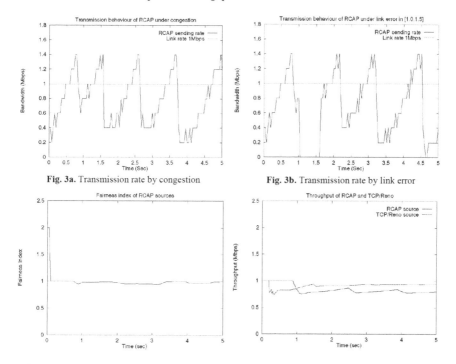

Fig. 3a. Transmission rate by congestion   **Fig. 3b.** Transmission rate by link error

Fig. 4a. Fairness of RCAP sources   **Fig. 4b.** Throughput of 1 RCAP source & 1 TCP/Reno

Figures 3a and 3b demonstrate the transmission behaviour of the RCAP protocol by congestion (3a) and link error (3b), respectively. In figure 3a, the congestion occurs at 0.6sec, 1.5sec, 2.6sec, 3.7sec, where the rate cross over the link bandwidth 1Mbps. The rate is adapted therefore accordingly. Figure 3b shows the case of a link error in the time interval [1.0sec,1.5sec]. During this time, the RCAP enters the backoff state and defers transmission.

The link error goes away after 1.5sec. The previous transmission rate (about 0.8 Mbps) is resumed, thus a high performance can be achieved. Figure 4a depicts the fairness of RCAP sources where the peak is due to the duration of the initial state (2*RTT). In the long term, a good fairness can be obtained, i.e. the fairness index approaches to the value of 1. Figure 4b compares the normalised throughput of a RCAP source with a TCP-Reno source. As shown, a fairness between flows is gained, i.e. the normalised throughput approaches 1 in long term.

5. Conclusion

The paper presents a rate control proactive scheme based on link bandwidth estimation and TCP-friendly congestion control for multimedia flows in wireless networks. With the bandwidth estimation method, not only the link state is predicted but also the wireless link available bandwidth can be estimated, thus the wireless link can be efficiently exploited. In case of a link error, the transmission is suspended in order to reduce the loss rate and the power use of wireless terminals. After the link is recovered, the previous rate is resumed, thus the performance is improved. By congestion, the control scheme behaves in a TCP-friendly fashion thus a fairness of different flows of different protocol types can be gained without starvation of other flows. The RCAP shows the comparable throughput with the TCP protocol.

6. References

H.Balakrishnan, V.N.Padmanabhan, S.Seshan, R.H.Katz (1997), "A Comparision of Mechanisms for Improving TCP Performance over Wireless Links", *IEEE/ACM Trans. On Networking*, Vol.5, No.6, Dec. 97.

S.Blake, D.Black, M.Carlson, E.Davies, Z.Wang, W.Weiss (1998), "An Architecture for Differentiated Services", *RFC 2475*, Dec. 1998.

D.Chalmers, M.Sloman (1999), "A Survey of Quality of Service in Mobile Computing Environments", *IEEE Communications Surveys*, Vol.2, No.2, 1999, also in *http://www.comsoc.org/pubs/serveys*.

J.Gomez, A.T.Campbell, H.Morikawa (1999), "The Havana Framework for supporting Application and Channel Dependent QoS in Wireless Networks", *IEEE 7th International Conference on Network Protocols (ICNP'99)*, November 1999, Toronto, Canada.

D-H.Hoang, D.Reschke, "A Proactive Concept for QoS Support in Wireless Networks", *NET.OBJECT-DAYS, MIK'2001*, Erfurt, Germany Sept. 2001.

V.Jacobson, "Congestion Avoidance and Control", *ACM SIGCOMM '88*, p314—329.

R.Rejaie, M.Handley, D.Estrin (1998), "RAP: An End-to-End Rate-based Congestion Control Mechanism for Real-time Streams in the Internet", *in Proc. of INFOCOM*, New York, NY, March 1999.

J.Padhye, V.Firoiu, D.Towsley, J.Kurosee (1998), "Modelling TCP Throughput: A Simple Model and Its Empirical Validation", *In ACM SIGCOMM'98*, Vancouver, Oct. 1998.

S.Shenker, C.Patridge, R. Guerin (1997), "Specification of Guaranteed Quality of Service", *RFC 2212*, Sept. 1997.

D.Sisalem, H.Schulzrinne (1998), "The Loss-based Adjustment Algorithm: A TCP-friendly Adaptation Schemes", *in Proc. of Intern. Workshop on Network and Operating System Support for Digital Audio and Video (NOSSDAV)*, Cambridge, England, July 1998.

J.Tang, G.Morabito, I.F.Akyildiz, M.Johnson, "RCS: A Rate Control Scheme for Real-time Traffic in Networks with High Bandwidth-Delay Products and High Bit Error Rates", *IEEE in Proc. of INFOCOM2001*, Alaska, April 2001.

B.Vandalore, R.Jain, S.Fahmy, S.Dixit (1999), "AQuaFWiN: Adaptive QoS Framework for Multimedia in Wireless Networks and its Comparision with other QoS Frameworks", *http://www.cis.ohio-state.edu/~jain/*.

Jitter control for interactive voice applications in mobile ad hoc networks

M.Benaissa[1], V.Lecuire[2] and F.Lepage[2]

[1] CRAN/LORIA, Université Nancy I
[2] CRAN, CNRS UMR 7039
Campus Scientifique - BP 239
54506 Vandœuvre-Nancy Cedex
e-mail: Mouna.Benaissa@loria.fr,{vincent.lecuire, francis.lepage}@cran.uhp-nancy.fr

Abstract

Mobility in ad hoc network affects packet jitter and leads to *handoff* delays. In this paper, we present a new *playout* delay adjustment algorithm of audio packets in mobile ad hoc networks for interactive audio applications. This algorithm has two modes of operation where *playout* delay is adapted differently, depending on whether or not a *handoff* has been detected. Interactivity constraints of audio applications are taken into account for the adjustments.

Keywords

Audio, Jitter, Ad hoc network, Mobility, *Handoff*, *Playout* delay.

1 . Introduction

One of the challenges of transmitting real-time voice on packet networks is how to overcome the variable inter-packet delay -the jitter- encountered as the packets cross the network. In order to compensate for these variable delays, packets are buffered at a receiver site and their *playout* is delayed for a period of time. Thus, most of the packets will have been received before their scheduled *playout* times (Moon et al.1998)(Clarck et al. 1992). In addition, *playout* delay must be maintained below a certain level that is considered to be quite acceptable in human conversation (less than 300ms) (ITU 2001)(Kitawaki and Itoh 1991). Although there are methods which use fixed *playout* delay throughout the duration of an audio call (Cho and Un 1994), recent research employs adaptive methods to vary *playout* delay during a call's lifetime (Moon et al. 1998)(Pinto and Christensen 1999)(Ramjee et al. 1994). These methods are used to overcome jitter problems in wide area networks. In this paper, we show that in mobile ad hoc networks, jitter phenomenon is different, and present a new algorithm that consider effects of mobility on jitter to adjust *playout* delay in such networks. The remainder of this paper is structured as follows. In section 2 we describe our study on the effect of mobility on jitter phenomenon in an ad hoc network; and we show that methods used to adjust *playout* delay in wide area networks lose some of their effectiveness in mobile ad hoc networks. In section 3, we present our new *playout* delay adjustment algorithm for mobile ad hoc networks. Evaluation results of this algorithm are discussed in section 4. Section 5 concludes this paper.

2. Jitter in ad hoc mobile networks

In the Internet, packets encounter a variable amount of inter-packet delay due to queuing and routing in the intermediate nodes, that changes the original periodicity (one packet every 20 ms) (Montgomery 1983). In order to smooth out such delay jitter, the initiation of periodic *playout* of received packets can be delayed for a length of time (Clarck et al. 1992). The receiver uses a *playout* buffer; also called a jitter buffer or smoothing buffer, to queue and hold each received packet for amount of buffer time that compensates for the network delay variance without excessively delaying the *playout*. Clearly, long delays are undesirable since they impair interactive application. Human conversation tolerates a maximum end-to-end delay of between 150 and 300 milliseconds (ITU 2001)(Kitawaki and Itoh 1991). However, packets which arrive after their scheduled *playout* time, are considered lost. We refer to "*playout* delay: d_i" of packet "i", the amount of time from when the ith packet is generated by the source until it is played out at the destination host. Previous studies (Bolot 1993)(Saghi et al. 1993)(Puigjaner 1996) have indicated that end-to-end delays fluctuate significantly in the Internet and have noted the presence of "*spike*" due to the congestion. A *spike* constitutes a sudden, large increase in the end-to-end network delay, followed by a series of packets arriving almost simultaneously, leading to the completion of the *spike*. Two *spike*s are illustrated in figure 1 and 2.

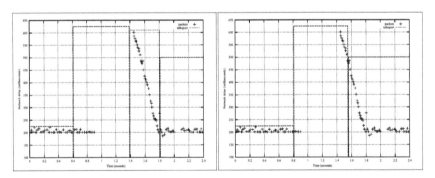

Figure 1: Spike contained within a talk-spurt　　　**Figure 2: Spike spanning two talk-spurts**

Adjustment *playout* delay algorithms for wide area networks are reported in (Ramjee et al. 1994) (Moon et al. 1998) (Pinto and Christensen 1999). The *playout* delay is adaptively adjusted from one *talkspurt* (periods of audio activity) to the next. In comparing four algorithms, (Ramjee et al. 1994) concludes that algorithm 4, which adapts to *spike* increases in packet delay, can achieve a lower rate of lost packets for a given average delay. This algorithm outperforms any existing adaptive algorithm in the presence of delay *spikes*. We refer to this algorithm in this paper as the *spike-algorithm*. The *spike-algorithm* has two modes of operation, depending on whether or not a *spike* has been detected. Existing adjustment *playout* delay algorithms are planned for problems of jitter in wide area networks.

In ad hoc networks, the jitter is not only related to the congestion. Ad hoc networks consist of a set of mobile hosts that communicate using wireless radios, without the aid of a fixed networking infrastructure. The topology of an ad hoc network changes due to the movement of mobile hosts (Johnson 1994). To identify characteristics of jitter in mobile ad hoc networks, we examined a series of delay traces obtained with the NS simulator (Greis 2001)(ISI 2001). In the scenario described in this paper, we introduced three mobility phases at different times within a topology of six ad hoc nodes. The DSR protocol is used for routing (Johnson and Maltz 1996)(Broch et al. 1999).

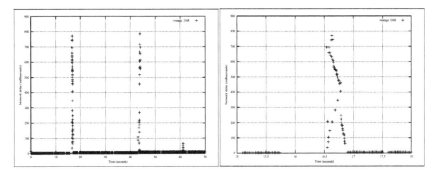

Figure 3: **Jitter in a mobile ad hoc network (routing protocol: DSR).**   **Figure 4**: **Jitter in a mobile ad hoc network: 1st handoff phase (routing protocol: DSR).**

The delay trace in figure 3 shows three phases where delay values (n_i) are very important, due to the three periods of mobility. The first period of mobility, illustrated in more detail in figure 4, shows that end-to-end delays fluctuate significantly from one packet to another. When a node moves, the flow transfer is interrupted during the *handoff* period, which is the delay required for a routing protocol to establish a new route towards the destination. Under normal conditions, end-to-end delays are low and rather stable (in the majority of simulated cases: $n_i - n_{i-1} < 1$). Mobility has a significant effect on the jitter and *playout* delay must therefore be adjusted according to these variations, when the nodes move with active connections. Using the *spike-algorithm*, we estimated the *playout* delay for the delay traces described in figure 3. Figures 5 and 6 show the estimated *playout* delay within the first and third *handoff* phases.

Compared to the packet delay "n_i" observed in figure 5, *playout* delay is excessively large. The *spike-algorithm* reacts to the presence of a *handoff* as if it were a *spike*. On the other hand, *playout* delay is under-estimated for the third *handoff* phase in figure 6 because the increase in packet delay is not large enough to be considered a *spike*. In figure 5, *playout* delay adjustment occurs late. This behaviour is also observed with *spikes* on wide area networks. A discussion about this behaviour can be found in (Moon et al. 1998). The *spike-algorithm* loses its effectiveness in ad hoc mobile networks and it is this which motivates our design of a new algorithm. In the following section, we describe a new algorithm based on these observations to adjust the *playout* delay according to jitter characteristics in mobile ad hoc networks.

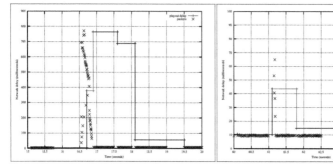

Figure 5: Estimated playout delay for the spike-algorithm in mobile ad hoc network: 1st handoff phase

Figure 6: Estimated playout delay for the spike-algorithm in a mobile ad hoc network: 3rd handoff phase

3. A playout delay adjustment algorithm in mobile ad hoc networks

Our algorithm has two modes of operation, depending on whether or not a *handoff* has been detected. For every packet that arrives at the receiver, the algorithm checks the current mode and, if necessary, switches its mode to the other. The estimated *playout* delay depends on the current mode. We have assumed that the network does not suffer from congestion. Thus, we do not consider here the effect of congestion on jitter. The operation of our algorithm is described in the following paragraphs.

3.1 Detection of the two phases: normal and handoff

Unlike in a normal phase, end-to-end delays are variable in *handoff* phases (see section 3). Through observing the level of the jitter, we can distinguish between the two phases. In order to achieve this, we check the delay between consecutive packets at the receiver. If end-to-end delay of the packets fluctuates significantly, the algorithm detects the beginning of a *handoff* event and switches the operation mode to HANDOFF. On the other hand, when the end-to-end delays become sufficiently stable, it detects the end of a *handoff* phase and switches back to NORMAL mode. In determining the number of packets which are necessary for the detection of the beginning and end of a *handoff* event, we found that the algorithm operates correctly when the two recent delay observations are used together with the current value n_i, i.e.:

If (abs($n_i - n_{i-1}$)>handoff_threshold) and (abs($n_{i-1} - n_{i-2}$)>handoff_threshold) then

mode = HANDOFF;

If (abs($n_i - n_{i-1}$)<normal_threshold) and (abs($n_{i-1} - n_{i-2}$)<normal_threshold) then

mode = NORMAL;

In our simulation, we set *normal_threshold* parameter to 1 because in the majority of simulated cases: $n_i - n_{i-1} < 1$ ms in an ad hoc mobile network during a normal phase. During some *handoff* phases, the end-to-end delays are not necessary very important, but only not stable. So, *handoff_threshold* parameter must be set to sufficiently low but still larger than the *normal_threshold* to react to the presence of such a *handoff* phase.

3.2 Playout delay estimation

Based on work already done on wide area networks (Ramjee et al. 1994), the *playout* point p_i for packet i, generated at time t_i by the sender, is computed as:

$$p_i = t_i + \hat{d}_i + a\hat{v}_i \qquad (1)$$

where $\hat{d}_i$ and $\hat{v}_i$ are estimates of the mean and variance in the end-to-end delay. The $a\hat{v}_i$ term is used to set the *playout* time to be far enough beyond the delay estimate; so that only a small fraction of the arriving packets should be lost due to late arrival. The computation of $\hat{v}_i$ (which in turn depends on $\hat{d}_i$) is defined in this equation:

$$\hat{v}_i = \alpha\hat{v}_{i-1} + (1 - \alpha)|\hat{d}_i - n_i| \qquad (2)$$

The mean estimation of network delay is based on the RFC 739 algorithm (Postel 1981), while the variance is estimated using a measure of the variation in the delays suggested by Van Jacobson in the calculation of the round trip estimates for the TCP retransmit timer (Jacobson 1988). The *playout* delay estimate for packet i is computed according to the current mode. It is not

```
n i = Receiver_ timestamp - Sender_timestamp;

if ( mode== normal) {   // handoff detection
  if (abs(n i - n i-1) > handoff_threshold) and  (abs(n i-1 - n i-2) > handoff_threshold ) {
     mode = handoff;
  }
}
else {  //  back to normal phase
  if (abs(n i - n i-1) < normal_threshold) and  (abs(n i-1 - n i-2) < normal_threshold ) {
     mode = normal;
     }
}

// compute the estimated playout delay
/ / only during the first talkspurt of an normal phase

if ( mode== normal ) {
     d i= (0.125 * n i + 0.875 * d i-1 );  }
else {  d i = 0.5 * n i + 0.5 * d i-1 ;  }   // phase handoff

v i= 0.125 * abs ( n i - d i) + 0.875 * v i-1 ;

if (d i + 4 v i) < max {  // Check of the boundary limit of interactivity
  update_playout (d i );  // the new values are taken into account
}
else {
  max_playout(d i );  // the estimated playout delay is set to maximum
}

n i-2 =n i-1 ;
n i-1 =n i-2 ;
```

Figure 7: **Pseudo code of the adjustment playout delay algorithm for mobile ad hoc network**

necessary to adjust *playout* delay during a normal phase because the jitter is very low. The estimated *playout* delay is only computed at the beginning of each normal phase, where this estimate is used by the subsequent packets. For this, packets which arrive at the beginning of a normal phase, take part in the estimation of *playout* delay, which is computed as:

$$\hat{d}_i = (1 - \alpha)n_i + \alpha\hat{d}_{i-1} \qquad (3)$$

This equation is basically a linear recursive filter and is characterised by the weighting factor α. In order to maintain a stable value, $(1 - \alpha)$ is set to be very low. In our simulations, received packets of the first *talkspurt* in each normal phase are used to compute the *playout* delay on normal mode. This is sufficient to lead to an average *playout* delay for all of the normal phase. While in *handoff* phase, we use a second weighting factor β. $(1 - \beta)$ is set to be high in the equation 4, in order to catch up quickly with a change in delays, caused by the significant jitter in this phase. In addition, excessive *playout* delay estimate is undesirable, and to avoid this $(1 - \beta)$ is set to be sufficient low. *Playout* delay is computed as:

$$\hat{d}_i = (1 - \beta)n_i + \beta\hat{d}_{i-1} \qquad (4)$$

$\hat{d}_i$ is computed for each packet received, although it is adjusted periodically within a *handoff* phase. The time for an adjustment period is chosen to be shorter than the length of a *talkspurt*. This will allow a better reaction to the end-to-end delays variations even if the *handoff* phase is contained within one *talkspurt*. Furthermore, this period must be large enough to keep the system stable. Note that only the increase in estimated *playout* delay is taken into account, in order to avoid collision when two consecutive packets are being played out. Lastly, the algorithm checks if the estimated *playout* delay exceeds 300 ms, the limit fixed for interactivity in audio applications. In this case, the *playout* delay is maintained at 300 ms. A pseudo code of this algorithm is given in figure 7 where α is fixed to the value of "7/8" and β to the value of "1/2".

4. Simulation and results

We applied our algorithm to the same scenario described in section 3, and varied the weighting factor β to determine the sensitivity of this algorithm to the value of β. For α, the algorithm's performance did not change because in normal phase the delays are almost the same. In our

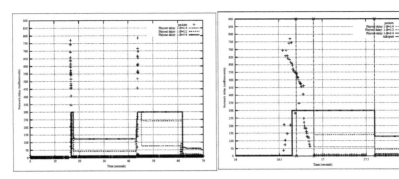

Figure 8: **Estimated playout delay in a mobile ad hoc network on all the session**   Figure 9: **Estimated playout delay in a mobile ad hoc network: 1st handoff phase**

simulations, α is set to 0.875. We performed a program which reads the sender and receiver timestamps of each packet from a trace and computes the estimation of *playout* delay using our algorithm. Packets which arrive before their deadline, are queued in the buffer to wait for delivery. Otherwise, the packet is dropped and considered lost. This program also calculates the loss percentage due to late arrivals.Figure 8 represents three graphs for the total estimated *playout* delay with our algorithm for three β values [1/4, 1/2, 3/4]. The estimated *playout* delay does not exceed 300 ms, the boundary limit for delays in interactive voice applications. The first *handoff* phase is shown in more detail in figure 9 where talkspurts are delimited by vertical dashed lines. The three graphs show that the algorithm reacts quickly to the presence of a *handoff*, even if the *handoff* begins within a *talkspurt*. The estimated *playout* delay is adjusted frequently during a *handoff* phase. In our simulation, the adjustment period in *handoff* phase is set to 100 ms. The loss percentage is almost the same with the three β values. At the beginning of a *handoff* phase the loss percentage is very important. In the first *handoff* phase, the loss percentage (96.5% of packets loss) is more important than it is in the second (46%); whereas there is no packet loss in the third *handoff* phase. This is not a serious problem because most of the packets lost at the receiver are those which exceed the boundary limit of 300ms.

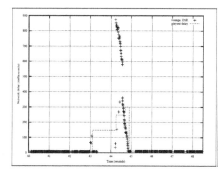 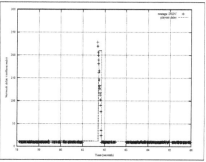

Figure 10: **Estimated playout delay in a mobile ad hoc network: zoom on a handoff phase (routing protocol: DSR)**   Figure 11: **Estimated playout delay in a mobile ad hoc network: zoom on a handoff phase (routing protocol: DSDV)**

This algorithm is not very sensitive to the variation of the value β, if we consider the loss rate alone. Human conversation tolerates a boundary limit of 300 ms for end-to-end delays but necessitates delays below 200 ms in order to be of a good quality. Therefore, the quality suffers when $(1 - \beta)$ is set to "3/4" (see figure 9). In addition, it is not desirable to set $(1 - \beta)$ very low in order to keep the system sufficiently stable. Thus the algorithm approaches good voice quality with the two values of $(1 - \beta)$: "1/2" and "1/4", but the system is more stable with the value of "1/2". Figure 10 and 11 represent the estimated *playout* delay with our algorithm for the two protocols: the reactive protocol DSR and the proactive protocol DSDV. The proactive approach requires to each node to maintain a view of the network topology with a cost for each link. The reactive approach uses the *source routing* before sending a packet. For the DSR protocol, the estimated *playout* delays are more important than those estimated for the DSDV protocol (see the handoff phases shown in figures 10 and 11). Our new algorithm reactscorrectly to the presence of *handoffs*. We obtained a better interactive quality when the weighting factor β is set to "1/2". This value gives the same importance to the previous estimated *playout* delay and the new end-to-end delays observed.

5. Conclusion

In this paper, we have focused on the effects of mobility on jitter in mobile ad hoc networks. We presented a new algorithm for *playout* delay adjustment for interactive audio applications in such networks. This algorithm correctly detects the two phases: *handoff* and normal. We evaluated its performance in ad hoc networks. Our proposal reacts correctly to the presence of *handoff* phases and computes *playout* delay according to the characteristics of jitter in ad hoc networks. Interactivity constraints of audio applications are taken into account for the adjustments. In addition, a good improvment to our algorithm would be to take into account the congestion phenomenon, which must be clearly distinguished from handoff phenomenon.

References

Bolot, J.(1993), Characterising end-to-end packet delay and loss in the internet, *J. of High-Speed Networks* pp. 305–323.

Broch, J., Johnson, D. B. and Maltz, D. A.(1999), The dynamic source routing protocol for mobile ad hoc networks, *draft-ietf-manet-dsr-03.txt*.

Cho, Y.-J. and Un, C.-K.(1994), Performance analysis of reconstruction algorithms for packet voice communications, *Computer Networks and ISDN Systems* **26**(11), 1385–1408.

Clark, D., Shenker, S. and Zhang, L.(1992), Supporting real-time applications in an integrated services packet network: architecture and mechanism, *SIGCOMM'92* pp. 14–26.

Greis, M.(2001), Tutorial for the network simulator "ns", *http://www.isi.edu/nsnam/ns/tutorial/*.

ISI(2001), The network simulator - ns, *http://www.isi.edu/nsnam/ns/*.

ITU(2001), List of itu-t recommendations, *http://www.itu.int/publications/itu-t/itutrec.htm*.

Jacobson, V.(1988), Congestion Avoidance and Control, *Proceedings, SIGCOMM '88 Workshop*, ACM SIG-COMM, ACM Press, pp. 314–329. Stanford, CA.

Johnson, D. and Maltz, D.(1996), Dynamic source routing in ad hoc wireless networks, *Mobile Computing, T. Imielinski and H.Korth, eds., Kluwer Academic Publishers*.

Johnson, D. B.(1994), Routing in ad hoc networks of mobile host, *IEEE Workshop on Mobile Computing Systemes and applications*.

Kitawaki, N. and Itoh, K.(1991), Pure delay effects on speech quality in telecommunications, *IEEE Journal of Selected Areas in Communications* 9(4), 586–593.

Montgomery, W.(1983), Techniques for packets voice synchronisation, *IEEE J. on Selected Areas in Communications*. pp. Sol.SAC–6, No. 1 pp. 1122 – 1028. http://www.cse.ucsc.edu/ rom/infocom2000.

Moon, S., Kurose, J. and Towsley, D.(1998), Packet audio playout delay ajustments: Performance bounds and algorithms, *ACM/Springer Multimedia System* pp. 17–18.

Pinto, J. and Christensen, K. J.(1999), An algorithm for playout of packet voice based on adaptive adjustment of talkspurt silence periods, *citeseer.nj.nec.com/pinto99algorithm.html*.

Postel, J.(1981), Transmission control protocol specification: Rfc 793, *ARPANET Working Group*.

Puigjaner, R.(1996), Performance modelling of atm networks, *ACM/Springer Multimedia System* pp. 3–7.

Ramjee, R., Kurose, J., Towsley, D. and Schulzrinne, H.(1994), Adaptive playout mechanisms for packetized audio applications in wide-area networks, *IEEE INFOCOM'94* pp. 680–688.

Sanghi, D., Agrawala, A., Gudhmundsson, O. and Jain, B. N.(1993), Experimental assessment of end-to-end behavior on internet, *citeseer.nj.nec.com/sanghi93experimental.html* pp. 867–874.

A Broadcasting Scheme to Support Fast-Forward Interaction in Video-on-Demand Service

Hon-Shing Ma, Tsun-Ping Jimmy To and Chi-Kwong Li

Department of Electronic and Information Engineering,
The Hong Kong Polytechnic University, Hung Hom, Hong Kong. *
e-mail: {enhsma, enjimmy, enckli}@polyu.edu.hk

Abstract

Periodic broadcasting can be used to support video-on-demand service for popular videos. To compete with existing video rental services, interactive functions are much preferred in the VoD service. Current studies of broadcast schemes mostly focus on the optimization of the usage of system resources, but seldom address the support of interactive functions. In this paper, we propose a new broadcast scheme called Short-Range Fast-Forward Broadcasting. The proposed scheme supports clients to perform fast forward interaction.

Keywords

Interactive Video-on-Demand, Broadcast scheme.

1. Introduction

Video-on-Demand (VoD) is an electronic form of video rental service. It offers clients a video library from which they can select a video programme to watch at any time. In the traditional broadcast TV system, a client is allowed to select from a group of parallel and competing TV programmes [Little and Venkatesh 1994]. Unfortunately, if a client misses the starting time of a programme, he/she needs to wait for another opportunity. This can mean hours in the case of a cable service, or weeks in the case of wireless broadcast TV channels. In contrast, VoD service makes all programmes available to the client without such restrictions.

A typical VoD system architecture consists of a local video server connected to clients via a communication network. The system can be part of a hierarchical video distribution system which consists of local and remote video servers [Mundur *et al* 1999]. The client's hardware consists of a set-top box (STB) with network interface for interacting with the system. Normally, a buffer is present inside the STB for smoothing of variable network delivery latencies and relaxing the coupling between the client and the server.

In the *Unicast* approach to provide VoD service, a private data stream is delivered to each client. This requires allocating network and server resources to each client. The serving of each client, including the handling of interactive functions, is mutually independent. This approach is non-scalable because the number of simultaneous clients that can be supported is limited by the network's or the server's capacities. The *startup latency*, i.e., the maximum delay that the client experiences in getting service, can easily be unbounded when the server runs out of resources.

* This work was partially supported by the Hong Kong Polytechnic University's internal research grants G-T229 & G-T042.

In *multicasting*, a new data stream is delivered to a pool of clients. How often a VoD server starts a data stream depends very much on the system design [Dan *et al* 1995, Dan *et al* 1996]. The server may start a new data stream when the number of waiting clients or the elapsed time reaches certain thresholds. Thus, the time intervals between starting of streams are not necessarily regular. The sharing of streams also means that one client's interaction can only be performed if other clients on the same stream are not affected. The support of interactive functions in multicast schemes has been studied to some extent [Abram-Profeta and Shin 1998, Almeroth and Ammar 1996, Liao and Li 1997]. In these studies, each client interaction are supported by a new data stream or by extra buffer in the server-side hardware. In short, extra system resources are needed.

In *broadcasting*, a new data stream to be shared by an unbounded number of clients is started at regular intervals. All the new clients who request for the same video will be grouped or batched together and simultaneously served by the same new data stream. The startup latency depends on the video's playback duration and the number of video streams that the VoD server has allocated to the video. In [Viswanathan and Imielinski 1996], the Pyramid Broadcasting (PB) scheme decreases the startup latency exponentially with the increase in the number of allocated channels. Based on PB, [Juhn and Tseng 1998] proposed the Fast Data Broadcasting scheme with smaller buffer requirement in the STB. In [Hua *et al* 1998], Hua exploited the client-side download bandwidth for more efficient video broadcast. In [Eager and Vernon 1998], the Dynamic Skyscraper Broadcasting scheme is proposed for lower client request rates and time-varying video popularities. In [Pâris 1999], the New Pagoda Broadcasting scheme is shown to require low transmission bandwidth. For VoD services delivered over cable and microwave technologies, broadcasting is often the only choice because in these scenarios the bandwidth is rigidly bounded.

Practically, most of the demand (80%) is for a few very popular videos [Dan *et al* 1996]. Broadcasting allows clients requesting the same popular video to be served economically. Unfortunately, broadcasting faces the same problem as multicasting in that one client's interaction affects all other clients on the same stream. Dynamic resources, required by solutions meant for multicasting, are unlikely to be available in broadcasting. This is because the extra network bandwidth needed is already fully exploited in broadcasting. With this difficulty, the provision of interactive functions in broadcast VoD systems has not been well addressed.

In this paper, we shall present a new broadcast scheme that supports clients to perform fast forward interaction. The remainder of this paper is organized as follows. We shall discuss our proposed broadcast scheme in Section 2 and its performance in Section 3. In Section 4, we shall provide a solution to improve the performance of the scheme. Finally, the conclusions will be given in Section 5.

2. Proposed Scheme: Short-Range Fast-Forward Broadcast Scheme

Fast-forward (FF) is a forward visible scan of the video at a rate higher than the normal playout rate. As a result, the video data will be consumed in a shorter time than its normal playback duration.

Pre-buffering is employed in all proposed broadcast schemes. The video data pre-buffered, however, may not necessarily be the data required in the immediate future and is not meant to support FF. Besides, the data transmission rate of *logical channels* (a collection of system resources required to deliver a data stream) in most schemes is the same as the video's normal playout rate. This means that the delivery rate of video data on a channel cannot be arbitrarily increased to the FF rate. Therefore, most previously proposed broadcast schemes are not designed to support fast-forward interactions. Based on these observations, we have designed a new broadcasting scheme called **Short-Range Fast-Forward Broadcasting (SRFFB)**. The theory behind SRFFB will be presented next.

2.1 Channel Allocation

Assuming that the server allocates B Mbits/sec network bandwidth to a video. The bandwidth is then divided into K logical channels, where $(K + 1) = \lfloor B/b \rfloor$ and b is the normal playout rate of the video. The bandwidth of the first logical channel is $2b$ Mbits/sec while the remaining $(K - 1)$ channels are b Mbits/sec. The logical channels are numbered starting with zero.

2.2 Video Segmentation and Allocation

In SRFFB, a video file is equally segmented into N *video segment blocks* (or *blocks* in short), where

$$N = 2^K$$

When the number of channels is increased by one, the total number of blocks is doubled. In other words, the size of a block is halved when K, the number of channels, is increased by one. Let X_j denote the jth block of the video ($j > 0$). The concatenation of all blocks, in the order of increasing block numbers, constitutes the whole video.

$$\text{video file} = X_1 \mid X_2 \mid X_3 \mid \dots \mid X_{N-1} \mid X_N$$

Figure 1 shows two examples of the segmentation of the same video in SRFFB. From the figure, we can see that there is a general relationship between the blocks under different segmentations. Denoting X^K_j as the jth block of the K-channel SRFFB scheme, we have

$$X^K_j = X^{K+1}_{2j-1} \mid X^{K+1}_{2j}$$

3-channel	1		2		3		4		5		6		7		8	
4-channel	1	2	3	4	5	6	7	8	9	10	11	12	13	14	15	16

Figure 1: Segmentation of a video under the 3-channel and 4-channel SRFFB schemes.

After the segmentation of the video, we shall decide how many blocks are to be put onto each channel for periodic broadcast. The allocation of blocks in SRFFB with K channels is defined by:

$$C(i) = \begin{cases} 2 & i = 0, \\ 2 & i = 1, \\ 2 * C(i-1) & 2 \le i \le (K-1) \end{cases}$$

where $C(i)$ is the number of blocks on channel i. Each block recurs on channel i every $C(i)$ timeslots. Thus, $C(i)$ is also referred to as the length of the **recurring period** of the blocks on channel i. Figure 2 shows an example of the broadcast schedule of SRFFB with three channels. The contiguous blocks on a channel are together referred to as a **video segment**. Let S_i denote the video segment on channel i. In general, the blocks that make up S_i are:

$$S_i = \begin{cases} X_1 + X_2 & i = 0 \\ X_{2^i+1}, X_{2^i+2}, \ldots, X_{2^{i+1}-1}, X_{2^{i+1}} & i > 0 \end{cases}$$

timeslot #	t0		t1		t2		t3		t4		t5		t6		t7	
channel 0	1	2	1	2	1	2	1	2	1	2	1	2	1	2	1	2
channel 1	3		4		3		4		3		4		3		4	
channel 2	5		6		7		8		5		6		7		8	

Figure 2: The broadcast schedule of SRFFB (3 logical channels).

2.3 Download Sequence

A **download sequence** refers to the way a client collects/downloads video data from the channels. In SRFFB, a new client has to catch the next appearance of the first segment S_1 of the target video. The timeslot at which downloading starts is referred to as the **starting timeslot**. Once downloading starts, consumption of S_1 also starts instantly. In the mean time, the client checks the **subsequent blocks** broadcast on the remaining channels until the last block of the video is downloaded. Denoting the block number of the current playing block as $N_{current}$, the block being checked is an instance of X_{check} with block number N_{check} and length of recurring period C_{check}. The block being checked needs to be downloaded if the following condition holds:

$$N_{check} - N_{current} \leq C_{check}$$

The value $(N_{check} - N_{current})$ is the *relative* playback time of X_{check} with respect to the current playing block. If the value is smaller than C_{check}, this instance of X_{check} is the last occurence of X_{check} on the channel before its normal playback time. If it is not captured, the client will experience a viewing discontinuity of the video. To support fast forward interaction, the equality part in the condition is crucial. If the equality part is not included, it is possible that a block is being downloaded while it is being viewed. This will rule out the possibility of fast forward operation. The equality part assures that pre-buffering of a subsequent block will always begin before consumption of the current block finishes.

Since $\sum_{j=0}^{i-1} C(j) = C(i)$, at least one instance of each block on channel i will appear (and be pre-buffered) before consumption of blocks on preceding channels completes. Hence, in any download sequence, every future block will have at least one of its instances being checked and downloaded before its consumption starts. One of the download sequences of SRFFB with three channels is illustrated in Figure 3.

timeslot #	t0		t1		t2		t3		t4		t5		t6		t7	
channel 0	1	2	1	2	1	2	1	2	1	2	1	2	1	2	1	2
channel 1	3		4		3		4		3		4		3		4	
channel 2	5		6		7		8		5		6		7		8	

Figure 3: A download sequence of SRFFB.

2.4 Fast Forward

SRFFB guarantees that a client can perform a *double-rate* fast-forward interaction within a range of two blocks at any point-of-play of the video. The correctness of the guarantee is given below.

Case 1. Fast-forward is performed at the beginning of the video.
At the starting timeslot, S_1, which is composed of two blocks X_1 and X_2, is downloaded at a rate twice of the normal playout rate. As a result, the downloading of S_1 is able to keep up with FF rate for two blocks.

Case 2. Fast-forward is performed during the consumption of the blocks of S_1.
Suppose FF is performed at time t and $|X|$ denotes the playback duration of one block. Hence, the downloading time of the remaining part of S_1 is $(|X| - t)$. At time t, only $t*b$ video data of S_1 is consumed and the size of the unconsumed part of S_1 is $(2|X| - t)*b$. The playback duration of the unconsumed part of S_1 in FF mode, being $(|X| - t/2)$, is longer than the downloading duration of the remaining part of S_1. In such download sequence, the downloading of S_2 will start either at the same timeslot as S_1 or just right after it. Therefore, during FF on S_1, the downloading of S_2 has already begun. In the worst case, the downloading of S_2 follows that of S_1. At such time, there is still $t*b$ amount of S_1 remaining in the client's buffer. During the consumption of these $t*b$ data, $t*b/2$ data of S_2 will be pre-buffered in the buffer. Similarly, during the consumption of the $t*b/2$ data of S_2, another $t*b/4$ data S_2 will be pre-buffered. Since the FF rate is twice of the delivery rate of S_2, the consumption will finally catch up with the downloading of video data such that no more readahead data in the buffer can be used to support FF. Within the FF period, the amount of video data consumed will be $(2|X| - t + t/2 + t/4 + t/8 + t/16 + \ldots)*b$, which converges to $2*|X|*b$, or the size of two blocks.

Case 3. Fast-forward is performed during the consumption of blocks other than that of S_1.
If no FF is performed during the downloading of S_1, then only X_1 is consumed and the full X_2 will be pre-buffered in the client's buffer. Meanwhile, the downloading of the remaining blocks starts concurrently at or after the starting timeslot. This implies that there will always be at least one block pre-buffered. Thus, the readahead video data in the buffer can at least support a FF period of $|X|/2$. With the same argument as stated in *case 2*, the downloading of video data is still in progress during the FF period. Therefore, the length of the FF period is $(|X|/2 + |X|/4 + |X|/8 + \ldots)$, i.e., the playback duration of one block. Since the FF rate is twice of the normal playout rate, the video data consumed in the FF period is also two blocks.

Summing up the above three cases, the range of FF supported in SRFFB is two blocks. The range of a second attempt will depend on the data accumulation level in the client's buffer and the then-shifted download sequence. However, SRFFB is extensible to a faster FF rate and a longer FF range.

3. Performance Analysis

3.1 Startup Latency
The startup latency is the time between occurrences of the first video segment of the video. For an M-minute video broadcasting in SRFFB with K logical channels, we have

$$Startup\ latency\ =\ (M/2^K)\ minutes$$

Figure 4 shows the startup latency of SRFFB for a 120-minute video. It can be seen that the startup latency decreases exponentially as the number of channel increases. With five channels, the startup latency can already be brought down to a few minutes.

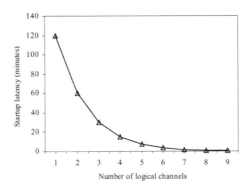

Figure 4: Startup latency of SRFFB

3.2 Client-side Buffer Requirement
Video segment blocks are pre-buffered in the client-side buffer in order to support FF. Maximum data accumulation occurs when all blocks of the video are downloaded concurrently in the shortest time. Thus, the shortest time to download all blocks is equal to the time needed to download the last segment which is the largest (of size 2^{K-1} blocks) among all segments. The number of blocks consumed during the downloading period will also be 2^{K-1}. Therefore, the client-side buffer requirement (in fraction of video file size) is:

$$Buffer\ size\ =\ \frac{2^K - 2^{K-1}}{2^K}$$
$$=\ 1/2$$

The client-side buffer requirement of SRFFB is half the size of a video.

4. Reduction of Buffer Requirements

To support FF interaction, apparently SRFFB requires a client-side buffer size of half of a video file. To be more competitive, next we shall show how this buffer requirement can be reduced by half.

In SRFFB, video segment blocks are pre-buffered into the client-side buffer. The buffer required reaches a peak when the blocks are all pre-buffered in the shortest time. If we can lengthen the length of such shortest download sequence (or shortest-length in brief), the number of blocks consumed during the lengthened downloading period will increase and hence the buffer requirement will decrease. The shortest-length is actually equal to the time needed to download the segment broadcast on the last channel. By making a larger segment out of the existing segments without violating the principle of pre-buffering, we can increase the shortest-length. To achieve this we can add one more logical channel to the K-channel SRFFB scheme. This extra channel (i.e., channel K) is used to broadcast the last segment again, but lagging behind channel $(K - 1)$ by a time difference of $C(K - 1)/2$ (i.e., 2^{K-3}) timeslots. This means that the last segment broadcast on channel K is shifted by 2^{K-3} timeslots relative to that on channel $(K - 1)$. The broadcasting pattern of segments on the other channels remains the same as before. We call this new scheme as **Small-Buffer SRFFB (SB-SRFFB)**. The broadcast schedule of SB-SRFFB with four channels is shown in Figure 5.

timeslot #	t0		t1		t2		t3		t4		t5		t6		t7	
channel 0	1	2	1	2	1	2	1	2	1	2	1	2	1	2	1	2
channel 1	3		4		3		4		3		4		3		4	
channel 2	5		6		7		8		5		6		7		8	
channel 3	7		8		5		6		7		8		5		6	

Figure 5: The broadcast schedule of SB-SRFFB (5 logical channels).

In Figure 5, we can see that the same video segment is broadcast on channel 2 and channel 3, but with a timeslot difference of two between them. The recurring period of the last channel is the same as that of the second-last channel. In the broadcast schedule of SB-SRFFB with $(K + 1)$ channels, there is always a new occurrence of S_{K-1}, either on channel $(K - 1)$ or on channel K, comes after each instance of S_{K-2} on channel $(K - 2)$. As a result, downloading of S_{K-1} can always start *after* that of S_{K-2} with no overlap. Since S_{K-2} is pre-buffered, S_{K-1} is consequently pre-buffered too. These two segments, S_{K-1} and S_{K-2}, can thus be viewed as a single large segment spread over two channels. As the pre-buffering principle is preserved, fast-forward interaction is still supported in the new SB-SRFFB scheme.

In SB-SRFFB with $(K + 1)$ channels, where $K > 2$, clients only need to download video data from the first $(K - 1)$ channels concurrently in the worst case since the last two channels are both used to deliver S_{K-1}. The shortest time to download all segments is equal to the sum of the delivery time of S_{K-2} and S_{K-1}, i.e., the delivery time of $(2^{K-3} + 2^{K-2})$ blocks. Hence, the client-side buffer requirement (in fraction of video file size) in SB-SRFFB is

$$Buffer\ size = 1 - \frac{2^{K-3} + 2^{K-2}}{2^{K-1}}$$
$$= 1/4$$

At the cost of one logical channel, the buffer requirement in SB-SRFFB can be drastically reduced to one quarter of a video file size, which is a saving of 50% relative to SRFFB.

5. Conclusions

Fast-forward (FF) operation consumes video data at a rate higher than the normal playout rate. To prevent buffer run out of data, the transmission rate of video data to clients has to be increased or a certain video data has to be pre-buffered before the interaction. Under these principles, the Short-Range Fast-Forward Broadcasting (SRFFB) scheme for VoD service is proposed in this paper. In SRFFB, only the first two video segment blocks are delivered to clients at a rate twice to the normal playout rate, while the others can be broadcast at the normal rate. As a result, a double-rate fast-forward operation can be economically performed at any point-of-play within the whole video.

References

1. Abram-Profeta, E.L. and Shin, K.G. (1998), "Providing Unrestricted VCR Functions in Multicast Video-on-Demand Servers". *Proceedings of the 1998 IEEE International Conference on Multimedia Computing and Systems*, Austin, T.X., 28 June-1 July, 1998, pp.66-75.
2. Almeroth, K.C. and Ammar, M.H. (1996), "The Use of Multicast Delivery to Provide a Scalable and Interactive Video-on-Demand Service". *IEEE Journal on Selected Areas in Communications*, Vol. 14, No. 6, pp.1110-1122.
3. Dan, A., Shahabuddin, P., Sitaram, D. and Towsley, D. (1995), "Channel Allocation under Batching and VCR Control in Video-on-Demand Systems". *Journal of Parallel and Distributed Computing*, Vol. 30, No. 2, pp.168-179.
4. Dan, A., Sitaram, D. and Shahabuddin, P. (1996), "Dynamic Batching Policies for an On-Demand Video Server". *Multimedia Systems*, Vol. 4, No. 3, pp.12-121.
5. Eager, D.L. and Vernon, M.K. (1998), "Dynamic Skyscraper Broadcasts for Video-on-Demand", *Proceedings of the Fourth International Workshop on Multimedia Information Systems*, Istanbul, Turkey, 24-26 September, 1998, pp.18-32.
6. Hua, K.A., Cai, Y. and Sheu, S. (1998), "Exploiting Client Bandwidth for More Efficient Video Broadcast". *Proceedings of the 7th International Conference on Computer Communications and Networks*, Lafayette, LA USA, 12-15 October, 1998, pp.848-856.
7. Juhn, L.S. and Tseng, L.M. (1998), "Fast Data Broadcasting and Receiving Scheme for Popular Video Service". *IEEE Transactions on Broadcasting*, Vol 44, No.1, pp.100-105.
8. Liao, W.J. and Li, V.O.K. (1997), "The Split and Merge Protocol for Interactive Video-on-Demand". *IEEE Multimedia*, Vol. 4, No. 4, pp51-62.
9. Little, T.D.C. and Venkatesh, D. (1994), "Prospects for Interactive Video-on-Demand". *IEEE Multimedia*, Vol. 1, No. 3, pp.14-23.
10. Mundur, P., Simon, R. and Sood, A. (1999), "Integrated Admission Control in Hierarchical Video-on-Demand Systems". *Proceedings of the 1999 IEEE International Conference on Multimedia Computing and Systems 1999*, Florence, Italy, 7-11 June, 1999, pp.220-225.
11. Pâris, J.F. (1999), "A Simple Low-Bandwidth Broadcasting Protocol for Video-on-Demand". *Proceedings of the 8th International Conference on Computer Communications and Networks*, Boston-Natick, MA, October 1999, pp.118-123.
12. Viswanathan, S. and Imielinski, T. (1996), "Metropolitan Area Video-on-Demand Service Using Pyramid Broadcasting". *Multimedia Systems*, Vol. 4, pp.197-208.

Efficient Voice Communications over IEEE802.11 WLANs Using Improved PCF Procedures

Eustathia Ziouva[1] and Theodore Antonakopoulos[2]

[1]Computers Technology Institute, Riga Feraiou 61, 26221 Patras, Greece
[2]Department of Electrical Engineering and Computers Technology
University of Patras, 26500 Rio - Patras, Greece
Tel: +30-61-997 346, Fax: +30-61-997 342, e-mail: antonako@ee.upatras.gr

Abstract

This paper presents a new dynamically adaptable polling scheme for efficient support of voice communications over different IEEE802.11 networks. The proposed polling scheme is simple to implement and does not require any modification on the existing access protocol. The analytical approach that models the proposed polling scheme, uses a discrete-time Markov chain and proves that the specific polling scheme, when silence detection is used at the wireless terminals, improves the capability of IEEE802.11wireless LANs for handling voice traffic efficiently.

Keywords

Wireless Networks, Centralized access control, Voice communication

1. Introduction

The IEEE802.11 standard (IEEE, 1997) for wireless local area networks (WLANs) covers the Medium Access Control (MAC) sub-layer and the physical layer of the Open System Interconnection (OSI) reference model. A group of wireless terminals under the control of a *Distributed Coordination Function* (DCF) or a *Point Coordination Function* (PCF) forms a *Basic Service Set* (BSS). A BSS can either be an independent network or an infrastructure network, in which an *Access Point* (AP) links the wireless terminals to a backbone network (like Asynchronous Transfer Mode, ATM), therefore extending their range to other BSSs via other APs. In a BSS, the wireless terminals and the AP can use either DCF for asynchronous data transmissions, or PCF for contention-free packet transmissions. In DCF mode, the network is in a *Contention Period* (CP) and the stations contend in order to gain access using the *Carrier Sense Multiple Access / Collision Avoidance* (CSMA/CA) access method. In PCF mode, the AP coordinates the medium usage and the network is in a *Contention-Free Period* (CFP). The medium can be alternated between CP and CFP according to the *Contention-Free Period Repetition* (CFPR) interval that is the reciprocal of the rate at which the AP initiates the CFP.

As the speed and capacity of WLANs increase, so does the demand for improving the quality of service (QoS) of real-time applications. (Zahedi and Pahlavan, 2000) used the DCF mode in order to provide real-time applications and showed that the performance is poor by considering the delay requirements. (Romans and Tourrilhes, 1998), (Deng and Chang, 1999) and (Liu and Wu, 2000) proposed modifications to the DCF mode in order to carry packet telephony traffic. (Sheu and Sheu, 2001) proposed a novel modified protocol to provide asynchronous and multimedia traffic over IEEE802.11 WLANs that is compliant with the IEEE802.11 standard. However, this protocol was not designed for real-time traffic exchange between stations belonging to different BSSs. For real-time traffic exchange between stations from different BSSs, all real-time packets have to be transferred to the AP of the BSS and thus a centralized access method like PCF is required. Although PCF introduces high overhead in each transaction, it can satisfy time-bounded requirements if it is properly adjusted. (Crow and *et al*, 1997) showed with simulations that polling is inefficient for handling on/off speech traffic. In (Ziouva and Antonakopoulos, 2001-1) we examined how PCF can efficiently be used to carry *Constant Bit Rate* (CBR) voice traffic between stations of the same BSS, while the DCF mode supports asynchronous data traffic. The number of voice users supported by PCF can be further increased by using silence detection at each voice user and a new management scheme on the AP's polling list, the so called Cyclic Shift polling process, that does not require any modifications on the wireless terminals access mechanism (Ziouva and Antonakopoulos, 2001-2).

In this work, we extend the Cyclic Shift polling process by adding a temporary removal procedure for stations that are in silent state. The AP's polling list does not remain constant during the lifetime of a conversation, but stations that enter silent state during their call are removed from the AP's polling list temporarily and are reinstalled on the polling list after a specific duration related to the *hangover* used by the silence detector. This dynamically adaptable management scheme implemented on the AP's polling list is called *Cyclic Shift and Station Removal Polling process* (CSSR). We consider voice activities between stations from different BSSs and we estimate an upper bound on the number of voice stations that a BSS can support, while keeping low voice packet delay and guaranteeing predetermined minimum bandwidth for data traffic. The CSSR polling process is evaluated by a discrete time Markov chain and is also compared with the Cyclic Shift polling process. Our studies were performed using 32 kbps *Adaptive Differential Pulse Code Modulation* (ADPCM) voice coding. For focusing on different aspects of PCF performance, we assumed an error-free channel.

Section 2 briefly describes the PCF operation for handling voice traffic while Section 3 presents the CSSR polling scheme and its Markov model. In Section 4, we evaluate the performance of the proposed scheme deriving the maximum number of voice stations handled by PCF. Finally, Section 5 discusses some numerical results.

2. Voice Traffic Management

We consider a number of BSSs interconnected via a backbone network. The AP initiates the CFP with the transmission of a Beacon frame and terminates it with the transmission of a CF-END frame. The CFP has a maximum duration that defines the maximum number of voice stations that can be supported. Due to the DCF traffic, the CFP may be stretched. Since the actual duration of CFP and CP may vary, the IEEE802.11 standard defines a maximum value of time that the CFP is stretched and a minimum duration for CP. All timing parameters that determine the coexistence of PCF and DCF are contained in each Beacon frame. Each voice station uses an ADPCM coder at 32 kbps and a silence detector. We exploit the silent periods of a voice source in order to increase the number of calls but at the expense of voice packets dropping rate. The used voice model is the well-known model proposed in (Brady, 1969). The durations of voice talk spurts and silence periods follow the exponential distribution with average d_t equal to 400 ms and d_s equal to 600 ms respectively (Sriram and *et al*, 1999), (Onvural, 1994). The silence detectors use a technique to avoid sudden end-clipping of speech and to bridge short speech gaps such as those due to stop consonants, the so called *hangover*. This technique results to silent gaps larger than the hangover duration. A voice packet is generated every CFPR interval when the CFP is scheduled to begin. A voice packet is transmitted over the network each time the station is being polled by the AP. If a new packet is generated before the previous packet has been transmitted, the older packet is discarded. All stations on the polling list are polled once during each CFP. The voice traffic management guarantees that the voice packet delay (Ziouva and Antonakopoulos, 2001-1) is less than the CFPR interval used by the AP. A station in talk spurt generates a voice packet (called *talk packet*) that is transmitted when the AP polls the station. A station in silent period does not generate any voice packets and transmits a NULL packet (called *silent packet*) when it is polled. When the AP takes control of the medium, it starts polling according to Figure 1.

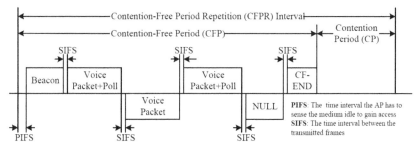

Figure 1. Voice transmissions in PCF mode

3. The CSSR polling process

The basic functionality of the dynamically adaptable polling scheme is the following: At the beginning of each CFP round, the AP cyclically shifts the stations on its polling list, so the first station at the previous round becomes the last station at the current round and all other stations advance one position towards the start of polling. At the beginning of each CFP round, the polling starts from the beginning of the shifted polling list. When the start of a silence period is detected for a station, the AP does not poll this station for a few PCF rounds. The PC maintains two polling lists, a *main polling list* that contains all stations having established connections, irrespective of their state and an *active polling list* (a subset of the main polling list) which contains only the stations that have to be polled at the next PCF round. Both polling lists are cyclically shifted in each PCF round. Whenever the AP cannot complete its active polling list during a CFP round, the AP starts its polling sequence with the first station on its polling list at the next CFP round. The advantages of the CSSR polling scheme are the following: The cyclic shift of the polling list spreads uniformly the dropped voice packet to all active stations in the network and therefore it increases the number of voice stations handled by PCF, compared to the case of using only silence detection (Ziouva and Antonakopoulos, 2001-2). The temporary station removal procedure provides more bandwidth for actual voice transmissions, thus the network performance is further improved. Finally, the AP's polling list management scheme does not require any modification on the wireless stations MAC protocol and is rather simple to implement.

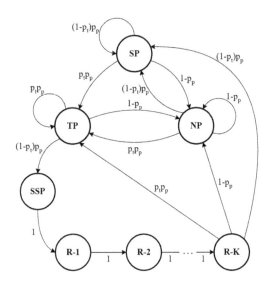

Figure 2. The CSRR polling process: Finite-state Markov chain for a voice station

For analyzing the CSSR polling scheme, a voice station is modeled as a discrete-time Markov chain that is shown in Figure 2. All state transitions occur at the end of a PCF round. During a CFP period, a voice station generates packets with probability p_t and may be polled with probability p_p. A voice station is in *Silent-Polled* (**SP**) state when it is polled and has no voice packet to transmit. The station leaves the SP state and enters the *Not-Polled* (**NP**) state when polling cannot be completed and the station is among the stations that are not polled. The station leaves the SP state and enters the *Talk-Polled* (**TP**) state when a voice packet is generated and the AP polls the station. A voice station remains in the TP state if it is in talk spurt and is polled continuously. If the station is in talk spurt and the AP does not poll it, the station moves to the NP state. If the station's talk spurt ends and the AP polls the station, the station transmits a NULL packet and moves to the *Start of Silence-Polled* (**SSP**) state and remains in this state until the next PCF round. Entering the SSP state, the station is removed from the active polling list for 1...K rounds and passes through the *Removed-i* (**R-i**) states. After K rounds, the station is repositioned on the polling list and, the station returns either to the NP, TP or SP state, depending on its position in the polling list and the transmission of a voice or a NULL packet. If Π_X is the steady state probability of a station being at state X, we can calculate the stationary distribution of the discrete Markov chain if the probabilities p_t and p_p are know.

$$\Pi_{TP} = \frac{P_p P_t}{1 + K p_p^2 p_t (1 - p_t)}, \quad \Pi_{SP} = \frac{P_p (1 - p_t)(1 - p_p p_t)}{1 + K p_p^2 p_t (1 - p_t)}, \quad \Pi_{NP} = \frac{1 - p_p}{1 + K p_p^2 p_t (1 - p_t)}$$

$$\Pi_{SSP} = \frac{p_p^2 p_t (1 - p_t)}{1 + K p_p^2 p_t (1 - p_t)}, \quad \Pi_R = \frac{K p_p^2 p_t (1 - p_t)}{1 + K p_p^2 p_t (1 - p_t)}$$

Π_R is the steady state probability of a station being removed from polling list for K PCF rounds. If $K = 0$ (a polling scheme without station removal) the CSRR polling process represents the Cyclic Shift polling process.

4. Performance Evaluation

In this section, an analytical approach is presented to derive an upper bound to the number of voice stations that can be handled by PCF, when silence detection and the CSSR polling scheme are employed.

4.1. The voice packet dropping probability

Since the CFPR interval can be selected so that the voice delay requirements are always satisfied, the parameter that defines the PCF performance is the probability of dropped packets P_{drop}. According to (Sriram and et al, 1999) and (Jayant and Christensen, 1981), 1 % of dropped voice packets loss can be tolerated. In this case, we can estimate an upper bound to the number of voice stations accommodated by PCF for various values of K, while the condition $P_{drop} < 0.01$ is satisfied. In order to decrease the number of rejected packets when a station is removed from the polling list, the duration of the station removal is limited to the hangover duration. Furthermore, for two connected stations A and B, when e.g. station A is in silent station B is usually in talk spurt, thus the AP of station A has to send the packets received by the AP of station B, to station A when this station is removed from its polling list. Under these circumstances, packets from station A are dropped either when it is in talk spurt and its AP does not poll it, or when the station is in talk spurt and is polled by its AP but the AP of station B does not poll station B, therefore the packets of station A are not delivered to station B. So, the probability of dropped voice packets is given by:

$$P_{drop}^{(A)} = \Pi_{NP}^{(A)} p_t + \Pi_{TP}^{(A)} \Pi_{NP}^{(B)} \tag{1}$$

Since, the steady state probabilities Π_X are functions of probabilities p_t and p_p and these two probabilities are considered equal for the two communication stations, the probability of dropped voice packets can be calculated if p_t and p_p are known.

4.2. The basic system probabilities

According to (Fine and Tobagi, 1986) and (Friedman and Ziegler, 1989), the probability p_t that a voice station is in talk spurt is given by $p_t = d_t/(d_t + d_s)$. If p_{np} is the probability that a station is not polled, then p_p will be derived by: $p_p = 1 - p_{np}$. The probability p_{np} depends on the number N of voice stations that form the main polling list (N stations generate $2N$ packets, uplink and downlink), the number N_r of stations that do not participate in the active polling list during a PCF round (remaining $2N - N_r$ packets to be exchanged) and the number N_p of stations that are polled during a PCF round. Let N_{tmax} denotes the maximum number of talk packets that can be handled by PCF. If $2N - N_r \le N_{tmax}$, every station is polled during a PCF round, but if $2N - N_r > N_{tmax}$, only N_p stations can be polled, the stations holding the first N_p positions on the active polling list, while the rest ($N - N_r - N_p$) stations are not polled. So the conditional probability $p_{np|Nr,Np}$ that a station is not polled during a PCF round when there are N_r and N_p stations is given by:

$$p_{np|N_r,N_p} = \left(N - N_r - N_p\right)/\left(N - N_r\right) \quad \text{if} \quad 0 \le N_r \le 2N - N_{tmax} - 1$$

For a given number N_r, the number of stations that can be polled has a maximum value N_{pmax} depending on the CFP length and the combination of the number of talk packets and the number of silent packets. The AP polls either N_{pmax} stations or $(N–N_r)$ stations, whatever of the two events happens first. Finding the probability $P_{Np|Nr}$ that the AP polls N_p stations given that it has removed N_r stations and the probability P_{Nr} that the AP has removed N_r stations, and using the total probability theorem and the above equation, we have that

$$P_{np} = \sum_{N_r=0}^{2N-N_{tmax}-1} \sum_{N_p=\lfloor(N_{tmax}-N_r)/2\rfloor}^{\min(N_{pmax},N-N_r)} \frac{N-N_r-N_p}{N-N_r} P_{N_p|N_r} P_{N_r}$$

Let assume that a station is removed from the polling list with probability p_r. Then the N_r stations during a PCF round have a binomial mass function and so

$$P_{N_r} = \binom{N}{N_r} p_r^{N_r} (1-p_r)^{N-N_r}$$

The probability p_r can be calculated by Π_R, where p_p is equal to $N_p/(N – N_r)$, since during a PCF round a station can be at one of the N_p first positions of $(N – N_r)$ stations on the active polling list. In order to find the probability $P_{Np|Nr}$, we must calculate the parameters N_{tmax} and N_{pmax}. The maximum number N_{tmax} of talk packets that the AP can handle depends on the CFP maximum duration and the talk packet transmission time T_t, which is equal to $T_{vp} + SIFS$, where T_{vp} is the transmission time of a voice packet including headers. Therefore:

$$N_{tmax} = \lfloor (T_{CFPR} - T_{maxFS} - PIFS - T_{Beacon} - SIFS - T_{CF-END} - T_{CP})/T_t \rfloor$$

where T_{CFPR}, T_{maxFS}, T_{BEACON}, T_{CF-END} and T_{CP} are the CFPR interval duration, the maximum time the CFP can be stretched, the Beacon and CF-END frame transmission time and the CP duration respectively. The different BSSs use the same CFPR interval duration, therefore the same transmission time is used for both uplink and downlink talk packets.

The maximum number N_{pmax} of stations that can be polled during a PCF round can be found when all exchanged packets are silent packets. Depending on T_t/T_s (T_s is the silent packet transmission time which equals the transmission time of a NULL packet plus the $SIFS$ time), a talk packet can be replaced by one or more silent packets. The AP defines the remaining CFP duration using time information from the previously transmitted packets, since it does not know if the next station in the list is in talk or silent state. The AP considers that the downlink and uplink packets of the last station that can be polled are talk packets and thus it guarantees that the maximum duration of the CFP is not exceeded. This explains why we subtract two talk packets from N_{tmax}. Finally, we have to subtract the N_r downlink packets that have to be sent to the removed silent stations. So N_{pmax} is given by:

$$N_{pmax} = \lfloor ((N_{tmax} - N_r - 2) T_t/T_s)/2 + 1 \rfloor$$

Finally, the probability $P_{Np|Nr}$ is determined by the number N_t of talk packets and the number $(2N_p + N_r – N_t)$ of silent packets during a CFP. Thus:

$$P_{N_p|N_r} = \sum_{N_t=0}^{\min(N_{tmax},2N_p+N_r)} \left[\binom{2N_p+N_r}{N_t} - g(N_p,N_r,N_t,N_{tmax}) \binom{2N_p+N_r-2}{N_t} \right]$$
$$\cdot p_t^{N_t} (1-p_t)^{2N_p+N_r-N_t} f\left(\lceil (2N_p+N_r-N_t)T_s/T_t \rceil + N_t - N_{tmax} \right)$$

where $f(x)$ and $g(x)$ are two functions that define the permitted combinations of N_t talk packets and $(2N_p + N_r - N_t)$ silent packets during CFP and are given by the following two equations:

$$f(x) = \begin{cases} 1 & \text{if} \quad x = 0 \\ 0 & \text{if} \quad x \neq 0 \end{cases}$$

$$g\left(N_p, N_r, N_t, N_{t\max}\right) =$$

$$= \begin{cases} 0 & \text{if} \quad 2N_p + N_r = N_{t\max} \lor N_t = 0 \\ & \lor N_t + 2N_p + N_r - N_{t\max} < N_{t\max} \\ & \lor \left(\left(N_t + 2N_p + N_r - N_{t\max} = N_{t\max}\right) \land \left(\left(N_t + 2\right)T_t + \left(2N_p + N_r - N_t - 2\right)T_s \leq N_{t\max}T_t\right)\right) \\ 1 & \text{if} \quad N_t + 2N_p + N_r - N_{t\max} > N_{t\max} \\ & \lor \left(\left(N_t + 2N_p + N_r - N_{t\max} = N_{t\max}\right) \land \left(\left(N_t + 2\right)T_t + \left(2N_p + N_r - N_t - 2\right)T_s > N_{t\max}T_t\right)\right) \end{cases}$$

5. Numerical Results

According to our analytical approach, the effect of CSSR polling scheme on the PCF performance is depicted in Figure 3. The supported number of voice stations increases when the proposed scheme is used along with silence detection in contrast to the case of CBR voice traffic. Furthermore, the throughput improves when the CFPR interval and the parameter K increase, but K must not exceed the hangover duration. The results of our analysis are derived considering the attribute values used by the high data rate extension of the IEEE802.11 standard at 5.5 and 11 Mbps. We also use the optional short physical header defined in the standard for reaching maximum throughput.

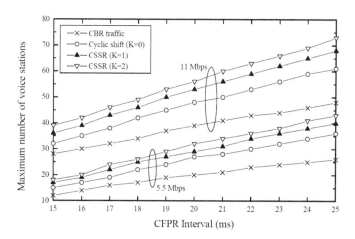

Figure 3. The effect of CSSR on the maximum number of supported voice stations

229

6. Conclusions

In this paper, we presented the CSSR polling scheme that can be used along with silence detection for increasing the number of supported voice communications over different IEEE802.11 WLANs. The proposed scheme improves the PCF performance by cyclically shifting the stations on the AP's polling list in each PCF round and dynamically removing stations that enter silence mode. The efficiency of the CSSR polling scheme is a function of the CFPR interval used by the network and the hangover duration of the silence detectors, which also determines the maximum duration of temporary station removal. Finally, the CSSR scheme can be easily implemented on the AP of an IEEE802.11 network, without requiring any modification on the wireless terminals access mechanism.

References

Brady, P.T. (1969), "A model for generating ON-OFF speech patterns in two-way conversation", *Bell System Technical Journal*, Vol. 48, No. 7, pp. 2445-2472.

Crow, B., Widjaja, I. Kim, J.G. and Sakai, P. (1997), "IEEE 802.11 Wireless Local Area Networks", *IEEE Communications Magazine*, Vol. 35, No. 9, pp. 116-126.

Deng, J. and Chang, R.S. (1999), "A Priority Scheme for IEEE 802.11 DCF Access Method", *IEICE Transactions Communications*, Vol. E82-B, No. 1, pp. 96-102.

Fine, M., and Tobagi, F.A. (1986), "Packet Voice on a Local Area Network with Round Robin Service", *IEEE Transactions on Communications*, Vol. COM-34, No. 9, pp. 906-915.

Friedman, E. and Ziegler, C. (1989), "Packet Voice Communications Over PC-Based Local Area Networks", *IEEE Journal on Selected Areas in Communications*, Vol. 7, No. 2, pp. 211-218.

IEEE, (1997), "Draft Standard for wireless LAN medium access control (MAC) and physical layer (PHY) specification", *IEEE P802.11*.

Jayant, N.S. and Christensen, S.W. (1981), "Effects of Packet Losses in Waveform Coded Speech and Improvements Due to an Odd-Even Sample-Interpolation Procedure", *IEEE Transactions on Communications*, Vol. COM-29, No. 2, pp. 101-109.

Liu, H-H. and Wu, J-L. C. (2000), "Packet Telephony Support for the IEEE 802.11 Wireless LAN", *IEEE Communications Letters*, Vol. 4, No. 9, pp. 286-288.

Onvural, R.O. (1994), Asynchronous Transfer Mode Networks: Performance Issues, Artech House, Boston.

Romans, C. and Tourrilhes, J. (1998), "A Medium Access Protocol for Wireless LANs Which Supports Isochronous and Asynchronous Traffic", *Tech. Rep. HPL-98-35*, Hewlett-Packard Com., Bristol.

Sheu, S.-T. and Sheu, T.-F. (2001), "A Bandwidth Allocation/Sharing/Extension Protocol for Multimedia Over IEEE 802.11 Ad Hoc Wireless LANs", *IEEE Journal on Selected Areas in Communications*, Vol. 19, No. 10, pp. 2065-2080.

Sriram, K., Lyons, T.G. and Wang, Y.T. (1999), "Anomalies Due to Delay and Loss in AAL2 Packet Voice Systems: Performance Models and Methods of Mitigation", *IEEE Journal on Selected Areas in Communications*, Vol. 17, No. 1, pp. 4-17.

Zahedi, A. and Pahlavan, K. (2000), "Capacity of a Wireless LAN with Voice and Data Services", *IEEE Transactions on Communications*, Vol. 48, No. 7, pp. 1160-1170.

Ziouva, E. and Antonakopoulos, T. (2001-1), "CBR Packetized Voice Transmission in IEEE802.11 Networks", in *Proc 6th IEEE Symposium on Computers and Communications*, pp. 392-398.

Ziouva, E. and Antonakopoulos, T. (2001-2), "Voice Communications over IEEE802.11 Wireless LANs Interconnected Using ATM Links", in *Proc. 26th Conference on Local Computer Networks*, pp. 620-629.

Study on the Architecture of IP telephony network

Tingxue Huang[1], Zhixiang Zhu[2] and Guanzhong Dai[1]

[1] Automatic Control Department, Northwest Polytechnical University Xi'an710072

[2] Research Institute of Communication Technology, Xi'an Institute of Posts & Telecommucation Xi'an710061

Abstract

In this paper the next-generation IP telephony network based on Internet is discussed. Therefore this paper provides one kind of architecture of next-generation IP telephony network. The architecture includes H.323 Zone layer and IPTel Zone (IP Telephony Zone) layer. The H.323 Zone is defined by H.323 recommendation and it is the basic organization unit of this architecture. The IPTel Zone is introduced in order that the IP telephony network can be realized and the characteristics of Internet, such as distributed feature and scalability, can be remained. It is the upper layer and includes one or several H.323 Zones. Moreover it adopts MPLS_VPN (MultiProtocol Label Switch_Virtual Private Network) technology to establish TELEPHONY_VPN. The TELEPHONY_VPN is established in order to achieve the security of the telephony network and make the architecture resolve all the business relationships among different entities including telephony providers, ISPs (Internet Service Providers) and customers. And the telephony network is manageable, scalable and available.

Keywords

IP telephony network, H.323 Zone, IPTel Zone, TELEPHONY_VPN

1. Introduction

IP telephony is one of the most popular research interests in the current communication field. Because the packet-based network can implement the multimedia communication and services very conveniently, introduce the new supplementary services very easily and possess scalable characteristic, IP telephony is becoming more and more attractive. The academic researchers, most IT companies and telecommunication service providers have kept eyes on IP telephony. Even some researchers predict that IP telephony will become the next-generation telephony system instead of the traditional PSTN telecommunication network.

Nowadays there are three popular IP telephony standards including H.323, SIP and H.248/Megaco. Because H.323 has been accepted by many companies and supported by many communication products, H.323 has been selected as the standard of IP Telephony in many countries including China.

H.323 recommendation specifies the packet-based multimedia communication system and is applied widely today in areas such as IP Telephony and IP videoconference. If IP telephony system can work like the traditional telecommunication several key issues such as the business relationships among all business entities must be resolved when using H.323

231

standards based on Internet. Therefore, this paper provides a kind of architecture with two layers and MPLS-VPN technology.

In this paper we introduce the issues which the next-generation telephony network is required to resolve in Section 2 and next explain two new concepts in Section 3. The two-layer architecture is discussed in Section 4. Then we discuss the TELEPHONY_VPN in Section 5. At last the concluding remarks are in Section 6.

2. The next-generation IP telephony network

The packet-based next-generation telecommunication network will take the place of the circuit-based PSTN at last. The current IP telephony is only a transitional system. It is an eclectic scheme according to the current situation.

First, all the current IP telephony providers provide services by building their own IP telephony network such as AT&T and China Telecomm. The private IP Telephony networks only carry its provider's telephony services. The carrying pattern can not fully utilize the network resource and the characteristics of IP network.

Second, the current IP Telephony calls partially use the packet-based network. In general, only the part of the toll call adopts packet-based communication and other parts including the ingress network and egress network still use the traditional circuit-based transmission.

The next-generation IP telephony network will regard Internet as the carrying network. So many telephony providers provide services through the same carrying network. And each telephony provider competes not through its monopolization and network layout but through the feature and quality of the services. Therefore some important problems need to be handled. Here is a summary of the relevant issues:

1) Quality of Service (QoS)(Blake,1998)(Braden and Zhang,1997): Because the telephony service is real-time and Internet is originally a best-effort service network, the next-generation IP telephony network should adopt some technology to acquire the satisfying QoS.

2) Security: Because Internet is fully distributed, the IP telephony network based on Internet must provide mechanisms to implement the security issues. Nowadays, in general IPSec (IP Security)(Kent,1998) or IPTunnel (IP Tunnel)(Cisco,2002) is used to guarantee the security. But because the technology need complete the encryption algorithm, it is not appropriate to perform the real-time service.

3) Telephony routing: In the traditional telecommunication network the telephony routing is simply because the network is private and based on circuit switch. In the next-generation telephony network the telephony routing will become anfractuous because Internet carries all kinds of services and in the customer's viewpoint the telephony service's operation should be like before.

4) Business relationships among the business entities: The business relationships among telephony providers, ISPs and customs will be complicated if Internet is considered as the carrying network.

3. New concepts

In order to discuss the architecture of the next-generation telephony network two new concepts are introduced. One is " IPTel Zone (IP Telephony Zone)", the other is " PZK (PhoneZonekeeper)".

1) IPTel Zone

IPTel Zone can be named "ITAD (Internet Telephony Administration Domain)". In each IPTel Zone the same set of Media Servers and Application Servers are used to provide the supplementary services and the same group of PSTN Gateways are used to access PSTN system. And the key mark of an IPTel Zone is that all the services of IPTel Zone are managed and controlled by a PhoneZonekeeper.

H.323 standard defines a concept named Zone (H.323 Zone). In general IPTel Zone is composed of several H.323 Zone. Within an H.323 Zone there is only one Gatekeeper. The Gatekeeper is in charge of the network resource and calls of the H.323 Zone. However, IPTel Zone mainly emphasizes that it is an administration domain. It manages the supplementary services, calls and routing among IPTel Zones and so on.

2) PZK (PhoneZonekeeper)

In each IPTel Zone there is a PhoneZonekeeper (PZK). PZK uses RAS (Registration Admission and Status) protocol to communicate with the Gatekeepers in the same IPTel Zone and the PZKs of other IPTel Zones. It is responsible for the management of the supplementary services and the distribution of the address template information. It still implements RADIUS (Remote Authentication Dial In User Service) to transmit the counting and authenticating information to the background servers.

4. The architecture of the next-generation IP telephony network

Because the next-generation telephony system works upon Internet, on one hand the characteristics of Internet such as distributed feature and scalable feature must be remained, on the other hand the functions of traditional telephony system can be implemented. This paper will introduce a kind of architecture with two-layer. The lower layer is H.323 Zone and the higher layer is IPTel Zone. H.323 Zone is the least organization unit. Several H.323 Zones form an IPTel Zone. Then all IPTel Zones will construct the entire telephony network. As for the telephony network of the different telephony providers, MPLS-VPN will be introduced to this architecture. The subject will be discussed in the next section.

4.1 H.323 Zone
As early as H.323v1 H.323 Zone was already defined(JONES,2001). Its construction is showed in Figure 1.

An H.323 Zone is the collection of all terminals (Tx), Gateways (GW), and Multipoint Control Units (MCUs) managed by a single Gatekeeper (GK). An H.323 Zone includes at least one terminal and may or may not include Gateways or MCUs. It has one and only one Gatekeeper. H.323 Zone may be independent of network topology. And it may be comprised of multiple network segments which are connected using routers (R) or other devices.

Here LAN is a shared or switched medium, peer-to-peer communications network that broadcasts information for all stations to receive within a moderate-sized geographic area, such as a single office building or a campus. The network is generally owned, used, and operated by a single organization.

The Terminal, Gatekeeper, MCU and Gateway show in Figure 1 are defined as H.323v4.

Router is a connection device. Because telephony network provides the real-time services and Internet is considered as the carrying network, Internet is required to provide the corresponding support. Therefore, a router should provide the functions of RSVP (Resource reSerVation Protocol) /Diffserv (Different Service) and MPLS. RSVP/Diffserv implements QoS to provide real-time voice services. MPLS constructs TELEPHONY_VPN in order to resolve the relationships among providers.

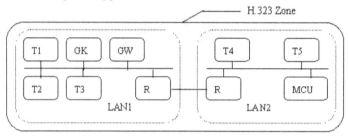

Figure 1 H.323 Zone

In Figure1, Tx--Terminal GK--Gatekeeper GW--Gateway R--Router MCU--Multipoint Control Unit

4.2 IPTel Zone

IPTel Zone is a new concept. H.323 standard has not description about it. It is the feature of the two-layer architecture. In section 3 IPTel Zone has been introduced in brief and its composing is shown in Figure 2.

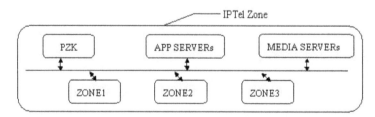

Figure 2 IPTel Zone

Here each component is described.

1)   PZK

PZK is the abbreviation of PhoneZonekeeper. It is specified in section 3.

2)   ZONEx

ZONEx is an H.323 Zone. All H.323 Zones are distributed and have not discrepancy in priority. They are managed by the PZK.

3) APP SERVER

APP SERVER is an application server. APP SERVER is responsible for the generation of the logicality of each supplementary service. Moreover, it still provides all kinds of API through which the third party can develop some new services. And it handles the interface signal of connecting PhoneZonekeeper.

4) MEDIA SERVER

MEDIA SERVER finishes the special services such as IVR (Interaction Voice Response), conference and FAX. When receiving the indication about implementing a service from an APP SERVER, a Media SERVER performs the service according to the logicality.

Through cooperating, APP SERVERs and MEDIA SERVERs provide all kinds of supplementary services for the IPTel Zone. In fact, an APP SERVER is a logical component and a MEDIA SERVER is an implementation component. The separating structure is more convenient to provide the supplementary services because the new service is provided more easily and the capability of providing services simultaneously is greatly improved.

The protocol reference point is shown in Figure 3.

1--RAS: RAS is adopted to finish address translation, admission control, status exchange and bandwidth management between a PhoneZonekeeper and an H.323 Zone.

2--H.323: Among H.323 Zones Gatekeepers and telephony terminals are compatible with H.323 recommendation group including H.225, H.245, H.450 and H.235.

3--RAS: A PhoneZonekeeper uses RAS to denote that an APP SERVER implements a supplementary service.

4--MGCP: An APP SERVER employs MGCP to indicate that a MEDIA SERVER completes a supplementary service.

5--RAS: A Gatekeeper uses RAS to indicate that an APP SERVER implements a supplementary service.

6--RTP: A MEDIA SERVER adopts RTP to transmit stream media to an H.323 Zone in order to complete voice prompt or VOD.

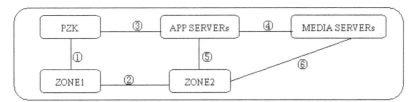

Figure 3 the protocol reference point of IPTel Zone

4.3 Telephony network

All IPTel Zones construct the entire telephony network. Although the telephony networks have many different scales, all of them are composed of IPTel Zone unlike the traditional telecommunication network mode with many layers. Then on one hand telephony network can fully take advantage of the distributed feature and scalability and availability of Internet.

On the other hand the size of IPTel Zone is flexible: IPTel Zone can be established according to necessity.

Another issue is counting. The different types of calls have different rates. Within an IPTel Zone there are a set of background servers. Let these servers implement authenticating, authorizing, counting and billing. The arrangement is very appropriate because all kinds of routing calls can be supervised.

The telephony network is composed as Figure 4. The following gives the brief description of its components.

1) Background Server

   The background servers include counting, authenticating and billing servers.

2) IPTel Zone:

   All IPTel Zones can be arranged according to many logical relationships such as the distributed model, hierarchical model and centralized model.

3) Agent

   The agents are the business agency of the telephony providers. They are responsible for all kinds of agent services such as user's registration, modification and unregistration.

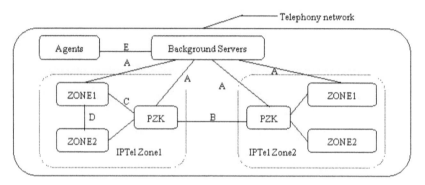

Figure 4 Telephony network

The protocol reference points are given.

A--RADIUS: RADIUS is used to transmit the information about counting and authenticating between Gatekeepers/PhoneZonekeepers and background servers.

B--IPTelRP (IPTel Zone Routing protocol): IPTelRP is a routing protocol among PhoneZonekeepers. Its main function is to exchange address template information.

C--H.323 and D--RAS: They have been discussed above.

E-- LDAP(Light Directory Address Protocol): The relationship between agents and background servers is Client/Server model. Therefore the general protocol between background units and front units can be used to transmit user's documents.

5. The management model of the provider's telephony network

The architecture provided in Section 4 can resolve the issues about the routing of telephony calls and providing telephony services on the Internet. However, a provider should consider the carrying relationships with other providers, ISPs and its customers. Only after these problems are resolved, a telephony provider can do a business.

Therefore the MPLS_VPN is introduced to the above architecture. As for MPLS_VPN technology, CISCO has a number of related white papers(Cisco,2002). Many IT companies are also very interested in it. Then, if MPLS_VPN technology is adopted there is too much research background. In this paper MPLS_VPN is used to build the telephony network manageable for the telephony providers.

In the telephony network the MPLS_VPN is called TELEPHONY_VPN or VOICE_VPN. The application is shown in Figure 5. Each IPTel Zone is an edge backbone network. Within an IPTel Zone a TELEPHONY_VPN is established. The TELEPHONY_VPN is named EDGE_VPN. Then all IPTel Zones commonly construct a TELEPHONY-VPN. It is called CORE_VPN. It should be noticed that the edge routers in an IPTel Zone have two statuses. They are not only P of EDGE_VPN but also PE of CORE_VPN.

As for the relationship among the telephony providers, the telephony providers can designate some routers (that is to say some sites) which are responsible for the exchange of communication. One way is to formulate the agreement between two providers through which the peer-to-peer relationship is built. The other way is to construct a VPN span many providers' telephony networks. The latter arrangement is recommended.

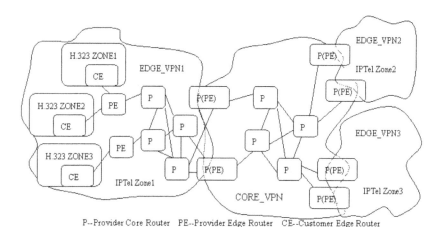

P--Provider Core Router   PE--Provider Edge Router   CE--Customer Edge Router

Figure 5 TELEPHONY-VPN

A company which has some separated branches can build its EDGE_VPN. Then its telephony network can use the overlapped IP addresses and the different service VPNs such as TELEPHONY_VPN, data VPN and education VPN can be separated very easily. Moreover, the security can be guaranteed on the network layer and the manageable and scalable features can be satisfied. It is more important that the telephony network based on Internet can be managed by the telephony providers. The architecture resolves all business relationships during carrying the telephony network.

1) The relationship among the telephony providers

First, the network architecture provides the support for communicating with each other. The method has been discussed above.

Second, H.323 protocol has to support it. Let us recollect that the procedure of establishing a call. At the beginning the telephony customer apply to the Gatekeeper for admitting, authenticating and routing. If the Gatekeeper can not authenticate this customer, it will apply to the PhoneZonekeeper. If the PhoneZonekeeper can not still complete it, it will apply to the background servers. These messages are transmitted through RAS(ITU-T,2000). Therefore RAS is required to modify. H225_AdmissionRequest need add an element named e_destinationproviderInfo which identifies the telephony provider of called terminal. After the authentication server receives the message it can make a decision. In addition, H225_AdmissionConfirm need add an element named e_outwardsiteInfo which denotes that the call should enter the backbone network through routing the corresponding site. Therefore the providers can manage the network and charge money very easily.

2) The relationship between the telephony providers and the ISPs

Telephony providers and ISPs are different business unities. They have business relationship. A telephony provider must be interrelated with many ISPs. In the same way, an ISP must be interrelated with many telephony providers. ISPs provides foundation network to providers. Moreover providers can still operate some functions on the network such as implementing policy services (for example providing many different quality services) for different customers. The above architecture can meet these requirements. ISPs can consider the traffic engineering and number of Label Switch Paths (LSPs) as commercial metrics with different telephony providers.

3) The relationship between the telephony providers and the customers

The future telephony customers first choose their ISP to access Internet. Telephony service is one of many services which the ISP provides. A customer can choose a fixed ISP and change its telephony provider. And a customer can choose a fixed telephony provider and change its ISP. From the relationship between ISPs and telephony providers we can see the above architecture meets the requirement. The telephony providers provide their feature services and high quality services to their customers through Gatekeeper, PhoneZonekeeper and a set of background servers. Customers can select their telephony provider through the service's categories, quality and feature.

6. Conclusion

This paper designs a two-layer architecture including H.323 Zone and IPTel Zone of telephony network. Moreover, MPLS-VPN is adopted. The architecture has two main advantages: First, the carrying telephony network can be established utilizing all characteristics of Internet; Second, that the QoS of telephony network can come true and the business relationships among different entities can be solved. Therefore, through the architecture all telephony providers can build their telephony network based on Internet. It is easily manageable, highly scalable and available.

However, as for the architecture there are two future tasks to do. One is to study the protocol on communication between PZKs. The other is to solve the problem of how the TELEPHONY_VPN traverses those existing VPNs. As long as they are solved, the two-layer architecture can be used widely.

References

Blake,S. (1998), "An Architecture for Differentiated Services ",*RFC2475*, IETF, pp96-101.

Braden,B. and Zhang,L. et al(1997), "Resource ReSerVation Protocol (RSVP) ", *RFC2205*, IETF,pp.111-125.

ITU-T(2000),"Call signalling protocols and media stream packetization for packet-based multimedia communication systems", *H.225v4*,ITU-T pp72-77.

JONES,P. (2001),"Packet-based multimedia communications systems", *H.323v4*,ITU-T, pp5-10.

Kent,S.(1998), " Security Architecture for the Internet Protocol",*RFC2401*,IETF, pp75-81.

http://www.cisco.com/warp/public/121/mpls_packflow.html(2002)

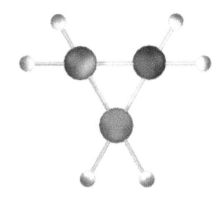

Chapter 4

Quality of Service

241

QoS Routing with Multiple Prioritised Constraints Using the Concept of the Analytic Hierarchy Process (AHP)

Abdullah M. S. Alkahtani, M. E. Woodward, K. Al-Begain and Abdullah N. Alghannam

Computing Department, University of Bradford, BD7 1DP, UK
e-mail: a.m.alkahtani@bradford.ac.uk

Abstract:

In this paper, we propose two algorithms; The first supports Quality of service Routing with Multiple and Prioritised Constraints (QRMPC). The second supports Quality of service Routing with Multiple Constraints (QRMC). Both algorithms apply the concept of the Analytic Hierarchy Process (AHP) which is a well-known model in the area of decision making with multiple objectives. We show how they work in general. We will see clearly how the final path decision changes as the priorities of the metrics change. The main novelty of this paper is the application of AHP approach which provides an opportunity to consider multiple constraints in the proposed algorithms.

Key words:

QoS routing, Multiple prioritised constraints, ATM, Routing algorithms, Communication networks, Analytic Hierarchy Process (AHP).

1. Introduction

Recent advances in high speed networking technology have created opportunities for the development of multimedia applications. These applications are characterised by multiple QoS requirements. One of the key issues in supporting QoS traffic is QoS routing, which is not only selecting a path for transmitting data from source to destination, but doing this to satisfy constraints dictated by the resource reservations and admission control. Because of the diverse QoS requirements, QoS based routing has been considered to be an NP-complete problem and cannot be solved by a simple and efficient algorithm (Wang and Crowcroft, 1996).

In general, routing consists of two basic tasks (Chen and Nahrsted, 1998): collecting the state information of the network and searching this information to find a feasible path, if one exists. In this paper we focus on the second task by assuming that the true state of the network is available to every node. Each link in the network is associated with multiple QoS parameters (metrics) such as residual bandwidth, loss probability, delay, delay variation (jitter) and security status.

The rest of this paper is organised as follows. In section 2, we give an overview of the QoS metrics and how they can be selected. In section 3, we review some of previous algorithms. In section 4, we give an overview of AHP.In sections 5 and 6, we present our proposed algorithms (QRMPC and QRMC) and show how they work based on a given example. Sections 7 and 8 contain the future work and the conclusion respectively.

2. QoS metrics

In this section we discuss various approaches that have been considered to deal with QoS characterisation. Namely, by using a single metric, a single compound metric or multiple metrics.

2.1 Single metric

In traditional data networks, routing protocols usually characterise the network with a *single metric* such as hop-count or delay, and use the shortest path algorithms for path computation. However, in order to support a wide range of QoS requirements, routing protocols need to have a more complex model.

2.2 Single compound metric

The basic idea of this is to combine several QoS parameters (metrics) in one representative value. Then use this value to take the routing decision applying any single metric algorithm.

One possible approach might be to define a function and generate a single metric from multiple parameters. For example, a compound metric M may be produced with bandwidth B, delay D and loss probability L with a formula $M(p) = B(p)/(D(p) * L(p))$ (Wang and Crowcroft, 1996). A path with a large value of M is likely to be a better choice in terms of bandwidth, delay, and loss probability.

A single compound metric, however, can only be used as an indicator at best, as it does not contain sufficient information to assess whether user QoS requirements can be met or not. Another problem has to do with combining parameters of different composition rules as will be explained in the next section (Wang and Crowcroft, 1996).

2.3 Multiple metrics

Multiple metrics can certainly model a network more accurately. However, the problem is that finding a path subject to multiple constraints is inherently hard. A simple problem with two constraints was considered as NP-complete (Wang and Crowcroft, 1996).

Resource requirements specified by the applications are often diverse and application-dependent. Moreover, the QoS parameters themselves have different natures of composition rules. Therefore, the problem in QoS routing is much more complicated.

The value of a metric over the entire path can be one of the following compositions (Wang and Crowcroft, 1996) (Al-Fawaz and Woodward, Jul 2000):

- *Additive metrics*: It can be represented mathematically as follows

$$m(p) = \sum_{i=1}^{LK} m(lk_i) \qquad (1)$$

  Where *m(p)* is the total of metric m of path *(p)*, lk_i is a link in the path *(p)*, *LK* is the number of links in path *(p)* and $i = 1,....,LK$.

  Delay, Delay variation (jitter), and cost are examples of this type of composition. Various factors that determine the delay in communication networks are reviewed in (Onvural, 1995).

- *Concave metrics:* It can be represented mathematically as follows

$$m(p) = \min(m(lk_i)) \qquad (2)$$

  Bandwidth is an example of this type of composition. The bandwidth we are interested in here is the residual bandwidth that is available for new traffic. It can be defined as the minimum of the residual bandwidth of all links on the path or the *bottleneck bandwidth*.

- *Multiplicative metrics*: It can be represented mathematically as follows

$$m(p) = \prod_{i=1}^{LK} m(lk_i) \qquad \textbf{(3)}$$

Loss probability (l), *indirectly*, is an example of this type of composition. Why indirectly? Loss probability metric can be easily transformed to its equivalent metric (the probability of successful transmission (st)) that follows the multiplicative composition rule (Wang and Crowcroft, 1996). Successful transmission (st) can be expressed as follows

$$st(lk) = 1 - l(lk) . \qquad \textbf{(4)}$$

$$st(p) = \prod_{i=1}^{LK} st(lk_i) \qquad \textbf{(5)}$$

Therefore, the loss probability metric (l) can be represented mathematically as follows

$$l(p) = 1 - \{[1 - l(lk_1)] * [1 - l(lk_2)] * ... * [1 - l(lk_{LK})]\} \qquad \textbf{(6)}$$

3. Previous works

In this section we summarise some previous works that investigate the problem of QoS-based routing.

3.1 Wang and Crowcroft Algorithms *(Wang and Crowcroft, 1996)*

These algorithms consider a number of issues in QoS routing. They first examine the basic problem of QoS routing, namely, finding a path that satisfies multiple constraints, and its implications on routing metric selection, and then present three path computation algorithms.

The first is a centralised algorithm that is suitable for source routing. Given bandwidth and delay constraints, the algorithm finds a path that satisfies both constraints. The second and third are distributed algorithms that are suitable for hop-by-hop routing.

3.2 Chen Algorithm *(Chen, 1999)*

In (Chen, 1999) a heuristic algorithm is proposed for the delay-cost constrained routing problem which is NP-complete. The main idea of this algorithm is to first reduce the NP-complete problem to a simpler one which can be solved in polynomial time, and then solve the new problem by either using an extended Dijkstra's algorithm or extended Bellman-Ford algorithm. The performance of the algorithm was studied by both theoretical analysis and simulation.

3.3 PNNI *(ATM-Forum, 1996)*

The abbreviation PNNI stands for either Private Network Node Interface or Private Network-to-Network Interface, reflecting these two possible usages. PNNI includes two categories of protocols:
- A protocol is defined for distributing topology information between switches and clusters of switches. This information is used to compute paths through the network. A hierarchy mechanism ensures that this protocol scales well for large wide-area ATM networks. A key feature of the PNNI hierarchy mechanism is its ability to automatically configure itself in networks in which the address structure reflects the topology. PNNI topology and routing is based on the well-known link-state routing technique.

- A second protocol is defined for signalling, that is message flows used to establish point-to-point and point-to-multipoint connections across the ATM network. This protocol is based on the ATM Forum UNI signalling, with mechanisms added to support source routing, crankback, and alternate routing of call setup requests in case of connection setup failure.

PNNI has the following characteristics: it scales to very large networks, supports hierarchical routing, supports multiple QoS routing metrics and attributes, uses source routed connection setup, provides dynamic routing, responsive to changes in resource availability and others.

3.4 Al-Fawaz-Woodward Algorithm *(Al-Fawaz and Woodward, Jul 2000)*

They propose a routing algorithm to find the shortest path between one source and one destination node while considering the criteria of multiple metric constraints. It has three goals to achieve, 1) sorting the QoS metrics according to the requested services, 2) Finding the possible routes between the source and the destination and 3) speed up the path determination by using sliding window and hierarchical clustering technique.

There are many other QoS routing algorithms. (Chen, 1999) gives a very comprehensive overview of such algorithms, compare them, and discuss their pros and cons.

4. The Analytic hierarchy process (AHP)

The Analytic Hierarchy Process (AHP), a multi-criteria technique developed by Saaty (Saaty, 1980) (Winston, 1994), is a robust and flexible multi-criteria decision analysis methodology. AHP is a decision-support procedure for dealing with complex, unstructured, and multiple-attribute decisions. Although most applications of AHP are in the area of socio-economic planning, there have been some applications in decisions related to road networks (Klungboonkrong and A. P. Taylor, 1998), petroleum pipeline networks (Dey and Gupta, 2000), Health service (Wang, 1999), project management (Al-Harbi, 2001) and telecommunications (Sato and Kataoka, 1996) (Andijani, 1998) (Douligeris and Pereira, 1994).

There are four basic steps in using AHP (Andijani, 1998) (Douligeris and Pereira, 1994):

1-The description of a complex decision problem as a *hierarchy*.

2-The use of *pair-wise comparisons* to estimate the relative weight (importance or priority) of the various elements to each other. This gives what is called the *priority weights*.

3-The use of pair-wise comparisons to estimate the relative weight (importance) of the various elements on each level of the hierarchy. Every element on each level is compared with adjacent elements in respect of their importance. This gives what is called the *score* of each level in each element.

4-The integration of these weights, from 2 and 3, to develop an *overall score* of decision alternatives. Then, the alternative with maximum overall score will be selected.

5. The first proposed algorithm (QRMPC)

5.1 Introduction

In this section we discuss situations in which the routing algorithm, QRMPC, chooses between different paths on the basis of how well the alternatives meet multiple *and* prioritised QoS constraints. For example, in determining which path to select QRMPC might choose between the alternatives by determining how well each path meets the following four constraints: Constraint-1 Residual Bandwidth (B), Constraint-2 Loss probability (L), Constraint-3 End-to-End Delay (D) and Constraint-4 Security (S=1 for secure or 0 for unsecure).

When multiple constraints are important to a routing algorithm, it is too difficult to choose between alternatives. (Chen and Nahrsted, 1998) and (Wang and Crowcroft, 1996) describe most of them as NP-complete. For example, one path may have the highest bandwidth (B), but the path may score poorly on the other three constraints. Another path may meet constraints 2-4 but have a low bandwidth (B). The proposed algorithm (QRMPC) provides a powerful tool that can be used to make decisions in situations involving *multiple* and *prioritised constraints*.

5.2   QRMPC functionality in general

To illustrate how the QRMPC works, consider the network (N) shown in Figure1. As can be seen from the Figure, there are seven paths from a source (s) to a destination (t). These seven paths are summarised in Table 1. Each path consists of more than one link. Each link has four metrics; Residual bandwidth *(b)*, loss probability *(l)*, delay *(d)* and security *(s)*.

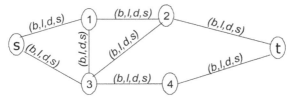

Figure 1: Example of a small network.

Path #	1	2	3	4	5	6	7
Links	s12t	s1234t	s132t	s134t	s34t	s32t	s312t

Table 1: The seven paths from (s) to (t).

Assuming that the overall metrics of each path are as given in Table 2. QRMPC must determine which path to be selected in order to satisfy *all* QoS constraints listed the last row of the same table. On top of that, *priorities* of the constraints have to be considered when making the routing decision. For this example the priority order is bandwidth (1), loss probability (2), delay (3) and security (4). The following steps illustrate, *in general*, how QRMPC works.

Path No#	Metrics			
	b	l	d	s
1	20	2e-6	20	1
2	10	1e-6	1	1
3	40	20e-6	2	1
4	80	10e-6	10	1
5	90	8e-6	5	0
6	100	28e-6	15	1
7	110	23e-6	32	1
REQ	20	25e-6	30	1

Table 2: Paths metrics and the QoS constraints

- **Step_A** QRMPC generates priority normalised weights, $prnw_i$ (i=1, 2, 3, 4) for the *ith* metric. For this example, the generated weights are shown in Table3. The weights indicate that bandwidth (*b*) is the most important constraint, followed by loss probability (*l*), delay (*d*), and security (*s*).

Priority NO#	1	2	3	4
Priority normalised weight (pmw)	0.4658	0.27714	0.16107	0.0959699

Table 3: priority normalised weight.

- **Step_B** QRMPC will find the "nominated" paths that satisfy all QoS constraints. These paths are P1, P3 and P4. P2 did not meet the bandwidth constraint (10 < 20), P5 did not meet the security constraint (unsecure), P6 did not meet the loss probability constraint (28e-6 > 25e-6), P7 did not meet the delay constraint (32 > 30).

- **Step_C** QRMPC will determine how well each path "scores" on each metric. For this example, the calculated *normalised* scores of each path on each metric are shown in Table 4. It can be seen that path 4 best meets the metric of a high bandwidth (*b*) but "scores" badly on all other metrics. It is worth mentioning here that these weights give accurate relative information about any path compared with all other nominated paths.

| Path | Metrics | | | |
No#	b	l	d	s
1	0.142857	0.769231	0.0769231	0.33333
3	0.285714	0.0769231	0.769231	0.33333
4	0.571429	0.153846	0.153846	0.33333

Table 4: Normalised path scores on each metric.

- **Step_D** given the priority normalised weights *(prnw)* form Table 3 and the score of each path on each metric from Table 4, QRMPC will calculate the *total score* of each path using this equation:

$$Total\ normalised\ score\ of\ path_j = \sum_{i=1}^{n} prnw_i * normalised\ score\ of\ path_j\ in\ metric_i$$

Computing each path's total score, we obtain

Path 1 total score = 0.32411

Path 3 total score = 0.3103

Path 4 total score = 0.365589

- **Step_E** now choose the path with the highest total score. Thus, the QRMPC would indicate that **path 4** should be selected.

5.2.1 Effect of changing priorities

If we change the priority of the metrics, The final path decision *may* change depending on how the total score will be after recalculations. Table 5 and Figure 2 (dark bars) represent these changes in two different ways. Moreover, Figure 2 compares QRMPC algorithm with a modified version in which prioritisation of constraints is disabled. The modified version will be discussed in the next section.

Changing priority is a natural action in order to meet some special requirements for certain traffic. For example, when routing delay sensitive traffic as in real-time applications, the delay metric will be the first priority while the loss metric will be in a lower priority level if not the least. In contrast, when routing loss sensitive traffic as in data transfer applications, the loss metric will be the first priority while the delay metric will be in a lower priority level if not the least.

Priorities	Total normalised Path Score			Selected Path
	P1	P3	P4	
BLDS	0.324	0.31	0.366	4
BLSD	0.341	0.282	0.377	4
BDLS	0.244	0.391	0.366	3
BDSL	0.215	0.407	0.377	3
BSLD	0.290	0.312	0.398	4
BSDL	0.245	0.357	0.398	4
LBDS	0.442	0.271	0.287	1
LBSD	0.459	0.243	0.298	1
LDBS	0.435	0.327	0.238	1
LDSB	0.447	0.330	0.223	1
LSDB	0.477	0.28	0.244	1
LSBD	0.481	0.248	0.271	1
DLBS	0.304	0.458	0.238	3
DLSB	0.316	0.461		3
DBLS	0.231	0.482	0.287	3
DBSL	0.188	0.353	0.269	3
DSBL	0.225	0.504	0.271	3
DSLB	0.266	0.491	0.244	3
SBLD	0.326	0.321	0.353	4
SBDL	0.281	0.366	0.353	3
SDBL	0.273	0.422	0.305	3
SDLB	0.314	0.408	0.278	3
SLBD	0.399	0.296	0.305	1
SLDB	0.395	0.328	0.278	1

Table 5: Effect of changing priority on the final path decision applying QRMPC algorithm.

6. The second proposed algorithm (QRMC)

For the sake of comparison, we modified the QRMPC algorithm in order to disable the constraint prioritisation. I.e. all constraints have the same level of importance or priority. The modified algorithm is called *QRMC*, Quality of Service Routing with Multiple Constraints. There are two possibilities in order to disable prioritisation; firstly, to remove the part of QRMPC algorithm that deals with the priority weighting. Secondly, to assign the same priority for all constraints, priority 1. Although, final results of both approaches are the same, We decided to choose the second approach because it needs less modification than the first one. Clearly, the priority normalised weights for all priorities will be *1/n* as can be seen from Table 6, where *n* is the number of constraints. The Normalised path scores on each metric will be exactly the same as QRMPC. See Table 7. As can be seen from Table 8 and Figure 2 (bright bars), changing priorities has no effect on the *total scores* of nominated paths and consequently has no effect on the final path decision when applying the modified algorithm, QRMC. Figure 2 also presents a comparison between QRMPC and QRMC algorithms.

Priority NO#	1	2	3	4
Priority normalised weight (pmw)	0.25	0.25	0.25	0.25

Table 6: priority normalised weights (no prioritisation).

Path	Metrics			
No#	*b*	*l*	*d*	*s*
1	0.142857	0.769231	0.0769231	0.33333
3	0.285714	0.0769231	0.769231	0.33333
4	0.571429	0.153846	0.153846	0.33333

Table 7: Normalised path scores on each metric.

Priorities	Total normalised Path Score			Selected
	P1	P3	P4	Path
BLDS	0.331	0.337	0.303	3
BLSD	0.331	0.337	0.303	3
BDLS	0.331	0.337	0.303	3
BDSL	0.331	0.337	0.303	3
BSLD	0.331	0.337	0.303	3
BSDL	0.331	0.337	0.303	3
LBDS	0.331	0.337	0.303	3
LBSD	0.331	0.337	0.303	3
LDBS	0.331	0.337	0.303	3
LDSB	0.331	0.337	0.303	3
LSDB	0.331	0.337	0.303	3
LSBD	0.331	0.337	0.303	3
DLBS	0.331	0.337	0.303	3
DLSB	0.331	0.337	0.303	3
DBLS	0.331	0.337	0.303	3
DBSL	0.331	0.337	0.303	3
DLBS	0.331	0.337	0.303	3
DLSB	0.331	0.337	0.303	3
SBLD	0.331	0.337	0.303	3
SBDL	0.331	0.337	0.303	3
SDBL	0.331	0.337	0.303	3
SDLB	0.331	0.337	0.303	3
SLBD	0.331	0.337	0.303	3
SLDB	0.331	0.337	0.303	3

Table 8: final path decision applying QRMC algorithm (no prioritisation).

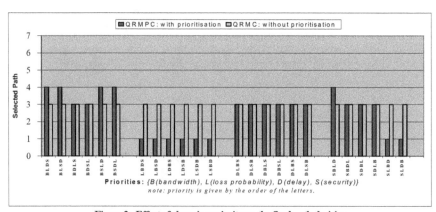

Figure 2: Effect of changing priority on the final path decision.

7. Future work

The proposed algorithms are still in their early stages of research and there are a number of issues for our future work:

1. Simulation experiments will be done on realistic topologies generated using well known tools, e.g. Waxman model for random network generation, in order to evaluate performance of the algorithms. The simulation will show us the behaviour of the proposed algorithms as the network size increases, scalability issue. Some preliminary results have been collected and they will be published nearly.

2. A comparison between the proposed algorithms and other proposed or published algorithms will be conducted in order to give them more credibility.

3. The algorithms applicability to wireless and mobile networks will also be investigated. For example to support QoS re-routing in the case of handover.

8. Conclusions

In this paper, we proposed two algorithms; The first one supports Quality of service Routing with Multiple and Prioritised Constraints (QRMPC). The second one supports Quality of service Routing with Multiple Constraints (QRMC). Both algorithms apply the concept of the Analytic Hierarchy Process (AHP) which is a very well known model in the area of decision making with multiple objectives. We showed how they work in general. We saw clearly how the final path decision changes as the priorities of the metrics change. The main novelty of this paper is the application of AHP approach which provides a convenient way to include multiple constraints in the proposed algorithms.

9. References

Al-Fawaz, M. M. M. and Woodward, M. E. (Jul 2000), "Fast Quality of Service Routing Algorithms with Multiple Constraints",*8th IFIP Workshop on ATM&IP,* Vol., No. pp 01/1-01/10.

Al-Harbi, K. M. A.-S. (2001), "Application of the AHP in project management",*International Journal of Project Management,* Vol. 19, No. 1, pp 19-27.

Andijani, A. A. (1998), "Buffer management of a switch for ATM networks: A multi-objective approach",*Computer Systems Science and Engineering,* Vol. 13, No. 6, pp 379-386.

ATM-Forum (1996), "Private Network Network Interface (PNNI) V1.0 Specifications", *ftp://ftp.atmforum.com/pub/approved-specs/af-pnni-0055.000.pdf,*5/4/2001.

Chen, S. (1999), "Routing Support for Providing Guaranteed End-to-End Quality of Service", PhD thesis, University of Illinois at Urbana-Champaign,*www.cs.uiuc.edu/Dienst/UI/2.0/Describe/ncstrl.uiuc_cs/*

Chen, S. and Nahrsted, K. (1998), "An Overview of Quality of Service Routing for Next-Generation High Speed Networks",*IEEE Networks,* Vol. 12, No. 6, pp 64-79.

Dey, P. K. and Gupta, S. S. (2000), "Decision-support system yields better pipeline route",*Oil and Gas Journal,* Vol. 98, No. 22, pp 68-73.

Douligeris, C. and Pereira, I. J. (1994), "A Telecommunications Quality Study Using the Analytical Hierarchy Process",*IEEE J. on S. A. in Communications,* Vol. 12, No. 2, pp 241-250.

Klungboonkrong, P. and A. P. Taylor, M. (1998), "A microcomputer-based- system for multicriteria environmental impacts evaluation of urban road networks",*Computers, Environment and Urban Systems,* Vol. 22, No. 5, pp 425-446.

Onvural, R. O. (1995) *Asynchronous transfer mode networks : performance issues,* Artech House, Boston.

Saaty, T. L. (1980) *The Analytic Hierarchy Process,* McGraw Hill, New York.

Sato, N. and Kataoka, H. (1996), "Selecting Network Services Based on Joint Assessment by Customer and Provider",*IEEE GLOBECOM 96 conference,* Vol. 1, No. pp 634-638.

Wang, N.-P. (1999), "The aplication of analytic hierarchy process in the selection of hospital",*Chinese Journal of Public Health,* Vol. 18, No. 2, pp 138-151.

Wang, Z. and Crowcroft, J. (1996), "Quality-of-Service Routing for Supporting Multimedia Applications",*IEEE Journal on Selected Areas in Communications,* Vol. 14, No. 7, pp 1228-1234.

Winston, W. L. (1994) *Operations Research : Applications and Algorithms,* International Thomson Publishing.

A Multicast Routing Algorithm for Multiple QoS Requirements

M. Kanbara, H. Tanioka, K. Kinoshita, K. Murakami

Department of Information Systems Engineering,
Graduate School of Engineering, Osaka University
e-mail: {kanbara, hideaki, kazuhiko, murakami} @ise.eng.osaka-u.ac.jp

Abstract

Multicast services have been used increasingly by various continuous multimedia applications. Most conventional multicast routing algorithms focus mainly on network cost optimization with or without delay constraint as a QoS (Quality of Service) requirement. In future multimedia communication services, however, it will be essential to satisfy multiple QoS requirements, such as jitter and error rate, in addition to delay. The new challenge is to build a multicast tree that delivers data from the source to all the members, so that multiple QoS requirements are satisfied, and the total network cost of the tree is minimized. In this paper, we propose a new multicast routing algorithm that not only satisfies multiple QoS requirements, but also efficiently reduces the total network cost of the multicast tree.

Keywords

Multicast routing, Multiple constraints, QoS routing, Dijkstra's algorithm

1. Introduction

Recent advances in optical fiber and switching technologies have resulted in high-speed networks. In addition, progress in audio, video, and data storage technologies has given rise to various multimedia applications that present diverse information in real time, e.g., news feeds, interactive games, video conferences, and VoD (Video on Demand). Multicast communication services have been used increasingly to provide such multimedia applications (Wang et al., 2000).

In multicast communications, instead of sending a separate copy of the data to each individual group member, a multicast source sends a single copy to all the members. To perform multicast communication, the nodes in the multicast group must be connected by a tree. Thus, the problem of conventional multicast routing in communication networks is equivalent to finding a tree T in a graph G such that T spans all vertices in the multicast group M (Sahasrabuddhe et al., 2000). Such a tree is called a *multicast tree*. There has been a lot of research in multicast routing algorithms. Most studies focus mainly on: (1) minimizing the total network cost of a multicast tree, e.g., (Kou et al., 1981; Shaikh et al., 1997) (*the Steiner tree problem*) (2) construction of the least-cost tree with bounded delay, e.g., (Salama et al., 1997) (*the constrained Steiner tree problem*) (3) finding the delay-constrained tree (construction of *the shortest path tree*).

However, many multimedia applications are QoS-sensitive in nature. It is therefore essential to support multiple QoS requirements such as end-to-end delay, jitter, and error rate. One of the key issues in providing such applications is to find feasible routes that satisfy multiple constraints. It is difficult to extend conventional multicast routing algorithms to handle multiple constraints. The new challenge is to build a multicast tree that delivers data from the source to all the members so that multiple QoS requirements are satisfied and the cost of the tree is minimized. Here, the cost may be the total bandwidth used and/or a monotonically nondecreasing function of network utilization. In this problem, given a set of constraints C in the form of delay bound, jitter bound and so on, multicast routing is a process of constructing, based on network topology and network state, a tree T that satisfies C and optimizes cost.

In this paper, we propose a new multicast routing algorithm for multiple QoS requirements. It satisfies multiple constraints and minimizes the cost of the multicast tree with small processing times. The proposed algorithm applies an enhanced Dijkstra's algorithm to find feasible routes that satisfy QoS constraints, and combines these routes to reduce the overall cost of the tree. In the proposed algorithm, we assume that the true state information of the network is available to every node, and that nodes use this information to construct trees.

2.   Classification of QoS Metrics

In QoS routing problems, the network is characterized with multiple metrics. The QoS metrics can be classified into three categories: additive, multiplicative, and concave metrics (Whang et al., 1996). Let $m(l)$ be defined as the performance metric for link l, for any path $P_T(u, v) = (u, i, j, \ldots, k, v)$ from node u to v.

- Additive metrics: A QoS metric is additive if

$$m(u, v) = m(u, i) + m(i, j) + \cdots + m(k, v).$$

  For example, the end-to-end delay $d(u, v)$ is additive and is equal to the sum of individual link metrics along the path.

- Multiplicative metrics: A QoS metric is multiplicative if

$$m(u, v) = m(u, i) \times m(i, j) \times \cdots \times m(k, v).$$

  For example, the probability, $1 - P_L(u, v)$, for a packet to reach node v from node u along $P_T(u, v)$ is multiplicative and is equal to the product of the individual link metrics $1 - P_L(i, j)$ along the path.

- Concave metrics: A QoS metric is concave if

$$m(u, v) = min[m(u, i), m(i, j), \ldots, m(k, v)].$$

  For example, the bandwidth $b(u, v)$, available along a path, is concave and is equal to the minimum bandwidth among the links on $P_T(u, v)$.

Note that a multiplicative metric can be converted to an additive metric by using logarithm and a concave metric can be ignored by removing the links that do not satisfy the constraint. Thus, it is sufficient to consider only additive QoS metrics.

3. Conventional Routing Algorithms

In unicast communications, the routing problem is defined as follows: given a source node s, a destination node d, a set of QoS constraints C, and possibly an optimization goal, find the best feasible path from s to d that satisfies C. This problem is known to be NP-complete (Whang et al., 1996), and many heuristic or approximate algorithms have been proposed to solve this problem (Chen et al., 1998; Korkmaz et al., 2001; Yuan et al., 2001). These algorithms can be applied to multicast routing. We now describe two multicast routing methods, which we call Parallel method and Serial method.

For each member, the Parallel method finds a route that satisfies the constraints, using a unicast QoS routing algorithm. This method can construct a multicast tree easily because it simply applies these feasible routes to the tree. However, the total cost of the tree may be large, as link sharing between the routes to each member is not taken into account.

On the other hand, in the Serial method, when a feasible route to a member is constructed with a unicast QoS routing algorithm, the cost of every link in the route is set to zero. The Serial method then finds the route to another member using the unicast routing algorithm. The process is repeated until the multicast tree is completed. This method can reduce the total cost of the tree efficiently since it considers link sharing. However, its processing time increases proportionally to the number of members. Therefore, it is not practical for larger-scale multicast communications.

4. Proposed Algorithm

In this section, we introduce a new multicast routing algorithm that not only satisfies multiple QoS constraints, but also minimizes the total cost of the tree in practical time. We use the enhanced Dijkstra's algorithm (here called ED) that we used in our proposed unicast QoS routing algorithm Fallback+ (Tanioka et al., 1998). We first introduce ED.

4.1. Enhanced Dijkstra's Algorithm

Dijkstra's algorithm solves *the shortest-path problem* (Dijkstra, 1959). The shortest path is the path for which the sum of the weights on the links along the path is minimized. In Dijkstra's algorithm, even though some tentative routes from one node to other nodes are generated before obtaining the final routes, the associated information is discarded. On the contrary, in ED, all tentative routes are preserved as available information.

We show an execution example of ED in Fig. 1. In this figure, the three numbers beside each link represent (*cost, delay, jitter*). Now we find the least-cost route from the source node 'S' to the destination node 'D' with ED.

First, the route 'S→D' is found and is preserved in the stack (Fig. 1(a)). Next, the route 'S→a' having the smaller cost is traced, and the route 'S→a→D' is found. The cost of this route is less than that of the route 'S→D'; therefore this route is preserved in the stack (Fig. 1(b)). Next, ED traces the route 'S→a→b' having the minimum cost

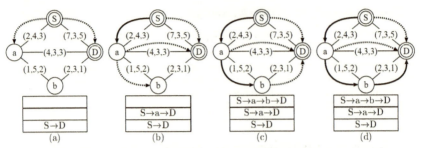

Figure 1: Example of execution of ED

of all the routes from 'S' to other nodes that are not yet traced, and then finds the route 'S→a→b→D'. The cost of this route is less than that of route 'S→a→D', and therefore this route is preserved in the stack (Fig. 1(c)). Finally, the route 'S→a→b→D' is traced (Fig. 1(d)).

When both the delay constraint and the jitter constraint are less than 10, Dijkstra's algorithm cannot find a feasible route because only the route 'S→a→b→D' is preserved and this route does not satisfy the delay constraint. On the other hand, ED can find feasible routes 'S→D' and 'S→a→D', since these routes are also preserved. Thus, ED can find many feasible routes because tentative routes are preserved.

Note here, that with both Dijkstra's algorithm and ED, one can find the shortest paths from the source to all nodes in a graph at the same time. In ED, tentative routes to all the members are also preserved in one calculation.

4.2. Multicast Routing with ED

In this subsection, we illustrate the procedure of the proposed algorithm. The proposed algorithm selects feasible routes from those found by ED with link sharing in mind.

First, the proposed algorithm solves the shortest path problems with respect to each metric (i.e., cost and all QoS metrics),using ED. Any feasible routes from all the routes to each member found by ED are preserved as candidates for objective routes.

Next, if a member is included in only one route, the proposed algorithm selects that route first, because this route is essential.

Then, until the tree is constructed, the proposed algorithm selects objective routes to other members one by one from the preserved routes to reduce the total cost of the tree. The specific approach is as follows. For every preserved route, let c denote the cost of the route, and m denote the number of members included in the route that are not yet added into the tree. Using this notation, we define a metric k to determine the priority as $k = c/m$. The proposed algorithm selects the route that has the minimum value of k and adds this route into the tree. Next, for every other preserved routes, the total cost c of the route is recalculated assuming that the cost of each link included in the selected route is equal to zero. In addition, the number of members m is also recalculated excluding the members that are included in the selected route. Then, the next objective route that has the minimum value of k is selected again in the same manner. These processes are repeated until the multicast tree is completed. Thus, the proposed algorithm minimizes the cost of the tree, because it can share links between the selected routes.

We show an execution example of the proposed algorithm. In Fig. 2, 'S' is the source node, 'M1' – 'M5' are member nodes and the values on each link denote (*cost, delay, jitter*). Let the QoS constraints be *delay, jitter* ≤ 10.

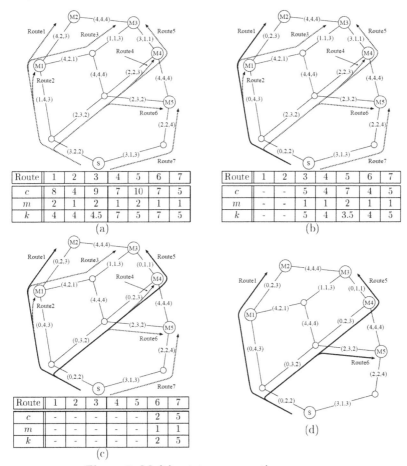

Route	1	2	3	4	5	6	7
c	8	4	9	7	10	7	5
m	2	1	2	1	2	1	1
k	4	4	4.5	7	5	7	5

(a)

Route	1	2	3	4	5	6	7
c	-	-	5	4	7	4	5
m	-	-	1	1	2	1	1
k	-	-	5	4	3.5	4	5

(b)

Route	1	2	3	4	5	6	7
c	-	-	-	-	-	2	5
m	-	-	-	-	-	1	1
k	-	-	-	-	-	2	5

(c)

(d)

Figure 2: Multicast tree generation process

ED is first applied with respect to all metrics (i.e., cost, delay, and jitter) and the seven routes 'Route 1' – 'Route 7' that satisfy both constraints are found (Fig. 2(a)). They are candidates for the objective route. Then 'Route 1', which is the unique route to the member node 'M2', is selected and for 'Route 3' – 'Route 7', each the total cost c of the route is recalculated assuming that the cost of every link on 'Route 1' is equal to zero. That is, c of 'Route 3' decreases from nine to five, that of 'Route 4' decreases from seven to four, that of 'Route 5' decreases from ten to seven and that of 'Route 6' decreases from seven to four. In addition, for 'Route 3' – 'Route 7', each m, the number of member nodes included in the route, is recalculated excluding 'M1' and 'M2' which are included in 'Route 1'. That is, m of 'Route 3' decreases from two to one. Then each k is also recalculated as shown in Fig. 2(b). 'Route 5', which has the minimum value of k, is now selected and c of 'Route 6' is recalculated assuming that the cost of every link on 'Route 5' is equal to zero, that is, c of 'Route 6' decreases from four to two. The remaining m values are also recalculated excluding 'M1' – 'M4', however, m values for 'Route 6' and 'Route 7' does not change in this case (Fig.2(c)). Finally, in the same manner, 'Route 6' which has smaller value of k, is selected and the proposed algorithm finishes as the multicast tree is completed (Fig.2(d)).

5. Performance Evaluation

In this section, we evaluate the performance of the proposed algorithm compared with the Parallel method and the Serial method. We chose Fallback+ (FB+) as the unicast QoS routing algorithm applied in both the Parallel and Serial methods.

5.1. Complexity Analysis

In this subsection, we show the worst-case time complexity of the Parallel method, the Serial method, and the proposed algorithm. Let V denote the number of nodes in a network, M denote the number of members in multicast communication, R denote the number of metrics (cost and QoS metrics) and P denote the number of feasible routes found by ED.

FB+ is based on Fallback algorithm (Lee *et al.*, 1995). In FB+, cost is chosen as an objective function first, and the shortest path problem is solved with ED. If any routes found by ED do not satisfy all constraints, a QoS metric is chosen as an objective function, and the same process is repeated until the route that satisfy all constraints is found. The time complexity of Dijkstra's algorithm is $O(V^2)$, and the time complexity of ED is also $O(V^2)$, because ED simply preserves routes that Dijkstra's algorithm discards. Therefore, the time complexity of FB+ is $O(RV^2)$, because FB+ applies ED R times in the worst-case (Tanioka *et al.*, 1998).

The worst-case time complexity of the Parallel method is $O(RV^2)$, because all routes to each member are selected by FB+ simultaneously with no overhead. On the other hand, the worst-case time complexity of the Serial method is $O(MRV^2)$, because it successively applies FB+ M times.

We now show the worst-case time complexity of the proposed algorithm. The time complexity of the process to find feasible routes by ED is $O(RV^2)$, because ED is applied with respect to all metrics. The time complexity of the selection process of the route having the minimum value of k (defined in section 4.) is $O(\log P)$. The time complexity of the calculation process for each cost and the number of members of routes $r \in F_r - S_r$, where F_r is the set of feasible routes found by ED and S_r is the set of selected routes, is $O(PV)$, because the maximum number of links included in one route is $(V - 1)$ (when all nodes are connected with each other). These processes are repeated up to M times. Therefore, the time complexity of the selection process of objective routes is $O(MPV)$. Note that $R, M \ll V$ and $P \propto RM$ because ED is applied R times to each member. We conclude that the worst-case time complexity of the proposed algorithm is $O(RV^2)$.

5.2. Simulation Experiments

To evaluate the mean tree cost and execution time, we performed simulation experiments. We generated ten graphs with 900 nodes using the algorithm proposed in (Waxman, 1988). A source node and group members on each graph were selected randomly. Each link was weighted by cost and four kinds of QoS metrics, and their values were assigned as random integers ranging from one to six. The number of members was changed between 10 and 90. We continued the experiments until 1000 feasible multicast trees were constructed by each algorithm on each graph. Note that, as we described in section 5.1, FB+ applies ED with respect to each metric (i.e., cost and all QoS metrics) in the worst-case. Therefore the probability of finding feasible trees with the Parallel method, and the Serial method is equal to that of the proposed algorithm.

Fig. 3 shows the average total cost of multicast trees created by the proposed algorithm and the Serial method as a function of the number of members. The values are normalized by the cost of multicast trees created by the Parallel method with a 95% confidence interval. We can see that the proposed algorithm reduces the total cost of multicast trees by about 7–8 % compared with the Parallel method. The Serial method reduces the total cost a little more than the proposed algorithm.

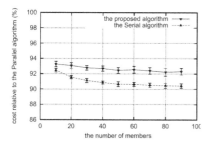

Figure 3: Tree cost

M	proposed	Parallel	Serial
10	1.3557	1.3507	19.2251
20	1.3884	1.3806	32.4363
30	1.4026	1.3902	45.3041
40	1.4160	1.3974	58.0174
50	1.4356	1.4095	71.0340
60	1.4526	1.4170	83.0665
70	1.4713	1.4252	94.1052
80	1.4946	1.4356	108.4759
90	1.5155	1.4440	117.4211

Table 1: CPU times (s)

We also measured the average computational time (CPU Time) of each algorithm when run on a Sun Ultra 80 workstations. Table 1 shows the result, where M denotes the number of members. From Table 1, it is clear that the CPU times for the proposed algorithm and the Parallel method are acceptable. On the contrary, the CPU times for the Serial method increase relative to the number of members. Therefore the Serial method cannot construct a multicast tree in a practical time in larger-scale multicast communications.

We conclude that the proposed algorithm reduces the total cost of multicast trees and that its computation time is small.

6. Conclusions

In this paper, we first showed that it was essential for multimedia application services to satisfy multiple QoS requirements such as delay, jitter, packet-loss probability. Next, we introduced a new multicast routing algorithm that not only satisfies multiple QoS requirements but also minimizes the total cost of the multicast tree. The proposed algorithm applies the enhanced Dijkstra's algorithm to find feasible routes that satisfy requirements and combines the routes to minimize the total cost of the tree. Finally, we have shown through some performance evaluations that the proposed algorithm reduces the total cost of multicast tree more than that of the Parallel algorithm with practical execution times equal to the Parallel method.

In future work, we try to support that an arbitrary node joins and/or leaves an ongoing multicast communication.

7. References

Chen, S. and Nahrstedt, K. (1998), "An overview of quality of service routing for next-generation high-speed networks: problems and solutions," *IEEE Network*, November/December, pp. 64–79.

Dijkstra, E. W. (1959), "A note on two problems in connection with graphs," *Numerische Mathematik*, Vol. 1, pp. 269–71.

Korkmaz, T. and Krunz M. (2001), "Multi-constrained optimal path selection," *IEEE INFOCOM*, pp. 834–843.

Kou, L., Markowsky, G. and Berman, L. (1981), "A fast algorithm for steiner trees," *Acta Informatica*, Vol. 15, No. 2, pp. 141–145.

Lee, W. C., Hluchyi, M. G. and Humblet, P. A. (1995), "Routing subject to quality of service constraints in integrated communication networks," *IEEE Network*, July/August, pp. 46–55.

Sahasrabuddhe, L. H. and Mukherjee, B. (2000), "Multicast routing algorithms and protocols: a tutorial," *IEEE Network*, January/February, pp. 90–102.

Salama, H. F., Reeves, D. S. and Viniotis, Y. (1997), "Evaluation of multicast routing algorithms for real-time communication on high-speed networks," *IEEE Journal on Selected Areas in Communications*, Vol. 15, No. 3, pp. 332–345.

Shaikh, A. and Shin, K. (1997), "Destination-driven routing for low-cost multicast," *IEEE Journal on Selected Areas in Communications*, Vol. 15, No. 3, pp. 373–381.

Tanioka, H., Kinoshita, K., Takine, T. and Murakami, K. (1998), "Fallback+: a routing algorithm subject to multiple qos constraints," *International Technical Conference on Circuits/Systems, Computers and Communications*, Vol. I, pp. 319–322.

Wang, B. and Hou, J. C. (2000), "Multicast routing and its qos extension: problems, algorithms, and protocols," *IEEE Network*, January/February, pp. 22–36.

Waxman, B. M. (1988), "Routing of multipoint connections," *IEEE Journal on Selected Areas in Communications*, Vol. 6, No. 9, pp. 1617–1621.

Whang, Z. and Crowcroft, J. (1996), "Quality-of-service routing for supporting multimedia applications," *IEEE Journal on Selected Areas in Communications*, Vol. 14, No. 7, pp. 1228–1234.

Yuan, X. and Liu, X. (2001), "Heuristic algorithms for multi-constrained quality of service routing," *IEEE INFOCOM*, pp. 844–853.

Endpoint study of Internet paths and web pages transfers

B. V. Ghita, S. M. Furnell, B. M. Lines, E. C. Ifeachor

University of Plymouth, Plymouth, United Kingdom
e-mail: bghita@jack.see.plymouth.ac.uk

Abstract

This paper presents the findings of a pilot study to provide information about the characteristics of current networks and data transfers. The main aim of the study was to infer the properties of a large number of network paths. In addition, the study produced statistics relating to the average size of a typical web page and both under the restriction of a single-point connection. The study was performed in two steps: trace collection followed by TCP per-flow analysis. The trace collection used the functionality of a random link generator, combined with an automatic HTTP retrieval tool. The TCP analysis was applied to the collected traces and it involved an offline TCP per-flow method developed in previous research.

Keywords

TCP connection analysis, Internet characteristics, web page size, web transfer features.

1   Introduction

The current status of the Internet is one of the issues being researched intensively. The first concerted initiative to evaluate the properties of the Internet belongs to Paxson. He deployed his Network Probe Daemon (NPD), established a measurement mesh to evaluate the characteristics of network paths, and generated and analysed the transfers running through this mesh (Paxson, 1999). Several bodies, such as the Active Measurement Project (AMP, 2002) and the National Internet Measurement Infrastructure, built on the concept of NPD) (NIMI, 2002) projects aim to describe the Internet from a holistic perspective by employing complex measurement infrastructures. A different view is embraced by passive traffic surveys, which capture and analyse data from backbone segments / endpoint networks (Thompson and Miller, 1997). The need for such information comes from both the research and commercial domains. The rationale is similar for the two cases: the marketing directions, as well as the improvements of current Internet-related technologies, have to be based on actual information rather than assumptions or previous studies.

All of the aforementioned measurement initiatives are very successful in their place, and they aim to answer the question 'How does the overall Internet behave?'. The study presented in this paper seeks to discuss the Internet characteristics from a different perspective: how the Internet is seen from an endpoint network and what are the characteristics of the data that may be retrieved from the Internet by other hosts connected to that respective endpoint network. Concluding, the question that this study aims to answer is 'How does Internet behave for *my* Internet traffic?', as would be asked by an endpoint network user / administrator.

2 Traffic collection

The study discussed by this paper presents analysis results based on two data sources: real traffic and artificially generated traffic. In both cases HTTP was used as the focused application for reasons of availability and convenience. It was observed before starting the experiments that most of the network TCP traffic is web browsing, which confirms the results of previous studies (Paxson, 1999). Also, as will be discussed later, artificial and random HTTP traffic was convenient to produce.

For the first option, i.e. capture real traffic, the hosts (approximately 15) within the Network Research Group (NRG) at University of Plymouth were used. The connectivity of the machines within the NRG is convenient for traffic capture, as they are all connected to a switch, and the capture machine was attached to the uplink of the switch through a hub. The traffic collection was performed continuously during spring 2002 for a period of two weeks and included only web traffic between the hosts in the NRG and hosts outside the UoP network. The second option, i.e. generate artificial traffic, allowed a more controlled approach to the data collection. The traffic was produced using the Random Yahoo Link page (RYL, 2002) from the Yahoo website, a CGI script that redirects a request to a random WWW page, taken from the Yahoo search engine database. The HTTP client used to perform the requests was wget (wget, 2002), a command-line HTTP retrieval tool, and the requests were controlled through a Linux shell script. The experiments in this case were also performed in two stages, but separately from the network segment traffic capture discussed above. It is known that at least one major event, in terms of network infrastructure changes, happened between the two experiments: an upgrade of the UoP network from a 100MB backbone / 10MB access speed to 1000MB backbone / 100MB access speed. As will be seen in the results section, all the network parameters (bandwidth, loss, delay) are improved for the second set of results. For both experiments, the traffic was captured using tcpdump (tcpdump, 2002), which was set to keep only the HTTP connections (using a *tcp and port 80* filter expression). The level of the monitored traffic was low in all cases and tcpdump did not report any dropped packets throughout the experiments. In all experiments, the traces were filtered offline in order to remove the unfinished or reseted connections, which could not be used for consistent analysis; the resulting figures are presented in Table 1.

Traffic type	Number of connections collected			
	2001		2002	
	Raw	Filtered	Raw	Filtered
Wget generated	15106	12469	16844	13674
Real	-	-	14288	11322

Table 1 – Capture statistics for the traffic collection experiments performed

3 Analysis

One of the aims of this paper is to advance the traffic analysis from an overall study, currently preferred for convenience and simplicity, to per-flow examination, in order to get an insight of the network conditions that are behind the traffic. The overall analysis studies present only the total figures of traffic (overall throughput in bytes, packets, or flows per second), the distribution of traffic per application (based on the port numbers), or the distribution of the packet lengths. The only concerted efforts in the area of TCP per-flow analysis were the ones made by Paxson in (Paxson, 1997a), (Paxson, 1999), which are quoted by most articles when discussing current characteristics of the Internet.

Two types of analysis were applied to the collected traces: network performance-related, to reveal the end-to-end network paths characteristics, and connection-related, to classify the web pages in terms of size and content. The network performance analysis was performed using a previously developed tool, described in (Ghita et al, 2001); the method employed is similar to other TCP flow analysers, like tcpanaly (Paxson, 1997b) and tcptrace (Osterman, 2002), with improvements for single point monitoring and network parameters inference. The connection analysis investigated the size and the content (object-wise) of the web pages for two reasons: to determine the average size of a page (together with the containing objects, e.g. images) and to establish the efficiency in practice of the HTTP 1.1 pipelining capabilities.

4   The Random Yahoo Link experiments - Results

4.1   Network topology

The UoP network is connected to the Internet, as mentioned before, via the UK academic network, JANET. As a result, the first 8 hops of all paths are part of the JANET infrastructure, and, implicitly, were common for all connections but the routes diverged at the exit from JANET, depending on the destination host. A separate experiment was carried out to estimate the number of individual paths explored within the performed experiments. A traceroute was run on a random subset of the sites (350 out of the 2744 unique servers which were used during the spring 2002 round of experiments) to see the number of different individual paths. The results are shown in Figure 1.

The number of routes differing by at least one hop was found to be as high as 180, figure that is approximately half of the number of hosts probed (the number of unique hops decreases towards the end of the graph due to path size, with an average hop count of 22.2 hops). Concluding, although the study was performed from a single point, this additional measurement indicates that the survey analysed a fairly large number of different Internet paths.

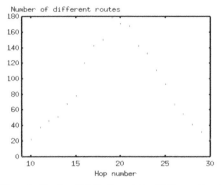

Figure 1 - Routing distribution, spring 2002 experiments

4.2 Round Trip Time results

The distribution of the RTT for the two sets of experiments is presented in Figure 2 (left). As can be observed, in both cases the average RTT values are very low for most of the connections, with an overall average of 200.5 ms for the first round of experiments and 136.5 ms for the second round. The difference between the figures may be associated with the network upgrade mentioned previously (unfortunately, there was no path information collected during the autumn 2001 experiments), as the shape of the distribution remained the same for the two sets of results.

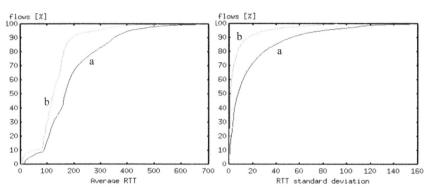

Figure 2 – left - RTT average [ms] cumulative distribution for: a) autumn 2001, b) spring 2002; right - RTT standard deviation [ms] cumulative distribution for: a) autumn 2001, b) spring 2002

Aside from the actual value of the RTT, the standard deviation of the RTT throughout a connection was calculated; the result is shown in Figure 2 (right). The average value of the standard deviation was 22.3 ms (10.4 % of the RTT averages) for the autumn 2001 round and 7.8 ms (4.7 % of the RTT averages) for spring 2002. The data results from spring 2002 indicate that, for 87% of the flows, the RTT standard deviation was 10 ms. This value is relevant as, at the moment, it is the default resolution for timers, at least for Linux based systems. Future work, aims to analyse the implications of these low figures for RTT estimation within the TCP clients, since the RTT variation plays an important role in the TCP retransmission mechanism (Jacobson and Karels, 1988). Since successive connections were made to different sites, conclusions could not be drawn with regard to the long / short term autocorrelation of either RTT average or RTT standard deviation.

4.3 Loss

Due to its self-adjusting behaviour (Jacobson and Karels, 1988), TCP performance is critically affected by loss. Nevertheless, previous studies (Paxson, 1997a) have shown that packet loss is low, at least for the analysed mesh of Internet paths. One of the purposes of this paper is to produce a similar study, but based only on traces collected from a single point and with no control over the senders. It may be argued that the survey carried out as part of this study was somehow limited, as the wget client does not support HTTP1.1. As a result, the objects from a page are downloaded in separate connections, which leads to smaller congestion windows. Further, the resulting figures for loss may be lower than the ones obtained for a long-lived connection, with larger congestion windows. The losses were split into visible retransmissions and inferred retransmissions. The first category, visible retransmissions, is represented by losses which are indicated by anomalies in the TCP segments sequence. The second category, inferred retransmissions, includes the losses that are not apparent from the sequence of succesive TCP segments (more details on this subject are given in (Ghita et al, 2001)). The second category was named *inferred* because the process of identifying a loss is not based on sequencing, but only on packet spacing. The technique is reliable for a simple HTTP 1.0 retrieval, where the reply is a single object. Additional problems arise if HTTP 1.1 is used, due to spacing introduced between retrievals of successive objects within the same connection. In this case, the method requires comprehensive information from the application layer; since this is currently under analysis, it is reserved for future work.

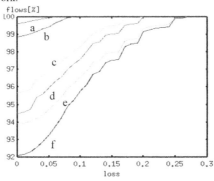

Figure 3 - Packet loss distribution for a) / b) visible retransmissions 2002 / 2001, c) / d) inferred retransmissions 2002 / 2001, e) / f) all losses 2002 / 2001

The distributions for both types of losses, as well as their sum, are displayed in Figure 3. The average figures for loss were: 0.18 / 0.83 / 1.1 % (visible / inferred / total) for the 2001 experiments and 0.16 / 0.47 / 0.63 % (visible / inferred / total) for the 2002 trace. It is noticeable that the inferred losses accounted for the vast majority of the total loss, which may be caused by the short-lived character of most connections. This may be due to the small number of packets / connection which, again, leads to low values for congestion window and, implicitly, too few acknowledgements returned for triggering a retransmission when a loss happens.

The short-lived connections have an additional undesired effect: the accuracy of the measurement cannot go beyond the granularity of the download due to the low number of packets exchanged. For example, having a transfer consisting of 10 packets, the minimum detectable loss is 0.1, a situation also described in (Paxson, 1997a). To reduce this error granularity, we calculated the loss based on the total number of packets. The year 2001 tests had a total of 137297 packets, with 295 visible and 1033 inferred retransmissions, producing the overall packet loss figures 0.21 / 0.75 / 0.96 % (visible / inferred / total). For the 2002 tests, a number of 297 packets were visible retransmissions and 604 packets were inferred retransmissions; comparing this with the total of 129404 packets, results in an overall packet loss of 0.22 / 0.46 / 0.68 % (visible / inferred / total).

4.4   Bandwidth

An estimate of the total bandwidth was produced for each connection. The estimate used delay between pairs of consecutive packets inferred to be sent in a back-to-back manner, and it was based on the method proposed by Keshav in (Keshav, 1991). The problems that may occur due to clock granularity were avoided by using a microsecond kernel timer, the Kansas University Real-Time Linux (KURT) (Niehaus, 2002). The obtained figure might be affected by the problems associated with packet-pair bandwidth inference but, due to the unknown behaviour of the senders, it was not possible to apply the Receiver Based Packet Pair as described in (Paxson, 1997a) to avoid these problems.

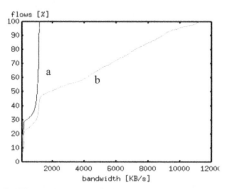

Figure 4 - Bandwidth cumulative distribution for a) autumn 2001 and b) spring 2002

From all network characteristics, the network upgrade mentioned earlier affected bandwidth the most. It can be noticed in the distribution from Figure 4 that bandwidth reached a maximum of approximately 1.2MB/s for the autumn 2001 round of experiments. This matches, in fact, the configuration of the network: at the time of the experiment, the connectivity of the desktops was 10Mb LAN. For the spring 2002, the maximum figure is 12MB/s, which reflects the tenfold increase in desktop bandwidth.

4.5   Congestion window analysis

The congestion window inference includes a high level of assumption in terms of TCP connection analysis. In our case, the task had an increased level of difficulty due to the characteristics of the monitored transfers: unknown senders, receiver-based capture, and no control over the endpoints / transfer. The fact that the senders use an unknown TCP implementation does not allow any inference in regards to profiling of the congestion window evolution. The intention was to produce a rough estimate of the congestion window, not to compete with *tcpanaly* (Paxson, 1997b), which includes more complex analysis but also requires traffic capture at / near the endpoints. The receiver-based capture brings with it uncertainty in regards to if, when, and as a response to what acknowledgement, the sender transmitted a data segment. Due to the variety of window increase policies and the uncertainty of which acknowledgements reached the server, the congestion window inference was based exclusively on timing between different trains of packets rather than acknowledgement dialogue. The actual method focused on isolating groups of packets that appear to be transmitted as part of the same round, based on the distance between successive in-sequence packets. The third problem, no control over the endpoints, differentiates the study from Internet measurement efforts (Paxson, 1999), (NIMI, 2002). Within measurement infrastructures, endpoints running dedicated clients transfer large files between them at regular intervals in order to determine the network characteristics. Within this study, all the senders were remote sites on the Internet and the objects transferred were various web pages residing on the servers; as a result, there was no control over the size / timing of the connections.

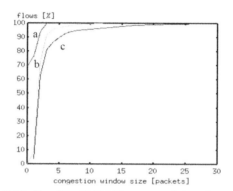

Figure 5 - Cumulative distribution of the a) initial, b) average, and c) maximum congestion window size

The resulting distribution is displayed in Figure 5. The average figures for the three variables (initial / average / maximum congestion window) were 1.91 / 3.47 / 4.95 for 2001 experiments and 1.77 / 3.16 / 4.52 for the 2002 experiments round. The difference between the figures can be attributed, again, to the network upgrade that reduced the packet loss and delay figures, as mentioned before.

5 The NRG network traces

5.6 Page content analysis

When the first round of experiments was run, the latest version at the time did not allow for a full download of the web pages (e.g. for a page with 4 images, only the HTML file was retrieved). At the second round of experiments, the newer version of wget had the facility to parse web pages and download the objects hosted on the same server with the page), which allowed a rough estimation of the actual content of the page. In the case of a HTTP1.1 client, these objects would be downloaded in a single connection. This gives an approximate indication of the actual length, in terms of size, of a connection.

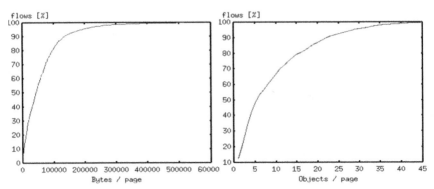

Figure 6 - Distribution of page content in bytes / page and objects / page

Figure 6 shows that most web pages have relatively large size (for some of his experiments, Paxson considered 100 KB files to be satisfactory for evaluating the properties of Internet). Also, from the distribution of objects per page, it may be concluded that full usage of HTTP 1.1 request pipelining would considerably reduce the overall time to retrieve the web page. The average figures for Figure 6 are 72607 bytes / page and 10.5 objects / page.

5.7   Connection analysis

Although a convenient and comprehensive tool, even the latest version of wget does not include some major functionality such as supporting frames and request pipelining (according to the author, there are no plans to expand it in the future in these areas). The set of traces captured from the traffic produced by the NRG members was therefore used for the connection analysis. The machines in the NRG were running either on a flavour of Linux (RedHat or SuSE) or Windows (NT4 or 2000 Professional), with Netscape Navigator 4.76-4.77 or Internet Explorer 5.0-5.5 as correspondent web clients. All the mentioned versions have HTTP1.1 enabled as standard, therefore they all should pipeline the requests whenever possible. The analysis of the captured traffic focused on the connection length, in order to determine the average length of an HTTP retrieval for the real traffic case. It may be argued that the amount of users involved in the study was relatively small; however, for future, it is aimed to compare these figures with results obtained from bigger, backbone collected traces. The result of the connection size analysis is displayed in Figure 7. It was observed that approximately three quarters of the flows had a download size of under 5KB with average numbers of 6220 bytes / connection and 7.12 packets / connection. These are very low figures, considering the previously estimated average of 72607 bytes / page obtained from the Random Yahoo Link experiments, and indicate that, in spite of the rich content of the Internet, the HTTP pipelining capabilities are not efficiently used.

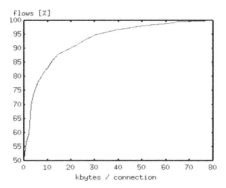

Figure 7 - Cumulative distribution of connection size

6   Conclusions

This paper presented the findings from an endpoint-based network per-flow trace analysis. In spite of its limited scope, the proposed analysis allowed characterisation of a fairly large number of network paths. The traffic was studied with a two-fold purpose: to evaluate the network conditions experienced by the flows and to determine the characteristics of a web page in terms of total content and number of elements per page. For the analysis, artificial traffic was mainly used. The experiment was carried out in two rounds: autumn 2001 and spring 2002. It used a random page generator combined with a command line HTTP retrieval tool, which was preferred instead of the real traffic due to the complexity in interpreting HTTP 1.1 pipelined transfers. Nevertheless, in order to evaluate the size characteristics of real transfers, a pilot traffic capture in a limited environment was performed.

The TCP analysis revealed a loss-free image of the Internet, with an average loss of 1.1% for the first round of experiments and 0.63% for the second round. The overall figures indicated even a smaller loss probability, of 0.96% and 0.96% respectively. The round trip delay values were also fairly low, with an average 200.5 ms for autumn 2001 and 196 ms for spring 2002 experiments and a standard deviation of 22.3 ms and 7.8 ms (4.7 % of the RTT averages) respectively. The page content analysis revealed that the average page size is approximately 70 KB, with an average of 10 objects / page that fully justify usage of HTTP 1.1 pipelining. However, the real network traffic showed much lower figures, of only 6220 bytes / connection and 7.12 packets / connection, which indicates that either the HTTP 1.1 pipelining mechanisms are inefficiently used or that current web pages are not suitable for pipelined requests.

For future work, it is primarily aimed to reduce the uncertainty of packet loss estimation and to expand the analysis towards connecting the TCP analysis with the HTTP retrieval, in order to be able to isolate individual retrievals of objects. Also, if possible, the per-flow analysis will be applied to larger traces to determine whether or not these findings are scalable and may be applied to traffic collected from core internet links.

7 References

AMP, The Active Measurement Project (AMP) homepage, http://moat.nlanr.net/AMP/, 2002

Ghita, B., Lines, B, Furnell, S., Ifeachor, E., "Non-intrusive IP Network Performance Monitoring for TCP flows", *Proceedings of IEEE ICT 2001*, 2001

Jacobson, V., Karels, M., 'Congestion Avoidance and Control', *Proceedings of SIGCOMM '88*, 1988

Keshav, S., "A Control-Theoretic Approach to Flow Control," *Proceedings of SIGCOMM '91*, pp. 3-15, 1991.

NIMI, The National Internet Measurement Infrastructure homepage, http://ncne.nlanr.net/nimi/, 2002

Niehaus, D., "KURT-Linux: Kansas University Real-Time Linux", http://www.ittc.ku.edu/kurt/, 2002

Osterman S., 'tcptrace homepage", http://www.tcptrace.org, 2002

Paxson, V., "Measurements and Analysis of End-to-End Internet Dynamics", PhD thesis, 1997

Paxson, V., "Automated Packet Trace Analysis of TCP Implementations", *Proceedings of SIGCOMM '97*, 1997

Paxson V., "End-to-end internet packet dynamics", *IEEE/ACM Transactions on Networking*, vol 7, no 3, 1999

Random Yahoo Link (RYL), Random Yahoo Link Page, http://random.yahoo.com/bin/ryl, 2002

tcpdump, tcpdump public repository, http://www.tcpdump.org/, 2002

Thompson K., Miller G.J. 'Wide-Area Internet Traffic Patterns and Characteristics', *IEEE network*, nov 1997

Wget, GNU Wget home page, http://www.gnu.org/software/wget/, 2002

G-Marking: Improved Marking Method for Multiple-Domain Differentiated Services

Seung-Joon Seok, Sung-Hyuck Lee and Chul-Hee Kang

Department of Electronics Engineering, Korea University, Seoul, Korea
e-mail : ssj@widecomm.korea.ac.kr

Abstract

End-to-end assured service may be provided by the combination of assured service models over multiple domains through service level agreements (SLA) between two neighbor domains. Many studies revealed that the current assured service model does not meet the target rate of large-profile flows in the presence of numerous small-profile flows and that it does not equally distribute the profile rate of an SLA with multiple flows that are included in the SLA. We proposed a marking rule, called G-Marking (Generalized Marking) in order to diminish these problems simultaneously. The G-Marking consists of an Ingress marking scheme (I-Marker) and an Egress marking scheme (E-Marker) that are performed in ingress and egress routers respectively. The E-Marker is responsible for distributing reservation rate to aggregated flows, while the I-Marker guarantees the target rate of SLA. Three experiments with the ns-2 simulator were performed: with E-Marker, I-Marker and G-Marking scheme respectively. Simulation results show that compared to other schemes, G-Marking can more greatly correct the current problems.

Keywords

Assured Service, Marking, Differentiated Services

1. Introduction and Architecture

Previous work reports that there are two types of unfairness in Assured Service (Heinanen et al, 1999). First, suppose that TCP flows with Assured Service path through the same bottleneck link. In particular, assume that the TCP flows has different traffic profile rate. Under these conditions, the flows expect to share the excess bandwidth of the bottleneck link to get its target rate. The target rate is the sum of traffic profile rate and equal share of excess bandwidth of the bottleneck link for all flows. This is called equal sharing target rate (Yeom and Reddy, 1999). However, several studies (Rezende, 1999)(Ibanez and Nichols, 1998) have found that TCP flows with large profile rate and/or long round trip time (RTT) barely meet their target rate in the presence of numerous flows with small profile rate. The reason of this problem is that current TCP additively increases its window size and multiplicatively decreases it when any packet is lost. This makes flows with large profile rate to have longer time to reach to its target rate after a packet loss or not to reach to. For convenience, this problem is herein referred to as *"inter-SLA unfairness"*. The unfairness is defined as excess bandwidth of a bottleneck link not being distributed equably among flows that go through the link.

A SLA may cover a set of flows. In this case, however, there exists unfair sharing reserved bandwidth or profile rate within aggregated flows. This unfairness between the aggregated flows is a serious problem in Assured Service model. The unfairness can be caused by differences in RTTs, in link capacities, or in congestion levels experienced by flows within the network, though the total throughput of the aggregation still reaches the target rate. This type of unfairness is herein referred to as *"intra-SLA unfairness"*. To balance or fix the unfairness, a sophisticated marking mechanism is required to distribute the profile rate fairly to the aggregated flows at edge routers (Yeom and Reddy, 1999)(Kim, 1999)(Andrikopoulos and Pavlou, 2000).

Today's Internet comprises of multiple interconnected autonomous domains, or administrative domains (Reichmeyer, 1998) and a packet from source generally reaches destination through several domains. In the backbone area of Internet, it is general that an upstream domain contracts a SLA with each downstream domain and the SLA includes all flows entering the upstream domain from different previous domains or users and going toward the downstream domain. Because the SLA is valid only within the entering new downstream domain, current DSCP (DiffServ Code Point) used in upstream domain should be changed to new DSCP used in downstream domain according to the SLA before entering the downstream domain.

There are several DiffServ marking rules to improve the two unfairness-problems. However no one considers two unfairness-problems simultaneously. Also almost rules are designed to be applied at source or near edge router close to source. (Wang et al, 2000) proposed an inter-domain flow control, called Random Early Demotion and Promotion (REDP). The main aspects of the REDP scheme are the provision of promotion of the demoted packets and marking the demotion/promotion process fairly using random detection scheme. When the aggregated incoming *GREEN* traffic exceeds the negotiated inter-domain service agreement, the edge router randomly demotes *GREEN* packets to *YELLOW* class at inter-domain interface. Otherwise, the edge router promotes *YELLOW* packets to *GREEN*. The provision of promotion enhances the performance of assured serviced traffic, whereas the early randomness in packet marking decision ensures the fairness of the proposed scheme. However this strategy does not support the two unfairness-problems as mentioned previously.

The main contribution of this paper is to propose a marking architecture to simultaneously correct the intra-SLA unfairness and inter-SLA unfairness that can be applied any DiffServ domain regardless of provisioning policy of DS domain and Internet Architecture. Therefore, we call this marking strategy "Generalized Marking" (G-Marking). G-Marking strategy is based structurally on the REDP. G-Marking also has two operation phases: demotion and promotion. The common idea behind G-Marking is that the marking results of previous edge routers are used as information representing the state of flow and arriving packets are remarked according to this information. This methodology is detailed more in next section.

2. Generalized Marking Scheme for Multiple-Domain Assured Service

G-Marking strategy consists of an "Ingress marking scheme" (I-Marker) and an "Egress marking scheme" (E-maker) that are located in ingress routers and egress routers respectively. We assume that two neighborhood domains agreed an SLA and that an E-Marker of upstream domain and an I-Marker of downstream domain that are located in opposite side on inter-domain interface are configured to the SLA. The upstream E-Marker and the downstream I-Marker are associated with each other to mark packets effectively based on the SLA between the two domains. The role of the upstream E-Marker is to distribute a reservation rate fairly among flows that are included in the SLA to reduce intra-SLA unfairness, while the downstream I-Marker guarantees the target rate of the SLA to reduce inter-SLA unfairness.

E-Marker should determine the drop precedence (colors) of packets that arrived from several different ingress routers within its domain so as to distribute traffic profile rate fairly to the flows aggregated in the SLA. However, it is difficult because all flows experience different path conditions such as different congestion level and round trip delay, and in particular because the flows have different source reservation rates. Figure 1 represents a simplified model of these cases. In these conditions, equal throughput or the strictly equal sharing profile rate, that are pursued by other studies, does not represent the fairness among aggregated flows. In this paper, thus, we redefine the "fairness" for aggregated flows as *how equably all flows have the excess throughput*. To achieve this fairness, the E-Marker should make *as many flows as possible over its reservation rate*.

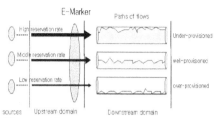

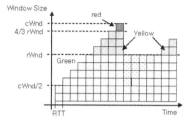

Figure 1. The aggregated flows with different congestion levels and reservation rates

Figure 2. The bandwidth guarantee three color marking

State information on all aggregated flows is necessary to determine marking rates of each flow. In this paper, E-Marker uses current packet distribution of each aggregated flow, especially the current *OUT* profile marking rate, as the only information used for remarking for a downstream domain. In other words, E-Marker uses a fact that a high *OUT* profile marking rate means that the flow is much over its reservation rate. In contrast, if the flow cannot get its reservation rate because of network congestion or competition with other flows, the *OUT* profile rate of the flow is very low. It is a proper assumption because an edge router can not have other information on each flow such as source reservation rates or a backbone link's congestion levels.

E-Marker operates in color-aware mode and has two operation phases: promotion phase and demotion phase. Also E-Marker performs two colors marking, but I-Marker three colors marking. It is necessary, thus, that E-Marker considers both *YELLOW* and *RED* packet as *OUT* packet and the I-Marker classifies packets into three colors. The promotion phase may occur when aggregated *IN* profile rates is less than the traffic profile rate of the SLA with downstream domain. Otherwise, the E-Marker may be in the demotion phase. In promotion phase some of *OUT* (*RED or YELLOW*) packets are promoted to the *IN* (*GREEN*) packets, and in demotion phase some of *IN* packets are remarked as *OUT* (*RED*). The E-Marker's basic methodology is increasing *IN* marking rate in reverse-proportion to the *OUT* profile marking rate of each aggregated flow in the promotion phase, but decreasing *IN* marking rates in proportion to the *OUT* profile marking rate of each aggregated flow in the demotion phase.

I-Marker aims to guarantee the target rate of SLA. As mentioned in section 1, the throughput of flow with large reservation rate hardly achieve its target rate because the small-profile flows greedy the excess bandwidth of bottleneck link. In G-Marking scheme, I-Marker modifies the marking result of upstream E-Marker using bgTCM (bandwidth guarantee three color marking) scheme in order to guarantee the flows' target rates. The bgTCM is proposed to reduce this inter-SLA unfairness in our previous study (Seok et al, 2001). bgTCM is a three-color marking scheme. Thus, it is required that core routers with domain support the three-color drop precedence. bgTCM rule marks arrival packets as *GREEN* by the profile rate, *YELLOW* between profile rate and 4/3 profile rate or *RED* over 4/3 profile rate which is called as extended profile rate. Figure 2 shows bgTCM marking operation. It is expected that almost *IN* (*GREEN*) packets marked by the upstream E-Marker may be not changed in I-Marker and some *OUT* (*RED*) packets may be remarked with *YELLOW* by 1/3 profile rate, if the G-Marking service is well provisioned. In addition, I-Marker has the added characteristic of avoiding non-responsive flows impact on the responsive flows. I-Marker first identified the flow type of arriving packets and does not apply the three-color marking rule to non-responsive flows, thus reducing the impact of non-responsive flows. However, how to detect the non-responsive flows is a current issue.

2.1 Implementation of Egress-Marker at upstream domain's egress edge

273

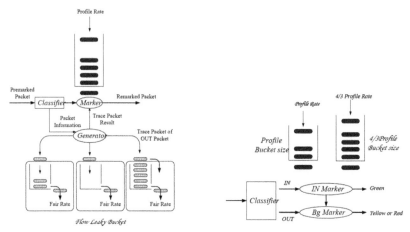

Figure 3. Egress-Marker Architecture   **Figure 4. Ingress-Marker Architecture**

Figure 3 shows an E-Marker's architecture. E-Marker is implemented using a token bucket and several leaky buckets. The token bucket is configured according to the traffic profile rate of the SLA and enforces *IN* marking rate of the aggregated flows to the profile rate. The presence of the token causes the promotion behavior of E-Marker. Conversely, the absence of the token represents the demotion phase. The leaky buckets are used to provide fair marking among the flows, and thus a leaky bucket is set up corresponding to each flow. E-Marker generates a trace packet for each *OUT (YELLOW or RED)* packet and inputs it into corresponding leaky bucket. Therefore, the occupancy of a leaky bucket can represent the state of the related flow. All leaky buckets have same output rates and bucket sizes. The leaky bucket rate is *"average out rate"* (aggregated out packet rate / the number of aggregated flows) and the leaky bucket size is as large as the burst packets absorbed.

The procedure of E-Marker is as follows: whenever a packet is arrived at the E-Marker, a classifier block pass the packet to a maker block and informs a generator block of flow identifier, packet size and marked type. The generator first creates a trace packet with the packet size and finds a leaky bucket representing the flow. If there is no leaky bucket, the generator creates a new leaky bucket. The generator then checks if the leaky bucket can accept the trace token and informs the maker of the result, either *"yes"* or *"no"*. If the leaky bucket has capacity for the trace packet and the packet type is *OUT*, it is entered into the leaky bucket by the generator. However, if the leaky bucket is full or the packet type is *IN (GREEN)*, the trace packet is discarded. The next operation of the marker block depends on the E-Marker operation phase. If there are enough tokens for the packet in token bucket, the promotion operation is carried out. Otherwise, the demotion operation.

- Promotion phase: If the packet type is *IN*, the marker consumes token from the token bucket and sends off the packet without change of service level, regardless of the answer from the generator. However, if the packet type is *OUT* and the answer is *yes*, token is consumed from the token bucket and the packet is remarked as *IN* and sent off. If the packet is not *IN* and the answer is *no*, the packet is remarked as *OUT (RED)* and sent off without consuming tokens.

- Demotion phase: If the packet type is *IN* and the answer is *yes*, the marker consumes token from the token bucket and sends off the packet without remarking, regardless of the capacity of the token bucket. Thus, the token current of the token bucket can have negative value temporally. Otherwise the packet is marked as *OUT* and sent off without consuming tokens.

2.2 Implementation of Ingress-Marker at downstream domain's ingress edge

Figure 4 shows an I-Marker's architecture. I-Marker is implemented using two token buckets. The first, called the profile bucket, is set up with the traffic profile of the SLA. The other, called the bg-bucket, is set up with extended profile rate. The extended profile rate has 4/3 profile rate and 4/3 profile bucket size. The classifier block classifies arrival packets into *IN* and *OUT* packets and passes these packets to the in-marker block and the bg-marker block respectively. When an *IN* packet is arrived and both token currents of the profile bucket and the bg-bucket are larger than the packet size, the in-marker block reduces the both token currents by packet size and passes out the packet without remarking. Otherwise the packet is passed on to the bg-marker block. The bg-marker checks whether or not the bg-bucket can support the packet size and wether or not the protocol is responsive flows. If both are true, the packet is remarked as *YELLOW* and the bg-bucket's tokens are reduced. Otherwise the packet must be marked with *RED* unconditionally. Note that I-Marker applies the bgTCM scheme to responsive flows, and so the non-responsive flows have only two colored packets.

3. Performance Study

In this section, we analyze the effectiveness of G-Marking scheme using ns-2 simulator. In the previous section, we claimed that G-Marking is composed of the I-Marker and the E-Marker, each playing a different role in the marking scheme. Thus, we qualify the effectiveness of these two components through two experiments and then overall evaluate G-Marking strategy when compared to other marking schemes: Proportional marking, Per Flow marking and Source only marking. Proportional marking is a color blind marking and does not maintain each flow state. Thus, *IN* marking rate of a flow is allocated in proportion to its sending rate. In Per Flow marking, the profile rate is distributed to all flows equally. In Source-only marking, packets are marked by only source node but do not be remarked by edge routers. The Source-only marking was considered for the purpose of comparing inter-domain and intra-domain cases.

3.1 Egress-Marker Test

E-Marker is designed to correct the intra-SLA fairness. Figure 5 depicts the experimental topology used to test the performance of the E-Marker. In this topology, all sources are assumed to be long-lived FTP sources using TCP Reno protocol. Flows originated from sources s1, s2, s3, s4 and s5 pass through domain1 and domain2 sequentially. Thus, these flows should be remarked by the SLA between domain1 and domain2 at the E1. The other flows are used for background traffic and assumed to arrive in the domain2 from different domains, except domain1. All sources have a source-integrated marker assigned its profile rate. Every router uses a RIO as multi-level dropping rule. The RIO parameter is [10/50/0.5, 60/80/0.02]. Flow1, 2, 3, 4 and 5 are routed through different routes in domain2 with different congestion levels and different RTT delays. To limit the investigation to E-Marker in this experiment, the egress node of domain1 conducts three aggregated marking schemes and the ingress nodes of domain2 do not remark arrived packets. We use a fairness index (equation 1) in order to compare simulation results among these aggregated marking schemes.

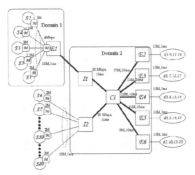

Figure 5. Experimental topology used to study the E-Marker

$$\frac{Max(Th./Src.profile)}{Min(Th./Src.profile)} \qquad (1)$$

where *Th.* and *Src.profile* denote a flow's throughput and source profile rate respectively. This index represents how fairly the excess bandwidth is distributed. The lesser the index value, thus, the greater the fairness among aggregated flows.

We consider two cases simulation where the profile rate of the domain1, x, is considered as 15Mbps and 7.5Mbps respectively. The first is promotion case and the second is demotion case. Figure 6 shows the results of this experiment. The results are denoted by throughputs of flows and deficits of difference between profile rate and throughput. The positive value of the deficit denotes that the flow has throughput over its marking rate. The fairness index values of E-Marker, Proportional Marking, Per-Flow marking, and Source only marking are 3.23, 5.66, 5.01, and 4.37 respectively in the first case. Also, E-Marker has the minimum fairness index value of 3.61 and the Proportional marking has the maximum value of 7.02 in the second case. In this case, source-only marking provides all flows with the most throughputs because the demotion operation is not carried out.

3.2 Ingress-Marker Test

In this experiment, we evaluate the effectiveness of I-Marker for the inter-SLA unfairness. Figure 7 depicts the experimental topology used for this experiment. In this topology, there are 10

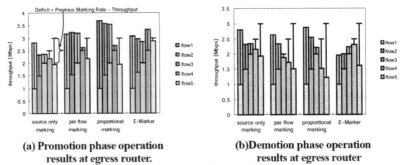

(a) Promotion phase operation results at egress router.	**(b)Demotion phase operation results at egress router**

Figure 6. The result of Egress-Marker Test

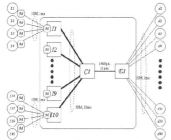

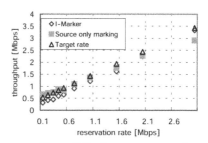

Figure 7. Experimental topology used to study the I-Marker

Figure 8. Performance comparison based on of the throughput

aggregations, each aggregation composed of four flows. All aggregations have its profile rate of 0.4Mbps, 0.8Mbos, 1.2Mbps, 1.6Mbps, 2Mbps, 2.8Mbps, 4Mbps, 6Mbps, 8Mbps and 12Mbps. All sources have a source integrated marker assigned a profile rate of aggregate profile rate / 4. Here, to limit investigation to I-Marker, the ingress nodes of domain conduct the only I-Marker scheme and all flows are assumed to arrive at the ingress node from different domains. In this topology, thus, I-Markers remark arriving packets from different upstream domains. In this experiment, the case using I-Marker is compared with using no ingress marking.

Figure 8 shows the simulation result which depicts the average rates of the aggregated flows. If there is no marking scheme at the ingress node but only source marking, low profile flows have larger throughput than its target rate but high profile flows have much smaller than its target rate. In the I-Marker, however, almost flows have approximated throughputs to the target rate. I-Marker can, therefore, obviously improve the inter-SLA unfairness.

3.3 End-to-End Performance Test via Multiple Domains

In this final experiment, we test overall the proposed G-Marking strategy composed of E-Marker and I-Marker. Figure 9 shows the experimental topology in which there are three DiffServ domains connected sequentially. Two neighborhood domains contract a SLA including the aggregated profile rate for all flows between two domains. All sources connect long-lived FTP connections to corresponding destinations using TCP-Reno protocol. In this simulation, a flow originated from s2 and passes through three domains is closely monitored. The other flows are injected for the purpose of cross traffic. Initially the flow2 from s2 starts at t=1s and then the flows from s1, s3, s6, s7, s4, and s5 start every 50sec sequentially. Thus, the egress marker at E1 always performs the promotion operation but the egress marker at E2 converts the promotion operation into the demotion operation at about 250sec. Figure 10 shows the throughputs of the flow2 in the cases of the four marking schemes. As a result, from these simulation results, we can observe that, compared with other schemes, G-Marking strategy can better provide congested flows with the stable and large throughput to the flow2.

4. Conclusion

In this paper, we proposed an inter-domain marking scheme, named G-Marking, for the assured service that can be applied regardless of DiffServ network model. The G-Marking strategy consists of Ingress marking scheme (I-Marker) and Egress marking scheme (E-Marker) that are carried out in the ingress routers and egress routers respectively. These two markers have different roles for the SLA at the inter-domain interface. E-Marker is responsible for distributing the

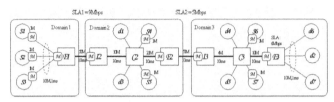

Figure 9. Experimental topology used to study the G-Marker

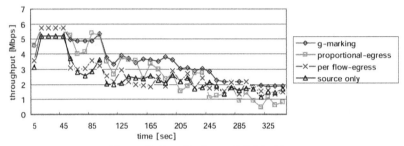

Figure 10. Benefit of overall G-Marking

marking rate fairly to the aggregated flows to improve the intra-SLA unfairness. E-Marker grasps the current states of the flows from the previous *OUT* marking rates of the flows and remarks the flows depending on the states. Several leaky buckets that input trace packet of *OUT* packet is used to model flow states and a token bucket to meter the aggregated traffic. The role of I-Marker is to guarantee the target rate of the SLA under competing with other flows for the excess bandwidth of the bottleneck link. I-Marker is a three-color marking scheme and implemented with two token buckets. In I-Marker, some *OUT* packets marked by the upstream E-Marker are remarked with *YELLOW* by 1/3 profile rate. This rate proportional *YELLOW* marking corrects the inter-SLA unfairness. We have simulated the E-Marker, I-Marker and G-Marking scheme using the ns-2 simulator. Results were compared with other marking schemes. From the simulation results, we have been convinced that G-Marking strategy can improve the two unfairness problem simultaneously and provide fair and stable performance in arbitrary DiffServ network.

5. References

Andrikopoulos, L. and Pavlou, G.(2000), "A fair traffic conditioner for the assured service in a differentiated service Internet", in Proc. IEEE ICC 2000.

Heinanen, J., Baker, F., Weiss, W., and Wroclawski, J.(1999), "Assured Forwarding PHB Group", RFC2597, IETF

Ibanez, J. and Nichols, K.(1998), "Preliminary Simulation Evaluation of an Assured Service", Internet Draft, IETF.

Kim, H.(1999), "A Fair Marker", Internet Draft, IETF.

Reichmeyer, F., Ong, L., Terzis, A., Zhang, L., and Yavatkar, R.(1998), "A two-tier resource management model for differentiated services networks", Internet Draft, IETF.

Rezende, J. F. (1999), "Assured Service Evaluation", in Proc. GLOBECOM'99, pp 100-104.

Seok, S. J., Lee, S. H., Lee, S. J., and Kang, C. H.(2001), "Bandwidth Guarantee Marking for TCP flows", Korea Univ. Technical Report.

Wang, F., Mohapatra, P., and Mukherjee, S.(2000), "A Random Early Demotion and 16. Promotion Marker for Assured Service", *IEEE Journal of Selective Area in Communications*, Vol. 18, No. 12, pp 2640- 2650.

Yeom, I. and Reddy, A. L. N.(1999), "Realizing Throughput Guarantees in a Differentiated Service Network", in Proc. ICMCS'99, pp372-376.

Yeom, I., and Reddy, A. L. N.(1999), "Impact of marking strategy on aggregated flows in a differentiated services network", in Proc. IWQoS'1999.

A QoS Dynamic Bandwidth Partitioning (Q-DBP) Using Fermi-Utility Functions

Chuang-Yueh Chen[1], Sandra I. Woolley[1], Andrew J. Forgham[2], Keith P. Jones[2]

[1]Electronic, Electrical and Computer Engineering, The University of Birmingham, UK
[2]Fujitsu Telecommunications Europe Ltd, Birmingham, UK
[1]e-mail: {C.Y.Chen, S.I.Woolley}@bham.ac.uk
[2]e-mail: {A.Forgham, K.P.Jones}@ftel.co.uk

Abstract

In order to manage network resources, class of service concepts were introduced in the Integrated Service (InServ) and Differentiated Service (DiffServ) architectures. In this paper, we propose a novel throughput-informed metric to quantify end users' perception of QoS in order to provide multi-class services.

To fairly allocate network resources when QoS is introduced, it is believed that pricing policies will be taken into account when defining principles of admission control and resource management. Since charges would be based on the level of received performance, it is important to preserve network resources to guarantee the level of service and satisfy the end users' expectations. Our proposed Fermi-Utility functions build on previous definitions of "Utility" (Breslau and Shenker, 1998; Rakocevic et al., 2001). Fermi-Utility functions are used to model end users' perceptual satisfactions, and are adopted into our definition of class of service. Using the proposed utility functions and definitions of class of service, a QoS Dynamic Bandwidth Partitioning (Q-DBP) algorithm is developed to optimize the total utility value over an end-to-end link.

The simulation result indicates an improved performance of resource management, i.e. metric fairness (Jain, 1991), compared to Rokcevic's algorithm.

Keywords

Resource management, bandwidth allocation, utility function, QoS, Class of Service.

Introduction

The internet currently supports only a Best-Effort (BE) service. However, many new types of multi-media and interactive applications require certain guaranteed minimum bandwidth to guarantee adequate performances. Many approaches have been proposed to prioritize traffic flows in order to avoid congestion, such as Integrated Service (InServ) and Differentiated Service (DiffServ). Both classify traffic flows at the ingress points of their domains, and classified packets then receive treatments based on their class of service specification.

279

In the future, end users will be charged for their usage of network resources in addition to the internet access fee. It is believed that introducing pricing policies will help to manage internet resources in order to attain the level of performance for multi-class services (Cocchi et al., 93; MacKie-Mason and Varian, 1995). Since users will pay based on the level of the received performance, it is very important to ensure maintenance of agreed QoS. We address this problem by using a novel and simple definition of class of service. From an engineering viewpoint, the level of provided service can be expressed by the level of loss, blockage, jitter, delay, and throughput. Alternately, the level of service could be judged subjectively by end users. In economic theories, the level of satisfaction can be represented by *utility* (Nicholson, 1989), which reflects the relative magnitudes of end users' happiness in terms of received service. We use utility functions to predict end users' level of satisfaction, and consequently define the provided class of service. In addition, we also propose a new utility function, the Fermi-Utility function, based on the Fermi-Dirac function (Pierret, 1987) to model stream-adaptive applications.

We also propose a QoS Dynamic Bandwidth Partitioning (Q-DBP) algorithm to optimize total utility over an end-to-end link, and satisfy the profile of each traffic flow. Q-DBP supports multi-class services.

Fermi-Utility Functions

Shenker (Shenker, 1995; Breslau and Shenker, 1998) introduced utility functions to describe QoS in terms of end users' perception. Shenker's papers consider the correlation between users' satisfaction and consumed bandwidth for different applications, and also proposed equations to model their relationships. In Rakocevic's work (Rakocevic et al., 2001), utility functions were adopted from Shenker's work and used to partition link bandwidth between two different types of traffic flows, *elastic* and *stream-adaptive* traffic. Rakocevic's results demonstrate improved utilization performance compared to complete partitioning and trunk reservation. However, the complex computation required to determine utility function parameters means that Rakocevic's approach cannot generate real-time utility functions for different stream-adaptive applications. In addition, Rakocevic's model supports only a single class of service and share bandwidth between two categories of traffic characteristics, elastic and stream-adaptive traffic. Our work builds on Rakocevic's algorithm and introduces support for multi-class services. The goal of our work is to maximize the total utility value. In addition, Fermi-Utility function is introduced to model stream-adaptive applications.

Microsoft has taken QoS issues into account in the design of Windows 2000©, which includes a Generic QoS (GQoS) interface developed to provide efficient information, such as average and peak rate, to describe applications. In addition, the GQoS interface is a means for applications to negotiate service levels with network resource brokers (Hua, 2001). The parameters of Fermi-Utility functions could be determined from the descriptions of traffic flows provided by the GQoS interface without any additional information. This reduces the necessary modifications while Q-DBP algorithm is used as a resource management principle.

In this work, two traffic types, elastic and adaptive-stream, are considered and two utility functions are used to model them. "Utility" values indicate end-users' relative levels of satisfaction, and vary between 0 and 1, where 0 is totally unsatisfied and 1 is completely satisfied. Utility values are calculated by using utility functions $U(bw)$. As shown in Figure 1a, the utility function of elastic traffic flow $U_e(bw)$ proposed by Rakocevic (Rakocevic et al., 2001), given in (1), shows decreasing utility marginal improvement when the consumed bandwidth bw is incrementally increased.

For elastic traffic flows:

$$U_e(bw) = 1 - e^{-\frac{k_e bw}{bw_{peak}}}$$

(1)

where bw_{peak} denotes the peak rate of the elastic traffic flow. Assuming that allocated bandwidth up to peak rates almost completely satisfies end users. Therefore, parameter k_e can be determined by

$$U_e(bw_{peak}) \cong 1$$

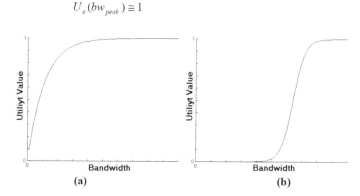

(a) (b)

Figure 1. Utility functions of (a) elastic (Breslau and Shenker, 1998) and (b) stream-adaptive (proposed Fermi-Utility function) application as a function of bandwidth

We propose new Fermi-Utility functions (2) to model stream-adaptive traffic flows, as shown in Figure 1b. At low and high-allocated bandwidths, the marginal utility is very slight while the allocated bandwidth is varied. In contrast, while the allocated bandwidth is around its average rate, the marginal utility is changed significantly.

For stream-adaptive traffic flows:

$$U_s(bw) = \frac{1}{1 + e^{(bw_{avg} - bw)/k_s}}$$

(2)

where bw_{avg} denotes the average rate of the stream-adaptive traffic flow. Again, assuming that allocated bandwidth up to peak rates of applications almost completely satisfies end users. Therefore, parameter k_s can be determined by

$$U_s(bw_{peak}) \cong 1$$

Class of Service

If customers are to pay for the subscripted internet service in addition to access charges, it is very important to evaluate and quantify the usage of internet resource of each class of service. Class of service definitions can be found and used in Integrated Service (InServ) (Wroclawski, 1997a) and Differentiated Service (DiffServ) (Blake et al., 1998).

- InServ supports three different classes of services; Best-Effort, Controlled-load (Wroclawski, 1997b), and Guaranteed (Shenker et al, 1997) services.

- DiffServ also defines three different classes of services; Best-Effort, Assured Forwarding (AF) (Heinanen et al, 1999), and Expedited Forwarding (EF) (Jacobson and Poduri, 1999) services.

The definitions of the classes of service in both InServ and DiffServ are conceptual. In order to realize these ideas into a practical network design, we propose a new definition to quantify QoS by using utility functions. This begins by considering the variation of QoS while the different bandwidth is allocated to an application.

The class of service received by an application is defined with the utility value, u. Utility functions $U(bw)$ express the satisfaction of end users in terms of the received bandwidth bw of their applications. We begin by evaluating performance in terms of allocated bandwidth for each traffic flow. Each class of service is defined with a lower bounded utility value. For example, the lower bound of the utility value for class $m-2$ is C_{m-2}, illustrated in Figure 2. In order to provide a class of service, m, we must guarantee that the traffic flow, either elastic traffic flow e_i or stream-adaptive traffic flow s_j, consumes more than a certain minimum bandwidth $\min(bw_{e_i,m})$ or $\min(bw_{s_j,m})$, respectively.

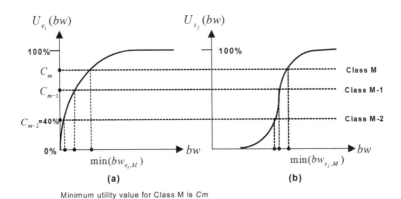

Minimum utility value for Class M is Cm
Minimum bandwidth requirement for Class M are $\min(bw_{e_i,M})$ and $\min(bw_{s_j,M})$

Figure 2. Class of service in terms of utility function of (a) elastic (b) stream-adaptive applications

$$u_{e_i} = U_{e_i}(bw_{e_i,m}) \geq C_m \qquad (3)$$

$$u_{s_j} = U_{s_j}(bw_{s_j,m}) \geq C_m \qquad (4)$$

$$bw_{e_i,m} \geq \min(bw_{e_i,m}) \qquad (5)$$

$$bw_{s_j,m} \geq \min(bw_{s_j,m}) \qquad (6)$$

Where u is the utility value, and $U(bw_{e_i,m})$ is the utility function of the elastic traffic flow e_i, which subscribes to a service of class m.

From the above definitions, an application assigned with a lower class might receive a higher-level quality of service when the link is lightly loaded.

QoS Dynamic Bandwidth Partitioning (Q-DBP) Algorithm

(Shenker, 1995) introduced a new goal of network design to maximize the total utility of architecture, referred as *"efficacy"*, V. In (Rajkumar, 1997), a general resource allocation model is described to maximize the overall system utility.

The goal of our Q-DBP algorithm is to allocate a portion of link bandwidth to each class of traffic flows in order to optimize efficacy, V (7). The aggregated traffic flow of each class contains both elastic and adaptive-stream traffic flows. In our utility model, the utility function of each application has been normalized. In order to reflect the scale of the utility value compared to other applications, a constant R is required. The values of R_e and R_s are equal to the average rates of the elastic and stream-adaptive traffic flows, respectively.

$$V = \sum_{n=1}^{M} \left(\sum_i R_{e_i} U_{e_i}(bw_{e_i,n}) + \sum_j R_{s_j} U_{s_j}(bw_{s_j,n}) \right) \qquad (7)$$

where $R_{e_i} = bw_{e_i,avg}$ and $R_{s_j} = bw_{s_j,avg}$

Link bandwidth BW is divided into M portions, which are assigned to different classes of traffic. The *partitioning parameter* α_n indicates the portion of the link bandwidth for class n.

$$BW = \sum_{n=1}^{M} \left(\sum_i bw_{e_i,n} + \sum_j bw_{s_j,n} \right) = \sum_{n=1}^{M} bw_n \qquad (8)$$

$$bw_n = \alpha_n BW \qquad (9)$$

$$\sum_{n=1}^{M} \alpha_n = 1 \qquad (10)$$

The aggregated traffic flows of class n can consume bandwidth $\alpha_n BW$. In order to determine the utility value gained by each traffic flow, the share of each traffic flow is assumed to be proportional to its average rate in the aggregated traffic flow.

$$bw_{e_i,m} = \frac{R_{e_i,m}}{\sum\limits_{n=1}^{M}(\sum\limits_{i} R_{e_i,n} + \sum\limits_{j} R_{s_j,n})} \alpha_m BW \qquad (11)$$

$$bw_{s_j,m} = \frac{R_{s_j,m}}{\sum\limits_{n=1}^{M}(\sum\limits_{i} R_{e_i,n} + \sum\limits_{j} R_{s_j,n})} \alpha_m BW \qquad (12)$$

By using the above equations and optimizing efficacy, V, partitioning parameters α can be calculated. In addition, an admission control mechanism is included to maintain the promised level of quality of service. A new incoming traffic flow will be accepted if and only if the reserved bandwidth of the class is able to accept this new request when the profiles of the existing traffic flows are still satisfied.

$$if\ (\ \alpha_m BW > \sum_i \min(bw_{e_i,m}) + \sum_j \min(bw_{s_j,m})\ )$$

Accept the new incoming traffic flow

else

Reject the request

Simulation Results

The fairness index is used to measure how fairly bandwidth is allocated in multi-user systems (13) (Jain, 1991). The value of fairness index has a value between 0 and 1, where 0 and 1 represent totally unfair and fair, respectively. If the pricing policy is not introduced, the value of fairness index is 1 when the same amount of bandwidth is allocated to each traffic flow.

$$f(x_1, x_2, ..., x_n) = \frac{(\sum\limits_{i=1}^{n} x_i)^2}{n \sum\limits_{i=1}^{n} x_i^2} \qquad (13)$$

We consider two examples of traffic flows, FTP and MPEG video, as elastic and stream-adaptive applications, respectively. In this case, Q-DBP only supports two classes of services. Each source node is connected to the ingress node of a single link. The link bandwidth is 10Mbps for each link between the source and ingress nodes. Class-Based Queuing (CBQ) is used on the ingress router. Each leaf class of CBQ is configured with the assigned bandwidth of the accepted service request. The maximum available bandwidth for a FTP traffic flow is no more than 10Mbps. The peak and average rates of the MPEG video traffic flow with 640x480 pixels 30 frames/sec are 8.25Mbps and 1.82Mbps (Roberts, 1995), respectively.

The result of the simulation, in Figure 3, shows an improved performance for Q-DBP. When traffic load is closer to the link bandwidth, the advantage of Q-DBP is not significant. However, using Q-DBP to fairly manage the bandwidth is much better then using Rakocevic's algorithm while the traffic load is very low. Mainly, the reason is that Q-DBP prevents traffic flows from accepting too many requests and bandwidth starvation.

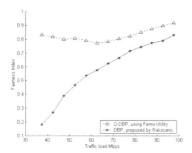

Figure 3. Fairness Indices for Rakocevic's and Q-DBP algorithms

Conclusions

The QoS Dynamic Bandwidth Partitioning algorithm (Q-DBP) is proposed to share bandwidth among incoming traffic flows and guarantee subscripted service profiles. Our algorithm builds on early works (Breslau and Shenker, 1998; Rakocevic et al., 2001) by using utility functions. We propose Fermi-Utility functions to model stream-adaptive applications. Fermi-Utility functions have the advantage of computational simplicity for real-time applications, and simple definition requiring only average and peak rate parameters. They can be more easily used by QoS interface mechanisms.

We introduce a novel definition to quantify and classify provided service from end users' viewpoints by the means of utility functions. By adopting the definition, Q-DBP can be used to realize differentiated service in the Internet.

Our simulation has shown that Q-DBP has an improved performance in terms of fairness. This is because Q-DBP not only partitions bandwidth in terms of traffic characteristics but also their service profile. Admission control over elastic traffic flows is necessary to avoid resource starvation amongst them.

References

Blake, S., Black, D., Carlson, M, Davies, E., Wang, Z., and Weiss, W. (1998), "An Architecture for Differentiated Services", *IETF RFC 2475*.

Breslau, L. and Shenker, S. (1998) "Best-Effort versus Reservations: A Simple Comparative Analysis", *ACM Computer Communication Review*, vol. 28, pp. 3-16.

Cocchi, R., Shenker, S, Estrin, D. and Zhang L. (1993), "Pricing in Computer Networks: Motivation, Formation, and Example", *proceedings in IEEE/ACM Transactions on Networking*, Vol. 1, No. 6, pp. 614-627.

Heinanen, J., Baker, F., Weiss, W., and Wroclawski, J. (1999), "Assured Forwarding PHB Group", *IETF RFC 2597*.

Hua, W (2001) "Winsock 2: QoS API Fine-Tunes Network APP Throughput & Reliability", *Microsoft MSDN Magazine*, Vol. 16, No. 4, http://msdn.microsoft.com/msdnmag

Jacobson, V. and Poduri, K. (1999) "An Expedited Forwarding PHB", *IETF RFC 2598*.

Jain, R (1991), *The Art of Computer Systems Performance Analysis: Techniques for Experimental Design, Measurement, Simulation, and Modeling*, John Wiley & Sons, New York, USA, ISBN 0-471-50336-3.

MacKie-Mason, J. K. and Varian, H. R. (1995), "Pricing the Internet", *Public Access to the Internet*, JFK School of Government, MIT press, pp. 269-314.

Nicholson, W. (1989), *Microeconomic Theory: Basic Principles and Extensions*, The Dryden press, Orlando, Florida, USA, ISBN 0-03-021669-9.

Pierret, R. F. (1987), *Semiconductor Fundamentals,* Addison-Wesley, New York, USA, ISBN 0-201-12295-2.

Rakocevic, V., Griffiths, J. M. and Cope, G. (2001), "Dynamic Partitioning of Link Bandwidth in IP/MPLS Networks", *proceedings in IEEE ICC2001*, vol. 9, pp. 2918-2922.

Rajkumar, R., Lee, C., Lehoczky, J. and Siewiorek, D. (1997), "A Resource Allocation Model for IETF Management", *Proceeding of IETF Real-Time Systems Symposium*.

Roberts, L. G. (1995), "Can ABR Service Replace VBR Service in ATM Networks", proceedings of the COMPON'95 – 40th IEEE International Computer Conference, Vol. 28, No. 5, pp. 346-348.

Shenker, S. (1995) "Fundamental Design Issues for the Future Internet", *IEEE Journal on Selected Area in Communications*, vol. 13, pp. 1176-1188.

Shenker, S., Partridge, C. and Guerin, R. (1997), "Specification of Guaranteed Quality of Service", *IETF RFC 2212*.

Wroclawski, J. (1997a), "The Use of IETF with IETF Integrated Service", *IETF RFC 2210*.

Wroclawski, J. (1997b), "Specification of the Controlled-load Network Element Service", *IETF RFC 2211*.

A Comparative Study of Explicit Congestion Notification Mechanism Effects in the Service Level of Differentiated Services Networks

Eliane Aureliana de Sousa Borges, Paulo Roberto Guardieiro

Faculty of Electrical Engineering, Federal University of Uberlândia, Brazil
E-mails: esousa@marbo.com.br, prguardieiro@ufu.br

Abstract

This article evaluates the effects of Explicit Congestion Notification (ECN) usage in the service level offered by Differentiated Services Networks (DiffServ). The main aspects that have been studied were: link efficiency, fairness of bandwidth sharing and discard, timeout and retransmission rates. The simulations study a wide range of provisioning scenarios for a varying number of active flows, not only for the proposed model, but also for the traditional one. The obtained results are compared in order to identify the solution that offers better performance and QoS. This comparative study permits understanding better the benefits of the combination of the two analyzed techniques. The simulations indicate that the use o ECN optimizes DiffServ performance for a great variety of scenarios. In particular, when the network is correctly dimensioned, the use of ECN, not only provides performance benefits, but also optimizes the excess bandwidth sharing, guaranteeing better distribution of available resources between the traffic sources. These characteristics are particularly evidenced when the total reserved bandwidth approaches the total link capacity.

Keywords

Internet, QoS, Traffic Management, DiffServ, ECN.

1 Introduction

With the rapid transformation of the Internet into a commercial network, and the dissemination of e-business, voice and multimedia applications, there has been an immense demand for mechanisms that can provide Quality of Service (QoS) in TCP/IP networks. Service differentiation and traffic management, which are considered key elements of quality of service, are the object of study of the work presented here. The evaluated technologies are: the Differentiated Services (DiffServ) architecture and the Explicit Congestion Notification (ECN) mechanism, both developed by IETF aiming to adapt the TCP/IP model currently utilized and optimize its performance.

The Differentiated Services (Blake *et al*, 1998) model has been playing an important role, standing out among current technologies that aim to improve QoS. In this architecture, packets are marked differently, and handled by the network according to this mark. This marking scheme creates a range of differentiated classes that allows traffic from different flows, having similar QoS requirements, to be mapped to the same service class. In addition to Best Effort (BE), where network resources are shared by applications with no service guarantees, the Assured Forwarding (AF) and Expedited Forwarding (EF) services classes were defined. These new classes require that a Service Level Agreement (SLA) be established between traffic sources and the network or between adjacent DiffServ domains. This agreement specifies the amount of traffic allowed to sources. While traffic is conformant with this contracted rate the packets are marked as in-profile (IN), when it exceeds this reserved bandwidth they are market as out-of-profile (OUT). The OUT packets have higher discard probability in the occurrence of congestion. When packets are dropped, the data flow control mechanisms implemented by TCP/IP (Postel, 1981) are triggered, and sources reduce their load. Thus, sources that are exceeding their target rate will be the first to reduce their rates, adapting to the SLA.

The Explicit Congestion Notification mechanism, proposed in (Floyd, 1994) and (Ramakrishnan et al, 2001), is a more efficient method of congestion signaling, that decouples TCP/IP traffic management from packet dropping. This mechanism provides a method for routers to convey direct feedback information of congestion to sources, allowing them to decrease their rates before packets actually need to be discarded. This strategy reduces packet losses and diminishes its negative effects. The implementation of ECN is achieved through the use of active queue management techniques, like Random Early Detection (RED) (Floyd and Jacobson, 1993) or Random Early Detection with IN/OUT (RIO) (Clark and Fang, 1998), which detect network congestion before the queue overflows, and are able to set a mark in the packet header indicating the imminence of congestion.

The organization of the rest of this article is as follows: Section 2 shows the problem statement and the motivation of this study. Section 3 presents the simulation model and it's parameters. The utilized metrics are shown in Section 4. Section 5 is dedicated to presenting and analyzing simulation results. Finally, Section 6 summarizes and concludes the article.

2 Motivation and Problem Statement

Although service differentiation provides the ability to transport heterogeneous services, it still relies on TCP/IP flow control techniques, and does not propose any mechanisms for improving traffic management. As the flow control algorithms utilized by TCP/IP are based on dropping packets, it increases the delays and does not achieve optimal performance, not being appropriate to the present scenario. Besides that, links with large delay-bandwidth are continually being deployed. In this new environment, the discard of packets is even more undesirable, as it wastes a great deal of bandwidth because of the time necessary for detecting and reacting to the losses. When the DiffServ architecture is deployed, the need for mechanisms that optimize its traffic management will be apparent. The Explicit Congestion Notification mechanism – recently approved by IESG as a proposed standard – is a promising technology, which can be utilized to improve DiffServ efficiency, providing higher levels of QoS that can better attend application needs. This approach focuses on traffic management, which is an important issue for achieving efficient deployment of QoS based solutions.

3 Simulation Model

The simulation model is presented in Figure 1. This topology consists of N traffic sources that send data through the link between routers R1 and R2 using the same AF traffic class. The traffic is unidirectional, that is, only the sources send data, the destinations send only acknowledgments.

The simulation parameters were defined according to the following patterns: a) all TCP sources are identical, implement the Reno flow control algorithm, and continuously send data, as long as it is allowed by the TCP window; b) to minimize the risk of synchronization, sources start at distinct intervals, delayed from each other by 5 s of simulation; c) all sources have the same contracted rate defined in their SLAs; d) the contracts were defined so that the total reserved bandwidth, which is the sum of all contracted rates, varies from 40% to 120% of the total link capacity; e) the RIO parameters were defined as: min_in = 12, max_in = 25, Pmax_in = 0,1 e min_out = 6, max_out = 12, Pmax_out = 0,1. Parameters that were not defined in this section are maintained in conformity with the patterns utilized by the network simulator NS version 2.1b5 and the DiffServ package for ns-2 (Murphy,1999).

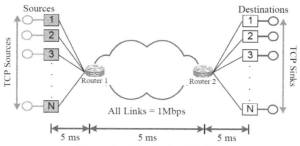

Figure 1. – Simulation Model.

4 Metrics

The main aspects that have been studied were: a) the service level achieved by sources; b) the total link efficiency; c) the fairness of bandwidth sharing; d) the packet discard rates and e) the *timeouts* and retransmissions rates. These metrics are defined below.

The service level SL_i, achieved by sources i, is calculated through the ratio between the throughput achieved by source i and it's actual reserved SLA. These parameters are represented in (1) by x_i and SLA_i.

$$SL_i = x_i / SLA_i \tag{1}$$

The link efficiency E, is defined in equation (2) where N is the number of active sources, x_i is the throughput achieved by source i and C is the total link capacity.

$$E = (\sum_{i=1}^{N} x_i) / C \tag{2}$$

The fairness of bandwidth sharing F is defined in (3) where, for the under and over provisioned scenarios, x_i corresponds to the difference between the throughput achieved by source i and it's reserved SLA. However, if the total reserved bandwidth is equivalent to the link capacity, x_i is equivalent to the throughput achieved by source i.

$$F = (\sum_{i=1}^{N} x_i)^2 / N \times (\sum_{i=1}^{N} x_i^2) \tag{3}$$

The AF, IN and OUT discard rates are respectively defined by equations (4), (5) and (6), where $AF_{dropped}$, $IN_{dropped}$ and $OUT_{dropped}$ correspond to the number of packets discarded and $AF_{arrived}$, $IN_{arrived}$ and $OUT_{arrived}$ are the number of packets that arrived to the router.

$$AF_{DR} = \frac{AF_{dropped}}{AF_{arrived}}$$

(4)

$$IN_{DR} = \frac{IN_{dropped}}{IN_{arrived}}$$

(5)

$$OUT_{DR} = \frac{OUT_{dropped}}{OUT_{arrived}}$$

(6)

5 Simulation Results

This section will present the simulation results. First, issues related to an over provisioned scenario, where the total contracted bandwidth is inferior to the link capacity, are going to be addressed. Then, the opposed situation is presented, and the total contracted bandwidth will exceed link capacity. Finally, to guarantee scalability and generality of results, the study is extended to a wide range of provisioning conditions and a varying number of active flows.

5.1 Over Provisioned Network

The simulations presented here evaluate the impact of using ECN in the performance of DiffServ networks in a scenario where the total contracted bandwidth only represents 40% of the total link capacity. A total of 10 traffic sources were used, and the target rate allocated to each source in their SLA is equal to 40 kbps. Table I presents the service level obtained by each source, the total link efficiency and the total fairness of excess bandwidth sharing on the last 40 s of simulation.

TABLE I – SERVICE LEVEL IN AN OVER PROVISIONED NETWORK

SLA (kbps)	Over Provisioned Network		Protocol Type		
	SLA Percentage Achieved			Throughput Achieved (kbps)	
	No ECN	ECN		No ECN	ECN
40	305%	252%	TCP	122	101
40	232%	252%	TCP	93	101
40	227%	255%	TCP	91	102
40	290%	250%	TCP	116	100
40	197%	247%	TCP	79	99
40	220%	257%	TCP	88	103
40	247%	245%	TCP	99	98
40	225%	242%	TCP	90	97
40	292%	220%	TCP	117	88
40	220%	267%	TCP	88	107
Efficiency	98%	100%		983	996
Fairness	94%	99%		94%	99%

Observing the presented results, it can be verified that despite the utilization or not of the ECN mechanism, all the sources have achieved the contracted SLA, and also have been able to obtain part of the exceeding bandwidth. These results demonstrate that DiffServ mechanisms are efficient, independently of the usage or not of ECN. However, it can also be seen that the use of ECN guaranteed better link utilization, improving the throughput of the majority of sources. Although this improvement does not have a high significance in terms of percentage, only 4%, it represents a gain of 20 kbps, which can be very important when considering the high monthly costs of long distance links.

The percentage of packet losses is another important factor to be analyzed. Table II shows the results of the main loss indicator parameters. The analysis of this table shows that the ECN mechanism was effective in minimizing packet losses, significantly reducing the discard, timeout and retransmission rates. This occurs because, when ECN is used, all unnecessary discards are avoided, and the starting of congestion management mechanisms is decoupled from the TCP timer, leading to a reduction in retransmissions and providing faster reaction to congestion situations. This behavior is more adequate to delay sensitive applications, which are continuously increasing their traffic volumes within the networks.

TABLE II - PERCENTAGE OF LOSSES IN AN OVER PROVISIONED NETWORK

	Over Provisioned Network	
	No ECN	ECN
AF Discard Rates	6,7%	< 0,1%
IN Discard Rates	< 0,1%	< 0,1%
OUT Discard Rates	8,5%	< 0,1%
Timeout Rates	1,6%	< 0,1%
Retransmission Rates	8,3%	< 0,1%

5.2 Under Provisioned Network

The simulations presented so far have shown the impact of ECN in the performance of DiffServ networks that were correctly dimensioned. Now we are going to present the results obtained in a situation where the total bandwidth contracted in the SLAs is superior to the link capacity. As in the previous scenario, the simulations have also used 10 traffic sources, although this time, each traffic source has 120 kbps of guaranteed bandwidth. This represents a total reservation of 120% of the link capacity. Table II presents the results of the last 40 s of simulation.

TABLE III - SERVICE LEVEL IN AN UNDER PROVISIONED NETWORK.

SLA (kbps)	Under Provisioned Network		Protocol Type		
	SLA Percentage Achieved			Throughput Achieved (kbps)	
	No ECN	ECN		No ECN	ECN
120	85%	94%	TCP	103	113
120	83%	70%	TCP	100	84
120	82%	74%	TCP	99	89
120	79%	74%	TCP	95	89
120	75%	95%	TCP	91	115
120	84%	81%	TCP	101	98
120	81%	83%	TCP	98	100
120	72%	88%	TCP	87	106
120	81%	80%	TCP	98	96
120	79%	87%	TCP	95	105
Efficiency	97%	100%		967	995
Fairness	96%	81%		96%	81%

The results show that none of the sources achieved the contracted SLA. This behavior was expected, once the total reserved bandwidth is superior to the link capacity. The analysis of the sources service level rates indicates that the performance degradation was homogeneous, demonstrating that the simulations achieved fairness on the sharing of the available bandwidth. This occurred for both simulations, and can be verified by the high indexes of fairness, achieved in spite of using or not ECN. It is important to emphasize that, although the simulation that implemented ECN achieved a smaller fairness index, it had guaranteed a better link utilization, and ended up offering a better overall throughput.

TABLE IV – PERCENTAGE OF LOSSES IN AN UNDER PROVISIONED NETWORK

	Under Provisioned Network	
	No ECN	ECN
AF Discard Rates	6,3%	< 0,1%
IN Discard Rates	0,5%	< 0,1%
OUT Discard Rates	22%	< 0,1%
Timeout Rates	2,2%	< 0,1%
Retransmission Rates	8,5%	< 0,1%

The examination of the loss indicators parameters, presented in Table IV, shows that, as in the over provisioned scenario, the utilization of ECN mechanism contributes to minimizing losses, reducing the discard, timeouts and retransmissions rates. This loss reduction guarantees all the benefits mentioned in the previous section, providing a behavior that is more adequate to the type of applications that are currently being disseminated.

5.3 Impact of Total Reserved Bandwidth

The objective of this simulation is to extend the results achieved in the simulations already performed to a wide range of provisioning conditions within the network. The percentage of contracted bandwidth was varied from 20% to 140%. The obtained results are presented by the graphs in Figures 2, 3 and 4, which will be analyzed next.

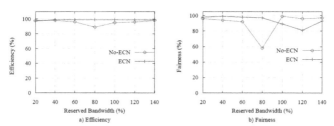

Figure 2 - Impact of Total Reserved Bandwidth in ECN Effects on the Efficiency and Fairness of Simulations.

The graphs presented in Figure 2 show the link efficiency and the fairness of bandwidth sharing achieved by each implemented simulation. The analysis of graph a) indicates that ECN usage guarantees a better utilization of resources, in spite of the network provisioning level. Graph b) shows that, when the network is correctly dimensioned, ECN usage results in higher levels of fairness, providing a better sharing of the available resources. However, when the network is under provisioned, this result is reversed.

Both graphs show that ECN benefits are highly evidenced when the total contracted bandwidth approaches, but does not reach, the total link capacity. This happens because, in this situation, the sources competition for the excess bandwidth is intensified. As ECN does not need to incur to discards to manage the competition, it can better control it, leading to a more stable behavior of sources which provides better performance levels.

Although the loss indicators parameters are not being presented here, the simulations have also demonstrated that the discard, timeout and retransmission rates of ECN sources were almost null, even when the contracted bandwidth exceeded the total link capacity, proving the effectiveness of ECN.

5.4 Impact of Number of Active Flows

The simulations presented in this section are intended to guarantee the scalability of results presented earlier. Different quantities of active sources were utilized, in simulations scenarios that represent two provisioning situations: one where the total contracted bandwidth corresponds to 40% of the link capacity, and other where the contracted percentage is of 120%, exceeding the total available bandwidth.

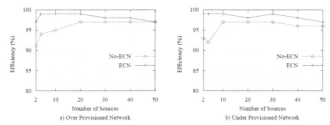

Figure 3 – The Impact of Number of Active Flows in the Link Efficiency Improvement Provided by ECN use for two Different Provisioning Scenarios.

Graphs in Figure 3 illustrate the link efficiency, both to the over provisioned and to the under provisioned scenarios. These graphs indicate that the ECN usage provided better performance, offering higher levels of efficiency for all the simulated quantities of active flows, independently of the network provisioning level.

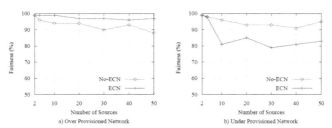

Figure 4 - The Impact of Number of Active Flows in the Fairness of Bandwidth Sharing Provided by ECN use for two Different Provisioning Scenarios.

A comparison between the fairness of bandwidth sharing, provided with and without the usage of ECN, can be observed in Figure 4. The presented graphs validate the results previously obtained, showing a better performance of ECN in the scenario where the network is correctly dimensioned. In this scenario, the increase in the number of sources degrades fairness of no ECN simulations in a more aggressive way than it degrades simulations that do use this mechanism. However, in the under provisioned scenario, the fairness index that is more aggressively degraded, is the one of the simulations that did utilize ECN.

The results presented in this section validate previous sections, and demonstrate that the performance benefits resulting from ECN usage are maintained, independently of the number of active sources.

6 Conclusion

This article implemented simulations with the objective of evaluating the proposal of utilizing Explicit Congestion Notification (ECN) mechanism to optimize the service level provided by Differentiated Services (DiffServ) networks. The obtained results demonstrate that the following benefits were achieved by the proposed model: a) increase in link efficiency for all the provisioning scenarios evaluated, in spite of the number of active flows; b) better distribution of excess bandwidth for correctly dimensioned networks and for the wide range of active flows analyzed; c) control of discards, resulting in reduced packet timeout and retransmission rates, which avoids unnecessary processing, prevents waste of bandwidth and diminishes queue occupation, reducing the delay and jitter of packets. These results lead to the conclusion that ECN mechanism provides performance benefits to the DiffServ architecture, thus making it possible for this mechanism to be used for improving QoS level of this model.

7 References

Blake, S., Black, D., Carlson, M., Davies, E., Wang, Z. and Weiss, W. (1998) *"An Architecture for Differentiated Services"*, IETF, RFC 2475.

Postel, J. B. (1981), *"Transmission Control Protocol – Darpa Internet Program Protocol Specification"*, RFC 793, University of Southern California / Information Sciences Institute.

Postel, J. B. (1981), *"Internet Protocol – Darpa Internet Program Protocol Specification"*, RFC 791, University of Southern California / Information Sciences Institute, September, 1981.

Floyd, S. (1994), *"TCP and Explicit Congestion Notification"*, ACM Computer Communication Review, V.24 N.5, pp 10-23.

Ramakrishnan, K., Floyd, S., Black, D. (2001), *"The Addition of Explicit Congestion Notification (ECN) to IP"*, IETF, RFC 3168.

Floyd, S., and Jacobson, V. (1993), *"Random Early Detection gateways for Congestion Avoidance"*, IEEE/ACM Transactions on Networking, V.1, N.4, pp. 397-413.

Clark, D. and Fang, W. (1998) *"Explicit Allocation of Best Effort Packet Delivery Service"*, http://diffserv.lcs.mit. edu/exp-alloc-ddc-wf.ps, 1998.

Murphy, S. (1999), *"Diffserv package for ns-2"*, http://www.teltec.dcu.ie/murphys/ns-work/diffserv/index.html.

An Approach for QoS Measurements in IP Multicast Networks
MQM - Multicast Quality Monitor

Falko Dressler

University of Erlangen-Nuremberg, Germany
email: falko.dressler@rrze.uni-erlangen.de / fd@acm.org

Abstract

MQM - Multicast Quality Monitor represents a new approach to measure QoS within an IP multicast environment. Existing tools stop at measuring some packet loss ratio or some reachability by producing there own low-rate measurement data streams. History has shown that there are a lot of interesting parameters to measure some multimedia transmissions such as one-way-delay, round-trip-time, packet-loss-ratio and others. Also, in a multicast environment, existing tools built for unicast measurements fail because of the very different communication model. The MQM tries to fill this gap by introducing methods as well as tools for reliability and QoS measurements.

In discussion are the most common problems such as the measurement of delays requires synchronized clocks and, much more important in the multicast environment, the scaling problem. Having a large number of measurement probes distributed over the network communicating to each other and measuring various QoS values using IP multicast results in some kind of flooding and overloading the network. Shown are approaches to minimize this effect as well as to examine really required parts of the network only.

Having in mind the reason for all the tests, the applications or services, also included is a short presentation of a model for multicast networks as well as the used services which builds a very basis for the measurements.

Keywords

IP Multicast, Quality of Service, IP Performance Measurements, Network Modeling

1. Introduction

In the last years, there have been different approaches to ensure a more reliable IP multicast network. Some are intended to check the reachability of different hosts and routers via IP multicast, some are going a little further. They try to measure the Quality of Service (QoS) of the IP multicast network as well.

The most interesting approach is the Multicast Reachability Monitor (MRM), formerly known as Multicast Route Monitor (Almeroth et al, 2001). The here presented Multicast Quality Monitor (MQM) is based on the ideas of the MRM. There are implementations of the MRM for Cisco IOS (ftp://ftpeng.cisco.com/ipmulticast/#MRM) and Sun Solaris (http://steamboat.cs.ucsb.edu/mrm/). An other implementation of a multicast quality monitor is the multicast beacon (http://dast.nlanr.net/projects/beacon/).

The MQM introduces different ways to measure the reliability (chapter 2) and the quality (chapter 3) of a IP multicast network. Very different from the MRM is the inter-probe communication (chapter 4). Based on these ideas, it became possible to do some measurement. But where to measure? Additionally, information is required to place every part of the measurement system properly within the network. This question should be discussed by presenting a model (chapter 6) for a whole IP multicast system.

2. Reliability measurement

For IP Unicast users as well as for management stations ICMP messages (Postel, 1981) are used to prove the connectivity of different IP end systems. Unfortunately there is no such tool for IP multicast connections. The MRM tries to solve this problem by defining a set of Test Senders (TS) and Test Receivers (TR). The TS send a (low bandwidth) stream of packets to a specified multicast group. The TR receive these packets and inform a central Management Station (MS) about these received packets. Basically, the MQM works like that. The MQM also uses - properly placed - probes which send MQM ping requests and act on incoming requests by replying with a MQM ping response.

Due to the principles of IP multicast, it is required to ping everyone from everywhere since it is not possible to use the information of A reaches B and C and, on the other hand, B and C both reach A via IP multicast to provide any information about the connection between B and C (this is true for IP unicast as well, but in IP multicast everyone gets each response but cannot detect the state of the network using these messages). A next version of the MQM may include a more intelligent system to prevent the transmission of additional pings if not required.

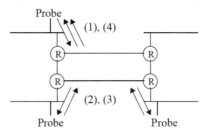

Figure 1: MQM ping mechanism

The MQM ping mechanism is shown in figure 1. For a single test, the probe sends a MQM ping request packet (1) to all the others to a well known multicast address. Other probes receive this request (2) and respond (3) back to the originator by sending a MQM ping response which is received (4) by the requesting probe. Each probe is required to send about 1 packet a minute to a well known MQM_PING IP multicast group. Lower rates do not refresh the states in the routers and result in indeterministic results. Higher rates are not required but increase the network congestion. To get more information about the state of the network, the use of unicast pings is required as well, either if there are failures in IP multicast connectivity or together with the IP multicast pings. For now, only the probes are able to do some reliability measurement of the IP multicast network. There are a few ideas how to summarize the information on a central point shown in chapter 4, MQM communication.

3. QoS measurement

The first step for QoS measurements of IP multicast networks is to define the term QoS in relationship to the multicast services and the multicast network. The most typical IP multicast applications are multimedia communications. Such real-time services depend on the current packet loss ratio, the absolute delay and the variation of the delay, the jitter. Most of these applications do use Real-time Transport Protocol (RTP) (Schulzrinne et al, 1996) as the transport protocol. This protocol already offers nearly all the information to measure the QoS of the network as it implements sequence numbers and time stamps into each packet. So RTP has been selected for the most QoS measurements.

3.1 Delay (one-way and round-trip)

The only measurement done by the MQM which is not based on RTP, is the delay. According to the research work of the IP Performance Metrics WG (IPPM) of the Internet Engineering Task Force (IETF), the most important information for real-time services is the one-way delay. The MQM introduces its own ping mechanism to measure both, the one-way delay (based on the work of the IPPM WG) in each direction and the round-trip time. Due to possible synchronization failures of the clocks of different probes, the correctness of the one-way delay may vary. This problem has been discussed at the IETF. The result was to make use of GPS clocks at each measurement probe. Nevertheless it should be possible to work with NTP synchronized clocks because most applications for which the tests are done do not depend on delays lower than 1 ms. Also GPS equipped probes would be very expensive.

The measurement of the delay is based on the reliability measurements. The same ping messages are used to calculate the one-way delay in both directions and the round-trip time. To ensure, that the ping response message belongs to the ping request sent from a particular probe (please note, every probe gets every ping message because they are multicasted through the network), the IP address of the requesting probe is included in both messages, the ping request as well as the ping response (see also chapter 6).

3.2 Packet loss and jitter

To measure packet loss and jitter, MQM makes use of RTP streams. There are two ways to do this: passive and active. Passive measurement means that the probes join an existing multicast session and decode the information of the received RTP packets. This procedure has no impact on the network but it is only useful if information about current sessions, active senders and their location is available. In the active way, the probes simulate typical transmissions with at least a little impact on the network. Simulating high bandwidth video transmissions may disturb other active IP connections (unicast and multicast) and raise the network congestion.

Using the model shown in chapter 6, it is possible to identify the parts of a particular network which are responsible for the most critical IP multicast applications. Based on these information, the probes can be placed properly within the network. It is necessary to distinguish between the two most important types of IP multicast communication: a broadcast from a single server (one-to-many communication model) and a conference between several end systems (many-to-many communication model).

A typical example of a broadcasting station is a video server (http://www.uni-tv.net). Such video broadcasts have some common properties. So they stream data mostly all the time at high data rates. If there are such services located in the network of interest, it would be a good idea to use this RTP stream to measure the packet loss ratio as well as the jitter. All the measurements are passive which means they do not affect the network if the probes are placed on the way of an active data transmission through the network. Figure 2 shows a typical situation. There is one sender which broadcasts a session to some receivers. If the probes are placed properly on the network, usually near the receivers, maybe somewhere in the path, it became possible to measure the current QoS without any impact on the network itself.

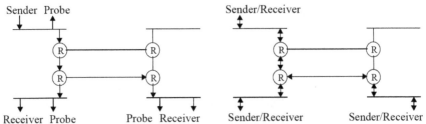

Figure 2: Passive QoS measurement   **Figure 3: A typical conference**

Most conferences are based on the following ideas: they last only for a short time, they are announced (start at well known times) and the location of the members is almost known but is expected to vary for different conferences. The idea is, to provide information about the current quality of the IP multicast network to all participants of a upcoming / running session. To allow this, it is required to configure all probes in involved parts of the network to simulate typical conference applications by sending simulated RTP streams. So all the probes do receive just the same traffic like if the real conference would be already active. So it is possible to simulate the traffic of a meeting and measure the QoS of the IP multicast network which allows to compute the expected QoS for the upcoming conference. In figure 3 an IP multicast network is shown which has been used by a typical conference. There is a number of participants. Everyone is sending and receiving traffic. Based on the knowledge about the network and the placement of the systems, it is possible to simulate this type of conference by configuring some intelligent probes to produce some simulated traffic and to receive and analyze it (see also figure 4). As well, the same configuration can be used to monitor a running conference.

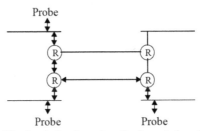

Probe

Probe   Probe
Figure 4: Active traffic simulation based on the knowledge about the conference

4. Inter-probe communication

The last two chapters have shown how to use intelligent probes to measure the reliability and the QoS of an IP multicast network. Not yet mentioned is the inter-probe communication. There are three different types of such communication:

4.1 Detecting new probes

The design of the MQM is based on the knowledge of the structure of the network and the used services. So the starting configuration will include some known probes. To provide a more flexible system, it should be possible to include more probes dynamically. The appearance of a new probe can be detected by listening to the MQM_PING multicast group. All the probes are required to periodically send ping requests to measure the reliability. The management station can join this group to detect new probes.

4.2 Starting the simulation of a RTP stream / starting analyzing a RTP stream

This is done using the same beacon mechanism as defined in MRM. The central management station can start and stop the QoS measurement via a beacon message sent to the same well known IP multicast group which is also used for the MQM_PING messages. Within this message, the manager tells the probes which RTP stream to analyze and, if required, which probe should simulate which type of traffic. Due to the use of the unreliable transport protocol UDP (Postel, 1980) for these beacon messages, they cover a maximum time to live (hold time) and the management station should send these beacon messages periodically.

4.3 Transferring the measured data to a central management station

All the described mechanisms allow the intelligent probes to measure the reliability and the QoS of an IP multicast network, partially controlled by a central manager. The idea of MQM is to let the probes save all these information locally. The transfer of these information to the management station should be done on a periodical base using the TCP protocol. The protocol ensures the reliable transport of the measured data. Not yet defined is who is required to start this transfer, the probes or the management station. Since it should be allowed to a user to force the presentation of the current situation of the network, the management station should be able to initiate this transfer. So, the current version of MQM is focused on the management station to control nearly everything, the QoS measurement (RTP analysis) and the transfer of the measured data from the probes.

5. Message format

The message format of the MQM uses the same principles as the MRM does. For the inter-probe communication, a separate header (MQM header) has been defined. Also, the beacon messages from the management station to the probes uses the MQM header. Table 1 shows the major MQM header format. Table 2 and 3 define header extensions for different MQM packet types. All values within the tables are in Byte.

Pos	Size	content
0	1	version
1	1	padding
2	2	type

Table 1: MQM Header format

Pos	Size	content
0	4	MQM header
4	4	IP address from the originator
8	4	timestamp sender
12	4	timestamp receiver

Table 2: MQM ping message format

Pos	Size	content
0	4	MQM header
4	2	hold time
6	2	message length
8	4	target probe address 1
12	4	multicast group address 1 (1st bit is used to specify if to receive or to transmit to this group)
...	4	target probe address n
...	4	multicast group address n

Table 3: MQM beacon message format

Currently, there are only three packet types: MQM_PING, MQM_PONG and MQM_BEACON. Since the transport of the measured data is an out-of-band mechanism which uses TCP for the communication, there is no MQM packet type for reporting messages. The MQM header is part of every MQM message. The encoding of the rest of the packet depends on the type value in the header. Not shown in the tables is some kind of example. The packet format has been included just to provide a more detailed view on the ideas of the MQM.

6. A model for IP multicast services

As shown in the previous chapters, it is very difficult to find proper places to deploy measurement probes and to use the computed results to provide better reliability and quality to these services.

6.1 Modeling IP multicast networks and services

One idea to solve this problem is to generate a model of the network including the overlying services. This chapter should give an overview to such a model (Dressler, 2001). The model should be able to include important functions from OSI Layer 1/2 (Physical and Link), Layer 3 (Network) and Layer 7 (Application, the services). The primary result of such a model is to find out which parts of a network are required for a particular service. This can be done by attaching various routing algorithms.

The basic objects for the model of the network are shown in figure 5. Based on these objects, it is possible to generate models of complex networks and to calculate a best route through the network. The current implementation includes the Dijkstra algorithm for route calculations. The objects are extensible to include parameters such as CPU load, bandwidth of an interface or a loss ratio of a link allowing a recalculation of the routes through the network based on more exactly information about the network.

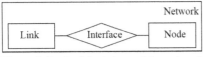

Figure 5: Basic objects to model a network

Figure 6: Example of service objects

Besides the model of the network, the representations for the services have to be modeled. Each object of class service stands for one multicast transmission which may use more than one multicast group (figure 6). Based on the concept of analyzing the most important services within the network first and using these information together with a detailed model of the underlying IP multicast network allows to extract the involved parts of the network.

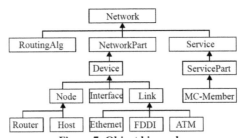

Figure 7: Object hierarchy

Summarizing the already presented objects and their capabilities, figure 7 shows the class diagram which has been used to implement the model in JAVA. This implementation called MRT (Multicast Routing Tool) has been done by Juan Ceballos-Mejia at the University of Erlangen-Nuremberg (Ceballos-Mejia, 2000) as a part of his masters thesis.

6.2 Using the model for measurements

In the last chapters an overview of a method to model an IP multicast network including the network itself, the applications / services and the participating hosts has been presented. Also, some real measurement tools have been introduced. The final question is 'How do I use this model to measure reliability and quality of IP multicast services?'.

The current implementation allows to model a network and check for optimum paths for IP multicast transmissions using the attached routing algorithm. To find the best way, the algorithm uses the constants out of the modeled objects such as bandwidth of a particular interface or the hop count. The following figures 8 and 9 show the mechanism. Using the information about the network and the service one can find out which parts of the network are used for this service.

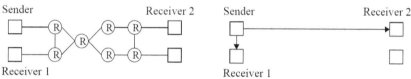

Figure 8: physical network   **Figure 9: logical data flow**

After all, this is only a first step to find all the required parts of the network for a particular service. Our implementation allows already to incorporate dynamic information about the current state of the network. The most interesting values are the state of a node, the state of an interface, the packet loss ratio from an interface and the load of a node. Also, the routing tables of the routers (IP unicast and IP multicast) have to be examined to get closer to the real behavior of the IP network. Based on these dynamic data and the knowledge about the network, the tool allows to find the used components and paths for the current situation and a particular service (figure 10). The current implementation includes an open interface to retrieve dynamic data. This includes also values such as the CPU load mentioned in chapter 6.1.

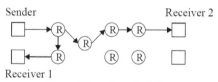

Figure 10: real packet flow

Describing the complete IP multicast network including the most critical services in this model, it is possible to use the attached routing algorithm to find proper places to implement the intelligent probes and to deploy the MQM measurements. The same model can also be used for offline analyzing of the used paths for the services and for offline simulation of the behavior of the network.

7. Summary

To summarize the introduction to MQM the most important common grounds and differences between MRM and MQM should be compared. This includes also some a summary of the functions of the MQM.

7.1 Common practices

Both, the MRM and the MQM use distributed probes (TRs and TSs). This allows to measure just these parts of an IP multicast network which are between these probes. Also, both tools are designed to measure some important QoS values like packet loss or the jitter by analyzing RTP streams.

7.2 Major differences

The first major difference is that the MQM design distinguishes between the test of functionality (reliability) and the measurement of the QoS of an IP multicast network. The first one is done without any involved central intelligence. This is very important because if there is a problem with parts of the network, the MRM is only able to detect the border of the problem but cannot look behind. With the MQM model, it is possible to check the function also behind the problem. Also, the measurement of the reliability of the MQM is done with only a very low impact on the network. Depending on the type of the IP multicast services, the additional congestion of the network may be very small if there are some broadcast services which can be used for the QoS measurement.

A real enhancement to the MRM is also the measurement of the one-way delay as a basis for real-time services. Another difference is the out-of-band transfer of the results of the tests. MRM uses the same mechanism to report to the management station as for all other communication between the MS and the TRs and TSs. So the probes became more intelligent and may act basically without any central supervision. The primary idea of the MQM is to measure the QoS depending to the services (applications) in the network. Using the model (Dressler, 2001), the deployment of the measurement probes became possible based on the requirements of a particular network. The model is not restricted for a local use only. It is designed to support distributed services as well. The same applies to the MQM.

8. References

K. Almeroth, L. Wei, D. Farinacci (2001), *"Multicast reachability monitor (MRM)"*, IETF draft.

J.-F. Ceballos-Mejia (2000), *"Design and implementation of a modeling tool for multicast networks"*, Master-Thesis, University of Erlangen-Nuremberg.

Falko Dressler (2001), "How to Measure Reliability and Quality of IP Multicast Services?", *Proceedings to 2001 IEEE Pacific Rim Conference on Communications, Computers and Signal Processing*, PACRIM'01, Victoria, B.C., Canada.

Falko Dressler (2002), "QoS considerations on IP multicast services", *Proceedings to International Conference on Advances in Infrastructure for Electronic Business, Education, Science, and Medicine on the Internet*, SSGRR 2002w, L'Aquila, Italy.

J. Postel (1981), *"Internet control message protocol"*, RFC 792.

J. Postel (1980), *"User datagram protocol"*, RFC 768.

H. Schulzrinne, S. Casner, R. Frederick, V. Jacobson (1996), *"RTP: a transport protocol for real-time applications"*, RFC 1889.

A Learning Approach to Quality-of-Service Routing in a Multimedia Environment

Ajoy Sharma[1], Himani Goyal[2],Dr. T S Bhatti[3] and Prof.D P Kothari[4]

[1]Military College of Telecommunication Engineering, Mhow, India
[2, 3, 4] Indian Institute of Technology, New Delhi, India
e-mail: himanigoyal@hotmail.com [2],dpk0710@yahoo.com [4]

Abstract

Multimedia applications such as digital video and audio often have stringent quality-of-service (QoS) requirements. In recent years, several new architectures have been developed for supporting such applications. In order to achieve the desired quality of service, an important element that must be incorporated into these architectures is QoS routing, namely routing based on QoS requirements. Routing protocols usually characterize the network with a single metric such as hop-count or delay. However to support a wide range of QoS requirements, there is a need to consider multiple metrics such as bandwidth, delay and loss probability while making routing decisions. The problem of determining a path that satisfies multiple constraints is computationally very demanding and in most cases, such problems have been shown to be NP complete. In this paper, we first examine the basic problem of QoS routing and then propose a new, efficient learning algorithm for selection of the optimum path. This algorithm is subsequently utilized to make routing decisions in various routing architectures.

Keywords

QoS Routing, NP Completeness, Source Routing, Hop-by-Hop Routing

1. Introduction

In order to support a wide range of QoS requirements, routing protocols need to have a more complex model where the network is characterized by multiple metrics such as bandwidth, delay and loss probability. The basic problem of QoS routing is then to find a path that satisfies multiple constraints. As current routing protocols are already reaching the limit of feasible complexity, it is important that complexity introduced by the QoS support should not impair the scalability of routing protocols. The problem of determining a valid path based on multiple additive constraints is known as the *Multiple Constrained Path* (MCP) problem .The MCP problem is known to be NP complete. In other words, there is no efficient polynomial time algorithm that can surely find a feasible path with respect to all constraints. A related, yet slightly different problem is known as the *Restricted Shortest Path* (RSP) problem in which the returned path is required to satisfy one constraint while being optimal with respect to the other. In this paper, we discuss briefly the previous work done in this field along with the research contributions of this paper.

2. Previous Work

To cope with the NP completeness of the MCP and the RSP problems, researchers have proposed several heuristics and approximation algorithms. One common approach to the RSP problem is to find k shortest paths with respect to cost function based on link weights and the given constraints, hoping that one of these paths is feasible and near optimal (Handler *et al*, 1984). If k is large, the algorithm has good performance but its computational cost is prohibitive. A similar approach is to enumerate all feasible paths (Aneja *et al*,1983) but this is computationally expensive. In an other approach (Widyono, 1994), a constrained Bellman Ford algorithm was proposed which performs a breadth first search by discovering paths of monotonically increasing delay while maintaining lowest cost paths to each visited node. Although the approach solves the RSP problem, its worst case running time grows exponentially with the network size. Jaffe considered the MCP problem and proposed an intuitive approximation to it based on minimizing a linear combination of link weights (Jaffe, 1979). However the computational complexity of this algorithm grows exponentially with the size of the network.

3. Research Contributions

In this paper we examine a number of aspects related to QoS routing. We first look at the complexity of determining a path that satisfies multiple constraints, and discuss the issue of appropriate metric selection. We discuss how metrics of one type may be conveniently converted into another type in order to determine a path satisfying the QoS requirements. We then present a learning algorithm that efficiently determines a path satisfying multiple constraints through an iterative procedure. The behaviour of the algorithm is analyzed to show that the algorithm almost always generates a valid path between Source and Destination nodes in a large asymmetric network provided such a path exists. Simulations performed corroborate the behavioural analysis of the algorithm. We then discuss the application of the learning algorithm to various routing architectures.

4. Metric Analysis and the Issue of Complexity

Path computation algorithms for a single metric, such as delay and hop-count are well known and have been widely used in current networks. However, multiple metrics model a network more accurately. Metrics may be categorized into additive, multiplicative and concave types (Wang and Crowcroft, 1996). The composition may be further reduced to two basic types: additive and concave, by appreciating the fact that multiplicative metrics may be transformed into the additive type by considering their logarithmic values. Parameters likely to be considered as routing metrics are delay, delay jitter, cost, loss probability and bandwidth. We notice that delay, delay jitter, and cost follow the additive composition rule while bandwidth follows the concave composition rule. Loss probability can be easily transformed into a metric (the probability of successful transmission), which follows the multiplicative composition rule. It has been shown (Wang and Crowcroft, 1996) that the problem of determining a valid path based on multiple additive, multiplicative or a combination of two or more additive and multiplicative metrics is NP complete. Therefore, a combination of one additive metric and one concave metric has been proposed. However it may not be enough to model the network behaviour using a combination of one additive and one concave metric or one multiplicative and one concave metric. We now present a learning algorithm that efficiently computes a path subject to multiple constraints. A composite metric is formulated by proportionate assignment of weights to each metric. These weights are revised iteratively and a valid path is computed based on the composite metric. We have observed that the algorithm quickly *learns* about the path that satisfies multiple constraints. We have considered additive metrics only for the formulation of the composite metric as multiplicative metrics may be transformed into additive metrics (as already brought out). Concave metrics have been discussed subsequently.

5. A Learning Algorithm to Compute a Path Subject to Multiple Constraints

Problem Formulation:

Consider a network $G = (N, A)$, n additive metrics $d_1(a), d_2(a), \ldots, d_n(a)$ for each $a \in A$, two specified nodes c, m, and n positive integers $D_1, D_2, \ldots D_n$ ($n \geq 2, D_i \geq 0$ for $i = 1, 2, \ldots, n$). We need to determine a simple, acyclic path $p = (c, d, e, \ldots, l, m)$ which satisfies the following constraints

$$d_i(p) \leq D_i \text{ where } i = 1, 2, \ldots, n$$

QoS Routing Algorithm: We now present a learning algorithm for QoS routing. The following steps describe the algorithm.

Step 1: Set $k = 0$ where k represents the iteration number. Formulate an ensemble of randomly assigned real weights

$$\phi^{(k)} = [\phi_1^{(k)}, \phi_2^{(k)}, \ldots, \phi_n^{(k)}] \qquad \text{such that}$$

$\phi_i^{(k)} \sim \text{Uniform}(0,1)$, $i = 1, 2, \ldots, n$

Compute the composite link costs $\sum_{i=1}^{n} \phi_i^{(k)} d_i(a) \; \forall \; a \in A,$

where $d_i(a)$ is the value(cost) of the ith metric for link a.
Determine a path $p^{(k)}$ such that

$$\sum_{i=1}^{n} \phi_i^{(k)} d_i(p^{(k)}) = \min_{p \in P} \{ \sum_{i=1}^{n} \phi_i^{(k)} d_i(p)\} \qquad \text{where}$$

$\sum_{i=1}^{n} \phi_i^{(k)} d_i(p) = \sum_{a \in p} \{ \sum_{i=1}^{n} \phi_i^{(k)} d_i(a)\}$, $d_i(p)$ being the value of the ith metric for path p and P the set of all simple acyclic paths between the source and destination nodes.

If $d_i(p^{(k)}) \leq D_i$ where $i = 1, 2, \ldots, n$ then *Stop* as $p^{(k)}$ is a desired path

Step 2 : Revise the ensemble $\phi^{(k)} = [\phi_1^{(k)}, \phi_2^{(k)}, \ldots, \phi_n^{(k)}]$ as follows

$$\phi_i^{(k+1)} = \phi_i^{(k)} + \mu [d_i(p^{(k)}) - D_i] I_{\{\phi_i^{(k+1)} \geq 0\}} \qquad (1)$$
$i = 1, 2, \ldots, n$

where μ is a positive real constant, which governs the learning process.

Set $k = k + 1$

Step 3 : Compute $\quad \sum_{i=1}^{n} \phi_i^{(k)} d_i(a) \ \forall \ a \in A.$

Determine a path $p^{(k)}$ such that

$$\sum_{i=1}^{n} \phi_i^{(k)} d_i(p^{(k)}) = \min_{p \in P} \ \{ \sum_{i=1}^{n} \phi_i^{(k)} d_i(p) \} \quad\quad\quad (2)$$

If $d_i (p^{(k)}) \leq D_i$ where $i = 1, 2, \dots, n$ then *Stop* as $p^{(k)}$ is a desired path
else
Go to step 2

Step 1 initializes the value of the weights and then determines the shortest path between the Source Destination pair using the composite metric developed. This path is checked for its validity. Step 2 revises the value of the weights if the path selected at the end of the kth iteration does not satisfy all the constraints. Step 3 computes the composite cost of the links based on weights determined in Step 2. The path having the lowest value of the composite cost is determined and this path is examined for its validity.

6. Simulations and Results

To evaluate the performance of the algorithm, a network with twenty nodes was considered for determination of a valid path between Source Destination pairs subject to four additive metrics. The network considered is given in Figure 1. Nodes 1 and 20 were selected as Source and Destination nodes respectively. A path is generated at the end of every iteration. Figure 2(a) depicts the behaviour of weights of metrics as the algorithm iterates. Figure 2(b) plots $d_i(p)$ - D_i for a path generated at the end of every iteration. Negative values of $d_i(p)$ - D_i for all metrics at the end of fourth iteration signify that the path generated at the end of the fourth iteration is a valid path.

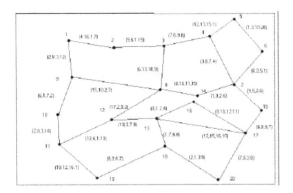

Fig1. A network of 20 nodes. The values of metrics for various links are enclosed in parentheses shown against the links.

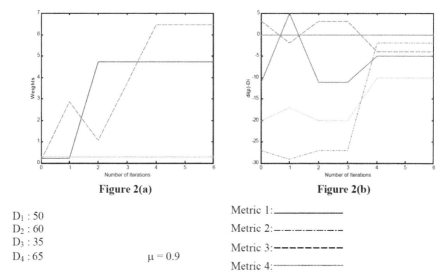

Figure 2(a)   Figure 2(b)

D_1 : 50   Metric 1:_____
D_2 : 60   Metric 2:_._._._._._.
D_3 : 35   Metric 3:_ _ _ _ _ _ _
D_4 : 65 $\mu = 0.9$ Metric 4:..............................

Fig 2(a) shows a plot of weights determined for every metric Vs the number of
iterations and Fig 2(b) shows a plot of $d_i(p) - D_i$ Vs the number of iterations when the
Source and Destination nodes were chosen to be nodes 1 and 20 respectively.

Iteration Number	Path at the end of Iteration	Status of Path
0	1 – 9 – 10 – 11 – 19 – 18 - 20	Invalid
1	1 – 9 – 8 – 12 – 13 – 18 - 20	Invalid
2	1 – 9 – 10 – 11 – 19 – 18 - 20	Invalid
3	1 – 9 – 10 – 11 – 19 – 18 - 20	Invalid
4	1 – 2 – 3 – 4 – 7 – 15 – 17 - 20	Valid

Table 1

7. Behavioral Analysis of the Algorithm

The weights are initialized and the algorithm determines a path with the initial value
of weights. If the path is valid, the algorithm terminates else the weights are revised
iteratively. The revision of the weights after the generation of an invalid path is done such that
the weights for those metrics, which were violated, are increased as per (1) and the weights for
those metrics, which were satisfied, are decreased as per (1). Thus we observe that metrics that
were violated more often and with larger margin, will have larger value of weights and their
contribution to the composite cost will be significant. Those metrics that were satisfied more
often and with larger margin will have lower value of weights and their contribution to the
composite cost will be relatively insignificant. The constant μ in (1) governs the learning
process and may be conveniently chosen. The algorithm makes use of the Dijkstra's algorithm
to determine the shortest path from the source to the destination using the composite cost.
Paths having a higher value of the metrics which are violated more often have a higher

composite cost compared to those having a lower value of these metrics and are naturally rejected in a minimizing operation given in (2). For a given Source Destination pair, a path is deemed to be invalid if any metric constraint is violated. We may classify the metrics into following types.

> *Type 1*: These metrics are those that are violated by all invalid paths
> *Type 2*: These metrics are those that are satisfied by all paths
> *Type 3*: These metrics are those that are violated by some invalid paths.

Theorem 1 proves that for a given Source Destination pair if only type 1 and type 2 metrics exist, then the algorithm determines a valid path in a finite number of iterations. However, when type 3 metrics are present, there may be situations where increase in the weight of a type 3 metric due to a generated path which violated that metric is countered by subsequently generated paths which although invalid, satisfied the metric in question causing its weight to decrease. Such situations may not lead to convergence and are more likely in smaller, sparsely connected networks with few paths between Source Destination pairs. In such cases, the behaviour of metrics is highly interdependent in that change in the weight of a specific metric may result in the change in weight of another specific metric in a fixed way. This may cause a progressive drift in the weights of these metrics without determining a valid path. However, in a large, asymmetric, well-connected network with multiple metrics and a number of valid and invalid paths between a given Source Destination pair, metrics may be assumed to behave independent of each other. The probability that the path at the end of kth iteration is valid may be defined as follows

$$P(\text{path at } k^{th} \text{ iteration is valid}) = P(d_1(p^{(k)}) \le D_1, \ d_2(p^{(k)}) \le D_2, \dots, \ d_n(p^{(k)}) \le D_n)$$

In large asymmetric networks with multiple metrics and a number of valid and invalid paths between a given Source Destination pair, due to the assumption of independent behaviour of metrics, the following product form approximation may be applied.

$$P(d_1(p^{(k)}) \le D_1, \ d_2(p^{(k)}) \le D_2, \dots \dots \dots, \ d_n(p^{(k)}) \le D_n) \cong \prod_{i=1}^{n} P(d_i(p^{(k)}) \le D_i)$$

For every metric i, $i=1, 2, \dots \dots n$, there exists at least one path which satisfies that metric else a solution does not exist. The algorithm endeavours to generate paths having lower value of metrics that have exceeded their D_i values frequently in the past. Due to this fact and the assumption of independent behaviour of metrics, we may say that for *any* iteration k,

$$P(d_i(p^{(k)}) \le D_i) > 0 \quad \text{for } i=1, 2, \dots \dots n. \qquad \text{Hence}$$

$$\prod_{i=1}^{n} P(d_i(p^{(k)}) \le D_i) > 0 \quad \text{for } i=1, 2, \dots \dots n.$$

i.e. every iteration has nonzero probability of generating a valid path. Therefore, assuming the product form approximation, the algorithm surely determines a valid path between a Source Destination pair as the number of iterations increase, provided a valid path exists. The same result was borne out by simulations discussed previously. The learning algorithm uses the Dijkstra's algorithm iteratively which has a computational complexity of $O(N^2)$. Since the number of iterations does not depend on network size but rather on the tightness of upper bounds, we believe that the learning algorithm has a computational complexity comparable to that of Dijkstra's algorithm.

8. Application of the Learning Algorithm to Various Routing Architectures

Source routing and Hop-by-Hop routing are the two basic routing architectures for data networks. Hop-by-Hop routing is the common form of general purpose routing in current networks while Source routing is mainly used for network diagnosis and special policy routes. In Source routing, a forwarding path is computed on-demand at the source and listed in the packet header. Packets are forwarded according to the path in the packet header. Source routing can be very precise, but a source must have access to full routing information of each link for path computation and packets have a larger packet header. Thus Source routing trades off specificity in routing for packet header size and extra overhead for control messages. The learning algorithm lends itself naturally to Source routing. Links that do not satisfy the concave metric requirement specified by the application may be ignored and the learning algorithm may be applied over the remaining network obtained by weeding out such links. Hop-by-Hop routing precomputes forwarding entries for every destination. Packets just carry the destination address and each router along the path can choose the next hop based on link states or distance vectors. The usual approach in current Hop-by-Hop algorithms is to compute the best path to every destination. The learning algorithm can be adapted for Hop-by-Hop routing by categorizing applications into a finite set. For each category of applications, the upper bound on the metric values i.e. D_is are laid down and the learning algorithm pre-computes a valid path to each destination node for that category of applications. Such a path is determined by weeding out links that do not satisfy the concave metric requirement and applying the learning algorithm over the remaining links. As and when an application arrives, it is mapped onto an appropriate category and the lookup table for that category is utilized to determine the next hop. Given a Source Destination pair, once a valid path is found, all intermediate nodes which lie on this path satisfy the given constraints as the metrics are additive. Thus a valid path from a source to a distant destination becomes valid for all the intermediate nodes also, reducing the computations further. Policy constraints can be introduced into routing decisions too by appropriately creating an additional metric and imparting high values of this metric to those links that must be avoided.

9. Conclusion and Future Work

In this paper we have examined a number of important issues in QoS routing and have presented a learning algorithm for determining a path subject to multiple constraints. The algorithm was found to be efficient and a path satisfying the constraints was quickly obtained in the simulations performed. The path selection problem was investigated using a complete knowledge of the network state. However, in practice, the true state of a network may not be known to all the nodes at all times due to network dynamics and latencies in the dissemination of state information. In future, we will focus on analyzing the MCP problem in the presence of inaccurate state information.

Theorem 1:   For a given Source Destination pair and specified upper bounds on the metric values, a valid path is determined in a finite number of iterations provided all metrics are of type 1 and type 2.

Proof :   For a given Source Destination pair and specified upper bounds on the metric values, the possible paths $p \in P$ can be divided into two disjoint sets, P^g containing valid paths and P^b containing invalid paths i.e. $P = P^g + P^b$. Assume the algorithm does not generate a valid path even after a large number of iterations k. This will imply that

$$\lim_{\substack{k \to \infty \\ j \in \text{type 1 metrics}}} \phi_j^{(k)} \to \infty \qquad \text{and}$$

$$\lim_{\substack{k \to \infty \\ j \in \text{type 2 metrics}}} \phi_j^{(k)} \to 0$$

For any $p \in P^g$ and $p' \in P^b$

$d_i(p) \le D_i$ and $d_i(p') > D_i$ Therefore, $d_i(p) < d_i(p')$ where $i \in$ *type 1 metrics*

Hence for finite metric values, there exists a finite k such that

$$\sum_{i \in \text{type 1 metrics}} \phi_i^{(k)} \{ d_i(p'^{(k)}) - d_i(p^{(k)}) \} > \sum_{j \in \text{type 2 metrics}} \phi_j^{(k)} \{ d_j(p^{(k)}) - d_j(p'^{(k)}) \} \qquad \text{or,}$$

$$\{ \sum_{i \in \text{type 1 metrics}} \phi_i^{(k)} d_i(p'^{(k)}) + \sum_{j \in \text{type 2 metrics}} \phi_j^{(k)} d_j(p'^{(k)}) \} > \{ \sum_{i \in \text{type 1 metrics}} \phi_i^{(k)} d_i(p^{(k)}) + \sum_{j \in \text{type 2 metrics}} \phi_j^{(k)} d_j(p^{(k)}) \} \qquad \text{Therefore,}$$

$$\sum_{\substack{i = 1 \\ p \in Pg}}^{n} \phi_i^{(k)} d_i(p^{(k)}) < \min_{p' \in Pb} \{ \sum_{i = 1}^{n} \phi_i^{(k)} d_i(p'^{(k)}) \}$$

Therefore some $p \in P^g$ will be selected which completes the proof.

10.   References

G Y Handler, I Zang (1984) ,"A Dual algorithm for the constrained Shortest Path Problem", *Networks*, 10:293-310.

H De Neve and P Van Meighiem (1988), "A multiple quality of service routing algorithm for PNNI", in *Proceedings of the ATM workshop*, pp 324-328, *IEEE*.

J Jaffe (1984), "Algorithms for finding paths with multiple constraints," *Networks*, vol 14, pp 95-116.

M Garey and D S Johnson (1979), " *Computers and Intractability : A guide to NP completeness*", Freeman, San Francisco.

R Widyono (1994). "The design and evaluation of routing algorithms for Real Time Channel", *Technical Report TR-94-024*, University of California at Berkley and International Computer Science Institute.

Y P Aneja *et al* (1983), "Shortest chain subject to side constraints", *Networks*, 13:295-302.

Zheng Wang and Jon Crowcroft (1996), "Quality-of-service Routing for Supporting Multimedia Applications", *IEEE JSAC*, vol 14, no 7.

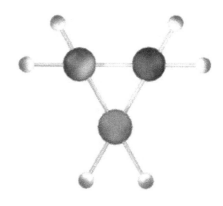

Chapter 5

Security and Privacy

Designing an Embedded Firewall/VPN Gateway[*]

Vassilis Prevelakis[1] and Angelos Keromytis[2]

[1] Department of Mathematics and Computer Science, Drexel University, Philadelphia, USA,
e-mail vp@drexel.edu
[2] Department of Computer Science, Columbia University, New York, USA
e-mail: angelos@cs.columbia.edu

Abstract

The widespread use of mobile computing and telecommuting has increased the need for effective protection of computing platforms. Traditional schemes that involve strengthening the security of individual systems, or the use of firewalls at network entry points have difficulty accommodating the special requirements of remote and mobile users. We propose the use of a special purpose drop-in firewall/VPN gateway called *Sieve*, that can be inserted between the mobile workstation and the network to provide individualized security services for that particular station. *Sieve* is meant to be used like an external modem: the user only needs to plug it in. Its existence is transparent to the user, requiring no modification to the workstation configuration. To function in this role, *Sieve* has been designed to be compact, low-cost, requiring little administration or maintenance. In this paper, we discuss the features and advantages of our system. We demonstrate how *Sieve* was used in various application areas (home, university environment, etc.) and describe our future plans.

Keywords

IPsec, VPN, credentials, embedded systems, OpenBSD.

1. Introduction

The recent advances in networking have created a situation where computers are practically always connected to the Internet. Cable modems and DSL lines for the SOHO environment and wireless networking for laptop and handheld computers ensure that the resources of the Internet are always accessible. Against the convenience of "always on" connections we must balance increased exposure to attacks.

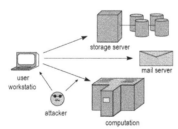

Figure 1: By accessing network resources, the user workstation runs the risk of having its communications intercepted, or being attacked by malicious third parties.

[*] This work was supported by DARPA under Contract F39502-99-1-0512-MOD P0001.

Traditional approaches for countering threats involve the use of firewalls (Cheswick and Bellovin 1994). Unfortunately firewalls are better suited to organizations that can afford to pay for the configuration and maintenance of such systems. Moreover, firewalls provide a hard shell protecting the soft core of the internal networks. This architecture does not protect against internal threats, nor does it protect mobile users, telecommuters, or users of wireless connections (see Figure 1).

Ioannidis et al (Ioannidis, Keromytis, *et al*, 2000) propose the use of a "distributed firewall," i.e. the integration of firewall functionality in every machine in the network. However, this approach requires that all computers in the network run appropriately modified operating systems and applications which, for the time being, is not feasible on a large scale basis. On the other hand, existing systems such as Windows NT (and its derivatives) and most Unix and Unix-like systems already provide security features that can be used to implement firewall functionality on every machine. The difficulty of securing general purpose operating systems has impeded the widespread use of this approach. Moreover, it is difficult to ensure that a secured system remains secure after the user has had the opportunity to install software and perform reconfigurations and upgrades.

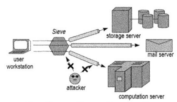

Figure 2: *Sieve* **provides firewall services and creates secure links to other servers in the network, establishing a secure overlay network that is inaccessible by third parties.**

Recognizing the futility of attempting to secure the user machines themselves, we propose the use of a portable "shrink-wrapped" firewall (which we have called *Sieve*). This is a separate machine running an embedded system that includes firewall capabilities and is normally placed between the general purpose computer and the network (Figure 2). The problem of securing the firewall becomes much simpler as the platform is a special-purpose one with a highly controlled architecture.

To avoid the need for labor intensive reconfigurations and to provide flexibility, we allow the security policy of this embedded platform to be downloaded from the network.

For a "shrink-wrapped" firewall to be effective, the following prerequisites must be satisfied:
- Low cost in terms of hardware, software, configuration and maintenance.
- While it may restrict some services, it must be totally transparent to authorized services.
- Offer secure connections to servers and other network assets, thus protecting the communications between the protected system and other resources.
- Be flexible: it should be able to accommodate various security policies and different types of network attachments (serial, Ethernet, wireless).
- Be resistant to tampering. Furthermore, in cases where there are indications that a station has been compromised, it must be easy to restore its original configuration.

- To simplify centralized management and troubleshooting, it must offer a standard platform for the execution of common network management and monitoring tools. Workstation users should not have access to the management information.
- Finally, regardless of the profile of the end user, the "shrink-wrapped" firewall must be able to be deployed with minimal overhead.

Existing commercial solutions do not offer the right mix of open standards and low price. In fact many solutions have a per node pricing model that is based on the assumption that remote locations are company branches. Thus, they have pricing structures that deal with tens or hundreds of nodes. Scaling them to networks with thousands of nodes produces outrageous prices. Thus, we decided to investigate an Open Source solution. The advantage of this approach is that it offers enormous potential for customization coupled with a low cost per node. Another benefit of using Open Source software is that, unlike proprietary solutions, the code can be freely audited thus providing security through openness.

3. System Architecture

Creating a system in-house has many pitfalls, mainly related to the fact that the platform design, implementation and support all have hidden costs that must be brought out into the open and accounted for. Just because a piece of software is free does not mean that its deployment in a production environment is without cost.

A lot of attention has to be given to the integration, large scale production, and maintenance of the nodes, in order that a usable system be achieved within the project's budget constraints.

The prime considerations in the design of Sieve have been simplicity and security. In this section we will elaborate on these two issues and examine their impact on the design of the operating environment. We will also present the major components of the Sieve platform and discuss the various design decisions.

3.1 Simplicity - Reliability

There are several good reasons to maintain low platform complexity:

- A complex design is difficult to verify and control. This implies that maintaining the security posture of the platform after its original roll-out will be difficult.
- A non-standard platform such as *Sieve* will have to be easy to master, otherwise new staff will not be able to support it.
- *Sieve* is intended for production use, thus the administrators must have confidence in the platform.

3.2 Operating System

From the very beginning, we wanted a platform that could accommodate tools for remote monitoring and management. The requirement that the station should operate in residential environments, without a monitor, keyboard or mouse effectively disqualified all Windows platforms. From the available UNIX or UNIX-like systems we eventually chose OpenBSD 2.9 for the following reasons:

- Built-in support for the transport layer security protocols (IPsec) that offer secure communication channels between stations. Since these channels are created by the networking code in the kernel, the encryption is transparent to applications. Thus, programs such as rlogin(1) that have no encryption facilities can take advantage of the built-in security offered by IPsec without any modifications to the application code.

- Like other free UNIX clones, a large number of programs such as tcpdump, snmpd, ssh, etc. are either supported in the base release or are available through the *ports* system.
- Good security. The designers of OpenBSD have paid a lot of attention to the security profile of the system, creating a robust environment.

3.3 IPsec

IPsec is a suite of protocols (Akinson, 1995) that provide encryption, authentication and integrity checking at the network layer. *Sieve* employs IPsec in tunnel mode with encryption (ESP) (Figure 3). Tunneling consists of encrypting and encapsulating a normal IP packet within an IPsec packet. Since both the header and payload of the original packet are encrypted, the internal structure of the private network is concealed from intruders (Shah and Holzbaur, 1997).

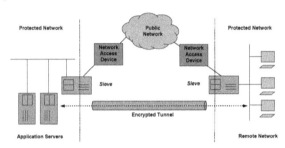

Figure 3: The IPsec tunnel provides a secure connection between the two local area networks over the public Internet.

The use of tunnel mode also allows us to use the *Sieve* nodes as routers sending packets from the remote home LANs to the main corporate network (Scott, Wolfe, *et al*, 1998). Under this scenario, addresses from the internal corporate network may be allocated to workstations at the employees' homes.

Another configuration (layer 2 VPN) utilizes bridging (Keromytis and Wright, 2000) rather than routing so that the remote node appears to be directly connected to the corporate network. This approach also allows the use of non-IP protocols such as LAN-Manager and Novel IPX/SPX.

Two sets of IPsec connections are maintained for each *Sieve* node. One carries the VPN data while the other is used for the management of the *Sieve* node itself. By using separate IPsec connections we ensure that users cannot access the management information or be in a position to contact other nodes through the VPN.

3.4 Key Management

Using IPsec with statically-defined Security Associations (SAs)[†] as we did in (Prevelakis, 1999), is equivalent to running the Internet with static routing tables. The resulting VPN is inflexible and keys are not changed as often as prudent cryptographic practice suggests, be-

---

[†] Security Association is the set of parameters for one-way communication between two nodes (cryptographic keys, choice of algorithm, etc.).

cause of the effort and disruption to service. Moreover, since SAs contain source and destination IP addresses, they have to be changed each time the IP address of one of the endpoints changes. Users that connect to the Internet via dial-up connections or even permanently connected users that are assigned IP addresses via *dhcp* cannot use statically assigned SAs. Workarounds to these problems exist and are discussed in detail in (Prevelakis, 1999). However, these solutions lack elegance and are not suitable for large-scale VPNs.

Purchases via credit cards provide a good analogy to the problem of setting up flexible SAs. When purchasing an item, the customer presents a credit card to the merchant. The merchant does not need to keep a record of all the people that have a VISA card in order to complete the transaction. Instead, the merchant contacts the credit card company and receives an authorization. In essence the credit card company vouches for the customer.

In the same way, one of the endpoints (A) of a VPN tunnel presents a certificate that is signed by a certification authority (CA) acceptable to the other side (B). There is no need for B to have previous knowledge of A since the certification authority vouches for the authenticity of (the certificate presented by) A.

There are two differences from the credit card example. The first is that there is no on-line communication with the CA during the negotiation. Endpoint B has the public key of the CA and can thus verify any certificate presented by A. The second difference is that A does not trust B and so B must also present a certificate to A. The second certificate must be signed by a CA acceptable to A. In our system all certificates are signed by the same CA, but this need not always be the case.

A serious issue with certificates is revocation, i.e., what happens if, for example, a *Sieve* node is lost or stolen. There are two mechanisms that can prevent compromised nodes from linking to the VPN: (1) certificates have limited lifetimes and so, unless renewed, become worthless after a specified interval, (2) by changing the policy file we can prevent nodes from accepting connections from blacklisted nodes.

3.5 Firewall

Sieve nodes must be able to allow traffic from the interior network to flow through the VPN to the other internal networks, while at the same time they should allow only a very restricted set of incoming connections. On the other hand, connections from other *Sieve* nodes must be accepted.

The VPN may be viewed as a transit network located between the end-user workstation and the internal network.

In the *Sieve* design we have used the packet filtering functionality of the OpenBSD kernel with a configuration that imposed three classes of restrictions:

- Public Internet.
  This refers to packets coming in from the interface that is connected to the public network. These packets are generally blocked except IPsec packets, since IPsec has its own security mechanisms. Moreover, we also allow ICMP echo and reply messages for network troubleshooting, but we block other ICMP messages.
- Transit packets flowing through the VPN.
  Packets received from the interface connected to the local (protected) network) and destined for the remote end of the VPN connection fall within this category of restrictions.

While allowing the packets to be routed through the VPN, we generally do not allow connections to the *Sieve* nodes themselves. Exceptions to this rule include services such as dhcp that are required for the operation of the node. We also allow certain types of ICMP packets for network troubleshooting.

- Traffic between the VPN nodes.
  In this category we have packets that are exchanged between the VPN nodes themselves. This kind of communication is mainly for management and node administration. Generally, no restrictions are placed to this type of traffic.

Given that we are enforcing no access restrictions within the VPN, we were extremely concerned about allowing access to the *Sieve* from the user workstation. When considering security mechanisms, there is always a need to strike a balance between security and convenience. Making life difficult for the end users would only mean that they would avoid using the VPN or find ways to disable or bypass various security mechanisms, thus compromising the security posture of the entire network. At the same time we did not wish to allow unsophisticated users access to the *Sieve* nodes.

In the end we decided that users may access their local *Sieve* node only from their own protected network. In this way only users suitably authorized would be able to access the configuration of their own *Sieve* nodes.

3.6 RAM-based system

In order to produce a simple and reliable system we decided to dispense with the hard disk. The reason behind this decision was twofold: reliability and support. Although disk drives tend to be reliable, they would have to operate continuously throughout the life of the *Sieve* nodes. In both home and mobile environments equipment tend to be subject to all kinds of abuse (knocked about, powered down without shutting down the system, relocated while in operation, etc.). Hard disks produce a fair amount of heat and noise and are also more prone to failure in these conditions.

The second and more important reason is related to the way that these machines are intended to be used. For our purposes, hard disks are already huge in terms of capacity and are getting bigger all the time. This free space can cause all kinds of trouble; for example, it may be tempting to fill it with data that should not be stored in the *Sieve* node in the first place. This means that stations can no longer be redeployed easily because this information must be backed up, or processed. Secondly, if a station is compromised, the intruders will be able to use this space as a bridgehead, transferring and installing tools that will enable them to attack other network assets.

On the other hand, diskless machines bring with them a whole collection of problems and administrative headaches. They are also basically incompatible with our objective of using standalone machines with encrypted tunnels for all communications over the public Internet.

Instead, we use a RAM-based system where the software is loaded once during boot and then the system runs entirely on the system main memory (RAM). The boot medium may be diskette, CDROM, or a solid state disk (e.g., Compact Flash). In our prototype system, we are using Compact Flash as the boot medium, so in the following paragraphs we use the term CF.

In order to produce a RAM-based system, we adopted the techniques used by the PICOBSD project which is a collection of FreeBSD configurations that can be accommodated within a single boot floppy (*http://www.freebsd.org/ ~picobsd*). The PICOBSD project provides configurations for a dial-up router, dial-in router (ISP access server), general purpose router and firewall. The PICOBSD technique links the code of all the executables that we wish to be available at runtime in a single executable using the *crunchgen* utility (da Silva, 1998). The single executable alters its behavior depending on the name under which it is run ($argv[0]$). By linking this executable to the names of the individual utilities we can create a fully functional /bin directory where all the system commands are accessible as apparently distinct files.

The aggregation of the system executables in a single file and the compression of the entire kernel allows a large number of facilities to be made available despite the small size of the boot medium. For example, in the *Sieve* distribution we include the following commands:

Category	Commands
Shell Commands (Korn Shell)	cat, chgrp, chmod, chown, cp, echo, kill, ln, ls, mkdir, more, pwd, rm, stty, telnet, test, w
Administration	date, dmesg, hostname, passwd, ps, reboot, update, vmstat
System Configuration	dev_mkdb, mknod, pwd_mkdb, swapctl, swapon, sysctl
Daemons	getty, inetd, init, login, snmpd, syslogd, telnetd, dhcpd
Networking	ifconfig, ipf, ipnat, ipsecadm, netstat, ping, route, traceroute, isakmpd, wicontrol, dhclient
Filesystem	mount, (cd9660, fdesc, ffs, kernfs, mfs, msdos, nfs, procfs), df, newfs, umount

The root of the runtime file system, together with the executable and associated links, are placed in a ramdisk that is stored within the kernel binary. The kernel is then compressed (using *gzip*) and placed on a bootable CF. This CF also contains the /etc directory of the running system in uncompressed form to allow easy configuration of the runtime parameters (Figure 4).

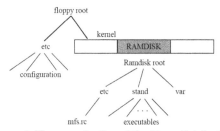

Figure 4. The organization of the Sieve distribution

At boot time, the kernel is copied from the CF disk to main memory, and is uncompressed and executed. The file system root is then located in the ramdisk. The CF boot partition is mounted and the /etc directory copied to the ramdisk. At this point the CF partition is unmounted and may be removed. The system is running entirely off the ramdisk and goes through the regular initialization process. Once the boot process is complete, user logins from the console or the network may occur. The CF is usually write-protected so changes in the system configuration do not survive reboots. If, however, the CF is not write protected, there exists a utility that can copy the contents of the ramdisk /etc directory to the CF boot partition, thus making the running configuration permanent. This organization places the files that are unlikely to change between *Sieve* nodes in the kernel where they are compressed, while leaving the configuration files in the /etc directory on the CF. Thus, these files can be easily accessed and modified. Moreover, a single image may be produced and the configuration of each station applied to it just before it is copied to the CF.

4. Prototype

In this section, we describe the *Sieve* prototype and three examples of its use: office desktop, wireless, and home gateway.

4.1 Office Desktop

Contrary to popular belief, internal networks in most organizations are not safe. Although protected by firewalls, these networks are vulnerable to internal attacks (e.g., by coworkers, worms and viruses from other infected machines, etc.). Our approach is to install *Sieve* stations between each sensitive desktop and the internal network. As it has been noted in (Prevelakis, 1999), the ability to manage these stations via a centralized Network Management System creates a safe and predictable platform from which user network problems can be diagnosed remotely.

We use the *Sieve* in bridge mode so that the desktop appears to be directly connected to the local area network.

4.2 Wireless network

Wireless networks, even with encryption activated (Stubblefield, Ioannidis, *et al*, 2002) are particularly vulnerable to intrusion attacks. A popular hacker pastime is to cruise around town with a laptop trying to connect to wireless networks. Wireless networks should be considered unsafe and thus always linked to the internal network via a firewall. In (Boscia and Shaw, 2000) the authors describe the difficulties in managing a wireless network (handing out addresses, opening connections through the firewall, etc.). They also include a number of solutions, but they admit that these solutions have weaknesses and, thus, they use them to provide access only to non-critical hosts in their network. Normally the system is used in bridging mode, although there were cases where the system administrators want to know which machines are on the wireless segment. The main difference with the desktop configuration is that in the wireless configuration all communication is carried over secure links. We use IPsec in tunnel mode (Figure 3) to link the workstation to the internal network. In this case, the public network of Figure 3 is the wireless network.

4.3 Home Network Gateway

Internet connections at home are seldom used by only one person or for only one task (e.g. work). By placing a *Sieve* between the home network and the ISP connection, we have the option of forcing everybody to go through the company network. This is not entirely without merit because it means that the home computers are shielded behind the company firewall. However, there may be cases where we wish to have access to sites or services that are blocked by the company firewall. In such cases, the *Sieve* can be configured to allow only certain PCs or network segments to be part of the VPN, while the rest work as if they were directly connected to the ISP. In this scenario, the *Sieve* can also perform the task of a NAT router, allowing the user to share a single ISP-provided IP address among multiple worksta-tions.

4.4 Hardware Platform

The VPN software runs on standard PC hardware. While most of the development was car-ried out on decommissioned PCs, the size, power requirements and, most importantly, the noise from the power supply fan, make such machines totally unsuitable for deployment in the field. Single board computers (SBCs) allow the creation of small-factor convection-cooled systems. These designs are mostly compatible with the PC motherboards and cards so that there is no need for software porting. Moreover, solid state storage in the form of Flash RAM may be added. Compared to ordinary hard drives, this offers improved reliability. After examining a number of products we chose the NetCARD system. This single board computer is about 14cm by 10cm and combines on board Ethernet interface, Compact Flash and 2 PC-CARD slots along with the usual PC-style interfaces (floppy, IDE disk, etc.). We used this system both with a floppy boot medium and with a Compact Flash. The on-board Ethernet interface was used to connect the VPN node to the network access device, while an Ethernet PC-CARD provided the inside-network connection. A wireless Ethernet card may be attached to the system, eliminating the need for fixed wiring.

4.2 Operation

As soon as power is applied and the power-on tests are complete, the PC BIOS loads the sys-tem from the boot medium and hands control over to the OpenBSD kernel. In order for the outside interface to be configured, the VPN node must find out the IP address provided by the ISP. If the IP address is always the same, then it can be included in the static configuration that is read off the boot medium. Otherwise, the system uses dhcp to configure its interface. The inside Ethernet interface uses a pre-assigned address from the private Internet range (RFC1918). The system also runs dhcpd on the inside interface so that workstations on the private network can be auto-configured. The system then runs the isakmpd daemon that cre-ates the IPsec tunnels. The packet filtering software ensures that the VPN is isolated from the outside world. The node may be powered down without the need for a shutdown procedure (e.g., sync).

5. Conclusions - Future Plans

The work presented in this paper is a continuation of the work described in (Prevelakis, 1999). In the previous project, a number of VPN stations were deployed within the University of Piraeus, in Greece, as part of a network of monitoring stations. The purpose of these Se-cure Network Stations (SNS) was to allow the creation of a secure network that allows ad-ministrators to manage and troubleshoot network elements such as routers, hubs, and switches deployed throughout the University campus. The SNS system has been in operation for more than three years. The SNS nodes have different configurations from the VPN nodes discussed in this paper because they serve different roles. For example, SNS nodes need to forward SNMP traffic from the network elements and allow connections from inside the secure net-work to reach network elements located outside the SNS perimeter. Moreover, the system uses static IPsec configuration, which necessitates the production and distribution of updated configurations on a regular basis. Nevertheless, the experience gained from their use helped in refining the requirements for the systems described in this paper. One notable decision that was directly influenced by the previous design was to have a fully connected mesh of IPsec tunnels linking every node to all the others. Most VPN solutions tend to link a central office with a number of remote locations with the IPsec tunnels arranged in a star. The many-to-many links allow the VPN to be resilient to failures of individual nodes and in the case where there is significant traffic between the remote nodes there is better utilization of the VPN resources as all packets go through at most one IPsec tunnel to their destination.

Another system that offers similar functionality to the one we have presented here is the Moat from the AT&T Labs (Denker, Bellovin, et al, 1999). Like our system, the Moat also utilizes small single board computers running a lightweight version of Linux and create VPNs allowing AT&T research personnel to telecommute. The Moat follows the one-to-many VPN layout probably because it is not envisaged that there will be significant traffic between employees working at home. Remote stations with floating IP addresses (as is the case of most dial-up Internet connections) are treated by dynamically rewriting the IPsec configuration files. This requires that a central cite is always operational so that the VPN nodes can get the information they need to create their configuration files. In our system, the use of certificates, allows any two stations to negotiate SAs and create IPsec tunnels. Additionally, the use of built-in facilities such as the isakmpd daemon make the system easier to maintain and port across Operating System releases.

As part of our future plans, we intend to improve the automatic configuration of our system. The goal is a system that explores the network it is connected to (discovering default routers, dhcp servers and so on) and configures itself accordingly.

References

Boscia, Nichole K.and Derek G. Shaw, "Wireless Firewall Gateway White Paper," NASA Advanced Supercomputing Division, Moffett Field, CA 94035

Cheswick, William and Steven Bellovin, *"Firewalls & Internet Security, Repelling the Wily Hacker,"* Addison-Wesley Professional Computing Series, 1994.

Denker, John S., Steven M. Bellovin, Hugh Daniel, Nancy L. Mintz, Tom Killian and Mark A. Plotnick, "Moat: A Virtual Private Network Appliance and Services Platform," *LISA '99: 13th Systems Administration Conference*, Washington, November 1999.

Ioannidis S., A.D. Keromytis, S.M. Bellovin and J.M. Smith, Implementing a Distributed Firewall, *Proceedings of Computer and Communications Security (CCS) 2000*, pp. 190-199.

Keromytis, Angelos D, Jason L. Wright, "Transparent Network Security Policy Enforcement," *USENIX Annual 2000 Technical Conference - Freenix Refereed Track*, San Diego, California, June 18-23, 2000.

Prevelakis, Vassilis "A Secure Station for Network Monitoring and Control," *The 8th USENIX Security Symposium*, Washington, D.C., USA, August 1999.

Atkinson, R. *"RFC-1825: Security Architecture for the Internet Protocol,"* Internet Engineering Task Force, August 1995.

Scott, Charlie, Paul Wolfe and Mike Erwin, *"Virtual Private Networks,"* O'Reilly & Associates, Inc. 1998.

Shah Deval and Helen Holzbaur, "Virtual Private Networks: Security With an Uncommon Touch," *Data Communications*, Sept. 97,

da Silva James, "Cruchgen," *OpenBSD User Manual*, 1998.

Stubblefield, Adam, John Ioannidis and Aviel D. Rubin, "Using the Fluhrer, Mantin, and Shamir Attack to Break WEP," *Proceedings of the 2002 Network and Distributed System Security Symposium*, San Diego, California February 2002

Measuring SSL and SET against e-commerce consumer requirements

Pita Jarupunphol[1] and Chris J. Mitchell

Information Security Group, Royal Holloway, University of London, UK.
P.Jarupunphol@rhul.ac.uk, C.Mitchell@rhul.ac.uk

Abstract

The threat of credit card fraud is arguably one of the most serious issues in e-commerce, since it makes consumers reluctant to engage in this alternative method of shopping. Most previous authors have focussed on technical and business issues, whilst virtually ignoring consumer confidence. If consumers are to lose their fears of e-commerce fraud, then it is important that the security solutions deployed address their concerns and not just the concerns of those building and operating the e-commerce infrastructure. According to Hassler (2000), Secure Socket Layer (SSL) and Secure Electronic Transaction (SET) are the two main industry standard means for securing Internet e-commerce communications. Currently, SSL is almost always used in preference to SET for Internet e-commerce security. SET was specifically designed to secure entire e-commerce transactions, but has been largely ignored. This paper assesses how well these existing security schemes meet consumer concerns, and hence how effectively they can increase consumer confidence. In addition, this paper also briefly considers how elements of these two protocols might be combined to offer both security and ease of use.

Keywords

Electronic Commerce (E-Commerce), Secure Socket Layer (SSL), Secure Electronic Transaction (SET), Transport Layer Security (TLS), digital certificate, digital signature.

1 Introduction

According to Jarupunphol and Mitchell (2001), there is a mismatch between real and perceived levels of risk for e-commerce consumers. There is thus a need for security measures to address both actual security threats and also customer perceptions of security threats. Most of the previous security analyses have focussed on the actual threats, whilst paying much less attention to the perceived threats. However, unless these perceived threats are successfully addressed, e-commerce will fail to meet its true potential because of continuing customer fears. According to Friedman et al. (2000), lack of financial confidence and security confidence are reducing consumer acceptance of this innovative online shopping technology.

Currently, the two main industry standard means for securing Internet e-commerce transactions are SSL, including the IETF variant TLS (Rescorla 2001), and SET (Merkow et al. 1998). However, for various reasons, including ease of installation, lower investment costs and the much greater complexity of SET, SSL is almost always used in preference to SET for Internet e-commerce security. This paper seeks to address the perceived threats, and assesses how well the two most commonly discussed approaches to securing e-commerce, namely SSL and SET, match up to the perceived threats. This paper also considers the feasibility of combining elements of these two protocols.

---

[1] Pita Jarupunphol was supported by the Rajabhat Institute of Phuket (Thailand).

2   Analysis of perceived consumer security requirements

A number of payment methods have been used in Internet e-commerce, including plastic (debit/credit) card, electronic cash (e-cash), and electronic cheque (e-cheque), (Oppliger 2000). In the business-to-consumer (B2C) context, the credit card is the most commonly used method of payment for e-commerce consumers, (Treese and Stewart 1998). According to an Internet shopping habits survey conducted by Survey.Net (http://www.survey.net), 36.0% of Internet users purchase goods by transmitting their credit card number via a secure form; the percentages for other payment methods are significantly lower.

Given that the debit/credit card is the primary means for consumers to purchase products or services online, the compromise of credit card numbers is clearly a serious threat to the consumer. Credit card numbers can be compromised in two main ways.

- Data transmission – financial information may be stolen by an interceptor.

- Data storage – financial information may be compromised by an intruder hacking into an e-commerce merchant website.

There is currently a mixture of consumer attitudes to e-commerce. Some people are happy to use this new method of shopping, whereas others perceive e-commerce as being too risky. According to a survey of consumer attitudes to Internet shopping conducted by Harris Interactive (http://www.harrisinteractive.com), security is arguably the main consumer concern. 57% of participants worry that their credit card numbers will be abused. Whilst fraud at the merchant, either initiated by the merchant or resulting from attacks on merchant servers, is not the foremost concern of users, it is nevertheless of importance. This is particularly the case since it could lead to large numbers of credit card details falling into criminal hands, and theft of credit card numbers is the most significant user concern (Tomlinson 2000). Hence, in our discussion below we consider the effectiveness of SSL and SET in protecting the privacy of credit card numbers both whilst communicated and while stored, e.g. in merchant servers.

3   Overview of SSL and SET

SSL, developed by Netscape, is a protocol that provides security for an Internet communications link. When used to protect an e-commerce transaction, all data sent from the customer PC to the merchant website will be encrypted in order to ensure data confidentiality, (Sherif 2000), (SET 1997), (also see Figure 1).

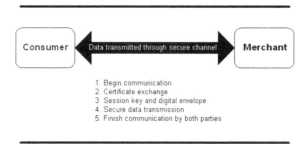

Figure 1: SSL security for e-commerce transactions

The SET scheme is, however, different from the SSL scheme; differences include the number of participants and the additional applications required to complete SET transactions. SET, invented by Visa and MasterCard (http://www.visa.com, http://www.mastercard.com), is designed to address security threats arising to both transmitted and stored data. Specifically, unlike SSL, SET provides protection for payment and order information both when transmitted and when stored at the merchant. In particular, the user account information is encrypted in such a way that it is only accessible to the Acquirer, thus preventing its compromise whilst stored at the merchant server. The main information flows in SET are shown in Figure 2, (Sherif 2000), (SET 1997).

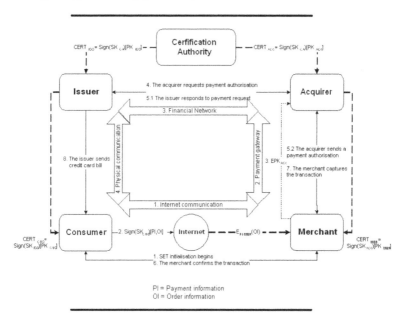

Figure 2: SET process in e-commerce transactions

4   Comparison: SSL versus SET

Table 1 compares SSL and SET in the context of e-commerce consumer requirements, based on a survey of consumer perceptions to Internet shopping conducted by the National Consumer Council (NCC 2000). Although a variety of possible risks are considered in the survey, we focus on those security issues of greatest concern to e-consumers. As a result, personal issues including the inability to touch goods, the absence of personal contact, delivery problems, and the dislike of shopping with a credit card, are excluded from the table.

Security issues of concern to e-commerce consumers	Within the scope	
	SSL	SET
Confidentiality of sensitive information		
• Afraid of credit card being stolen online	Y	Y
• Afraid of personal data being abused	Y/N	Y
Merchant Integrity		
• Afraid of fraudulent suppliers	Y/N	Y
Payment Integrity		
• Hidden charges	N	Y

Table 1: SSL and SET versus security issues of concern to e-consumers

As can be seen from Table 1, significant differences exist between SSL and SET with respect to the issues of concern to e-commerce consumers. Two of the differences highlighted in the table are with respect to the abuse of personal data, since SET protects personal information stored on merchant servers whilst SSL does not, and with respect to trustworthiness of sellers. Since abuse of personal data is apparently one of the two most important issues of concern to consumers (NCC 2000), these differences are potentially significant. Payment integrity is also a significant difference. We now consider these three main differences between SSL and SET in a little more detail.

4.1   Confidentiality of sensitive information

In order to conduct e-commerce, consumers need to submit their credit card numbers to merchant websites through the Internet. Many consumers are concerned that their credit card numbers might be stolen during data transmission. There exist well-established cryptographic techniques that can be used to address this threat; see, for example, (Ghosh 1998, Hassler 2000). Both SSL and SET employ well-established secure techniques for data encryption in order to provide confidentiality for transferred e-commerce data.

Although both SSL and SET seem to provide sufficient security to protect the data transmission process, there is a difference in the level of assurance for consumer payment information after it has been sent to a merchant web server. We have seen that a significant number of consumers are concerned about the trustworthiness of their merchant. Hence countermeasures that deny merchants access to sensitive customer information will potentially be of value in allaying customer fears.

As far as data storage is concerned, there is a significant difference between SSL and SET. When SSL is used, order and payment information are stored at a merchant web server and then the merchant will pass payment information, which contains the consumer credit card details, to the acquiring bank. Therefore, the merchant has access to consumer payment information, which may be a serious cause of concern to e-commerce consumers.

By contrast, in SET, different types of transaction information will be separately transmitted to specific recipients. The order information is encrypted in such a way that it can be decrypted by the merchant, while payment information is encrypted using an acquiring bank's public key and hence is not available to the merchant. This means that merchants will only be able to access order information, whilst payment information will be forwarded directly to the acquiring bank in encrypted form.

We can conclude that SET seems to be much more effective in preventing merchant fraud than SSL, since SSL, by its nature as a communication security protocol, cannot offer any protection for order and payment information stored at the merchant web server.

4.2 Merchant integrity

As opposed to the situation for most conventional debit/credit card transactions, there is no face-to-face contact in Internet shopping. Consumers are often concerned that the merchant that they communicate with may not be valid. As a replacement for photos and signatures used for conventional face-to-face authentication, digital certificates or digital IDs based on X.509 public key certificates (ITU-T 2000), have been widely used in both SSL and SET to authenticate principals in cyberspace.

In both SSL and SET, as part of the transaction process consumers and merchants authenticate each other using public key certificates. However, there are some significant differences between SSL and SET in terms of the institutions issuing certificates.

In SSL, consumers and merchants can obtain the necessary certificates from any trusted third party acting as a Certification Authority (CA). The CA public key needed by the consumer to authenticate the merchant's certificate will typically be embedded in the consumer's web browser, and will be distributed with the browser software. Handling of certificate revocation will depend on the facilities offered by the web browser (currently, this is typically a process not widely supported).

Note that, since the merchant's certificate is issued by a third party, all that is being achieved in SSL is entity authentication, and the user gains no guarantees about the reputability of the merchant. Finally, note also that, in SSL, only the merchant actually needs a certificate, as authentication of the consumer to the merchant is optional.

In SET, consumers (cardholders) can apply for digital certificates from their issuing bank, while the acquiring bank will be responsible for issuing digital certificates for merchant e-commerce (SET 1997). In this case and as opposed to the case for SSL, consumers can be assured that there is a financial institution certifying the merchant before making a transaction.

4.3 Payment Integrity

Payment information sent from cardholders to merchants must remain accurate and not be modifiable. Consumers need to be sure that the payment made will not be altered. Payment integrity services mean that if there is a change in payment information such as the details of the order, the recipient will be aware that the information was altered in transit. Digital signatures can be used in the electronic environment to replace conventional signatures for proving that a message originated with the signer and guaranteeing its integrity.

SSL and SET both use well-established cryptographic techniques to assure the integrity of e-commerce messages. SSL and SET thus both provide payment integrity services for transmitted data. However, there is a difference in the integrity protection provided for stored data between SSL and SET. With the use of SSL, the integrity protection only applies to the communications path between users and merchants. However, in SET the security critical parts of the transaction are protected using digital signatures that can be verified by the acquirer. As a consequence, the use of SSL does not provide any integrity protection for stored data, whereas SET does.

5 Current status of SSL and SET

As previously stated, SET potentially offers a higher level of security protection for e-consumer transaction information than does SSL. Despite this, SSL is widely used to protect e-commerce transactions whereas SET has not really taken off. Some of the reasons for this are as follows.

- Unlike SSL, SET initialisation is complicated. In particular, key pairs need to be established for each entity (and public keys certified), (SET 1997). According to Lieb (1999, p.2), 'the effort to obtain digital certificates has held up deployment of SET technology'.

- Interoperation of SET requires special software to be installed by every participating entity, whereas there is no need for additional software when using SSL.

- SET is somewhat inflexible in that, since digital wallets need to be present in the consumer PC, performing e-commerce transactions from third party PCs (e.g. in airport lounges, Internet cafes, etc.) is difficult, (Rescorla 2001).

- Implementing SET is costly since special applications are required to implement it (unlike SSL, which is built into commonly used web software).

- SET has not been adopted to any great extent, and is widely perceived as being 'dead'.

- The low speed and high complexity of transactions is another commonly made criticism of SET that reduces its attractiveness to both merchants and consumers, (Sherif 2000).

6   Combining SSL/TLS with SET

As stated earlier, SSL provides security purely for a communications link, and hence its use fails to address many of the security issues for an e-commerce transaction. By contrast, SET can provide integrity, confidentiality, and authentication services for entire e-commerce transactions. Although SSL is much simpler to implement and use, SET still appears to be the most appropriate scheme for Internet e-commerce security, given that many consumers remain very concerned about the threat of credit card fraud. We now concentrate on the possibility of combining elements of the two protocols; one being popular, lightweight and in widespread use and the other being comprehensive in its security coverage.

One way in which SSL and SET might be combined would be by focussing on the e-commerce transaction relationships. This might enable us to replace SET with SSL in the areas causing most implementation difficulties.

Electronic payment or e-payment systems generally comprise four main relationships: consumer and merchant, merchant and acquirer, acquirer and issuer, and issuer and consumer. When a consumer purchases products or services from a merchant, consumer financial information will pass in several stages via the merchant, an acquirer, and an issuer until the consumer receives a confirmation of the transaction from the merchant, and ultimately a bill is physically sent from the issuer to the consumer. In what follows, we focus on the relationship between consumer and merchant, since this is both the link of potentially highest security criticality and is also the source of many of the implementation issues with SET. One existing step in this direction is the 3D SET scheme, which we now describe. Note that this is by no means the only possible way in which elements of SET and SSL can be combined, although we do not explore this issue further here.

6.1   3D SET

One reason that SSL/TLS has been so widely adopted is that it offers a measure of security without requiring the consumer to perform any initialisation process (apart from installing a web browser). However, one problem with SSL/TLS is that merchants do not authenticate the cardholder. Remedying this defect inevitably appears to require the user to have security credentials of some kind, which implies an initialisation process of the type required by SET. One possible way to make SET much simpler for e-commerce consumers would be to remove the requirement for consumers to store certificates on their PC, and instead give this responsibility to the issuer, who communicates with the merchant's bank (acquirer) directly. This is precisely the approach adopted by 3D SET (Bounie and Vaninetti 2001), proposed by Visa as an alternative version of the SET scheme. 3D SET operates between the three domains in an e-commerce transaction, namely the acquirer, issuer, and interoperability domains. When consumers order products or services under 3D SET, all payment facilities, including consumer certificates, are securely stored at the issuer secure server. SSL could be used to secure consumer payment information when sent between consumer and merchant.

7 Conclusions

The use of both SSL and SET has clear benefits to e-consumer and merchant. Although SSL is very convenient to use to protect Internet e-commerce transactions, SET obviously addresses the lack of consumer confidence in e-commerce rather better than does SSL. However, the complexity of SET scheme has restricted its adoption by e-commerce end-users. The 3D SET technology appears to be a possible means to reduce the complexity of SET implementation at end-users. Furthermore, the possibility of combining SSL and SET is also likely to encourage consumers to participate in e-commerce, offering both convenience and confidence. In a further paper we will consider the future of SET in e-commerce.

8 References

Bounie, D. and Vaninetti, L. (2001), "E-Payments: Which Systems in Europe for the Coming Years?", *ENST*, August.

NCC Report (2000), "E-Commerce and Consummer Protection: Consumer – real needs in a virtual world", *National Consumer Council*, August.

ITU-T (2000), *Recommendation X.509 (03/00) – Information technology – Open Systems Interconnection – The directory: Public-key and attribute certificate frameworks*, March.

Friedman, M., Kahn, P. H. and Howe, D. C. (2000), "Trust online", *Communications of the ACM*, Vol. 43, No. 12, pp34-40, December.

Ghosh, A. K. (1998), *E-Commerce Security, Weak Links, Best Defences*, John Wiley and Sons, New York.

Hassler, V. (2000), *Security Fundamentals for E-Commerce*, Artech House, Massachusetts.

Jarupunphol, P. and Mitchell, C. (2001), "Actual and perceived levels of risk in consumer e-commerce", In *Proceedings of 2nd International We-B Conference*, November, pp.207-216.

Lieb, J. (1999), "Getting secure online – an overview", *CommerceNet – The Strategies Report*, Vol. 1, No. 3, pp1-4, July.

Merkow, M. S., Breithaupt, J., and Wheeler, K. L (1998), *Building SET Applications for Secure Transactions*, John Wiley and Sons, New York.

Rescorla, E. (2001), *SSL and TLS – Designing and Building Secure Systems*, Addison-Wesley, Boston.

SET (1997), *Secure Electronic Transaction Specification – Book 1: Business Description*, SetCo.Org, May.

Sherif, M. H. (2000), *Protocols for Secure Electronic Commerce*, CRC Press, Florida.

Tomlinson, M. (2000), "Tackling e-commerce security issues head on", *Computer Fraud and Security*, Vol. 2000, No. 11, pp10-13, November.

Treese, G. W. and Stewart, L. C. (1998), *Designing Systems for Internet Commerce*, Addison-Wesley, Boston.

A Secure Multicast Architecture Based on Policy

Sun Wei-qiang, Li Jin-sheng, Hong Pei-lin, Xiong Ji-ping, Liao Xiao-fei
Information Networks Lab, University of Science and Technology of China
Email: sunwq@mail.ustc.edu.cn

Abstract

As link speed and device throughput are increasing rapidly in recent years, broadband service such as video-on-demand and remote education run all the way to commercialization. But the open characteristics of current multicast mechanism provide no means to ensure data secrecy and integrity. In this paper we introduce a method to enhance multicast security and explain that application level authentication is not enough to ensure multicast security. Then we present our policy-based multicast access control architecture. The two building blocks are introduced in detail, together with the messages exchanged between them. We further explain that our scheme is flexible and scalable.

Keywords

Multicast-Aware-l2-Switch, multicast security, policy

1. Introduction

The link speed and device throughput on the Internet have been growing rapidly due to the development of such technologies as ASIC, WDM, and optical switching. This gives ISPs wider space and more choices to provide bandwidth-consuming services such as video-conferencing, video on demand and remote education. To make use of bandwidth effectively, the traffic of such services should be transported to the user by multicast.

But the current widely deployed multicast mechanism provides no security measures to ensure the secrecy and integrity of multicast traffic (Moyer and Rao, 1999). Any host with network access can send UDP packets to particular multicast group. And in a multicast enabled network, networked hosts can also join any multicast group and then receive all subsequent traffic of that group. This open characteristic of multicast makes it very difficult to provide commercial broadband services that need to be carried by multicast. Figure 1 illustrates the basic principle of current multicast transport mechanism and its security problems.

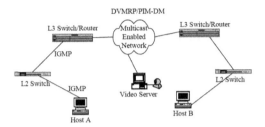

Fig. 1. Basic Multicast Service Model

Fig 1. shows a typical multicast enabled MAN configuration. L3 switches are connected to the metro core through 1000Mpbs link. Each L2 switch has a 100Mbps uplink and provides 10Mbps switched ports to home users. Here port allocation is on a per-user basis, e.g. one port for each broadband user. To join a multicast group, host A first sends a IGMP request to the network. The IGMP request is intercepted by L2 switch that is capable of IGMP snooping. It configures the corresponding user port to forwarding multicast traffic and forwards the IGMP request further to the network until it finally reaches an L3 switch. The L3 switch puts the corresponding interface into the multicast group and delivers subsequent traffic of that multicast group to this interface. If host B (not authorized though) sends some UDP packets, which will be called multicast noise in the rest parts of this paper, destined for that multicast address, these packets will be delivered to all the members in that group. This can bring two problems to the multicast receivers. First, since normal multicast traffic, along with noise traffic, are send to the receiver, the receiver may have problem dealing with them (e.g. error in video/audio decoding). This may result in degradation of quality of service. Second if the noise traffic is something like flood, all the group members may suffer from port congestion, which may bring down overall network QoS.

In this paper we introduce a method to enhance multicast service security and explain that application level authentication is not enough to ensure multicast security. Then we present our scheme that can effectively increase the secrecy and integrity of multicast traffic by rendering a policy-based multicast user access control on L2 switches. The two building blocks are introduced in detail, together with the messages exchanged between them. We further explain that our scheme is flexible and scalable.

2. Enhancing Security of Multicast Service by Application Level Authentication

Every network user who knows the multicast address of a certain service can retrieve/send data from/to the multicast group. We can make things a little better by changing the basic service model in Fig.1. As show in Fig.2, an authentication server is added (Cisco, 2001). The new model now works as follows.

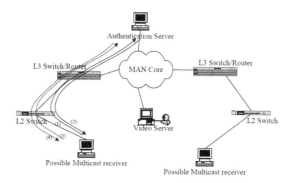

Fig. 2. Add application level authentication to multicast service model

First, a possible multicast receiver sends a request to the authentication server (1). Upon receiving the request, the authentication server (AS in brief) check its local database whether this user is authorized. If the user is authorized, AS will respond with available program list. Each entry of the list contains the name and a brief introduction of the program, but NOT the network parameters such as IP address and transport level port number (2). If the user is interested in one of the program, he/she will use the entry to generate another request to the AS (3). AS will check whether the user is authorized for the particular program and respond with either a positive answer or a negative one (4). If the user is authorized for the program, multicast client on the user host will automatically join the multicast group and start to receive data from the network. Otherwise the user will not get the multicast address or the port number used by this multicast service. A possible optimization is to merge this two-stage authentication, depending on service policy.

In this model, we try to provide multicast service in a transparent way, thus rendering more secrecy in multicast transportation and less possibility of been sneaked or attacked. This model also provides a means to do accounting on a per-user basis. This model works well at first glance. But problem will arise again if the multicast address and port number are stolen. By now it is obvious that authentication at application level may increase the security of multicast service, but cannot ensure it.

3. Policy Based Secure Multicast Delivery

We know from above that application level authentication is not enough to ensure the multicast service security. A strict access control mechanism must be applied to the group members and multicast source. A lot of research is going on in msec WG of IETF (Harney and Colegrove et al, 2001)and smug, gsec WG of IRTF(Hardjono and Canetti, 2000)(He and Hardjono, 2001). Among them, msec WG have introduced key building blocks (BBs) of a secure multicast architecture: data security transforms functional building block, group key management and group security association (GSA) functional building block, Group policy management functional building block. These researches are under progress and no Internet standard is available by now.

Starting from the basic idea of application level authentication, we suggest a policy based secure multicast architecture with the support of MAS (Multicast-Aware-l2-Switch). The proposed architecture makes use of the current multicast transportation infrastructure and is suitable for various multicast applications.

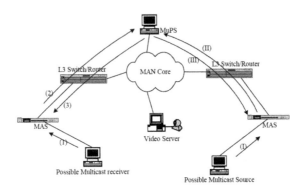

Fig. 3. A Policy Based Secure Multicast Architecture

The network configuration in Fig. 3 is pretty much the same as the one in Fig.2 only that AS in Fig.2 is replaced by MuPS (Multicast Policy Server) and ordinary L2 switches are replaced by MASes (Multicast Aware l2 Switches), which are two functional building blocks of this architecture. In the following parts we will talk about this architecture in detail.

3.1. Multicast User Access Control

As mentioned above, any user who wants to join a certain multicast group will send an IGMP request to the network ((1) in Fig. 3). In traditional networks, this IGMP request will be intercepted by the L2 switch and later forwarded further to the network. L2 switches use the information in the IGMP request to configure its local interface. In our scheme, MAS, in much the same way of a L2 switch, will intercept the IGMP request sent by user. But MAS will not forward this request further before it is authenticated. Upon receiving the request, MAS will generate a (User IP Address, Port Identifier, Requested Multicast Address) 3-tuple and send them in a policy request to MuPS (2). MuPS will check the request against the rules in its policy database. If the user, either identified by the Source IP address or Port ID, is authenticated, MuPS will return a positive policy, telling the MAS to accept the user and server him/her in a traditional way. Otherwise a negative policy will be sent to the MAS and user access to the particular multicast group will be denied (3). In this way, even an unauthorized user gets the multicast address and port number of the corresponding multicast service, he/her is still unable to get anything out of that group.

3.2. Control Over Multicast Source

In traditional networks, any user who knows the multicast address is free to send data to that group. In our scheme, we suppose one user gets the multicast address and begins to pour data to that group. These data will arrive at MAS ((I) in Fig.3). Once MAS finds that there is a noticeable amount of multicast traffic from the user port, it will issue a policy request to MuPS (II), containing the 4-tuple (Source IP address, Port Identifier, Multicast address, estimated bit-rate of incoming multicast flow). MuPS will authenticate the user upon receipt of the policy request and respond with a positive or negative policy according to authentication result (III). MAS will block the multicast flow on that user port if the user doesn't pass the authentication otherwise no further action is needed.

3.3. Messages Exchanged and Actions Taken

Some important messages that are needed are listed below and discussed in detail. In the following messages, a network user is called a valid user for a certain multicast group if he/she passes the required authentication to receive multicast traffic, otherwise he/she is called an invalid user for that group. And a network user is called a valid source if he/she is authorized to send data to that group, otherwise he/she is an invalid source.

1) JoinGroupRequest

This is a policy request issued by MAS. An IGMP join group request may be the first one from the user during this multicast session or simply a keep-alive message. In the former case, upon receipt of the request, MAS send a JoinGroupRequest message to MuPS. The parameter of this message is a 3-tuple (User IP Address, Port Identifier, Requested Multicast Address). It is desirable that the number of multicast services provided on the network is more than one so Multicast Address must be provided during policy request. In the later case, MAS only refresh the maintained status of corresponding multicast group on that port and forward this request uplink. No policy request is issued.MuPS checks the policy request against its policy database after it receives the request. If the user is authorized for the group, MuPS replies with a positive policy. Otherwise a negative policy is send to MAS. Here both Source IP Address and Port Identifier is required because some Internet Service Provider may use DHCP for address allocation and users can only be identified by port numbers.

2) SendDataRequest

This is a policy request issued by MAS. MAS sends this message to MuPS when MAS detects a possible multicast noise on a particular port. Here MAS also maintains the status of multicast input on each port. If one port is authorized and active, then no alarm is triggered locally and no policy request is sent to MuPS. Otherwise a SendDataRequest containing the 4-tuple (Source IP address, Port Identifier, Multicast address, estimated bit-rate of incoming multicast flow) will be send to the MuPS.

3) SolicitedValidUser

This is a positive reply of message 1). This reply will be sent to MAS if the user has passed required authentication.Upon receipt of this message, MAS will configure the corresponding port LISTEN_ENABLED for that group and forward the IGMP request from user further to the network. When traffic for that group comes from uplink, MAS will forward it to the ports that have been marked LISTEN_ENABLED.

4) SolicitedInvalidUser

This is a negative reply of message 1). This reply will be sent to MAS if user hasn't passed required authentication.Upon receipt of this message, MAS simply discard the IGMP request and mark the corresponding port LISTEN_DISABLED for that group.

Note that both 3) and 4) take the triple (Source IP Address, Port Identifier, Requested Multicast Address) as their parameter.

5) SolicitedValidSource

It is a positive reply to message 2). MuPS will issue this reply if user passed required authentication. Upon receipt of this message, MAS marks the corresponding port to SEND_ENABLED for that group and begins to forward multicast traffic from that source.

6) SolicitedInvalidSource

It is a negative reply to message 2). MuPS will issue this reply if user didn't pass required authentication. MAS marks the port SEND_DISABLED for that group and blocks subsequent multicast traffic for that group.Note that both 5) and 6) take the quadruple (Source IP address, Port Identifier, Multicast address, acceptable bit-rate) as their parameter only that in 6) MAS will ignore the last element.

7) UnsolicitedValidUser

Same to 5) only that it is not a reply.

8) UnsolicitedInvalidSource

Same to 6) only that it is not a reply.

Here message 7) and 8) are needed for flexible considerations. 5) and 6) can be considered as "dynamic" configuration but 7) and 8) are static ones. Which one should be used for a certain multicast service can be determined by the service characteristics and service policy. For example, ISPs may choose to configure corresponding ports when users are being registered for a certain multicast service. This will reduce the service delay caused by user authentication.

4. Conclusion

In this paper we present a policy based secure multicast architecture. In this architecture, two important building blocks are introduced. The necessary messages exchanged and actions taken are discussed in detail. As seen in the previous sections, our scheme is application independent. Multicast users are not required to encrypt their data since it will be totally invisible to unauthorized users (here we assume ISPs are reliable). Neither new protocol nor changes to existing multicast protocols are needed. MuPS can be implemented using COPS plus an AAA server that can run on the same machine. MuPS can also be distributed if applicable. So our scheme well meets the scaling of a metro area network under the condition that L2 switched ports are allocated on a per-user basis. Even changes to L2 switches are minimal. Some of the L2 switches already have ACLs (Access Control List) that can provide some user access control functions and a little extension is needed to fully support the requirements of an MAS. Some link layer chips (LSI, 1999) also support multicast filtering, which can also be easily used to implement functionalities required by an MAS. Authentication between MuPS and MAS can be imported if necessary. It can be implemented using widely used security measures such as AH and ESP.

Our scheme well meets the security need in a metro-area network, which has a homogenous network configuration. It is also easy to adapt complex network to share the security provided by our scheme.

References

Cisco Systems (2001), "New Features in IPTV v3.2", www.cisco.com

Haixiang He ,Thomas Hardjono and Brad Cain (2001), "Simple Multicast Receiver Access Control", draft-irtf-gsec-smrac-00.txt

H Harney, A Colegrove, E Harder, U Meth and R Fleischer (2001), "Group Secure Association Key Management Protocol", draft-ietf-msec-gsakmp-sec-00.txt

LSI Logic (1999), "Quad 100/10 Mbps Ethernet Controller with RMON/SNMP Management Counters", www.lsilogic.com

Matthew J. Moyer , Josyula R. Rao and Pankaji Rohatgi (1999), "A Survey of Security Issues in Multicast Communications", *IEEE Network*, Dec. 1999, pp12-23

T. Hardjono and R. Canetti (2000), "Secure IP Multicast: Problem Areas, Framework and Building Blocks", draft-irtf-smug-framework-01.txt

Internet smartcard, a device for solving security issues over Internet

Pascal Urien[1]

[1]SchlumbergerSema Smartcard Research Center, 36-38 rue de la Princesse,
BP 45, 78431 Louveciennes Cedex France
email: Pascal.Urien@louveciennes.sema.slb.com

Abstract.

This paper suggests using smartcards as Internet nodes, including HTTP servers and client protocols. Because XML is the emerging standard for data syntax, we propose to describe smartcards cryptographic resources by DTDs, and to access to these objects through URLs or XML messages. We underline that according to their computing capacities, smartcards could support classical Remote Procedure Call paradigms (using CGI like mechanisms) or implement trusted proxies performing authentication operations and computing session keys. These components could realise Authentication, Authorisation and Accounting features (AAA) needed in the next Internet generation, for example to ensure VoIP security operations or to negotiate and to charge QoS services.

Keywords.

Security, Internet, Smartcard.

1. Introduction.

The microprocessor based smartcard (SPOM - Self Programmable One chip Microcomputer) was born at the beginning of the 80s. This silicon chip realises (Guillou & al, 1992) five operations types: data input and output (in-going and out-going orders), reading and writing in a non-volatile memory (E²PROM), and cryptographic algorithms computation. Limited storage size (few dozen of Kb) and relatively low computing capacities (around one MIPS) led to software architectures based on a classical remote procedure call paradigm. In other words the *middleware* associated to smartcards realises most of software processing. Furthermore cryptographic embedded procedures or memory data structures are deduced in an implicit way (for example a SIM card works inside mobile phone) or by means of information printed on the PVC rectangle on which the silicon chip is stuck.

The convergence of several factors could contribute to modifying smartcard deployment in information technologies, particularly in fixed and mobile networks. The number of communicating devices continuously increases, for example, mobile phones, personal computers using wired or wireless networks, personal assistants, and so on. The data exchange between these digital entities, often portable, creates new requirements and markets for user authentication and software download. It becomes more and more complex to develop and support middleware dedicated to an heterogeneous set of devices.

Converging public and private networks is a trend today (Zuidweg, 2000). The IP protocol is more and more popular for network information exchange. As a consequence wired or wireless devices usually include a TCP/IP stack and are configured for Internet access. Smartcard chips' computing and memory capacities are increasing and will probably follow the More's Law. Today they may support communication stacks that are compatible with the IP protocol. Such a smartcard works as a highly secure Internet node.

It directly exchanges data with remote Internet servers, according to various Internet protocols specified in RFCs, such as HTTP, LDAP, SIP, and others. The smartcard can act as a Web server and a TCP client.

A secure die is a silicon rectangle, whose surface is typically smaller than 25mm². See Figure 1. This area is imposed by flexion constraints generated by the plastic card that supports the chip. It also results from a compromise between physical security (chip integrity control, temperature measurement, and so on) and logical complexity. A SPOM is organised around a CPU that exchanges data through an interconnection bus with several memory blocks (ROM, E²PROM, RAM), and an IO block managing a serial link.

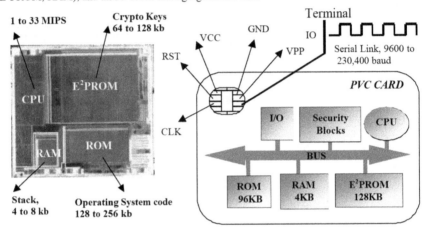

Figure 1. Smartcard components.

The memory size of a smartcard ranges between 128 and 256 Kb for ROM (with a relative surface 1), 64 and 128 Kb for E²PROM (with a relative surface 4), 4 and 8 Kb for RAM (with a relative surface 16). According to these technological constraints RAM size is rather small; while E²PROM block occupies most of chip surface. Classical 8 bits processors exhibit computing capacities ranging from 1 to 3 MIPS, but this parameter is greater than 33 MIPS for new architectures based on 32 bits RISC processors (Tual, 1999)

Smartcard is a *tamper resistant* device, designed to resist attacks, which aim at reading data, such as cryptographic algorithm keys, stored in the non-volatile memory. It is generally consider as the best secure system dedicated to information storage and cryptographic algorithms calculation. We classify attacks against smart cards into three types (Kommerling and Kuhn, 1999), *logical breaking* of the micro-controller (exploiting hardware defaults), *physical attacks* (chip reverse engineering), and *sophisticated analysis techniques* like differential power analysis (Kocher, 1999).

ISO 7816 standard (ISO 7816) specifies the communication interface between smartcard and its associated terminal. A terminal supplies a smartcard with energy and clock through a card reader. Information is exchanged via a serial link whose throughput is between 9600 and 230,400 bauds. Terminal produces a request (APDU). According to *T=0* 7816 protocol, the request contains at least 5 bytes (CLA INS P1 P2 P3) and optional bytes. The P3 gives the length Lc of the optional bytes. The card delivers a response that includes optional data and ends by a two bytes status word. When the response size is unknown, a status word *61 Le* gives the message length. Once this parameter is known, the terminal issues a *Get Response* command (CLA C0 00 00 Le) in order to collect the response.

Smartcard applications require a software interface to generate APDUs in order to invoke embedded resources. Figure 2 illustrates the win32 system architecture for interfacing user applications to smartcard secure procedures. Applications use *CryptoAPI* services to interface with one or more *cryptographic service provider (CSP)*. The CSP's provide cryptographic resources like ciphering/enciphering or keys generation. These components deliver such functions either by software way (through DLLs), or by smartcards means (*SCSP – Smartcard CSP*). In this last case the PC/SC stack (PS/SC, 1996) manages data exchange between smartcard and *CryptoAPI*. Invoking *CryptoAPI* from a navigator or from electronic mail software can transparently use smartcard embedded services.

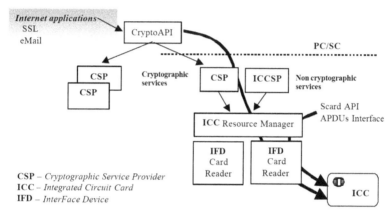

Figure 2. Smartcard integration in win32 systems.

2. Smartcard as an Internet node.

As mentioned above, smartcards communicate through APDUs. An application intending to use smartcard must generate APDU commands. Meanwhile more and more applications exchange data transported by TCP/IP packets and work with higher level protocols (like HTTP) defined by RFCs. If smartcard becomes an internet node, for example, using a reduced set of TCP ports, applications could easily interact with its secure embedded resources.

The Internet smartcard concept aims at using smartcard as network node. The secure chip runs server and client applications (defined in conformance with RFCs). Smartcard includes an Http server. Every embedded resource is identified by an URL. A smartcard can access a remote Internet server, either for internal reason (for example for data swapping), or for managing an authentication procedure.

Because it's not possible today to integrate physical communication resources in small silicon chip, the communication stack is distributed between terminal and smartcard. Furthermore a single IO pin is available for serial link. ISO 7816 transport protocols are half- duplex and work according to a request/response paradigm. Consequently a protocol like SLIP (Serial Line IP) is not applicable to smartcards. Although Internet protocols, such as HTTP, LDAP, and SIP, use half duplex data exchange, dialogue rules follow a request/response model. In fact full duplex requirements are induced by the TCP protocol, in which ACK packets may be asynchronously received during data packets transmission.

Several (HTTP) server architectures have been proposed for smartcards,

❑ *HTTP proxy server* (Barber, 1999). Software running in a terminal implements an HTTP server and is customized for each smartcard. It translates an incoming HTTP request as an APDUs set which select and read an embedded smartcard resource.

❑ *TCP server* (Rees, 2000). A subset of TCP and HTTP protocols is implemented in a smartcard. A tunnel software running in terminal forwards TCP/IP packets encapsulated in APDUs to/from smartcard.

❑ *Protocol bridge* (Urien, 2000). A software agent located in terminal translates TCP network packets as SmartTP packets (another transport protocol), which are sent/received to/from smartcard and carried by APDUs.

The CITI (Rees 2000) architecture deals with a fix IPv4 address. In this case, the smartcards only work in a particular Internet sub-network. In general, with today's Internet service capacities, it is unrealistic to assign billions of smartcards with Ipv4 addresses. IPv6 addresses are more attractive because it is possible to allocate a unique address for very embedded applications. Furthermore the Application Identifier (AID) of each embedded application is a 16 bytes number. The size of the AID is identical to that of an IPv6 address.

We have designed an architecture based on the SmartTP protocol (SmartTP, 2001). This architecture fits well to smartcard computing and communication capacities. It allows both server and client features. Although current implementation uses SmartTP over APDUs, we plan to deploy SmartTP over IPv6 for data exchange between smartcard and terminal. This will enable to identify smartcards applications by IPv6 addresses. It should be noticed that a terminal IPv4 address could be extended to an IPv6 format.

3. SmartTP architecture.

In our approach, the smartcard and the terminal share the terminal's TCP/IP stack and Internet access configuration, such as DNS server. Smartcard uses the terminal IPv4 address and is associated to well known TCP ports. TCP protocol is translated into a simpler one, SmartTP, at the terminal. The SmartTP adapts to ISO 7816 constraints. APDUs transport SmartTP between terminal and smartcard.

SmartTP (figure 3) can be thought as a light TCP version. Its packets have a five bytes header and up to 240 optional data bytes. The header includes source and destination references that are equivalent to TCP ports, and a flag field for session management (open, close, blocking calls). Autonomous software entities, named agents, perform on terminal side protocol conversion between TCP (server or client state machine) and SmartTP. Inside smartcard agents implement (HTTP) server or client features, such as LDAP and SIP. The agents communicate with Internet by means of sessions opened with terminal agents. The smartcard agents and terminal agents exchange information by SmartTP PDUs.

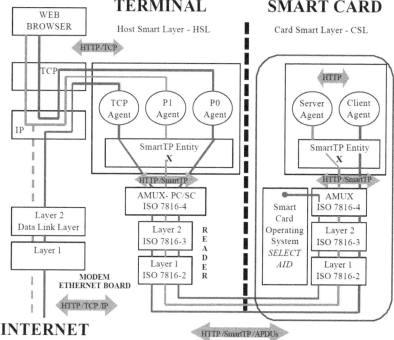

Figure 3. Internet smartcard & SmartTP architecture.

A terminal agent associated to TCP port P0 (P0=8080) gives access to smartcard embedded HTTP server. A smartcard WEB agent realizes the HTTP server. A terminal agent using TCP port P1 (P1=8082) translates HTTP messages in APDUs commands addressed to smartcard operating system, for example in order to select a particular embedded application. A smartcard agent, implementing client protocol, exchanges data with a remote internet server by using services offered by a terminal TCP agent. We hope to standardize P0 and P1 ports, in order to widely deploy smartcards in TCP/IP environment.

We have defined two URLs types for embedded resources identification and cryptographic procedures invocation,
- ❑ URLs for smartcard embedded application detection and selection, for example http://127.0.0.1:8082/write?format=gif&value=00A40400054A54455354 selects an JTEST applet ('5A' '54' '45' '53' '54'), and returns either an HTTP error status, or upon success a gif file of which download can be detected by a javascript . We called this technique *cardbug* (Urien, 2001).

❑ URLs giving access to secure resources, for example
http://127.0.0.1:8080/DES?Key1=69DA379EF99580A8 returns the ciphered value of an
height bytes number 69DA379EF99580A8 according to a DES algorithm using *Key1* key.

We should notice that an embedded resource identifier is made up of four elements, an
application name (AID), the terminal IP address, the TCP port P0, and the resource name with
optional call parameters.

4. Working with Internet smartcards.

There are two ways to use smartcards in information technologies.

❑ In the first approach, smartcard resources are invoked through a classical remote
procedure call paradigm. In a manner similar to distributed computing over internet
network, working with *common gateway interface* or similar methods, smartcard data or
cryptographic functions are identified by URLs. The URLs may optionally include call
parameters. These URLs can be deduced from the format generated by HTML forms,
which includes a procedure name and input fields. The procedure processes incoming data
and its name ends by a ? character. The input fields are separated by & character. As an
example a procedure call like function(parameter1,parameter2) is encoded as
http://127.0.0.1:P1/function_name?parameter1=value1&parameter2=value2.
The return value format is generally a set of ASCII characters (either a text string or an
hexadecimal number).

❑ Second approach uses smartcard as trusted proxy. An embedded Internet client application
is started from an incoming HTTP message. In this case the smartcard connects with a
remote Internet server, in order, for example, to realize an authentication procedure and to
deduce from it an ephemeris session keys that may be used by terminal for privacy and
integrity purposes. This operation mode is quite similar to the one that is used by SIM
cards in mobile phone. The SIM cards perform subscriber authentication and compute an
optional enciphering key. This process may ensure security for many emerging internet
services, such as authentication in wireless 802.11 networks, quality of service
management (QoS) or voice over IP architectures (SIP, H323,...). Smartcard is an
appropriate place to store authentication keys (either symmetric or asymmetric), to
generate cryptographic random numbers or to compute session keys.

5. XML and Internet smartcards.

XML syntax describes an information tree. The tags, including optional attributes, identify
nodes in the tree. A DTD (*Data Type Document*) file depicts the XML authorized structure.
An XML document is made of entities identified by URLs and transported by the HTTP
protocol. Because Internet smartcards natively support this protocol, they can be easily
integrated to XML technologies. Various XML components like DTD parts or XML entities
may be stored in internet smartcards. There is a real need for smartcard files identification and
standardization of messages used by embedded cryptographic functions. XML is a convenient
and elegant solution for solving these issues, first by using well known DTDs for information
description, and second by expressing messages in XML syntax. Figure 4 illustrates a process
for smartcard content definition. A service provider first defines a set of entities required for,

❑ Customer identification, a USERNAME entity specifies the card bearer name.
❑ Customer authentication, an AUTHENTICATION_PROC entity gives a pointer to an
authentication procedure.

❏ Session key determination, a KEY_PROC entity identifies a session key, computed from a previous authentication procedure.

Inside the secure chip, smartcard.dtd file establishes a correspondence between service entities and smartcard data and procedures. From this DTD, it is then possible to deduce of set of three URLs which are used for embedded resource invocation,

❏ http://127.0.0.1:8080/name.txt, is the service customer identifier.

❏ http://127.0.0.1:8080/F?x=1234, calls an authentication function F with an input parameter 1234 and returns the result expressed in an hexadecimal format.

❏ http://127.0.0.1:8080/Fkey, returns a session key computed during the authentication process.

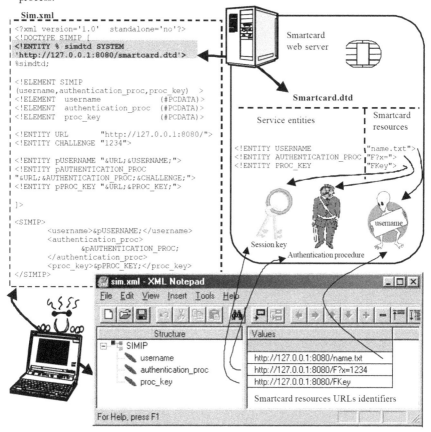

Figure 4. XML use in internet smartcard.

In this example internet smartcard is used as a server storing XML entities. An alternative is to implement an AUTHENTICATE procedure in smartcard. The procedure manages the connection to the remote authentication server, performs all needed operations and returns a key session value. Furthermore, by introducing an XML parser in smartcard (Urien, 2001) its possible to describe these interactions in XML scripts. The XML script is an executable file. It can invoke procedures through messages using an XML dialect. There are two main motivations for organising an internet smartcard around a central XML parser,

- ❑ First reason is flexibility; XML script offers a high level description of services, which are offered by smartcards. Embedded resources are described by specific DTDs, which guaranties that *well formed* scripts can be correctly executed.
- ❑ Second reason is supporting an open object distributed architecture. Embedded object messages are expressed in XML syntax, which is independent from any smartcard operating system.

6. Acknowledgments.

I would like to thank Karen Lu for its careful reading and helpful suggestions.

7. Conclusion.

In this paper we presented various perpectives for internet smartcard integration in emerging technologies dealing with internet wired or wireless networks. The characteristics of this device in terms of memory size and computing capacities make it suitable as security coprocessor, using the IP address and a specific TCP port of the host machine to which it is connected. Security is a key parameter for services transporting sensitive information or involving payment mechanisms. Although most of Internet protocols natively integrate security features, they usually do not specify an interface for smartcards. We underline that the definition of profitable and secure models for the net economy could be the mainspring for smartcard communication stack and data schemes standardization.

8. References.

Barber, J. (1999) "The Smart Card URL Programming Interface", *Proceedings of Gemplus Developer Conference GDC'99.*

Guillou, L.C. and Ugon, M. and Quisquater, J.J.(1992), "The smard card: A standardized security device dedicated to public cryptology", *Contemporary cryptology - The science of information integrity , G. J. Simmons, Ed., IEEE Press,* pp. 561-613.

ISO/IEC 7816, "Identification cards - Integrated circuit(s) card with contact". *International Organization for Standardization.*

Kocher, P.and Jaffe, J.and Jun,B. (1999) "Differential Power Analysis" *Proceedings of CRYPTO'99, Springer-Verlag,* pp 388-397.

Kommerling, 0. and Kuhn, M.G. (1999) "Design Principles for Tamper-Resistant smartcard Processors" *Proceedings of the USENIX Workshop on Smartcard Technology Smartcard'99,* pp 9-20.

PC/SC (1996) "Interoperability Specification for ICCs and Personal Computer Systems", © *1996 CP8 Transac, HP, Microsoft, Schlumberger, Siemens Nixdorf.*

Rees, J. and Honeyman, P. (2000),"Webcard: a Java Card web server". *Proceeding of Smart Card Research and Advanced Application Conference CARDIS'2000.*

Tual, J.P. (1999) "MASSC : A Generic Architecture for Multi application Smart Cards", *IEEE Micro journal,* N°0272-1739/99.

Urien, P. (2000) " Internet Card, a smart card as a true Internet node", *Elsevier Science Computer Communication,* volume 23, issue 17.

SmartTP (2001) "SmartTP, smart transfer protocol" *internet draft, draft-urien-SmartTP-00.txt.*

Urien, P., Saleh, H., Tizraoui, A. (2001) "XML Smartcards", *LNCS 2093,* IEEE International Conference on Networking, ICN'01.

Urien, P. (2001) "Programming internet smartcard with XML scripts", *LNCS 2140,* e-Smart 2001.

Zuidweg, J. (2000) "Software architectures for next generation networks", *Protocols for Multimedia Systems PROMS 2000 ISBN 83-88309-05-6,* pp 513,527.

Subscriber Authentication for Mobile Phones using Keystroke Dynamics

N.L. Clarke[†], S.M. Furnell[†] B.M. Lines[†] and P.L. Reynolds[‡]

[†] Network Research Group, Department of Communication and Electronic Engineering, University of Plymouth, Plymouth, United Kingdom.
[‡] Orange Personal Communications Services Ltd, Bradley Stoke, Bristol, United Kingdom.
Email: nrg@plymouth.ac.uk

Abstract

With the introduction of third generation phones, a technological transition is occurring in which the devices begin to have similar functionality to that of current personal digital assistants. The ability of these phones to store sensitive information, such as financial records, digital certificates and company records, makes them desirable targets for impostors. Current security for mobile phones is provided by the Personal Identification Number (PIN), which has weaknesses from both technological and end-user perspectives. As such, non-intrusive and stronger subscriber authentication techniques are required. This paper details the feasibility of one such technique, the use of keystroke dynamics. This feasibility study comprises a number of investigations into the ability of neural networks to authenticate users successfully based upon their interactions with a mobile phone keypad. The initial results are promising with individual users' classification performing as well as 0% false rejection and 1.3% false acceptance

1 Introduction

Mobile phones are becoming an ever-increasing part of our lives, with users becoming more reliant upon the services that they can provide. The evolution has been directed towards the provision of data services, by increasing data rates through technologies such as the General Packet Radio Service (GPRS) and the emerging third generation networks, which will enable a broadband service of up to 2Mbps (UTMS Forum 1998). With this increase in information capability, the mobile phone will begin to acquire many of the uses a personal computer has today. Access security currently takes the form of a Personal Identification Number (PIN), a secret-knowledge approach that relies heavily on the user to ensure its validity. For example, the user should not use the default factory settings, tell other people their PIN, or write it down. Apart from the technological arguments, a recent survey into attitudes and opinions of mobile phone customers found that 45% of respondents thought the PIN to be inconvenient and did not use the facility (Clarke et al. 2001). The findings also demonstrated the user's awareness of the security implications, with 81% of respondents overwhelmingly in supported for more security. Therefore the protection against unauthorised access and use of mobile phones is currently questionable – not because users do not want protection, but because they do not like the current method by which it is achieved.

It is clear that an alternative means of subscriber authentication is required to replace the PIN, but at the same time, other forms of secret knowledge-based approach are likely to be regarded as similarly inconvenient. It is, therefore, considered appropriate to examine the potential of a fundamentally different strategy. Amongst the most powerful approaches to facilitate this are biometrics, which are based not on what the user *knows*, but who the user *is*. Biometrics can include physiological characteristics, such as fingerprints and hand geometry, and behavioural traits, such as voice and signature. Another behavioural biometric is keystroke dynamics, which measures the typing pattern of a user. This paper presents the findings of an investigation into the feasibility of using keystroke dynamics to authenticate users on a mobile handset, according to the way in which they use the keypad.

2 Background Concepts

The principal concept behind keystroke dynamics is the ability of the system to recognise patterns, such as characteristic rhythms, during keyboard interactions. A significant amount of prior research has been conducted in this domain, dating back to the 1980s (Legett and Williams 1988; Joyce and Gupta 1990; Monrose and Rubin 1999). However, all of these studies, have focused upon alphabetic inputs from a standard PC keyboard. Little work to date has considered the feasibility of assessing numeric input as the basis for authentication (Ord 1999), and to the best knowledge of the authors, no work has evaluated the application of the technique to a context such as a telephony handset (although the idea was previously proposed by Furnell et al. (1996)).

The assessment of keystroke dynamics can be based upon the more traditional statistical analysis or relatively newer pattern recognition techniques, and previous published studies have incorporated both approaches. The results generally favour the effectiveness of the pattern recognition, with neural network approaches having been shown to perform well (Cho et al. 2000). The network configurations of particular interest are the *Feed-Forward Multi-Layered Perceptrons (MLP)*, as they have particularly good pattern associative properties and provide the ability to solve complex non-linear problems (Bishop 1995).

The size of the neural network in terms of number of layers, and number of neurons per layer, plays a key role in the processing ability of the network. However, in the design of neural networks very few, if any, solid rules exist to govern the size of neural networks, with respect to problem complexity. As such, concerns over network size are solved in this study through an iterative process of review and modification. For more information about the design, structure, training and implementation of neural networks, see reference (Bishop 1995; Haykin 1999).

As with other biometric techniques, the performance of the neural network classification for keystroke dynamics is measured using two error rates, the False Acceptance Rate (FAR) and False Rejection Rate (FRR). The former represents the level to which impostors are authorised by the network, and the latter is the likelihood an authorised user being rejected. However with keystroke dynamics, as with all biometric techniques, a threshold must be chosen for the error rates. The trade-off exists between high security/low user acceptance (a threshold value that provides a low FAR and high FRR) and low security/high user acceptance (a threshold value that provides a high FAR and low FRR). It is generally held as being infeasible to simultaneously achieve zero as they share a mutually exclusive relationship (Cope 1990). The point at which the FAR and FRR errors coincide is termed as the Equal Error Rate (EER) (Ashbourn 2000) and is often used as a performance measure when comparing biometric techniques. These measures are used as the basis for evaluating the practical experiments discussed in this paper.

3 Experimental Procedure

The eventual application of keystroke dynamics to a mobile phone would ideally authenticate a user by monitoring his or her continuous use of the phone, during activities such as the entry of telephone numbers, use of the menu system, and composition of text messages. However the objective at this stage is to investigate the feasibility of the technique rather than to provide a complete solution to the problem. As such, the initial study has been confined to two types of data, namely:

1. PIN code, representing a 4 digit number plus the enter key (i.e. 5 key presses in total).
2. Telephone Number, including area code, representing a 10/11 digit numerical number plus the call key (i.e.11/12 key presses in total).

From these sets of data, three investigations were designed, which sought to assess the ability of a neural network to classify users based upon:

1. Entry of a fixed four-digit number, analogous to the PINs used on many current systems. The users entered the same four-digit code thirty times. Twenty of these inputs were utilised in the training of the neural network, with the remaining ten used as validation samples.
2. Entry of a series of telephone numbers. Fifty mock telephone numbers are entered per user. The classification of inputs was expected to increase inter-sample variance, and thereby make it harder for the network to classify. Thirty samples were used in the training of the network, with the remaining twenty used as validation samples.
3. Entry of a fixed telephone number in order to facilitate a comparison against the results from the second experiment. As with the fixed four-digit investigation, there are thirty samples, twenty for training and ten for validation.

A total of sixteen test subjects provided the input data required for all three investigations. The neural networks in all investigations were trained with one user acting as the valid authorised user, whist all the other users are acting as impostors.

A specially written application was used to collect the sample data. However, it was considered that the standard numerical keypad on a PC keyboard would not be an appropriate means of data entry, as it differs from a mobile handset in terms of both feel and layout, and users would be likely to exhibit a markedly different style when entering the data. As such, the data capture was performed using a modified mobile phone handset, interfaced to a PC through the keyboard connection. Figure 1 shows a screenshot from the data capture software that was used.

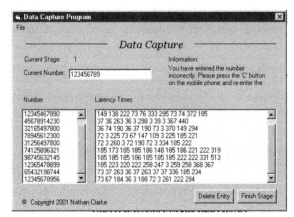

Figure 1 : Data Capture Software

Due to the limitations of data collection, the input data required for training and testing of the authentication system had to be collected in a single session. Ideally, the data would be collected over a period of time, in order to capture a truer representation of the users typing pattern. For example, by asking the user to type in 50 telephone numbers all at once, could result in an exaggerated learning curve.

4 Results

The analysis of the input data allows an insight into the complexities of successfully authenticating a person from a single input vector of latency values. The problem is that latency vectors observed from a single user may incorporate a fairly large spread of values. This spread, otherwise known as variance, is likely to encompass input vectors that closely match other users. Because users' latency vectors do not exist on clearly definable classification regions, the problem is made that much more complex for the neural networks.

Two types of variance exist in the latency data:

- inter-sample variance, which ideally would be zero, so that every sample a user inputs would be identical and therefore easier to classify.
- inter-user variance, a measure of the spread of the input samples between users, which would be ideally as large as possible in order widen the boundaries between classification regions.

An initial analysis of the inter-sample variance indicates that they are not ideal by any means, however some users obviously have smaller inter-sample variances than others. The graphs in Figure 2 illustrate the inter-sample mean for each of the users in each investigation. Significant differences can be noted between the three sets of results, such as generally smaller standard deviations and the lower average latency for the fixed telephone number tests when compared to those from the test in which varying numbers were used. This was expected, in the sense that users would become used to entering the fixed telephone number, and therefore the inter-sample variation would progressively decrease. However, the 4-digit PIN investigation shows the lowest inter-sample variance, possibly indicating strong classifiable regions.

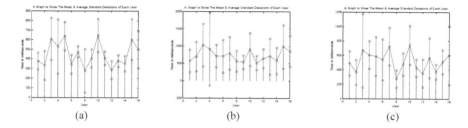

(a)   (b)   (c)

Figure 2 : Mean & Standard Deviation of User's for (a) 4-digit PIN, (b) varying telephone numbers, and (c) fixed telephone numbers

It is interesting to note that the inter-user variance is not considerably larger than the inter-sample variances, as would be favourable, indicating that less well defined classification boundaries exist.

Analysis of individual network performances shows unfavourably large error rates, with some users experiencing FAR/FRR pairs of 41%/20% and 37%/60% in the telephone number investigation. The large error rates suggests there are groups of users with more similar typing characteristics than others, thus making it difficult for the networks to classify them correctly. In particular, two groups of users were identified as having high false acceptances as each other. One such group is illustrated in figure 3(a), with figure 3(b) illustrating a group of dissimilar user inputs. However, in constrast, some users exhibited much more encouraging FAR/FRR figures, such as 1.3%/0% and 4%/10%, both of which were observed in the PIN code investigation. Results such as these suggest that keystroke characteristics can indeed be used to facilitate correct classification, but further development is required in improving network sensitivity and generalisation in other cases.

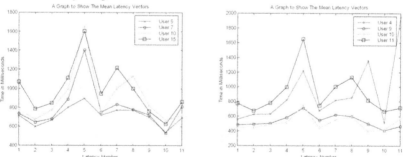

Figure 3 : (a) Similar User Input Latency Vectors (b) Dissimilar User Input Latency Vectors

The overall performances of the neural networks are illustrated in figures 4(a), (b) and (c). The optimum configurations for the MLP's were 11 inputs, 22 neurons for both the 1st and 2nd hidden layers, and 1 neuron in the output layer (i.e.11-22-22-1) for the telephone number based investigations, while the configuration for the PIN based investigation was 4-8-8-1. Unsurprisingly the fixed input networks of the PIN and fixed-telephone investigations performed substantially better than the pseudo-random telephone investigation. The difference between the two telephone investigations are an improvement in the FRR of over 50% and 35% in the FAR. Interestingly, the results indicate that the neural networks can classify the 4-digit PIN input at least as well as an 11-digit fixed telephone input. It would be normal to assume the more information a system has, the better it is able to classify the inputs.

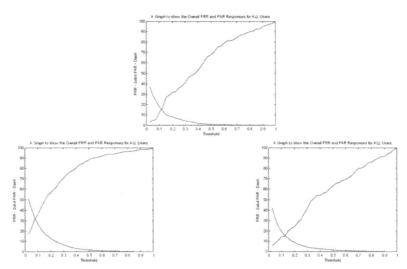

Figure 4 : Overall FRR & FAR for the (a) PIN Code Input Neural Network (b) Pseudo-Random
Telephone Neural Network (c) Fixed Telephone Neural Network

The exclusivity of the FA and FR rates are clear, as one error rate decreases the other increases. The equal error rates (EER) for this study are shown in table 1. The threshold value assigned to the network is the level at which the network operator considers that the compromise between security and convenience has been established. For this study, the threshold level was kept constant throughout each of the networks per investigation to enable comparison. Both the PIN Code and mock telephone number networks were given static thresholds of 0.1, and the fixed telephone a threshold of 0.125. Tables of results for a static threshold level can be seen in table 1.

Investigation	FAR (%)	FRR (%)	EER (%)
PIN Code	18.1	12.5	15
Varying Telephone	36.3	24.3	32
Fixed Telephone	16	15	15

Table 1 : Investigation Results

5 Discussion

The investigations have shown the neural networks ability to classify valid and invalid users with a relative degree of success. The networks ability to classify users entering a varying series of telephone number was, as expected, the weakest of network configurations. The classification of fixed 4-digit input suggests that the entering of a PIN number has a quite unique dialling pattern of its own. The reason for this might lie in the fact that users become familiar with typing the 4 digit PIN quite quickly, enabling improved classification. The fixed telephone number has more digits, so while the entry is more consistent than for a variable series of phone numbers, it is not as fluid as the PIN code. However, more practice would probably improve this. Additionally, the 11-digit input has a longer feature set, making it more difficult for an impostor to duplicate.

From the two investigations surrounding the telephone number input, it can be seen that improvements in the inter-sample variance experienced between the varying and fixed telephone numbers has provided a proportionality higher improvement in network performance. However, it should also be noted that the inter-sample and inter-user variances are not the only relationships that determine the neural networks ability to classify users. For instance, the inter-sample variance of User 8 in the PIN investigation is one of the largest in the user group and covers the input latency range of other users, indicating a small inter-user variance. Yet, User 8 has the best FAR and FRR of all the users.

From the analysis of the individual network performances, it is clear that some networks perform far better than others. For instance User 9 in the PIN investigation has an FAR of 90% with Users 11 and 13. This could indicate one of two problems. Firstly, the typing patterns of those users are just too similar and no network would be able to successfully classify those users on a regular basis, or, more likely, it may be the case that the network is not sensitive enough to users data and through further training of the networks with those users with similar responses will help increase network sensitivity. Either way, this error rate is completely unsatisfactory and any further development will need to monitor the individual user performances, not just the average. Conversely, it is worth noting that individual networks performed as well as 0% FRR and 1.33% FAR, indicating that user typing patterns can be classifiable with a good degree of accuracy.

The FAR and FRR errors indicate how often a valid and invalid user will be authenticated onto the system. The trade off between the inconvenience of valid users not being accepted and invalid users being accepted means ideally a level has to be chosen at which these are both minimised. However the likelihood is one error rate will be minimised over another. From the results, if the FAR were to be set in the 2% range this would translate to having an FRR of approximately 55% for the PIN code and fixed telephone inputs. Inversely, setting the FRR in the 5% range (lowest FRR level) corresponds to approximately an FAR of 40%. It would be likely that a level in between theses extremes would be chosen by the network operator, to ensure the impact on legitimate users is minimised, but keeping a practical and useable level of security.

6 Conclusion

This paper has presented an investigation into the feasibilty of using keystroke analysis as a means of enhancing subscriber authentication on mobile handsets. Although the mis-authentications observed at this stage indicate that a practical implementation would prove too error prone, the nature of the investigtions, and the controlled environment in which they were carried out, are believed to be large contributing error factors (as well as actually being necessary to establish a worst case senerio).

The implementation employed in this study has adapted the neural network approach to determine the feasibility of a keystroke-based technique. As such, several areas for possible further research and experimentation can be identified. The first would be to obtain more representative input data, which would ideally incorporate all user input data from the mobile phone (including keystrokes relating to SMS text message entry and menu interactions), and be obtained over a reasonable period of time, in order to ensure a truer representation of users normal behaviour.

From an analysis perspective, further developments could include:

- Removal of outliers from the source input. A quick analysis of the user input data shows a small number of anomalies, which could be unfavourably biasing the network. This will have the effect of reducing the inter-sample variance.
- Increased network sensitivity by training the network using impostor input data that closely matches that of the authorised user, rather than training with all impostor input data.
- Use of generalisation techniques, such as early stopping and regularisation, to optimise the training of the network.
- Analysis of network structure, in terms of network interconnections and transfer functions. Although feed-forward backpropagation networks are amongst the best pattern associators at present, this need not be the case. A structure may exist that is better able to classify this particular problem.
- Updating network configuration over time through re-training.

However, no matter how accurate keystroke analysis becomes, the mutually exclusive relationship between false acceptance and false rejection rates would mean that it is unlikely that 0% can be achieved for both simultaneously. Therefore the study suggests the best implementation of a keystroke analysis authentication technique would be as part of a larger hybrid authentication algorithm, involving two or more non-intrusive biometric authentication techniques for normal authentication.

The technqiues discussed here will be the focus of futher research and practical experimentation by the authors.

References

Ashbourn, J. 2000. *Biometric. Advanced Identity Verification. The Complete Guide.* Springer.

Bishop, M. 1995. *Neural Networks for Pattern Recognition.* Oxford University Press.

Cho, S., Han, C., Han, D., Kim, H., 2000. *Web Based Keystroke Dynamics Identity Verification using Neural Networks.* Journal of Organisational Computing & Electronic Commerce, Vol. 10, No.4, pp 295-307.

Clarke, N., Furnell, S., Rodwell, P., Reynolds, P. 2001. *Acceptance of Subscriber Authentication for Mobile Telephony Devices.* Computers & Security. (In press)

Furnell, S.M.; Green, M.; Hope, S.; Morrissey, J.P. and Reynolds, P.L. 1996. *Non-Intrusive Security Arrangements to support Terminal and Personal Mobility.* Proceedings of EUROMEDIA 96, London, UK, 19-21 December 1996. pp167-171.

Haykin, S. 1999. *Neural Networks. A comprehensive Foundation. Second Edition.* Prentice Hall.
Cope, B. 1990. "Biometric Systems of Access Control", *Electrotechnology,* April/May: 71-74

Joyce, R., Gupta, G., 1990. *Identity Authorisation Based on Keystroke Latencies.* Communications of the ACM, 33(2): 168-176, February.

Legett, J., Williams, G., 1988. *Verifying User Identity via Keystroke Characteristics.* International Journal of Man-Machine Studies, Vol 28, pp 67-76.

Monrose, F., Rubin, A., 1999. *Keystroke Dynamics as a Biometric for Authentication.* Future Generation Computer Systems, 16(4) (2000) pp 351-359.

Ord, T. 1999. *User Authentication Using Keystroke Analysis with a Numerical Keypad Approach.* MSc Thesis, University Of Plymouth, UK.

UMTS Forum. 1998. *The Path Towards UMTS – Technologies for the Information Society.* Report Number 2. http://www.utms-forum.org/reports.html

Anomaly Intrusion Detection System Based on Online User Recognition

Alexandr Seleznyov, Oleksiy Mazhelis, Seppo Puuronen

Computer Science and Information Systems Department
University of Jyväskylä
P.O. Box35, FIN-40351, Jyväskylä, Finland

E-mail: {alexandr,mazhelis,sepi}@it.jyu.fi

Abstract

In this paper we present first results of the intrusion detection project aimed at development of an efficient and portable anomaly intrusion detection system. The system detects masqueraders by comparing current user behavior with his behavioral model stored in a profile. The model of user behavior in each profile is represented by a number of patterns that describe sequential and temporal behavioral regularities. This paper also discusses implementation issues, describes our solutions and provides performance results of the prototype.

Keywords

Network Security, Anomaly Intrusion Detection, User Profile, Online Verification

1 Introduction

An explosive spread of computers and computer networks has resulted in a society that is increasingly dependent on information stored on them. Benefits, provided by the connection of a computer system to a network, create at the same time almost unlimited opportunities for malicious persons, which using software applications' and operating systems' vulnerabilities may successfully penetrate a networked computer system. To eliminate potential devastating consequences caused by breaches in computer systems more and more attention is paid to this issue. However, despite of these efforts, occurrences of security violations in the computer networks became increasingly frequent.

If an attack is successful, it turns into an intrusion and traditional security tools are not capable to deal with the problem. Therefore, there is a need to implement an additional level of protection, such as a dynamic behaviour tracking, which can act as burglar alarm in respect of computer system.

In this paper we present an approach to anomaly intrusion detection. Here we intend to improve main parameters of the anomaly detection: maximize percentage of detected attacks and minimize the rate of false positives. Our approach is based on matching encoded patterns against current stream of events to find deviations from normal behaviour. Analyzing these deviations, an intrusion detection system decides whether it is intrusion or normal user behaviour changes. It relies on the background assumption that user's behaviour includes sequential and temporal regularities that can be detected and coded as a number of patterns. The information derived from these patterns could be used to detect the abnormal behaviour and to learn the intrusion detection system.

The rest of the paper is organized as follows. Section 2 provides all necessary definitions followed by the description of a user profile. Section 3 describes the architecture of the implemented IDS prototype, section 4 provides experimental results of prototype's performance and compares them with results of other approaches. Finally, in Section 5 concludes this work.

2   User Profile

In this section, an anomaly detection methodology, used in our prototype, is briefly described (for details see (Seleznyov *et al.*, 2001)). This work aims at improving anomaly detection abilities by covering as fully as possible different aspects of user behavior. It may be achieved by defining and then discovering more kinds of patterns in user behavior that characterize this behavior in a more complete way. We define two kinds of patterns: sequential and temporal. *Sequential pattern* describes a sequence of events where they repeat time after time in the same consecution. *Temporal pattern* contains regularities that may be observed among events' time lengths and time intervals between them. We would like to note that this division into sequential and temporal patterns is very relative and used for clarity purposes only.

Here we consider the process of user profile creation as a search for regularities in user's activities through analysing audit trails. These regularities are aggregated into a user profile on a higher abstraction level, which is source-independent abstract behavioral model. To represent the behavior regularities we use temporal intervals (actions) connected by relations (derived from Allen's temporal relations (Allen, 1983)). Below we introduce class and instance notions used to build the behavioral patterns.

Action class is a general concept describing one of the possible kinds of actions. Action class contains descriptions of events that start and end that action and possible events between them. A number of all possible actions is limited by operation system tools and installed programs, therefore, the number of action classes is finite and known beforehand.

An *action class instance* is a record that describes a certain group of actions that belong to the same action class and have similar temporal characteristics. By similar temporal characteristics, we imply temporal distances (time lengths) that characterize actions. These distances must be distributed normally in order to be grouped into a same instance. Instances are described by their statistical parameters - μ and σ. Since an action has a beginning and an ending, it is described by a temporal interval that has length T (action's length).

Similarly concepts of *relation class* and *relation class instance* are defined. Relation class describes one of possible relations between actions, meanwhile the relation class instance describes a set of relations that have similar temporal characteristics - the of temporal distance between actions - t and belong to the same relation class.

The instances of action and relation classes are needed in order to store in the profile statistical information about temporal characteristics of user's actions. To store sequential patterns a temporal-probabilistic tree is used (Seleznyov *et al.*, 2001). Nodes of the tree correspond to the action instances, while the edges reflect the relations between them.

3   System Architecture and Simulation Results

During implementation of the prototype we had to address the following issues:

1. Every system has a unique configuration of software that makes it almost impossible to have a consistent test environment.

2. There is no any comprehensive definition of what a "system load" is, therefore it is necessary to define it for our own case.

3. One of important requirements to intrusion detection systems is minimum performance impact, but nowhere is defined what "performance" means. Some people choose CPU load, others choose response time, etc.

We defined the "system load" and "performance" for our case in a way that it would allow us to compare our results with evaluation results of other intrusion detection systems. The tests described below are aimed at showing the possibility of usage and possible benefits of discovering and employing behavior regularities for user recognition. The prototype has been developed to serve as a proof of concept implementation of the model.

3.1 Application Architecture

Software we have implemented to support the classification process contains numerous classes, each providing a different functionality. Some part of it had to be implemented on an operating system level, other on an application level. Below we will concentrate on some important design details.

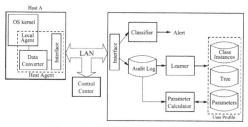

Figure 1: Prototype architecture.

Figure 1 depicts main components of the implemented prototype. The architecture consists of three main components, which are interacting with each other: detection server, control center, and host agents.

3.2 Exchanging Information Between System's Modules

The external representation of actions is designed as a straightforward syntax that directly reflects their structure and provides user id, computer id, class name, start and end time of the action. These specifications may be stored in a file and maintained as encrypted strings. Events are collected by a local agent, transformed into actions by a data converter, prepared for sending and encrypted by a network interface.

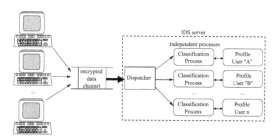

Figure 2: Data flow inside the prototype during online classification.

In the Figure 2 an information flow in the prototype is depicted. As can be seen information comes from different sources - workstations. A single user may be logged into a single work-station, or several remotely/locally logged users may share it. All collected information is assembled into a single stream of events and comes to a detection server through an encrypted data channel, which protects private information from outside eavesdropping.

In our prototype we have used host agents compiled for several *nix type of operating systems. They were implemented as a loadable kernel modules. When an operating system starts on a local workstation the host agent is loaded into memory. Then it is reports to the control center that it is loaded and goes into standby mode waiting activation and synchronization from the control center.

The detection server instantiates an independent application server (classification process) for every active user. Every process encapsulates necessary information about normal behavior of a single particular user (it is taken from a user profile). All received by the detection server information is decrypted and dispatched to different application servers, each of which tracks and analyses the behavior of a specified user as described in (Seleznyov *et al.*, 2001).

3.3 Learning

In order to use the system it has to be trained first. The training period consists of two phases: training itself (approximately 80% of the training period) and calculation of thresholds (20%). During the first phase, the system has to create profiles for all users. Those profiles have to be detailed enough in order to allow the system to perform a classification with an acceptable accuracy. In other words, the first phase has to be long enough to allow the system to learn a number of patterns in user behavior (otherwise it will make numerous classification errors). Also, this phase cannot be too long. It is difficult to submit only "good" cases during long period of time, the longer time interval the higher probability that there will be "bad" cases among a training set that may increase a false positives rate. Additionally, the long training phase may cause some over-training: it is possible that the system learn too many unnecessary behavioral details rather than patterns, which will result in growth of a false negatives rate.

During the second phase, the system calculates individual thresholds for every profile. It is done to increase the accuracy of the classification. For these calculations, system submits positive cases (taken from a stream of events of a same user, which were not present in the training set on the first phase) to a classifier and defines the detection threshold according to classification results.

Figure 3: An example of a pattern.

There is a concept drift issue when dealing with behavioral models: users' behaviors tend to change with time, therefore the effective lifetime of a static user profile is limited. To deal with this issue we developed our methods in a way that they constantly update user profiles making new information to appear and old to disappear for the profiles. To test the ability to successfully update the user profiles we took all users' history in our experiments. Some users' data was containing up to 20000 actions covering more then six months of user activity. During this time the behavior was changing in one or another way. In our experiments the system was trained during the learning phase (first few weeks of the user data) and then tested on the rest of the covered by the user data interval (sometimes more then six months), updating profiles when necessary. Therefore, all our experiments were conducted on the dynamic profiles and results described here represent system's performance in a real word environment.

For the implementation we decided to chose chains (figure 3) to represent behavioral patterns. Every state in the chain is connected with another one by a basic temporal relation (Seleznyov *et al.*, 2001) (in our case solid line represents *after* relation, and dotted line - *during*). Each chain consists of two parts: conditions of transaction and possible destination states. The conditions of the chain are expressed by several actions connected by relations. In our example (figure 3) we have two actions: class "2"(instance 1) *after* class "1" (instance 2). It is possible to increase the number of conditions, which in turn will increase patterns' descriptive precision, but at the same time, it may increase a rate of false negatives, since the patterns will describe too many details instead of behavioral trends.

Second part of every chain is a set of actions. These actions represent possible actions that a user may chose after performing those described in the condition part. In our example there are following possibilities: 64% that the user will perform action from class "4" (instance 1) after finishing previous action, 26% and 10% that action class "4" (instance 2) and "7" (instance 2) respectively, will start before the previous action will be finished. Temporal parameters that are stored with action and relation instances help to determinate how much time should pass between previous action's end and next action's beginning in the first case (for *after* relation), and in the second case they show how the previous and the next action overlap each other (for *during*). Oversimplifying, it is possible to say that the chain's structure is an *if-then* rule, which contains extensive sequential and temporal statistical information. Also, these chains may be assembled in a tree, for example for manual profile control.

4 Performance

The experiments described in this section were performed on an AMD 1.4 GHz workstation with 512MB of memory running RedHat Linux 7.1 under light load. Host agents collected the audit from different operating systems: RedHat Linux 6.1, RedHat Linux 7.1, Debian GNU Linux 2.0, FreeBSD 4.1. Logs of 16 different users were collected for the experiments.

Here in addition to the traditional accuracy characteristics we employ maximum *time-to-alarm* measurement. It should be short enough in order to detect hostile activities fast, but long enough so that normal work is interrupted by false alarms as rare as possible. In this work we define the time-to-alarm as a maximum time interval during which an anomaly will be detected if it is present in the current behavioral sequence.

For our experiments we collected output streams that were produced by host agents for different users. Later those outputs were given as an input for profile building techniques. Lacking traces of intrusive behavior, we tested approache's viability on the task of differentiating different valid users. Anomalous situations were simulated by testing one valid user's data against another user's profile. This testing approach does not cover all possible misuse scenarios, but it gives a possibility to evaluate the viability of the our approaches.

4.1 Space Requirements

Here we consider possible space requirements for user profile storage. For our experiments, we have tried from one up to for conditions for all users. For example, for two conditions the mean size of the profile is 18362 Bytes and the size of profile varies between 4176 Bytes and 34476 Bytes. Considering a case when our prototype is monitoring 10 000 users, we can approximate that we will need to reserve in order to store all profiles about 175.1 Mb.

There are two factors that may affect significantly the average size of the profile: the number of classes and the number of conditions for the patterns. According to our observations the number of classes does not affect the size of profile as much as the number of encoded conditions. Therefore, fixating the number of conditions (with two conditions we can get more or less reasonable size of the profile) we are able to keep the size of the profile in a certain range, and, thus, estimate space required to store profiles.

4.2 Accuracy

There is a number of different parameters that may affect classification accuracy. Here we try to carefully select those in a way that minimize an overall error rate. Each profile was tested against the corresponding test set for each user. A test against user's own profile allows us to examine false negative (false rejection FR) alarm rates, while testing against other profiles allows us to determine false positive (false acceptance FA) rates. Below we are going to determine suitable parameters for our approach. Firstly, it is necessary to determine a number of conditions in patterns in our prototype.

After trying different number of conditional states we concluded that two states are sufficient to provide acceptable accuracy. When the number of conditions is one, patterns encode too general model of behavior, therefore the false positive rate is high. With growth of conditions number, the patterns will become more and more specific. They will describe small unnecessary detail rather then trends in user behavior. As a result we will encounter more false negative cases.

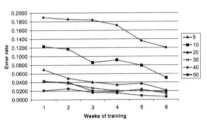

Figure 4: Dependence of the overall error rate on the length of the training period for different window lengths

After this it is necessary to determine a sliding window length. This length implicitly affects time-to-alarm rate: the longer window the longer a time-to-alarm interval. We observed that during eight hours working day a system receives in average 369 actions per user. Average time between actions is about 78 seconds per user. This means that if we take the window length as 20 actions our system will have minimum 26 minutes time-to-alarm, which is, in our opinion, is quite suitable. Thus, since the system determines the length of the window during the learning stage, we established the minimum length of 20 actions and the maximum of 60 (time-to-alarm lies in [26,78] minutes interval). The length depends on user activity and size of patterns in user profile. We would like to point out that in our experiment the system was choosing the window length to minimize the overall error rate. However, in real life some additional requirements, such as shorter time-to-alarm, may be applied during this process.

The Figure 4 shows that the length of the sliding window, which was chosen at the beginning of this section, is quite suitable for a temporal-probabilistic tree. The system is ready to use after approximately two weeks of training. After this its error rate will be not higher than 8%. The accuracy results achieved during our experiments are quite promising, however they should be treated with some skepticism since . We cannot be sure that they will be constant in the future since we cannot simulate all possible variants of user behavior.

There is differential analysis has been put as a foundation of user behavior classification, in which the detection accuracy does not depend on the number of profiles in the system (in contrast with to absolute analysis). We learn the system giving it only "good" examples, i.e. only event sequences of a single user for which we are building a profile. Then during the classification each classification process has a profile of a single user and compares only this user actions with his profile. Therefore, growth of the number of profiles in the system will increase a number of classification processes working in parallel, but not the error rate.

4.3 Timing Results

In order to measure classification time we have created an audit file that contains 14625 actions. We applied our approach on this audit log eight times. The result consists of two parts: classification time for actions inside of a sliding window and time necessary to update coefficient of reliability before moving the window. Obviously that the former one depends on window length and it forms variable overhead. The latter one is based on certain formulas, thus it does not depend on classification parameters and forms fixed overhead.

We observed that the classifier has spent $61.06\mu s$ to classify a single action (for 20 actions window length). Consider the extrapolation of these results to estimate the performance in real settings (for 10 000 users in the system). If they are all active the system will get 461 540 actions per hour. In this situation, a classifier will take 28.2s to classify all actions. This is about $\approx 1\%$ of the CPU's hourly activity.

4.4 Analysis

In this section, we analyze how the selection of different hardware could affect the results described. This gives us a possibility to make comparisons with other systems.

Faster system. If these experiments were run on a faster system then the classification time will slightly decrease. However, according to our observations, the CPU overhead due to classification processes is insignificant. If the detection server is devoted for a classification (as in our experiments) then it handles 10 000 users without any problems and therefore, making the system faster does not dramatically improve the overall performance.

Faster network connections. The amount of information sent over a local network depends only on the number of active users. Our prototype receives in average 40 bytes per one action. Therefore, for 10 000 users the network traffic overhead will be 513 bytes per second, which is insignificant amount for modern networks. Thus, we can conclude the main factor that may significantly affect the system's performance is a number of users that are active at the moment.

We took performance results of five different anomaly detectors to compare our results with. *Instance-based Learning.* The approach for the anomaly detection based on the instance-based learning was developed by T. Lane and C. Brodley (Lane and Brodley, 1997), (Lane and Brodley, 1999). Eight users were used to evaluate this approach and all false positives as well as false negatives were identified. The classifier's detection accuracy lies in (0.7,1) interval.

Neural Networks Approach. Here we take a report on experiments where neural networks were used for statistical anomaly intrusion detection (Zhang *et al.*, 2001). A classifier was build to detect anomalies in network traffic. Five types of neural networks were tested: perceptron, backpropagation, perceptron-backpropagation, fuzzy ARTMAP, and radial-basis function. The studies showed that backpropagation and perceptron-backpropagation networks have similar performance and both networks perform better then the other three types. The results for these networks: mean squared root errors (0,0.2) and misclassification rate (0,0.09).

NIDES based Frequentist Detector. This and the following two anomaly detectors were implemented and described in (Ali, 2001). To test these three approaches eleven test data sets were generated with different amount of noise and an alphabet size of six. Then 160 anomalies were injected into each of these sets. The frequentist detector is a statistical anomaly classifier, which takes frequencies of various components in the training data as a measure of normalcy of the data. For this approach the hit rate varied between 0.8 and 1 depending on the level of noise in the training data. However, the false alarm rate was sometimes quite high - up to 0.4.

A Data-mining based Detector. The detector was based on RIPPER (Lee *et al.*, 1999) which is a rule learning program. System call traces and *tcpdump* data was used to evaluate the approach. In this experiment the detector had negligible rate of false alarms (almost 0.00001), however, the hit rate of the detector was surprisingly low - up to 0.25. That shows that the detector cannot probably be used alone in an IDS.

A Generic Programming based Detector. This is a classifier built for supervised learning. All experiments were performed with population size 50, number of generations 20 and maximum depth of the GP tree of 45. Pattern size was varied from three to twelve during the tests. Author claims that the best results were achieved for pattern sizes nine and twelve. The hit rate was in the (0.5,1) interval and the false alarm rate - (0,0.55) for the best case.

To summarize this section we would like to note that it is very difficult to find experimental performance results of different anomaly detectors. In publications only accuracy results are provided, and if there is some extra information - it is given in relative values, which are very difficult to compare with absolute values obtained from our experiments. Moreover, we have not seen nor actual profile size, neither classification time analysis for anomaly detector. Therefore, we cannot provide any comparison here. But from the comparisons we were able to make it is possible to see that our classifiers perform sometimes slightly, sometimes significantly better, supporting our initial claim that this work improves aspects of current anomaly intrusion systems.

5 Conclusions

In this paper we outlined main problems and our solutions during implementation of the IDS prototype. We presented here a possible architecture for an anomaly detector employed for online user verfication. Here we have showed that there are temporal patterns in user behavior and they may be used as well as sequential ones to efficiently detect anomalies in user behavior, moreover the temporal patterns may support the anomaly detection significantly increasing the probability of correct classification. Also we proposed an efficient way to build and maintain user profiles keeping resource consumption on a reasonable level. In our experiments we were able to keep an overall error rate (false negatives + false positives) below 8% level without consuming much resources.

References

Ali, S.: 2001, Adventures in anomaly detection, www.cs.cmu.edu/ ~ cheeko/ intrusion/final.ps.gz.

Allen, J.: 1983, Maintaining knowledge about temporal intervals, *Communications of the ACM* **26**, 832–843.

Lane, T. and Brodley, C.: 1997, An application of machine learning to anomaly detection, *20th Annual National Information Systems Security Conference*, Vol. 1, Baltimore, Maryland, USA, pp. 366–380.

Lane, T. and Brodley, C.: 1999, Temporal sequence learning and data reduction for anomaly detection, *ACM Transactions on Information and System Security* **2**(3), 295–331.

Lee, W., Stolfo, S. and Mok, K.: 1999, A data mining framework for building intrusion detection models, IEEE Press.

Seleznyov, A., Mazhelis, O. and Puuronen, S.: 2001, Learning temporal regularities of user behavior for anomaly detection, *International Workshop on Mathematical Methods, Models and Architectures for Computer Networks Security*, St.Petersburg, Russia.

Zhang, Z., Li, J., Manikopoulos, C., Jorgenson, J. and Ucles, J.: 2001, Neural networks in statistical intrusion detection, *5th World Multi-Conference on Circuits, Systems, Communications and Computers (CSCC 2001)*, Crete Island, Greece.

Identifying security vulnerabilities through input flow tracing and analysis

S.D.Xenitellis

Information Security Group, Royal Holloway University of London, Egham,
Surrey TW20 0EX, United Kingdom
e-mail: S.Xenitellis@rhul.ac.uk

Abstract

A software system can be considered as a collection of data and procedures that are separated from the environment and interact with it through channels of communication. If we assume that the system does not contain any Trojan horse code, then the only way it can be attacked is during the processing of input through interactions with the environment. While most methodologies attempt to identify security vulnerabilities in the local context, we propose the use of complete input tracing that identifies all possible input sources, traces the input flow from the source until termination of use and compares the flow segments for known security vulnerability constructs. This paper discusses input flow tracing and its benefits such as the provision of metrics for security assurance, complete vulnerability assessment and the ability to examine combinations of vulnerabilities.

Keywords

Security, static analysis, input, flow tracing and analysis

1. Introduction

In the early days of computing, security vulnerabilities were not a major issue in software engineering. Computers were not as powerful as today, they were not generally networked and programmers were more concerned in delivering software that was reliable and worked with the existing hardware limitations.

In the seventies, software reliability was becoming increasingly a popular issue. In (Meyers, 1979) it is shown that to ensure the correctness of software, there are generally two methodologies to apply, black-box testing and white-box testing. The former is carried out by the automatic input of data to the software being tested and the observation of the results. By knowing what the correct result is, one is able to determine if the software functions correctly or not without requiring access to the source code. The latter is carried out by the automatic verification of the software with inspection of the source code and examination of all branches of execution. The concept of white-box testing is that if we inspect all combinations of flows of execution, we can have a good degree of certainty that the software is reliable.

On the one hand, black-box testing cannot be carried out in its general form as the number of all possible input combinations is extremely large. On the other hand, white-box testing is even more difficult to implement efficiently. We first need to know how the application should function and then we could write controlling software that checks the target application for conformity. However, if we first can produce a correct reference application, then we can use that instead of the application we are trying to test. It is very difficult to apply either black-box or white-box testing in their general form to tackle software reliability issues.

Over the years, the solution has been to work on partial solutions by making priorities on the issues that we want to examine. In the case of black-box testing, test cases are used to capture as much of the usage patterns of the end-users. By ensuring that the software operates correctly for a reasonably large number of test cases, one can ensure to a moderate degree that the software is correct. In the case of white-box testing, flow analysis is used in a local scope instead of the entirety of the application. However, although these partial solutions may be adequate for software testing and software reliability, they are not adequate for software security and assurance as a single mistake can compromise the security of the whole system.

In this paper, we follow the elements of white-box testing methodology and propose the use of complete input flow analysis in order to identify security vulnerabilities. To tackle the inherent complexity in white-box testing where the number of branches is unmanageable, our analysis is driven by the input that an attacker can manipulate.

The significance of following the input flow of data lies in the fact that we can get a level of assurance that for given software the attacker cannot compromise the security exploiting specific types of vulnerabilities.

We target software written in the C/C++ programming languages where buffer overflow (Smith, 1997) and format string vulnerabilities (Newsham 2001 and Scut, 2001) exist. In addition, we target software that has been written over time and although it is in heavy use, no substantial new development takes place.

In sections 2 and 3, we provide the background and the related work respectively. In section 4, we present the methodology. In section 5, we give a practical example of the examination of source code. Finally, in section 6, we provide conclusions and future research directions.

2. Background

A buffer overflow relates to memory management where areas of memory are overwritten (Aleph, 1996 and Smith, 1997). It is commonly associated to programming languages that do not offer buffer bounds checking support and it is left to the programmer to ensure that no case of overwriting is possible. However, due to a variety of reasons, such cases tend to occur often (Miller, 1995).

An example of a buffer overflow is depicted in Table 1.

If the user uses a string longer than 22 bytes, the *buf* buffer of the program is overrun and important memory structures of the running application are overwritten.

Since this specific program would typically execute with no extra privileges, it merely exhibits a software reliability problem. If we assume that it is a privileged application (such as a set-user-id application owned by the superuser, in Unix terminology), then the buffer could be overwritten with specially crafted data that would enable the attacker to execute his own malicious code under the elevated privileges (Aleph, 1996). In this case, the software reliability problem is a security vulnerability.

```
int main( int argc, char** argv )
{
       char buf[20] = "Hello ";

       strcat( buf, argv[1]);
       printf( buf );
}

% ./example1 World
Hello World
%
```

Table 1 – C program with buffer overflow and format string vulnerabilities

A format string vulnerability is a type of security vulnerability where the attacker can place crafted data in a format string of a privileged application written in the C programming language (Newsham, 2001 and Scut, 2001). To demonstrate format string vulnerabilities, we reuse the example in Table 1. The first argument of the *printf* function in the source code is also used for the format string material and a potential attacker has access to it through the command line interface. By carefully selecting the contents of the format string, the attacker can make the application execute malicious code.

Although in small applications it is quite straightforward to find security vulnerabilities, in bigger ones it is quite difficult to establish whether a suspicious operation can indeed result in security vulnerability.

3. Related work

Currently one of the most successful methods of finding and eliminating security vulnerabilities is manual security audit of the source code by security experts (De Raadt, 2002). Although the results are quite impressive, there is no published security audit methodology or guidelines in the literature.

Security vulnerabilities are not evenly distributed in the source code of software. There are typically specific programming constructs that tend to attract vulnerabilities. An example of this is string management functions that do not check the size of the buffers they work on. Based on this fact, programs such as flawfinder (Wheeler, 2001), RATS (Secure Software Solutions, 2001), Splint (Evans and Larochelle, 2002) and ITS4 (Viega et al., 2001) can signal those dangerous constructs so that a security auditor can draw her attention to them.

In (Wagner, 2000), the problem of detecting buffer overflows is converted into a range analysis problem; the source code is analysed, the code related to memory management is identified and the cases that can result in the range of a buffer being bypassed are identified.

In (Engler et al., 2001), the execution flow is analysed in a local context by examining the source code, and segments of it are compared with known constructs that produce security vulnerabilities. To enable the easier analysis of the source code, they use the GNU GCC compiler (GCC, 2002) suite that parses the source code and delivers an intermediate form. This intermediate form is then checked to see if it contains problematic segments of execution.

4. The input flow tracing methodology

We start with the requirements of the methodology and continue with the inputs to the software system that an attacker can manipulate. Subsequently, we describe the vulnerability constructs that we search for, and finally we identify those cases that do result in a security vulnerability. We end when all flows of data input reach the end-point of their execution.

4.1 Requirements

Apart from the requirement of the availability of the source code, the source code of system and auxiliary libraries may be needed. In addition, the source code of the kernel may also be needed.

4.2 Inputs to the system

Typical inputs to a software system include (Wheeler, 2002)

- Command line input (through the *argc* and *argv* parameters),
- Environment variables (through the *envp* parameter or the *getenv* function),
- File descriptors from already open files,
- File contents,
- Input from the network (through the Web, from cookies and so on),
- Locale selection,
- Events from event-driven systems (Xenitellis, 2002b),

We then need to assess which of the above inputs the target application is using and the attacker can access. This important step can reduce the complexity of the analysis.

To illustrate the procedure of the selection of inputs, we provide an example. A word processor that is used to create documents on a standalone computer does not open foreign documents and thus does not have inputs that an attacker can manipulate. However, if it is used to open documents obtained from a hostile environment such as the Internet, then the content of the files are the input to the system. Note that we do not refer to macro viruses that may exist in the documents; we refer to vulnerabilities such as buffer overflows. An example of such a vulnerability used to exist in Microsoft Windows (Microsoft, 2000). An oversized keyword in a crafted RTF (Rich Text Format) file (an example of such a RTF file can be found in http://lists.insecure.org/vuln-dev/1999/Nov/0092.html) would cause a buffer overflow in the RTF document processing system library.

4.3 Vulnerabilities

Among the vulnerabilities that static analysis of the source code can detect when analysing the input flow are:

- Buffer overflow vulnerabilities
- Format string vulnerabilities
- Part of event-driven system vulnerabilities (Xenitellis, 2002b)

In addition to individual types of vulnerabilities, by following the data flow we are able to detect security vulnerabilities arising from combinations of the individual types.

For example, suppose an event-driven application takes as command line parameter a description text. The attacker can place exploit code so that the running application will have it in its address space. We assume that the buffer that holds the description text has adequate size and no buffer overflow takes place. However, using a vulnerability found in an implementation of an event-driven system, we are able to execute this code.

4.4 Example

We use the *dip-3.3.7o* (available at ftp://sunsite.unc.edu/pub/Linux/system/network/serial/dip) communication package as an example of locating a specific security vulnerability by tracing the input flow. Since the source code is available, we are able to investigate known and documented security vulnerabilities.

We identified a vulnerability by examining the CERT-1996-13 security advisory (CERT, 1996). From this advisory, we managed to identify that the security vulnerability is a buffer overrun (Aleph, 1996) that can be exploited by the careful manipulation of the command line parameters of the *dip* application. *Dip* is a set-user-id application which means that it is executed under the privileges of its owner, the superuser.

The offending line in the source code is

```
sprintf(buf, "%s/LCK..%s", "/usr/sbin/lockd", path);
```

Both the *buf* and *path* buffers are 128 bytes long. However, when the above function constructs the contents of the *buf* buffer, it adds characters from the format string (second argument) and an additional string (third argument). If the path (fourth argument) is over 106 bytes, it causes a buffer overflow.

The input flow is depicted in Table 2. Section A of the table shows the available input sources to the application that an attacker can manipulate. The next section, B, shows how the input is passed to the *path* variable that is 128 bytes long. The only restriction for the content of *path* is that no NULL bytes can be present. Finally, in section C, it is shown how the path overflows the *buf* variable. As a solution, *path* should be restricted to 106 bytes or *sprintf()* should have been replaced with *snprintf()*.

A. Input sources	Comments
`int argc;` `char** argv;`	Command line parameters
B. Input flow tracing "main()"	**Comments and code fragments**

the_argv: char**
the_argv = argv
	global variable
	`char *the_argv = (char **)0;`
	Initialisation (in main)
	`the_argv = argv;`

... (Omitted for clarity)	

path: char[128]
path = optarg (derived from argv)
	local variable (in main)
	`char path[128];`
	Initialisation
	`strncpy(path,optarg,sizeof(path));`
	examine buffer operation: safe

... (Omitted for clarity)	
Invocation of function new_kill_dip(path)	*path* is 128 bytes long, has user supplied data
C. Input flow tracing "new_kill_dip()"	**Comments and code fragments**
... (Omitted for clarity)	

buf: char[128]
buf = string operation involving path
	local variable
	`char buf[128];`
	Initialisation (in main)
	`sprintf(buf,        "%s/LCK..%s",`
	`"/usr/sbin/lockd", path);`
	examine buffer operation: unsafe

Table 2 – Following the input flow in the dip-3.3.7o application

5. Benefits

There are several benefits from the examination of security vulnerabilities through input flow tracing and analysis.

Firstly, we are able to identify combinations of basic types of vulnerabilities that are exploited together to produce combined vulnerability. By tracing the flow of input, we can cut down on the possible combinations to those that can actually take place.

Secondly, we can discern whether a specific vulnerability can result in a denial of service attack or it can further lead to execution of malicious code. Since we follow the input flow, we can identify the limits to the input data that previous processing may have imposed. For example, a string that carries malicious code may have had its contents converted to capital letters. In this case, the attacker would have to insert assembly instructions that do not contain small letters. In some cases, these requirements may make the restrictions to the input code so high that the chances for execution of remote code are minimised.

Thirdly, we can explain how a security vulnerability was caused in a straightforward way since we can show clearly the type of compromise. This can both enable the appropriate parties to identify the problem that needs to be addressed and help them to produce an appropriate fix.

Finally, by examining the input flow we are able to obtain a good level of assurance that the software does not contain specific types of vulnerabilities.

6. Conclusion

It is a difficult task to find security vulnerabilities in the source code of an application. To solve this problem, a method is to establish all possible inputs to the application and then examine the flows of input data to the software that an attacker can potentially manipulate. Following the flow of data, we signal the relevant code fragments as suspicious and then analyse.

In addition, in this paper we provide an example of a manual source code input flow trace for security vulnerabilities using as target a commonly used network application. This manual investigation helps in highlighting aspects of data flow tracing and enables us to experiment with different software engineering models to aid the automatic inspection. One implementation method of automatic inspection is to mimic the process of manual inspection. This involves the use of software engineering techniques found in artificial intelligence such as the blackboard model (Xenitellis, 2002a). The purpose of this paper is to approach security auditing in a way that can be formalised and carried out automatically with those artificial intelligence techniques.

Finally, we presented the benefits that arise from the use of input flow tracing. We have a complete analysis of the vulnerability, assess its real severity, detect combinations of several vulnerabilities and eventually have a level of assurance about the security of the software.

Acknowledgements

The author would like to thank Vorapranee Khu-Smith, Chris Mitchell and the anonymous reviewers of INC2002 for their comments on this paper.

The author's studies are funded by the State's Scholarship Foundation (S.S.F.) of Greece.

7. References

Aleph, O (1996), "Smashing the stack for fun and profit", *Phrack*, Vol. 49, No. 7.

CERT, 1996, "CERT Advisory CA-1996-13", *http://www.cert.org/advisories/CA-1996-13.html*, Computer Emergency Response Team.

Dawson, S. and Jahanian, F. and Mitton, T. (1997), "Experiments on six commercial TCP implementations using a software fault injection tool", *Software - Practice and Experience (SPE)*, Vol. 12, No. 27, pp1385–1410.

De Raadt, T. et al. (2002), "The OpenBSD free operating system", *http://www.openbsd.org*

Engler, D, et al. (2001), "The Meta-level Compilation (MC) project", *http://hands.stanford.edu/*, Stanford University.

Evans, D. and Larochelle, D. (2002), "Improving security using extensible lightweight static analysis", *IEEE Software,* IEEE.

GCC (2002), "GNU Compiler Collection", *http://gcc.gnu.org/*

Microsoft, (2000), "Security Bulletin (MS00-005): Frequently Asked Questions" *http://www.microsoft.com/technet/treeview/default.asp?url=/technet/security/bulletin/fq00-005.asp, Microsoft.*

Miller B.P. and Lee C.P. and Maganty V. and Murthy R. and Natarajan A. and Steidl J. (1995), "Fuzz revisited: A re-examination of the reliability of Unix utilities and services", *Technical report*, Computer Sciences Department, University of Wisconsin.

Myers, G.J. (1979), "The art of software testing", *Business Data Processing,* John Wiley and Sons, New York.

Newsham, T. (200), "Format string attacks", *http://www.guardent.com/docs/FormatString.PDF*, Guardent, Inc.

Scut, (2001), "Exploiting format string vulnerabilities", *http://teso.scene.at/articles/formatstring/*, TESO.

Secure Software Solutions, (2001), "Rough Auditing Tool for Security (RATS)", *http://www.securesw.com/rats/*

Smith, N. P. (1997), "Stack smashing vulnerabilities in the Unix operating system", http://destroy.net/machines/security/nate-buffer.ps

Viega, J. and Bloch, J.T. and Kohno Y. and McGraw G. (2001), "ITS4: A static vulnerability scanner for C and C++ code", *Proceedings of the 16th Annual Computer Security Applications Conference (ACSAC'00),* IEEE.

Wagner, D.A. (2000), "Static analysis and computer security: New techniques for software assurance", *Ph.D. dissertation,* University of California at Berkeley.

Wheeler, D.A. (2001), "?aw?nder", *http://www.dwheeler.com/?aw?nder/*

Wheeler, D.A. (2002), "Secure Programming for Linux and Unix HOWTO", *http://www.dwheeler.com/secure-programs/*

Xenitellis, S. (2002a), "Applying the Blackboard Model to the Security Field", *2nd Hellenic Conference on Artificial Intelligence (SETN-02)*, Hellenic Artificial Intelligence Society (EETN) and Department of Informatics Aristotle University of Thessaloniki, Thessaloniki, pp531-536.

Xenitellis, S. (2002b), "Security vulnerabilities in Event-Driven Systems", *In Proceedings of Security in the Information Society: Visions and Perspectives*, IFIP TC11 17th International Conference on Information Security, Kluwer Academic Press, pp147-160.

Partially sighted signatures on large documents

F. Bergadano[1], D. Cavagnino[1] and L. Egidi[2]

[1]Dipartimento di Informatica, Università di Torino, Torino, Italy
[2]Dipartimento di Informatica, Università del Piemonte Orientale, Alessandria, Italy
e-mail: {bergadan, davide}@di.unito.it, lavinia@mfn.unipmn.it

Abstract

The paper deals with the problem of signing for approval a large amount of data, when it is impossible for the signer to examine all of them (because of their sheer amount or for privacy reasons). The non-standard signing procedure we propose allows the signer to see only a small random sample of what she is signing, yet guaranteeing that with high probability the data she has seen is representative of the contents of the whole file.

The signature is not altogether blind but the signer has only a partial (randomized) vision of the data submitted.

We present a set of interactive protocols to deploy the signing procedure in different settings, discuss their reliability and propose some applications of our methodology.

Keywords

Signatures, large files, confidentiality, percentual signature.

1 Introduction

Bulky files are created daily and need to be approved or made official or must gain some legal validity status, in order to be of some use; in other words, they must be certified. The procedures involved in this validation phase on the one side are complicated by the size of the files, on the other concur in disclosing private information to a few authorities with all the related risks.

In this paper we propose new techniques designed to address both issues: a validation procedure requiring only a partial exam of the contents. The idea is that the authority checks only a limited number of records chosen at random, and signs the hash of the file binding it to the records checked, only if she finds them valid.

This means that the files approved are valid *with high probability*, i.e. there can be a very low percentage of unacceptable records in the file, and yet the file is approved by the authority. Therefore the technique is useful in cases in which it doesn't matter if a few records don't comply to the specific requests.

In general, problems that benefit from the techniques we present can be described by four requirements: there is some interest in signing the file; the file is too large to transfer or thoroughly examine, or it cannot be disclosed in its entirety for privacy reasons; the file consists of records and the correctness of each record is independent of the contents of others; it is acceptable that a very low percentage of the records are not compliant to the specific regulations or format that is guaranteed by the signature. The files might be, for instance, large log files, or records of transactions of some large company.

The properties that the signing authority can certify with high probability include: the format is correct; records don't disclose sensible information; records don't breach (customers') privacy; records don't include forbidden material; the contents are correct (with respect to some specified parameters); the contents are truthful; the contents are up to date. We describe interactive protocols that, if properly deployed, lead to a validation in the sense specified above.

We introduce (in Section 2) the technique in the simple framework, in which the signing authority doesn't participate to the construction of the file she signs, and prove the soundness of the technique. Also, we relax the validity constraints on the contents of the file to be validated. In Section 3 we consider the different setting in which the construction of the file must be somehow supervised by the signer, either to make sure that the file was built properly or to check the contents synchronously with the construction of the file. An auditing agency that must certify frequency of access to a web server, for instance, faces typically the latter more complex situation. Finally (Section 4) we mention some areas of application of the techniques presented and discuss related work.

2 The vanilla protocol

The techniques we describe can be applied to files that consist of records. In the simplest situation (and a reasonably common one) the records are numbered in increasing order. Each record is labelled by an integer, in the range $\{1, \ldots, \text{MAX}\}$, where MAX is the total number of records in the file. S is the signer. A needs a signature on the file F. The protocol is the following:

1. A→S: $H(F)$, MAX (A computes the hash $H(F)$ of the file F and sends it to the signer S, along with the total number of records MAX)

2. S→A: $l_1, \ldots, l_N$ (S computes N random numbers $l_1, \ldots, l_N$ in the range $\{1, \ldots, \text{MAX}\}$ and sends them to A)

3. A→S: $\text{Rec}[l_1], \ldots, \text{Rec}[l_N]$ (A responds with the N records labelled $l_1, \ldots, l_N$)

4. S checks that the records received are correctly labelled $l_1, \ldots, l_N$ and checks their contents; if the latter are not "acceptable" the protocol is terminated

5. S→A: $\sigma = \text{Sig}_{K_S}(H(F)||\text{MAX}||\text{Rec}[l_1]\ldots\text{Rec}[l_N])$ (S appends MAX and the records to the hash of the file, signs the resulting string and sends the signature σ to A)

6. A stores F, σ and $l_1, \ldots, l_N$,

where F is the file to be signed, H is a secure hash function (like RIPEMD-160 or SHA-1), MAX and $l_1, \ldots, l_N$ are as above, $\text{Rec}[n]$ is the record labelled n and $\text{Sig}_{K_S}(M)$ is the signature of M with S's private key K_S.

A must communicate to S the total number of records in the file, so that S can generate random numbers in the appropriate range. S binds the number MAX communicated by A to the hash of the file in the signature so that it can later be checked that it is the actual number of records in the file. Indeed, A might communicate a number L lower than the actual number MAX of records thus making sure that S doesn't ask to be shown the last MAX-L records.

In order to verify the signature σ, both the file F and the labels $l_1, \ldots, l_N$ must be available. The verifyer V must take the following steps:

1. V computes the hash of the file and appends the length of the file, MAX, to it and the records $\text{Rec}[l_1]$ through $\text{Rec}[l_N]$, to obtain a string τ;

2. V uses S's public key K_P to check that σ is a valid signature of τ.

Notice that A can be trusted to store the unsigned numbers $l_1, \ldots, l_N$; indeed, if A maliciously stores a different sequence of numbers $n_1, \ldots, n_N$, the verification will fail, since the records included in the signature are labelled exactly $l_1, \ldots, l_N$ (before signing, S checks that this is so). Therefore even if the records $\text{Rec}[n_1] \ldots \text{Rec}[n_N]$ have exactly the same contents as those sent to S in Step 3 of the protocol, yet they have a different label, and the signature verification will expose that difference.

Let us stress that the verification of the signature completes the correctness check of the authority. S has never seen the whole file and cannot even be sure that the records it received in Step 3 are actually the requested records as they appear in the file. S doesn't even know whether the number of records in the file is actually MAX. Upon verification of the signature, the correct records are extracted from the file and appended to the hash of the file along with the length MAX of the file. If either the length of the file or the selected records as communicated to S were incorrect, the verification fails.

The probability to fail detection of a forgery of at least one record, may be made as small as desired by sampling a specific number of records.

Theorem 1 *Let β be the ratio of bad records over all the records in F. For any $\epsilon > 0$ there is an N_β (which depends both on β and on ϵ) such that, if S requests to see N_β records chosen at random among the MAX records of the file, the probability that no one of them is bad is less than ϵ.*

Proof: Let us denote with k the number of bad records, i.e. $k = \text{MAX} \cdot \beta$. The probability P_F to fail detection of, at least, a bad record is:

$$P_F = \left(1 - \frac{k}{MAX}\right)\left(1 - \frac{k}{MAX - 1}\right) \cdots \left(1 - \frac{k}{MAX - (N_\beta - 1)}\right) \qquad (1)$$

Some algebra yields $P_F \leq e^{-\beta N_\beta}$, which proves the theorem. QED

Notice that, for files of any size, with $\beta = 0.1$, if only $N_\beta = 60$ records are checked the probability of detecting a bogus record is very close to 1.

The protocol can be adapted to the more general situation in which the set of labels is uniformly distributed over (say) an initial segment of the natural numbers (or over any set that can be bijectively and efficiently computed from an initial segment of the natural numbers) and is efficiently recognizable. Let δ be the density of the set of legal labels over the appropriate initial segment of $\mathbb{N}$, i.e. the probability that a number in the proper range is a legal label. Then, in Step 2, S chooses $1/\delta \cdot N$ random numbers (to make sure that she will be shown roughly N records), and in Step 5 she includes in its signature the numbers that A declared not to correspond to any record, along with the records that A sent her. It must be noted, though, that if the density is too low, the size of the signature explodes.

In some applications it may be too restrictive that all the sampled records are found to be acceptable, for example because a record is not valid for a reason not imputable to the owner of the file. We propose, for a similar situation, a *percentual signature* i.e. a signature that guarantees the characteristics of the file specifying the percentual of records that are valid, with a certain probability. Specifically (as follows from the Central Limit Theorem):

Proposition 1 *Let γ be the ratio of valid records found in a sample of size n. Then a percentual signature with confidence $100(1-\alpha)\%$ certifies that with probability $1-\alpha$ the proportion of valid records in the file is in the range*

$$\left[\gamma - z_{\alpha/2}\sqrt{\frac{\gamma(1-\gamma)}{n}}, \gamma + z_{\alpha/2}\sqrt{\frac{\gamma(1-\gamma)}{n}} \right] \tag{2}$$

where Z is a standard normal.

3 Variations

It might be impossible to check the authenticity, or truthfulness, of records in the file after they have been appended to the file. Consider for instance the example of a log file that is modified as events occur in the system. In general, the only way to establish whether an entry in the log file is bogus is to have a reliable log file to refer to.

In a similar situation, the signing authority would have to be informed of all events as they occur so that it can record them on a file of its own for future reference. The problem is of course that it is impractical that the authority follows and logs all activity at one site, especially if it is providing the same service to many customers.

This scenario is not merely speculative. In the practical situation of the auditing of web accesses to a server, for instance, it is not only vital that the construction of the log be monitored by the authority, but also that the authority check the contents of the records in real time.

We first address the simpler case in which the construction of the file must be supervised by the authority, and then add in Section 3.2 the further constraint that the checks be performed in real time.

3.1 Supervised construction

A is now equipped with some tamper resistant hardware (which we call Box) installed by S at A's site. It could be a standard tamper resistant device or preferably one capable of warning S in case it is tampered with, like in (Håstad et al., 2000). It is installed so that all information to be recorded must pass through it. The task of the Box is labelling each record with an order number and attaching to the record a MAC (for instance HMAC with SHA-1) for future reference.

Therefore the file to be signed consists of records numbered 1 through MAX to each of which a MAC is appended. The MAC guarantees to the signing authority that the contents of the record have not been modified after the Box has seen the data, and that no record has been fabricated. The signing protocol is then as follows:

1. A→S: $H(F)$, MAX

2. S→A: $l_1, \ldots, l_N$

3. A→S: $\text{Rec}[l_1], \ldots, \text{Rec}[l_N]$

4. S checks the labels of the records, checks the records against their MACs and checks the contents of the records; if any step of the verification fails the protocol is terminated

5. S→A: $\sigma = \text{Sig}_{K_S}(H(F)||\text{MAX}||\text{Rec}[l_1] \ldots \text{Rec}[l_N])$

6. A stores F, σ and $l_1, \ldots, l_N$.

The verification of the signature is exactly as for the vanilla protocol (Section 2).

Notice that the proof in Section 2 guarantees that the probability of exposing a fraud on A's part can be made arbitrarily large by choosing a big enough N. In particular, in this setting the remark applies both to the contents of the records and to fabrication or modification of data: if A has modified a significant percentage of records, N can be chosen so that with high probability S will receive in Step 3 some record that doesn't have the right MAC appended to it. Besides, the secret key of the MAC doesn't need to be disclosed by the authority at any moment in the deployment of the protocol. Indeed, if the file passes the probabilistic check performed by S, it is considered valid at all later times, on the basis of the above considerations.

3.2 Real time check of contents

Suppose that the check on the contents of a record can only be carried out at the moment in which the event recorded takes place, or it is much more convenient to do so.

A typical situation in which this happens is the auditing of web accesses to a server. Various techniques have been developed to solve this problem, see (Naor and Pinkas, 1998; Blundo et al., 2001). The application of the protocol we are going to present is discussed in (Bergadano and Cavagnino, 2000). One of the main characteristcs of the protocol discussed is its efficiency, in the sense that the performance of the web server (and of the service to the client) is not affected by the check. The reason lies in the fact that the check is not performed on each record added to the file but just on a few records chosen randomly, and with a low frequency.

Again, a tamper resistant device installed by S at A's site is necessary.

This time the Box is programmed so that it randomly chooses records on which S must perform the real time check. S is thus capable of checking the authenticity of the information that is going to be recorded. If it receives any records that contain bogus data, it considers A unreliable and will not sign any files for A in the future. If all randomly chosen records are truthful, S is willing to sign log files of activity at A's site. Before the final step of the protocol, A doesn't know which records are checked and stored by the authority.

Without loss of generality, we assume that the records in the file are numbered 1 through MAX. It can be requested that the Box itself attaches the numbers to the records. The protocol is much simpler, because in this case S has already chosen and checked random records via the Box:

1. A→S: $H(F)$, MAX

2. S checks that MAX≤M, where M is the number of records seen by the Box; if not, the protocol is terminated

3. S computes $\sigma = \text{Sig}_{K_S}(H(F)||\text{MAX}||\text{Rec}[l_1]\ldots\text{Rec}[l_N])$

4. S→A: $\sigma, l_1, \ldots, l_N$

5. A stores F, σ and $l_1, \ldots, l_N$.

The check in Step 2 is necessary because otherwise A might add records to the file prior to sending its digest to S, and of course would be sure that the new records have not been checked by S. Since A doesn't know which records have been checked by S until after the file has been signed, the strength of this variation of the signature scheme can be proved again as in Section 2.

4   Applications and related work

Applications of our protocols include validation of the contents of a large database in a particular instant of time (here the requirement of timeliness is in conflict with the large amount of data to be transferred and processed); validation of the contents of log files of a server, like a web server, whose owner is paid by banner insertionists depending on the number of page views by different users (here a potentially large log file must be validated, and the contents of the file must be verified during its construction); validation of contents and quality of a movie (in this case, our technique has a characteristic similar to the image authentication technique described in (Xie et al., 2000), since both accept a certain degree of modification of the content certified); approval of large records of economic transactions (here there is interest in avoiding to disclose to the signer the whole document for privacy reasons while exposing with high probability faults in single transactions, if the illegal operations were not occasional).

The problem posed by privacy is addressed throughout literature from classical works like (Chaum, 1983; Chaum, 1985; Chaum, 1988) to recent applications like, for instance, (Shields and Levine, 2000; Reiter and Rubin, 1988). In the spirit of the latter papers, our validation protocols would allow to disclose only a small percentage of a list of IP addresses of clients connecting to a web site.

In analogy to Chaum's blind signatures (Chaum, 1983; Chaum, 1985), our authority doesn't know what she is signing (she never even sees the whole file), but the blinding is here natural, since the files are in general too large to be transferred, and, again, it is partial, because it's a *validation* scheme and therefore has an implication on the contents. Besides, the authority, in contrast to Chaum's scheme, might here release an invalid signature, in case the other party didn't follow correctly the protocol (which of course would be exposed upon verification). The theoretical foundations of this scheme resemble those of our non-standard signing procedure in the enrichment of the blind signature technique described in (Schneier, 1996)(pages 113-115).

The idea of the random selection of entries for a check of correctness is also in (Yacobi, 1999), in the setting of theft in electronic payment transactions, to reduce verification costs.

Large files and low bandwidth or costly communication are also concerns that cannot be disregarded. (Gennaro and Rohatgi, 1997; Bergadano et al., 2001) propose signature and multicast authentication protocols useful to authenticate large amounts of data, even when transmitted in real time, by means of efficient signature and MAC schemes. In (Gennaro and Rohatgi, 1997), though, the accepted scenario is one in which the whole file has eventually to be transferred, no matter how bulky. Their techniques aim at efficient signing and verification, both to adjust the necessity of on-line operation and continuous authentication of data.

The situation considered in (Bergadano et al., 2001) is yet different. In a videoconference, the continuous exchange of data is authenticated as it flows. Again, all the data is eventually transferred. The issues here are speed of signing and verification, and compactness of the authentication data.

In contrast, we consider situations in which the transferral of the whole file is either impractical or undesirable, and thus our protocols are designed to minimize communication requirements.

In a sense, a closer stand is taken in (Schneier and Kelsey, 1999) in which, for verification of integrity of log files, the authors try to minimize the amount of data to be exchanged between a trusted machine and the verifier. The basic scheme (discussed in (Schneier and Kelsey, 1998)) with no special attention to bandwidth problems, prescribes that the seals of integrity (again MACs) are computed and attached to the log files by an untrusted machine, thus proposing a setting in which the certification of authenticity itself is delegated. In the specific application, this is doable, since the untrusted machine is precisely an "unsecure" machine: it is assumed that it can be penetrated by an attacker. The scheme doesn't apply when one cannot trust even normal operation.

Our techniques can also be used for the metering of accesses to web sites. It is a hot issue due to the common practice of supporting web sites via banner advertising. See for instance (Reiter et al., 1998; Franklin and Malkhi, 1997; Naor and Pinkas, 1998) or the totally different approach of (Jakobsson et al., 1999).

The motivation of (Schneier and Kelsey, 1997) is the certification of high scores in computer games, although the framework proposed is also suitable for different applications like the metering of visits to a web page or the use of a database with a pay-per-page access policy, and others. The solutions proposed need a tamper resistant device installed on the customer's computer, that communicates with the trusted computer of the certifying authority. This setting is very similar to what we propose in one of the variations of our protocol, except that our interest is centered on the novel type of certification protocol which we propose (in (Schneier and Kelsey, 1997) there's no reference to whichever the certification procedure might be, suggesting a standard one).

References

Bergadano, F. and Cavagnino, D. (2000). Certificazione di accessi a server web. In *Proc. of AICA 2000*, pages 287–298.

Bergadano, F., Cavagnino, D., and Crispo, B. (2001). Chained stream authentication. In *Proc. of Selected Areas in Cryptography 2000, LNCS 2012*, pages 144–157. Springer.

Blundo, C., Bonis, A. D., Masucci, B., and Stinson, D. R. (2001). Dynamic multi-threshold metering schemes. In *Proc. of SAC 2000, LNCS 2012*, pages 130–143. Springer.

Chaum, D. (1983). Blind signatures for untraceable payment. In *Proc. of CRYPTO'82, Springer*.

Chaum, D. (1985). Security without identification: transaction systems to make big brother obsolete. *Communications of the ACM*, 28(10):1030–1044.

Chaum, D. (1988). The dining cryptographers problem: Unconditional sender and recipient untraceability. *Journal of Cryptography*, 1:65–75.

Franklin, M. and Malkhi, D. (1997). Auditable metering with lightweight security. In *LNCS 1318*, pages 151–160. Proc. of Financial Cryptography 97, Springer.

Gennaro, R. and Rohatgi, P. (1997). How to sign digital streams. In *LNCS 1294*, pages 180–197. Proc. of CRYPTO'97, Springer.

Håstad, J., Jonsson, J., Juels, A., and Yung, M. (2000). Funkspiel schemes: an alternative to conventional tamper resistance. In *Proc. of the 7th ACM Conf. on CCS*, pages 125–133.

Jakobsson, M., MacKenzie, P. D., and Stern, J. P. (1999). Secure and lightweight advertising on the web. In *Proceedings of WWW8*.

Naor, M. and Pinkas, B. (1998). Secure and efficient metering. In *Proceedings of Advances in Cryptology - EUROCRYPT '98, LNCS 1403*, pages 576–590. Springer.

Reiter, M. K., Anupam, V., and Mayer, A. (1998). Detecting hit shaving in click-through payment schemes. In *Proc. of the 3rd USENIX Workshop on Electronic Commerce*, pages 155–166.

Reiter, M. K. and Rubin, A. D. (1988). Crowds: Anonymity for web transactions. *ACM Transactions on Information and System Security*, 1(1):66–92.

Schneier, B. (1996). *Applied Cryptography, second edition*. John Wiley & Sons, Inc.

Schneier, B. and Kelsey, J. (1997). Remote auditing of software outputs using a trusted coprocessor. *Journal of Future Generation Computer Systems*, 13(1):9–18.

Schneier, B. and Kelsey, J. (1998). Cryptographic support for secure logs on untrusted machines. In *Proc. of 7th USENIX Security Symposium, USENIX Press*, pages 53–62.

Schneier, B. and Kelsey, J. (1999). Minimizing bandwidth for remote access to cryptographically protected audit logs. In *Proc. of RAID '99*.

Shields, C. and Levine, B. N. (2000). A protocol for anonymous communicaton over the internet. In *Proc. of the 7th ACM Conf. on CCS*, pages 33–42.

Xie, L., Arce, G. R., Lewis, A., and Basch, E. B. (2000). Image enhancement towards soft image authentication. In *Proc. of Int. Conference on Multimedia and Expo*, New York City, USA.

Yacobi, Y. (1999). Auditable metering with lightweight security. In *LNCS 1648*, pages 62–71. Proc. of Financial Cryptography 99, Springer.

A Hybrid Approach to Group Key Management

H. Seba[1], A. Bouabdallah[2], H. Bettahar[2], N. Badache[3], and D. Tandjaoui[4]

[1]Institut National d'Informatique (INI), Alger, Algeria
[2] Heudiasyc-UMR CNRS 6599, Université de Technologie de Compiègne, France
[3] Département d'Informatique, USTHB, Alger, Algeria
[4]Centre de Recherche sur l'Information Scientifique et Technique (CERIST), Alger, Algeria
e-mail: seba@utc.fr

Abstract

In this paper, we study the importance of group characteristics in the design of group key management protocols. As a case study, we consider the heterogeneity in group dynamism and trust issues within a multicast group. We distinguish between fixed and dynamic members with different trust considerations. We present an appropriate group key management protocol that combines the scalability of sub-grouping based approaches and the efficiency of logical key tree based approaches. This hybrid approach achieves better 1 affects n scalability, alleviates the workload associated to the management of mass joins and mass leaves and reduces the communication cost of rekeying.

Keywords

Group key management, 1 affects n scalability, Group characteristics, Logical binary trees.

1. Introduction

The large deployment of the internet in this last decade has greatly stimulated the development of many applications combining text video and voice over IP. A non exhaustive list of such applications includes teleconferencing, distance education, collaborative work and distributed interactive games. Based on a group communication model, these applications deserve several domains but share a same feature: the necessity of transmitting each group message to all the members of the group. Multicast routing (Deering, 1988) is an efficient and scalable solution to group communication since only one transmission is needed to reach all members. However, the multicast service currently supported in the internet does not offer any provisions for restricting delivery of data to a specified set of receivers. Any host can join a multicast group and start receiving data sent to the group. So, every one can listen to all traffic of a specified multicast group. This characteristic raises concerns about privacy and security of multicast applications. As a result, securing multicast communications becomes a critical network issue. To run secure multicast sessions, cryptographic techniques are applied. Group messages are protected by encryption using a chosen key (group key). Only those who knows the group key are able to recover the original message. However, key management, i.e. establishing and securely distributing the group key to valid members, is a complex problem. One of the issues that has to be addressed is the need for backward and forward secrecy (Menezes et al., 1997). In other words, new members joining a group should not be able to access previously multicast data and old members should not be able to continue to access data multicast after they have left the group. Thus, the group key needs to be changed on each membership change and securely redistributed to the current members of the group. This is referred to as group re-keying. Key management must be also scalable, i.e. key distribution overhead should be independent of the size of the multicast group. The scalability of the rekeying process is generally termed 1 affects n scalability. A rekeying protocol exhibits a 1 affects n scalability if it does not allow the action of one member (join or leave) to affect the entire group.

Several group key management approaches have been proposed in the literature (Wallner et al., 1999; Steer et al., 1988; Wong et al., 1998; McGrew and Sherman, 1998; Dondeti et al., 1999a; Waldvogel et al., 1999; Kim et al., 2000; Perrig et al., 2001; Mittra, 1997; Li et al., 2001). However, these approaches construct the group key without caring about the type of the group itself. We believe that more efficient key management may be obtained only if we consider the different characteristics of the multicast group. In current group key management approaches, the only group characteristic that is considered as a major factor is whether the group is autonomous or administered by a central server. Autonomous groups or dynamic peer groups are small groups where all members are equal. The key management protocol, which is a key agreement protocol in this case, asks each group member to contribute an equal share to the common group key computed as a function of all members' contributions. With groups administered by a central server, the key management problem is reduced to a key distribution problem where the central sever generates and distributes the group key. In the same way many other group characteristics should be considered in group key management as the group dynamism, the way members join the group, the size of the group and its composition, the periodicity of the group, the security characteristics of the group and more importantly and also most neglected by existing schemes the heterogeneity in characteristics between members of the same group.

In this paper, we investigate the issue of including different multicast group characteristics in key management in order to achieve efficiency. To prove the importance of group characteristics in group key management, we present a case study of the heterogeneity in group dynamism and trust issues where we distinguish between fixed and dynamic members with two levels of trust. We present an appropriate protocol that achieves better 1 affects n scalability than existing protocols and alleviates considerably handling of mass joins and mass leaves. Furthermore, the proposed scheme allows flexibility in defining different security scenarios for the same group.

The rest of the paper is organized as follows. Section 2 is dedicated to related work. In Section 3, we present group characteristics and formulate the problem of exploiting these characteristics in group key management. In Section 4, we discuss a case study, by taking the heterogeneity in group dynamism and trust issues as examples of important group characteristics. We present an appropriate key management protocol in this case. In Section 5, we evaluate the results of the proposed approach and compare its performance with existing key management protocols. Section 6 brings our remarks concluding the paper.

2. Related Work

We focus here on approaches that address the need for frequent group key changes and the associated scalability problem. They are mainly hierarchical approaches.

To address scalability, Iolus (Mittra, 1997) decomposes a large group of users into many subgroups and employs a hierarchy of group security agents (GSA). Each GSA generates and maintains a subgroup key. Each GSA receives data encrypted with its parent's subgroup key, decrypts them, recrypts them with its own subgroup key and multicasts the resulting message in its subgroup. Iolus achieves $O(1)$ messages for keying a subgroup before a join and $O(c)$ messages, where c is the average size of a subgroup, to rekey a group after a leave. This approach is scalable but requires many trusted entities and several levels of decryption/encryption to transmit data.

DEP (Dondeti et al., 1999b) is an extension of Iolus that avoids the use of trusted third parties at the cost of an additional level of encryption and unicast communications established between the source and each group member. During these unicast communications a KEK (Key Encryption Key) is

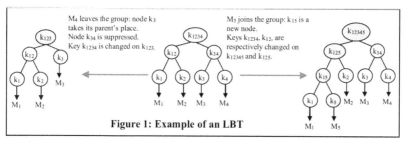

Figure 1: Example of an LBT

transmitted to group members. GSAs that are not group members do not receive the KEK. The KEK is used to encrypt the group key. Thus, non members GSAs can not read group messages.

Another hierarchical approach consists on using a Logical Binary Tree (LBT) of keys (see Figure 1). Internal nodes of the tree are KEKs used to simplify the rekeying process. Leaf nodes hold the keys associated to group members. Each member maintains the key associated to its leaf and all the KEKs corresponding to each ancestor node in the path from its parent node to the root. All group members share the key held by the root of the LBT (it is the group key). Two management approaches of LBTs exist in the literature:

1) Centralized LBT based protocols (Wallner et al., 1999; McGrew and Sherman, 1998; Wong at al., 1998; Perrig et al., 2001): a key distribution center (KDC) which is a trusted member or a third party maintains the tree, generates the keys, updates them and distributes them. The disadvantage of this approach is the reliance on a single entity that becomes a center of failures and attacks.

2) Distributed LBT based protocols (Steer et al., 1998; Kim et al., 2000; Waldvogel et al., 1999; Dondeti et al., 1999a): the tree is maintained by each member. Each member generates the key associated with its leaf and contribute to the generation of the keys in the path from the node to the root of the tree. This approach avoids the problems with the single point of trust and failures. Because all members participate in the computation of the group key, distributed LBT based protocols are said contributory protocols.

In both cases, for a balanced tree of keys, each member stores $\log_2 n + 1$ keys, where n is the number of members. This hierarchy achieves better performance when updating keys (Figure 1 shows basic operations on an LBT). When a new member joins the group or an old one leaves the group, only the keys in the path from the new member (or the departing one) to the root, i.e. $\log_2 n$ keys, must be updated. The message complexity of these approaches during rekeying is $O(\log_2 n)$. Using group characteristics, we propose to combine the scalability of subgrouping based approaches with the efficiency of LBT based approaches.

3. Group Characteristics

A multicast group G is a set of nodes participating in the same multicast session. Several characteristics (Canneti et al., 1999; Bettahar and Bouabdallah, 2001) of G may influence group key management.

– *Group Size:* The expected size of the group, the number of senders, the number of receivers are important factors in the keying/rekeying scheme. For example, contributory protocols are more suitable for dynamic peer groups with few members.

– *Group Dynamism:* The group membership may be static and known in advance. It also may be dynamic. In this last case, only joins may be possible or also leaves. Frequency of membership changes may also be known or estimated. In many multicast groups, senders or receivers may be fixed (known, subscribed) or dynamic (Visitors). This is the case for example in a tele-education session, where the audience may consist of subscribed known teachers and students of the class (fixed sources and receivers) and other visitors (dynamic sources or receivers) who can occasionally join the group. We will discuss the influence of such heterogeneity in the dynamism of the group in Section 4. Another important issue in group dynamism are cascaded events. A cascaded event occurs, in its simplest form, when one membership change occurs while another is being handled. Mass joins and mass leaves are particular cascaded events. The frequency of rekeying becomes a primary bottleneck for scalable group rekeying when cascaded events occur. So, dealing with such events is an important issue in group key management.

- **Session Type:** A session may be one-to-many, few-to-many, many-to-many, join only or join-leave.
- **Security requirements:** The main security concerns is typically access control. Other concerns include source authentication and clogging attacks.
- **Trust Issue:** group members may trust each other or suspect each other. In several multicast group scenarios, exists a single entity (member of the group or a third party) trusted by all the members to perform keying tasks. We may also have heterogeneity in trust considerations. For example, in the tele-education group, communications between teachers should not be readable by students.
- **Volume and type of traffic:** Volume of communication, allowed latency, available bandwidth, delay of communications for real time sessions may influence the choice of the rekeying protocol.
- **Underlying Routing Protocol:** For example, it may be relevant to know if all routing is done via a single server or it is distributed, how the routing protocol constructs the routing tree, etc. In (Ballardie, 1996), the author presents a group key management protocol that uses the CBT (Core Based Tree) multicast tree.
- **Life time of the group:** A multicast group may be permanent, periodic, or temporary. In each case, a different keying/rekeying approach should be applied.
- **Underlying group communication tools:** Several group key management protocols use the capabilities of an underlying group communication service that offers reliability, fault tolerance and other interesting properties (Amir et al., 2001; Kim et al., 2001).
- **Heterogeneity:** The members of a group may have different computing and storage capabilities, different dynamism and trusting issues (as described above), different roles and different security requirements.

We note that this list may be completed by many other group characteristics that may also influence group key management. We cite here only important ones. Because of the diversity of group characteristics, Canneti et al. (Canneti et al., 1999) claim that it is unlikely that a single group key management solution will satisfy all multicast group scenarios. We agree with them and think that, because of heterogeneity of characteristics within the same multicast group, it is unlikely that a single solution will reach the intended efficiency. This does not systematically imply that new solutions are needed but simply re-structuring, hybridization, and integration of group characteristics within existing solutions.

4. Case Study: Semi-Dynamic Groups

4.1. Architecture

We consider here a multicast group G that exhibits heterogeneity in dynamism and trust considerations. G has two types of members:
- Static members (SMs): They are quasi-permanent members. Generally, known or subscribed members. They join the group early and rarely leave it before the session is closed.
- Dynamic members (DMs): or unknown members who may join or leave the group at any time.

SMs are equal. They may or may not trust each other but do not trust DMs. However, DMs have complete trust in SMs. We aim to construct an efficient keying/rekeying scheme for G. The efficiency of the presented scheme may be measured by its 1 affects n scalability and its ability to undertake mass joins and mass leaves of DMs. To achieve better efficiency than LBTs based approaches while preserving forward and backward secrecy, we propose an hybrid approach that uses several LBTs and two keying levels. The first level consists on keying the set of SMs. The second level consists on keying DMs. This solution is motivated by the dynamism and trust characteristics of the group. SMs have the same role. They can use a contributory key management protocol (say P_s) to generate a key. Every SM handles key management for a subset of DMs with a centralized or distributed LBT based approach, say P_d. If SMs join the group early, they first establish a key between them using P_s. This does not exclude DMs to join as early as SMs. Each SM can simultaneously establish key materials within a sub group of DMs. Let n_s be the number of SMs, $n_d=n-n_s$ the expected number of DMs. Each SM controls an LBT tree of n_d/n_s DMs. Figure 2 describes the global architecture. The flexibility of the presented architecture is the possibility of using different keying schemes. P_s may be different from P_d. Furthermore, different P_d protocols may be used in response to particular characteristics in the subgroup attached to each of the SMs.

4.2. Basic Operations

In this Section, we describe the basic algorithms for join and leave operations without using specific P_s and P_d protocols. We rely only on the idea that P_s is a contributory key management protocol (hierarchical or not). A good choice for P_s is the protocol of Dondetti et al. (Dondeti et al., 1999a) because it is completely distributed, no member has a particular role. P_d is an LBT based key management protocol. Because of the difference between centralized and distributed LBT based protocols in key generation, we assume for simplicity of the description that P_d is a centralized LBT based protocol. A good choice for P_d is the extension of LBT based protocols presented in (Rafaeli et al., 2001) that reduces message size.

Dynamic members' Join/leave operations: To join the group, a DM D_i multicasts a join request to the SMs of the group and waits for the first positive response. SMs that can handle the additional workload of another member in their LBT respond to the request. An other approach consists in all SMs respond by giving the number c of DMs in their underlying subgroup. D_i chooses the SM that handles the smallest number of DMs. In the two cases, the concerned SM, verifies D_i's authorization capabilities, associates D_i to a leaf, rekeys its LBT and gives D_i its keying material according to P_d (generates and distributes $\log_2 c$ keys).

When a DM D_i leaves or is removed from the group, the corresponding SM removes the leaf associated to D_i as well as its parent node from the LBT. It gives the sibling node of D_i the parent's place in the LBT. The SM initiates the rekeying process according to P_d. Several joins and leaves may be handled simultaneously without decreasing the group performance. If p is the probability of occurrence of m simultaneous joins or leaves, the probability that a particular SM handles them is p/n_s.

Static Members' Join/leave operations: Join and leave events in the set of SMs are rare but possible. Leaves more likely due to possible failures. When a latecomer SM joins the group, a new group key must be established between SMs according to P_s. Only SMs are affected. The new SM receives from the other SMs (the nearest one) the access control list of the group and starts its activity with an empty LBT.

When an SM S_i fails, keying material of its subgroup of DMs is lost. These DMs must rejoin the group. If S_i leaves the group, it transmits the control of its subgroup to the nearest SM, say S_j. S_j merges the two LBTs as described in Figure 3: it rekeys the received LBT, creates a new root key, multicasts it in the received LBT (encrypted with the root key it attributed to the received LBT) and in its own LBT (encrypted with the old root key). Note here that If SMs are trusted, rekeying after joins and leaves are not necessary.

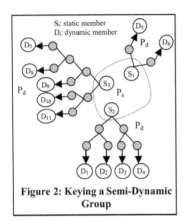

Figure 2: Keying a Semi-Dynamic Group

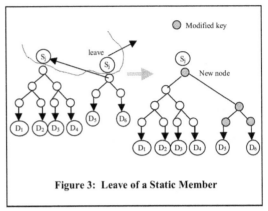

Figure 3: Leave of a Static Member

For data transmission, each SM decrypts received messages and recrypt them before forwarding them.

5. Comparison with Existing Protocols

To the best of our knowledge, none of the existing group key management protocols combines the scalability of subgroups based approaches (such as Iolus and DEP) and the efficiency of LBT based approaches. In this section, we evaluate the performance of this hybrid approach and compare it to LBT based protocols (only some of them because of space limitation) and subgrouping based protocols existing in the literature. We focus on 1 affects n scalability, communication and storage costs at the level of each group member. Table 1 summarizes the obtained results. The main contribution of the hybrid approach is its 1 affects n scalability. It exhibits an 1 affects n scalability equivalent to the scalability of subgrouping schemes ($c \approx n_d/n_s$). For join operations, the results of the hybrid scheme are equivalent to the results of LBT based schemes for SMs and better for DMs since $\log_2 n_d < \log_2 n$. But the hybrid scheme loses out to the subgrouping schemes that achieve a communication cost of $O(1)$ at joins. For leaving operations, again the hybrid scheme achieves better than the other schemes regarding the number of messages required: $\log_2 n_d$ is smaller than c and $\log_2 n$. Regarding the total number of encryption operations necessary to transmit data, the hybrid scheme uses two encryption operations which is better than $t \geq 2$ encryption operations involved in subgrouping schemes. It however loses out to LBT based schemes that use only one encryption operation. Storage overhead, involved in the hybrid scheme, is also acceptable when compared to the other schemes.

6. Conclusion

In this paper, we focused on using group characteristics to achieve better efficiency in group key management. To prove the importance of group characteristics in group key management, we presented a case study of the heterogeneity in group dynamism and trust issue within a multicast group where we distinguish between fixed and dynamic participants and trust considerations between them. We presented an appropriate protocol which achieves better 1 affects n scalability and alleviates the management of mass joins and mass leaves of dynamic members.

Our scheme requires $\log_2 n_d/n_s$ messages for join/leave operations (n_d is the number of dynamic members and n_s is the number of static members). It considerably alleviates the management of mass joins and leaves. If p is the average number of joins or leaves that have to be handled simultaneously, p

	Centralised LBT based protocols.	Distributed LBT based protocols	Mittra, 1997 (Iolus)	Dondetti et al., 1999b (DEP)	Hybrid Approach
1-affecte-?	n	n	c	c	n_d/n_s
Dynamic joins and leaves	yes	yes	yes	yes	yes
Centralised entity required	yes	Dondeti et al., 1999a: no Steer et al., 1988, Kim et al., 2000: variable	yes	yes	no
Trust third party	no	no	yes	no	no
Nbr. Keys at controller	$2n-1$	–	$c\,K_{SGRP-x}$ $+1\,K_{SGRP}$	$c\,KEK$ $+1\,DEK$ $+1\,K_{SGRP}$	–
Nbr. Keys at sub-controllers (GSA)	–	–	$c\,K_{SGRP-x}$ $+1\,K_{SGRP}$ $+1$ parent K_{SGRP} $+1$own K_{SGRP-x}	$\pm1\,KEK$ $\pm1\,DEK$ $+1$parent K_{SGRP} $+1\,K_{SGRP}$ $+1$ private key	Static member $\log_2 n_s +1$ $+(2n_d/n_s -1)$
Nbr. Keys at member	$\log_2 n +1$	Steer et al., 1988: n Others: $\log_2 n +1$	$1\,K_{SGRP-x}$ $+1\,K_{SGRP}$	$1\,KEK$ $+1\,DEK$ $+1\,K_{SGRP}$ $+1$ private	Dynamic member $\log_2 n_d/n_s +1$
Nbr. messages at join	$\log_2 n$	Steer et al., 1988: 2 Kim et al., 2000 with a KDC: 3 Dondeti et al. 1999a: $\log_2 n$	1	1	P_s: distributed LBT P_d: $\log_2 n_d$
Nbr. messages at leave	$\log_2 n$	Steer et al., 1988: 2 Kim et al., 2000 with a KDC: 3 Dondeti et al., 1999a: $\log_2 n$	c	c	P_s: distributed LBT P_d: $\log_2 n_d$
Total Encryption	1	1	t	t+1	2

n : group size. t: depth of the hierarchy of sub-grouping. n_s : number of static members. n_d: number of dynamic members, $n_d = n-n_s$. P_s : protocol used for keying static members. P_d: protocol used for keying dynamic members. c:average size of a subgroup. K_{SGRP}: subgroup key. K_{SGRP-x}: key between a sub-group controller and a member x in the sub-group. KEK: key encryption key. DEK: data encryption key or group key.

Table 1: Comparison with Existing Key Management Protocols

is divided by n_s in the hybrid scheme. Additionally, the hybrid scheme requires the storage of only $\log_2 n_d/n_s +1$ keys at the level of each dynamic member and $\log_2 n_s +(2n_d/n_s)$ keys at the level of each static member.

One area of future work is to simulate the proposed approach, together with the discussed related protocols, in a common environment. Such experiment not only can bring valuable performance results, it can also give a sound platform on which to build a wide range of efficient hybridized, group characteristic based protocols.

7. References

Amir, Y., Kim, Y., Nita-Rotaru, C., and Tsudik, G. (2001), "On the Performance of Group key Agreement Protocols", *TR CNDS-2001-5*, John Hopkins University, Baltimore.

Ballardie, T. (1996), Scalable Multicast Key Distribution", *RFC 1949.*

Bettahar, H. and Bouabdallah, A. (2001), "Qos Routing for the Generalized Multicast Routing Problem (GMRP)", *In proc. of the 1st Intl. Conf. On Networking*, ICN2001, France, LNCS2093, pp. 630-639.

Canneti, R., Garay, J., Itkis, G., Micciancio, D., Naor, M., and Pinkas, B. (1999), "Multicast Security: A Taxonomy and Some Efficient Constructions", *In Proc. of the INFOCOM99*, Vol.2, pp. 708-716, USA.

Deering, S. E. (1988), "Multicast Routing in Internetworks and Extended LANs". *In proc. of the ACM SIGCOMM'88.*

Dondeti, L. R., Mukherjee, S., and Samal, A. (1999a), "A Distributed group key management Scheme for secure many-to-many Communication", *T.R. PINTL-TR-207-99*, University of Nebraska-Lincoln.

Dondeti, L. R., Mukherjee, S., and Samal, A. (1999b), "A Dual Encryption Protocol for Scalable Secure Multicasting", *Proc. of IEEE Intl. Symposium on Computer Communication*, Egypt.

Kim, Y., Perrig, A., and Tsudik, G. (2000), "Simple and fault-Tolerant Key Agreement for Dynamic Collaborative groups", *Intl. Conf. on Computer and Comm. Security*, pp. 235-244.

Kim, Y., Perrig, A., and Tsudik, G. (2001), "Communication-Efficient group Key Agreement", *Proc. of IFIP SEC.*

Li, X. S., Yang, Y. R., Gouda, M. G., and Lam, S. S. (2001), "Batch Rekeying for Secure Group Communication", *Proc., of the 10th Intl. WWW Conference*, China.

McGrew, D. A., and Sherman, A. T. (1998), "Key Establishment in Large Dynamic Groups Using One-Way Function Trees". *T.R. TR-0755, TIS labs at Network Associates, Inc.*, Glenwood, MD, may, 1998.

Menezes, A. J., Van Oorschot, P. C., and Vanstone, S. A. (1997). "Handbook of Applied Cryptography", *CRC press series on Discrete mathematics and its Applications*, ISBN 0-8493-8523-7.

Mittra, S. (1997), "Iolus: A Framework for Scalable Secure Multicasting", *Proc. ACM SIGCOMM*, pp. 277-288, France.

Perrig, A., Song D., and Tygar J. D. (2001), "ELK, a New Protocol for Efficient Large-Group Key Distribution", *Proc. of IEEE Security and privacy Symposium*, S&P2001.

Rafaeli, S., Mathy, L., and Hutchison, D. (2001), "EHBT: An Efficient Protocol for Group Key Management", *3rd Intl. Workshop on Networked group Communication*, NGC2001, London.

Steer, D., Strawczynski, L. L., Diffie, W., and Weiner, M. (1988), "A Secure Audio Teleconference System", *CRYPTO88.*

Waldvogel, M., Caronni, G., Sun, D., Weiler, N., and Plattner, B. (1999), "The Versakey Framework: Versatile Group Key Management", *IEEE Journal on selected Areas in Communications (Special Issue on Middleware)*, 17(9), pp. 1614-1631.

Wallner, D., Harder, E., and Agee, R. (1999), "Key Management for Multicast: Issues and Architectures", *RFC 2627.*

Wong, W., Gouda, M., and Lam, S. (1998), "Secure Group Communication using Key Graphs", *Proc: of the ACM SIGCOMM'98 Conference on Applications, Technologies, Architectures, and Protocols for Computer Communication*, pp. 68-79.

Securing the Network Client[*]

Victoria Skoularidou[1, 2] and Diomidis Spinellis[1]

[1]Department of Management Science and Technology,
Athens University of Economics and Business (AUEB),
Patission 76, GR-104 34, Athens, Greece
Tel: +30 108203682, Fax: +30 108203685
http://www.dmst.aueb.gr/dds/, mailto:dds@aueb.gr

[2]Development Programmes Dept., INTRACOM S.A.,
Hellenic Telecommunications and Electronics Industry,
19.5 Km Markopoulo Ave., GR-190 02, Peania, Greece
Tel: +30 106690347, Fax: +30 106830312
http://www.intracom.gr/, mailto:vsko@intracom.gr

Abstract

We enumerate and compare a number of security-enabling architectures for network clients. These architectures, either proposed as methodologies or currently implemented in software and/or hardware, are capable of protecting the client's software integrity and its environment. The most important methodologies include the reference monitor model, firewalls and virtual machines. Software implementations are the Java sandbox and the code signing concept. Hardware that can be used includes smart cards. We describe their most important features and provide a review and comparative study based on a number of criteria. We believe that ongoing research can empower these mechanisms for protecting network clients in a more effective way.

Keywords

Security-enabling architectures, Network clients, Client software integrity.

1. Introduction

Despite effort being expended to secure network clients, these are increasingly and continuously succumbing to viruses, worms, and Trojan horses. As the same client is nowadays trusted to conduct financial transactions or store and process sensitive personal information, its users deserve to be assured of a higher level of security than what is currently the norm. In this paper we review, from an architectural standpoint, methodologies and technologies that can be used towards this end.

According to (Ghosh, 1998) the security of Web-based systems should be ensured in four fronts: Web client, data transport, Web server and operating system security. In this survey paper, we focus on the network client side and examine a number of architectures and technologies that can be used for protecting the integrity of the client and its environment. With the term "client" we refer to web clients, e-mail clients, access clients (like ftp and/or

---

[*] This work was partially funded by the IST Project mEXPRESS (IST-2001-33432).

telnet), and similar applications. These architectures have either being proposed as methodologies, presented in section 2, or are actual implementations (in software and hardware) currently in use and described in sections 3 and 4. Section 5 draws the lessons of this study and compares the security-enabling architectures that were studied.

2. Methodologies

From the theoretical security models in existence, some have been realized in commercial product implementations while others were abandoned and exist only as concepts in the research community. In the first category we can identify the notion of *firewall* and *virtual machine* while the *reference monitor* model falls in the second one. We provide a description of these models in the following paragraphs.

2.1. The Reference Monitor Security Model

The *Reference Monitor* was based on the abstract modeling efforts of (Lampson, 1971) and was also described by (Anderson, 1972). It is depicted in the figure below (Stallings, 1995):

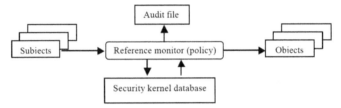

Figure 1: The Reference Monitor Concept.

The reference monitor is a controlling element in the hardware and operating system of a computer that regulates the access of *subjects* (e.g. users, processes, etc.) to *objects* (e.g. files, programs, etc.) on the basis of their security parameters. It has access to the *security kernel database* that lists the access privileges of each subject and the protection attributes of each object. Any detected security violations and authorised changes, are stored in an *audit file*.

One major problem of the reference monitor concept is that it is too complex and requires the developer to start with a totally new operating system (and probably hardware) design (Lobel, 1986). Another problem is that early attempts to reproduce it in actual hardware and software met with only minimal success, primarily because of unexpectedly high overhead and/or system performance degradation. One historical example is the operating system MULTICS (Organick, 1972), developed in the late 1960s by MIT, Bell Labs, and Honeywell.

However, supposing that the reference monitor was implemented as a part of a system, then a network client could be protected in the following way: Let's imagine that a UNIX system user navigates with his web browser into a number of web sites. According to the RM's policy, as a subject, the only privilege he has is the capability of saving web pages, files, etc. in the directory "internet_files" of his mounted hard disk (the corresponding object). If a malicious applet is downloaded on his machine and tries to gain root privileges by e.g. executing a SUID program, it will simply fail since the reference monitor will deny access, according to the previous security policy. The same applies with the user's mail client. If the user is only allowed to save attachments on his disk storage then a rogue program could not harm his system, as the reference monitor would prevent any compromise.

2.2. The Firewall Concept

Properly configured firewalls can constitute an effective type of network security. They prevent the dangers of the Internet from spreading into the internal network by restricting access at a centrally managed point.

Firewalls are classified into three main categories (Cheswick and Bellovin, 1994): packet filters that drop packets based on their destination address and port, circuit gateways that relay TCP connections, and application-level gateways where special-purpose code is used for each desired application (making it easy to log and control all incoming and outgoing traffic).

Application-level gateways can provide a centralized point for monitoring the behavior of an electronic mail system and they can analyze and record traffic and content looking for information leaks. Their principal disadvantage is the need for a specialized user program for most services provided. Also, the use of such gateways is easiest with applications that make provision for redirection, such as email, otherwise new client programs must be provided.

2.3. The Virtual Machine Concept

A Virtual Machine is a piece of computer software designed to reproduce a specific set of computer behaviors and capabilities other than the ones native to the computer or operating system on which the software itself is running. Some virtual machines are *emulators*; Others produce behaviors and capabilities of a machine that doesn't necessarily exist as an actual piece of hardware but may only be a detailed specification. More modern examples include the specification of the Java Virtual Machine (JVM) (Lindhorn and Yellin, 1997) and the Common Language Infrastructure (CLI) of the Microsoft .NET initiative. These allow diverse computers to run software written to that specification; the virtual machine software itself must be written separately for each type of computer on which it runs. Other virtual machines let one operating system run on top of another on the same machine like (VMware Inc, 2000).

The virtual machine design has two advantages: a) *system independence*, since any application will run the same in any virtual machine, regardless of the hardware and software underlying the system, and b) *security*, because the virtual machine has no contact with the operating system, hence there is little possibility of a program damaging other files or applications. The virtual machine can be used to sandbox applications since it stands between the real hardware or another operating system layer (the virtual machine is often an operating system). This, of course, has a downside concerning efficiency, because operating system calls and privileged instructions of programs running in a virtual machine have to pass through the virtual machine layer. Thus, virtual machines like JVM and VMware also provide a restricted environment in which programs may operate. Errant applications should only be able to cause damage to the virtual machine, thus leaving the real system intact.

3. Software Implementations

Here, we present network client security architectures currently implemented in software that allow the secure execution of downloadable executable content (i.e. mobile code).

3.1. The Java Sandbox

The Java Sandbox is Java's security model, by which any untrusted Java applet must abide. It is a technological solution to prevent malicious code behavior, thus protecting a network client from possible attacks. For example, if a user downloads via her Web browser an applet that tries to erase her hard disk, it will fail because the sandbox restricts its operation, since it is untrusted. The Java sandbox is enforced by three technologies: the *Bytecode Verifier,* the *Applet Class Loader,* and the *Security Manager* (McGraw and Felten, 2000).

The Java sandbox is quite complicated but it is one of the most complete existing security models. The problem is that the three technologies comprising the model work in concert to prevent an applet from abusing its restricted privileges. They are highly interdependent and non-overlapping. Because each one provides a different function, a flaw in one can break the whole sandbox (McGraw and Felten, 1997). So, their design must be solid, and their implementations must not be flawed. The complexity of the functions that each technology provides makes a correct implementation a difficult goal to attain. The Java security problems found to date are a direct result of flaws in these functions implementations (Ghosh, 1998).

3.2. Code Signing

Modern component-based software is a lot harder to secure because: a) someone cannot assume that all the modules are trustworthy, b) someone cannot assume that all the modules are written well enough to work in every possible configuration, and c) the operating system is not there to deal with (a) and (b), since modern components talk to each other directly, not through the operating system, so any built-in safety features simply do not apply. Several general methods for dealing with this security problem have been tried, like *Code Signing.* The programmer signs components and the user decides, based on the signatures, which components to allow on his computer. Sun's Java and Microsoft's ActiveX Controls provide code-signing features.

The *Java sandbox* very simply and strictly prevents Java applets downloaded from the network from using sensitive system services. The security policy for untrusted applets is *black-and-white* (Ghosh, 1998): if applets are downloaded across a network connection, they must abide by the strict constraints of the sandbox; if they are loaded from the local file system, they are completely trusted and given free rein of the system, as Java applications do.

To provide greater flexibility to run Java applets in a trusted environment, JavaSoft has provided the ability to sign applets using JDK's 1.1 Crypto API. It provides the ability to digitally sign applets with unforgeable proof of identity (Gritzalis et al., 1998). In this way, applets access system resources based on who signs them. The *black-and-white* security policy for executing applets in JDK 1.1 changed to a *shades-of-gray* model in JDK 1.2 where more fine-grained access control is supported.

ActiveX is a framework for Microsoft's software component technology that allows programs encapsulated in units called controls to be embedded in Web pages (Ghosh, 1998). Unlike

Java, ActiveX is language independent but platform specific. The controls can be written in several different languages but can be executed only on a 32-bit Windows platform. Since ActiveX controls have the ability to execute much like any other program on a computer, they may be used to forge e-mail, monitor Web usage, send files over Internet, write files, interact with other programs, etc.

Microsoft's response to addressing ActiveX technology security problems is *Authenticode* (Microsoft Corp., 2001). This does not prevent ActiveX controls from behaving maliciously but it can be used to prevent automatic execution of untrusted ones. Authenticode can provide two checks before executing ActiveX controls: it can verify a) who signs the code, and b) if the code has been altered since it was signed. Authenticode provides verification of the identity of the person who signed the control and integrity checks of the software to ensure it has not been altered since it was signed. However, the signature provides no assurance that the control will not behave maliciously. Authenticode technology works solely on a trust model and there is no middle ground to let the control execute in a constrained environment where it can be observed before granting full access.

The key difference in security between ActiveX controls and Java applets is that ActiveX security is based wholly on the trust placed in the code signer, while Java applet security is based on restricting the behavior of the applet (Ghosh, 1998). One is a *human judgment-based* approach to security, while the other is a *technology-based* approach using the sandbox solution. *Java applets signing* has been also introduced by JavaSoft as a policy based on trust and human judgment. Signed applets have the ability to access system resources based on who signed them, but untrusted ones can still execute, albeit with the sandbox limitations.

4. Hardware Implementations

So far, security-enabling architectures that were proposed as methodologies or are based on software implementations were examined. In this section, we describe hardware-based ones.

4.1. Smart Cards

A smart card stores and processes information through the electronic circuits embedded in silicon in the plastic substrate of its body. There are two basic kinds of smart cards (Chen, 1998): An *intelligent smart card* contains a microprocessor and a memory chip and offers read, write, and calculation capability. A *memory card* contains only a memory chip, is meant only for information storage and can only undertake a predefined operation. Smart cards can carry all necessary functions and information on the card, so they do not require access to remote databases at the time of the transaction. Their benefits of increased storage, security and portability have made them very popular against magnetic stripe cards, that are not so secure, require a host system to store and process all data and cannot make data universally accessible (Coleman, 1998). By putting sensitive information like passwords and encryption keys into a central point like the card and, thus, outside of the client's environment, the client becomes less vulnerable to malicious attacks. On the other hand there also exist problems: if a hacker takes the control of the client he could force the card to do something the client does not want like giving his credit card information to a malicious site (Balfanz and Felten, 1999). Typically any application requiring authentication can benefit from a smart card. Smart cards can be used for authentication and as a secure, convenient portable storage mechanism. With the advent of the Java Card (a smart card capable of running Java bytecodes) limitations like the portability of applications and the flexibility of downloading applications into the card are eliminated, since a single Java application can run on all smart cards (Coleman, 1998). Since one of the fundamental problems in securing computer systems is the need for tamper-resistant storage of keys, smart cards can provide this functionality so that the private key of the network client can be placed on it and the access control on the card is offered via a proper Personal Identification Number (PIN). Smart cards provide also the ability to upgrade security solutions when they become compromised, e.g. if a hacker cracks the security of smart-card enabled digital satellite systems new cardlets – Java Card applications) could be sent.

The fact that smart cards now employ public key encryption to both encrypt data and digitally sign messages to provide unforgeable proof of identity, makes them ideal for integrating into them applications like social security card, access control to Web sites or online databases, digital signatures for e-mail and Web transactions, public keys for encrypting data transactions, credit/debit cards, e-cash, etc. (Ghosh, 1998). Smart cards importance has been identified by major credit card organizations like Visa, which has recently announced its Chip Migration Plan (Visa International, 2001) involving the substitution of credit cards with new ones with a microchip, more suitable for e-banking and e-commerce applications.

5. Review and Comparison

After presenting the various types of security-enabling architectures, in this section we review them and use them as a basis for a comparative study.

First, we identify the protection these mechanisms offer against specific security threats. Generally, security threats to computer systems, fall into the following broad classes (Gritzalis and Spinellis, 1997), (Meyer et al., 1995):

- **Leakage (Disclosure):** The acquisition of information by unauthorized recipients (loss of confidentiality or privacy).
- **Tampering (Modification):** The unauthorized alteration of information (loss of integrity).
- **Resource stealing:** The unauthorized use of system facilities.
- **Repudiation:** Loss of attribution.

Table 1 summarizes the protection against these security threats offered by the described technologies. Malware and user ignorance have been added, since they also comprise serious threats to a computer system:

	Leakage	Tampering	Resource stealing	Repudiation	Malware	User ignorance
Reference monitor	✓	✓	✓		✓	✓
Firewalls	✓	✓	✓		✓	✓
Virtual machines	✓	✓	✓		✓	✓
Java sandbox	✓	✓	✓		✓	✓
Code signing				✓		
Smart cards	✓	✓	✓		✓	✓

Table 1: Protection against security threats.

Apart from the level of protection and the security service these mechanism provide, we also compare them against a number of non-functional characteristics (Sommerville, 2001), summarized in Table 2:

- **Complexity.** It is not enough to just allege that a certain methodology provides security. On the contrary, security attributes need to be easily verified thus should not be complex. Simplicity is a fundamental hint of computer systems design (Lampson, 1983).
- **Ease of use.** This is another important attribute, since usually system administrators and users do not want to use awkward systems.
- **Incorporation into existing applications.** How easily these mechanisms could be ported into existing systems.

	Level of protection and security service provided	Complexity	Ease of use	Incorporation into existing applications
Reference monitor	Offers a high level of protection by residing at the lowest system layer. Adding security to the lowest level automatically secures all the above layers (Saltzer et al., 1984).	Very complex since it needs new operating system design.	A new operating system with system calls based on the reference monitor would be difficult to use.	Presumes a new operating system (and maybe hardware) design.
Firewalls	Best solution for separating the internal network but cannot provide protection against malicious insiders. An application-level gateway can provide better protection than a packet filter because since it does not rely only on addresses and ports.	Their installation requires the configuration of a number of devices.	They need installation and configuration procedures.	Their configuration can be easily provided.
Virtual machines	They provide separation and isolation of processes.	Realization requires the installation of a proper package.	They need installation and configuration procedures.	Can be easily installed on a system in order to make it capable of accessing another one.
Java sandbox	Ideal for mobile code since it can protect the integrity of the client environment by confining the use of resources.	Its complexity lies in the strong interdependence of its three basic components.	It needs only knowledge of the proper packages.	It is ready for operation whenever mobile code (Java applet) needs to be executed on a client machine.
Code signing	Ideal for mobile code since it can protect the integrity of the client environment by confining the use of resources.	A signature that accompanies the component is needed.	It needs only knowledge of the proper packages.	The only thing needed is a proper toolkit for being able to sign the code produced.
Smart cards	Perfect for authentication provision.	Complexity lies in the familiarization with the accompanying features (reader, use of a PIN, etc.).	The user uses them as a black box and the programmer creates the proper application.	In order to operate a proper reader needs to be used and the smart card to be programmed.

Table 2: Non-functional characteristics of the described technologies.

These technologies can be combined in order to provide more fine-grained protection. E.g., in the case of a Java Card, the Java sandbox and/or the code signing mechanism need to operate in order to prevent malicious Java Card applications from being downloaded to a smart card. Similarly, if a firewall lets applets to be executed on the client's machine the Java sandbox and/or code signing features should be also used to prevent a possible malicious behavior.

6.   Conclusions

There exist a lot of technologies for securing network clients. Ongoing research in sandboxing applications can be found in (Prevelakis and Spinellis, 2001) and (Fu et al., 2000) while (NSA, 2001) investigates architectures for providing operating system security mechanisms. Firewall vendors should consider more the ease of configuration while virtual machines need to be enhanced in order to provide better performance. Code signing is an improvement in controlling software origin but the fact that it is based on human judgment poses the need to use it in combination with sandboxes. Smart cards seem to be a very promising technology for client protection. Protecting network clients becomes an imperative as users rely more and more on them in order to conduct sensitive operations (e.g. e-commerce transactions). We believe that in the forthcoming years research in this area will empower their security.

7.   References

Anderson, J. (1972), Computer Security Technology Planning Study", *ESD-TR-73-51*, HQ Electronic Systems Division (AFSC), L. G. Hanscom Field, Bedford, Mass., October 1972, vols. 1, 2.

Balfanz, D. and Felten, E. (1999), "Hand-Held Computers Can Be Better Smart Cards", *Proceedings of the 8th USENIX Security Symposium*, Washington, D.C., USA.

Chen, Z. (1998), "Understanding Java Card 2.0", *Javaworld Magazine*.

Cheswick, W. and Bellovin, S. (1994), *"Building Internet Firewalls"*, Addison-Wesley, USA.

Coleman, A. (1998), "Giving currency to the Java Card API", *Javaworld Magazine*.

Fu K., Sit E., Smith K., and Feamster N., (2000), "MAPbox: Using Parameterized Behavior Classes to Confine Untrusted Applications", *9th USENIX UNIX Security Symposium*, Denver, Colorado, USA.

Ghosh, A. (1998), *"E-Commerce Security: Weak Links, Best Defenses"*, Wiley Computer Publishing, USA.

Gritzalis S., and Spinellis D. (1997) "Addressing Threats and Security Issues in World Wide Web Technology", *3rd International Conference on Communications and Multimedia Security*, pp. 33-46, Athens, Greece.

Gritzalis, S., Aggelis, G., and Spinellis, D. (1998), "Programming Languages for Mobile Code: A problems viewpoint", *1st International Network Conference INC '98*, pp. 210-217, Plymouth, UK.

Lampson, B. (1971), "Protection", *5th Princeton Conference on Information Science and Systems*, Princeton.

Lampson, B. (1983), "Hints for Computer Systems Design", *9th ACM Symposium on Operating Systems Principles*, Bretton Woods, New Hampshire, USA.

Lindhorn, T. and Yellin, F. (1997), *"The Java Virtual Machine Specification"*, Addison-Wesley, USA.

Lobel, J. (1986), *"Computer Security and Access Control: Foiling the System Breakers"*, McGraw-Hill, USA.

McGraw, G. and Felten, E. (1997), "Understanding the keys to Java Security", *Javaworld Magazine*.

McGraw, G. and Felten, E. (2000), *"Securing Java"*, Wiley Computer Publishing, USA.

Meyer K., Schaeffer S., Baker D., and Manning S. (1995) "Addressing Threats in World Wide Web Technology", *11th Annual Computer Security Applications Conference*, pp. 123--132".

Microsoft Corp. (2001) *"Code Signing with Microsoft Authenticode"*, MSDN Library Online.

NSA (2001), *"Security Enhanced Linux"*, available on-line at http://www.nsa.gov/selinux/.

Organick, E. (1972), *"The Multics System: An Examination of Its Structure"*, MIT Press.

Prevelakis, V. and Spinellis, D. (2001), *USENIX 2001 Technical Conference*, USENIX Association.

Saltzer J., Reed D., and Clark D. (1984), "End-to-end arguments in system design", *ACM Transactions on Computer Systems*, Vol. 2, No. 4, pp. 277-288.

Sommerville I. (2001), *"Software Engineering, 6th Edition"*, Addison-Wesley, USA.

Stallings, W. (1995), *"Network and Internetwork Security: Principles and Practice"*, Prentice-Hall, USA.

Visa International (2001), *"Chip Migration Plan"*, available online at http://www.visa.com

VMware Inc. (2000), *"VMware GSX Server"*, available at http://www.vmware.com/pdf/gsx_whitepaper.pdf.

Security Risk Analysis e-Commerce

[ψ]M Warren and [Ω]W Hutchinson

[ψ]School of Computing and Mathematics,
Deakin University,
Geelong, Victoria, Australia, 3217.

[Ω]School of Computer and Information Science
Edith Cowan University,
Mt Lawley, Western AUSTRALIA, 6050.

Email contact: mwarren@deakin.edu.au

Abstract

E-Commerce security is a complex issue, it is concerned with a number of security risks that can appear at either a technical level or organisational level. This paper uses a systemic framework, the Viable System Model (VSM) to determine the high level security risks and then uses baseline security methods to determine the lower level security risks.

Keywords

e-Commerce, Security, Security Risk Analysis and Baseline Security.

1. Introduction

Information systems are now heavily utilized by all organizations and relied upon to the extent that it would be impossible to manage without them. This has been encapsulated by the recent development of e-Commerce in a consumer and business environment. The situation now arises that information systems are at threat from a number of security risks and what is needed is a security method to allow for these risks to be evaluated and ensure that appropriate security countermeasures are applied.

2. Security Methods

The aim of the research was too combine a information systems modeling method with a baseline security method to form a hybrid security method. This method could be used to evaluate high and low level security risks associated with e-Commerce. The methods used in this model are the Viable System Model (VSM) and Baseline Security approach. The VSM is used to model an organisation's basic functions and associated data flows, whilst the Baseline Security approach is used to implement appropriate security countermeasures.

2.1 The Viable System Model (VSM)

The Viable System Model (VSM) developed by Stafford Beer (Beer, 1985), uses the principles of cybernetics. It has been successfully used to diagnose existing organisational structures and design new ones. It is the generic nature of the VSM that allows it to be used in a number of different situations (Hutchinson and Warren, 2000). In terms of this paper the model will be used to analyze potential security vulnerabilities to an organisation's information systems at a high level.

Before using the VSM, it is essential to understand the dynamics of its applicability and a diagrammatic representation is shown at Figure 1. The VSM consists of five subsystems, or functions. These are:

- *Implementation* (S1): this function consists of semi-autonomous units, which carry out the operational tasks in the system. These are the functions that are basic to the existence/purpose(s) of the system. They interact with their local environment, and each other. Each unit has its own local management, which is connected to wider management by vertical information flows. This function is the 'doing' part of an organization. The VSM has a recursive element, and each S1 has another VSM embedded in it.

- *Co-ordination* (S2): this function co-ordinates the S1 units to ensure that each S1 unit acts in the best interest of the whole system, rather than its own. This could be represented by something as simple as a timetable, or as subtle as morale among the workforce.

- *Internal Control* (S3): this function interprets policy information from 'higher' functions (S4), and 'lower' functions. It is the function, which controls the operational levels. Its function is not to create policy, but to implement it. Information arriving from the S1 function must periodically be audited for its quality and correctness. This is the S3* audit function.

- *Intelligence and Development* (S4): this function acts as a filter of information from the S3 function and the overall outside environment. Its purpose is to ensure that the policy making function (S5) is adequately briefed, and decisions are transmitted to S3.

- *Strategy and Policy* (S5): this function is responsible for the direction of the whole system. It must balance internal and external factors.

The data flows between S1 and S5 and the environment are shown in Figure 1. These flows show the potential points of vulnerability to a 'computer based attack'. With this conceptual model of a viable system (organisation), strategies and tactics can be developed to make the system 'non-viable' or dysfunctional. The logic being that investigating functional shortcomings can be used to improve an organisation and show its weaknesses, but also, to show possibilities for attack.

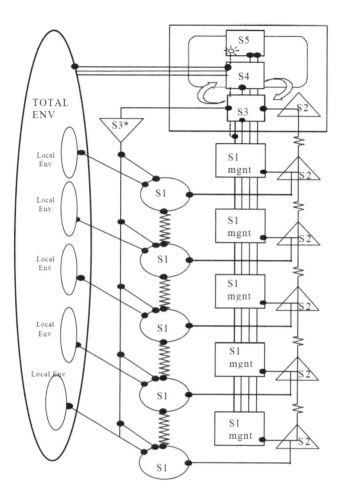

(Note: Env = Environment, mgnt = management)

Figure 1: The Viable System Model

2.2 Baseline Security Approach

The aim of risk analysis is to eliminate or reduce risks and vulnerabilities that affect the overall operation of organisational computer systems. Risk analysis not only looks at hardware and software, but also covers other areas such as physical security, human security, and business and disaster protection. In practice, there are major problems with the use of risk analysis; the time taken to carry out a review; the cost of hiring consultants and/or training staff. To overcome these negative aspects, baseline security approaches were developed. Baseline security offers an alternative to conventional risk methods as they represent the minimally acceptable security countermeasures that an organisation should have implemented. These countermeasures are applied in a generic manner, for example, every organisation should have the same baseline security countermeasures implemented.

The advantages of using baseline methods include (Warren and Hutchinson, 2000):
- cheap to use;
- simple to use;
- no training is required to use the method;
- it is quicker then undertaking a full security review.

Commonly used baseline methods include: the Australian and New Zealand AS/NZS 4444 standard (Australian and New Zealand Standard Committee, 1998), the British BS7799 standards (British Standards Institute, 1995 & 1998) and German BSI standard (BSI, 1994).

The authors decided to develop a security assessment method by which baseline security techniques could be applied.

3. Duality Risk Analysis Model

The aim of the duality risk analysis security model is to develop a security method that combines the strength of VMS and baseline approaches. Another aim is to overcome the weaknesses associated with baseline security models and allows for the VMS approach to be used in a security environment.

The stages of the duality risk analysis model are:

Stage 1 - VMS Stage
This stage of the model is concerned with using the VMS model to determine the impacts and risks that a particular security threat would have upon an organisation The impact can be assessed upon the whole organisations as shown by figure 1. Vulnerabilities of the various functions (S1 to S5) are used to examine various options for attack. The authors have developed software to assist in this task as shown by figure 2.

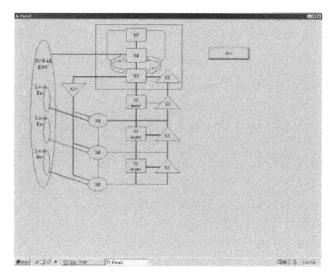

Figure 2. Software Developed by authors to model VSM Situations

Stage 2 -Baseline Stage
The appropriate baseline countermeasure are selected to reduce the security threat as defined in stage 1.

The authors have created special advisory software that allows for appropriate countermeasures to be selected e.g. what are the BS7799 guidelines that relate to computer viruses.

Stage 3 - Evaluation of Impact
The stage 1 process is repeated but this time the impact of the security countermeasure is evaluated. This will allow for the evaluation of the security countermeasure and show its effectiveness across the whole organization. The information provided by this will allow management to determine of effectiveness of security countermeasures.

This approach can by used to evaluate any security risk associated with e-Commerce. This type of approach will allow an organisation to model what it perceives are the important security risks and how they could relate to their organization.

4. Validation of Research

To validate the model the authors looked at a number of security risks that could impact organisations in relation to e-Commerce. In this section we will look at the impact of viruses. The type of virus attack that is being modeled would be a 'Word macro' virus infection similar to the 'Lovebug' virus.

Stage 1 - VMS Stage

Figure 1 illustrates the different levels of a sample organisatons. The impact of the virus attack upon that sample organization would be:

S1 Implementation

During the attack the S1 operating units will be affected. Within an organization each S1 might well have their own IT infrastructure as part of the overall organization's system. A virus outbreak would focus upon the communication infrastructure of the S1 unit. The impact will be that e-mail servers will crash under the extensive volume of data and possibly cause a cascade effect through the S1 unit by the increase of email traffic caused by the viruses. For example, if the mail server crashes what else would crash? Therefore a macro virus attack might affect S1 units' ability to interact from their operating (local) environment as well as disconnecting them from other S1 units and separating them from management functions. The attacks on the S1 unit will decrease the efficiency of the whole organization because of the disruption it will have upon the operational aspects.

S2 Co-ordination

There would be a dramatic impact upon the coordinating function of the S1 units. Because of the impact of the macro viruses S2 would not be able to work due to the isolation of the S1 units. There is also a chance that the S2 function would be affected by viruses spreading from the S1 units and therefore become isolated causing the coordination function to collapse.

S3 Internal Control

The internal control of the information system will be disrupted because of the chaos at the lower levels. It is therefore difficult to implement policy when structure of the information system infrastructure to be neutralized

S4 Intelligence and Development/S5 Strategy and Policy

The virus will not directly impact the S4 and S5 functions, unless the cascade effects of failures were dramatic to affect these higher level systems or unless the S4 and S5 functions were identified for attack and they would then become isolated from the rest of the organization.

Stage 2 - Baseline Security Stage

The decision support security software would be used to pick an appropriate baseline security countermeasure. Figure 3 shows a screenshot from the baseline security tool.

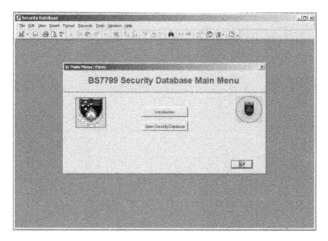

Figure 3: Security Baseline Tool

The software will work by the user selecting an appropriate baseline security countermeasure that could be implemented. The user would use the Security Baseline Tool Software (as shown by figure 3) and find an appropriate security countermeasure that would relate to computer viruses. The software would then show the appropriate baseline security countermeasure such as:

"Implement appropriate virus protection strategy"

The user can select this as being the security countermeasure that they wish to asses.

Stage 3 Re-evaluation of Impact

The user reviews the situation with the existing new countermeasure in place, using the VMS approach:

S1 Implementation
The virus protection strategy localises the damage to a few S1 units, assuming that some S1 units do not effectively implement a proper virus protection system for example, virus checkers out of date.

S2 Co-ordination
There would be localised disruption of a few S1 units. Co-ordinations functions can be adapted to overcome these localised difficulties until the problem is quickly resolved.

S3 Internal Control
No direct impact.

S4 Intelligence and Development/S5 Strategy and Policy
No direct impact.

Stage 2 and Stage 3 can be repeated if a security countermeasure does not have the required effect in reducing a security risk to an acceptable level.

5. Conclusion

The paper has shown that hybrid security risk analysis models can be used to model complex security solutions in relation to e-Commerce. The aim of the research is not to fully replace detailed security risks analysis methods but to offer an easier alternative that can be used to model different e-Commerce security risks and determine the impact of appropriate security countermeasures.

6. References

Australian and New Zealand Standard Committee (1998), *AS/NZS 4444.1 Information Security Management*, Australia.

Beer S (1985) *Diagnosing the System for Organisations.* Wiley, Chichester.

BSI. (1994). *Information Technology Baseline Protection Manual.* Bundesamt fur Sicherheit in der Informationstechnik, Germany. http://www.bsi.bund.de

British Standards Institute (1995) BS7799 - *Code of Practice for Information Security Management*, UK.

British Standards Institute (1998), *BS7799-2, Information security management, Specification for Information Security Management Systems,* UK.

Hutchinson, W. and Warren, M. (2000) Using The Viable Systems Model To Develop An Understanding Information System Security Threats To An Organisation, *1st Australian Information Security Management Workshop*, Deakin University, Geelong, Australia, November.

Warren, M. and Hutchinson, W (2000), *The Australian & New Zealand Security Standard AS/NZS 4444*, New Zealand Journal of Computing, Volume 8 (1/2), pp 37-43, November, New Zealand.

IS Security, Trust And Culture: A Theoretical Framework For Managing IS Security In Multicultural Settings

Dr Jill Slay

School of Computer and Information Science, University of South Australia, MAWSON
LAKES, SA5095, Australia
email: Jill.Slay@unisa.edu.au

Abstract

System security today focuses on the design of safe and secure information systems and their operation. In the analysis of any information system, whether small or large, one observes within it a "set of human activities related to each other so they can be viewed as a whole" (Checkland, 1981, p.47). If one particularly focuses on security aspects of large information systems, and then considers the many layers of complexity comprising the human activity systems within them, it becomes apparent that one of these layers, or subsystems, is a cultural one. This paper proposes that the perspective gained on the impact of culture in such a system by the application of Kline's (1995) systems theory, augmented by perspectives supplied by worldview theory, is helpful in designing appropriate learning environments for multicultural settings

Keywords
IS security management, culture.

1. Introduction

Internationally, governments and the commercial sector are being challenged by the exponential growth in high technology and computer-related terrorism and crime. Of particular concern is the growing number of attacks on supposedly secure computer systems, such as that of the White House and Pentagon. These kinds of attacks first predominated within e-commerce. However, such attacks have become even more of a problem as government and the military begin to offer many more of their services online, or rely more heavily on distributed information systems to provide their operating data.

System security today focuses on the design of safe and secure information systems and their operation. Various system components are analysed and then steps are taken toward making not only the single components, such as operating system, databases, communication channels and user interfaces secure, but also in ensuring the security of the interfaces between these components. Risk and requirements analysis techniques also contribute to making systems more secure and multilevel system security and more advanced cryptographic protection of transactions have already impeded the progress of intruders.

Organisational aspects of Information Systems (IS) security become important, making it clear that technology alone cannot lead to an adequate solution. A proper analysis of security requirements reveals that the issue of system security has to be dealt with at different levels. One hypothesis is that these levels follow the phases of the software design process; others group security requirements according to the ISO-OSI or IEEE network architecture models. Both approaches do however only cover the ICT architecture and infrastructure of a company. They do not deal with the related organisational issues. One of the major organisational issues to face is the human factor within IS security. Although media focuses on external attacks, it is recognised that up to 40 % of IS security related crime arises from malice or error from staff of the organisation (Davey, 2001).

Many secure systems rely on pin numbers or passwords. Systems become very vulnerable where employees, either deliberately or inadvertently, disclose such passwords to others. There are many different reasons why an individual might choose to disclose a password (even when he had she had a very good understanding of the sensitive nature of the data within the protected system). This can be seen as an issue of trust.

The **aim** of this research is to model the relationship between trust (as exemplified in the disclosure of a password to a secure system) and culture. The **outcomes** will be an understanding of the correlations between self-identified belief system, gender and trust.

2. Theoretical Model

Computer and information scientists have become accustomed to the use implicit use of multidisciplinary frameworks within their own area. Many researchers have attempted to deal with cultural issue but they have tended to draw on frameworks that rise from psychology. This research draws on anthropological frameworks and methodologies that are well established in science education.

Human Computer Interactions and Intelligent Tutoring Systems draw so strongly on frameworks from cognitive psychology that these foundations in psychology are not usually made explicit. Artificial Intelligence (AI) and knowledge representation draws on logical frameworks developed by the philosopher Aristotle (Sowa, 2000). AI has attempted to address cultural issues and cultural algorithms have been developed (Reynolds, 1994) which focus on the shared understanding of cultural phenomena. These "memetic algorithms" similar to genetic algorithms "address the evolution of culture in terms of evolution of ideas". Khaslavasky (1998) attempts to define culture and considers its role in the design of "internationalized" user interfaces.

Finkelstein and Fuks (1989) draw on viewpoint analysis, the interaction of various perspectives, in the specification and design of large, complex distributed systems. They see their approach as one, which "works on specification with advances in foundations of logic, linguistic philosophy, distributed AI and the use of social metaphors in computing" and they develop tools to support their approach.

This research is based on soft systems methodologies that allow us to identify internet-mediated distributed systems as complex socio-technical systems since they can be idealised as open systems which depends on the technology, the sentiments of the members, and the organisational environment (Checkland, 1981). Although the system is organised to focus on a primary task (electronic commerce or military communications) this cannot be separated from the environment and the social factors, including cultural ones.

Checkland also notes that a reasonable method for gaining an understanding of such a system is to produce an overview of the system from several perspectives. It allows us to incorporate subjective and objective impressions of the system into a bricolage, a rich picture, which allows us to include the human agents, the problems, conflicts and other seemingly "soft" aspects of the system so as to determine the areas, which need improvement. Informal models are made of problem areas within a system to allow new conceptual models to be built and compared and evaluated against the problem in the rich picture. Formalisation of these conceptual models allows for solution of the problems within the system

We turn to Kline (1995) who also gives us an understanding of how to derive credible perspectives on the complex system under examination. He maintains that three foundational perspectives of a multifaceted and hierarchical system are a synoptic, a piecewise and a structural perspective.
- A synoptic view is an overview, which takes a top down approach to extract and synthesise and thus map a desired property of the system.
- A piecewise view is one that looks at the smallest portions of a system that might be relevant in providing information to aid in the solution of any particular problem.
- A structural view is one that provides details of how a particular system fits together within its hierarchy and provides information on the relationship between local and global effects within the system.

The definition of culture that is most commonly found in the literature of science and engineering (Cobern, 1991; Waldrip & Taylor, 1995) is that of Clifford Geertz who indicates that " The concept of culture I espouse ... is essentially a semiotic one. Believing.. that man is an animal suspended in webs of significance he has spun, I take culture to be those webs, and the analysis of it to be therefore not an experimental science in search of law but an interpretive one in search of meaning (Geertz, 1973, p.3). Geertz' definition is one which proposes that a person's knowledge of his or her world, is essentially mediated by signs, and it is the structure of these signs which establishes reality for an individual or a group.

.The term 'world view' (Cobern, 1991) has two different connotations in English and is firmly linked to culture. The first has a philosophical meaning and involves a person's concepts of human existence and reality; the second is an individual's picture of the world that he or she lives in. The term 'world view' as used in anthropology refers to the 'culturally-dependent, implicit, fundamental organisations of the mind (Cobern, 1991, p.19). Kearney's (1984) model of world view presumes a logical and structural integration of presuppositions within any individual and therefore the model is known as a logico-structural one. He then identifies seven logico-structural categories contained within a given individual's world view:
- The Other
- Classification
- Causality
- Relationship
- Self
- Time & Space

These categories serve as a framework for analysis of a world view. Kearney (1984, p.65) draws the parallel between these factors of an individual world view and the categories a doctor uses for the diagnosis of a patient's disease. In order to determine the world view of an individual, his or her understanding of the seven categories of Other, Self, Time & Space, etc., need to be identified and integrated to produce a picture of the complete world view.

In previous well-established research in science education, Cobern (1993) used Kearney's logico-structural model to examine students' attitudes to the Other. In this case, he determined that the Other was everything that an individual did not identify as Self, and in his study concentrated on that part of the Other that could be defined as Nature, or the natural world. He felt that his research raised additional questions and opened further areas of research.

I am choosing to follow Cobern's methodology, with his support, and to apply it within the area of holistic approaches to IS security, examining the relationship between IS students and and the effect of their trust in the Other, as represented by a parent, sibling, close friend , or partner, on the disclosure of passwords to secure systems. Cobern adapted a methodology that is already well established within social science and recently applied it to cross-cultural research in science education in America. This paper extend the methodology into the modelling of human factors within IS security as a precursor to fieldwork which will implement the methodology.

3. Applying Kline's Analysis Of Complex Systems

Kline's hypothesis, (Kline 1995) is that at least three views are needed for a reasonably good understanding of hierarchically structured systems with interfaces of mutual constraint: synoptic, piecewise and structural.

3.1 Structural View

Arguably, the most common type of architecture view is the structural view in which a system is depicted as a set of inter-related elements. Examples include:
- blue-prints used by the architects of buildings and engineers in general;
- organisation charts used to depict the authority/responsibility structures in institutions.

A structural view of a typical IS would therefore show the way all the elements within the system fitted together.

3.2 Piecewise View

Another common view is the piecewise view that depicts the smallest relevant parts of a system for a particular problem. Examples include:
- detailed wiring diagrams produced by electronic and electrical engineers that show the smallest components of the devices with which they are concerned and the way that they are inter-connected;
- musical scores used by composers to depict the notes to be played by the instruments in orchestras;

A piecewise view of an IS would therefore include all the individual people involved in its creation, use and maintenance

3.3 Synoptic View

A less common type of architecture view is the synoptic view. Synoptic views treat systems as an atomic entities or wholes. They selectively emphasise characteristics of the system that are deemed to be salient in a given context and suppress information that is not pertinent in these respects. Examples include:

- the synoptic weather charts used in television and newspaper weather reports.
- topographic al, political, climatic, demographic etc. maps.

4. Integrating The Three Views

This is best illustrated by considering a lifelike to scenario introduced previously. Let us assume a large Australian company is developing a joint venture with a Chinese company and is looking for interoperability with its partner as they seek to extend their distributed networking via the internet. It has a major need to protect the integrity of its system and will need to consider how its IS security policy will be affected by this development

When we use Kline's analysis we can readily obtain a structural view of both the Australian and Chinese information systems. We can also develop a piecewise view of all the players, the professional staff, administrative staff and technicians who will be working together, to conceptualise, design, develop, administer and program the system. Worldview theory gives an opportunity to begin to identify where cultural factors begin to come into play and thus enable the development of a cultural synopsis of the system by the use of the general categories identified by Kearney:

- The Other
- Classification
- Causality
- Relationship
- Self
- Time & Space

When we begin to investigate the concept of Trust and its effect on IS security and then consider relationship to the Other, within this context. then factors which need to be taken into considerations are:

Attitude to authority: does one culture behave in a more authoritarian way to the other (can an older person "force" respect or trust from a younger one)

Attitude to age and youth: does one culture value the contribution of older people with more respect than the other

Value of loyalty and previous working relationship: does one culture place higher regard on personal loyalty to the other

Formality in relationship: will one culture value a more formal relationship than the other

Gender differences: Is there a difference in the role women play – are females trusted in different ways in this culture

Each of these factors might increase the risk of breaches IS security when working cross-culturally

We can look then at Causality and ask:

> *Does each culture understand causality in the same way:* are there strong religious or philosophical beliefs that will cause individuals to explain issues in "non scientific" ways? Is superstition an issue? Does each culture espouse a western scientific explanation for natural phenomena?

5. Conclusion and Further Work

The development of these three views of any given human activity system provides valuable advice to an enterprise seeking to examine its own cultural makeup and the potential impact of this on IS security, particularly while working cross-culturally both inside and outside of Australia. When considering the possibilities of merging institutional cultures or international expansion (and thus forming a system of systems), it is important to recognise that each institution or will bring a different group worldview (whether a western scientific one or a non-western one), and individual perspectives which will produce a lack of uniformity within the system. This preliminary analysis shows that enterprises could be guided in their internal, external and global expansion and maintenance of there is security by the application of Kline's type of analysis, supported by insights drawn from anthropology as encapsulated in world view theory.

Further work will be carried out structured interview techniques and an anonymous survey to examine the relationship between belief system, gender and degree of trust in a significant other. It will specifically examine individuals who have been brought up within a belief system that they self-identify as Confucian (generally Asians of Chinese racial origin from China and any other part of the Chinese Diaspora) and others who self identify Western (non – Confucian). It will examine the probability of their disclosure of secret passwords to a parent of same and other sex, same and other gender sibling, close friend or partner.

6. References

Checkland, P, (1981), *Systems Thinking, Systems Practice,* Wiley, Chichester, UK.

Cobern, W.W,(1991) *World view theory and science education research,* NARST Monograph No. 3. National Association for Research in Science Teaching, Manhattan, KS,.

Cobern, W.W,(1995) *World view - reality as viewed by students: A synopsis of methodology,* Paper presented at annual meeting of the National Association for Research in Science Teaching, San Francisco, CA.

Davey, J., (2001), *Information Warfare and Cyber Warfare: More than just software tools*, Second World Conference on Information Security Education, Perth.

Finkelstein, A., & Fuks, H, (1989), *Multi-party Specification*, 5th Int. Conference on Software Secification and Design.

Geertz, C,(1973), *The interpretation of cultures*, Basic Books, New York.

Kearney, M, (1984), *World View* Chandler & Sharp. Novalto, CA .

Khaslavsky, J., (1998). Culture and International Software Design, CHI 98,

Klein, H,A, Pongonis, A,, & Klein, G, (2000), *Cultural Barriers to Multinational C2 Decision Making*, Proceedings of the 2000 International Command and Control Research and Technology Symposium, Monterey, CA.

Kline, S.J, (1995), *Conceptual Foundations for Multidisciplinary Thinking*, Stanford University Press, Stanford, CA, USA.

Reynolds, R.G (1994), "An introduction to Cultural Algorithms", *Proceeding of Evolutionary Programming*, San Francisco, CA

Network Security & Data Protection Analysis

C. G. Cuevas[1], J. U. Quevedo[2] and S. H. S. Huang[2]

[1]School of Computer Science, Universidad Autónoma de Guadalajara, Jalisco 44100, México

[2]Department of Computer Science, University of Houston, Houston, TX 77204-3010, U.S.A

e-mail: ccuevas@uag.mx

Abstract

In this paper, we present a network security and data protection analysis to try to stop some hacker's attacks and provide valuable information on how to improve security and protect data. Data availability is very important for every company. If for any reason data was not available when needed, a company could lose important amounts of money. A common type of attack called "Denial of Service" (DoS) has greatly increased lately. We will use the norm IEEE P802.1Q to prevent and stop some of this kind of attack.

Keywords

Network security, Data protection, Quality of Service, Class of Service.

1. Introduction

It is amazing and almost unbelievable that agencies like the FBI, The Pentagon and, NASA, with state of the art infrastructure and vast amounts of money have been the victims of hackers. Moreover, it is worse now that the Internet allows you easy access to source code and tools created by hackers that allow you to attack systems and deny services. If these kinds of events happen to these giants, do we stand a chance against hackers in a medium or small company with a little budget? Most of the corporate network implementations use the TCP/IP protocol. Our analysis focuses on the weaknesses of this universal protocol. TCP/IP communication uses a special *port number*, which it connects to. These port numbers determine the kind of service the sender wants to communicate to the receiver of information. Some well-known port numbers are:

21 - FTP (File Transfer Protocol)
22 - Telnet
25 - SMTP (Simple Mail Transfer Protocol)
80 - HTTP (Hyper Text Transfer Protocol)

"A lot of the attacks on computers which are connected to the Internet exploit the design and implementation of the TCP/IP protocol." (Norman Data Defense Systems, Inc.,2001). Another important issue (ASUS Emagazine Inc., *2001*) is that "even now, most firms still rely on firewalls and anti-virus programs such as Norton Anti-virus, to protect their Intranets from hackers. However, research shows that attacks from internal sources seem to occur more often and result in more severe damages than those caused by external parties. "

2. Related work

2.1 Attacks against weaknesses in the TCP/IP protocol

Research done by The Norman Company (Norman Data Defense Systems, Inc.,2001) tells us that these kinds of attacks work by using a special port number to get a service. One thing is clear; the number of different attacks is increasing. The reason why is probably because TCP/IP has become very popular, and there are a lot of people who are familiar with this protocol's strengths and weaknesses. This will result in a lot more of the *Denial-of-Service* attacks against companies and other organizations in the future. Some of these attacks may be severe for those involved. That means that if we can manipulate those ports we can control who can log on in our network and keep it under control. See figure 1.

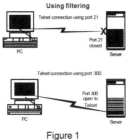

Figure 1

2.2 Network Insecurity with switches

This paper (Turner , 2000) discusses the common misconceptions and poorly publicized issues regarding the use of switches for security policy enforcement. Due to the fact that there are hundred of models of switches to choose, this paper will concentrate on the Cisco Catalyst Ethernet switches, which in the author's opinion, are the most widely used corporate switches today. The conclusions tell us that the only way to guarantee the network boundaries will be properly enforced is to use physically separate hardware to support each LAN. See figures 2 and 3.

Figure 2   Figure 3

The main problem of this kind of equipment (Cisco switches) is that the switch software does not provide any IP filtering options to prevent attacks. Our proposal includes the use of a layer 3 switch that includes this feature (IP filtering) from IEEE.

2.3 The top ten most critical security vulnerabilities in Internet

The main focus of this paper (Marchany, 2000) is to help a network administrator to find out quickly the weakness of his system, especially UNIX and how to fix them (Chaddock, 2000) by providing the correct steps. This document shows us that the attacks target the use of services through special port numbers and some system daemons. This tell us that our proposal can be mixed with the suggestions of this document to improve network security & data protection on UNIX, BSDI, Solaris and LINUX systems, etc. Our IP filtering can be used at the same time to stop the hacker's attacks.

2.4 A virtual private Intranet architecture for Georgetown University

In this project Mr. Richard M. Kogut "Chief Information Technology Architect office of Information Services Georgetown University (Kogut, 1998); introduced Virtual Private Intranet (VPIN) this infrastructure was designed to allow remote users and internal users to access the campus network and their services with strong security polices. VPIN's was an effective solution to supply different kind of services to different type of users providing a manageable and scalable approach of network security. . In our proposal we can make use of all those techniques plus quality of service (QoS), class of service (CoS), Layer 3 Switching and, Wire speed all in the same box (switch), simplifying the administration and using standards from the IEEE committee.

2.5 The future of web server security

In our global business environment if a company does not have a Web site, it is basically not a participant in today's economy (Hollander, 2001). However, this race to participate in the Internet has created an environment where Web an e-commerce sites are multiplying at an astonishing pace. A major threat is that as fast as e-commerce site are being constructed, hackers are developing techniques to deface them and steal the data that exist on the Web server. This proliferation of hacking information on the Web allows even a novice to break into a system, deface a Web site, access confidential information and launch Denial of Service (DoS) attacks to take down a server. The 2000 CSI/FBI Computer Crime and Security Survey http://www.gosci.com, which included

643 respondents, reported that approximately 19% of them reported that their Web sites had suffered unauthorized access or misuse in the last 12 months. The total losses reported by the survey respondents between 1997 and 2000 were $646 million.

Firewall are not enough to protect Web servers, because in order for e Business systems to function, ports within the firewall have to be left open, allowing hackers to get in. Using all this information, we can conclude that our proposal, which makes use of IP filtering, can bring under control the port services that deny access to unauthorized users.

3. System implementation

3.1 IEEE P802.1Q
(IEEE Standards for Local and Metropolitan Area Networks: Virtual Bridged Local Area Networks), (Jarvis, 2002).

The MAC Bridge standardization activities that resulted in the development of ISO/IEC 10038: 1993 introduced the concept of Filtering Services in the Bridged LANs, and mechanisms whereby filtering information in such LANs may be acquired and held in a Filtering Database.

ISO/IEC 15802-3, a revision of ISO/IEC 10038, extends this concept of Filtering Services in order to define additional capabilities in Bridged LANs. This Standard makes use of the concepts and mechanisms of VLAN Bridging that were introduced by ISO/IEC 15802-3, and defines additional mechanisms that allow the implementation of Virtual Bridged LANs.

3.2 Practical application

The Filtering service concepts introduced in this standard came to improve the network security and data protection. To obtain this kind of benefits we must use Virtual Bridged LANs.

This Filtering tools will allow us to verify:

- The source and target MAC address.
- The Protocol and service used.
- The priority packed.
- The type of application.

Network devices using this standard will be able to define any kind of filters, helping the network administrator on security and data issues.

Here you will find an example of how useful the Filtering service IEEE P802.1Q can be. In this case we used a switch 3COM 3500.

Antecedents:

The company X, which is dedicated to electronic products of advanced technologies, has a confidential area, which deals with critical information. If this information gets out of this area, the company could in a blink of an eye lose important amounts of money.

General requirements:

To administering this network we need an isolated network for this critical area (CA), with high level of security on access, services and applications. This special group CA must be sharing the backbone with the general area (GA) in the same network device.

Specifications:

1. We need 2 subnetworks, using TCP/IP protocol only.

2. The subnet 1 will be type "C", with IP address: 68.49.120.X, the subnet 2 must be type "C" with IP: 68.49.122.X. Both subnets with subnet mask: 255.255.255.0

3. The subnet 1 will be assigned to attend all the requirements of GA including the work stations and must have the following connectivity without restriction from/to:

   • All stations and servers in the subnet 1,

   • All servers/applications of an external site 10 miles away.

   • All servers/applications from Corporate in U.S.A.

4. The subnet 2 will attend all the requirements from CA and their stations. All the stations cannot get out of this subnet.

It is restricted for the stations of the subnet 2 to get out of their network under any protocol or service (ej. ping, telnet, ftp, etc.). And any atempt of communications from an external network must be blocked. All this conditions apply to all stations in the subnet 2 with this exceptions:

   • The server with IP : 68.49.122.51, must have a full communications with the stations in the sunbet 2, must have external access to the following IP addresses: 68.49.240.90, and 68.49.112.67. The connection must be using FTP or TFTP service.

Two stations from subnet 2 with IP address: 68.49.122.98 and 68.49.122.99, must have full access to all the stations in the subnet2, they only must have communications to the IP addresses: 68.49.240.90 and 68.49.112.67 to use the SAP applications using TELNET service.

Proposal:

Implementation of two bridged subnetworks using VLANs with different IP address, isolated traffic (Filtering **QoS** (Quality of Service), **CoS** (Class of Service)), internal hardware routing (Switching level 3).

(1) Create 2 Vlans under TCP/IP protocol. (2) Vlans will be a subnet type "C". (3) The Vlan 1 will attend all requirements of GA without restrictions. (4) Vlan 2 will attend all the requirements of CA, all stations could be connected between them and their servers. The stations of this VLAN will not have any external communication under any protocol or service (Telnet, FTP, TFTP), any intend of communications from an external to Vlan 2 will be restricted. A very well defined internal IP addresses will have an external full communication to some specifics IP address using FTP, TFTP and Telnet services.

TESTING SCENARIOS

Following you will find real life scenarios and examples of how this standard can help us to improve our network security and the data protection using the Filtering service from IEEE P802.1Q. To implement this kind of security, we had to create a filter to allow or deny a service; this filters are designed by the network device 3COM CB 3500, these filters are kept in an internal database; when a VLAN2 member (CA) tries to use this service, the device checks in its Database of filters and executes or denies the service. Once we have created all the filters, we can proceed to make connectivity tests using a PC member of VLAN2 with the server using different services (telnet, ftp , tftp, etc). We find that the only way to get communication with the server was using "telnet"; we try to reach a PC or server from VLAN1 and all the time we were refused. This tells us the high efficiency of these filters to improve the network security and data protection. When the filters are ready, we can proceed to make connectivity tests using some services (telnet, ftp,tftp,etc) in different PCs members of VLAN2 and we prove the communication from PCs to the server.

Then we try to reach some server or PC from VLAN1 and all communications were denied. We try to get connection with the external servers (68.49.240.90 y 68.49.112.67) and just the ftp service was able to get connected and the rest of services were refused. This is a very interesting test and shows us the benefits of the use of a network device. In this case a 3COM CB 3500 that came with the IEEE P802.1Q standard. Both networks reside in the same box (CORE), but thanks to the Filtering services we have isolated the traffic with high efficiency, low cost an easy administration. One of the most important general requirements was the ability to isolate traffic, especially from the critical area CA.. And we meet all requirements; no body from VLAN1 had access to VLAN2 due to all filtering services created to reach this high level of security.

A remote user that is using the remote access service by modem to logon in our network,

SERVICES	STATUS (Open / Denied)
Ftp	Denied
Tftp	Denied
Telnet	Open only to IP address 68.49.122.51
Rlogin	Denied
Rsh	Denied
Http	Denied
Xwindows	Denied
Smtp	Denied
Nfs	Denied
Rpc	Denied
Snmp	Denied

Table 1: 6.8 Access of a VLAN2' s user (CA restricted)

SERVICES	STATUS (Open / Denied)
	Open to:
ftp	All the stations of VLAN2 and IP 68.49.240.90 y 68.49.112.67
Tftp	All the stations of VLAN2.
Telnet	All the stations of VLAN2
Rlogin	All the stations of VLAN2
Rsh	All the stations of VLAN2
http	All the stations of VLAN2
Xwindows	All the stations of VLAN2.
Smtp	All the stations of VLAN2
1Nfs	All the stations of VLAN2
Rpc	All the stations of VLAN2
Snmp	All the stations of VLAN2
Etc.	

Table 2: 6.9 VLAN2 Server (CA restricted)

automatically is detected and classified like a member of the VLAN1 and will apply all filters to this kind of users. See table 3. With these scenarios we meet all the requirements from the client and we demonstrate the useful of the IEEE P802.1Q standard. This standard helps us to improve the network security and data protection from intrusions in an easy and reliable way.

SERVICES	STATUS (Open / Denied)
Ftp	Access Denied to VLAN2
Tftp	Access Denied to VLAN2
Telnet	Access Denied to VLAN2
Rlogin	Access Denied to VLAN2
Rsh	Access Denied to VLAN2
Http	Access Denied to VLAN2
Xwindows	Access Denied to VLAN2
Smtp	Access Denied to VLAN2
1Nfs	Access Denied to VLAN2
Rpc	Access Denied to VLAN2
Snmp	Access Denied to VLAN2
Etc.	

Table 3: 6.10 VLAN1' Member (GA)

SERVICES	STATUS (Open / Denied)
ftp	Access denied to VLAN2
Tftp	Access denied to VLAN2
Telnet	Access denied to VLAN2
Rlogin	Access denied to VLAN2
Rsh	Access denied to VLAN2
Http	Access denied to VLAN2
Xwindows	Access denied to VLAN2
Smtp	Access denied to VLAN2
Nfs	Access denied to VLAN2
Rpc	Access denied to VLAN2
Snmp	Access denied to VLAN2
etc.	

Table 4: 6.11 Remote Access User (external)

4. CONCLUSIONS

As we have explained, some of the most common Denied of Services (DoS) attacks use service ports of the TCP/IP protocol to penetrate into networks and systems. These weaknesses of the TCP/IP protocol can be neutralized by using the IEEE P802.1Q norm, creating filters to control the access to networks and systems and thus helping us to improve the network security and data protection.

Some Institutes and companies focused on Network and data security have been doing research about these topics due to the rapidly growing pace of the Internet and its expansion around the world. Some new products and techniques have been developed as a result.

Sophisticated products, real-time applications with ability to look at very sophisticated traffic in order to sniff out malicious activity are available today to help the network administrator improve the network security and protect his data.

A mixed of this techniques (hardware, software, network infrastructure planned will provide a high protection against DoS attacks.

ACKNOWLEDGMENTS

Our gratitude to: Ricardo Arrazate for his support and contributions to our research.

5. REFERENCES

Chaddock, M. M. (10/11/2000), *Finding the most critical security vulnerabilities guide*, SANS Institute, Abilene, TX, U.S.A http://www.selseg.com/informes/breakdown

Hollander, Y. PhD,(2001), *The Future of Web Server Security*, San Jose, CA, U.S.A. http://www.entercept.com/products/entercept/whitepapers/downloads/wpfuture.pdf

Kogut, R. M. (10/26/1998), *Virtual Private Intranet Architecture for Georgetown University.* Georgetown, U.S.A http://www.georgetown.edu/technology/ois/itarchitct/guvpin.htm

Marchany, R. (2000), *The TOP ten critical security vulnerabilities internet*, Virginia Tech, v1.1 , S. Northcutt (Ed.) December, 2000, U.S.A. http://www.sans.org/audio/sanstop10presentation.pdf

Norman Data Defense Systems, Inc.(2001), *Attacks against weaknesses in the TCP/IP protocol, U.S.A.* http://www.norman.no/documents/wp_smurf.shtml.

Norman Data Defense Systems, Inc.(2001), *Security on the Internet,* U.S.A http:///www.norman.no/internet.shtml

SUS Emagazine*(2001), IP Security: Tactics for LAN protection*, U.S.A. http://www.asusemag.com.tw/latest/ch5/ch5-1.htm

The Institute of Electrical and Electronics Engineers, inc. (1998*), "IEEE Standards for Local and Metropolitan Area Networks: Virtual Bridged Local Area Network", IEEE Std 802.1Q-1998* , U.S.A. http://standards.ieee.org/getieee802/download/802.1Q-1998.pdf

Turner, A. (8/29/2000), *Network Insecurity with switches*, Information Security Reading Room, SANS Institute, Boston, MA September 5-12, 2001 U.S.A. http://www.sans.org/infosecFAQ/switchednet/switch_security.htm

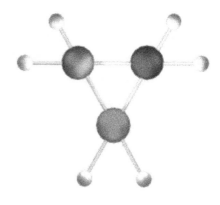

Chapter 6

Distributed Technologies

Transparent Process Migration for Distributed Applications in a Beowulf Cluster

Mark Claypool and David Finkel
Department of Computer Science
Worcester Polytechnic Institute
Worcester, MA 01609 USA
{claypool | dfinkel}@cs.wpi.edu

Abstract

Powerful, low-cost clusters of personal computers, such as Beowulf clusters, have fueled the potential for widespread distributed computation. While these Beowulf clusters typically have software that facilitates development of distributed applications, there is still a need for effective distributed computation that is transparent to the application programmer. This paper describes the design and development of the PANTS Application Node Transparency System (PANTS), which enables transparent distributed computation. PANTS employs a fault-tolerant communication architecture based on multicast communication that minimizes load on busy cluster nodes. PANTS runs on any modern distribution of Linux without requiring any kernel modifications.

1. Introduction

Cluster computing offers several benefits to application programmers and to users. A large class of computations can be broken into smaller pieces and executed by the various nodes in a cluster. However, sometimes on a cluster it can be beneficial to run an application that was not designed to be cluster-aware. One of the main goals of our research is to support such applications.

We have developed a system for distributed applications running in a cluster environment. Our system automatically detects which nodes of the cluster are overloaded and which are underloaded, and transfers work from overloaded nodes to underloaded nodes so that the overall application can complete more quickly. Two fundamental design goals of our system are that its operation should be transparent to the programmer and to the user of the distributed application, and that the system should impose only minimal overhead on the system.

Our system is called PANTS, an acronym for the PANTS Application Node Transparency System. It runs on a Beowulf cluster, which is a cluster of PC-class machines running a free/open-source operating system, in our case Linux, and connected by a standard local area network.

PANTS is designed to be transparent to the application as well as the programmer. This transparency allows an increased range of applications to benefit from process migration. Under PANTS, existing multi-process applications that are not built with support for distributed computation can now run on multiple nodes by starting all the processes of the application on a single node and allowing PANTS to migrate the individual processes of the application to other nodes. As far as the application is concerned, it is running on a single computer, while PANTS controls what cluster computatio n resources it is using.

The PANTS design provides a method for minimal inter-node communication and for fault tolerance. In a Beowulf system, the network is most often the performance bottleneck. With this in mind, PANTS keeps the number of message sent between machines low and also uses a protocol that does not exchange messages with nodes that are busy with computations. Built- in fault tolerance allows the cluster to continue functioning even in the event that a node fails. In the same way, nodes can be added or removed from a cluster without dramatic consequences.

2. The Design and Implementation of PANTS

2.1 Beowulf and Distributed Applications

In general, a Beowulf cluster is a collection or cluster of personal computers connected by a private network (Sterling et al, 1998). The principal goal of the development of Beowulf clusters is to build low cost, scalable systems using relatively inexpensive personal computers and networks in order to support distributed parallel applications. Our Beowulf cluster consists of seven Alpha personal computers, connected by a private Ethernet. Many Beowulf clusters are much larger (Becker and Merkey).

There are many libraries designed to simplify the creation of distributed parallel applications for Beowulf clusters:
- PVM, Parallel Virtual Machine, is a runtime message-passing system that is easy to use, portable, and widely popular on parallel systems. It has been designed so that users without system-administration privileges could install the software and run parallel jobs from their shell accounts (PVM).
- MPI, Message Passing Interface, provides a complete library specification for message-passing primitives and has been widely accepted by vendors, programmers, and users (MPIF).
- DIPC, Distributed IPC, provides distributed program developers with semaphores, messages and transparent distributed shared memory (Karimi).
- BPROC, Beowulf Distributed Process Space, allows a node to run processes that appear in its process tree even though the processes are not physically on the node itself (Hendriks).

While these libraries are very effective for writing distributed applications, they also require that the programmer explicitly implement the communications between nodes, and write the applications for a specific library. One goal of PANTS is to overcome these limitations by creating an environment where load sharing of multi-process applications can take place automatically, without the need for the application programmer to think about the details of working in a cluster environment.

2.2 PANTS and Process Migration

Process migration can be preemptive or non-preemptive. In preemptive process migration, processes can be migrated while they are running. In non-preemptive process migration, processes are only eligible for process migration when they are first initiated. There is more overhead in supporting preemptive process migration since the run-time state of the process must be migrated. On the other hand, preemptive process migration would seem to have more potential to improve performance, since there are more opportunities to migrate processes. Previous research has suggested (Eager et al, 1998) that non-preemptive process migration can provide significant performance improvement with lower overhead than preemptive process migration.

A preliminary version of PANTS (Moyer) provided a tool for distributed applications on an Intel-based Beowulf cluster through preemptive process migration. It was implemented by making changes to the Linux kernel. A crucial step was the use of EPCKPT, a Linux process checkpointing utility (Pinheiro). Thus, processes at a busy node could be stopped in mid-computation, checkpointed, and moved to another, less busy, node, without intervention or even the knowledge of the user.

After the development of this preliminary version, there were two issues we wanted to address. First, the use of kernel modifications meant that the PANTS software might have to be modified with each new kernel release. To avoid this version chasing, we wanted to eliminate the need for kernel modifications. Second, since there were many Intel-specific aspects to EPCKPT, the use of the EPCKPT utility restricted the use of the system to Intel systems. In order to make PANTS platform-independent, we wanted to remove the dependency on EPCKPT. This required us to restrict our system to non-preemptive process migration.

2.3 The Load-Balancing Algorithm

An important aspect of any process migration scheme is how to decide when to transfer a process from a heavily loaded node to a lightly loaded node. We call this the load-balancing algorithm. Many load-balancing algorithms for distributed systems have been proposed; there is a summary in (Wills and Finkel, 1995). We have implemented a variation of the multi-leader load-balancing algorithm proposed in (Wills and Finkel, 1995).

In this algorithm, one of the nodes is required to be the leader. The leader can be any node in the cluster, and is chosen randomly from among all of the nodes. The leader has three basic responsibilities: accept information from lightly-loaded ("available") nodes in the cluster, use that information to maintain a list of available nodes, and return an available node to any client that requests it. In the current project, for fault tolerance, we implemented an election procedure to select a new leader in case the leader node fails.

An available node is one that is lightly loaded, as measured by CPU utilization. When any node in the cluster becomes available, it sends a message to the leader, indicating that it is free to accept new work. If a node becomes unavailable, for example if it begins a new computation, it sends another message to the leader. Thus, the leader always knows which nodes are available at any time. If a node wants to off-load work onto another node, it need only ask the leader for an available node, then send the process to that node.

The actual implementation is a variation of the multi-leader policy described in (Wills and Finkel, 1995) and implemented in (Moyer). In many other load-balancing algorithms, either nodes that are available or nodes that need to off-load work broadcast their status to all the nodes in the cluster. These broadcast messages frequently need to be handled by machines that are heavily loaded ("busy machines"). The multi-leader algorithm avoids these "busy-machine messages" by sending messages only to the leader multicast address.

We modified the Wills-Finkel policy (Wills and Finkel, 1995) to simplify the implementation and improve fault tolerance, at the cost of a small increase in the amount of network traffic. In PANTS, there are two multicast addresses. One of the addresses is read only by the leader; both available nodes and nodes with work to off-load send to the leader on this address. Because the leader is contacted via multicast, the leader can be any node in the cluster, and leadership can change at any time, without needing to update the clients. Available nodes receive on the other multicast address. This address is only used when the leader needs to discover, for the first time, which nodes are available. Because multicast is used to communicate with available nodes, busy nodes are not even aware of the traffic.

Leader Multicast Address

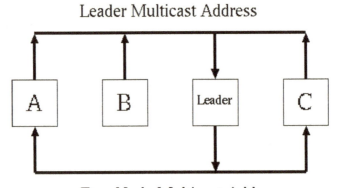

Free Node Multicast Address

Figure 1: PANTS Multicast Communications

Figure 1 depicts the multicast communication among PANTS nodes. There are four nodes in this Beowulf cluster, one of which is the leader. Nodes A and C are "free" nodes, having little computation load and Node B is a "busy" node. All Nodes can communicate with the leader by sending to the leader multicast address. The leader communicates with all free nodes, A and C in this example, by sending to the free node multicast address. Node B is not "bothered" by messages to the free nodes since it is not subscribed to that multicast address.

2.4 PANTS Implementation

PANTS is composed of two major software components, the PANTS daemon and PREX, which stands for PANTS remote execute. The PANTS daemon is responsible for coordinating the available resources in the cluster. It communicates among nodes to determine which nodes are available to receive processes. PREX intercepts the execution of a process, queries the PANTS daemon for an available node and remotely executes the process to distribute load among the nodes in the cluster.

Using the multicast policy described in Section 2.3, the PANTS daemon can respond quickly to a request from PREX for an available node.

PREX is made up of a library object called `libprex.o` and a remote execution program called prex. The library object is designed to intercept programs when they are initially executed and then send them to the prex program.

The way libprex works with the C library allows it to intercept processes transparently. To enable libprex, the Linux environment variable LD_PRELOAD is set to reference the `libprex` library object. Doing this causes the library functions in libprex to override the usual C library functions. When programs call the execve function to execute a binary (for example, when a user executes a binary from a command line shell), our version of `execve()` is used instead of the original one. Inside of our `execve()` function, the real C library `execve()` is invoked to execute `prex`, whose arguments are the process name, followed by the original arguments for that process. `prex` can then use `rsh` to remotely execute the process.

When prex is invoked for a process, the process is checked for migratability, which is determined by flags set within the binary. Several user-defined bits within the flag area of the binary's header signal whether the process should be migrated. If the binary is migratable, `prex` queries the local PANTS daemon to determine if the local machine is busy with other computations. If the process is not migratable, or the local machine is not busy, the binary is executed on the local machine by calling the original version of `execve()`. If the local machine is busy, `prex` queries the local PANTS daemon for an available node. If a node is returned, prex calls `rsh` to execute the process on that node. If all nodes are busy, the process is executed locally.

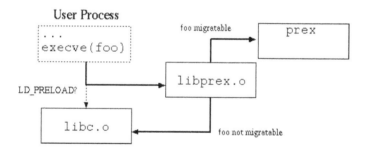

Figure 2: PREX Functionality

Figure 2 depicts the functionality of PREX. When a process calls `execve()` and the environment variable LD_PRELOAD is set, `libprex.o` intercepts the lbc.o version of `execve()`. If the executable file is migratable, `libprex.o` invokes `prex` to communicate with the PANTS daemon to find a free node and migrate the process. If the executable is not migratable, `libprex.o` invokes the normal `libc.o` version of `execve()`.

One of the more difficult responsibilities of PANTS is determining whether or not each node is busy with a computation or available to receive a task. The original version of PANTS used a periodic check of the percentage of CPU utilization to make this decision. However, CPU load is not the only possible way to measure load. A process can require large amounts of memory, or I/O activity, which can limit its performance. The current version of PANTS considers CPU, memory, I/O and interrupts in making load decisions. For each load component, a threshold is chosen, and any node with utilization greater than the threshold of any one component is considered "busy," while others are "free." More details on PANTS load measurements can be found in (Nichols and Lemaire, 2002).

3. Results

The PANTS system has been fully implemented and is running on our Beowulf cluster of Alpha processor workstations. Our cluster consists of seven 64-bit Alpha 600 MHz workstations connected on a private subnet via a 100 Mbps switch. Each machine has between 64 and 512 MB of RAM and at least one SCSI hard drive. The PANTS system was thoroughly tested and found functionally correct and small scale testing showed a nearly linear speed-up with PANTS for a computation-intensive numerical application.

In order to further evaluate the performance and transparency of PANTS, we used compilation of the Linux kernel as a benchmark and ran it on our Beowulf cluster. In order to enable PANTS migration, we marked the `gcc` binary as migratable. The Linux kernel version used was 2.4.18 (the same Linux kernel version our cluster was running), with 432 files with a mean file size of 19 Kbytes.

Our first test was a compile where the Linux source tree was stored on the local hard disk without PANTS running. The second test was a compile where the Linux source tree was stored on the NFS mounted disk. The third test was a compile where the Linux source tree was stored on the NFS disk and PANTS was running, but was forced to never choose to migrate the process. The fourth test was a compile where the Linux source tree was stored on the NFS disk and PANTS was running with migration enabled. We ran each test 5 times and computed the average compile time in seconds. The results are depicted in Figure 3.

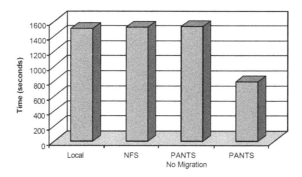

Figure 3: Linux Kernel Compile Time

The local compile took 1520 seconds (about 25 minutes). Accessing the Linux source tree over NFS added about 20 seconds to the total compile time, approximately a 2% overhead. Adding PANTS without migration added an additional 5 seconds to the NFS compile time, approximately a 0.5% overhead. PANTS, fully enabled with migration, reduced the compile time to about 670 seconds, approximately a 55% reduction in compile time.

We have also demonstrated that PANTS is compatible with the distributed interprocess communications package DIPC (Karimi). The use of DIPC requires the programmer to include DIPC-specific code in the program, and thus compromises our transparency goal of not requiring any special code for the distributed application. However, the use of DIPC does allow the programmer to use a wider range of interprocess communication primitives, such as such as shared memory, semaphores, and message queues, than would otherwise not be available (Szelag et al, 2001).

4. Future Work

Although PANTS shows significant potential in distributed processing, there are a number of ways that we see PANTS growing into a more mature cluster environment.

Preemptive migration is the act of moving a process from one node to another when it is already running. It has been shown in (Barak et al, 1996) that there are situations where preemptive process migration can give a significant performance benefit over a simple remote execution scheme. Specifically, when distributed applications are executed on a shared network of workstations, rather than on a single-user cluster of dedicated nodes, preemptive migration allows more flexible use of idle workstations. As discussed above, the original version of PANTS implemented preemptive migration for the Intel platform only, and in the current version we decided to implement the non-preemptive, but platform independent, PREX. BPROC, the Beowulf Distributed Process Space, supports preemptive process migration on many platforms (Hendriks). Thus, the capability for preemptive migration could be added back to PANTS without affecting platform independence, by borrowing generously from BPROC.

A project with similar goals to our project is the MOSIX system (Barak). MOSIX provides preemptive process migration in a MOSIX Linux cluster. The process migration is transparent to the programmer. As in our system, a user can start multiple processes on a single node and allow the process migration system to relocate the processes on other nodes to improve performance. In the future, we hope to compare the performance and capabilities of PANTS with MOSIX.

5. Conclusions

Distributed computation has grown in popularity recently, earning attention from scientists and even corporations. Accompanied with the dramatic growth of Linux, Beowulf clusters provide a cost effective solution to today's large computation needs. PANTS and its use of transparent load sharing takes another step in the direction of ever more powerful cluster technology. PANTS is designed to run on any system running a modern distribution of Linux regardless of the underlying hardware architecture. Transparency, reduced busy node communication, and fault tolerance make PANTS a viable solution for more effective use of a Beowulf cluster.

Acknowledgements

This research was supported by equipment grants from Alpha Processor, Inc. and from Compaq Computer Corporation. The authors would also like to thank the following WPI students who have contributed to various phases of the PANTS project: Jeffrey Moyer, Kevin Dickson, Chuck Homic, Bryan Villamin, Michael Szelag, David Terry, Jennifer Waite, Marc Lemaire and Jim Nichols.

References

Barak, A., "MOSIX – Scalable Cluster Computing for Linux", Online at:
http://www.cs.huji.ac.il/mosix/

Barak, A., Braverman, A., Gilderman, I. and Laden, O. (1996), "Performance of PVM with the MOSIX Preemptive Process Migration Scheme", In *Proceedings of the 7th Israeli Conf. on Computer Systems and Software Engineering*, June.

Becker, D. and Merkey, P., "The Beowulf Project", Online at: http://www.beowulf.org/

Eager, D., Lazowska, E. and Zahorjan, J. (1998), "The Limited Performance Benefits of Migrating Active Processes for Load Sharing", In *Proceedings of ACM Measurement & Modeling of Computer Systems (SIGMETRICS)*, pp. 63-72, May.

Hendriks, E., "BPROC: Beowulf Distributed Process Space", Online at:
http://www.beowulf.org/software/bproc.html

Karimi, K., "Welcome to DIPC", Online at: http://www.gpg.com/DIPC/

Moyer, J., "PANTS Application Node Transparency System", Online at:
http://segfault.dhs.org/ProcessMigration/

MPIF, "Message Passing Interface Forum Home Page", Online at:
http://www.mpi-forum.org/

Nichols, J. and Lemaire, M. (2002), "Performance Evaluation of Load Sharing Policies on a Beowulf Cluster", *Major Qualifying Project MQP-MLC-BW01*, Spring. Online at:
http://www.cs.wpi.edu/~claypool/mqp/pants-load/

Pinheiro, E., "EPCKPT - A Checkpoint Utility for Linux Kernel", Online at:
http://www.cs.rochester.edu/u/edpin/epckpt/

PVM, "PVM: Parallel Virtual Machine", Online at:
http://www.epm.ornl.gov/pvm/pvm_home.html

Sterling, T., Salmon, J., Becker D. and Savarese, D. (1998), *How to Build a Beowulf*, MIT Press, Cambridge, Massachusetts USA.

Szelag, M., Terry, D. and Waite, J. (2001), "Integrating Distributed Inter-Process Communication with PANTS on a Beowulf Cluster", *Major Qualifying Project MQP-DXF-0021*, Spring. Online at:
http://www.cs.wpi.edu/~claypool/mqp/pants-dipc/

Wills, C. and Finkel, D. (1995), "Scalable Approaches to Load Sharing in the Presence of Multicasting", *Computer Communications*, 18(9), pp. 620-630, September.

431

ActorServer: A Java middleware for programming distributed applications over the Internet

Angelo Furfaro, Libero Nigro, Francesco Pupo
Laboratorio di Ingegneria del Software
Dipartimento di Elettronica Informatica e Sistemistica
Università della Calabria, I-87036 Rende (CS) – Italy
e-mail: a.furfaro@deis.unical.it, {l.nigro,f.pupo}@unical.it

Abstract

This paper proposes ActorServer, a Java middleware for programming general distributed, possibly time-dependent, applications over the Internet. ActorServer allows an exploitation of heterogeneous computing platforms. Actors are reusable components which can directly be programmed in Java. They have location-transparent names and can migrate from a computing node to another. The paper introduces the programming level and the runtime of ActorServer and shows its practical use through an example.

Keywords

Middleware, distributed programming, Internet, mobile actors, synchronizers, Java.

1. Introduction

The aim of the work described in this paper is the development of language abstractions and a runtime infrastructure for the construction of distributed applications running on a Internet-based virtual computer. These issues are at the basis of known industry-relevant tools and methodologies for open distributed systems, like CORBA (OMG, 1997) and Java related efforts, notably Java RMI (JavaSoft, 1996), Jini (Waldo, 1998) and JavaSpaces (JavaSoft, 1998). CORBA aims at facilitating interactions between object-based, interoperable applications running on heterogeneous environments. Java technologies are able to transform a network of heterogeneous machines in a network of homogeneous virtual machines. Sun Jini has a goal similar to CORBA. It depends on Java RMI and JavaSpaces which uses a Linda-like (Carriero and Gelernter, 1990) model to share, coordinate and communicate tasks in Jini-based distributed systems.

This work argues that the Actor model of computation (Agha, 1986) has the necessary expressive power to program general distributed systems and to support nowadays Internet-based mobile computing paradigms (Gray et al, 2000). Actors are concurrent units which communicate and synchronize to one another exclusively by asynchronous message passing (Varela and Agha, 1998). Actors lend themselves to be easily extended to support migration and dynamic reconfiguration operations. In addition, coordination structures can be defined to constrain message reception in group of actors (Ren et al, 1996)(Nielsen et al, 1998)(Varela and Agha, 2001)(Nigro and Pupo, 2001).

An experimental tool supporting the notion of actor/agent is ActorFoundry (Astley, 1999) which permits the development in Java of distributed applications executing on possibly heterogeneous computing platforms. SALSA (Simple Actor Language, System and Applications) (Varela and Agha, 2001) is a more recent achievement which fosters a minimal yet powerful programming style for building open and re-configurable applications over the Internet.

This work proposes ActorServer, a novel middleware which is based on a variant of the Actor model designed and implemented in Java for the development of distributed and time-dependent applications over the Internet. A distinguishing factor of ActorServer is the adoption of a runtime executive which can be customized to operate according to an application tuned message control structure which can be time sensitive. ActorServer enables message passing in group of actors to be constrained by *synchronizers* (Ren *et al*, 1996). As in SALSA and ActorFoundry, ActorServer actors have the ability to behave as mobile agents so as to facilitate dynamic (re)configuration and the expression of patterns of mobile computing. ActorServer relies on a network class loader for loading on-demand the bytecode of a required actor, message or other dependent class.

The ActorServer project is intended to be practically used for high-performance, mobile, real-time, multimedia, and discrete-event simulation applications.

2. System architecture

The following describes an architectural framework that makes it possible to integrate heterogeneous platforms in a computing model which offers naming, communication, migration (of data and code) and coordination support to basic software components (actors).

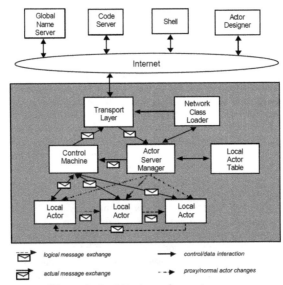

Figure 1: Architecture of an actor server

The allocation unit at the system level is the Actor Server, which provides the execution environment (including an instance of the Java Virtual Machine) for a collection of local actors. The architecture of an actor server is depicted in Figure 1. A fundamental component is the Control Machine, i.e. a runtime which orchestrates the execution of the local actors. The Control Machine transparently filters the exchanged messages among the actors, buffers them into one or more message queues (Message Pending Set), and dispatches messages according to a proper control strategy which can be timed or untimed. The message is the unit of scheduling and dispatching.

Remote communications with partner actor servers are handled by the *Transport Layer* component, which is TCP based. A TCP Transport Layer ensures reliable FIFO channels among interacting actor servers. In addition, an UDP transport can be required by some applications, e.g. data streaming in a multimedia session. The Transport Layer component is interfaced with the *Actor Server Manager* which receives an external message or actor and enforces admission control on the basis of an authentication check and a security management policy. To authenticate actors a digital signed code technique can be used. An incoming accepted actor will be handled for execution by the local runtime. An external message gets scheduled on the runtime Message Pending Set.

At any point in time, all the local executing actors are kept in the *Local Actor Table* (an hash table), where the key is the actor name. Actor names are implicitly assigned by the actor servers as unique identifiers (strings) at the actor instantiation time. The Local Actor Table memorizes tuples <actor name, actor reference>. An actor server is characterized by its pair <URL, Port>, e.g. <asp://apollo.lis.deis.unical.it, 4444>.

The operation of an actor server naturally requires some code to be dynamically loaded on-demand, for instance the class of an external received message or actor. To support class loading at runtime, a *Network Class Loader* is used. The Network Class Loader consults the site of a *Code Server* over the Internet for retrieving the necessary code. The Code Server is identified by its pair <URL, Port>, e.g. <nclp://argo.lis.deis.unical.it, 7777>.

2.1 Actor model

Actors (Agha, 1986) are encapsulation units which hide a *state* and have a *behaviour* for responding to a given *message interface*. Actor behaviour is modelled as a finite state machine. An actor is a reactive object which responds to an incoming message on the basis of the current state and message contents. Message reception is implicit. An actor is at rest until a message arrives. Message processing triggers a state transition and the execution of an atomic action. Messages can be unexpected in the current state. Their processing can be postponed by remembering them in local data or in states of the life cycle. Basic actor operations are

- *new*, for creating a new actor
- *become*, for changing the actor state
- (non blocking) *send* for transmitting messages to *acquaintance* actors (including itself)
- *defer*, for postponing an unexpected message in a local deferred message queue.
  Deferred messages are received again by the actor as soon as it changes its current state.

Differences from the Actor model are:

- an absence of an internal thread in actors. Actors are instances of a (passive) class which extends directly or indirectly the Actor base class. Life cycle is provided by a message *handler* which is invoked by the control machine at message dispatch time. Non thread based behaviour is a key for timing control and custom scheduling
- an absence of the mail queue per actor. Rather, a single message queue is introduced by the control machine upon which sent messages are scheduled, selected and dispatched according to a suitable control structure
- source of concurrency among actors in a same subsystem is *action interleaving* ensured by the control machine dispatching scheme. Concurrency among actors allocated on different processors is true parallelism.

Listing 1 shows the Java schema of a typical user-defined actor class.

```
import it.unical.deis.lis.as.*;
public class UserActor extends Actor{
    //message interface
    public static class Init extends Message{...}
    public static class Start extends Message{...}
    ...
    //local variables
    ...
    //internal states
    protected static final int CREATED=0, INITIALIZED=1, OPERATING=2, ...;
    //constructor
    public UserActor(){ become( CREATED ); }
    //behaviour
    public void handler( Message m ){
        switch( currentStatus() ){
            case CREATED:
                if( m instanceof Init ){ initialize; become( INITIALIZED ); } break;
            case INITIALIZED: ...
                ...
        }
    }//handler
}//UserActor
```

Listing 1: The schema of an actor in Java

Messages are programmed as static inner classes which extend the *Message* base class. The Message class introduces the *receiver* actor. The initialisation of an actor is the responsibility of an *Init* message. The Init parameters can include the *acquaintances*, i.e. the set of known actors to which messages can subsequently be sent. Knowledge of other acquaintances can be learnt dynamically by receiving messages. The actor behaviour is programmed in the *handler(Message)* method which gets as parameter the incoming message. The provided response depends in general on the current status and the particular arrived message. An actor changes its current behaviour by setting the next status with the *become()* method. The following exemplifies the creation and initialisation of an actor:

```
UserActor a=new UserActor();
a.send( new UserActor.Init( init_parameters ) );
```

The notation is simplified when the receiver is the actor itself:

```
send( new Compute( Compute_parameters ) );
```

An actor can be migrated to a given destination as follows:

```
a.migrate( actor_server_destination [, activation_message] );
```

The *migrate* method requires the URL and port of the destination actor server and, possibly, an activation message which will be sent to the actor after its arrival. Migration and network message passing are currently based on a customisation of the Java serialization mechanism.
A user-defined message class can include a reply message (*token*) to be used, after being possibly filled with suitable data, for carrying back an answer to the sender. Since the receiver of the reply message can freely be defined, the token can actually be transmitted to a proper

delegate actor. This mechanism can be exploited to reproduce in ActorServer all the continuation-based control structures of SALSA (Varela and Agha, 2001).

2.2 Location transparent naming

An actor is always created as a local object of the hosting actor server. Its Java reference persists when the actor is migrated to a different actor server. The notion of a *proxy actor* is used. A proxy actor is an non active version of the actor which acts as a *forwarder*. Dispatching a message to a proxy has the effect of automatically forwarding it to the remote actor server (*hop*). The approach ensures that at most one incarnation of an actor, in proxy or normal form, can exist within any actor server during the execution. Actor migration implies the relation proxy/normal of its acquaintances to be reviewed according to the receiving actor server. Some acquaintances become proxies since the corresponding actors reside in a remote actor server, e.g. that from which the mobile actor originated. Other acquaintance references can change from proxy to normal in the case the referred actor is local to the migrated site. The update operation is accomplished with the help of the Local Actor Table and by using location information carried by the migrated actor.

Knowledge about the execution location of an actor can be refreshed by consulting the authoritative source of information which is the *Global Name Server* which is updated at every actor migration.

When a migrated actor comes back to an actor server where there is a proxy of itself, the proxy is replaced by the arrived actor (i.e., it receives its computational status) but the local actor reference (existing in the Local Actor Table) is retained. The Global Name Server is identified by its pair <URL, Port>, e.g. <gnsp://zeus.lis.deis.unical.it, 8888>.

2.3 Coordination and synchronization

ActorServer naturally supports the expression of crosscutting concepts or aspects (Furfaro *et al*, 2002). The concept of *synchronizer* (Ren *et al*, 1996)(Nielsen *et al*, 1998) is adopted as an useful abstraction for capturing and applying synchronization constraints in groups of actors. Whereas in (Ren *et al*, 1996)(Nielsen *et al*, 1998) synchronizers are viewed as special entities capable of expressing synchronization constraints declaratively, in (Nigro and Pupo, 2001)(Varela and Agha, 2001) and in ActorServer, synchronizers are programmed almost as normal actors. They can be regulated by a state machine. The guarded group of actors of a synchronizer constitutes its set of acquaintances. A synchronizer intercepts messages destined to controlled actors and takes some action based on the *"safe progress, unsafe block"* semantics, in the sense that the synchronizer can temporarily store or drop the message if releasing it for scheduling would cause violation of constraints in the future.

3. An example using parallel matrix multiplication

As an example, ActorServer was applied to a parallel algorithm for matrix multiplication (see (Fox *et al*, 1988), pag. 169). The algorithm splits the two multiplicand matrixes A and B into $\sqrt{P}$ sub-blocks of square matrixes each of $(N/\sqrt{P}) \times (N/\sqrt{P})$ elements, where P is the number of processors. The sub-blocks $A_{i,j}$, $B_{i,j}$ are initially allocated to processor $P_{i,j}$. The algorithm for computing the sub-block $C_{i,j}$ of the product matrix consists in iterating $\sqrt{P}-1$ times the following three phases: *broadcast* of a selected sub-block $A_{i,j}$ to all the processors in row i, *computing* $C_{i,j}=C_{i,j}+T*B_{i,j}$ where T is the A sub-block defined in the broadcast phase (see below), and *rolling upwards* the sub-block $B_{i,j}$ along the column j of B. Both broadcast and rolling upwards consider the involved matrix as a toroid. At each iteration, only one processor $P_{i,j}$ in each row i of matrix A is actually responsible of broadcasting, i.e. sending its sub-block $A_{i,j}$ to all the remaining processors in the row. During a broadcast phase, either a processor broadcasts its sub-block or expects a sub-block. Broadcasting is efficiently accomplished by piping: a processor which receives a sub-block $A_{i,j}$ propagates it to the next processor. Every processor communicates only with its nearest neighbours.

```
import it.unical.deis.lis.as.*;
public class LogicalProcessor extends Actor{
    //message interface
    ...
    //local variables
    int i,j /*processor coordinates*/, it=0 /*iteration counter*/, broadcastIteration;
    int p; //number of processors per row/column
    long startTime;
    double [][]a,b/*assigned sub-blocks*/, t, res /*computed sub-block of product matrix*/;
    LogicalProcessor above, right;
    Master master;
    //internal states
    static final int CREATED=0, BROADCAST=1, COMPUTE=2, WAIT_B=3, STOP=4;
    public LogicalProcessor(){ become( CREATED ); }
    public void handler( Message m ){
        switch( currentStatus() ){
            case CREATED:
                if( m instanceof Init ){
                    Init msg=(Init)m; above=msg.above; right=msg.right;
                    i=msg.i; j=msg.j; p=msg.p; master=msg.master; a=msg.a; b=msg.b;
                    res=new double[a.length][a.length]; broadcastIteration=(i-j+p)%p;
                    if( it==broadcastIteration ) send( new AMsg( a, i, j ) );
                    become( BROADCAST ); startTime=System.currentTimeMillis();
                }else defer( m );
                break;
            case BROADCAST:
                if( m instanceof AMsg ){
                    AMsg aMsg = (AMsg)m; t=aMsg.a;
                    if( aMsg.j!=((j+1)%p) ) right.send( m );
                    send( new Compute() ); become( COMPUTE );
                }else defer( m );
                break;
            case COMPUTE:
                if( m instanceof Compute )
                {compute();++it; above.send( new BMsg(b) ); become( WAIT_B );}
                else defer( m );
                break;
            case WAIT_B:
                if( m instanceof BMsg ){
                    BMsg bMsg=(BMsg)m; b=bMsg.b;
                    if( it==p ){ send( new Stop() ); become( STOP ); }
                    else{ if( it==broadcastIteration ) send( new AMsg(a, i, j) );
                        become( BROADCAST ); }
                }else defer( m );
                break;
            case STOP:
                if( m instanceof Stop )
                { long ctime=System.currentTimeMillis()-startTime;
                  master.send( new Master.Report( ctime, res, i, j ) ); }
        }//switch
    }//handler
    private void compute(){ //compute res=res+t*b }
}//LogicalProcessor
```

Listing 2: An ActorServer implementation of parallel matrix multiplication algorithm

Listing 2 depicts an implementation of the algorithm according to ActorServer. A logical processor understands the public *Init* message carrying the initialisation data (including the master actor which is in charge of system configuration and final collection of the computed sub-blocks of the product matrix), *AMsg* and *BMsg* messages respectively for broadcasting and rolling upwards an A sub-block and a B sub-block, and the private (self-sent) messages *Compute* which triggers a compute phase and *Stop* which finishes the local algorithm.

The use of the *defer()* method in Listing 2 should be noted. It allows postponing the processing of an early received sub-block.

3.1 Distributed execution experiments

The matrix multiplication algorithm was executed using four instances of the LogicalProcessor class equally split between two actor servers running respectively on a Sun UltraSparc 10 (Solaris) and a Pentium III (Win98) platforms, interconnected by a dedicated 100 Mbps fast Ethernet. The worst-case execution time (wall clock time) required by the distributed application was measured along the four logical processors. Figure 2 portrays, with the matrix dimension varying from 50 to 1000, the speedup, i.e. the ratio between the execution time of a sequential version of the program (based on the classical three-nested for loops) executed on the fastest machine (Sun UltraSparc 10) and the execution time of the distributed ActorServer version of the program.

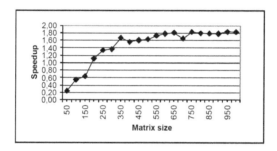

Figure 2: Speedup vs matrix size (2 physical processors)

4. Conclusions

This paper proposes ActorServer, a novel middleware based on a variant of the Actor model (Agha, 1986) designed for programming distributed and time-dependent applications over the Internet. ActorServer is 100% Java, is totally portable and can exploit heterogeneous computing platforms. Research issues which deserve further work include the following.

- Improving the transport layer by replacing Java serialization, at least for application messages, with a custom marshalling/unmarshalling process for better controlling dynamic memory management and Java garbage collections.
- Implementing dynamic load balancers which try to enhance processor occupation by migrating objects between processors according to a customisable policy.
- Porting on ActorServer a Time Warp mechanism (Beraldi and Nigro, 2001) suited to general distributed simulation.

- Defining and implementing a SALSA-like high-level language (Varela and Agha, 2001) on top of ActorServer.

Acknowledgments

This work was partially supported by italian Consiglio Nazionale delle Ricerche under the contract no. CNRC002FE3_004 of CNR-Agenzia2000.

5. References

G. Agha (1986). *Actors: A model for concurrent computation in distributed systems*. MIT Press.

M. Astley (1999). The Actor Foundry. University of Illinois. http://osl.cs.uiuc.edu.

R. Beraldi, L. Nigro (2001). A time warp mechanism based on temporal uncertainty. *Transactions of the Society for Modelling and Simulation International*, **18**(2), June, pp. 60-72.

N. Carriero, D. Gelernter (1990). *How to write parallel programs*. MIT Press.

A. Furfaro, L. Nigro, F. Pupo (2002). Aspect oriented programming using actors. *Proc. 2nd Int. Workshop on Aspect Oriented Programming for Distributed Computer Systems* (AOPDCS 2002), July 2-5, Vienna.

J. Fox, M. Johnson, G. Lyzenga, S. Otto, J. Salmon, D. Walker (1988). *Solving problems on concurrent processors*. Vol. **1**, Prentice-Hall Int. Editions.

R. Gray, D. Kotz, G. Cybenko, D. Rus (2000). Mobile agents: motivations and state-of-the-art systems. Dartmouth College Computer Science Department, *Technical Report TR2000-365*. ftp://ftp.cs.darthmouth.edu/TR/TR2000-365.ps.Z.

B. Nielsen, S. Ren, G. Agha (1998). Specification of real-time interaction constraints. *Proc. of 1st Int. Symposium on Object-Oriented Real-Time Computing*. IEEE Computer Society.

L. Nigro, F. Pupo (2001). Schedulability analysis of real time actor systems using Coloured Petri Nets. *Concurrent Object-Oriented Programming and Petri Nets – Advances in Petri Nets*. G. Agha, F. De Cindio, G. Rozenberg (Eds.), Springer, LNCS 2001, pp. 493-513.

Object Management Group (1997). CORBA services: Common object services specification version 2. *Technical report, Object Management Group*, June. www.omg.org/corba/.

S. Ren, G. Agha, M. Saito (1996). A modular approach for programming distributed real-time systems. *J. of Parallel and Distributed Computing*. Special issue on Object Oriented Real Time Systems.

Sun Microsystems Inc. JavaSoft (1996). Remote Method Invocation Specification. www.javasoft.com/products/jdk/rmi/.

Sun Microsystems Inc. JavaSoft (1998). JavaSpaces. www.javasoft.com/products/javaspaces/.

C. Varela, G. Agha (1998). What after Java ? From objects to actors. *Computer Networks and ISDN Systems: The Int. J. of Computer, Telecommunications and Networking*. Vol. **30**, pp. 573-577, April.

C. Varela, G. Agha (2001). Programming dynamically reconfigurable open systems with SALSA. *Proc. of OOPSLA '01*.

J. Waldo (1998). Jini Architecture Overview. www.javasoft.com/products/jini/

GRID Talk: Connecting Grids

Virupatchan Maheswaran[1] and Nick Antonopoulos[2]

[1,2] Software Agents Research Group, Department of Computing
University of Surrey, United Kingdom
m.virupatchan@surrey.ac.uk and *n.antonopoulos@surrey.ac.uk*

Abstract

A new breed of advanced network-based applications is emerging, prominent from today's Web browsers and other standard Internet applications by a coordinated use of networks and end system computers. These applications require services not provided by today's Internet and Web: they need a "GRID" that both integrates new types of resource into the network and provides enhanced "middleware" services. The initial step is to outline the existing situation and the requirements. Then, we propose a peer-to-peer structure as opposed to the existing hierarchical and the central-server structures, which will enable GRID interoperation for information search and retrieval. Further, we also show the object-oriented model of the structure and prove by both statistical analysis and simulation that the model is efficient in limiting the network data traffic over time.

Keywords

GRID, Peer-to-Peer, Networks, Interoperability, Distributed Processing

1. Introduction

The term "the GRID" (Fo, Ke, and Tu, 2001) was invented in the mid 90s to denote a proposed distributed computing infrastructure for advanced science and engineering. Considerable progress has since been made on the construction of such an infrastructure, but the term "GRID" has also been conflated, at least in popular perception, to embrace everything from advanced networking to artificial intelligence. One might wonder whether the term has any real substance and meaning. Is there really a distinct "GRID problem" and hence a need for new "GRID technologies"? If so, what is the nature of these technologies, and what is their domain of applicability? While numerous groups have interest in GRID concepts and to a significant extent share a common vision of GRID architecture, we do not see consensus on the answers to these questions.

The concept of GRID is about coordinated resource sharing and problem solving in dynamic organizations. The sharing that we are concerned with is not file exchange, direct access to computers or software but the direct communication of resource/non-resource components.

2. GRID And Heterogeneity

A GRID is simply a mechanism or concept for integrating or sharing physical or logical things, which can be considered as a single unit. A GRID can also be thought of as a continuum (Foster and Kesselman, 1999).

Some important services that GRID systems provide (Kr, Bu and Ma) include: location of resources which involve persistent storage such as databases to manage and access resource information; creation of processes, which involve job scheduling and management of resources; low-level communication between processes, which involve protocols that can be used to build higher-level messaging systems. A key aspect of GRIDs is the composition of resources in a sense that goes beyond simply interconnecting them.

Research is being carried out both in the industry and academia with the aim of defining the architecture of an "ideal GRID". Three of the well-established examples are Globus (Foster and Kesselman) from Argonne National Labs, Legion (Lewis and Grimshaw, 1995) from the University of Virginia and Globe (St, Ho, and Ta, 1999) from Vrije University. Due to the development carried out by many research groups with the same objective but using different methodologies, GRID systems vary widely with services and functionalities. This is a real and a specific problem in the GRID domain, which demands a resolution.

Since GRIDs tend to be thought of as "units", they tend to involve some level of unified management. The management consists of rules, policies, and mechanisms. GRID management might also come in many forms (central authority, de-centralized, democratic, etc.). As a result of a GRID being a unit with compositional properties, there can be more than one GRID. (i.e. there can be local and global GRIDs, or a hierarchy of GRIDs and larger GRIDs can be constructed by composing smaller (perhaps local) GRIDs. It may be possible for local GRIDs to operate independently from larger GRIDs of which they may temporarily be a part. This issue of interoperability has not yet been addressed properly and is an essential necessity for a global network of GRIDs. This paper aims to provide a framework which will address the issue of GRID interoperability enabling various heterogeneous GRIDs to share resources. In the following sections we describe a model which will function as a connector for existing varied GRID systems.

3. A Model to Support Heterogeneous GRID Interoperability

We propose an agent based peer-to-peer model as opposed to the commonly existing hierarchical and the central-server models (Texar Corporation), arguing that the peer-to-peer model introduces flexibility and deeper control of components in the organisation. Every agent acts as a standalone element in the peer-to-peer organisation and they are called GRID Talk agents (GT). Every GT agent represents a GRID (its owner) in the organisation. GT acts as an interface to external heterogeneous GRID(s) for the owner GRID (i.e. a gateway) enabling them to communicate to each other hence referred to as, GRID Talk.

Common requirements of a GRID states the following dedicated tasks for a GT agent to function effectively in a peer-to-peer setting; a communication mechanism from the GRID to the GT agent for control purposes, an internal automation process to carry out routine management tasks, a member policy management system, a group management facility, a translation unit to exchange messages to and from the GRID, a database for information storage, search/discovery facility, an advertisement routine and a job distribution functionality.

Figure 1 shows a logical view of the structure, modelling the above stated requirements with the appropriate representative components.

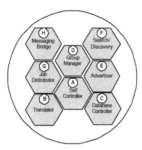

Figure 1: GT agent Model Diagram

- **Self Controller:** (A) takes care of the internal automation processes and controls other GT components.
- **Translator:** (B) translates messages from one GRID format to the GT's logical format, since GT is independent of the GRID framework.
- **Database Controller:** (C) stores member data, policy rules, and other control information.
- **Group Manager:** (D) maintains the profile of members and monitors member behaviour. (D) also controls policies of individual members depending on their status. Possible policies depend on the type of GRIDs, the owning GRID will accept/support.
- **Advertiser:** (E) is an active process, which broadcasts the owner's existence and capacity.
- **Search/Discovery Unit:** (F) is responsible for discovering and querying other members for resources.
- **Job Distributor:** (G) optimiser decides the division of job submissions. This will enable a job to be submitted to multiple different GRIDs based on the reachable resources. Distribution plan is formulated based on the rules in the database.
- **Messaging Bridge:** (H) is the gateway to the GT and is a dual thread process to handle external and the owner GRID's requests and responses.

Main features of the GT agent to operate in a totally peer-to-peer environment are as follows:

- **Group(s) per GRID, each GRID also acts as a Group of its own interest(s)**
  Each peer manages its own group(s) (i.e. a collection of peers grouped or not grouped into categories depending on their services. A peer may also provide a number of services, hence will be listed under different groups). The owner decides whom to invite or whom to grant access to the group. If the owner of the group requires a service, either a broadcast can be sent out or the GT can seek already registered members. The first point of contact will be the already registered members with the GT and, if they cannot provide the requirement, a broadcast is sent out to non-registered external GTs.
  Disadvantages: Broadcasting introduces the problem of excess network data traffic.
  Advantages: A GRID has total control over its own group(s). Due to the lack of resources in smaller GRIDs, GT will enable that GRID to participate in a wider organisation with many resources shared by the surrounding GT community. The proposed model reduces the broadcasting to a negligent level over a period (*See Section 6: Broadcasting Behaviour*).

- **Policy management by the originating GRID**
  As opposed to hierarchical management, peers manage their own rules of interaction. As a group is individual based, policies will be bi-directional, i.e. each of the participating GRID will hold its own policy during the interaction.
  Disadvantages: Inability of setting up a common high-level policy for all the peers and hence the absence of a centralised policy management architecture
  Advantages: Both the owners get to decide whom to accept and whom to avoid, hence every individual peers will have the power of defining their own rules of interaction.
- **Total peer-to-peer interaction**
  Peers contact each other directly without travelling via a route of mediators. A broadcast must be sent out when a GT agent first comes into existence. GT gradually builds up contacts as it becomes more functional in its environment.
  Advantages: No isolation due to node breakdowns and no need for a centralised administration

It is clearly evident that the advantages of our proposed peer-to-peer model overrides the hierarchical and the central-server models for the setting of interconnecting GRIDs.

4. Model Behaviour

The GT agent has to carry out four main tasks in order to ensure a smooth operation. These tasks also introduce us to the object-oriented view of the proposed architecture. GT's focal tasks are: internal automation operations; search/discovery operations; task of adding a member and job submitting operations. As GT emerges into existence on a GRID administrative domain, standard operations are performed to configure and set up the environment. A relationship with the owning GRID and the outside world is formed. Messages passed between the components also fall into three primary categories. This division helps us to understand the workflow with greater clarity. The three message types are:

Control Information	M_c	*Messages sent to invoke an activity on a component*
Data	M_d	*Messages resulting due to an activity/request*
Job Query	M_{jq}	*Job query information generated by a GRID*

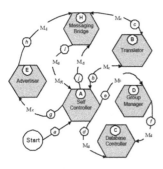

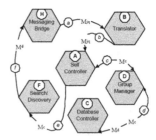

Figure 2: Automation   Figure 3: Search/Discovery

As Figure 2 illustrates, as soon as the GT is initiated (*a*), a message is sent to the GRID requesting its profile via (B), (*b, c*). The information is received, a profile is entered in (C) (*d*), and the information is passed to (D) to set up policies and a group(s) (*e, f*). This profile acts as the identity of this GT to other GTs. As the set up phase is now complete, advertisement of position and profile begins (*g, h*). At this stage external GRIDs may start to respond (*i*), hence reply to responses (*j*) as appropriate. This described scenario is GT's automation related operation.

Once the GT is configured, the owning GRID may start sending resource querying requests to the GT. Figure 3 shows the behaviour of such a search/discovery operation. A request is received via (B) in need for a specified amount of resources (*a, b*). First, (D) is consulted for members who can satisfy the need (*c, d*). If appropriate members exist then the request is sent to them, otherwise a broadcast is sent out (*e, f*).

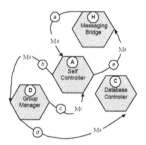

Figure 4: Add a Member   Figure 5: Submit a Job

When an external GRID shows an interest in processing a requested job, it must first be made a member of the requester GRID before proceeding with any further interaction. For this reason the requester GRID's policies have to be satisfied by the external responder. After a successful validation, the responder is made a member of the requester's GRID. As Figure 4 illustrates, a positive response arrives (*a*) from an external GRID. (D) validates the external response (*b*). If the validation is satisfied then the responder's details are added to the member's database (*c, d*). An acceptance message is sent back to the responder (*e*). For a job submission, the job data is sent to the GT from the GRID via (B), (*a, b*). (D) is consulted regarding members location/profile (*c, d*). (G), based on certain rules on member's resources, sends the job to the target member (*e, f*). Figure 5 shows this scenario.

This demonstration of GT's activities further establishes the sub-components, functionalities and their necessity. The type of messages and the order of interactions show the workflow pattern in the GT agent. Further, the modular design enables the "Black Box" Approach (Prowell, 1999), where we regard the specified objects (A - J) as Black Boxes. The implementation of the objects will be transparent to each other apart from the required interfaces for communication. For example if we consider (D) as a Black Box, (A) can use D's capabilities without the underlying knowledge of D. Due to this development procedure any component can be modified and updated subject to any new modification requirement.

5. Object Oriented View

The next level down to the modular description is the object-oriented architecture. Figure 6 shows the inheritance hierarchy of the model. This hierarchy can be divided into 3 levels according to operations of the GT as described in section 5. **Level one:** The GT base class, this specifies the core functionality, which defines the GT. One of the sample implementations can be the *IResourceManager* interface, whose capability is required by the Translator and the Group Manager to access command and policies resource files respectively. **Level Two:** The Self Controller, this class specifies the core functionality of the GT itself and contains automation threading and interfaces to communicate to other classes. **Level Three:** Rest of the classes: these are sub specifications intended to carryout a task. These classes are used by the Self Controller to initiate an activity.

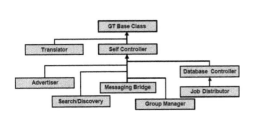

Figure 6: Class Hierarchy   Figure 7: GT View

In terms of messages being passed, the GT base class handles the communication with the GRID itself and hence the Self Controller and the Translator inherit from this base class. These components depend on (M_c, M_d, M_{jq}) from the GRID to function properly. The Messaging Bridge handles both the GT specific commands and the GRID commands and hence inherits from the Self Controller. Likewise, the Advertiser and the Search/Discovery components exchange (M_c) with the Self Controller and don't handle (M_d). The Group Manager exchanges (M_c) with the Self Controller and (M_d) with the GT base class and hence inherit from the Self Controller. The Database Controller handles members, job distribution (M_d) and requires interfaces from the Self Controller, as this is the primary information provider to the GT. The Job Distributor depends on the Database Controller for (M_d) for decisions on distribution algorithms. This discussion shows the reliance of the GT's components on each other in an object-oriented assessment. The object-oriented view is the abstract design with higher-level classes and descriptions which leads us to the implementation phase.

Figure 7 shows the initial prototype of the GT agent. The prototype provides important proposed functions of broadcasting and discovering other peer GTs and it's currently being tested on the university network for resource sharing. Current activities are based on a generic message query interface that can be used by third party GRIDs to communicate to remote GRIDs via GT for resource querying.

6. Broadcasting Behaviour

We have used broadcasts as a way to announce a particular GT and discover other GT peers. Broadcasting will be the initial starting point for a new isolated GT. We have proposed a framework which keeps the broadcasting at a minimum level to reduce the excess amount of network data traffic.

In order to prove our concept of reduction in network data traffic over a period of time as the GT builds up more and more member GTs, a simple simulation is performed. Assumptions also have to be made to control the behaviour in relation to the stated model. The main parameters of our analysis are: n, number of GRIDs; p, probability of requests from a GRID; a, average no of resources per GRID; q, probability of responses from external GRIDs; r, probability of responder also wishing to become a member and s, probability of responses from member GRIDs. On the first iteration, the number of broadcast messages are $ap(n-1)$. The external response for these messages is $q(n-1)$ and the external response with an interest of becoming a member is $qr(n-1)$. Provided that an initial set of members have been added to the member list after the first iteration, then on the second iteration; the number of broadcast messages will be $ap(1-s)(n-1)(1-qr)$. The new total of members is the sum of newly added members and the previous set of members, $qr(n-1)+qr[(n-1)-qr(n-1)]$. Summarising the number of generated broadcast messages over 5 iterations gives,

$$BroadcastMsgs_1 = ap(n-1)$$
$$BroadcastMsgs_2 = ap\bar{s}(n-1)(1-qr)$$
$$BroadcastMsgs_3 = ap\bar{s}(n-1)(1-2qr+qr^2)$$
$$BroadcastMsgs_4 = ap\bar{s}(n-1)(1-3qr+3qr^2-qr^3)$$

From these results, it can be noted that over iterations, number of responses with the interest of becoming a member reduces as the power of probabilities qr increase. To view the physical outcome of these results, a simulation was performed. We assume that the number of participating GRIDs (n), average number of resources per GRID (a) and the probability of requests (p) are constants. As time increases, GT's members will gradually increase and the probability of responses by members, s will increase. At the same time, probability of external GRIDs promising to become members qr will decrease due to the reduction of external non-members. This behaviour is stated as one of the main properties of the proposed model. According to this, collective probability qr and s are obtained from random number generators, in the interval of 0 to 1. The factor qr will be in the decreasing order from 1 to 0 and s in the increasing order from 0 to 1.

n=10	a = 5	p=0.5
Iterations	**BroadcastMsgs**	
1	11.046462	
2	6.4703774	
3	2.461256	
4	1.6050186	
5	0.99702865	

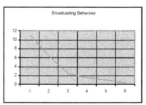

Figure 8: Broadcasting Behaviour

The output is shown on Figure 8, for 10 GRIDs; with an average number of resources of 5 and a probability p of 0.5. The claim does not state that the broadcasting will completely vanish, but it will reduce to a level where it is almost negligible.

7. Conclusions

Computational GRIDs is an emerging technology, which mainly aims to improve distributed resource sharing and utilisation through peer-to-peer algorithms and computer networks. A number of tools have been developed to facilitate the development of GRIDs, the most notable being Globus and Legion. Although these tools are necessary components of the GRID technology, they introduce the problem of interoperability. Currently no two GRIDs built with different tools can communicate with each other and share computational power.

In this paper, we attempted to address this issue and presented the GRID Talk agent (GT) architecture to support GRID interoperability. The GT agent architecture follows the main premise of the GRID technology, which is peer-to-peer interaction. We have also shown that our model greatly reduces the network data traffic caused by the peer-to-peer design. In conclusion, the GT architecture provides a simple peer-to-peer framework to enable distributed, specialised GRIDs to share information and resources. Such architecture is needed to ensure that the GRID technology will fulfil its expectations of providing global sharing of computing power in a heterogeneous environment.

References

Foster, I. Kesselman, C. Tuecke, S. 2001. *"The Anatomy of the GRID"*. Intl J. Supercomputer Applications.

Foster, I. Kesselman, C. 1999. *"The GRID: Blueprint for a New Computing Infrastructure"*. Morgan Kaufmann publishers, USA.

Foster, I. Kesselman, C. *"The Globus Project"*. A Status Report. http://www.globus.org

Krauter, K. Buyya, R. Maheswaran, M. *"A Survey and Taxonomy of Resource Management Systems for GRID Computing"*. Technical Report, Computer Science Department, University of Manitoba

Lewis, M. Grimshaw, A. 1995. *"The Core Legion Object Model"*. Computer Science Technical Report, University of Virginia

Prowell, S. May 1999. *"Developing Black Box Specifications Through Sequence Enumeration"*. Proceedings of the Harlan Mills Colloquium, IEEE

Steen, M. Homburg, P. Tanenbaum, A.S. 1999. *"Globe: A Wide-Area Distributed System"*. IEEE Concurrency

Texar Corporation. *"Peer-to-Peer Computing: Issues and Opportunities in Information Sharing"*. White Paper

Software Component Assembly Prediction — or how to predict the unpredictable

Holger D. Hofmann, Marcel Dix

ABB Group, Corporate Research Center, Ladenburg, Germany

e-mail: holger.hofmann@de.abb.com

Abstract

Composing entire information systems from pre-built software components, sometimes called 'commercial off-the-shelf (COTS) software', has gained significant interest as a way for creating software products faster and cheaper. Independently developed software components are assembled to form applications for specific domains. This raises the problem of component collaboration, i.e., how self-contained computational entities use each other's functionality without prior knowledge of semantics and signatures. The ease with which this can be solved highly depends on the granularity of software components to be assembled. Fine granular components such as GUI elements can be assembled very easily while high-level components or even entire applications provide own functionality, for example, for data storage or transaction management, which cannot easily be reused on a cross-component basis. ABB provides an architecture (Industrial IT architecture, see www.abb.com) which facilitates the assembly and collaboration of large-grained software components. In this article, we describe ABB's approach and in addition outline the work that has been started in a joint project of the ABB Group and the Software Engineering Institute at Carnegie Mellon University to predict some of the extra-functional properties (performance, reliability, etc.) of such integrations. The underlying idea is to equip software components with certifiable quality attributes and reason about a composition based on analytical models. We describe the steps taken in applying the concepts developed in this collaboration to the ABB Industrial IT architecture.

Keywords

Software component, assembly, prediction, ABB Industrial IT

1. Introduction

The ABB Group is an organisation producing the full range of equipment with and without software needed to handle extremely large integration projects, such as the engineering, installation, deployment and operation/decommissioning of an entire paper production plant. However, ABB is also involved in such diverse activities such as the propulsion control-system in vessels and power plants. Apart from being responsible for integrating these kinds of systems, the company also creates many of the components used in-house, while other components are bought from third party suppliers.

Most components are in one form or the other intended for integration. However, integration can take place at many levels. Traditionally, systems are integrated at the mechanical and electrical levels. Today, systems are usually integrated into a control and automation communication architecture such as the Foundation Fieldbus and Profibus. It is then up to the integrating company, such as ABB, to integrate products in other aspects, such as plant control, spare parts handling, maintenance planning, and safety systems. In this process, architectural mismatch (Garlan, 1995) challenges are common, resulting in lost time and money.

In this paper, we focus on integration issues of software components representing the physical components to be integrated and acting as a software driver-like interface to a common system architecture.

2. ABB's Industrial IT

The whole is more than the sum of its parts.
— *Aristotle, Metaphysica 10f-1045a*

In order to make the most out of the resources, buyers of systems want to integrate their devices into as many as possible of their existing systems. To decrease total cost of operation, the heavy duty industry currently integrate life cycle asset management systems and ERP systems with their plant operation systems. The popular phrase is 'see the sensor in the boardroom'. This causes even more integration challenges. To be able to cope with the aforementioned integration challenges, a common IT platform has been developed and deployed within ABB: *ABB Industrial IT*. In this architecture, a real-world object is represented by a software object (see Figure 1).

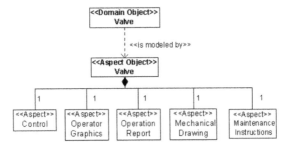

Figure 1: Mapping of Real-World Objects to Computational Objects

Aspects represent user-oriented views on a real world object. The software object (the Aspect Object) holds pointers to aspects of the object, similar to an HTML page referencing other HTML pages. For example, an object can have a documentation aspect, an error log aspect and a replacement availability aspect. Each aspect holds a particular type of data belonging to the complete system, rather than the individual application (called Aspect System) that operates on the data. For example, a spare parts aspect could have a URL as its only data, and a Web browser could be the Aspect System that operates on the data. The structure of Aspect systems can be seen in Figure 2. An Aspect System defines one or several aspect types, each representing the implementation of a certain aspect (collection of COM components). Of each aspect type, one or more aspect categories can be defined as different specialisations. For example, the aspect system Graphics implements the aspect types Graphic Display, Faceplate, and Display Element, where the aspect type Graphic Display includes the categories Overview, Group, and Object Display. A discussion of all conceptual elements of ABB Industrial IT would go far beyond the scope of this paper (for more information, refer to (Preiss, 2001) or (Preiss, 2002).

The Aspect Object model represents a very special approach since it differs from the traditional approaches in component-based software engineering in which an application is assembled from lower-level software components (see Szyperski, 1998). Industrial IT rather uses pre-built high-level components that may range from a word processor such as Microsoft Winword up to a complete SAP R/3 system. Figure 3 shows the different between 'traditional' component-oriented software engineering and the approach used within ABB Industrial IT.

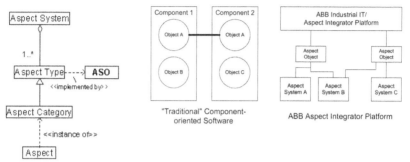

Figure 2: Structure of Aspect Systems

Figure 3: Traditional Componentware vs. ABB Aspect Integrator Platform

While the collaboration of fine-granular components requires the sharing of a common object model (see also Hofmann, 1998), the integration of software components using ABB Industrial IT integrates even independently developed systems. The architectural backbone of ABB Industrial IT is represented by the Aspect Integrator Platform. This architecture allows the plugging-in of Aspect Objects holding references to Aspect Systems. While the Aspect Integrator Platform defines common interfaces and offers a standard set of services, Aspect Systems can be completely independent of one another. Within the Aspect Integrator Platform, different levels of component integration are available:

i.) *Aspect User Interface Wrapping* – the application provides its user interface as an ActiveX control, ASP/HTML page, Active Document, OLE Server, or Windows application.

ii.) *Aspect User Interface Integration* – the application recognises itself as an Aspect System, and it supports basic Aspect operations, such as Create/Delete. When one navigates to the Aspect, he or she ends up in a context that is relevant to the current Aspect Object.

iii.) *Aspect Navigation Integration* – the Aspect system recognises the fact that there are also other Aspect Systems. It supports context menus, making it possible to navigate to other Aspects directly from within the application. It also provides contents for other Aspect Systems to include in context menus.

iv.) *Aspect Engineering Integration* – the Aspect System supports all Aspect operations, including Copy/Paste, Export/Import, Inheritance, and Version Handling. The Aspect System has knowledge about object type libraries and structures.

v.) *Aspect Administration Integration* – the Aspect System supports integrated administration, including install, backup/restore.

vi.) *Aspect Data Management Integration* – the Aspect System supports life-cycle management, and transaction handling with rollback.

vii.) *Aspect System Integration* – a combination of the aforementioned integration options allowing the interaction of 3rd party tools with the Aspect Integrator Platform.

The last integration realises functionality similar to a device driver of an operating system. This is, for example, necessary for the integration of tools such as SAP R/3, Autocad, or Microsoft Winword. Only the integrating Aspect System (the 'driver') has the knowledge about the component's semantics while the collaborating Aspect Systems are completely decoupled.

Physical objects in the Industrial IT architecture can have relations to other physical objects. For example, they can have location relations (same room/different rooms), they can participate in same/different production processes. In the software representation, an object can participate in different structures such as the location structure, and the process structure. The idea of placing the same object in multiple structures is based on (IEC 1996; IEC, 1997). It is easy to add new structures. For example, one may want an electrical structure to keep track of which power consuming devices are attached to the same energy generators.

During operation, a plant operator (or, a vessel captain, or a mill maintenance staff-member) is presented with an object-oriented view of the real-world objects. An example is shown in Figure 4. This view is completely customisable, because the usability needs may differ very much between different user groups. For example, a plant control operator may need to access much more information than the engine room operators on a naval vessel.

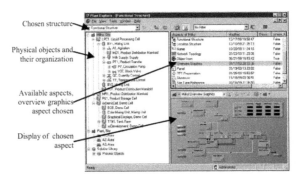

Chosen structure

Physical objects and their organization

Available aspects, overview graphics aspect chosen

Display of chosen aspect

Figure 4: Example of one Operate^{IT} workplace

For commercial reasons, the Aspect Integrator Platform is based on the Microsoft Windows 2000 (Win2k) platform. COM (Box, 1998) is used as component model, and OPC (OLE for Process Control (OPC, online)) is the main means of communication with hardware from various manufacturers. Win2k provides the security platform, a component model, connectivity, installation/deinstallation features and support for multiple screens.

The use of component technologies has a particular advantage for system-integrating organisations, such as ABB: It simplifies the outsourcing of some functionality, as a COM component by definitions has defined interfaces.

3. Prediction-Enabled Component Technology (PECT)

For our discussion of prediction-enabled component technology (PECT; see Hissam, 2001), we will use the following basic definitions (Hofmann, 1997):

- A software component is pieces of software with one or more well-defined interfaces that are configurable, integrable, and immutable.

- Componentware is a set of collaborating software components.

- A componentware architecture describes how software components are built, managed, and how they interoperate with other software components».

Similar to a chain that is only as strong as its weakest link, the quality of an assembly of independently developed software components is only as good as the quality of the component with the lowest quality. If, for example, all software components in an assembly implement security functionality for data transmission but one component does not, the whole inter-component communication can be regarded as to be not secure. For assessing a component assembly, interface or syntactical compatibility is not sufficient since it does not give an insight on a component's behaviour in a particular environment. A stronger form of syntactical compatibility is protocol compatibility (Yellin, 1997), but this only guarantees operations to be executed in a defined order. The semantics of these operations is neither defined nor checked. For a detailed discussion of challenges in building componentware refer to (Hofmann, 1998) and (Hofmann, Zeidler, 2000).

Software quality in component-based systems covers the quality of single components and the quality of the assembly, which does not has to be conformant with the rule mentioned above. The questions in this connection arising are:

- How can software component quality be measured and specified?

- How can the quality of a component assembly be inferred (predicted) from the quality of the components used?

A collaborative project between ABB Corporate Research and the Software Engineering Institute at Carnegie Mellon University is to focus on these questions and to develop a solution that is applicable to the ABB Industrial IT Platform.

PECT complements a componentware architecture by an analysis technology (see Figure 5). It is concerned with the rapid assembly of systems from components where components have certified properties providing the basis for predicting properties of the resulting assemblies. This is being provided by analysis technology, which allows the analysis and prediction of assembly-level properties prior to software component assembly, or even prior to component acquisition. The goal of PECT is not to analyse arbitrary designs for any application domain, but to restrict those to an analysable sub-set. Component properties of interest are, for example:

- Reliability (fault-tolerance, i.e., avoidance of single points of failure),
- Scalability (from 100 objects up to 200,000 or more objects),
- Distributability (realise several distribution transparencies: location transparency, access transparency, ...),
- Openness (interoperability, integrability, ...),
- Predictability for reliability, availability and performance of real-time process control solutions,
- Integrity (provide security mechanisms),
- Reusability (of partial and entire solutions), and
- Controlled Evolution (new functionality incrementally added).

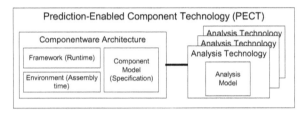

Figure 5: Elements of Prediction-Enabled Component Technology

A component supporting PECT provides two types of interfaces: behavioural interfaces and analytic interfaces supporting component properties. While behavioural interfaces provide a component's functionality to other components, analytic interfaces provide a hook-in for tools applying analysis technologies to an assembly of components. The analysis model defines the property theory underlying the analysis technology as well as a set of properties a component has to provide. Figure 6 shows the relation between the component model and the analytic model. For each constructive model, an analytic counterpart exists, which can be validated.

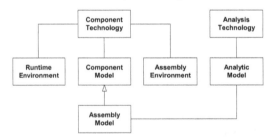

Figure 6: PECT Component Model and Assembly Model

Component property specification takes a central role in PECT since the accuracy of analytic models highly depends on these. Simplistic analytic models only taking into account, for example, the memory footprint of software components or their latency can easily specify component properties. But how can properties such as reliability in a particular environment (e.g., version X of operating system Y on computer Z) or component security be specified so that the property definitions of different component vendors match each other?

Another aspect is that trust in component properties and their evaluation has to be established. On principle, one can distinguish between two types of component properties: pre-defined and parameterised properties. While the former specify immutable traits of a software component, such as the security algorithms used to encrypt data, the latter focus on the behaviour of a component in a particular environment. This is particularly of interest to the evaluation of runtime parameters.

Parameterised component properties can be determined at runtime on a per-component basis. Pre-defined component properties raise the problem of trust levels, i.e., does the user of a component trust a property value, or not. In this connection, certification authorities such as known for security certificates (see, e.g., www.verisign.com) are required to establish a common level of trust for component properties.

4. PECT within ABB

Applications being based on ABB Industrial IT integrate complex high-level applications called Aspect Systems in mostly very demanding or restrictive application domains such as power plant automation, power transmission, upstream oil & gas, substation automation, and pulp & paper automation. Thus ABB Industrial IT's freedom to assemble even independently developed software components can have disadvantages in terms of product quality. In the collaborative project Predictable Assembly of Certifiable Components (PACC), CMU and ABB are to develop a PECT application to ABB Industrial IT. This means that Aspect Systems to be integrated on the basis of AIP have certified properties for particular application domains for which well-defined analysis technologies and models exist.

The integration of PECT to ABB's Industrial IT has been subdivided into four phases:

(i)   demonstrate PECT feasibility with COM components,

(ii)   port COM components developed in (i) to ABB Industrial IT,

(iii)   integrate PECT into real-world, existing Industrial IT solution, and

(iv)   integrate PECT into ABB's Industrial IT architecture.

(i) is to demonstrate the feasibility of PECT application to Microsoft COM technology. This is to show that the prototypical Java Beans-based (Sun Microsystems, 1997) PECT implementation. (ii) represents a port of the formerly developed COM components to AIP. This can be done by the previously described AIP integration techniques. (iii) is an integration of PECT into a 'living' ABB Industrial IT system that is to show the inherent benefits of PECT. A feasible model problem and thus potential application is described in (Preiss, 2001). (iv) represents and integration of PECT into the AIP.

The integration of PECT into ABB Industrial IT raises mainly two questions: at which conceptual level should PECT be integrated? And how should the integration be realised on the technical side? This is not trivial since one Aspect System can hold different relations to other Aspect Systems and can provide different functionality in the form of Aspect Types belonging to particular Aspect Categories.

The software components (i.e., COM components) realising the Aspect behaviour and data management are the Aspect System Objects (ASO, see Figure 2). ASOs define the set of COM components realising an Aspect Type's behaviour. Hence, the basic approach to combine the PECT ideas with the AIP is to annotate ASOs with quality attributes and define whatever analytical model is used based on ASOs and their higher level concepts. Figure 1 is to illustrate this. An Aspect Type's ASO consisting of a component implementing the interface *IAfwASOBasicView* is augmented by a component implementing the *IPrediction* interface. The straightforward usage of PECT is shown in the C++/COM ATL (Microsoft Active Template Library) pseudo code below.

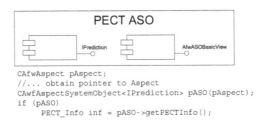

```
CAfwAspect pAspect;
//... obtain pointer to Aspect
CAwfAspectSystemObject<IPrediction> pASO(pAspect);
if (pASO)
    PECT_Info inf = pASO->getPECTInfo();
```

Figure 7: Implementation of AIP/PECT Integration

First, a pointer to an Aspect has to be available. With it, a pointer to the corresponding ASO can be obtained. The instantiation of an object of the class *CAfwAspectSystemObject* with the interface to be returned (*IPrediction*) as a generic parameter returns a pointer to the ASO or NULL if the interface is not supported.

With the PECT interface being available, one can read a component's properties or initiate the collection of empirical data required for assembly prediction. For each particular property available, a specific component can be implemented to be integrated with the ASO.

5. Conclusions and Outlook

ABB Industrial IT is a component-based distributed architecture allowing the integration of even independently-developed high-level software components including entire applications such as Autocad or SAP R/3. Conceptually, introducing the concepts of Aspects and Aspect Objects breaks down the complexity of these systems. A real-world object is modelled by an Aspect Object that can have different Aspects. Aspect can be realised by one or more Aspect Systems. The freedom to integrate nearly arbitrary sets of Aspect Systems into a common application environment can on principle negatively influence the software quality. A technology being developed in a collaborative project between ABB and CMU/SEI is to cope with this problem: Predictable Assembly of Certifiable Components (PACC). In PACC, prediction-enabling component technology (PECT) is to be integrated into the ABB Industrial IT architecture. This will help to determine the shaping of particular quality attributes of a defined assembly of Aspect Systems prior to the actual assembly, will help to shorten development costs, and will also help to shorten the development time of complete solutions.

Acknowledgement

The authors would like to thank Dr. Manfred Schölzke (ABB Corporate Research Germany), Dr. Martin Hollender (consultant, www.hollender.de), and Otto Preiss (ABB Corporate Research Switzerland) for their constructive criticism and their support.

6. References

Box, D. (1998) *Essential COM*. Addison Wesley.

Bratthall, v.d.Geest, Hofmann, et al. (2002), *Integrating Hundred's of Products through One Architecture – The Industrial IT architecture*. International Conference on Software Engineering/ISCSE, May 2002.

Garlan, D., Allen, R., Ockerbloom, J. (1995) *Architectural Mismatch or Why it's hard to Build Systems out of Existing Parts*. In: Proc. of 17th International Conference on Software Engineering, Seattle.

Hissam, S., Moreno, G., Stafford, J., Wallnau, K.C. (2001) *Packaging Predictable Assembly with Prediction-Enabled Component Technology*. Technical Report, CMU/SEI-2001-TR024, Software Engineering Institute, Carnegie Mellon University.

Hofmann, H.D. (1997). *Componentware — Integration of Software Components in Distributed Computing Environments*. M.Sc. Thesis, Cork Institute of Technology.

Hofmann, H.D. (1998), *Implementation Reuse and Inheritance in Distributed Component Systems*. Proceedings of Twenty-Second Annual International Computer Software and Applications Conference (COMPSAC'98), Vienna/Austria.

Hofmann H.D, Zeidler, C. (2000) *Prevalent Challenges in Building Componentware*. Conference/Workshop on Component-Based Software Engineering 23-24 August 2000 - ABB Corporate Research Center, Daettwil, Switzerland.

IEC Standard 61346 (1996) *Structuring principles and reference designations*.

IEC Standard 61355 (1997) *Classification and Designation of documents for plants, systems and equipment*.

OPC Foundation. www.opcfoundation.org.

Preiss O., Wegmann A. (2001) *Towards a Composition Model Problem Based on IEC61850*. 4th ICSE Workshop on Component-Based Software Engineering, Toronto, Canada, May 13-14.

Preiss O, Naedele M. (2002) *Architectural Support for Reuse: A Case Study in Industrial Automation*, chapt. 16 in I. Crnkovic, M. Larsson (edts.): Building Reliable Component-Based Systems, Artech House.

Sun Microsystems (1997) *JavaBeans Specification. Version 1.01*. Hamilton, Graham (ed.), Moutain View, CA, USA.

Szyperski, C. (1998) *Component Software*. Addison Wesley.

Yellin, D.M.; Strom, R.E. (1997) *Protocol Specifications and Component Adaptors*. ACM Transactions on Programming Languages and Systems, 19(2), pp. 292-333.

Garbage collection for Java distributed objects

A.Dancus[1][*] and D. Finkel[2]

[1]Network Storage Group, Sun Microsystems, Nashua, NH, USA
[2]Department of Computer Science, Worcester Polytechnic Institute, Worcester, MA, USA
e-mail: andrei.dancus@sun.com, dfinkel@wpi.edu

Abstract

Distributed programming in a language that relies on garbage collection, like Java, requires support for distributed garbage collection. We present a distributed garbage collection algorithm for a particular distributed object model, Java Support for Distributed Applications (JSDA). Our algorithm could also be used for any other Java-based distributed object models that use the stub-skeleton paradigm. The solution could also be used with other languages that provide the necessary means for interacting with the local garbage collector.

1. Introduction

The Java language is well suited to distributed programming because of its orientation towards simplicity in network access. Various distributed object models have been proposed for Java. Java Support for Distributed Application (JSDA) (Teodorescu and Dancus, 1999) is one such model.

Since Java relies on garbage collection, the automatic reclamation of heap-allocated memory after its last use in a program, distributed object models in Java must also provide garbage collection. This paper describes the design and implementation of distributed garbage collection for JSDA.

The Reference Objects (java.lang.ref) API, introduced in Java 1.2, provides limited functionality for programs to interact with the built-in Java garbage collector. We use this functionality to design and implement distributed garbage collection in JSDA.

Section 2 provides some background and related work in the fields of distributed programming and garbage collection. Section 3 uses these concepts to describe our algorithm; we discuss the Reference Objects API and describe how we used it to implement our algorithm. Section 4 summarizes presents the conclusions of our work – it summarizes our achievements and it suggests some possible directions for future work.

2. Background and Related Work

2.1 Distributed Programming in Java

Several approaches are available for distributed programming in Java. Java Remote Method Invocation (Java RMI) (Sun, 1999) provides support for distributed programming, but does not transform Java into a distributed programming language – such as Emerald (Black, 1986),

Linda (Linda Group, -), Orca (Bal, 1994) – since the user is exposed to underlying concepts such as RMI stubs and skeletons. CORBA (Common Object Request Broker Architecture) (OMG, 2001) is a general purpose distributed programming platform, which can be used with any programming language. A third approach is used in frameworks such as Jade (Bellifemine et al, 1999), which provides tools for implementing agent technologies.

Although these and other approaches have been used for developing distributed applications, they are difficult to use. They require the Java programmer to understand a new programming model and to become familiar with (usually many) new classes; Jade, for example, contains 29 packages. Moreover, they do not make Java a distributed language, since they do not propose extensions at the language level.

JSDA (Java Support for Distributed Application) (Teodorescu and Dancus, 1999) is an approach for distributed programming that focuses on simplicity and ease of use, while still providing flexibility. The primary goal in designing JSDA was to provide distribution capabilities at the language level. This could be done either by rewriting the JVM (Java Virtual Machine) – one such approach is used by (Aridor et al, 1999) – or by adding a pre-processing step for parsing the applications written in a Java "distributed style". JSDA falls in the second category, which has the advantage of portability on any system that has a standard JVM and the JSDA platform (which is entirely written in Java). The remainder of this section provides a brief description of JSDA architecture and concepts.

2.2 Overview of JSDA

The distributed object model in JSDA has similarities with RMI and CORBA. The idea is that a distributed object consists of a *master object* (that resides on a machine that we call the *owner* of that object) plus *ambassador objects (stubs)* that provide access to the master object from any host in the distributed system.

One of the key differences between JSDA and RMI or CORBA is that master objects are associated to physical machines *at runtime* in JSDA. This is a natural consequence of the fact that JSDA tries to encourage and simplify distribution at the language level. On the other hand, RMI and CORBA are better suited to the idea of server objects that offer specific services on designated machines.

A JSDA distributed application is launched from a particular machine, called the *server host* for this application. Each machine that is willing to participate in this application logs onto the server host. When the distributed application is launched, a program called the *JSDA Kernel* or *runtime* runs on every participating host; the JSDA runtime is responsible for associating each master object with one of the machines that has joined the application. The other machines in the application receive *ambassador objects (stubs)* for this object when they need them. Thus a distributed object consists of one master object plus the stubs on other machines.

An ambassador object (stub) has several key roles:
1. It provides read/write access to the fields of the master object
2. It can execute methods of the master object on the local machine
3. It can initiate the execution for methods of the master object on any other machine

4. It provides synchronization features using the master object as a synchronization object

A special field – named *owner* – in each distributed class specifies the name of the machine where the master object was built, marking the difference between master and ambassador. This approach makes it possible to deal with distributed objects in a homogenous way; the code generated by JSDA does not have to distinguish between ambassadors and masters. JSDA decides at run-time whether a remote access is necessary or not and takes the necessary actions.

To keep the programming model as simple as possible, only two directives were added to the standard Java; their meaning is to force the execution of the an instruction (or block of instructions) on the specified host(s).

The two types of directives accepted are:
- **on <machine_name>** - this directive will force the execution of the following instruction or block on machine *<machine_name>*
- **foreach <machine_class_name>** - this directive will force the execution of the following instruction or block on all machines belonging to class *<machine_class_name>*

JSDA directives are embedded in Java as comments. The reason for choosing this syntax was to give the programmer the ability to run the code, without modification, on a single machine for debugging purposes. When the programmer is ready to run the code in a distributed manner, it is run through a JSDA Parser, which translates the directives into the necessary distributed code.

2.3 Garbage Collection

Garbage collection is the automatic reclamation of heap-allocated storage after its last usage by a program. An object is *garbage* if there are no longer any references to the object.

There are two main properties that ensure the correctness of a garbage collection algorithm:

1. **Liveness** – All objects that are no longer usable will be collected eventually.
2. **Safety** – No objects are still in use will be collected.

A **cycle** consists of a group of objects that refer to each other, but none of them is accessible from the application (they are all garbage). If the group spans multiple distributed spaces, this is a **distributed cycle**. A **conservative** garbage collector is one that does not enforce immediate reclamation of unreachable data. This is usually done for performance reasons, but it results in temporary **floating garbage**.

Some desirable properties of an ideal garbage collector are:
- Completeness – all objects (ideally including components of cycles), that are garbage at the start of a collection cycle should be reclaimed by its end
- Safety
- Concurrency – neither the application program nor the garbage collector should be suspended; distinct distributed collection processes should run concurrently.

- Efficiency – time and space costs should be minimal

Depending on the technique used, some of these features will be hard (or even impossible) to accomplish.

2.4 Distributed Garbage Collection

The main differences between non-distributed and distributed garbage collectors are caused by the main difference between local and distributed systems: the presence of a message passing mechanism in distributed systems. Message-based communication (over potentially unreliable connections) results in the following issues, which are specific to distributed garbage collectors:

- Race conditions.
- Additional overhead due to the message passing.
- Distributed cycles.

All these issues must be considered, but the first one mentioned above is particularly important since the correctness of the distributed algorithm depends on it.

3. Garbage Collection for JSDA

As mentioned in Section 2.2, JSDA uses a distributed object model that is based on stubs and skeletons (skeletons are called *master objects* in JSDA) – an approach similar to other popular architectures like CORBA and RMI. The functionality of a stub is basically to send and receive remote requests involving the object they are associated with.

3.1 Artificial References

JSDA creates **artificial references** to objects. These references are created by the JSDA runtime and are totally unrelated to the semantics of the distributed application and the user is not aware of them. Their existence prevents *any* object from being garbage collected. We will describe now how exactly the artificial references occur in JSDA.

The JSDA framework consists of two main components – a parser and a kernel (runtime). The parser generates distributed versions of all the Java classes required by the user's application (this includes the classes written by the user as well as the required classes that come with the Java platform). The JSDA Kernel is responsible for keeping track of the correspondence between global and local references by means of a global reference or id internal to JSDA which uniquely identifies each stub object on a host as part of a distributed object. This creates artificial references to each object in the system; these references will prevent them from being garbage collected. Thus there are data structures inside the JSDA Kernel that – unless modified – will prevent any garbage collector (local or distributed) from reclaiming JSDA objects.

3.2 Java Reference Objects

Java comes with a built-in local garbage collector, since the language does not allow explicit deallocation. In order to find a solution to the problem described above, we investigated the tools provided by the Java language to allow the programmer to obtain information about the garbage collection process.

Java platform version 1.2 came with a small new package (*java.lang.ref*) whose only goal was to provide some hooks to the garbage collector, using **reference objects**. A reference object is an object that does not prevent another object referred by it – called the **referent** – from being garbage collected once the local collector determined it is not reachable through normal references.

Besides reachable and unreachable objects, the Reference Objects API gives us strengths of reachability. We can have softly, weakly and phantomly reachable objects and gain a limited amount of interaction with the garbage collector according to the strength of reachability. Details of these can be found in (Pawlan, 1998) or in the full version of this work, (Dancus, 2001). We will refer to objects that are reachable by standard references as **strongly reachable**. We will call **weakly reachable** any object which is neither strongly reachable nor unreachable, since the differences among soft, weak, and phantom references are not essential to our discussion. We will refer to the corresponding references as **strong references** or **weak references**.

When a Reference object is created, two things may be specified:
1. The referent object (this is mandatory)
2. A **ReferenceQueue** object (optional)

If a reference object is registered to ReferenceQueue, the local Java collector will place the reference object in this queue when the reference field is cleared (is set to *null*). The reference field is the field that stores the link to the referent. Reference queues are used to find out when an object becomes weakly reachable so the program can take some action based on that knowledge.

3.3 The JSDA Garbage Collection Algorithm

Our goal is to use Reference Objects to implement distributed garbage collection. As discussed in Section 3.1, there are data structures inside the JSDA kernel that prevent JSDA objects from being garbage collected. The key idea is to use weak references instead of strong references whenever artificial references are created in JSDA. This rule alone does not solve the problem; applying it without additional mechanisms would solve the liveness problem but not the safety problem. We will need to create additional mechanisms to enforce the safety property. The following discussion presents a simplified version of our algorithm. A more complete discussion can be found in (Dancus, 2001)

Each master object has an associated reference list (a bitmap) that stores information about remote reachability for the object. More precisely, there will be one bit for each host in the system, and each host holding a reference to a stub for this object will have the corresponding bit in the reference list to be set to 1. When a stub for an object P is created on a host X, a **dirty** message is sent to the owner of P in order to set to 1 the corresponding bit (the bit for X) in P's master reference list. Similarly, a **clean** message will be send to P's owner whenever JSDA detects that a local garbage collector collected a stub for P, and the bit for X will be set to 0.

An Object Table on each host stores information about stubs and master object on that host. Entries for objects are identified as local (for masters) or non-local (for stubs) and indexed by the object ID. For stub objects, each entry also stores the host ID for the machine that owns the object and either a strong reference or a weak reference to the stub, and a counter that counts the number of on-going remote calls that passed this stub as a parameter. Entries for master objects also have a field that indicates whether the master object is weakly or strongly reachable via the Object Table, and a reference list (a bitmap) corresponding to the list of hosts that hold strong references to this stub.

The hosts holding stub objects for a given object send update messages to the host with the master object, so the entry in the Object Table for the master object will accurately reflect the status of the stub objects on the various hosts.

When the entry for an stub object indicates that there are no outstanding remote method calls related to this stub, the local JSDA runtime changes the reference to the stub from a strong reference to a weak reference. If there are no other references to the stub from the application, then the stub will eventually be garbage collected by the local Java garbage collection,. The JSDA runtime will be notified that the stub has been garbage collected through the ReferenceQueue. When the stub is garbage collected then, as mentioned above, the local JSDA runtime sends a clean message to the host owning the corresponding master object. In response to this message, the JSDA runtime on the owner host updates the reference list (bitmap) for this object.

The JSDA runtime on the host owning a master object examines the bitmap for the master object to determine if all of the stub objects on other hosts have been garbage collected. If this is the case, then this object is no longer in use at any of the other hosts, and the reference from the Object Table to the master object can be changed from strong to weak, allowing it to be garbage collected.

In order to prevent a master object from being garbage collected while a dirty message is en route from another host, indicating that the ambassador object is now in use, the Object Table keeps strong references to all stubs passed as parameters of ongoing remote calls until those calls return. This ensures that if a stub needs to created on some host as part of remote call, then the corresponding dirty message will reach the owner host before a clean message from the host originating the call. In multithreaded applications, it is likely that there will be simultaneous calls involving the same stubs; therefore strong references to stubs must not be changed *automatically* to weak references upon returns from remote calls involving the stubs. The counter field mentioned earlier is inspected in order to make sure that there are no threads currently manipulating the object. Only if there are no such threads is the reference to that object's stub changed to weak.

Thus the use of Reference Objects allows the JSDA runtime to exercise control over when the local garbage collectors collect stub and master instances of distributed objects.

4. Conclusions and Future Work

We have designed a distributed garbage collection algorithm for Java and implemented it in the JSDA framework. The full version of this work (Dancus, 2001) describes testing and a proof of correctness for this algorithm. Our algorithm does not collect distribut ed cycles; we believe that this functionality cannot be obtained with the current functionality available in Java.

As a result of this implementation, we have demonstrated that the limited interaction with the local collector offered by the java.lang.ref package is sufficient to build a distributed garbage collector. In addition, this algorithm can be implemented for any object-oriented language offering features similar to the Reference Objects API.

We have designed the algorithm to be efficient in terms of network and CPU overhead. Accurate performance measurements will be desirable as a future step of the evaluation of our approach. The fault tolerance of the algorithm should also be investigated.

5. References

Aridor, Y., Factor, M., Taperman A. (1999) "cJVM: a Single System Image of a JVM on a Cluster", *Proceedings of the 1999 International Conference on Parallel Processing*, 4-11, Wakamatsu, Japan

Bellifemine, F., Poggi, A., Rimassa, G. (1999) "JADE – A FIPA-compliant agent framework", CSELT Internal Technical Report, available at *http://sharon.cselt.it/projects/jade/*

Black, A., Hutchinson, N., Jul, E. and Levy, H. (1986) "Object Structure in the Emerald System", *Proceedings of the 1986 Conference on Object-Oriented Programming Systems, Languages, and Applications (OOPSLA)*, Portland, OR, USA

Dancus, A. (2001) "Garbage Collection for Java Distributed Objects", M.S. Thesis available at *http://www.wpi.edu/Pubs/ETD/*. Worcester Polytechnic Institute, Worcester, MA, USA

Linda Group, *http://www.cs.yale.edu/Linda/linda.html*

OMG (Object Management Group) (2001) "The Common Object Request Broker: Architecture and Specification. Rev.2.6", available at *http://www.corba.org*

Pawlan, M. (1998) "Reference Objects and Garbage Collection", available at *http://developer.java.sun.com/developer/technicalArticles/ALT/RefObj/*

Sun Microsystems (1999) "Java Remote Method Invocation Specification. Rev.1.3.0", available at *ftp://ftp.java.sun.com/docs/j2se1.3/rmi-spec-1.3.ps*

Teodorescu, R., Dancus, A., and Handorean, R. (1999) "Java Support for Distributed Applications (JSDA)". *Graduation Thesis. Politehnica University of Bucharest (PUB)*, Bucharest, Romania

The design of a Reliable Multipeer Protocol in Java for Internet based Distributed Virtual Environments.

Gunther Stuer, Jan Broeckhove, Frans Arickx

University of Antwerp
Department of Mathematics and Computer Sciences
Groenenborgerlaan 171, 2020 Antwerp, Belgium
gunther.stuer@ua.ac.be

Abstract

We present the design and implementation of a Reliable MultiPeer Protocol (RMPP). This protocol is suitable for applications in the area of distributed virtual environments and is written in JAVA. Motivation, protocol classification, design goals and the error recovery algorithm are discussed. Furthermore, some implementation issues are listed. This paper concludes by presenting two possible applications of the RMPP.

Keywords

Java, Distributed Virtual Reality, Reliable Multipeer

1.Introduction

One of the main bottle–necks in virtual environments has always been the availability of sufficient network bandwidth to allow the participating objects to communicate with each other (Zyda, 1996). With the introduction of multicasting this problem was partly solved, but traditional multicast protocols are all based on best effort approaches, i.e. message delivery is not guaranteed. In order to achieve this guarantee, reliable multicast protocols were introduced (Hall, 1994). Although there are already many such protocols, none is optimised for distributed virtual environments (DVE) (Birman, 1999). The most important problem is that in a typical DVE many nodes are simultaneously sending and receiving each other's information (Sato F, et al., 1999) and classic reliable multicast protocols are not designed to handle this situation. For this reason, the development of a Reliable Multipeer Protocol (RMPP) is an important contribution to the development of large DVEs. The RMPP is a member of the multipeer protocol family. This family generalizes the traditional multicast – one sender, many receivers – to the situation of many senders as well as many receivers (Wittman R., et al., 2000).

This paper describes the RMPP, in particular the algorithms involved in the protocol and a number of aspects of its design and development. In addition some applications of the RMPP are discussed.

2.Protocol Classification

In the classification of reliable multicast protocols (Obraczka, 1998), the one presented here is most closely related to the *Transport Protocol for Reliable Multicast* (TPRM) (Sabata B. et al, 1998). RMPP is a message based protocol which means that there is no stream between sender and receivers, but rather that a number of independent messages are transmitted. Every message consists of one or more packets, each one transmitted as a UDP datagram. The most important difference with TRPM is that RMPP is a multipeer protocol.

If one classifies on error correction schemes, RMPP is a *receiver–initiated* protocol (Levine B.N. et al, 1998), i.e. possible errors are detected by the receiver which informs the sender hereof through a negative acknowledgement (NACK). On reception the sender will re–transmit the erroneous or missing packets.

This type of protocol has two important drawbacks. The first one is the danger of a NACK implosion which can happen when multiple recipients detect that a packet is missing. They will all send a NACK for the same packet with a serious regression in network performance as a result. This problem can be solved by making all receivers wait a random amount of time before actually sending the NACK. If during this delay, they receive a NACK sent by another receiver, they drop their own request. A consequence of this solution is that all NACK requests and NACK responses have to be multicasted to warn all interested recipients.

The second problem is that in theory these protocols need an infinite amount of memory because you never can be sure whether all receivers correctly received a certain datagram. This problem is solved heuristically by assuming that in a virtual environment old messages have lost their importance and can be dropped.

The opposite of *receiver–initiated* protocols are *sender–initiated* protocols where the sender is responsible for handling errors or missing packets. To do this, the sender maintains a list of all clients and after each transmission every client has to send an acknowledgement (ACK). If one is missing, an error has occurred and unacknowledged datagrams are re–transmitted. This type of protocol does not exhibit the two problems stated above, but is not very scalable due to the large amount of ACKs.

3.The Protocol

When one wants to recover from an erroneous or missing packet, it is very important to have a way to uniquely identify this packet. In the RMPP this is done in three steps.

The first one is at the level of the VR–participants. Each one is identified by a unique ID, which is basically a random 32–bit number generated during construction. Every datagram transmitted will contain this ID. In this way the receiver can determine which VR–participant sent the datagram. Every datagram also contains a *message sequence number* (MSN) which uniquely identifies every message sent by a given participant. So, the combination (*nodeID, MSN*) uniquely identifies every message in the system. The third level of identification is the *packetNr*. This one uniquely identifies every packet within a message. As such, the 3–tuple (*nodeID, MSN, packetNr*) uniquely identifies every datagram in the system.

Whenever a gap is detected between messages received from the same node, or between two packets from the same message, a *NACK–request* is sent for every message involved. When a whole message is missing, the *NACK–request* contains its *MSN,* and the requested *packetNr* is set to 1, since there is always at least one packet in every message. When one or more packets from a certain message are missing, the *NACK–request* contains this messages *MSN* and a list of all missing *packetNrs*. The sender will re–transmit all packets it receives a *NACK–request* for. These are known as *NACK–response* packets.

When the first packet of a given message arrives, a new empty message is created at the receiver side and its timer is set to *receiveTimeout*. Whenever another packet for this message arrives, it is added to the message and the timer is reset. When the timer reaches zero, the RMPP assumes all unaccounted packets lost and sends a *NACK–request* for them. If however all packets were received, the message is considered to be complete.

When a *NACK–request* is sent, the timer of the error producing message is set to *nackTimeout*. If no *NACK–response* is received before the timer ends, another *NACK–request* is sent. This goes on until *maxRequests NACK–requests* have been transmitted after which the message is considered lost and removed from the system. If on the other hand a *NACK–response* is received, the timer is reset to *recvTimeout* and the algorithm starts all over agin.

The sender keeps every message in memory for *sendTimeout* seconds. This timer is reset with every incoming *NACK–request*. When it reaches zero, the sender assumes that all receivers did receive the message correctly and removes it from memory. Figure 1 describes the protocol.

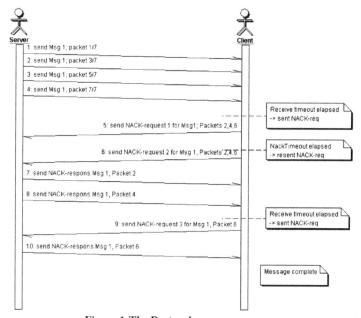

Figure 1:The Protocol

Each of the timers *RecvTimeout, NackTimeout* and *SendTimeout* is responsive to the frequency with which timeouts occur. If timeouts are frequent the timeout–interval is lengthened. If on the other hand the timer is frequently reset while there is a significant amount of spare time left, the timeout–interval is shortened. This approach matches the timeout–interval to current operating conditions and optimized responsiveness. This is also the technique that ensures that fluctuations in the responsiveness of Java due to garbage collection and datastructure optimizations do not destabilize the protocol.

4.Design Goals

The primary goal of this research project was the creation of a reliable multipeer system optimized for distributed virtual environments written in Java. As a reference platform we used VEplatform (Demuynck, 2000), a 100% distributed VR–framework developed in C++ at the university of Antwerp. Note that the 100% distributability rules out the use of tree–based reliable multicast protocols like TRAM developed by Sun Labs (Chiu D.M., et al., 1998) which is a part of Sun's JRMS–project (Hanna S., et al., 1998). The secondary goal was to emphasise on good design. We considered the architectural aspect to be more important than top notch performance. To achieve this, we extensively used object oriented techniques, UML (Pooch G. et AL, 1999) and design patterns (Grand M, 1998).

The fact that this protocol is tuned for virtual environments has three interesting consequences:

1. The frequency with which VR–nodes send updates has a maximum of 30 messages a second (Brutzman D.P., et al, 1995) because this implies one message for every screen update. When one uses dead–reckoning algorithms it is possible to reduce the update frequency to an average of 1 message a second (Demuynck K, 1998). This maximum and average value allows for the optimization of the data–structures.
2. The size of a typical VR–message is usually less than 1 KB because only the position, orientation and some state information is transmitted. This made it possible to optimize buffer sizes.
3. After a certain amount of time, an update message is of no importance anymore since the object that sent it probably already altered one or more of the transmitted parameters. This is why *old* messages may be dropped.

As an implementation language we had to choose between C++, the language used to implement VEplatform, and Java. After carefully considering the benefits and drawbacks of both, we chose for Java. Its benefits are:

1. Java is a very expressive language with many standard class libraries. This allows for the construction of complex applications with much less code than C++.
2. Java's syntax and semantics are much more clear than those of C++ which enhances the quality of the produced code.
3. Java has built in features such as threading and dynamic class loading that are extensively used in our design.

The drawbacks of using Java are:

1. Java applications are not the most performant. Although serious advances have been made, C++ is still faster. It is however our belief that this obstacle will slowly resolve as better compilers and interpreters become available.
2. Java was never intended for real–time applications. This can be observed when monitoring the behaviour of the garbage collector and the collections framework. The RMPP depends heavily on timers to decide when to take action. Java however gives no guarantees whatsoever about their correct behaviour. The specifications state e.g. that the method *sleep(x)* will cause the thread to sleep *at least* x milliseconds. In situations where one needs an immediate response to some action, such as handling a NACK, the garbage collector and collections framework overhead can be very problematic. However, a solution to this problem has been found and will be discussed in the next section

5.Implementation Problems & Solutions

In this section, the different pitfalls one can encounter when constructing an RMPP will be described. In four subsequent revisions, design and implementation solutions to problems encountered were accounted for. The current version seems to perform as expected.

5.1 Initial design

The very first design was conceptually the most pure one. Every message had its own thread (Kleiman S., et al., 1996) which took care of this object's timer. This strongest points of this design were its pureness and transparency. But unfortunately, some problems were encountered that led to erratic behaviour.

The first one is that the creation of a Java thread takes about 1.5 ms (Lewis B., Berg D.J., 2000). Let *st* be the *sendTimeout*, ms_i the *maxSending* value of node i, *n* the amount of nodes and *rt* the *receiveTimeout*, then the following formula tells us how many threads are active in the system

$$st * ms_0 + rt * \sum_{i=1}^{n} ms_i$$

at any given moment. A very plausible situation is that there will be 10 nodes, each sending 30 messages a second. Typical values for *sendTimeout* and *recvTimeout* are respectively 30 seconds and 1 second. One can see that in this case, the system contains 1200 threads, of which each second 330 die and 330 new ones are created. If it takes 1.5 ms to create a single thread, the RMPP spends half of its time constructing threads.

The second problem is that there are many differences between threading libraries on different platforms. The most important differences are in the area of thread scheduling. Since the protocol depends on quick responses when e.g. a *NACK–request* is sent, this can have a devastating effect on protocol stability.

This is why this initial design attempt can best be seen as a *proof of concept implementation* (Stuer G., et al, 1999).

5.2 The thread pool

To solve the thread creation problem mentioned above, a thread pool was used. When the application starts, the size of the thread pool is determined and it is populated with sleeping threads. Whenever a thread is needed, one is removed from the pool and reinserted when no longer needed. When additional threads are requested, the pool is expanded.

With these changes, the RMPP became much faster (Stuer G., et al, 2001), but stability remained an issue. Whenever the protocol was tuned for one OS, its behaviour was problematic on other platforms.

5.3 A new design

To solve the stability problem, a whole new design was necessary (Stuer G., et al, 2001). Instead of assigning one thread to each message, the RMPP now has a *Timer–Thread*. All messages wanting to be notified after some period of time can register themselves with this timer. When the requested period is over, they are informed of this using a call–back mechanism. However, this *timer* turned out to be a bottle–neck because the data structures used to construct it were not fast enough to handle the large amount of requests needed.

With this new design, the protocol was stable under all tested operating systems, but due to the bottlenck not as performant as it could be. The drawback is that part of the original design elegance is gone.

5.4 A Final Optimization

By taking into account the fact that most VR–messages are small and fit in a single datagram, a final and important optimization could be achieved. On reception of such a message, the *recvTimeout* notification can be omitted since we already have the complete message. By doing this, the last remaining bottle–neck is solved because the load on the *Timer–Thread* is now significantly reduced.

6.Applications

In this section we will discuss two possible applications of the RMPP. Both are components to be used in a highly dynamical distributed virtual environment.

6.1 Probe Classes

The best technique to make a virtual environment scalable is to make sure that each participant only receives the information it is interested in. One way to do this is to divide the world in regions where each region has its own multicast group (Morse K.L., 1996). All objects in the same region transmit their updates on the same multicast group. Another, still experimental, but better method is described in what follows.

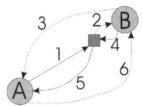

Figure 2:Probe classes

Consider virtual world that are not divided in fixed regions, but where objects cluster dynamically dependent on some criteria. This can be implemented using a fuzzy clustering algorithm (Looney C., 1999). Each cluster then corresponds to one multicast group. Participants decide periodically which set of objects they are interested in, and thus to which multicast groups they should listen.

The technique that makes this approach possible is that of *probe–classes*. The protocol is described in figure 2. An object (A) multicasts a probe–class (1) to all participating objects (B). The probe–class gives B information about A so that B can decide whether it wants to listen to A (3) or not. After this, the probe–class receives information from B so it can decide whether A would be interested in B or not. If so, the multicast address of B is transmitted to A (5) and A starts listening (6). This technique allows for asymmetric interests, e.g. it is possible for A to listen to B, but not the other way around.

Every time a parameter used in the decision making process changes out of a preset range, an updated probe–class is fired to notify all objects of the change in state. As an example one can assume a three dimensional system. Two objects are interested in each other when their distance is less than 100 units. An object launches a new probe whenever it moved 10 units from its previous launch position. An example of an asymmetric interest would be when one participant is looking through a binocular while the other is not.

6.2 Object Mirroring

Object mirroring is a possible strategy to minimize communications in a distributed virtual environment. One can use the RMPP to multicast the VR–objects to all interested nodes. With the use of Java classloading it is possible to create a local object from this stream of bytes. This local object serves as a *proxy* for the original one. Figure 3 illustrates this principle where object A gets replicated to objects A' at the receiver sides.

Figure 3: VR–Object Mirroring

All communication between the original object and its proxies also relies on the RMPP system. An XML message is transmitted which consists of two parts. The first one identifies the target object and the second part contains the actual message. Using this technique, the virtual world is extremely expandable because each type of object (e.g. table, avatar, room, ...) can define its own message scheme. This way one does not need to specify the complete protocol when designing the virtuel environment.

7.Conclusions

Our contribution in this paper has been to develop a Reliable MultiPeer Protocol (RMPP). This protocol is geared towards applications in the area of multi user DVEs. To achieve our design goals – in particularly scalebility and 100% distributability – a receiver initiated protocol was used. We have found that the advantages of implementing the RMPP in Java outweighs the disadvantages. The performance penalty was well within the targeted limits.

8.References

Birman, K.P. (1999), "A Review of experiences with reliable multicast", *Software – Practice and Experience*, Vol. 29, No. 9, pp 741–774.

Booch G., Rumbaugh J., Jacobson I. (1999), "The Unified Modeling Language User Guide", *Addison–Wesley*.

Brutzman D.P., Macedonia M.C., Zyda, M.J. (1995), "Internetwork Infrastructure Requirements for Virtual Environments", *proceedings of the 1995 symposium on Virtual Reality modeling languages*.

Chiu D.M., Hurst S., Kadansky M., Wesley J. (1998), "TRAM: A tree–based Reliable Multicast Protocol", *Sun Research Technical Report TR–98–66*.

Demuynck K., Arickx F., Broeckhove J. (1998), "The VEplatform system: a system for distributed virtual reality", *Future generation Computer Systems*, No 14, pp 193–198.

Demuynck K. (2000), "The VEplatform for distributed virtual reality", *PhD. Thesis*, University of Antwerp, Belgium.

Grand M. (1998), "Patterns in Java, volume 1", *John Wiley & Sons*.

Hall, K.A. (1994), "The implementation and Evaluation of Reliable IP Multicast", *Master of Science Thesis*, University of Tennessee, Knowville, USA.

Hanna S., Kadansky M., Rosenzweig Ph. (1998), "The Java Reliable Multicast Service: A Reliable Multicast Library", *Sun Reseach Technical Report TR–98–68*.

Kleiman S., Shah D., Smaalders B. (1996), "Programming with threads", *SunSoft Press*.

Levine B.N., Garcia–Luna–Aceves J.J. (1998), "A comparison of reliable multicast protocols", *Multimedia Systems*, Vol. 6, pp. 334–348.

Lewis B., Berg D.J. (2000), "Multithreaded programming with Java technology", *Sun Microsystems Press*.

Looney C. (1999), "Fuzzy Clustering: A new algorithm", *Proceedings of INCOSE'99*.

Morse K.L. (1996), "Interest Management in Large–Scale Distributed Simuations", *Irvine University of California Technical Report* ICS–TR–96–27.

Obraczka K. (1998), "Multicast Transport Protocols: A survey and taxonomy", *IEEE Communications Magazine*, pp 94–102.

Sabata B., Brown M.J., Denny B.A. (1998), "Transport Protocol for Reliable Multicast: TRM", *Proceedings of IASTED International Conference on Networks*, pp. 143–145.

Sato F., Minamihata K., Fukuoka H., Mizuno T. (1999), "A reliable multicast framework for distributed virtual reality environments", *proceedings of the 1999 International Workshop on Parallel Processing*.

Stuer G., Broeckhove J., Arickx F. (1999), "A message oriented reliable multicast protocol for a distributed virtual environment", *Proceedings of Incose'99*.

Stuer G., Broeckhove J., Arickx F. (2001), "Design & Implementation of a reliable multicast protocol for distributed virtual environments written in Java", *Proceedings of EuroMedia2001*.

Stuer G., Broeckhove J., Arickx F. (2001), "Performance analysis of a reliable multicast protocol for virtual environments in Java", *Proceedings of the 2001 International Conference on Parallel and Distributed Processing Techniques and Applications*.

Wittmann R., Zitterbart M. (2000), "Multicast Communications", *Academic Press*, chapter 2.

Zyda, M.J. (1996), "Networking Large–Scale Virtual Environments", *Proceedings of Computer Animation'96*.

Distributed Genetic Algorithm with Multiple Populations using Multi-Agent for the TSP

Jung -Sook Kim[1]

[1]Dept. of Computer Science, Kimpo College
San 14-1, Ponae-ri, Wolgot-myun, Kimpo-si, Kyounggi-do, 415-870, Korea
e-mail : kimjs@kimpo.ac.kr

Abstract

Distributed genetic algorithms with multiple populations are difficult to configure because they are controlled by many parameters that affect their efficiency and accuracy. Among other things, one must decide the number and the size of the populations (demes), the rate of migration, the frequency of migrations, and the destination of the migrants. In this paper, I develop two dynamic migration window methods that control the size and the frequency of migrations. Increasing dynamic window size starts with 1, whenever the migration occurs, the window size increases the fixed number until the size is equal to 20% of population size. Second, whenever migration occurs window size varies at random from 1 to 20% of population size. In addition to this, I design new two genetic migration policies that select the destination of the migrants among the slave agents. Two genetic migration policies are reciprocal migration, and heuristic migration policy.

Keywords

Distributed genetic algorithm, Multi-agent, TSP(Traveling Salesman Problem), Multiple populations, Migration window size, Migration frequency, Migration Policy

1. Introduction

In the traveling salesman problem, a set of N cities is given and the problem is to find the shortest route connecting them all, with no city visited twice and return to the city at which it started. In the symmetric TSP, $distance(c_i, c_j) = distance(c_j, c_i)$ holds for any two cities

c_i and c_j , while in the asymmetric TSP this condition is not satisfied.

Since TSP is a well-known combinatorial optimization problem and belongs to the class of NP-complete problems, various techniques are required for finding optimum or near optimum solution to the TSP(Gerhard, 1997). The dynamic programming and the branch-and-bound algorithm could be employed to find an optimal solution for the TSP. In addition to the classical heuristics developed especially for the TSP, there are several problem-independent search algorithms which have been applied to the TSP for finding near optimum solution, such as genetic algorithm(David, 1998; Zbigniew, 1995), ant colonies, neural networks and simulated annealing(Colorni et al.; Terry and Stephanie, 1995). And parallel and distributed systems have emerged as a key enabling technology in modern computing. During the last few years, many distributed algorithms are designed in order to reduce the execution time for the TSP with exponential time complexity in the worst case(Erick, 1995; Erick, 1997a; Macro).

Software agents can be classified in terms of a space defined by three dimensions of intelligence, agency and mobility. Currently agent systems generally do not exploit all the capabilities classified by three dimensions. For example, multi-agent systems of distributed artificial intelligence try to execute a given task using a large number of possibly distributed but static agents that collaborate and cooperate in an intelligent manner with each other(http://www.cs.tcd.ie/research_gropus/aig/areab.html).

Under the right circumstances, I propose a new distributed genetic algorithm with multiple populations using master-slave multi-agent model for the TSP. Distributed genetic algorithm is based on the distributed population structure that has the potential of providing better near optimal value and is suited for parallel implementation. And distributed genetic algorithm executes a conventional genetic algorithm on each of the distributed populations. But the distributed genetic algorithm with multiple populations is difficult to configure because they are controlled by many parameters that affect their efficiency and accuracy. Among other things, one must decide the number and the size of the populations, the rate of migration, the frequency of migrations, and the destination of the migrants. In this paper, I develop two dynamic migration window methods that control the size and the frequency of migrations. In addition to this, I design new two genetic migration policies that select the destination of the migrants among the slave agents.

The rest of this paper is organized as follows. Section 2 presents the related works and section 3 explains two dynamic migration window methods, and section 4 describes the two genetic migration policies. Section 5 summarizes the methods of the experiments. The remaining section presents the conclusion and outlines areas for future research.

2. Related works

2.1 Genetic algorithm

The classification of parallel genetic algorithms is the global parallelization, coarse-grained parallel genetic algorithm and fine-grained parallel genetic algorithm. The coarse-grained parallel genetic algorithm is divided into multiple populations or demes that evolve isolated from each other most of the time, but exchange individuals occasionally. This exchange of individuals is called migration and, as we shall see in later chapters, it is controlled by several parameters(Erick, 1997b).

The studies on genetic algorithms for the TSP provide rich experiences and a sound basis for combinatorial optimization problems. Major efforts have been made to achieve the following. 1. Give a proper representation to encode a tour. 2. Devise applicable genetic operators to keep building blocks and avoid illegality. 3. Prevent premature convergence. Permutation representation has an appeal not only for the TSP but also for other combinatorial optimization problems. This representation may be the most natural representation of a TSP tour, where cities are listed in the order in which they are visited. The search space for this representation is the set of permutations of the cities. For example, a tour of a 17-city TSP $1 - 2 - 3 - 4 - 5 - 6 - 7 - 8 - 9 - 10 - 11 - 12 - 13 - 14 - 15 - 16 - 17$ is simply represented as follows: <1 2 3 4 5 6 7 8 9 10 11 12 13 14 15 16 17>. The strength of genetic algorithms arises from the structured information exchange of crossover combination of highly fit individuals. Until recently, three crossovers were defined for the path representation, PMX(Partially-Mapped), OX(order), and CX(cycle) crossovers. OX proposed by Davis builds the offspring by choosing a subsequence of a tour one parent and preserving the relative order of cities from the other parent. During the past decade, several mutation operators have been proposed for permutation representation, such as inversion, insertion, displacement, and reciprocal exchange mutation. Reciprocal exchange mutation selects two positions at random and swaps the cities on these positions. The reproduction simply copies the selected parents of all genes without changing the chromosome into the next generation. Selection provides the driving force in a genetic algorithm, and the selection pressure is critical in it. In rank selection, the individuals in the population are ordered by fitness and copies assigned in such a way that the best individual receives a predetermined multiple of the number of copies than the worst one. TSP has an extremely natural evaluation function: for any potential solution (a permutation of cities), we can refer to the table with distances between all cities and we get the total length of the tour after $n-1$ addition operations.

2.2 Multi-agent

The various agent technologies existing today can be classified as being either single-agent or multi-agent systems. In single-agent systems, an agent performs may communicate with the user as well as with local or remote system resources, but it will never communicate with other agents. In contrast, the agents in a multi-agent system not only communicate with the user and system resources, but they also extensively communicate and work with each other, solving problems that are beyond their individual capabilities. Distributed problem solving is applied to a multi-agent system in order to solve the coordination and cooperation problems central to the society of agents. Moreover, negotiation, which plays a fundamentals role in human cooperative activities, is required to resolve any conflicts that may arise. Such conflicts may arise while agents are trying to complete against each other or trying to collaborate with each other to build a shared plan, thus giving rise to two different types of agents participating in a multi-agent systems, competitive agents and collaborative agents. Competitive agents : Each agent's goal to maximize its own interests, while attempting to reach agreement with other agents. Collaborative agents : In contrast to the above, collaborative agents share their knowledge and beliefs to try maximize the benefit of the community as a whole.

3. Two dynamic migration window methods and the frequency of migrations

A new distributed genetic algorithm with multiple populations using master-slave multi-agent model for the TSP is illustrated in Figure 1.

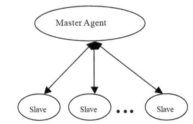

Figure 1: Distributed genetic algorithm structure

In the master-slave multi-agent model, master agent generates the population and divides them into subpopulations and then sends them to slave agents. The slaves execute a conventional genetic algorithm on their subpopulation and periodically return their best partial results to the master process. And the master agent applies the genetic migration policies to select the destination of the migrants and controls the dynamic migration window size. Then master agent sends the results to slave agents. The migration occurs per a fixed number of generation rather than each generation to reduce the communication time. The number of slaves is variable for large population in order to get more near optimal

solution. Good individuals migrate and the migrants replace bad individuals.
Two dynamic window methods are following.

3.1 Increasing dynamic migration window

The starting dynamic window size for the migration is 1, whenever the migration occurs, the migration window size increases a fixed number until the size is equal to 20% of population size.

3.2 Variable dynamic migration window

Whenever the migration occurs, dynamic window size varies at random. The variation is from 1 to θ. The θ value is generated at random within 20% of the population size per each migration. For example, first window size is 3 and second is 5, etc.

3.3 Frequency of migrations

There is interesting question being raised : when is the right time to migrate? If migration occurs too early during the run, the number of correct building blocks in the migrants may be too low to influence the search on the right direction and we would be wasting expensive communication resources.

In the distributed genetic algorithm, migration occurs at predetermined constant interval and occurs after the demes converge completely, but I experiment with a "delayed" migration scheme. As the number of generation increase, migration interval is short in order to alleviate the problem of converging prematurely to a solution of low quality.

4. Two genetic migration policies

I design new two genetic migration policies that select the destination of the migrants among the slave agents. Two genetic migration policies are reciprocal migration policy and heuristic migration policy.

4.1 Reciprocal migration policy

The reciprocal migration policy operates similar to a reciprocal exchange mutation in genetic algorithm. It selects two slave agents at random and then migrates the individuals on these agents.

4.2 Heuristic migration policy

Step 1. Pick up λ slave agents at random.
Step 2. Generate neighbors according to all possible permutations of the selected agents.
Step 3. Evaluate all neighbors and select the best one as destination of the migrants.

5. Experiments

The hardware used is a collection of the PCs connected with a 100Mbit/sec Ethernet and all communications are implemented using C. This is a rather slow communication environment. The parameters of the genetic algorithm described in this experiment are shown in Table 1.

	Size and rates
Population size	Variable size
The number of generation	Variable size (50-100)
Crossover rate	0.6
Mutation rate	0.1
Inversion rate	0.1

Table 1: Parameters

TSP instances are taken from the TSPLIB. In the experiment, dynamic migration window size starts with 1, after the first migration, window size increase 1. So, window size become 2, continue until window size is equal to 20% of population. The second method, whenever migration occurs, the dynamic migration window size varies at random from 1 to a θ. The θ value is generated at random within 20% of the population size. The λ size is 3. And migration occurs per 30, 20 or 10 generations in order to reduce communication time rather than each generation.

I obtain slightly better results from variable dynamic migration window method than increasing dynamic migration window method. Table 2 shows the results using reciprocal migration policy.

Migration rates	0.1	0.2
Near optimal rates	1.0	1.01

Table 2: The result using reciprocal migration policy

Table 3 shows the results using heuristic migration policy.

Migration rates	0.1	0.2
Near optimal rates	1.0	1.02

Table 3: The result using heuristic migration policy

The choice of migrants is a greater factor in the convergence speed than the choice of replacements.

6. Conclusions and future works

TSP is a well-known combinatorial optimization problem and belongs to the class of NP-complete problems, various techniques are required for finding optimum or near optimum solution to the TSP.

This paper design a distributed genetic algorithm in order to reduce the execution time and obtain more near optimal using master-slave multi-agent model for the TSP. Distributed genetic algorithms with multiple populations are difficult to configure because they are controlled by many parameters that affect their efficiency and accuracy. Among other things, one must decide the number and the size of the populations, the rate of migration, and the destination of the migrants. In this paper, I develop two dynamic migration window methods that control the size and the frequency of migration. Also I design new two genetic migration policies that select the destination of the migrants among the slave agents.

In the future work, I will find more optimal dynamic migration window size, θ, and more efficient migration policy.

7. References

Colorni, M. Dorigo, F. Maffioli, V. Maniezzo, G. Righini, M. and Trubian, "Heuristics from Nature for Hard Combinatorial Optimization Problems", *Int. Trans. in Operational Research*, 3, 1, 1-21.

David, E.G(1998), *Genetic Algorithms: in Search and Optimization*, Addison-Wesley, pp.1-125.

Erick, C.P. and David, E.G(1995), "A Summary of Research on Parallel Genetic Algorithms", *IlliGAL Report No. 95007*.

Erick, C.P.(1997a), "Designing Efficient Master-Slave Parallel Genetic Algorithms", *IlliGAL Technical Report No. 97004*.

Erick, C.P.(1997b), "A Survey of Parallel Genetic Algorithm", *IlliGAL Technical Report 97003*.

Gerhard, R.(1994), *The Traveling Salesman Computational Solutions for TSP Applications*, Springer-Verlag, Berlin.

http://www.cs.tcd.ie/research_groups/aig/iag/areab.html, "Distributed Problem Solving in Multi-Agent Systems".

Marco, T., "Parallel and Distributed Evolutionary Algorithms : A Review", *http://www-iis.unil.ch*

Terry, J. and Stephanie, F.(1995), "Genetic Algorithms and Heuristic Search", *International Joint Conference on Artificial Intelligence*, January.

TSPLIB, *http://www.iwr.uni-heidelberg.de/iwr/comopt/soft/TSPLIB95/ATSP.html*.

Zbigniew, M.(1995), *Genetic Algorithms + Data Structures = Evolution Programs*, Springer-verlag, Berlin, pp. 209-237.

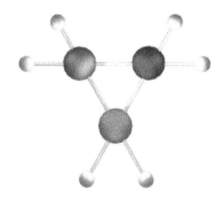

Chapter 7

Mobility

Protocol Stack Design for 3rd Generation Mobile Systems – UMTS Core Network

Theodore Stergiou, Professor Roger J. Green, Dr. Mark S. Leeson

Communications and Signal Processing Group, School of Engineering, University of
Warwick, Coventry, United Kingdom
e-mail: {esrua, rjg, msl}@eng.warwick.ac.uk

Abstract

In this paper we illustrate a new protocol stack, namely the FCNS (Future Core Networks System), primarily designed for carrying signalling information in the UMTS core network packet switched domain that will provide interoperability with the circuit switched domain and greater flexibility, robustness and security than the proposed schemes from the telecommunications community.

The paper is divided in sections, as follows. In the first section an introduction is given as to the current research undergoing by academic and commercial organisations and committees. We then move to analyse the proposed approaches depicting their disadvantages that constitute the motivation behind our work. A detailed overview of the FCNS architecture is given explaining its features, capabilities and services offered. Finally we give some comparisons and description of the current work undergoing for the protocol and possible future enhancements.

Keywords

UMTS, core network, security, protocol design, FCNS

1. Introduction

Universal Mobile Telecommunications System (UMTS) is the de facto standard that will be used in order to introduce the third generation (3G) mobile systems to the subscribers. It constitutes the platform where services such as high-speed data, multimedia applications, videoconferencing, m-commerce and international roaming will be deployed.

UMTS is composed of three main sub-systems or components, which will together provide for the efficient and worldwide access to services by the users. These include the satellite system (defined as S-UMTS), the generic air interface (described in terms of the access network) and the fixed network (referred to as the core network). The latter, which is the network our research work is based upon, is comprised of systems such as optical networks, the Internet, telephony system, Local Area Networks (LANs) and ISDN systems.

Currently, there exist two architectures for the core network defined by the European Telecommunications Standards Institute (ETSI) and the Third Generation Partnership Program (3GPP), the Release 99 (3GPP,1998) and Release 4/5 (3GPP,2001). Release 4/5 is the all-IP version of the UMTS core network that will not be on effect until 2005, where UMTS services will be offered to home users after migrating from the currently used second generation (2G) systems. Release 99 on the other hand, whose architecture is depicted in

Figure 1, is based on the General Packet Radio Service (GPRS) platform allowing operators to fully utilise the capabilities and investments made for that system.

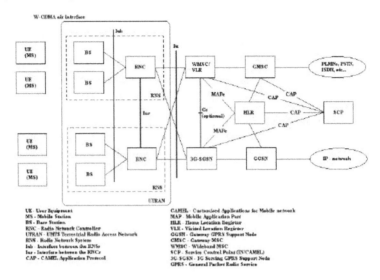

Figure 1: UMTS core network architecture, Release 99, reproduced by [1]

The proposed protocols to support the transfer of signalling information between the UMTS core network elements include the Mobile Internet Protocol (MIP), the Stream Control Transmission Protocol (SCTP) and Asynchronous Transfer Mode (ATM) protocol. In the following section we introduce the main disadvantages of these protocols, especially MIP/IP and further analyse the reasons for which the need of a new approach has been imperative.

2. Work Motivation

In the first part of this section we provide readers with a brief overview of MIP/IP (Ollikainen,1999) and the proposed protocols to act as its transport means, followed by the analysis of the problems associated with these standards.

2.1 MIP/IP overview

MIP is an enhanced version of IP optimised for use within mobile environments, where sophisticated routing mechanisms are required to support mobile hosts' connection throughout a call's duration. It defines procedures required to support the hosts of a mobile system irrespective of their point-of-attachment to the network and without altering their IP address. These techniques that ultimately compose what is known as triangular routing, forward the host's packets to its permanent home environment, which in turn forwards them to the network where the host belongs at the time. The packet routing is done via tunnelling, where modified IP packets encapsulating additional headers indicating the packets' original source and destination address are advanced between the agents, which are responsible for the forwarding of the user data.

Advantages of this approach include the case of the IPsec architecture, where encapsulation and tunnelling are governed by the use of the Authentication Header (AH) and Encapsulation Security Payload (ESP) protocols, which enhance packet security against malicious attacks, by authenticating and encrypting the IP packet's contents (Kent,1998).

For the UMTS core network there may be the need of using additional protocols in order to support the MIP broadband backbone mechanisms during the exchange of information between different networks. ATM and SCTP are two well-defined standards that commercial organisations may adopt if it is required that speeds greater than the primary rate (i.e. well above 2Mbit/s) need to be supported.

SCTP is a general-purpose transport protocol initially designed to support telephony signalling over unreliable networks, such as IP. Its services include multihoming enabling network to maintain a connection (association in SCTP terms) even when a route fails and a certain degree of protection against resource attacks by implementing a four-way connection establishment (handshake) mechanism. Its advantages over TCP are explained in (Steward et al,2000) with the most important being the message-based orientation of the protocol in contrast to TCP, which is connection-oriented, ensuring a more reliable and flexible transmission of small amounts of data, like signalling information.

2.2 Standard weaknesses

MIP has disadvantages associated with its performance when operating in a mobile environment, mainly during handoff sessions and when interoperability with other protocols is necessary. One of the main concerns of the Internet community is the triangular routing and the necessity of periodically advertising routing information to the nodes and agents present in the network. The authors in (Yap et al,2000) describe these problems in details proposing an enhanced version of MIP (Itinerant IP - IIP) that in a sense does not make use of mobile agents eliminating problems such as bottlenecks and delays that may be imposed during handoffs.

IIP makes use of the Point-to-point protocol (PPP) for internetworking purposes as well as the Dynamic Host Configuration Protocol (DHCP) servers in order to acquire IP addresses on demand, when a mobile node or the mobile station is on move. Both protocols have security flaws already exploited by their use in the computer systems, which makes them a less attractive solution for use in UMTS.

Furthermore location update procedures do not incorporate any kind of security mechanisms in order to ensure the authentication of the information passed to the base home register from the mobile node nor that between the register and the correspondent node. This may result in the information being compromised by an attacker who may for example wish to attack the correspondent node or even impersonate it.

ATM is a protocol designed for variable bit rate environments, operating at high speeds where network elements or nodes exchange real-time data, like video and audio. Its features include the capabilities of maintaining a connection via the Operation and Maintenance cells (OAM) and the choice between various service classes of service. ATM though does not incorporate any kind of security functions to ensure the secured packet flow in the network nor does it integrate a standard fault detection and correction mechanism for the mapping of IP/IIP or other messages into the ATM cells (Stergiou,1999). Additional protocols would add extra overhead to the messages and would also introduce the problem of interoperability with the ATM platform.

SCTP on the other hand makes use of enhanced handshake mechanism than TCP or ATM ensuring greater protection against potential attacks. Although SCTP is a protocol more suitable for use in mobile systems from the performance and security point of view, we have identified several deficiencies arising from its design and possible methods of implementation.

The handshake mechanism used in the connection establishment phase ensures that a node wishing to connect to a peer, really wants to establish the communication. The mechanism though does not ensure protection against passive attacks, where an attacker could monitor the channel and exploit the contents of the messages, which are sent unencrypted. Furthermore the protocol does not support protection against attacks targeting the Domain Name Server (DNS), which an attacker can overflow in order to gain access to the host names included in the INIT messages. Additionally, alert mechanisms are also sent unsecured and could be used by an attacker to exploit the network's vulnerabilities. Moreover man-in-the-middle attacks could be successful, where an intruder could be able to intercept and ultimately alter the messages exchanged in a communication. The protocol does not offer any kind of protection against such attacks that could result in a whole connection to be compromised. The use of IPsec and AH specifically could prevent, to a degree, the effect of such attacks, but there are problems associated with the IPsec architecture (Ferguson and Schneier,1999) that would also introduce delays and inter-operational problems due to the use of encapsulation. For protection against other attacks ESP could be used to ensure the security of the messages, yet as analysed in (Bellovin,1996) certain vulnerabilities (session high jacking attacks is typical example) degrade protocol's performance.

From our analysis we have concluded that there is a need for a protocol stack to support the transfer of signalling information in the UMTS core network that would offer greater flexibility, robustness and security than the proposed solutions.

3. FCNS protocol stack

In the following sections we present our solution, FCNS, outlining its architecture and design principles followed to realise the protocol. Its main advantage is that its implementation will result in vital information passed through the UMTS core network being sent securely in contrast to the Release99 platform, where data such as secret keys are sent in plaintext form, increasing potential security risks.

3.1 Architecture and layers analysis

FCNS is a packet-based protocol stack designed according to the OSI 7-layer model principle, decomposing the protocol into several layers, each of which performs specific tasks, which are independent from the other layers' tasks.

The protocol has not been designed solely for use within the UMTS core network; instead it can be used as the means of establishing a communication between users in any environment that is supported by the protocol. For this reason FCNS is composed of 5 layers, namely the User Defined layer (composed of the User-Defined presentation layer - UDpres, User-Defined session layer - UDses), Transmission layer (tx_layer), End-to-end layer (ee_layer), Security layer (sec_layer) and the physical layer (phys_layer). The relationship and interconnection of these layers is depicted in Figure 2.

The User-defined layer serves as the means of establishing a connection between two users belonging to a different network and environment, where both the semantics of the data to be exchanged must be defined as well as a session between these users, in order to enforce the necessary synchronisation and QoS functions for the data stream.

The Transmission layer has the job of ensuring the secured and reliable end-to-end transfer of signalling information between nodes belonging to different subnetworks. The functions supported by this layer include explicit flow control, QoS maintenance for a particular connection, segmentation and reassembly, if that is required, as well as security for the particular level of the connection, which the layer is responsible for. The message that is passed onto the End-to-end sublayer is encrypted according to the specifications and algorithms dictated by the Security layer. FCNS does not support connectionless operation of the network and includes mechanisms to support resynchronisation of the data stream. Typical examples of use are the transfer of information between a mobile node and its correspondent belonging in a different domain or network.

The End-to-end layer is similar to the network layer defined by the OSI model, responsible for the routing of FCNS packets between different subnetworks, checksum calculation for the error detection and correction mechanisms, error control, segmentation and reassembly, as well as providing for the links' and messages' security. The latter feature is again governed by the security layer that initiates the necessary mechanisms in order to secure the intermediate links between the end nodes. The End-to-end layer is also responsible for the signalling of errors to the system concerning the underlying subnetworks supporting a connection. Also, because Release99 is composed of a Circuit Switched Domain in addition to the Packet Switched Domain, this layer is responsible for the correct function calls to SS7 supporting a circuit switched connection.

The physical layer is a layer acting as an interface between the physical medium protocols and standards for data transmission and FCNS, more like the data link layer defined by the OSI 7-layer model. It is responsible for identifying the various communication media and appropriately format and synchronise the data stream before passing it onto the physical link. It is also responsible for monitoring the transmission of packets and ensures that they are delivered in the same order they have been sent.

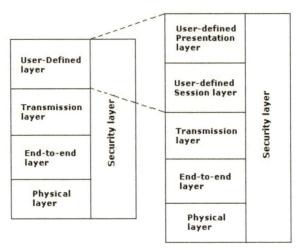

Figure 2: FCNS architecture

Finally, the security layer is the layer responsible for identifying and validating (authenticating) the nodes participating in a communication, as well as initiating, monitoring and terminating the security functions used for the communication links security. It also controls the encryption and decryption mechanisms for the various messages and packets exchanged either internally in FCNS or between network nodes, ensuring the secure update of mobile node information between its home and serving environment. It is the layer that acts as the interface between FCNS and the various network elements of the UMTS core network where all messages are authenticated prior to their transmission or upon their reception. Its simplicity and well-defined structure provides network operators with the advantage of ease in use and implementation of the layer within FCNS.

3.2 Advantages

In this subsection we present the advantages of our approach based on comparisons made with the protocols described in Section 2. Performance, flexibility, robustness and security are the main areas FCNS addresses and, hence, all evaluations of our protocol with the proposed standards are focused in these issues.

Security performance is the main issue for which FCNS has been designed in order to overcome the problems associated with SCTP, MoIP and ATM. Its strength lies in the security layer, which provides for the necessary functions and mechanisms, ensuring the secure functioning of the protocol under any operational environment.

FCNS does not suffer from the effects of man-in-the-middle attacks like SCTP where an adversary can intercept any message present in the communication link and either alter its contents or even deny the forwarding of that message to its intended destination. This is achieved by encrypting all the routes of the network, both on an end-to-end and link basis. Traffic padding functions enforced by security layer protect the network from passive attacks and hence possible interceptions. A 10-way handshake mechanism on the same time ensures the authentication of the hosts present in a communication further enhancing the protocol's capability of overcoming attacks targeted at the communication establishment time. FCNS makes use of the HLR/AuC of the UMTS core network in order to obtain all the information necessary to efficiently identify a host initiating or requesting a connection. The link security mechanisms enable the secure transfer of that information to the Visited Location Register (VLR) when the mobile host changes its environment during a handoff procedure. The use of the security layer is not limited to securing the communication links between the different nodes and subnetworks or to enforce the handshake mechanism during connection setup phase. The layer is responsible for ensuring that all messages generated by the FCNS error protocol are sent encrypted and never unsecured. This measure ensures that an attacker, if able to overcome the traffic padding mechanisms, could not be easily able to obtain information as to the contents of the messages and hence use those to manipulate with the protocol.

Another strength of the protocol is that the internal messages or service primitives are sent encrypted between the different layers of FCNS. 160-bit encryption keys are used in order to scramble the messages and provide an adequate level of security for the protocol. This approach has the advantage over attacks aimed at the protocol itself, where an attacker could manipulate the FCNS messages and be further able to force unauthorised requests for connection establishment or tearing down procedures.

Furthermore, FCNS as a protocol stack provides for a solid and robust architecture for use not only with the UMTS core network, but with any other architecture that is needed to be supported. FCNS is defined in layers that can either be used as single protocols or together forming the FCNS protocol stack. The need of interoperation with different protocols is eliminated, reducing the network's complexity and cost that would be required for the addition of extra logic and switches in a network topology. Moreover mapping procedures of messages created by different protocols require extra fault detection and correction mechanisms to guard the process, which may deemed unsuccessful under heavy network load.

Finally, the support of different addressing schemes makes FCNS compatible with most of the existing technology and hence an attractive solution for network operators wishing to enhance the security and overall performance of a given network.

4. Current status and future developments

Our research focuses on the development of FCNS and its comparison with the proposed protocols for the UMTS core network. The work involves the simulation of the UMTS core network using the IP based solution and then the FCNS solution. The comparisons and tests focus on performance and security issues, such as congestion, delays in the transmission, link errors and bandwidth (BW) limitations, timeouts and synchronisation issues, as well as authentication and encryption measures.

Such measurements include the relative efficiency of the protocol given for the various layers of FCNS, together with the representation of its overall performance. The calculated overall FCNS efficiency has been 92% (total of 676 bytes) for systems under normal operational modes.

Currently the protocol is subject to simulation-based evaluation separated in two phases. The first phase includes the simulation of FCNS in a computer environment to obtain a first set of measurements and then the second phase will utilise a more sophisticated test-bed emulating the UMTS core network Release99, in order to check the performance of the protocol in situations where shifting between the circuit- and packet-switched domains is necessary. There are measurements completed for packet delay times, round-trip delays and so on, with results pending on the efficiency and the quality of service offered by FCNS, as well as its security features compared to IPsec and relevant architectures.

The authors believe that FCNS is a strong candidate for use within the UMTS core network Release 99, which could be used instead of the various architectures and proposals made by the telecommunication society. An example of such a suggestion is given in (Kaaranen, 2001) where IP and the GPRS Tunnelling Protocol (GTP) are used in order to form the User Plane Protocol stack for the UMTS packet switched domain. The problems observed at the design of the Release 99, as mentioned in the sections 2 and 3, are, in part, associated with the use of various protocols for the different planes of the UMTS core network, which may lead to interoperability problems and reduced system's flexibility. FCNS as a solid and robust design could replace these proposals and form a more flexible and efficient architecture that could be further used in order to allow for the migration to the all-packet-switched philosophy of the Release 4/5. Its advantages and increased security performance over the proposed protocols, together with the delay in deploying the UMTS platform, could provide the opportunity of modifying the anticipated stacks and hence utilize all the features of FCNS, resulting in a stronger and more secure 3G mobile system.

5. References

3GPP (1998), Third Generation Partnership Program Specifications, "Technical Recommendation (TR) 21.101: 3rd Generation Mobile System Release 1999 Specifications", *Technical Specification Group Services and System Aspects.*

3GPP (2001), Third Generation Partnership Program Specifications, "Technical Recommendation (TR) 21.103: 3rd Generation Mobile System Release 5 Specifications", *Technical Specification Group Services and System Aspects.*

Bellovin, S.M. (1996), "Problem areas for the IP security protocols", *Proceedings of the 6th Usenix UNIX Security symposium*, San Jose, CA, U.S.A.

Ferguson, N., Schneier, B. (1999), "A Cryptographic evaluation of IPsec", *Counterpane Internet Security Inc.*, Counterpane Labs, California, U.S.A.

Kaaranen H., Ahtiaien A., Laitinen L., Naghian S., Niemi V. (2001), "UMTS Networks, Architecture, Mobility and Services", John Wiley & Sons Ltd., Chichester, England

Kent, S. (1998), "Security Architecture for the Internet Protocol", *IETF Request for Comments 2401*, Network Working Group, The Internet Society.

Stergiou T. (1999), "Fault detection in heterogeneous ATM/SDH systems", *MSc dissertation thesis*, University of Essex

Steward, R., Xie, Q. et al (2000), "Stream Control Transmission Protocol", *IETF Request for Comments 2960*, Network Working Group, The Internet Society.

Ville Ollikainen (1999), "Mobile IP explained", *Seminar on Multimedia*, University of Technology, Helsinki, Finland.

Yap, C.N., Kraner, M. et al (2000), "Novel and enchanced Mobile Internet Protocol for third generation cellular environments compared to MIP and MIP-LR", *IEE 3G Mobile communication technologies conference*, No. 471

An Enhanced Handoff Mechanism for Cellular IP

Jong-deok Kim, [1] Kyung-ah Kim, [1, 2] JaeYoon Park[2], Chong-kwon Kim[1]

[1] School of Electrical Engineering and Computer Science, SNU, Seoul, Korea
[2] Korea Telecom, Seoul, Korea
e-mail : kimjd@popeye.snu.ac.kr

Abstract

Handoff is one of the most important factors that may degrade the performance of TCP connections in wireless data networks. In this paper, we present a lossless and duplication free handoff scheme called LPM (Last Packet Marking) for improving Cellular IP semisoft handoff. LPM signals the safe handoff cue by sending a specially marked packet to mobile hosts. With this control packet, MH can adapt to network dynamics simply and efficiently. Our performance study shows that LPM achieves lossless packet delivery without duplication and increases TCP throughput significantly.

Keywords

Micro Mobility, Cellular IP, Hard Handoff, Semi-soft Handoff, Last Packet Marking

1. Introduction

Currently, there are many efforts underway to provide Internet services on integrated wireless and wireline networks. Supporting efficient IP mobility is one of the major issues to construct IP-based wireless access networks. Mobile users will expect the same level of service quality as wireline users. Even though access point of mobile user changes, IP connections should be maintained transparently. The Mobile Internet Protocol (Perkins, 1996, Johnson and Perkins, 2000) is the current standard for supporting global IP mobility in simple and scalable manner. But, in processing frequent handoffs in cellular based wireless access networks, Mobile IP has some limitations. After each migration, a new local address called the care-of address must be obtained and registered to a possibly distant home agent. This incurs increasing handoff latency and load on the global Internet, and mobile users suffer service degradation during the handoff period.

A number of solutions (Cambell, et al, 2000, Ramjee, et al, 1999, Mankin and Soliman, 2000) have been discussed to overcome these problems. These approaches are extending Mobile IP rather than replacing it. To handle local movement of mobile hosts without interaction with the Mobile-IP-enabled Internet, they adopt a domain-based approach. That is, these intra-domain protocols are used for establishing and exchanging the state information inside the wireless access networks, so as to get fast and efficient intra-domain mobility or *micro-mobility* control

Among these intra-domain mobility protocols, Cellular IP (Cambell, et al, 2000) attracts special attention for it's seamless mobility support in limited geographical areas. Since COA(Care-of-Address) is not changed in local mobility control, it eliminates the load for location update in the global Internet. And by using paging concept, Cellular IP provides simple location tracking scheme called cheap passive connectivity, which imposes neither traffic nor processing load on the global network as long as the host is idle, and preserves the power reserves of mobile nodes.

A previous study (Seshan, et al 1997) showed that the performance of TCP degrades significantly due to packet losses in frequent handoffs in small cell wireless networks. Cellular IP introduces *semisoft* handoff mechanism to reduce the number of lost packets. It establishes a routing path to the new BS (Base Station) before handoff, and temporarily bi-casts data to the both old (current) and new BS. The throughput of TCP using semisoft handoff is much better than that of hard handoff. Nonetheless, packet loss or packet duplication still can occur in Cellular IP semisoft handoff, which results in the degradation of TCP performance.

In this paper, we propose a simple handoff scheme called LPM (Last Packet Marking) for Cellular IP. LPM gives exact cue to mobile host for safe handoff to remove packet loss or packet duplication. This paper is structured as follows. In section 2, we briefly preview the Cellular IP handoff mechanism. In section 3, we describe last packet marking method for improving Cellular IP semisoft handoff. In section 4, we verify LPM by computer simulations. Finally, we conclude in section 5.

2. Review of Cellular IP

In Cellular IP, a group of BSs (Base Stations) forms one access network. Each access network attaches to the Internet via a gateway router. A BS, which provides wireless access service to MHs (Mobile Hosts), is a special-purpose router with mobility-related functions. Cellular IP assumes the tree network topology to simplify routing within an access network. An MH which visits a certain access network uses the IP address of the gateway router as its care-of-address. Within the access network, the MH is identified by its home address. Since COA (Care of Address) is not changed in local mobility control, Cellular IP eliminates the load for location update in global Internet.

Let us examine Cellular IP handoff schemes briefly. Cellular IP proposes *hard* and *semisoft* handoff. The *hard* handoff scheme, the basic handoff mechanism of Cellular IP, makes a new route to the new BS after real handoff. Hard handoff suffers from severe packet losses and results in performance degradation. To provide adequate performance to both TCP and UDP traffic while maintaining the lightweight nature of the base Cellular IP protocol, Cellular IP introduced a new handoff method called *semisoft* handoff. Prior to make a real handoff, an MH makes a brief connection to a new BS and sends a *semisoft request* packet. The semisoft request packet is forwarded toward the gateway router and eventually it reaches a crossover router which is a branching point of the path to the old BS and the path to the new BS. Receiving the semisoft request packet, the crossover node updates its route cache by adding the path to the new BS and starts to buffer packets destined to the MH in a delay device. The MH makes a real handoff after a pre-determined "semisoft delay". The MH issues a *route update* packet to the crossover node after the real handoff. The crossover node updates the route cache and transmits packets buffered in a delay device and packets arrived thereafter.

Since optimal semisoft delay cannot be predicted accurately, Cellular IP fixes the semisoft delay proportional to the maximum mobile-to-gateway round-trip delay. On various network topology and network traffic, applying constant semisoft delay may cause an MH to receive duplicated packets or to suffer packet losses. Duplicated packet does not disrupt many applications, but packet loss limits TCP's performance severely. To eliminate the packet loss, Cellular IP temporarily introduces a constant delay along the new path between the crossover node and the new BS using a delay device on the crossover node. So, just after a handoff, most MH suffers packet delay or duplication, which can cause quality degradation of real time traffic or can trigger TCP congestion control.

3. Last Packet Marking

We develop a new handoff scheme called LPM which can signal exact handoff initiation time to an MH. Overall LPM procedure is similar to the semisoft handoff in many aspects. As in Cellular IP, an MH sends a semisoft request packet to the new BS before making a real handoff. Receiving the semisoft request packet, a crossover node creates a mapping for the new path and forwards it to the gateway. LPM makes a distinction in that the crossover node sends a special control message called the *semisoft reply* to the old BS before multicasting data packets to both the new BS and the old BS. As the semisoft reply assures the MH that it has received all the packets that can be received only through the BS and it can receive following data packets from the new BS. So the semisoft reply can be used as a trigger for safe handoff by the MH. Therefore, receiving the semisoft reply through the old BS, MH initiates real handoff immediately rather than waiting for the expiration of constant semisoft delay as in Cellular IP.

Cellular IP introduces the crossover delay to synchronize the delay difference between the new path and the old path from the crossover node in case the new path is shorter than the old path. However this may introduce undesirable additional delay in many situations. LPM makes another distinction in that the crossover node sends data packets to the new BS immediately instead of buffering packets in its delay device for the constant crossover delay. In case packets sent to the new path arrive the new BS before the handoff, the new BS buffer them for fast delivery after handoff. This approach eliminates undesirable packet delay and packet duplication in many cases.

Cellular IP does not place any restriction on delaying a real handoff for the constant semisoft delay. However delaying a handoff would be restricted in real situations. Therefore there would be situations that an MH should make a real handoff even if it does not receive the semisoft reply, or it could make a real handoff only after it has received several data packets after the semisoft reply. The former case may result in the packet loss and the latter case may result in the packet duplication. To overcome these, we propose packet forwarding to the new BS by the old BS for the former case, and packet duplicate elimination at the new BS for the latter case. The old BS uses the semisoft reply as a delimiter for the packet forwarding to the new BS. That is, packets arrived at the old BS after the last packet mark will not be forwarded, which alleviates the forwarding overhead compared to the general forwarding mechanism proposed. As there is no sequence number in IP Header, the new BS uses a hash function to identify and eliminate the duplicated packets from its buffer.

Compared to Cellular IP, LPM only introduces a simple handoff signal, semisoft reply, that enables MH to adapt to the network topology and dynamics instead of using fixed parameters like semisoft, crossover delays, which results in no packet loss and duplication. In case delaying a handoff is constrained, which is not considered in Cellular IP, LPM makes use of efficient packet forwarding and duplicate elimination mechanisms which help to recover from packet loss and duplication.

4. Simulation Results

We used computer simulation for performance analysis. 2 network topologies are considered. One is shown in Figure 1-(a) where all possible MH-to-Gateway delays are same, and possible MH-to-Crossover node delays are also same before/after handoff. Determining proper parameters for semisoft delay and crossover delay would not be difficult in this situation. Actually, this topology is used for the performance study of Cellular IP (Cambell, et al, 2000). Another topology is shown in Figure 1-(b) where neither possible MH-to-Gateway delays nor possible MH-to-Crossover node delays before/after handoff are not same. Considering dynamic network delay due to short burst characteristics of data traffic and competing backgrounds traffics, we assert that this one would be more realistic.

N1 through N5 are Cellular IP nodes and N0 is the gateway. Each transmission delay of links is 5 ms. CN (Correspondent Node) transmits UDP or TCP traffic to MH from time 3. An MH oscillates between BS1 and BS5 at the constant speed from time 5. The MH stays for about 10 seconds before moving to the next BS. Cellular IP semisoft delay is fixed to 50 ms, and crossover delay to 20 ms.

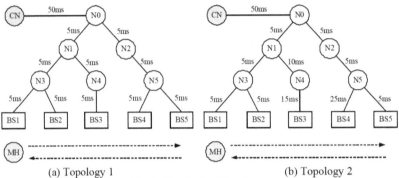

(a) Topology 1   (b) Topology 2

Fig. 1. Simulation Topologies

4.1 UDP Results

Table 1 and Table 2 show the number of lost packets and duplicated packets for UDP traffic in the topology 1 and the topology 2 each. The CN transmits a UDP packet every 5 ms. We compared the numbers of lost packets and duplicated packets of LPM with those of hard handoff and semisoft handoff. Note that LPM has no packet loss or duplication in both topologies. In hard handoff, it always suffers from the packet loss. The number of lost packets is proportional to the sum of the transmission delay from the new BS to the crossover node and the transmission delay from the crossover node to the old BS. Semisoft handoff shows no packet loss in topology 1. However it still suffers from packet duplication in topology 1. These packet duplications are caused by the crossover delay in the crossover node. With the longer crossover delay, the number of packet duplication would increase. Though it is not shown at the tables, end-to-end delay of each packet during handoff is also increased by the crossover delay, which is not suitable for the real-time multimedia application. In topology 2, the performance of semisoft handoff get aggravated, it suffers either from the packet loss or from the packet duplication. As fixed semisoft and crossover delay do not adapt to the network dynamics, they are too small (packet loss) in some cases and too large (packet duplication) in other cases.

Type	BS1→ BS2	BS2→ BS3	BS3→ BS4	BS4→ BS5	BS5→ BS4	BS4→ BS3	BS3→ BS2	BS2→ BS1
Hard	4/0	6/0	8/0	5/0	4/0	9/0	6/0	4/0
Semisoft	0/2	0/2	0/2	0/2	0/2	0/2	0/1	0/2
LPM	0/0	0/0	0/0	0/0	0/0	0/0	0/0	0/0

Table 1 : UDP Number of Lost and Duplicated packets on Topology1 (Lost/Duplicated)

Type	BS1→ BS2	BS2→ BS3	BS3→ BS4	BS4→ BS5	BS5→ BS4	BS4→ BS3	BS3→ BS2	BS2→ BS1
Hard	4/0	9/0	15/0	8/0	9/0	16/0	9/0	4/0
Semisoft	0/2	0/3	3/0	3/0	0/3	4/0	2/0	0/2
LPM	0/0	0/0	0/0	0/0	0/0	0/0	0/0	0/0

Table 2 : UDP Number of Lost and Duplicated packets on Topology2 (Lost/Duplicated)

4.2 TCP Results

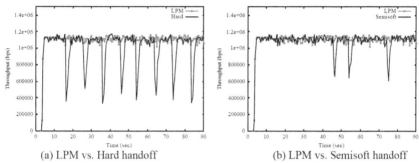

(a) LPM vs. Hard handoff   (b) LPM vs. Semisoft handoff

Fig. 2. TCP throughput on Topology 1.

Figure 2(a) shows TCP connection throughput of hard handoff and LPM as a function of time on topology 1. On every handoff, hard handoff shows abrupt drops caused by lost packets. It is well known that a packet loss decreases the TCP performance significantly due to the TCP congestion control. Figure 2(b) shows TCP connection throughput of semisoft handoff and LPM as a function of time on topology 1. Although semisoft handoff improves the number of abrupt drops, semisoft can't get rid of all drops. On the other hand, LPM shows no throughput drops on every handoff.

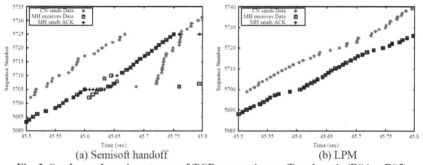

(a) Semisoft handoff   (b) LPM

Fig. 3. Sender and receiver traces of TCP connection on Topology 1. (BS4 to BS5)

In figure 3(a), TCP packet traces of the sender and the receiver around 45.6 are shown. Abrupt drops of throughput on semisoft handoff are caused by duplicated packets, which had been buffered in crossover node. An MH receives packets which had been received from old BS. Although UDP shows duplicated packet at most 2, TCP traffic is relatively burst than

UDP traffic, the number of packet duplication is more than UDP. As TCP uses the accumulated ACK mechanism, rather than relying only on the time-out mechanism, it uses sequential duplicate ACKs more than 3 as an indication of packet loss. If a TCP receiver receives packets which had been already received, it may generate duplicate ACKs that trigger the congestion control of the sender. The MH starts real handoff at 45.6 and starts receiving packets from the new BS at 45.61. Through 45.61 and 45.63, the MH receives packets that had already received from old BS and sends more than 3 duplicate ACKs to CN. CN interprets these duplicated ACKs as a signal of packet loss, it sends that packet again and starts congestion control at 45.68. Whereas semisoft suffers packet duplication, LPM shows no duplication (figure 3(b)).

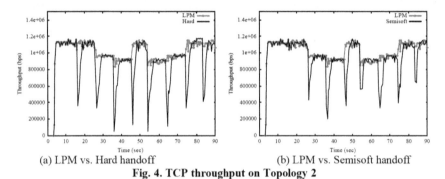

(a) LPM vs. Hard handoff   (b) LPM vs. Semisoft handoff

Fig. 4. TCP throughput on Topology 2

Figure 4 shows the TCP connection throughput on topology 2 as a function of time. The throughput of LPM drops from 1100 Kbps to 940 Kbps at time 25. This is because the RTT increases by 30ms as the MH moves from BS2 to BS3. TCP throughput decrease as the RTT increases. Hard and semisoft handoff shows more rapid drops of throughput than in topology 1. All hard handoff suffers from packet drops. Except handoff from BS1 to BS2, all semisoft handoff shows abrupt drops of throughput. Remember that semisoft handoff suffered from packet duplications as well as packet losses during handoffs. Duplicated packets may also decrease throughput by triggering the TCP fast recovery mechanism. Because LPM is free from packet loss and duplication, its throughput is only affected by the variance of RTT.

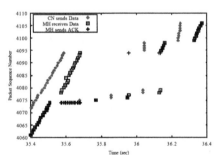

Fig 5. Handoff from BS3 to BS4 : Packet Loss
Semisoft delay is shorter than the sum of new and old path transmission delay

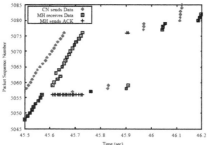

Fig 6. Handoff from BS4 to BS5 : Packet Loss
New path transmission delay is far shorter than that of old path.

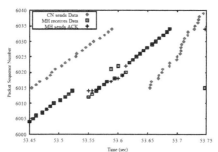

Fig. 7. Handoff from BS5 to BS4 : Packet Duplication
New path transmission delay is longer than that of old path

Throughput degradation of semisoft handoff can be classified as 3 categories. For each case, TCP sender and receiver traces are shown in figure 5, 6, 7. The first case is shown in figure 5. When MH handoffs from BS3 to BS4, semisoft delay (50ms) is shorter than the sum of new path transmission delay and old path transmission delay (65ms). When MH makes real handoff to BS4, although crossover node multicast data packets to both the new and old path, there still are unicast packets on old path which MH doesn't receive yet. These packets (packet 4075, 4076 and 4077) are destined to loss after handoff and incur TCP congestion control. But to get rid of this condition, setting up longer semisoft delay is not advisable. Link layer connection may be disconnected if real handoff is delayed too long. Handoff from BS4 to BS3 shows same result.

In the second case shown in figure 6, new path transmission delay is far shorter than that of old path. New BS receives multicasted packets long before old BS receives the same packets. Crossover delay is not sufficient to delay these packets. Before the MH hands off to the new BS, packet 5057 through 5059 are already arrived to the new BS and these packets are lost. But increasing crossover delay is not advisable too. Because on other conditions like further new path, increasing crossover delay incurs more duplicated ACKs, that degrades TCP performance severely. Handoff from BS3 to BS2 shows similar results.

In the third case shown in figure 7, new path transmission delay is longer than that of old path. At 53.55, real handoff is finished. Crossover node forwards packets, which had stayed more than crossover delay, to the new BS. The MH receives these packets from 53.55 to

53.59, which the MH already received from old BS. So, the MH sends more than 3 duplicated ACKs to CN and this incurs packet retransmission and congestion control. Handoff from BS2 to BS3 shows similar result.On the contrary, for every case, LPM shows no duplication, no loss of packets and no throughput degradation. An MH hands off safely for TCP connection. Packet sequence number increase stably and the result pattern is similar to figure 2 (b). We omit the TCP sender and receiver traces of LPM because of space limitation.

We studied the performance of LPM where delaying a handoff is restricted, where we complement the basic LPM with the packet forwarding and duplicate packet elimination mechanism described in Section 2. It also showed similar results. However due to the space limitation, we omit the result too.

5. Conclusion

We have proposed a simple handoff scheme called LPM for Cellular IP that signals an MH the exact cue to handoff on optimal time point for micro-mobility. We also proposed efficient packet forwarding and duplicate packet elimination mechanism for the situation where delaying a handoff is restricted.

We studied the performance of LPM using computer simulation. Our simulation study showed that LPM received all packets without duplication in case of UDP traffic. Also in case of TCP traffic, the throughput of LPM is significantly better than those of semisoft handoff and hard handoff.

6. References

Andrew T. Campbell, Javier Gomez, Sanghyo Kim, Andras G. Valko, Chieh-Yih Wan, "Design, Implementation, and Evaluation of Cellular IP", *IEEE Personal communication*, Vol. 7, No.4, Aug. 2000, pp 42-49

D.B. Johnson, C. Perkins. "Mobility Support in Ipv6", *IETF Internet Draft*, draft-ietf-mobileip-ipv6-12.txt, Apr. 2000

Karim El Malki, Hesham Soliman, "Fast Handoffs in Mobile IPv4", *IETF Internet Draft*, draft-elmalki-mobileip-fast-handoffs-03.txt, Internet Draft, Sept 27, 2000.

C. Perkins, editor, "IP Mobility Support", *IETF RFC 2002*, Oct. 1996

R. Ramjee, T. La Porta, S. Thuel, K.Varadhan and S. Wang, "HAWAII: A Domain-based Approach for Supporting Mobility in Wide-area Wireless networks", *International Conference on Network Protocols*, ICNP'99

S. Seshan, H. Balakrishnan, and R.H. Katz, "Handoffs cellular wireless networks: The Daedalus implementation and experience," *Wireless Personal Communications*, Vol. 4, No. 2, 1997, pp. 141-162.

Security for IP multimedia services in the 3GPP third generation mobile system

G. Horn, D. Kröselberg, K. Müller

Siemens AG, Corporate Technology, D-81730 München, Germany
e-mail: {guenther.horn, dirk.kroeselberg, klaus.mueller}@mchp.siemens.de

Abstract

This paper surveys the security architecture of the IP multimedia core network subsystem (IMS) of the third generation mobile system which is known in Europe as UMTS. Security procedures for the IMS are expected to be stable by June 2002. The main features of the security architecture include user specific features protecting the access of the IMS user, such as authentication and key agreement when a user registers and integrity protection of IMS access signalling, but also features for the user independent protection of SIP signalling in the IMS core network Authenticated registration is given an in-depth treatment.

Keywords

Third generation mobile system , 3GPP, IP, multimedia, IMS, registration, authentication, integrity, SIP, IPsec

1. Introduction

3GPP (Third Generation Partnership Project), a partnership of international standardisation bodies, specifies a global third generation mobile system, known in Europe as UMTS (Universal Mobile Telecommunications System). UMTS has evolved from the second generation mobile systems GSM (Global System for Mobile Communications). Compared to GSM, UMTS offers, among many other things, enhanced security features. What is new in UMTS is the introduction of countermeasures against threats involving active attacks to masquerade or eavesdrop, and the increased focus not only on the vulnerable radio interface but also on other parts of the system, such as the signalling infrastructure in the core network. A survey of the basic 3GPP security architecture, specified in (3GPP TS 33.102, 2002) can be found in (Horn and Howard, 2000).

The third release of UMTS (the so-called 3GPP Release 5, due to be finalised in June 2002) contains an IP multimedia core network subsystem (IMS). Using the services of the UMTS packet domain for IP connectivity, the IMS provides the possibility to set up multimedia sessions by means of the SIP (Session Initiation Protocol) protocol specified by the Internet Engineering Task Force (IETF) in (Rosenberg and Schulzrinne, 2002). The architecture of the IMS is designed such that it may use mechanisms for IP connectivity other than those provided by the UMTS packet domain in future releases. It is the aim of 3GPP to make the protocols specified for the IMS IETF-compatible.

This paper is structured as follows: following a section on the security requirements for the IMS, an outline of the security architecture is given. Then it is described in detail how an IMS user is authenticated when registering with the IMS. The following section shows how the session keys derived in the authentication are used to protect the integrity and confidentiality of IMS signalling messages on the first hop. The paper continues to describe how IMS signalling messages are protected further inside the network by user-independent means. The paper concludes with an overview of likely future developments in IMS security.

2. IMS security requirements

It is well known that the Internet protocol itself does not offer any security in terms of authentication, integrity or confidentiality. And it is also well known that the Internet engineering task force spends more and more effort on security issues, cf. e.g. (Schiller, 2002).Clearly security for UMTS is an important prerequisite for its success.

From the beginning, security has been an integral part of the IMS architecture. It aims at protecting the access to multimedia services by users. The protection of user data is not in the scope of the current work on IMS security.

The requirements that were seen for securing IMS signalling can be divided into two sets. One set of requirements relates to the authentication of mobile users, and the security of signalling transmitted over the air interface. One basic assumption here is that the IMS does not rely on security mechanisms within the underlying IP transport (in Release 5 this will be the security provided by the General Packet Radio Service (GPRS) of the UMTS packet domain). Rather, it independently uses its own mechanisms to allow other means for providing IP transport in the future, e.g. IEEE 802.11 (Wireless Local Area Networks, WLAN), and therefore achieve access network independence. The second set of requirements relates to the security of IMS signalling messages that are transported through the core network.

It was clear from the beginning that for IMS signalling mutual authentication and key agreement as well as integrity protection of the signalling messages - at least over the particularly vulnerable air interface - must be provided as a mandatory feature. Encryption of IMS signalling data will not be implemented for Release 5 but is likely to become an optional feature for later releases.

For authentication and key agreement (AKA) between mobile users and the network side, a protocol fulfilling specific delegation requirements is needed, such that it becomes possible to run authentication between the mobile user and the home network, and to delegate subsequent signalling protection to the visited network. The latter implies that the derived session keys have to be provided to the visited network by the home network.

Besides the pure security requirements, the limited computing power of the mobile devices and the limited bandwidth of the air interface pose additional constraints on the security solutions. For these reasons, security will be based on symmetric instead of more costly asymmetric (public-key) mechanisms.

As the IMS uses the IETF SIP protocol for signalling, an important requirement on the IMS security architecture is its conformity to the work of the relevant IETF workgroups. Therefore all security mechanisms used for SIP in the IMS shall at least not conflict with the IETF SIP architecture, and should as far as possible be aligned with the IETF. The role of 3GPP can therefore be seen as one driver for SIP security in the IETF.

A draft collecting the overall requirements of the IMS has been submitted to the IETF, which also contains a section on security (Garcia et al, 2002).

3. IMS security architecture

Figure 1 gives an overview of the IMS security architecture. It distinguishes between

- IMS access network security which provides the security features for a secure access of a user to the IMS network (indicated by the solid lines) and

- IMS network domain security which provides protection between the IMS network nodes indicated by the dashed lines. Protection of the IMS messages is provided on a hop-by-hop basis between the involved entities.

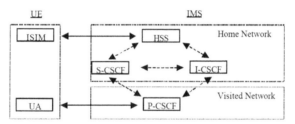

Figure 1: IMS security architecture

The User Equipment (UE) contains the SIP user agent (UA) and the ISIM (IP Multimedia Services Identity Module). The ISIM is a term that indicates the collection of IMS security data and functions. The following implementation options are permitted:

- Use of a distinct ISIM application on a smart card platform which does not share security functions with the USIM (User Services Identity Module);

- Use of a distinct ISIM application on a smart card platform which does share security functions with the USIM;

- Derivation of IMS security parameters from a USIM application on a smart card platform. The USIM is the logical entity containing the permanent keys and the functions required to perform the

UMTS AKA protocol in the UMTS circuit switching and packet switching domains, cf. (3GPP TS 33.102, 2002).

The P-CSCF (Proxy - Call Session Control Function) is a SIP outbound proxy to support the UA. It is assigned after the mobile has connected to the access network. The serving CSCF (S-CSCF) is a SIP proxy server, which also acts as a SIP registrar. The interrogating CSCF (I-CSCF) may act as the first entry point for SIP signalling to the home network and may decide (with the help of location servers) which S-CSCF to assign to a particular user. The Home Subscriber Server (HSS) contains IMS subscriber authorisation information and the IMS authentication centre.

IMS access network security is user specific and provides the following security features:

- Mutual authentication and key agreement between ISIM and home network:
  HSS and ISIM of the user's UE share a long-term secret authentication key. The S-CSCF receives the appropriate security parameters from the HSS so that it can check the correctness of the authentication response from the ISIM. The session keys are forwarded in the course of an authentication procedure from the ISIM to the UA and from the HSS via the S-CSCF to the P-CSCF.

- Integrity protection of SIP messages between UA and P-CSCF in the visited network using the received session keys.

IMS network domain security is user independent and provides the following security features:

- Mandatory integrity and confidentiality protection by using IPsec (Kent and Atkinson, 1998) for links which cross the boundaries of networks (e.g. links between a P-CSCF and an I-CSCF).

- For intra-network links protection is up to the network provider. If protection is applied then IPsec has to be employed.

4. Authentication between IMS user and home network

For the protection of a user's access to the IMS, an authentication and key agreement mechanism is required that provides mutual authentication between the user and the IMS home network and the derivation of session keys for the protection of SIP messages on the first hop to and from the UA. An analysis of IMS system and security requirements showed that the mechanisms specified for SIP (Rosenberg and Schulzrinne, 2002) were not appropriate. They were either too heavy-weight due to their use of public-key techniques (Internet Key Exchange IKE, Transport Layer Security TLS), did not support the User Datagram Protocol UDP (TLS), did not provide key agreement (http basic and digest authentication) or did not provide the required level of security (http basic and digest authentication). As the UMTS AKA mechanism (used to protect the UMTS network on the bearer level) fulfilled all the IMS security requirements it was decided to re-use it for authentication and key agreement in the IMS (called IMS AKA), possibly with different keys.

Before a user can get access to IMS services, he needs to be initially registered. As a successful registration is only valid for a certain period of time, which is negotiated as part of the registration procedure, re-registrations are required from time to time. It was decided in 3GPP to integrate the IMS AKA mechanism into the initial registration and the re-registration procedures, respectively.

Figure 2 shows a simplified version of an information flow for an initial registration procedure with successful authentication and key agreement using the IMS AKA. The simplified flow only shows the messages which are relevant for security purposes. (More details can be found in (3GPP TS 33.203, 2002) and (3GPP TS 23.228, 2002). The appropriate flows for re-registrations are very similar and can also be found there.)

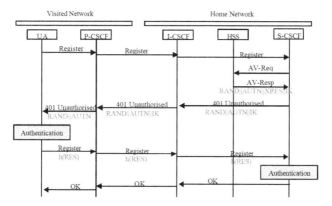

Figure 2: Registration with successful authentication and key agreement (simplified)

The user sends a SIP REGISTER request to the assigned P-CSCF in the visited network. This REGISTER message is forwarded via an I-CSCF in the home network of the user to an appropriately selected S-CSCF. Then the S-CSCF requests from the HSS an authentication vector which contains the user specific security parameters. These security parameters are derived from a user specific long-term key shared between the user and its HSS. They may be derived in the HSS in real time, but they may also be pre-computed. The authentication vector containing the security parameters is sent from the HSS to the S-CSCF.

An authentication vector consists of a random number RAND, the authentication token AUTN used for the authentication of the network to the user, an expected response XRES used for the authentication of the user to the network, a session keys IK for integrity protection between UA and P-CSCF. XRES is stored in the S-CSCF. The S-CSCF indicates to the user that authentication is required by sending a 401 Unauthorised message which includes the other security parameters RAND, AUTN and IK. They are forwarded via the I-CSCF to the P-CSCF. The P-CSCF stores the session key IK and forwards RAND and AUTN to the UA. The ISIM authenticates the network by verifying AUTN and calculates a response parameter RES. A hash of RES is sent with a second REGISTER message to the S-CSCF, which now authenticates the user by comparing the hash of the stored value XRES with the received hash of RES. In case of a successful authentication an OK message is send back to the user.

The integration of the IMS AKA parameters into the SIP registration flow uses the HTTP digest framework specified for SIP and is described in (Niemi, Arkko and Torvinen, 2002). Because of this particular approach, only hash values of RES are compared at the S-CSCF.

With the procedures described above, authentication of a user is only possible in the course of registration and re-registration procedures, and both can only be initiated by the user himself.

It is a desirable feature of GSM and UMTS Release'99 that the network can flexibly decide when to authenticate a user, e.g. when chargeable events occur. It was seen as a requirement within 3GPP that this kind of flexible authentication policy should also be available for the IMS. In order to avoid the introduction of unwarranted complexity in the IMS by integrating the authentication mechanism also into other SIP methods (e.g. into the INVITE method used for session set-up), it was decided that it shall be possible for the S-CSCF on which the user is registered to initiate an authenticated re-registration of a user at any time. Details of the mechanism are omitted here.

5. Integrity and confidentiality for IMS signalling

As already mentioned in section 3, the security architecture splits into two parts employing different means of protection, network domain security and access network security. The different integrity and confidentiality mechanisms for SIP messages in these two parts of the IMS will be treated in some more detail in this section.

5.1 Integrity and Confidentiality in the Network Domain

All IMS signalling in the network domain can be protected transparently at the network layer, by using IPsec ESP (Encapsulating Security Payload) (Kent and Atkinson, 1998) between two adjacent IMS nodes, independent of any security association with the user. Automated negotiation of the security associations required by ESP is provided by the IKE (Internet key exchange) protocol (Harkins and Carrel, 1998).

For setting up secure ESP tunnels between IMS nodes, key management will be required, as IKE uses long-term keys for authenticating the initial Diffie-Hellman key exchange between the tunnel endpoints. These long-term keys can be simple pre-shared secrets, or public/private key pairs.

It is only mandated to secure IMS signalling between the core networks of different operators. It is left to the discretion of network operators whether to secure their network internal communication (although this seems clearly advisable). Thus IPsec will, as a minimum, be implemented at specific entities at the network borders. These entities, called security gateways (SEG), will maintain IPsec tunnels with the SEGs of other network operators, see figure 3. As there may be few SEGs in the initial stages of IMS deployment, keying with pre-shared secrets may be feasible.

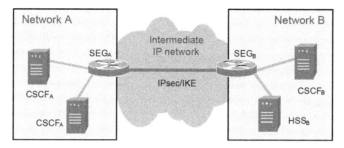

Figure 3: IPsec secured tunnel between network operators

For future IMS networks that will grow in complexity it is most likely that public key based authentication and Public Key Infrastructure (PKI) based key management are required to provide better scalability.

5.2   Integrity and Confidentiality in the Access Network

3GPP decided to provide integrity protection at the network layer by using IPsec ESP. Confidentiality protection is foreseen for later releases.

Since the P-CSCF will be the first hop from the UE perspective, it is possible to apply ESP network layer protection here. IPsec offers a secure mechanism that only adds a relatively small overhead to signalling traffic. The session key for integrity protection by means of IPsec ESP is provided by the authentication and key establishment protocol AKA described in section 4. The parameters needed for the IPsec ESP security association are negotiated by means of the security mode set-up procedure, described in the following subsection 5.3.

5.3   Security mode set-up

It is necessary for the UE and the P-CSCF to agree on specific parameters like the cryptographic algorithms to be used, prior to sending protected messages. Such parameters are required in addition to the session integrity key IK provided by the IMS AKA protocol.

For setting up the IMS security parameters, the mechanism described in (Arkko et. al., 2002) is used. The specification of this mechanism originates from 3GPP but was submitted to the IETF as a generic mechanism allowing to negotiate different integrity protection and encryption mechanisms for SIP, including TLS and http digest. The messages of the protocol described in (Arkko et. al., 2002)are integrated into the SIP messages exchanged during the registration and authentication procedure described in section 4.

6. Future aspects of IMS security

The above sections have shown how an IMS user is authenticated when registering, and how integrity and confidentiality protection can be provided for SIP messages in the IMS. It is expected that IMS security will be developed further in future 3GPP releases. Two possible directions of such developments can be discerned today:

- Other authentication schemes in addition to IMS AKA may be introduced.
- Support for end-to-end security for user data may be introduced.

7. Conclusions

The employment of IP transport in the UMTS IMS and its connections to the public Internet make the IMS system more vulnerable to attacks. Therefore the IMS has to be protected by appropriate security means. The security services offered include user-specific security mechanisms where authentication is based on a secure hardware token, but also include mechanisms for the user-independent protection of SIP signalling in the IMS core network.

Specifications for the protection of the UMTS IMS are expected to be finalised in June 2002.

8. Acknowledgements

The authors have actively contributed to the specification of IMS security in 3GPP SA3. But, needless to say, the specification of IMS security as a whole draws from contributions by numerous other parties working in that group.

9. References

3GPP TSG SA WG2 Architecture (2002), "IP Multimedia (IM) Subsystem - Stage 2", 3G TS 23.228, v5.4.1, April 2002, http://www.3gpp.org/specs/specs.htm.

3GPP TSG SA WG3 Security (2002), "Security Architecture (Release 4)", 3G TS 33.102 v4.3.0, January 2002, http://www.3gpp.org/specs/specs.htm.

3GPP TSG SA WG3 Security (2002), "Access security for IP-based services", 3G TS 33.203 v5.1.0, March 2002, http://www.3gpp.org/specs/specs.htm.

Arkko, J., Torvinen, V., Haukka, T., Sen, S., Valerius, L. (2002), "Security Mechanism Agreement for SIP Connections", *IETF Internet Draft draft -sip-sec-agree-00.txt,* April 2002, http://www.ietf.org.

Franks, J. et al (1999), "HTTP Authentication: Basic and Digest Access Authentication", *IETF RFC 2617,* http://www.ietf.org.

Garcia, M. et al (2002), "3GPP requirements on SIP", *IETF Internet Draft* draft-garcia-sipping-3gpp-reqs-03, March 2002, http://www.ietf.org.

Harkins, D. and Carrel, D. (1998), "The Internet Key Exchange (IKE)", IETF RFC 2409, http://www.ietf.org..

Horn, G. and Howard, P. (2000) "Review of third generation mobile system security architecture", *Proceedings of ISSE 2000, Barcelona, 27-29 Sept 2000.*

Kent, S. and Atkinson, R. (1998), "Security Architecture for the Internet Protocol", IETF RFC-2401, http://www.ietf.org.

Kent, S. and Atkinson, R. (1998), " IP Encapsulating Security Payload (ESP)", IETF RFC-2406.

Niemi, A., Arkko, J., Torvinen, V., "HTTP Digest Authentication Using AKA", *IETF Internet Draft, draft-niemi-sipping-digest-aka-00,* February 2002, http://www.ietf.org.

Roach, A. (2002), "Event notification in SIP", *IETF Internet Draft, draft-roach-sip-subscribe-notify-05.txt,* February 2002, http://www.ietf.org..

Rosenberg, J. and Schulzrinne, H. et al (2002), " SIP: Session Initiation Protocol", *IETF Internet Draft, draft-ietf-sip-rfc2543bis-09.txt,* February 2002, http://www.ietf.org.

Schiller. J. (2002), "Designing secure protocols", http://jis.mit.edu/sectutorial/.

Please note that Internet-drafts and some of the referenced 3GPP specifications are work in progress and may evolve over time.

A Vision of the Internet in 2010
(The Mobile Internet)

Paul Reynolds

Orange PCS & University of Plymouth, United Kingdom
e-mail: Paul.Reynolds@orange.co.uk

Abstract

This invited paper presents a vision of the Internet eight years from now (i.e. in the year 2010). The study was performed in two steps: the definition of requirements and drivers together with an extrapolation of technology developments, and, an articulation of the vision. The vision is a direct result of the authors extensive experience with working with the development of the internet including his technical leadership of the Mobile Wireless Internet Forum (MWIF) and a contributor to the Internet engineering Task Force (IETF).

Keywords

Internet, Mobile Internet, Personal Mobility, Terminal Mobility, Session Mobility, Code Mobility, Access Network, Core Network Service Network.

1. Background

In this paper I articulate a vision of the Internet in 2010 i.e. eight years from now. The vision is one that fully supports mobility including personal, terminal, session and code. It is, in effect, a Mobile Internet.

The 2010 Internet will be characterised by a move away from intelligence within the network (3rd Generation mobile network architecture) or at the edges (current Internet architecture) to intelligence everywhere. The 2010 Internet will have an all IETF protocol based access, core and service networks with effective quality management. It will be underpinned by Mobile-IPv6 which is adaptable to mobile networks, having adequate addressing capacity, multicast management, security mechanisms, and mobility management.

2. 2010 Internet Requirements

The 2010 Internet will be required to support:

- terminal, personal, session and code mobility;
- roaming and fast-hand-off between different access networks;
- quality comparable with telecommunications networks;
- global and seamless service provision;

- data rates starting at 2Mbit/s and ranging up to 1Gbit/s;
- highly distributed terminals;
- managed Quality of Service (QoS);
- any air interface specification that may be required to achieve higher bit rates and improve spectrum utilisation;
- capacity for several radio interfaces depending on the context; and
- "smart antenna" processing.

3. Extrapolating Technology Trends to a Vision

One method to provide a vision for the 2010 Internet is to extrapolate from current technology trends, the most significant for the next 8 years being:

- more technology in the user space, not less;
- increased user literacy;
- more open, and less standardised, interfaces;
- greater impact of nomadic computing as terminal devices become more portable;
- Internet and telecommunications convergence supporting QoS management;
- software dominance over hardware;
- greater transparency to technology complexity;
- automated and autonomously initiated machine-to-machine interactions;
- much reduced time to market;
- shorter service life cycles;
- smaller, and faster, micro-chips;
- smaller and smarter user terminals; and
- commodity networks.

These trends are supported by a number of enabling technologies including:

- low cost embedded, even disposable, radio microchips and software defined radio systems supporting dynamic configuration of the air interface and dynamic spectrum allocation, i.e. possibly no operator ownership of unique spectrum;
- mobile software agents, supporting personal profiles and personalisation of data, and, intelligent agents learning, adapting and acting on behalf of a user even pre-empting their needs and wishes. These agents will require minimal user involvement, i.e. the technology complexity is hidden from the user;
- pervasive network of sensors, ad-hoc networking, distributed mobility management, middleware to support homogeny, autonomous adaptive networks that self manage their structure to meet ever changing demands; and
- software defined network elements.

4. Drivers to Achieve the Vision

The vision for the 2010 Internet will not be incarnated without a sense of purpose or drive from the user community. These users will demand:

- applications that require "extreme bit rates" such as the 1Gbit/s;
- applications that are "mobile aware";
- not just "IP technology", also "IP thinking";
- user-centric, bespoke services;
- ubiquitous computing and context awareness;
- distributed mobility management including inter and intra technology hand-off;
- ad-hoc networking;
- open architectures for re-configurabilty of all layers of the management;
- enhanced privacy and security;
- soft networking;
- scalable middleware deployments;
- flexible and reconfiguarble radio architectures; and
- radically improved battery technology.

The drive for the distribution of intelligence will result in:

- intelligence on the move (mobile agents);
- virtual-home environments;
- service provisioning based on software downloading; and
- cognitive radio systems.

5. 2010 Internet Vision

Based upon the above requirements, trends and drivers it is possible to envisage the Internet in the year 2010. It can be perceived as comprising three parts: an access, a core and a service network.

5.1 2010 Internet "Access Network"

The 2010 Internet access network will be characterised by an improved capacity from the available spectrum and a move away from a cellular-only system to one that integrates broadcast, cellular, cordless, Wireless LAN, point-to-multipoint, and fixed access technologies. There will be a need to support more elaborate radio access technologies and allow, for example, adaptive signal processing at both the base station and terminal. The access network will:

- have a mixed mode radio interface with rapid adaptation to bursty traffic, for example, to support a digital terrestrial television return channel and its adaptation to asymmetrical bit rates;

- use smart antennas at both the base station and terminal. The radio interface will be designed to take advantage of them, for example, include signalling to allow enhanced antenna processing;
- support dynamic allocation of spectrum as loading demands;
- use of spread spectrum techniques;
- use Internet Engineering Task Force (IETF) protocols for mobility and hand-off management with consequence of openness towards radio networks, with a generic "IP over wireless" interface, that can be adapted to several radio interfaces.

There will be a need to relieve the expensive 3rd Generation Mobile Network spectrum whenever possible, and, to offer higher bit rates to nomadic customers when they are in a static situation by way of unregulated spectrum, for example, Wireless LAN.

The 2010 Internet will integrate broadcasting services, notably "IP push" services. Different degrees of integration will be possible with an "intelligent" server hiding complexity to the user and server. This approach raises considerable technical and regulatory challenges because it implies co-operation of heterogeneous networks that may be operated by different enterprise entities.

The use of broadband coverage of specific areas or "hot spots", for example, hotels, congress centres, airports, etc., will be provided albeit at the cost of a restricted mobility data access with techniques derived from wireless local area networks.

Complementary fixed access networks, for example, ADSL, and the domestic cordless networks can be expected to be found in most households by 2010. For example, a Bluetooth access point connected to an ADSL modem will allow mobile terminals to connect to a mobile network without loading the air interface of the mobile network, i.e. ADSL provides a tunnel to the mobile network. The mobile terminal will have become a universal terminal, for example, supporting telephony, remote controls, etc.

5.2 2010 Internet "Core Network"

The 2010 Internet will comprise a single universal network that will be capable of supporting all types of access, fixed and mobile. Mobile operators will find that their core networks will evolve towards more open and universal solutions capable of supporting fixed, mobile and broadcasting, allowing them to inter-work more deeply than they do today.

Intelligent mobile agents will exist throughout the network and in user devices and will act continually to simplify tasks and ensure transparency

5.3 2010 Internet "Service Network"

For the user, Service Network will be capable of supporting:

- access to services via the best access route, in terms of cost and bit rate, without the need to manage several environments;
- access too much higher bit rates in "static" situations and when the required information is not personalised, i.e. broadcast;
- "capacity-aware" accesses that adapt to, and make use of, the available bit rate, for example, to synchronise files in relation to a distant computer, to download attached files etc. when the availability of a broadband network has been detected
- access to the same services via variable data rates by way of content adaptation or application transcodeing. This will entail the adaptation of service presentation before being transmitted so that its size can be adapted to the bit rate available. This implies variable rate coding for voice and video, but also variable contents format or even service adaptation, for example, deleting or reducing images, deleting access to certain applications.

6. Discussion

The 2010 Internet can be defined as a simplified access for the user to all of their services across multiple radio technologies and networks. Their services adapting, notably to the available bit rate, without forcing them to manage the consequential complexities.

The 2010 Internet will be delivered over time. Starting with the introduction of nomadic services, for example, broadband access in "hot spots" via a WLAN connected to a fixed network; access to the mobile network via a home radio interface and a "tunnel" through the fixed network. Later, it will evolve towards a more generic solution making the support for services by different networks easier, including:

- the implementation of QoS management protocols and parameters recognisable by all types of networks; each network being able to map the QoS protocols and parameters to its own requirements, for example, radio resource allocation;
- generalisation of IPv6 and the emergence of consistent solutions for IPv4/IPv6 interworking;
- convergence of security policies, for example, based on an AAA (Authentication, Authorisation, and Accounting) architecture on the network side and the SIM card on the terminal side.

It will be possible to use differing technologies to support services in a way to optimise performance and cost trade-offs. These technologies include:

- auto-adaptation of services to the available bit rate and to the terminal capabilities;
- flexible access networks capable of easily integrating new radio interfaces, allowing the implementation of higher performance radio solutions, for example, increased user peak bit rate, increased physical layer spectral efficiency, more efficient resource allocation;
- continuous connection to the mobile network via radio access technologies optimised for different contexts, for example, indoor-outdoor, new frequency bands, etc.
- applications taking advantage of the changes in communication conditions – for example, to automatically carry out certain heavy tasks when the available bit rate is increased;
- universal core network, evolution of fixed IP networks;
- multi-interface terminals, programmable at the radio level.

Along with this evolution, the 2010 Internet will need to deal with:

- the degree to which operators can control services and service access when terminals are becoming more powerful;
- different business models between mobile operators, ISPs and WLAN "hot spot" operators;
- regulatory hurdles, including, limitations and ambiguities on the use of wireless LAN frequencies for access to a public network; and using broadcasting frequencies for combining telecommunications and broadcasting services.

7. Conclusions

The 2010 Internet will be able to support the mobility. The division of mobile telecommunication networks and the Internet will be bridged and a single unifying technology IETF protocols will support mobility and ubiquitous computing.

Acknowledgements

In developing the vision for 2010 the author has had many discussions and brainstorming sessions with his Orange colleagues from around the world. As such it is difficult to acknowledge them all by name. However, he would like to single out Mr Combelles, from France Telecom, for his significant contribution.

Towards a smooth handoff for TCP and real time applications in wireless network

D.Tandjaoui[1] and N.Badache[1] and H.Bettahar[2] and A.Bouabdallah[2] and H. Seba[2]

[1] Basic Software Laboratory, CERIST
3, rue des Frères Aissou, Ben Aknoun, BP 143, 16030
Alger, Algeria
[2] Heudiasyc-UMR CNRS 6599, Université de Technologie de Compiègne,
BP 20529, 60200, Compiègne cedex France.
e-mail: dtandjaoui@mail.cerist.dz

Abstract

In this paper, we propose a new solution to guarantee the arrival of ordered packets to the mobile node after a handoff. It also minimizes the delay of forwarding buffered packets which is very important for real time and multimedia applications. Our solution is based on buffering mobile node's packets at a *cross over router* before a handoff instead of buffering them at the old foreign agent. We define the *cross over router* as the low intersection between the paths from the old foreign agent and the new one to the root of the hierarchy. This new solution ensures that real time and TCP applications will not be disturbed.

Key words

Mobile IP, Smooth handoff, Micro-mobility, cross over router buffering

1. Introduction

The integration of mobility in the Internet network has lead to many problems. One of them is that IP protocol is not adapted to support host mobility. Mobile IP is a protocol proposed by Perkins (Perkins, 1996) to support mobility. It is not specifically planned to support micro-mobility and it has not been considered to be a good solution for network level micro-mobility (Brown and Sing, 1996)(Caceras and Padmanabhan, 1998)(Campbell *et al*, 1999) (Mysore and Bharghavan, 1997). So several micro-mobility proposals with and without Mobile IP have been introduced (Campbell *et al*, 1999)(Ramjee *et al*, 1999)(McCann *et al*, 1999). For all these proposals, different handoff protocols have been presented. Most of them try to reach a seamless handoff. The principle objective of a seamless handoff is to ensure a fast and smooth handoff. Fast handoff tries to reduce the latency during a handoff. For the latency problem, regional registration seems to be a good alternative to hide the mobility from the home agent inside a domain. Different techniques were studied in order to get a fast handoff (Tan *et al*, 1999)(Caceras and Padmanabhan, 1998).

To achieve a fast handoff we shall employ good mechanisms of movement detection. A mobile node entering a new subnetwork will detect its movements by the reception of an unknown advertisement. There are different methods that allow detecting the movement of the mobile node from one foreign agent to another. With the Lazy Cell Switching (LCS) method (Fikouras *et al*, 1999), when a mobile node registers a care-of address (CoA) with its home agent, it holds on it until the agent life time is expired. This occurs when the mobile node misses three advertisements. Eager Cell Switching (ECS) method (Fikouras *et al*, 1999) is more efficient than LCS, it tends to function in a way opposite to that of LCS. The mobile node initiates a handoff immediately upon discovering a new agent. Hinted Cell Switching (HCS) (Fikouras and Gorg, 2001) method is very efficient. It bases its functionality on link layer information, termed as hints, with purpose to indicating when a link layer handoff occurs.

If fast handoff is necessary for mobile node to provide continuous connectivity with less disruption to ongoing traffic, it does not guarantee no packets loss and ordered packets. To avoid these problems, besides ensuring fast handoff, we must also ensure smooth handoff that guarantees no packets loss and ordered arrival of packets. Furthermore, packets loss and mis-ordered packets arriving to a mobile node could adversely impact both audio and TCP applications (Ramjee et *al*, 1999). In (Tan *et al*, 1999) and (Mysore and Bharghavan, 1997), the authors propose to multicast all the packets destined to a mobile node to the foreign agent and to all its adjacent foreign agents. Adjacent foreign agents buffer arriving packets. When the mobile node finishes handoff, it receives the buffered packets from the new foreign agent. This method guarantees no packets loss, but the scheme has two drawbacks. First, the scheme has to handle the IP multicast address management issues across the network (Tan *et al*, 1999). Second, the mobile node may receive duplicated packets that disturb TCP applications. (Perkins and Wang, 1999), (Perkins, 1996) and (Wang *et al*, 2001) propose to buffer packets at the foreign agent. After the handoff, the old foreign agent forward buffered packets to the new one where the mobile node has moved. However, this solution can lead to delayed and mis-ordered packets. The arrival of delayed and mis-ordered packets to a mobile node also disturbs audio and TCP applications. Furthermore, when using the forwarding solution from the old foreign agent to the new one, packets delay may reach 500ms. This delay is not acceptable for real time application such as telephony, which expect end to end delays below 300ms (Kraner *et al*, 2000).

In this paper, we propose a new solution to guarantee the arrival of ordered packets to the mobile node after a handoff. It also minimizes the delay of forwarding buffered packets. Our solution is based on buffering mobile node's packets at a *cross over router* before a handoff. We define the *cross over router* as the low intersection between the paths from the old foreign agent and the new one to the root of the hierarchy. By using this technique, we avoid to have multiple streams of mis-ordered packets arriving to the mobile node. Indeed, buffered packets of the mobile node at the *cross over router* are forwarded before that new mobile node's packets follow the new path to the new foreign agent. This manner of forwarding buffered packets gives two advantages. First, It ensures that older packets and newer packets will arrive to the mobile node in order. Second, it minimizes the delay of forwarding process. It is clear that forwarding buffered packets from the old foreign agent to the new one takes more time than forwarding the same buffered packets from the *cross over router* to the new foreign agent. With this solution, we must determine the new foreign agent before the handoff in order to define the *cross over router*. To do this, we propose two methods to select the *cross over router*. The first method consists on informing all adjacent foreign agents about the current foreign agent of the mobile. Each adjacent foreign agent looks for the low intersection between its paths and the path of the current foreign agent to the root of the hierarchy. This intersection defines the *cross over router*. The second method consists on using one of the movement detection techniques, which allows predicting the new foreign agent before a handoff. Thus, it is possible to define the *cross over router*.

The rest of the paper is organized as follows. Section two presents an overview of mobile IP. In section three, we present the macro and micro-mobility approaches. Section four describes the hierarchical solution for micro-mobility and presents problems of delayed and mis-ordered packets encountered after the forwarding. Our solution is introduced in section five. In section six, we present our handoff protocol. Section seven concludes the paper.

2. Mobile IP Overview

Mobile node (MN) is a host that can changes its point of attachment from one network or subnetwork to another without changing the IP address. It may continue to communicate with other Internet nodes called correspondent nodes (CN) at any location using the same home IP address. A home agent (HA) is a host in the home network of a MN. A foreign network is any other network that can be visited by the mobile. A foreign agent (FA) is a host in a foreign network. It provides routing services to the registered MNs in the foreign network.

TCP/IP was designed for fixed hosts, so it does not support host mobility. Mobile IP is a new protocol proposed to provide mobility support for hosts connected to Internet without changing their IP Addresses (Perkins, 1996). While roaming, a mobile node maintains two IP Addresses. A permanent home address and a topologically correct care-of address (CoA) that reflects the current point of attachment. When a mobile node moves to a new location, it obtains a new care-of address from the FA to which it is currently connected. The mobile node registers its current care-of address with its HA. The HA maintains a mobility binding that maps the mobile node home address to its care-of address. When a CN sends packets to the mobile node, they are intercepted by the HA and forwarded to the MN's care-of address by encapsulation (Perkins, 1996). The FA then decapsulates the packets and delivers them to the MN. Basically, there are two major drawbacks with routing in mobile IP making it inefficient: latency and packet loss during handoff.

2.1 Handoff

A handoff is the procedure and signaling executed when a mobile node moves from one network or wireless cell to another. In mobile IP, a handoff is an event that occurs between communicating FAs and a MN. At least three nodes are involved in a handoff; one is the MN and the other two are the old and the new FAs. Thus, a handoff is the process during which a node is "*handed over*" between two designated FAs (Fikouras *et al*, 1999).

2.2 Latency and packet loss during handoff

Every time the mobile host changes its CoA, It must register with its HA. If the HA is very far from the mobile node, this registration take a long time during which the MN cannot communicate. This latency could lead to packets loss and degrade both audio and TCP applications.

3. Micro and Macro Mobility

Future networks will include small wireless cells, which offer high aggregate bandwidth, support low powered mobile transceivers and provide accurate location information. In these kinds of networks, users will often carry devices across cells boundaries in the midst of data transfer. A handoff mechanism is needed to maintain connectivity as devices move, while minimizing disruption to ongoing communication. However mobile IP introduces significant latency when used in a cellular environment, simply because handoffs occur frequently and registration messages may travel long distances to the HA before packets redirection. If handoff is frequent, then the traffic perturbation for the MN will be intolerable. To avoid these drawbacks, it is important to divide the mobility into two approaches micro-mobility and macro mobility. Micro-mobility manages the movements of the MN across different subnets within a single domain or region. In such domain, the movements of the MN occurs relatively less frequently. Micro-mobility is currently handled by many protocols such as cellular IP, HAWAII, TELEMIP. Macro mobility manages movements of a MN among different domains or geographical regions. At present, Mobile IP handles the macro mobility.

4. The hierarchical approch

Inside a domain, when a handoff occurs, a MN does not need to update the association between its CoA with its home address at the HA. All MN's updates are done inside the domain. To do so, (Perkins and Wang, 1999), propose an approach based on hierarchical FAs. All FAs within a domain are organised into a hierarchy (more precisely a tree of FAs) to handle local movements of the MN inside the domain. The root of the hierarchy is connected to the Internet as shown in Fig 3. Each FA includes in its agent advertisement a vector of CoA, which are the IP Addresses of all its ancestors FAs as well as its own.

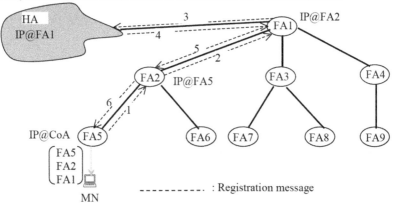

Fig 3 : The hierarchical model

When the MN enters in a foreign domain, it first registers with its HA by sending a registration request to its current FA. As shown in Fig 3 the request travels hop by hop the hierarchy (1,2,3), until it arrives to the HA. The HA creates a binding to the MN home address with the corresponding address of FA1 and sends a reply. The registration reply from the HA agent traverses the reverse path to reaches the MN (Fig3: arrows 4, 5 and 6). Upon the receipt of the reply, FA1 creates a binding to the MN with the corresponding FA2. FA2 creates a similar binding of the MN with the corresponding FA5. When a packet for the MN arrives at its home network, the HA tunnels it to the root of the hierarchy FA1. FA1 forwards these tunneled packets to its next lower level FA. When the lowest level FA receives these packets, it delivers them directly to the MN. When the MN moves to a new FA, it receives a new vector of care-of addresses from the new FA. This vector contains IP addresses of the new FA and all its ancestors. The MN compares the new vector with the old one. It chooses the lowest-level FA that apperas in both vectors, and sends a regional registration request to that FA. Any higher level agent needs not be informed of this movements since the other end of its forwarding tunell still points the current location of the MN. During the periode between the initiating a handoff and performing a regional registration, the MN is *handed over* between the old FA and the new one. During this time, it may miss newer packets, which will be lost. To avoid this packets loss during handoff, buffering mechanism at the foreign agent is used. The old FA delivers packets to the MN and also buffers them. When the handoff finishes, the new FA sends notification to the old one. Upon receiving this notification, the old FA forwards buffered packets to the new FA. The forwarding of buffered packets from the old foreign agent to the new one has two drawbacks. First, it creates multiple streams of mis-ordered packets. Second, the MN may receives delayed packets(Ramjee *et al*, 1999) (Fikouras *et al*, 1999).

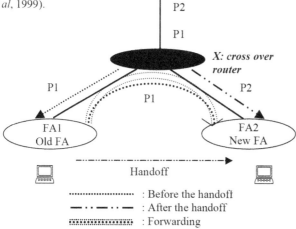

Fig 4 : Mis ordered and delayed packets

Fig 4 shows two streams of packets P1 and P2 arriving to the *cross over router* X. At the same time, the MN moves from FA1 to FA2 and sends a regional registration to the *cross over router* X. Before the mobile node terminates its registration, the stream of packets P1 are forwarded to FA1. FA1 sends these packets to the MN and also buffers them. When the MN registration finishes, it adds a new forwarding entry at the *cross over router* table that results in new stream of packets P2 being diverted to FA2. FA2 sends notification to FA1 informing it about the handoff. FA1 sends an acknowledgement and forwards the buffered packets to FA1. This order of updating entries at the *cross over router* and the forwarding leads to the creation of multiple streams of mis-ordered packets arriving to the MN. During a handoff period, newer packets diverted by the *cross over router* may arrive to the MN before older packets forwarded by FA1. Furthermore, the stream of packets P1 must follow the path to FA1, which forwards them to FA2. This triangular path of forwarding leads to receiving delayed packets by the MN.

5. Buffering at the *cross over Router*

Major side effects of forwarding buffered packets of a MN from the old foreign agent to the new one after handoff are mis-ordering and delaying of packets, specially when handoff lasts for a long period of time. To avoid these effects, we propose to buffer the packets destined to the MN at the *cross over router*. We define the *cross over router* as the first node at which the two paths P1 and P2 intersect. Where P1 is the path from the old foreign agent to the root of the hierarchy and P2 is the path from the new foreign agent to the root of the hierarchy. However, to select the *cross over router*, it is important to detect the new foreign agent before handoff. There are two advantages of buffering packets at the *cross over router*. First, it ensures that packets arriving to the MN are ordered. Indeed, when the MN does a handoff and sends a request for regional registration to the *cross over router*, the *cross over router* forwards the buffered packets to the MN immediately. The *cross over router* also adds an entry for the MN in its routing table. By doing so, all new packets destined to the MN will be diverted to the new foreign agent. It is clear, that such packets forwarding mechanism from the *cross over router* to the new foreign agent ensures that packets arrive to the MN in order. Second, the forwarding of packets from the *cross over router* to the new foreign agent takes less time than the forwarding of the same packets from the old foreign agent to the new one. Thus, our solution minimizes the delay of forwarding buffered packets.

We will use the scenario shown in fig 5 to explain our solution. In the hierarchical micro-mobility approach, FA includes in its advertisements a vector of care-of addresses, containing the IP Addresses of all its ancestors. For example, when the MN arrives at FA5, it stores the path P1={FA5, FA2, FA1} and it registers with all foreign agents in these path (see section 4).

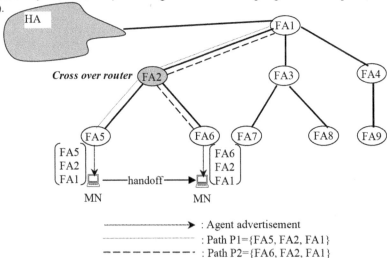

Fig 5 : Buffering at the *cross over router*

Assuming that the MN moves to FA6, hears advertisement from FA6 and decides to do a handoff to FA6. FA5 sends notification to FA6 containing the IP address of the MN and the path P1={FA6, FA2, FA1}. When the foreign agent FA6 receives this notification, it performs the low intersection between its path P2={FA6, FA2, FA1} and the path P1={FA5, FA2, FA1}. The result of this intersection defines the *cross over router* FA2. FA6 sends a message, which contains the IP address of the MN to FA2. This message will trigger buffering MN's packets at FA2. FA2 continues forwarding packets to FA5. Referring to the scenario shown in fig 5, FA2 buffers the recent few packets sent to the MN. When the MN does a handoff and registers with FA6. It receives a new vector of care-of addresses from FA6. It looks for the low intersection between the old vector and the new one, which is equal to FA2. It sends regional registration request to FA2. This request contains the IP ID of the last forwarded packet received by the MN from FA5. When FA2 receives this request, it creates a new binding for the MN with the correspondent FA6. This new binding will divert the path to FA6 and forward the buffered packets to the MN, starting with the packet IP ID.

6. Handoff protocol

In our protocol, one issue is how to define the new foreign agent before handoff in order to select the *cross over router*. We present in this section two methods. The first one is based on informing all adjacent FAs by the FA where the MN is attached (Tan *et al*, 1999). The second method uses link layer information to predict the new FA before initiating a handoff (Elmalki *et al*, 2001).

6.1 Informing adjacent FAs

We associate to each FA at the leaf of the hierarchy a path P. This path is a set of all ancestors of the FA. It begins with this FA and finishes with the FA at the root of the hierarchy. When a MN roams into foreign agent FA_i. FA_i informs all physically adjacent FA_j by transmitting a message containing the IP address of the MN and the path $P_i=\{FA_i,...,FA_k,...,FA_1\}$ as shown in fig 6.

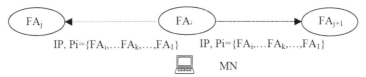

$$IP, Pi=\{FA_i,...FA_k,...,FA_1\} \quad IP, Pi=\{FA_i,...FA_k,...,FA_1\}$$

MN

Fig 6 : Informing adjacent FAs

Each FA_j which receives this message performs the low intersection between its associated path $P_j = \{FA_j,...,FA_k,...,FA_1\}$ and the path P_i received from FA_i. The result defines the *cross over router*:

$$low(P_i \cap P_j) = FA_k$$

Where **low** is an operator selecting the low intersection between two paths. In fact, FA_j knows the *cross over router* FA_k, it can send a message to inform FA_k to begin buffering packets which are destined to the MN. When the MN does a handoff and leaves FA_i to FA_j, it sends a regional registration request to the *cross over router* FA_k containing the IP ID of the last forwarded packet from FA_i. The *cross over router* FA_k adds a new binding to the MN in its routing table. This binding consists of the association between the MN home address and the address of the next lower level FA. The *cross over router* FA_k also sends buffered packets to the MN. When the handoff finishes, FA_j sends a notification to FA_i. Upon receiving this notification, FA_i sends an acknowledgement to FA_j and informs all its adjacent FAs except FA_j that the MN has moved. Each foreign agent which receives this information sends a message to its *cross over router* with FA_i, informing it to stop buffering for the MN and to dump the buffer associated with the MN.

6.2 Predict the new FA

In this method, communication between link layer and network layer must happen to predict the new FA. The movement detection method Hinted Cell Switching (HCS) is used. It is based on link layer information termed as hints, with the purpose of indicating when a link layer handoff occurs (Fikouras and Gorg, 2001). the receipt of link layer hints will cause the MN to broadcast an agent sollicitation which in turn forces all adjacent FAs to respond with an unicast agent advertisement. The MN is in the position to promptly determine the identity of FA_j regardless of the advertisement periods. It transmits this information to FA_i. FA_i sends then a message to FA_j containing the path $P_i=\{FA_i,...,FA_k,...,FA_1\}$. FA_i is the current foreign agent of the MN. FA_j performs the intersection between its path P_j and P_i. The result defines the *cross over router*. In this case, the handoff protocol changes. In fact, there is one *cross over router*, which buffers MN's packets and forward them to the MN.

7. Conclusion

we have presented a handoff scheme with a hierachical mobility management to handle real time applications in wireless environments. We have proposed a new solution to ensures an efficient handoff for TCP and real time applications. It consists on avoiding that mobile nodes receive mis-ordered and delayed packets at the time of forwarding mobile node's buffered packets. To reach our goal, we have proposed to buffer MN's packets at the *cross over router* instead of buffering them at the old foreign agent. By doing so, the forwarding from the old foreign agent to the new one is replaced by the forwarding from the *cross over router* to the new FA. This solution minimizes the forwarding delay. Indeed, the forwarding of MN's buffered packets from *cross over router* to the new foreign agent takes less time than the forwarding of the same buffered packets from the old foreign agent to the new one. It also guarantees that the MN receives the buffered packets in order. However, it was important to select the *cross over router* before a handoff. We have adopted two methods. The first one consists on informing all adjacent foreign agents by the current foreign agent. This way, each adjacent foreign agent selects the *cross over router*. The second uses link layer information to predict the new foreign agent.

In this paper, we proposed a general framework for an efficient handoff scheme. We plan to do further work, mainly by adapting our scheme to existing hierarchical solution as HAWAII. We also plan to do simulation on mobile platform to compare performance of our approach with other ones.

8. References

Brown, K. and Sing, S. (1996), "M-UDP: UDP for mobile networks", *ACM computre communication Review*, 26(5) : 60-78.

Caceras, R. and Padmanabhan, V.N. (1998), "Fast and scalable wireless handoff in support of mobile internet audio", *ACM journal on mobile and applications*, 3(4).

Campbell, A. Gomez, J. Wan, C.Y. Turanyi, Z. and Valko, A. (1999), "Cellular IP" internet Draft.

Elmalki, K. Calhoun, R. and Hiller, T. (2001), Low latency handoffs in mobile Ipv4. *Internet Draft.*

Fikouras, N.A. and Gorg, C. (2001), "A complete comparaison of algorithms for mobile IP handoff with complex movements patterns and internet audio", In *Proceedings of the Fourth Internation Symposium on Wireless Personal Multimedia Communications (WPMC)*, Aalborg, Denmark,

Fikouras, N. El Malki, K. Cvetkovic, S. and Smythe, C. (1999), "Performance of TCP and UDP during mobile IP handoffs in single agent subnetwork", *In IEEE wireless communication and networking conference, WCNC.* page 1258-1262.

Fikouras, N.A. El Malki, K. and Cvetkovic, S.R. (1999), "Performance analysis of mobile IP handoffs", *Proceedings IEEE APMC'99* Asia Pacific Microwave Conference, Singapore.

Kraner, M. Yap, C.N. Cvetkovic, S. and Sanchez, E. (2000), "Can mobile IP used as a link between IMT 2000 technologies and operators?", *Karlsruhe Workshop on Software Radios, University of Karlsruhe*, Germany.

McCann, P. Wang. T.H.J. Casati, A. Perkins, C. and Calhoun, P. (1999), "Transparent hierarchical mobility agents (THEMA)" Internet Draft.

Mysore, J. and Bharghavan, V. (1997), "A new multicasting based architecture for Internet host mobility", *In mobicom 97 Budapest Hunguary*, pages 161-172.

Perkins, C. (1996), "IP mobility support", RFC 2002 Updated by RFC *2290*. Status : Proposed standard.

Perkins, C. (1996), "IP encapsulation within IP", Net. Network working request for comments 2003.

Perkins, C. and Wang, K.Y. (1999), "Optimised smooth handoffs in mobile IP", *In the fourth IEEE symposium on computers and communications*, page 340-346.

Ramjee, R. Porta, T.L. Thuel, S. Vradhan, K. and Salgarelli, L. (1999) "IP micro-mobility support using HAWAII", Internet draft.

Ramjee, R. La Porta, T. Thuel, S. Varadhan, K. and Wang, S. (1999), "HAWAII: A Domain-based Approach for Supporting Mobility in Wide-area Wireless Networks", *Proc. IEEE Int'l. Conf. Network protocols.*

Tan, C. Pink, S. and Lye, K. (1999), "A fast handoff scheme for wireless Network", *In 2nd ACM international workshop on wireless Mobile multimeda (WowMo'99)*. Seatle, washington page 83-90.

Tan, C.L. Pink, S. and Lye K.M. (1999) "A Fast handoff sheme for wireless network", *In 2nd ACM International Workshop on Wireless Mobile Multimedia (WoWMoM'99)*, seatle, Washington, page 83-90.

Wang, K. Wei, Y. Dutta, A. and Young, K. (2001), "Performance of IP micromobility management schemes using host based routing", *Wireless Personal Multimedia Communications 2001*, September.

A Hierarchical Mobile Multicast Communication Protocol

Kwang-Hui Lee, and Tae-Soo Kim

Department of Computer Engineering Changwon National University, South Korea
e-mail : khlee@sarim.changwon.ac.kr

Abstract

One of the problems in handoff procedure of mobile multicast communication is that the efficient multicast path establishment is not easy without any special mechanism. If handoff procedure can be treated ahead of handoff event for candidate MSS(s) of mobile host to establish the new efficient path for multicast data transmission, mobile users can get good quality service with minimum handoff transition time. In order to provide good quality service to mobile hosts, we have proposed an efficient hierarchical architecture for multicast in mobile computing environment and functionality of each level. Active and passive path concepts in order to handle frequent handoff are introduced. Also we proposed mobility prediction mechanism for efficient mobility management.

Thus we found out an efficient solution that MSS joins multicast group on behalf of mobile host like an agent. With active and passive path concept and proper reservation period, it has been achieved to reduce waste of network bandwidth and transition time in handoff procedure.

Keywords

Mobile communication, multicast, group communication, routing

1. Introduction

Recently, dynamical expansion of wireless networking technology relating with generalization of mobile computer makes mobile communication environment to be realized. In this environment, many researches have developed various services for mobile users, for instance mobile multicast communication service. The multicast service provides n:m communication facility, saves the communication bandwidth in general and makes user be able to develop various applications. The multicast protocols have been designed and implemented in many research projects (Ballaride, 1997) (Estrin et al, 1998) (Waitzman, 1988) (Moy, 1998).

But, in mobile computing environment, frequent handoff may cause not only overweight procedure of handoff itself but also frequent change of the multicast path. It can be one of the hindrance to support continuous service with efficiency for multicast. One of the problems in handoff procedure of mobile multicast communication is that the efficient multicast path establishment and management is not easy without any special mechanism. If handoff procedure can be treated ahead of handoff event itself for candidate MSS(s) (mobile support station or base station) of mobile host to establish the new efficient path (it is the passive path concept explained in section 2), mobile users can get the continuous service with minimum handoff transition. In this paper, the candidate means that MSS, SH or MH has the passive path to the multicast source. If it is possible that the MSS expected to be the next MSS of moving MH can make a new path before the mobile host actually

* *This work was supported by grant No. (2000-1-51200-003-2) from the Basic Research Program of the Korea Science & Engineering Foundation*

moves into, the MH can get the continuous service during the handoff procedure. For this we have proposed a mobile multicast mechanism that has a hierarchical structure in this paper.

The rest of this paper is organized as follows. Section 2 is devoted to the description of the concepts of mobility management and hierarchical mobile communication model. In section 3, the operation of this model is mentioned in detail. Finally, we conclude in section 4.

2. The Proposed Architecture

In this section, we describe an efficient hierarchical architecture for multicast communication service in mobile computing environment and functionality of each level. Active and passive concepts mentioned. Also, an efficient mechanism for mobility prediction is described.

2.1 3-level hierarchy architecture

Traditional architectures for mobile networks view the system as a two-level hierarchy, that is, mobile hosts (MH) comprising the lowest level and mobile support Stations (MSS) providing network connectivity to the MH (Achary and Badrinath, 1996). It was found that traditional two-level architecture couldn't be well suited for mobile multicast services because MSS have too great a burden. Therefore, as shown in figure 1 b), the three-level hierarchy model has been adopted in our system similar to that of RelM (Brown and Singh, 1998).

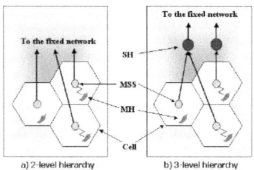

a) 2-level hierarchy   b) 3-level hierarchy

Figure 1. A hierarchical architecture

At bottom level, there are mobile hosts (MH) that can move from cell to cell. A MH can dynamically join and leave the specific multicast group. Also, it can send and receive a multicast message at any time.

At the middle level, there are Mobile Support Stations (MSS – which is connection point for the mobile host) - one a cell. A MSS provides mobile hosts connectivity to MH(s) in its cell. In this paper, it has been assumed that a MSS knows the identities of adjacent MSS(s). Also, a MSS can join a multicast group on behalf of the MH(s) resided in its cell. A MSS has to solicit adjacent MSS(s) to join multicast group on behalf of the member MH(s). That is, when a MSS has to join the group, the MSS lets the candidates make a passive path to the source. This passive path is the inactive path, but ready to be active in the case of handoff event (section 2.2). MSS has to know the status of MH(s) in its cell and filter the multicast datagrams depending on the status (section 3).

At the top level, a group of MSS(s) are controlled by an assigned supervisor machine, called Supervisor Host (SH). A SH is a part of the wired network and has a multicast capability among SHs. A SH does not have any direct relation with MH(s). SH and MSSs are directly connected by wired link. Each SH maintains the information on the group of MSSs to provide the multicast service among them. A SH, therefore, has to know the status of MSS(s) in its area and filter the multicast datagrams based on the information of status.

In this paper, we propose the method that the corresponding MSS joins the multicast group on behalf of MHs like an agent. A SH keeps the information of member MSS(s) while a MSS maintains the status of member MH(s) in its cell. Therefore, the localization of MH's mobility can be achieved. However, if the related cells are included in different SHs when a mobile host moves from one cell to other cell, the operation of handoff would give the effect on the SH level.

2.2 Active and Passive Path

In this paper, active and passive concept has been introduced for handling the handoff. The similar concept has been used at MRSVP (Talukdar et al, 1997) to offer QoS reservation to mobile node. This concept has been modified and extended in our system as follows.

Active: At MSS's level, if the MH sends and receives a message actively, the state of the path between the MH and MSS is active. It means that the MSS sends a message to and receives the incoming message from the MH. At SH's level, the path between the SH and MSS is active if messages are exchanged actively using this path. It means that there is more one member MH.

Passive: At MSS's level, if there is any active MSS in adjacent MSSs, this MSS should be passive. It means that this MSS is one of the candidates for the corresponding MH which maybe moves into this cell. The passive MSS is not sending and receiving the message, but it is ready to send and receive the message if the MH moves into this cell. At SH's level, the similar mechanism can be applied.

When a MSS receives multicast messages from SH, the MSS has to send it to only *active* MHs in its cell. When a SH receive multicast datagram from sender or other SH, SH has to send it to only *active* MSSs in its area. Both SH and MSS need to keep the *membership status table (Mstable)* for the status information.

2.3 Mobility Prediction Mechanism

2.3.1 Reservation Period

Considering mobility characteristics, a certain MH does not handoff during a multicast communication session. That is, the MH does not move or roams within the scope of its cell. Rather, in this case, it wastes precious network resources to make several passive join for the MH. If it starts handoff after long times freeze or it is frozen after short term moving, it can make a waste of resources.

In this paper, in order to minimize the wasting resource, we proposed the method that adjacent MSSs do not make passive join immediately after MH join in a group but they make passive join when the MH occur handoff event. That is, it can be regarded as a moving MH since a MH occurred the first handoff. Therefore, this mechanism may reduce wasting resource from the MH that does not move or roams within its cell during multicast session. Also, if a MH has stopped moving after handoff occurred, passive join may waste network resource. So, it is necessary to assign proper period of reservation for the MH.

In general, a MH moving with high speed has short handoff interval while a MH with low speed or stationary state has long handoff interval relatively. In other words, the handoff interval can be expressed as the residence time in a cell. MH's residence time in a cell is proportional to the diameter of the cell and proportional to the inverse of the average speed the cell. So, the proper period of reservation for the MH can be expressed as follows.

$$RT \propto \frac{D_c}{S_{avg}}$$

$$RT_{avg} = k \frac{D_c}{S_{avg}}$$

RT ; Residence Time
RT_{avg} ; Average Residence Time
D_c ; Cell Diameter
S_{avg} ; Average Speed
k ; Constant value

Figure 2. Equation of Average Residence Time

We can compute *Average Residence Time* using this equation. RT_{avg} value means expectation time of the next handoff. Thus, adjacent MSSs may reserve passive path for the MH during RT_{avg}. For example, if there is the cell that diameter is 2km and average speed is 50km/h, the next handoff is happened after 140 seconds because RT_{avg} is 140 seconds. If a MH moves faster than average speed, handoff event may happen before RT_{avg}. The remainder of the reservation time withdraws at the time when handoff occurs. On the other hand, if a MH moves slower than average speed or does not move, MSS maintains passive path during RT_{avg} and then MSS release the passive path for the MH. So, this mechanism may reduce wasting resource from the MH that does not move or roams within its cell or moves so slowly during multicast session.

2.3.2 Selection of MSSs

It is hard to know which neighbor MSS a MH moves to. To solicit all of adjacent MSSs to join multicast group on behalf of the MH can provide high probability of good service. However wasting resource will be increased because of many unused passive connections. A mobility prediction mechanism, therefore, has been developed to minimize the redundant overhead. In this paper, we proposed a mobility prediction method that predicts next direction using movement history of MHs. That is, a MSS solicits two or three MSSs elected with probability to passive join correspondent multicast group.

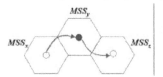

| Figure 3. Example 1 | Figure 4. TMI Table | Figure 5. Today's CMI Table |

For example, as shown in figure 3, let's suppose that MH_i moves from MSS_x to MSS_z via MSS_y. As MSS_y receives handoff request message from MSS_x for MH_i, MSS_y adds an entry $(mh_i, mss_x, ?)$ to *TMIT(Temporary Mobility Information Table)* after the handoff confirm message is sent. This information describes that MH_i migrated from MSS_x (figure 4). And then, if MH_i moves to MSS_z, MSS_y updates the entry to (mh_i, mss_x, mss_z) after handoff confirm message received. It means that MH_i moved to MSS_z via MSS_y.

To maintain movement history MSS_y increases the count value of correspondent filed at *CMIT*(*Cumulative Mobility Information Table*)(figure 5) and deletes the entry of MH_i at *TMIT*.

If MSS_y cannot fill into "*To MSS*" field because MH_i left the group in its area and multicast session is disconnected, MSS_y deletes MH_i's entry at *TMIT* because it cannot trace the direction of MH_i. Also, we used four kinds of *CMIT* (*CMIT*$_{today}$, *CMIT*$_{yesterday}$, *CMIT*$_{lastweek}$, *CMIT*$_{lastmonth}$) and *Weight* (W_t, W_y, W_w, W_m) in order to get higher accuracy. And each weight value has to satisfy below conditions.

$$W_t + W_y + W_w + W_m = 1$$
$$W_t > W_y > W_w > W_m$$

As show in figure 6, let's suppose that MH_1 moved from MSS_4 to MSS_7. Using follow equation (Figure 7), we can compute each probability that MH_1 moves to which of adjacent *MSSs*. Thus, in this paper, we chose two MSS with a high probability (P) as candidate MSS for next handoff.

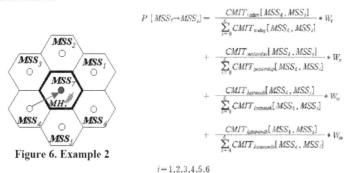

Figure 6. Example 2

$$P\,[MSS_7 \rightarrow MSS_i] = \frac{CMIT_{today}[MSS_4, MSS_i]}{\sum_{i=0}^{6} CMIT_{today}[MSS_4, MSS_i]} * W_t$$
$$+ \frac{CMIT_{yesterday}[MSS_4, MSS_i]}{\sum_{i=0}^{6} CMIT_{yesterday}[MSS_4, MSS_i]} * W_y$$
$$+ \frac{CMIT_{lastweek}[MSS_4, MSS_i]}{\sum_{i=0}^{6} CMIT_{lastweek}[MSS_4, MSS_i]} * W_w$$
$$+ \frac{CMIT_{lastmonth}[MSS_4, MSS_i]}{\sum_{i=0}^{6} CMIT_{lastmonth}[MSS_4, MSS_i]} * W_m$$

$$i = 1,2,3,4,5,6$$

Figure 7. Equation of Probability

3. The Proposed Mechanism

In this section, the operation procedures of the proposed protocol are described in brief. Some of service and protocol primitives and several related functions for mobile multicast communication are given.

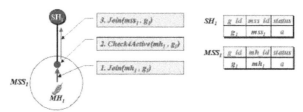

Figure 8. Join Mechanism

3.1 Join

As shown in figure 8, MH_1 sends a join message to MSS_1 for participating in the group g_1. MSS_1 checks whether any members of g_1 already exist or not in the corresponding cell with *MStable*. If it is first, MSS_1 adds an entry of the table with the appropriate values (*group_id* = g_1, *mh_id* =mh_1, *status=active*). After that, MSS_1 sends a join message to the SH_1 on behalf of the MH_1.

3.2 Handoff

Figure 9 presents the handoff mechanism. When MSS_1 receives *handoff request* message from a MH_1, the MSS_1 sends handoff request message to the following MSS_3.

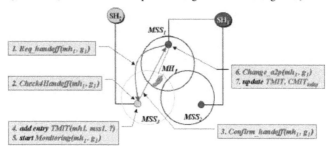

Figure 9. Handoff Mechanism

MSS_3 checks whether any *MH* participating in the group g_1 exists in *MStable* or not. If there is no *MH* involving in the group g_1, MSS_3 sends a *join* message to SH_2 and then creates an entry composed of $(g_1$, mh_1, *active*) at *MStable*. But, if there is at least a *MH* involving in the group g_1, MSS_3 checks again whether *passive MH₁* participating in the group g_1 exists or not. If there is passive MH_1 participating in g_1, MSS_3 changes into active status for MH_1 and then sends a *State_Notification(mss₃, g₁, active)* message to SH_2. On the contrary, if there is no passive MH_1, MSS_3 checks whether any active *MH* participating in the group g_1 exists in *MStable* or not. If there is no any active member, MSS_3 sends a *State_Notification(mss₃, g₁, active)* message to SH_2 and then adds an entry composed of $(g_1$, mh_1, *active*) at *MStable* because MSS_3 is *passive* status. But, if there is at least an active *MH* involving in g_1, MSS_3 adds entry $(g_1$, mh_1, *active*) for MH_1 to the *MStable* and then delivers multicast datagrams.

And then, MSS_3 sends a *Confirm_handoff* message to MSS_1 and adds entry (mh_1, mss_1, ?) to the *TMIT* and starts *Monitoring* function for MH_1. The operation of the *Monitoring* function is described in bellow subsection. When MSS_1 receives it, MSS_1 stops monitoring for MH_1. And then, MSS_1 changes the MH_1's status into passive. If there is no active *MH*, MSS_1 sends a *State_Notification(mss₁, g₁, passive)* message to SH_1. Also, in order to predict mobility, MSS_1 updates *TMIT* corresponding $MH_1$and $CMIT_{today}$.

3.2.1 Monitoring

As shown in section 2.3.1, during RT_{avg} periods, *MSS* monitors *MH* until receiving handoff request or leave message from the *MH*. As we can see from figure 10, MSS_1 periodically sends a *passive* message to the expected *MSSs*(MSS_3 and MSS_7 in this example) for them to prepare multicast service to MH_1 with minimum handoff transition delay. In this case, MSS_3 and MSS_7 have the passive path during RT_{avg} periods.

After RT_{avg} periods, a *MSS* does not monitor for the *MH*. Consequently, there is a possibility that the handoff transition delay become longer. However, by reason of the hierarchical architecture, in the case of inter-MSS handoff in the same *SH* domain, the handoff transition delay may not very long because the upper level *SH* have been received a multicast datagram already.

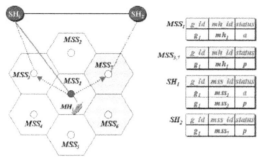

Figure 10. Monitoring Mechanism

As $MSS_{3,7}$ receive passive messages, they check *MStable* for the previous MH_i participated in the same group. If it is not the first member of the relating group, $MSS_{3,7}$ add an entry which consists of $(g_1, mh_1, passive)$ to the *MStable*. If it is the first, $MSS_{3,7}$ add entry which consists of $(g_1, mh_1, passive)$ and then send passive join message to $SH_{1,2}$ on behalf of the MH_1. And $MSS_{3,7}$ send *Status_Notification(mss_i, g_i, passive)* message to the upper level $SH_{1,2}$. In this way, $SH_{1,2}$ can get the information whether $MSS_{1\sim7}$ status are *active* or *passive*.

The basic idea of monitoring function is that the *MSS* or *SH* can keep the *passive* connection between *MSS* and multicast source. Therefore, when *MH* moves into other domain, *MSS* or *SH* provides the continuous service to the *MH* through *passive* connection.

3.2.2 Timeout

The function of timeout is to release the passive path for the resource saving if the passive path was not activated by certain period. *MSS* receives the passive message from the neighbor *MSS* periodically (ΔT). Then, *MSS* starts $Timer(\Delta T+n)$. The period of timeout, that is value of n, has not been determined yet. But we can get the value of this parameter with simulation and operation of this protocol. If a *MSS* receives passive message again before the *Timer* expires, *MSS* restarts the *Timer*. If the *Timer* expired, *MSS* deletes the entry of the *MH* in *MStable*. After that, if there are no members in this area, *MSS* sends a leave message to the upper level *SH*.

3.3 Leave

When *MSS* receives a *leave* message from the *MH*, it deletes an entry of the corresponding *MH* in *MStable* and stops $Monitoring(mh_i, g_i)$ function. If there is no more active or passive *MH*, *MSS* sends a leave message to the upper level *SH*. Otherwise, *MSS* sends a *State_Notification(mss_i, g_i, passive)* message to the upper level *SH*.

3.4 Send

In Figure 11, we show how a MH sends and receives a multicast datagram. When MSS_1 receives multicast datagram from MH_1, MSS_1 checks *MStable* for active *MH* participated in the group g_1. If there is any active member MH involving in the g_1, MSS_1 delivers the multicast message to all active MHs included in this cell ($MSS\_Backward$) and forwards it to the upper SH_1. SH_1 sends this message to all members of $MSSs$ of group g_1 by referencing the table in SH_1 ($SH\_Backward$).

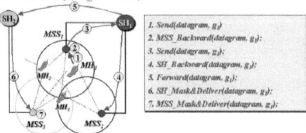

1. Send(datagram, g_1)
2. MSS_Backward(datagram, g_1);
3. Send(datagram, g_1);
4. SH_Backward(datagram, g_1);
5. Forward(datagram, g_1);
6. SH_Mask&Deliver(datagram, g_1);
7. MSS_Mask&Deliver(datagram, g_1);

Figure 11. Send Mechanism

When SH_2 receives multicast datagram from SH_1, SH_2 checks $MStable$ for active MSS participated in the group g_1. If there is any active $MSS(s)$ of group g_1, SH_2 selectively forwards the datagram to the only active $MSS(s)$. Otherwise, SH_2 does not forward it to passive $MSSs$ and drops message ($SH\_Mask\&Deliver$). Similarly, MSS_3 delivers it to the only active $MH(s)$ in its cell ($MSS\_Mask\&Deliver$). Therefore, by using $active$ and

4. Conclusions

In this paper, we proposed a hierarchical multicast protocol architecture in mobile computing environments. We found out efficient solution that fixed MSS joins in multicast group on behalf of mobile host. As the MH moves from one cell to other cell, the MSS joins the corresponding multicast group and leaves it. With using active and passive concept and proper reservation period, it has been achieved to reduce waste of network bandwidth, transmission delay and transition time in handoff procedure. The simulation model has been built and now the simulation is under way.

References

Acharya, A. and Badrinath, B.R. (1996), "A Framework for delivering multicast messages in networks with mobile hosts", *Journal on Mobile Networks and Applications*, Vol. 1, No. 2, pp. 199-220.

Ballaride, A. (1997), "Core Based Trees Multicast Routing Architecture", *RFC2201*.

Talukdar, A., Badrinath, B. and Archaya, A. (1997), "MRSVP: A reservation protocol for an Integrated Services Packet Networks with Mobile hosts", *Technical report, TR-337*.

Estrin, D. et al (1998), "Protocol Independent Multicast-Sparse Mode (PIM-SM): Protocol Specification", *RFC2362*.

Waitzman, D., Partridge, C. and Deering, S.E. (1988), "Distance Vector Multicast Routing Protocol", *RFC1075*.

Moy, J. (1994), "Multicast Extensions to OSPF", *RFC1584*.

Brown, K. and Singh, S. (1998), "RelM: Reliable Multicast for Mobile Networks", *Computer Communications*, Vol. 21, pp. 1379-1400.

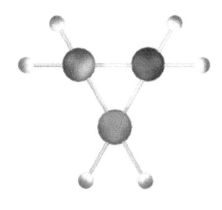

Chapter 8

Applications and Impacts

My Information Broker

A Next Step to overcome the Information Problems in the Internet

Robert Loew[1,2], Udo Bleimann[2], Brendan Murphy[1], Joerg Preuss[1,2]

[1] Department of Mathematics and Computing, Cork Institute of Technology, Ireland
[2] Institute of Applied Informatics Darmstadt (aida),
University of Applied Sciences Darmstadt, Germany
e-mail : robert@loew.com

Abstract

In this paper the information problems in the Internet are addressed via a new concept : My Infobroker. My Infobroker is like a personal assistant for all the information problems of a client. An Infobroker is implemented as a man-machine-cooperation. Some interesting details are discussed in the paper : What is a Personal Infobroker, how to find an Infobroker, how Infobrokers are organised, how to form communities and what would an Infobroker look like ?

Keywords

Infobroker, Information Broker, Information Brokering, Information Overload

Introduction

Today the Internet offers a massive amount of information and services that are no longer manageable. Often search engines, which return a huge quantity of information, are not able to deliver the requested information. Also there is no guarantee on the quality of the returned information, so it is hard for the user to have a high degree of trust in every information source.

What Internet Users really want, is to be able to express their needs for information or services to somebody that can help them with their problem.

In practice with the Internet the situation of users has declined by comparison to the former situation where expert advice was offered at every store. In an Internet store there is normally no advice.

Information Brokerage

A possible way out of the information overload problem could be an Information Broker (called Infobroker or IB) which offers quality proofed information and services and will be paid for this.

Infobrokers form a network and work together to offer information and services from all specialities.

To date the term "Infobroker" describes the profession of registrars and other people who are professional dealing with information.

Several organisations are offering contact to Infobrokers, e.g. AIIP (aiip website), EIRENE (eirene website) and DGI (dgi website).

These organisations are normally offering a web-based Infobroker directory where a Client can search an Infobroker. There is no communication model offered - there is only contact information provided. The specialities of every Infobroker are described as free-text or as the DGI does, there are a variety of specialities to choose from.
If one Infobroker wants to communicate with another Infobroker, he has to use the same web-site to find him.

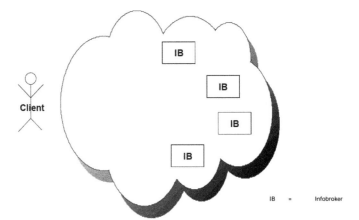

Figure 1 : Situation Today

We would like to extend this Infobroker in some aspects which will be described in the next section.

Our Concept : Personal Infobroker or My Infobroker

Every client has a Personal Infobroker, who manages his requests. A Personal Infobroker has to manage the profiles of each client. In these profiles, the preferences of a client are managed.

In general we can say that a Personal Infobroker is a modern type of secretary or personal assistant out-sourced in the Internet.
A mutual trust relationship must be built up between the client and his personal Infobroker.
When this relationship exists, the client gives his personal data to his Infobroker.

Of course, an Infobroker is not a specialist in every field, he has to find out which of his colleagues are specialists in the requested area. The Personal Infobroker then generates a task which describes the client's request. This task will be transferred to his colleague. After the colleague fulfills the task, he informs the Personal Infobroker as well as the client.

If a client is satisfied with his Personal Infobroker, then he will be more inclined to do all his business with him.

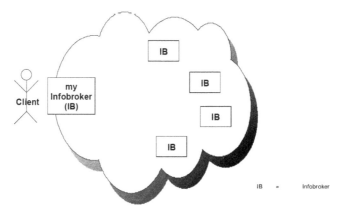

Figure 2 : Personal Infobroker (My Infobroker)

We would now like to look more in detail and address the following aspects within our concept:
1 How to find an Infobroker (IB Directory)
2 How Infobrokers are organised
3 How to form communities for clients and Infobrokers
4 What would an Infobroker look like

1 How to find an Infobroker (IB Directory)

The Infobroker community is growing, and there are only a few methods used to find a broker. At first a contact address can only be found by using a normal search engine like Altavista, Fireball, Google, etc. This is a very annoying job, because of the thousands of links that may be found. Then you can try one of those organisational Infobroker search engines from AIIP (aiip website), EIRENE (eirene website), DGI (dgi website) and some others.

So what is needed is a global search engine where all Infobrokers are stored, wherever they are globally located. Even the usability is the same and there are well defined points in the Internet, where you can start your query. No searching where to find a place for search - only search for your contact.

Which technology is used for such a search engine ?

The kind of search discussed, is a sort of browsing in the yellow pages. This simplifies the choice of technology to be used. A directory service needs to be developed.

There are some possibilities for setting up a directory service. The most preferred way is to use LDAP - the Lightweight Directory Access Protocol from IETF (Wahl et al, 1995). It is a light version of X.500 which originates from ITU. The hierarchical tree structure in LDAP (see Figure 3) is useful for placing all Infobrokers' information in the directory.

LDAP is supporting us in making the directory more secure. LDAP even offers the possibility to distribute the directory over many different machines. In the case of a fast growing Infobroker community, a standalone-system will be not enough to handle all the possible requests in a reasonable time. With LDAP the traffic can spread over many machines to achieve better result times.

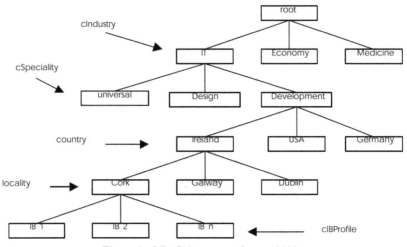

Figure 3 : LDAP Structure (Preuss, 2002)

Where do all the Infobrokers come from ?

First of all Infobrokers are needed to fill the directory. A possible solution is to bring several organisations together e.g., AIIP (aiip website), EIRENE (eirene website) and DGI (dgi website). Another possibility is to create a new organisation, which handles all those Infobrokers.

The way is, to register those Infobrokers - even to ensure their offer and quality. To register an Infobroker, the person has to specify a business category that he would offer and any specialities that the person has, along with any personal data needed. By personal data is meant information like postal-, e-mail and web-addresses. Because of the fact that the Infobroker has to fit his preferred business category and speciality into the given ones, he may specify some aspects of his business in his own words - those entries we will call skills further on.
All registered brokers will be included in the directory.

How will the search engine be used ?

A user visits a special web-site dedicated to searching for Infobrokers. There are two possibilities for such searches.

• The first possibility is, the user fills out a form with search attributes, such as the business category and specialty for which an Infobroker is needed. The user can narrow the search to only defined countries and/or cities if locality is necessary. The directory service will then show the results. If more than one broker is found, the list will be sorted alphabetically. Each result entry can be opened by the user to check the broker's profile and skills (included within the profile).

• The second possibility is to browse through the Infobroker tree to find a matching contact. This is similar to using the yellow pages. The user has to decide which business category and specialty he wants supported. He also can specify a locality.

Who is able to use this system ?

The Infobrokers themselves are able to use that special search engine. They have overall access possibilities. But not only the Infobrokers, even the Clients who are searching for an Infobroker may use this system, to find a contact. Although their possibilities are not as extensive as Infobrokers have themselves.

2 How Infobrokers are organised ?

A communication infrastructure is used for all communications between clients and their personal Infobrokers, or for communication between two or more Infobrokers.

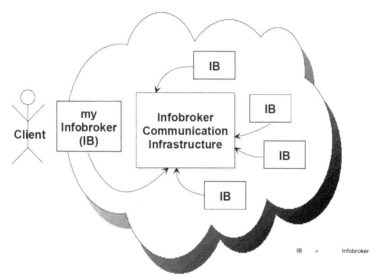

Figure 4 : Infobroker Communication Infrastructure

Knowledge Management System (KMS)

The Infobroker network creates a Knowledge Management System available to all Infobrokers.

Using a simple tool, every Infobroker manages the structure and the content of their own data within this Knowledge Management System. All his knowledge could be managed in his own words and own structure. For example, for every client a profile is created and is managed dynamically. Every profile has a different structure that can be extended dynamically.

An Infobroker can describe every part of his/her information as public domain, for personal use only or for payable use.

In a standard KMS all information is designed for public use. It takes by far more time for the author to produce this than writing only for some experts working in his area or for the author only.

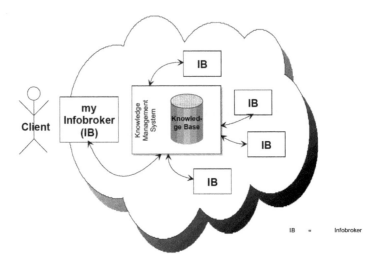

Figure 5 : Infobroker Knowledge Management System

External Experts and Services

Infobrokers use external Experts and Services. For example, a service can be a special bookseller that sells academic books - the person guarantees the quality of the books that are offered. An expert offers knowledge.

Every Infobroker manages his contacts to experts and services using the Knowledge Management System because it is to difficult to automate the communiaction totally.

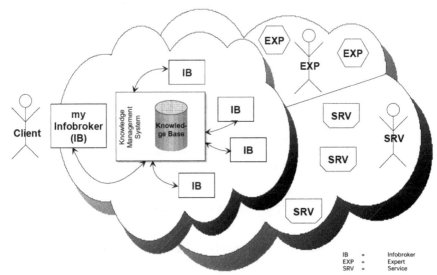

Figure 6 : Infobroker Architecture with Experts and Services

3 How to form communities for Clients and Infobrokers

Often it's better to know somebody with the same interests or research areas than reading hundreds of documents. A background system in the Infobroker Architecture scans the client's profile and compares their interests to their requests. A contact between two (ore more) Partners will be offered to them if their Interests seem to be similar. So a Community can be established. This has of course to follow some regulations :
a) All partners are anonymously asked whether they are interested in such a communication.
b) If accepted by all communication partners, a communication can then be established.

To support these Communities the Infobroker communication infrastructure offers methods for instant communication e.g., chatrooms, teamrooms and secure point-to-point communication between two members of the community. Of course community members can exchange contact information and manage their communication with one another themselves.

An example of such a community approach is the "RAVEN" project from IBM / Lotus (Kajmo and Hunter, 2000).

4 What would an Infobroker look like

Man-machine-cooperation

An Infobroker could be implemented in a machine using artificial intelligence. But this approach has failed in many projects. Another possibility is solely man based because it is the most flexible solution. But this is too expensive.
Because of the complexity of the different requirements e.g., search problems, ordering problems from our point of view the solution will be based on man-machine-cooperation. We think this is the best balance between costs and flexibility.

Standard requests are answered in the first step by an automated process, due to the fact that human resources are expensive. As an example client A started a request which had been answered for Client B a short time before. The results for Client B could be transferred to client A with the extension that he is asked whether this answer is OK or whether he wants more information. If he needs more information a communication with his personal Infobroker must be established.

How to implement such a cooperative system

At present we are developing a generic information logistics architecture which could be used for different applications. This architecture is based on an application server. It uses web services, XML, SOAP, CORBA, DCOM and proprietary technologies like EntireX for access to backend systems (Fuchs and Glogowski, 2002).
Within our team we are working as well on mobile agent technology (Stengel et al, 2002). With this technology we want to support the clients and the Infobrokers with personal agents which will assist in fulfilling their tasks.

Summary and Outlook

This paper proposes a new concept to overcome the information problems in the Internet. An Infobroker works like a personal assistant and could fix all information problems for a client. We will implement an Infobroker as a man-machine-cooperation.

This is a joint research project which will address security and additional man-machine-cooperation aspects in the future. We are also working on the financial part of the concept which investigates several billing procedures.

The whole concept will be presented as an animated multimedia presentation at the aida website.

References and further readings

aida website, Institute of Applied Informatics Darmstadt (aida),
http://www.aida.fh-darmstadt.de

aiip website, Association of Independent Information Professionals,
http://www.aiip.org

Bachmann, J. (2000), Der Information Broker, Addison-Wesley Verlag, München (in German)

dgi website, Deutsche Gesellschaft für Informationswissenschaft und Informationspraxis e.V., http://www.dgd.de (in German) / http://www.dgd.de/english/index.html (in English)

Davenport, H. and Prusak, L. (2000), Working Knowledge, Harvard Business School Press

eirene website, European Information Researchers Network EIRENE,
http://www.eirene.com

Fuchs, C. and Glogowski J.-M. (2002), A Model for a web-based Information Logistics Concept, Diploma Thesis, aida, University of Applied Sciences Darmstadt (in German)

Kajmo, D.; Hunter, K. (2000), Introduction to Raven,
http://media.lotus.com/devcon/BUS111.pdf (last Access May 2001)

Preuss, J. (2002), Information Brokerage - A Communication Model for Infobrokers, Diploma Thesis, aida, University of Applied Sciences Darmstadt (in German)

Stengel, I.; Bleimann, U.; Stynes J. (2002), A Virtual University using Mobile Agent Technology, *Proceedings of International Network Conference (INC 2002)*, Plymouth / UK

Tiwana, A. (2000), Essential Guide to Knowledge Management, The: E-Business and CRM Applications, Prentice Hall Computer Books

Tiwana, A. (2000), Knowledge Management Toolkit, The: Practical Techniques for Building a Knowledge Management System, Prentice Hall

Wahl, M.; Howes, T.; Kille, S. (1995), LDAP v3,
http://www.faqs.org/rfcs/rfc2251.html (last Access December 2001)

Information Provision to Individuals and User Profiles

M. Konstantopoulos[1,2], J.S. Darzentas[1], T. Spyrou[1,2], J. Darzentas[1]

[1]Department of Product and Systems Design
University of the Aegean, GR 84100 Hermoupolis, Syros, Greece,
[2]Department of Information and Communication Systems
University of the Aegean, GR 82300 Karlovassi, Samos, Greece,
email: {mpk, jennyd, tsp, idarz}@aegean.gr

Abstract

Information provision to individuals is a possibility nowadays partly due to the technological advances that permit a high degree of customisation and instant delivery at a low cost. In this paper, information provision is defined as the provision of digital content through a network to a user of a digital access device. It is our belief that the provision of information services to individuals outside the organizational boundaries is changing the type of information circulated and consequently the users' profiles. We discuss the user profiling techniques of the GUARDIANS project designed to handle the delivery of content to the user. We debate on reasons that already deployed user profiling systems and techniques may not be adequate for current information provision systems

Keywords

Information Provision, User profiles, Multi-organisational applications

1. Introduction

IS theory has for long has a strong connection to the organisational environment (see for example Avgerou, 2000 for the thematic areas of IS discipline) while IS implementations usually take place in these or similar environments. The treatment of information in IS theory is analogous. Eaton and Bawden (1991) reflecting on the nature of information, note that in information management theory, 'the idea that information is a resource, to be managed on behalf of the organization it belongs, is now well entrenched'.

Eaton and Bawden conclude that for a number of reasons to do with the special characteristics of information – be it termed 'value', 'consumption,' 'dynamics', 'life-cycle' or 'individuality' of information - it should not be treated as a typical resource, a commodity to be measured similarly with others in the organisational environment. Ten years on their observations seem even more acute. Much of current discussions on 'the Information Society' revolve around the issues of information production, circulation of information and expectations from it. In the vision of the information society, individual citizens are required to act in both an organizational environment and a societal level making use of advanced informational services.

The fact that individuals are nowadays information consumers not only in connection with their organizational role but also at their societal one is changing the way the related information has to be modelled and delivered. The notion of the Information Society supposes that individuals are making use of information for the fulfilment of their social role and their "digital citizenship". This means an end to considering a user merely as an individual within an organisation, playing an organisational role. Being that information is thus considered central for the fulfilment of an individual's social role, the individual's access to digital services, and remote information resources is generating new uses of information and the equivalent systems to support such utilization.

A common and generic case is examined in this paper, that is, the provision of digital informative content, as required for instance in the online delivery of distance learning programmes. Digital informative content is defined as any piece of instructive and informative content. The next section discusses the individual's relation to information. Section 3 presents a business model of the GUARDIANS project, for information provision to individuals. Section 4 proposes a framework for information to individual modeling for business related activities. Finally section 5 discusses open issues and conclusions.

2. Information and its relation to individuals

There is much discussion today on the relations between data-information and knowledge that have been theorised as following a pyramidal model, where knowledge is produced by information, which is produced by data. Many have noted deficiencies in this model (summarised in Newman, 2001). But there is also a wide acceptance of it, and theories based on the fact that information has been separated from data because information is related to an information consumer, usually a human. The path from data to information has been concisely defined by Mylopoulos (1998) who describes information modeling as the area of research "concerned with the construction of computer-based symbol structures which capture the meaning of information and organise it in ways that make it understandable and useful to the people". He considers information modeling as encompassing such techniques as knowledge representation, data modeling and requirements analysis.

Although there is a debate about whether humans are able to capture and conceptualise objectively, ideally, 'data' is the term used for an objective fact, free of any semantic dimension. Moreover data are not considered tied to transmission but they are defined as events waiting to be retrieved or discovered. This of course is not totally true because data capturing is already a transformation procedure and data modelling, which is the "art" of data representation, has to make some assumptions on human knowledge representation in order to produce efficient structures and relationships for data.

Information is commonly then being defined with regard to objects and subjects. It is usually understood as the meanings appointed to an objective event (fact) by people (Hirschheim, Klein, Lyytinen, 1995) or put another way, the conceptualisation of an event by a human. Especially in socio-technical environments and equivalent disciplines information is closely related to the subject describing it. Information modeling concerns both the formalisation of the object (data) and the determination of its relation to the subject. Therefore, when discussing information modelling, the important parameter to be kept in mind is the consumer of information i.e. the human.

The issue is now how the human is modelled in practice. Due to the fact mentioned previously that information was of value in an organisational environment, this had, as a direct consequence, that the consumers of information are organisational users, and the human 'subjects' of the information are usually not thought of as individuals but as organisational roles (the manager, the accounts department, the logistics, etc.). Moreover they are supposed to be located in a certain place (office) from where they have access to organizational information. Usually software implementations make the assumption that the humans involved with data have an organisational role to play. Such an approach downgrades the generic definition of an individual as an entity to that of an organisational role and this may not be adequate for the case of a user who is not part of an organisation but rather an external entity - a client in the broad sense.

The 'networkers' community has also inherited its modelling techniques from the business world. This is also probably a consequence of the introduction of networks as business value adding tools. What was needed then was a business profile of the user, his/ her function within an organisation, his/her rights to the organisational resources. The first representation of users in a networking environment trying to make up a user profile can be considered to capture such information (OSI/ISO, 1993). Other efforts were only partial and function oriented in such a manner that any other use was excluded (e.g. operating system user profiles/ accounts).

However, now as the use of networks is changing, as new quests for the development of social or global level applications are coming to the fore, new models for the user profiles are required. Our scenario is one where a user is a potential consumer of a wide range of information related services and thus a customer of information providers and brokers. We can also envisage an "information society" environment where a user is coping with governmental and community level equivalent services. A user is a digital citizen with the need to access, and be provided with, information and exploit the vast amount of information resources in an efficient manner (i.e. navigate the information space), to have the capability of fulfilling various roles and make use of various service providers. The quest is now not the correlation of users with organisational data but rather the profiling of individuals in order to be able to make use of information services from multiple non-binding providers, securely and through various access means.

3. An information usage business model

This section, presents the overall architecture for information provision of the GUARDIANS (Gateway for User Access to Remote Distributed Information and Network Services) project. The GUARDIANS project (GUARDIANS, 2000) identifies the technology for the next generation of Information Management tools and specify how the required infrastructure will allow distributed components to interwork Information Management in this context is taken to have a wider meaning than just the content that is of interest to users. It encompasses:

- Rich, diverse and interactive content drawn from both web resources intended to be delivered over the Internet and interactive digital broadcast content;
- Metadata describing these diverse resources;
- User profiles describing user preferences, both on content and access configuration;
- Advanced search and notification services (traditionally called Selective Dissemination of Information SDI);
- Information Object Agent technology capable of comparing resources and their metadata descriptions to identify related materials;
- Distributed software technology for dynamic management and update of metadata, with specific reference to problems related to availability and accessibility of multimedia resources.

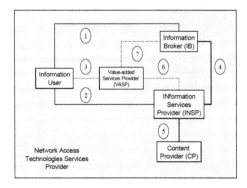

Figure 1 – GUARDIANS Business Model

A brief description of the roles played in the GUARDIANS environment is shown in figure one and explained below. Depending upon the situation, different organizations or individuals involved in a GUARDIANS session can take on different Roles.

Information User: equivalent to an individual making used of advanced information services, is at the heart of the GUARDIANS Business Model. The "user" is the entity wishing to discover the existence and location of an information resource and/or actually participating in a GUARDIANS information session. It could also be a software agent, or an information brokerage service. The user is characterised by his/her/its profile, which provides a common point for the structured consolidated storage of information about a user – their background, experience, preferences, etc. This profile may be partially held to the information broker, INSP or an independent third party (VASP).

Network Access Technologies Services Provider: consists of the organisation/s providing the physical links and network services required to link the various actors playing GUARDIANS roles together. By its very definition the GUARDIANS environment is distributed.

Information Broker: can be defined as an on-line service that mediates in the discovery of items available from a variety of vendors, or information about such items, to users wishing to find out more and then use/purchase the items. In the GUARDIANS environment the items are information resources (either as discrete components or packaged in an integrated way). The user wishes to discover the existence of an information resource, or set of information resources, meeting his/her/its user defined search criteria.

INformation Service Provider (INSP):, which is the entity that houses and controls access to the information resources. It is also likely that the INSP controls the interactive interface, management, delivery, administration and presentation of the information resources. The INSP is characterised by its profile which provides information on Service Providers and is useful in targeting content to user profiles by the Information Broker

Value Added Service Provider (VASP): there are various intelligent components and services that may be developed on such an environment. It may be independent profiling services for users to the other GUARDIANS components or it may be a niche market component like provider of some very specific information.

Content Provider: is the individual or organisation actually producing and/or making available the information content via the INSP's.

In addition to the roles described above, the inter-role business relationships between the previously described GUARDIANS roles are described below. These business relationships are depicted in Figure 1 as the lines identified by circled numbers. Solid lines represent primary relationships and dashed lines represent secondary relationships concerning the VASP role:

1) **User – Information Broker***:* the user engages the services of the Information Broker to discover the existence of information resources based on a user profile and any additional search criteria supplied.

4) **Information Broker - INSP***:* the Information Broker will initiate search requests on behalf of the User to the INSP's. All search operations are directed via the Information Broker.

2) **User - INSP***:* the relationship between the user and the INSP for the delivery of selected information will be that of a client-server relationship. The user connects to the INSP and if necessary gains authorisation to proceed before using any of the INSP's information resources. The INSP will at all times control delivery and interactions.

5) **INSP - Content Provider***:* the business relationship between the INSP and the content provider will cover the provision of digital information from the content provider to the service provider/s. It will also cover the reward of the content provider for the use of such material as specified in the business agreement between the two roles.

3) **User – VASP***:* Depending on the functionality of the VASP, the User may select to use the functionality of the VASP to create and maintain a profile of himself/herself/itself or make use of the specialised information services (the example case).

6) **INSP - VASP***:* There are again two cases of correlation between an INSP and a VASP. One is that the INSP registering with GUARDIANS may select to have a detailed service provider profile adequate enough to enable efficient searching of its information resources. The second that the VASP is a reseller of INSP information.

7) **VASP – Information Broker**: the VASP role may be the concept of the Information Broker using User and INSP profiles to match users to INSP resources or the concept of the Information Service Provider for specialised services.

4. The Information User profile

There is then a new environment characterised partly by its multi-organisational structure. Multi-organisational environments permit operations to take place in a global scale with multiple service levels and imply that users have to be considered outside their usual organisational environment.

In this context there is a challenge of how to build the appropriate user profile. The typical case is that every network user is identified by others based on a profile. This is usually an electronic record stored somewhere containing the characteristics of the user. Each user daily handles a set of records to make use of the digital or network services. User and mail accounts, digital subscriptions or more advanced digital "passports" to services are components of the daily network user life.

Users and service providers are asking for a concentration of the various services, to promote ease of handling the various accounts and profiles. The scenario of building a scalable profile in a service provider is one case. The other is the scenario of building a profile shared across multiple providers. A joint scenario may contain both and this the one promoted by the GUARDIANS project. The GUARDIANS project is trying to exploit the current informational infrastructures of the Internet and those of the providers' in order to achieve a scalable and efficient user profile for the provision of multiple services.

4.1 The existing model

Internet is a peer to peer network but from a certain point of view, that is, the naming scheme of it, it provides a hierarchical structure. This assumption has been considered necessary for the stake of simplicity, as the expression of full relational schemas like the ones depicted in databases would produce an administrative nightmare to implementers. This hierarchy introduced and used by the DNS (Domain Name Service) is more recently adopted for user manipulation by X.500 (OSI/ISO, 1993) and lastly the Lightweight Directory Access Protocol –LDAP (Wahl at al., 1997). Supposing a global directory infrastructure, each user is associated with a unique account and an accompanying profile. Such a profile may provide access to various services ranging from access to content to special service provision characteristics (like QoS), with the use of some basic functions (authentication, definition of access rights, etc.). The LDAP protocol has inherited from its predecessor (X.500) some assumptions about the user and what it is. A hierarchy of classes for the representation of user information is indicative of what the Internet user is considered to be.

At the core of this user information are the demographic personal details of the user. At a second level come the business details of the user. The user is modeled in an organisational role. At a third level, class developers are working on applications that extend this user model to an application specific profile, enhancing it with more information. This hierarchy is shown in Figure 2. Examples of implementations based on this model are numerous, a typical and one of the latest being Internet2's initiative EduPerson (Gettes, 2001) where a similar hierarchy has been proposed for users of academic institutions in US.

4.2 The GUARDIANS model

GUARDIANS has modified this hierarchy by in the first place adding an information client role and secondly transferring the user's model of an organizational role to the application level. There is a substantial reason for performing such a change. Users need to be and feel autonomous from organisations in the information and network space. Users want to be able to change or share application providers without substantial loss in the service provision to them. Typical examples are in the vocational training business, where a trainee is able to take courses from different institutions in parallel or sequence and at the end to be able to get a degree, or mobile user profiles (directories, settings etc.), that users would like to carry across various service providers.

While in the common previous modeling schemata, applications had an intranet organisational nature, in this case the applications are supposed to reside in different organisations and most importantly are usually more complex. In our GUARDIANS case example, the information broker client may find information about a learning services provider and then register in order to follow courses or take a qualification. The learning services provider is the application level provider and its profile captures the organisation related information. This describes current real world scenarios. In the learning technology area, the standardisation of user profiles is quite more complex since the learning service provider has to follow the user activity in multiple actions. Typical schemas for learning profiles are the ones proposed from IEEE (the PAPI profile, see IEEE, 2000) and the one from IMS (LIP schema, see IMS, 2001). These schemas are complex and contain learning organisation and learning process specific information.

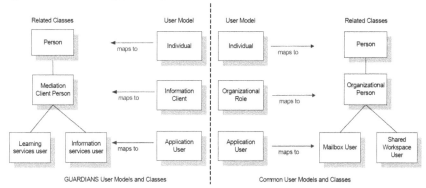

Figure 2 Guardians compared with Common user models and implementation classes

The fact that the information consumer may operate in a multi-organisational environment cannot, of course, be considered accomplished with only a user model. It also requires an environment organised to carry out such a function. For example, information providers and learning organisations nowadays are moving in such a direction. For the first a typical example is the registration to various news agencies through a mediation service like Yahoo! (http://my.yahoo.com/). For the second the exchange of learning modules (franchise) between institutions (http://www.international.university.ttm.bg/univer.html).

4.3 The structure of GUARDIANS user profiles

The GUARDIANS project is a successor of the GESTALT project (GESTALT, 2000) and as such, it has inherited a learner standpoint in the usage and management of information. An information consumer is considered a potential learner; information is considered a tool in the learning process. Our user community also typically refers to academic institutions. Therefore the application level is considered to consist basically in learning technologies applications. In our example implementation, the application level profile is based upon an implementation of IMS LIP schema (IMS, 2001).

The conceptual model analysed earlier on, has been implemented using an LDAP server. Our core profile is a typical user person profile similar to the ones common in directories (see for example M. Wahl, 1997; Smith, 2000; Zeilenga 2001). This information is contained in any directory and can be considered multi-domain, multi-environment. At the next level, the information appropriate to the information client is captured. This information does not have any organisational information in it. It is instead, sets of data related to user's preferences, interests, qualifications and goals. A typical information broker maintains such information. But any information linked with user's relation to institutions is portrayed at the third level. For example, affiliation information or user's progress regarding a qualification (degrees etc.).

This architecture ensures that the information broker has sufficient information for fulfilling user's information needs, a user does not lose any critical information when making use of multiple application service providers and the application service providers keep private the information critical for their service and the those data that add value to it. It is expected that the related business players (basically the broker and the service provider) have their own directory servers. One may suppose that organisations like information brokers and application service providers can exchange profile information of their common users if they have users' consent in order to increase efficiency and accuracy of their service.

Level 1	Common to all directories. Transferable across multi-
Level 2	Specific to MS Short Gup
Level 3	Specific to Learning Environment (INSP) LIP based GUP

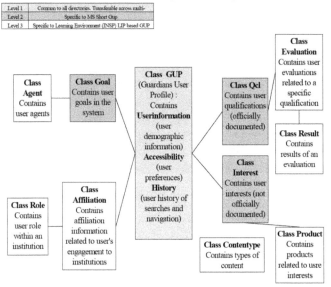

Figure 3. A three level architecture for user profiles

5. Conclusions and future directions

The GUARDIANS project introduces an information provision environment for individuals of the network age, making use of digital materials provided through the network and comprising business roles for brokers, information and content providers. Individuals are mainly considered clients of these information provision services and thus an effort has been made to profile them according to this special role. Emphasis has been given to the fact that any such effort has to be conceptualised bearing in mind the currently prevalent information society vision. The assumptions of early implementations on this issue, basically the fact that a user must be modelled as a business role have been left behind. The fact that the Information Society gives a role to the individual is pushing designers to create more generic models appropriate to a more societal role. The design is tending towards trying to capture at the first level an individual's needs when acting as a network based users of services and less the business needs an individual is associated with. This function is accomplished at a second level.

An important issue is always the effectiveness of a profile for the targets of the individual it is supposed to model. To succeed in the design, the individual should be modelled integrally (or at least paying close attention to) with the information content –or otherwise data- associated to it and keeping in mind issues of user machine interaction. The picture is replenished when the environmental parameters are taken into consideration. In our case these are mainly what is concisely called Information Infrastructures, which comprise digital public services, procedures and regulations.

An open issue is what is the societal role an individual will be called on to fulfil using networks in the future. These roles will be accomplished probably by different organisations and institutions and the users will need to move between them, seamlessly, without reregistering and yet without loss of privacy and security.

Acknowledgments

This work has been partly supported by the European Union through the IST Programme GUARDIANS (Gateway for User Access to Remote Distributed Information and Network Services): IST 1999-20758 http://www.fdgroup.com/GUARDIANS

References

Avgerou, C. (2000). Information Systems: what sort of science is it?, Omega, 28 (2000), pp. 567-579.

Eaton, J.J., Bawden, D. (1991). What kind of resource is Information? International Journal of Information Management (11): 156-165. Butterworth-Heinemann Ltd

Federal Public Key Infrastructure Steering Committee (1998). Access with Trust. September 1998 (http://www.gits.gov).

Gettes, M. R (2001). A Recipe for Configuring and Operating LDAP Directories. Georgetown University. Georgetown Institute for Information Assurance. Version 1.5 (2001/02/13). Available at: http://www.georgetown.edu/giia/internet2/ldap-recipe/

GESTALT Project Partners Consortium (2000). Final Report. Work Package 1. Deliverable. Reference: A367/KYR/WP02/DS/P/001/b2.

GUARDIANS Project Partners Consortium (2000). GUARDIANS. Gateway for User Access to Remote Distributed Information and Network Services. Technical Annex. Reference IST-1999-20758.

GUARDIANS Project Partners Consortium (2001). Requirements Specification. Work Package 2 – Deliverable D3. Reference IST-1999-20758/FDE/WP02/D3/v3.2.

Hirschheim, R., Klein, H., Lyytinen, K. (1995). Information Systems Development and Data Modeling: Conceptual and philosophical foundations. Cambridge University Press.

Horn, R. (1999). Information Design: Emergence of a new Profession. In Information Design (eds. R. Jacobson). Massachusetts Institute of Technology. 1999.

IEEE, (2000). Draft Standard for Learning Technology —Public and Private Information (PAPI) for Learners (PAPI Learner). IEEE P1484.2/D7, 2000-11-28. (http://www.edutool.com/papi)

IMS, (2001). IMS Learner Information Packaging Information Model Specification. Final Specification Version 1.0. Available at: http://www.imsproject.org/profiles/index.html)

Mylopoulos, J. (1998). Information Modeling in the Time of the Revolution. Information systems 23(¾): 127-155, 1998.

Newman, J. (2001). Some Observations on the Semantics of "Information". Information Systems Frontiers 3:2, pp. 156-167, 2001. Kluwer Academic Publishers.

OSI, ISO/IEC 9594-1, (1993). The Directory: Overview of Concepts, Models and Services. Recom. X.500.

Smith, M. (2000). Definition of the inetOrgPerson LDAP Object Class. Request for Comments, 2798. The Internet Society (2000).

Wahl, M. (1997). A Summary of the X.500(96) User Schema for use with LDAPv3. Request for Comments, 2255. The Internet Society (1997).

Wahl, M., Howes, T., Kille, S., (1997). Lightweight Directory Access Protocol (v3). Request for Comments, 2251. The Internet Society (1997).

Zeilenga, K. (2001). LDAPv3: A Collection of User Schema. Internet-Draft. Available at: http://search.ietf.org/internet-drafts/draft-zeilenga-ldap-user-schema-00.txt

Peer Acceptance in a Virtual Community – The Impact of the Web on Surfing

Andy Phippen, Ben Beadman

School of Computing, University of Plymouth, UK
Email: andy@jack.see.plymouth.ac.uk

Abstract

The impact of the Internet in social contexts opens up a vast amount of research questions yet to be addressed by studies into web technologies in a work context. This paper describes a research project assessing the impact of web technologies upon existing groups of common interest, namely surfing communities. A survey-based approach provides a quantitative assessment of the impact, and highlights significant differences between anecdotal opinion and empirical study. Such evidence justifies the aims of the research and encourages further study into the area of user acceptance in virtual communities.

Keywords

Virtual community, WWW, empirical research.

1. Introduction

The advent of the Internet as a domestic community phenomenon, rather than one based around an organisation or business, has changed the landscape of computer use. Accounts of communities such as the WELL (Rheingold, H., 2000) and Blacksburg Electronic Village (Carrol et al., 2001) show how new varieties of computer-based human activity have emerged, based not around work but around geographical communities and communities of common interest. Such communities are recognised as having great potential for reversing the long history of decline in community life (Putnam R, 1996).

However, the advent of this new form of computer use has raised a wide range of research questions. Brown et al., 1999 identify the need for multi-disciplinary research involving computer science, sociology, social psychology and human centred systems design to inform the design of online communities. In particular:

> "Designing measuring and evaluating online communities requires well-established techniques to be modified and some new techniques to be developed…. Research is needed to develop participatory, community-centred design and evaluation techniques. Approaches are needed to ensure that account is taken of different (functional requirements) and access needs. Methods, techniques and tools are needed to measure online activities and to understand how online communities differ from geographical communities." Preece, 1999 (8.1.5)

This research project is part of a larger study examining the role of the internet in social contexts, namely whether technologies can aid in the greater integration of geographically distributed but socially isolated communities. These projects should assess the suitability of such electronic forms of interaction in a community environment and inform the design process of future services intended to support community, rather than organisation or business.

This particular project examines how the web has impacted upon a specific community and how it has been accepted. Such acceptance is crucial within the development of virtual communities - their existence relies on user participation. Such acceptance has been discussed in both anecdotal (Dery (Ed.), 1994) and academic literature (Preece, 2000). Drawing from the above quote, it is acknowledged that there is a lack of empirical work examining issues related to virtual communities. In contributing to the field, this project aims to consider how the introduction of web based services to an already established community of common interest can affect community composition and dynamics. In order to study such an aspect of virtual community use, it was necessary to have a suitable study group. In the case of this project such a group was evident in a community familiar to the authors – namely surfing.

2. Surfing Communities

While surfing can, essentially, be seen as a sport, a community ethic emerges from its nature. Surfing communities exist as collections of like-minded people, from regionally specific, but distributed locations. While there is a lack of rigorous academic data regarding these communities, there has been some study into social aspects of surfing (e.g. Crawford, 1995, Hull, 1976, Angeli, 1992, Flint, 1999). All acknowledge the community aspect of the sport, and the concept of inclusion and exclusion within such communities. While these studies are generally carried out in the US, such communities can also be seen to exist in the UK. For example, the North Cornwall surfing community encompasses a geographical distribution from Bude around to Newquay. The community is defined by the common interest of its participants (i.e. surfers or bodyboarders from the region) and an interest in shared knowledge relating to the surfing conditions within their community. The most important information to these groups relates to the forecasting of surf – which locations are going to be best, at what time of day, etc. Traditionally, such communities rely on amateur meteorology, word of mouth and, to a growing extent, mobile phones to communicate local knowledge among the community. These communities tend to be localised to specific locales.

In such a community, the use of web technologies seems, on the surface, to be ideal – it enables the communication of information, generally in a real time context, across a distributed environment. This exactly mimics the current information flows with the community, but provides the facilities to carry out the communication in a far faster, richer way.

The use of web technologies among surfing communities is becoming widespread – web sites offering services such as surf reports, web cameras to specific beaches and forecasting are all prevalent and their use is widespread among such communities. The facilities offered by sites such as A1Surf (www.a1surf.com) offer a truly integrated service to a virtual community of surfers. Surfers visit the site to look at surf forecasts and reports, follow links to meteorological data and web cameras and participate in discussions centred on both the sport and culture of surfing.

However, rather than wholly embracing the new technologies, debate among community peers rages as to whether such technologies are a good or a bad thing. Flint (1999) commented on the impact of the Internet on the sport and how its introduction could result in an "institutionalisation" of surfing – ruining its cultural and community aspects. Within surfing communities, some are of the view that they make it easier in choosing where to surf while others feel that in exposing information about local breaks, information is too freely available. Secret spots only known by a few knowledgeable locals are held in sacred regard by members of the community, and their whereabouts are closely guarded secrets. There is a fear among some members of such communities that web sites offering services that show real time information about local surfing locations will encourage the dissemination of knowledge regarding such secret spots.

Such opposition to the use of technologies was amply demonstrated at the start of this project. One aspect of this project is the installation of a new web camera at a surfing beach on the south coast of devon - Bantham. This intention was stated on the published survey, and respondents were invited to comment on the need for such a service. Within days of the publication of the survey, a discussion page was set up on a local surfing website (www.localsurfer.co.uk) stating opposition to the proposed camera and encouraging others to comment in a similarly negative way. The quotes below are representative of the opposition to such a service:

a webcam is just gonna advertise the existence of the place to all those weekend surfers who usually breeze on by, to cornwall, oblivious that bantham even exists, let alone might get good swell, which is only ever gonna increase the (already) big crowds it's starting to attract. Bad idea. Bantham doesn't even have a surf shop or desperate tourisim excuse in order to attract people, and will only give the **** in the carpark hut another excuse to raise his car park prices. Say no to the webcam!

Say no :-0 to the webcam so we dont got half assed kooks, weekend surfers, students and crowds. If we all tell the guys who want to put the cam up to **** off then maybe they'll get the message. And if they do put it up, well......vandalise it

However, the discussion also reflect a more positive approach to such a service:

Say Yes to Bantham Webcam! Say no to selfish surfers who only believe in 'Local Surf' for 'Local Surfers'! Come on, Get your webbed thumbs out of yer backsides and think.. Bantham is no secret, it will always be busy! If you think the biggest problem against it, is an increase in the amount of weekend surfers - your wrong. A lot of surfers, surf at weekends because they have jobs during the week.. and webcam or no, your bound to get more surf traffic during the summer. Anyway, only the serious surfers would bother checking the forecasts properly before they left the house and do you think there aren't any forecasts for Bantham right now? The only major difference a webcam would make to surfing at Bantham would be to surfers pockets... it would definitely save my wasted petrol money!

Also, the discussions did not last for a prolonged period or have a large amount of participants. After a few days and seven postings to the discussion group, all went quiet. This does highlight an issue when considering the acceptance of such technologies within a community – opposition is generally voiced whereas acceptance is not.

Therefore, as well as providing an interesting aside to the study, this feedback did provide us with further justification for the project. Word of mouth discussion will generally provide a less than representative result, as some voices will be louder than others. In our own research, we wished to examine the opinions of a representative sample across the communities, and to assess every opinion in the sample, not just those with the strongest concerns.

3. Research Method and Target Audience

A web-based survey was chosen for a number of reasons. Firstly, it enables the fast propagation of the survey through the distribution of the survey URL via email. It also enables a large distribution at low cost. The survey approach enabled a breadth of opinion while providing a controlled, measurable response from all respondents.

We positioned the survey from the negative viewpoint expressed by some members of surfing communities – that is, the web has an adverse effect on the sport and community, effectively allowing undesirable[1] people to gain greater knowledge and therefore destroying the "sacred" nature of some surfing locations. We wished to determine what sort of people used the web and how it was used in order to test this negative viewpoint.

Questions were closed and all feedback was quantitative in nature. The questions were grouped into three general categories, detailed below:

- **Use** – How does the respondent use web services related to their community?
  Do you use the World Wide Web to check the surf forecasts?
  Do you only use the WWW, or do you combine other facilities, or do you simply use other means?

- **Facilities** – what facilities, out of those offered, do they use?
  Which, out of these facilities do you also use for forecasting your surfing location?
  From this list, which other services on the WWW, apart from the surf forecasts, do you use to predict your location (BBC On-line, Wave Buoy Sites, Met Office, Web Cameras)?

- **"Acceptance"** – their opinions on the use of web facilities, and the personal impact of the web on their surfing
  On a scale of 1 - 10, how reliable to you believe the WWW is for forecasting?
  Do you believe that you have become reliant upon the facilities of the WWW?
  Do you believe that you could accurately predict the forecast without the WWW?
  Do you believe that the WWW has encouraged or discouraged your surfing, or neither?

4. Feedback and Results Analysis

As both authors are members of local surfing communities, selecting suitable respondents was straightforward. Members of the communities were emailed with the survey URL, asked to carry out the survey and to forward the URL onto other suitable respondents. Overall, a sample set of fourty-four respondents was obtained out of a potential group of sixty. This shows an extremely high response rate (73%), reflected the effective nature of web based

---

[1] By undesirable we are referring to people perceived by community member to be "unworthy" of such knowledge, such as those people who don't respect the coastline or fellow surfers – the "weekend" surfers described in the discussion group

surveying. All respondents were from the south west of the UK and were active members of surfing communities.

The most basic question assessed how many respondents actually used web services related to surfing. This was an important question – a criticism that could be levelled at the survey approach was that in using electronic means to distribute the survey, you would skew the sample to those that would, in general, use the World Wide Web. However, as the results illustrated in table 1 show, there was a small, but significant, amount of respondents who did not use the web:

Yes	79%
No	21%

Table 1 - Do you use the web to help predict surf locations?

For those respondents who did use the web, we firstly wished to determine the nature of its use. There are, essentially, two ways of use web facilities – one is the assumed "easy" use, which is met with most opposition from some surfers - that is the use of reports and other people's forecasts for determining best locations. This can be seen as easy because it requires none of the knowledge considered by many in the communities to be important in being member – to understand meteorological conditions and to have local knowledge in order to inform choices on where to surf. However, it can be argued that the web does provide the facilities to provide the "real" surfer with the sort of information they required to make their own informed decisions. It was certainly the authors' own experience that reports and forecasts were only used as a general guide, and certainly not the sole use of the web. Faculties included wave buoy information (WB)[2], meteorological information such as weather and pressure charts (provided by BBC Online (BBC) and the UK Meteorological Office (MO)), and web cameras (WC). Figure 1 illustrates the responses:

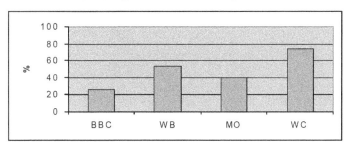

Figure 1 - Services additional to forecasts and reports

As can be seen, in two cases (wave buoy information and web cameras), over 50% of respondents are using information resources to inform their own choices, rather than relying

---

[2] Wave buoy information is generally used in shipping and meteorology – buoys positioned at locations in the sea provide large amounts of data such a wind speed and direction, swell size, swell direction, sea temperature, etc. Such information, if read by a knowledgeable user, can also greater aid surf forecasting.

on the opinions of others. There are also a significant proportion of respondents who also use meteorological data.

In further considering the way the web was used by members of surfing communities, a simple test was to analyse how many replaced "traditional" approaches with web services, and how many used them to compliment existing techniques. Table 2 shows the results of this analysis, demonstrating the extremely high proportion of community members who use the web in combination with other techniques, rather than opting for the perceived "easier" approach of relying on web based forecasts.

WWW Only	13%
Combination	87%

Table 2 - Web only or a combination of services?

As a final, more focussed, analysis, we wished to determine whether there was any difference in the type of traditional services used between web and non-web users. In the case of this survey, we considered weather services (WS), telephone reports (T), coastguard reporting (C), wave buoy information (WB) and friends (F). Figure 2 illustrates the response:

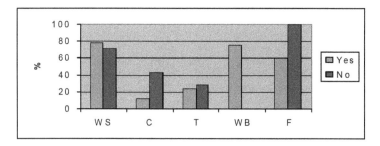

Figure 2 - Comparison of services used between web and non-web users

As can be seen from the figure, using web technologies does not replace any of the traditional activities. The reduction in community members using friends does demonstrate a reduction in the use of "word-of-mouth" communication, but the most significant difference is the use wave buoy data. None of the respondents who did not use the world wide web used wave buoy data – the use of web technologies open up the means to access this extremely useful data whereas before it tended to only be available to shipping and meteorologists.

In addition to this analysis, we wished to consider the level of acceptance among community members – whether members felt that their use of the web is effective and whether they have become reliant upon the services offered. The aspect of reliance is a good way of determining acceptance – if members have become reliant on the services offered it can be argued that the services have become implicit within the community.

Our first question aimed to determine how effective those who used the web for forecasting felt it was. The respondents were asked to rate the quality of forecasting, detailed in table 3.

Mean	7.11290 3
Min	1
Max	10
Std. Dev.	1.80605 3

Table 3 - Effectiveness of web based forecasting

While there were a few extreme values, the mean of just over seven and a standard deviation of 1.8 shows a reasonable level of faith in the services offered to the community by the web. In further considering the level of acceptance of the web, we considered two other aspects – whether respondents considered themselves to be reliant on the web for informing their choices on where to surf, and whether they felt they could effectively forecast surf conditions without the services offered by the web. Tables 4 and 5 illustrate the responses.

Yes	65%
No	35%

Table 4 - Are you reliant on the web for surf forecasting?

Yes	65%
No	35%

Table 5 - Can you accurately predict without the web?

The responses show a conflict of opinion between those who feel they are reliant on the web and those who feel they can predict surf conditions without it (i.e. they are not reliant on the web). If 65% of respondents felt they were reliant on the web, one would expect 65% to be unable to predict surf conditions without it. However, only 35% of respondents stated such an opinion. Figure 3 considers the responses of those who feel they can predict surf conditions without the web against the responses of those who felt they were reliant on the web for forecasting.

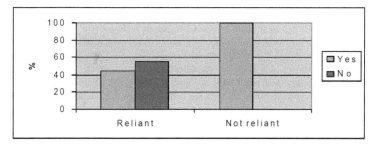

Figure 3 - Reliance on the web against ability to predict without it

100% of those respondents who did not consider themselves reliant on the web felt they could predict surf conditions without the services offered by the web. However, 45% of those respondents who said they were reliant on the web felt they could accurately predict surf conditions without the web. We can consider this response in terms of community membership and usage of the web – firstly, while respondents like to use web services, they still have the requisite knowledge to effectively determine surf conditions without it. Only a small proportion of the overall respondents is totally reliant on the web for forecasting. This contrasts with the opinion that the web attracts people without the requisite knowledge to "respect" the surfing community.

5. Consideration of response and conclusions

We can consider the aim of this research project to be an empirical assessment of the impact of virtual services on an established distributed community. The analysis of feedback from community members enables us to draw quantifiable conclusions regarding the impact of such services. The most significant aspect of the feedback we have received in this survey is the positive opinion of most of the respondents. This contrasts with our assumptions drawn from informal discussion with community members, where most voice opposition to web services. Additionally, the feeling that such services will introduce the "uneducated" into communities is not reflected either. In general, respondents used the services offered over the web to augment prior knowledge, i.e. it would be difficult for a person without such knowledge to make best use of web based surfing services. For example, the web provides the means for community members to access meteorological data such as weather charts and wave buoy data – both useful in predicting surf. However, without prior understanding of such information, the web would offer no benefit to the user. This does demonstrate the fact that these web sites do offer services to the existing community, rather than opening the community to those without the requisite knowledge.

Anecdotal opinion had suggested that the introduction of such technologies would make the forecasting of surfing "easy" and therefore spoils the membership of surfing communities. If this was to be the case, we should assume a great deal of opposition to the technologies. However, our findings show the technologies being used in a complimentary manner. The technological introduction essential opens up information resources for the informed user rather than making life easy for casual users.

Finally, our research does demonstrate the value of empirical techniques in this research area. A lot of key texts within the virtual communities area (for example, Rheingold, H., 2000, Smith and Kollock, 1997) are still anecdotal in nature while being held up as definitive opinion on the area. Our empirical work has shown a conflict between the perceived opinion of a community, based upon anecdotal and informal evidence, and the real opinion of the community. The implications of these findings have implications for the study of any virtual community – there is a need to move away from assumed authority without the support of empirical evidence. Quantitative methods such as those discussed in this paper provide the mean to quantify opinion from a cross section of community members. Additionally, we would like to see further qualitative study within community to study the impact of technologies at a far more detailed and richer level. Further research from our own group should continue with such assessment.

6. References

Angeli M. (1992). Beach Culture. Esquire; July 1992 v118 n1 p58(10)

Brown, van Dam, Earnshaw, Encarnação, Guedj, Preece, Shneiderman, Vince (1999). "Human-Centered Computing, Online Communities and Virtual Environments" Report on the First Joint European Commission/National Science Foundation Advanced Research Workshop, June 1-4, 1999, Chateau de Bonas, France

Carroll, Rosson, Isenhour, Ganoe, Dunlap, Fogarty, Schafer, Van Metre (2001). "Designing our Town: MOOsburg". International Journal of Human-Computer Studies 54, 725-751.

Crawford. (1995). Waves of Transformation. [online]
http://206.102.92.130/ses/surf/papers/home.html

Dery (Ed.) (1994). "Flame Wars – The Discourse of CyberCulture". Durham: Duke University Press.

DTI (2000). "Closing the Digital Divide: Information and Communications Technologies in Deprived Areas – A Report by Policy Action Team 15". February 2000.

Flint (1999). Popular Culture – Surfing.
http://molasar.blackmagic.com/ses/surf/papers/essay1/home.html

Hershman Leason (1996). "Clicking In – Hot Links to a Digital Culture". Seattle: Bay Press.

Hull S. (1976). A Sociological Study of the Surfing Subculture in the Santa Cruz Area. (thesis) in [online] http://206.102.92.130/ses/surf/papers/home.html

Preece (1999). Apprearing in Brown et. al.. (1999)

Preece (2000). "Online Communities: Designing Usability, Supporting Sociability". John Wiley & Sons.

Putnam R (1996). "The Strange Disappearance of Civic America" The American Prospect 24, 34-49.

Rheingold, H. (2000). "The Virtual Community: Homesteading on the Electronic Frontier: Second Edition". Reading, MA:Addison-Wesley.

Schuler, Douglas (1996). "New Community Networks: Wired for Change". Reading: Adison-Wesley.

Smith and Kollock (1997). "Communities in Cyberspace: Perspectives on New Forms of Social Organizations". Los Angeles: University of California Press.

Information superiority and the role of an organisation's network

W. Hutchinson[1] and M.Warren[2]

[1]School of Computer and Information Science
Edith Cowan University, Mt Lawley, Western Australia 6050
email: w.hutchinson@ecu.edu.au

[2]School of Computing and Mathematics
Deakin University
Geelong, Victoria, Australia 3217
email: mwarren@deakin.edu.au

Abstract

This paper examines the concept of information superiority and how it relates to the exploitation and administration of computer networks. The roles of management and network administrators are investigated in this context.

Keywords

Information warfare, netwar, net centric warfare, information superiority, network administration.

1. Information Superiority

Information superiority has been the aim of commanders since the dawn of warfare. However, the modern concept derives from the Gulf War in the early 1990s (Campden, 1992). It involves the use of integrated electronic communications and computer networks plus the use of sophisticated satellite and airborne surveillance to totally dominate the battle-space. This is a two way process. Not only is the C4I (command, control, communication, computers and intelligence) system capable of providing better information for one's own actions, but this very advantage often allows the enemy's C4I system to be degraded. This degradation of the opponent's abilities is caused by the capability to monitor and disrupt data communication, and also to manipulate and fabricate data. Thus, the adversary knows 'what you want them to know'. This concept has also been exploited by the US in both the conflicts in Kosovo (Ignatieff, 2000) and Afghanistan. All this tends to lift the 'fog of war' (see Owens, 2000). In other words, the information confusion caused in all dynamic battlefield situations is alleviated to some degree.

Other commentators (Arquilla and Rondfeldt, 1996) have seen this trend merge with the development of networks in the organisational and societal contexts. All this is facilitated by information technology. Hence, there is also a trend for the effective use of networks in a competitive sense to diffuse from the military into the commercial and governmental areas.

A simple version defined in Alberts *et al* (1999) is illustrated in figure 1. Here, it can be seen that information superiority is defined in terms of timeliness, relevance, and accuracy of the information supplied to the commander (manager). Coupled with this, is the assumption that the information is given to correct manager, is in an easily comprehensible form, and that the manager acts on the information presented. In conventional, contemporary organisations, network management might not take on the responsibility of the relevance of information but should ensure the timely delivery of it, and also its accuracy (although only in terms of its transmission rather than its original source).

The concept of information warfare both in its offensive and defensive (security) modes is closely aligned with information superiority. This is has been well documented by authors such as Denning (1999), Knetch (1996), Hutchinson and Warren (2001), Waltz (1998), and Schwartau (1996).

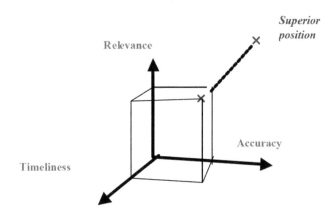

Figure 1: Information Superiority
(after Alberts et al, 1999, p.34)

2.   The Nature of Information

In the context of information superiority, a useful definition can be derived in the model proposed by Boisot (1998). Here, data is associated with a *thing*, and discriminates between different states of the thing it describes. It consists of attributes of the events or objects it describes. On the other hand, knowledge is an attribute of an *agent*. Knowledge is a set of interacting mindsets about data activated by an event. (Mindsets are the groupings of dynamic cognitive models unique to each individual by which the human 'knows' the world). Hence, in most circumstances the word 'agent' means a human being or a group of people. Information is the set of data filtered by the agent within the bounds of the knowledge held by the agent; it establishes a link between the agent and the data. The use of knowledge within a certain situation is done within a *context*.

The definition of data is fairly simple to understand. Events or items have attributes and descriptions of these attributes are data. However, a human agent decides knowledge. The history of the person (for example, by education, culture, age, and sex) and the context of the problem establish it. It is this characteristic which makes the idea of 'truth' in information problematic. However, there might be general agreement about data. As Alberts and Garstka (2000) put it: "Information is where reality and cognition collide". The concept of information superiority assumes an environment of conflict. Hence, information must be considered as both a weapon and a target in that conflict be it business, crime, or war. From the above definition, it can be seen that people, communications, computer hardware/software, and data are all players.

The concept of information superiority assumes an environment of conflict. Hence, information must be considered as both a weapon and a target in that conflict be it business, crime, or war. From the above definition, it can be seen that people, communications, computer hardware/software, and data are all players in that conflict. Figure 2 illustrates how the components involved in information production can be attacked. The objective of these attacks is to either deprive the competitor of information (by denying access to data, equipment, or communications) or to distort the information created (by altering data and or the context in which it is interpreted).

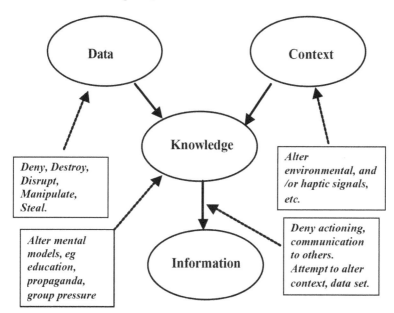

Figure 2: The relationships between data, context, knowledge, information; and the methods by which each element can be attacked.

3. The Involvement of Networks and their Administrators

It can be seen from both figures 1 and 2 that the need for a stable, reliable, and fast network with high integrity is essential to enable all the components in information production to function effectively. It is also apparent that these components must be secured.

Denning (1999) uses a different approach to define the potential elements in information systems that are prone to attack and exploitation. She categorises these elements.

- **Data stores**: for example, computer and human memories.
- **Communication channels**: for example, humans, telecommunication systems.
- **Sensors/input devices**: for example, scanners, cameras, microphones, human senses.
- **Output devices**: for example, disk writers, printers, human processes.
- **Manipulators of data**: for example, microprocessors, humans, software.

Hence, networks are essential to communicate timely, accurate, and relevant information (as in figure 1). In conventional organisations, network administrators are only responsible for the running of the systems rather than its use. Although with the advent of 'firewalls' and the implementation of Internet misuse policies, a monitoring/surveillance function has evolved. However, the conventional network administrator must ensure the security of communications, the integrity of data, the physical security of equipment, and the denial of invalid access to the systems. By inference, this includes all the components listed by Denning (op cit). It does not include those elements directly concerned with knowledge (hence, humans). Therefore, the only components that network administrators are concerned with are data and equipment. Is this about to change?

4. Information Superiority as the Organisational Paradigm

Information superiority in the military context is easy to comprehend. There is an enemy; the concepts of information as a weapon and target are relatively obvious. However, are the same principles applicable in the modern commercial environment? What 'enemies' do companies have? The first that come to mind are commercial competitors. However, there are not so obvious candidates including criminals, dysfunctional/disgruntled staff, suppliers, hackers/crackers, intelligence services, foreign and domestic governments, the law, the media, clients, and pressure groups (often these groups are competing for the same resources, for example, environmental groups compete with logging companies for the same forests). The corporate environment does not look so safe when viewed from this perspective.

The need to protect the integrity of the corporate database and its delivery and storage systems is obvious. This is the traditional security paradigm. However, the concept of information superiority takes this further. If information (that is corporate data plus the knowledge in its staff) is power, then lack of it is weakness. Therefore, the **fundamental** aim of the organisation must be to **exploit** its own information to its fullest extent, and to **deprive** its 'enemies' of the same resource. Thus, the energies of an organisation should be concentrated in the exploitation of information. The delivery, security, and integrity of information are essential, but **subservient**, **service** activities in the Information Age organisation.

In this context, the conventional network administrator is providing a support service for the decision-makers. Is this really the case? As Schwartau (2001) points outs, the network administrator is the core functionary in the operational life of an organisation. Network management and their decisions determine an organisation's strategic positioning. Yet the function is rarely managed properly or given its rightful place in the corporate hierarchy. Coupled with this, is a lack of any knowledge of upper management of how networks actually work. Hence, a lack of correct monitoring occurs. Skills' shortages also ensure a lack of staff vetting or aptitude testing.

Figure 2, illustrates the vulnerability of data. Network administrators have privileged access rights and could cause organisational havoc. Schwartau points out that most network administrators in the US are contract staff and the majority of them are foreign nationals. All of this adds to the possibility of corporate espionage, and other security breaches. It is obvious that at an operational level, network managers/administrators are pivotal.

At a strategic level network managers are critical to the development of a superior information positions. Networks might not develop information (except their own, of course) but without them the efficient transmission of data to create information is impaired.

5.   Conclusion

In the Information Age, the concept of information superiority is the determining factor of an organisation's success.   At present, the effective delivery of data to decision makers is assumed. The vehicle for this is the corporate network. Both corporate management and network staff do not fully appreciate it vital function. As a result, organisations that do not realign the functions within their structure to make allowance for this new paradigm might find themselves floundering. Network staff should appreciate their part in this process and not remain immersed in the technology, and upper management should be encouraged to understand the technology to better manage it within the new world of information superiority and, by implication, inferiority.

6.   References

Alberts, D.S. and Garstka, J. (2000) Information Superiority and Network Centric Warfare, talk given at *InfoWarCon2000*, Washington, September, 2000.

Alberts, D.S. and Garstka, J..J., Stein, F.P. (1999) *Network Centric Warfare*, CCRP, Washington.

Arquilla, J. and Ronfeldt, D. (1996) *The Advent of Netwar,* RAND, Santa Monica.

Boisot, M.H. (1998) *Knowledge Assets.* Oxford University Press, Oxford.

Campen, A.D. (ed) (1992) *The First Information War*, AFCEA International Press, Fairfax.

Denning, D.E. (1999). *Information Warfare and Security*, Addison Wesley, Reading: Mass.

Hutchinson, W.E. and Warren, M.J. (2001) Concepts in Information Warfare, *Journal of Information Warfare*, 1,1:1-7.

Ignatieff, M. (2000) *Virtual war*, Chatto and Windus, London.

Knecht, R.J. (1996) Thoughts About Information Warfare, in: Campen, A.D., Dearth, D.H., Thomas Godden, R (eds) *Cyberwar: Security, Strategy, and Conflict in the Information Age,*. AFCEA International Press, Fairfax.

Owens, B (2000) *Lifting the Fog of War*, FSG, New York.

Schwartau, W. (1996). *Information Warfare – second editio,* Thunder's Mouth Press, New York.

Schwartau, W. (2001) *Whom Do You trust?* A talk given at the 2nd Australian Information Warfare and Security Conference, Perth, Australia. 30 November, 2001.

Waltz, E. (1998) *Information Warfare – Principles and Operations.*,Artech House, Norwood.

Privacy Management– A New Era in the Australian Business Environment

Vidya Moghe

618 King Georges Rd., Penshurst, N.S.W. Australia 2222
email: vidyamoghe@hotmail.com

Abstract

People all over the world are increasingly concerned about the privacy issues surrounding the personal information collected by the governments, private organizations and employers. Privacy relates to issues surrounding collection, secure transmission, storage, authorized access, usage and disclosure of personal information. Australian businesses for the first time will need to comply with the new privacy law coming into effect on 21st December 2001. This paper briefly discusses the privacy and related management issues in the Information Age in general, and privacy related legal requirements in Australia in particular. It further discusses IT-centric measures that need to be undertaken for the purposes of compliance of the Act and provides an overview of enabling technology currently available.

Keywords

Networks, Privacy, Australia, Law, Management, P3P, Conferences, Papers

Introduction

With the advent of Internet, technology has enabled government and commercial entities to collect, use and disclose vast amounts of personal information with or without the consent of people. This information is used for the commercial gain by many organizations e.g. Direct, and targeted marketing, cross-selling of information, e-mail Spam. The use of the Internet by governments and organizations has raised concerns about the privacy of staff e-mail and web browsing activities of employees. Australian organizations in private sector face a big challenge in getting ready to comply with the new Act. Discussion in this paper is based on a review of Privacy Act related information published by the Office of the Federal Privacy Commissioner, survey of the published information related to the organizational preparation to comply with the new Act and enabling technology tools currently available.

Privacy Concerns

Findings from various market research conducted (GVU 10th WWW user survey1998, Forrester Research 1999, Consumer Privacy Survey 1999, Internet Policy institute July 2000, NFO Interactive 2000, Consumers International 2001) indicate that people care deeply about the collection, usage and dissemination of personal information such as name, postal and email address, martial status, income, credit card numbers and medical information by the organizations. (Crompton M, 2001) One of the first international efforts to address these concerns was the Guidelines adopted in 1980 by the Organization for Economic Cooperation and Development (OECD) for the Protection of Privacy and Transborder Flows of Personal

Data. Many OECD member countries have since then adopted privacy laws such as New Zealand, Hong Kong, Canada and many European nations.

Privacy Legislation in Australia

Privacy legislation came into existence in Australia in 1988. The Commonwealth *Privacy Act 1988* laid down strict privacy safeguards which Commonwealth (federal) and ACT government agencies must observe when collecting, storing, using and disclosing personal information. This Act also gave individuals access and correction rights in relation to their own personal information. The Act applied to the wider community (including the private sector and state and local governments) only in relation to specific categories of information: tax file number information and consumer credit information. The Act (About Australia's privacy laws, 2001) gave effect to Australia's agreement to implement OECD guidelines as well as to its obligations under Article 17 of the International Covenant on Civil and Political Rights. In 1997, the Telecommunications Act came into effect, which specified rules for the use and disclosure of personal information held by carriers, carriage service providers and others. The Telecommunications Act also provides a scheme under which industry can develop codes dealing with a range of consumer protection and privacy issues. Although, since 1988, Commonwealth and ACT government agencies had to comply with the privacy regulations, private sector was by and large free of such obligation in Australia. This discrepancy was removed in 2000 by the Federal government. Individual states also passed parallel Acts, most notable of which are the Victorian Information Privacy Bill and the Health Records Act passed in November 2000 in Victoria regulating the handling of personal information, except personal health information, in the public sector and the handling of personal health information in both the public and private sectors of Victoria respectively.

Privacy Amendment (Private Sector) Act 2000

Australian Federal Parliament passed the Privacy Amendment (Private Sector) Act 2000 on 6/12/2000 to come into effect on 21/12/2001. This Act has empowered Australians for the first time; giving individuals the right to know what information private sector organization holds about them and a right to correct that information if it is wrong. The key components of the Act are: What personal information (PI) is protected, standards for handling PI, dispute resolution framework and coverage and exemptions from the Act (Kirk G, 2001).

Impact of the Privacy Amendment

The Act applies to organizations (including not-for-profit organizations) with an annual turnover of more than AUS$3 million and to all health service providers from 21 December 2001. It applies to all federal government contractors and organizations that have been prescribed under legislation. It also applies to small businesses (annual turnover < $3 million) that trade in PI from 21/12/2002. The Privacy Act exempts from its coverage State or Territory authorities; political parties and acts of political representatives in relation to electoral matters; acts or practices in relation to employee records of an individual if the act or practice directly relates to a current or former employment relationship between the employer and the individual; and acts or practices of media organizations in the practice of journalism. (Information sheet 12, 2001)

Act Compliance

The new Act regulates the way private sector organizations collect, use, store and disclose personal information requiring them to comply with ten National Privacy Principles (NPPs) laid down as the cornerstones of the Act. The NPPs cover collection (NPP 1), use and disclosure (NPP 2), data quality (NPP 3), data security (NPP 4) openness (NPP 5), access and correction (NPP 6), identifiers (NPP 7), anonymity (NPP 8), Transborder flow of data (NPP 9) and sensitive information (NPP 10). NPPs establish a nationally consistent approach to handling of personal information in the private sector that is to be applied across jurisdictions and across industries. The NPPs are drafted in a way that is technology neutral. The result is that the NPPs apply equally to conventional, electronic and digital environments. The Privacy Act also gives organizations the option of adopting a privacy code. Once approved by the Privacy Commissioner a privacy code effectively replaces the NPPs for those organizations bound by it. NPP 3 (Data quality on use and disclosure), 4, 5, 7, 9 apply regardless of when information is collected and other NPPs apply to the information collected after effective date (21/12/2001).

Getting Ready

In an article published in the periodical 'elaw Practice', author (Fraser H, 2001) mentions that survey commissioned by the Privacy Commissioner found that as of May/June 2001, 74 % of business had not started preparing for the new law and 91% of businesses felt they had inadequate information on the new law to commence their preparations. Following is the summary (Information sheet 2, 2001) of 'Things to do' for organizations in order to be ready by 21 December 2001:

- **appoint privacy officer** to be responsible for developing and implementing a privacy policy that suits the organisation's business and complies with the law.
- ensure that relevant members of the organisation **become familiar with the NPPs**
- **conduct a privacy audit** using internal or external resources to work out what sort of personal information the organisation collects and holds, uses and discloses.
- **compare practices (outcome of the above audit) with requirements in the NPPs** develop a plan to address any areas that do not comply with the NPPs.
- **Consult relevant people to develop the plan**
- **develop an effective complaints handling process** - an important part of managing privacy risks within an organisation. It helps an organisation to identify (and address) any systemic or ongoing compliance problems; increase consumer confidence in the organisation's privacy procedures; build the good reputation of the organisation; and address complaints quickly and effectively. (Information Sheet 2, 2001)
- **develop Privacy policy and procedures**
- **train staff** on privacy procedures and the organisation's privacy policies. A number of training packages in 'ready to roll' format are available.
- After the development of Privacy Plan, **organization will need to make changes** in business practices, day-to-day procedures and systems (manual and IT) **to become NPP compliant.** Compliance being an ongoing commitment, **periodical review of the process** and training should take place.

IT-Centric Measures

The inherent limitations of paper-based systems provide a certain level of privacy protection. The migration of records of personal information to IT systems has made possible a far greater range of uses of personal information and has made it easy to transfer information. Information and communications technology including e-mail and the Internet access in the workplace raises questions about the supervision of its use. Commonwealth agencies covered by 1988 Act need to comply with the transparency and openness Guidelines based on the Information Privacy Principles (IPPs). IPPs (Guidelines for Federal and ACT Government World Wide Websites, 2000) apply to emails, which contain personal information and logging of activities on the networks. For private sector and other organizations not covered by privacy legislation, the Guidelines are recommended as good privacy practice. However, the Privacy Act for the private sector will apply to logs of staff web browsing activities and staff emails that contain personal information other than "employee records" in certain circumstances. (Guidelines on Workplace E-mail, Web Browsing and Privacy, 2000). NPP compliance by organizations can be largely achieved by making IT systems compliant. This may involve in-house development efforts, implementing commercial product tools or combination of both.

Workplace Privacy Management

The computers and internal network involved are controlled by the organization and management has the responsibility for issuing instructions as to their proper use. Most software used to operate networks, including web servers, mail servers and gateways, logs transactions and communications. These logs will normally include the e-mail addresses of senders and recipients of e-mail and the time of transmission. The content of e-mails themselves would not normally be logged but may be stored on mail servers. Similarly, web server logs record information on the sites that people visit. The keeping of these logs is usually necessary for the routine maintenance and management of networks and systems. System administrators are also capable of reading the contents of e-mails sent and received by the corporate network. Most staff do not expect to completely sacrifice their privacy while at work which includes the access to the computer network including storage space for their files. While it is acknowledged that access to staff emails and browsing logs by system administrators may be required in certain circumstances, it is unlikely that pervasive, systematic and ongoing surveillance of staff e-mails and logs should be necessary. To assure staff that the privacy of their communications will be respected as long as they abide by the organization's stated policy, organizations need to develop and implement Information Security policy and the Privacy Policy. The policy should be reviewed on a regular basis in order to keep up with the accelerating development of the Internet and Information Technology. The policy should be re-issued whenever significant change is made. This would help to reinforce the message to staff. Excerpts from Guidelines published on the Web by the Privacy Commissioner (Guidelines for workplace privacy, 2001) are given below:

1. The policy should be clear. Management should ensure that it is known and understood by staff. Ideally the policy should be linked from a screen that the user sees when they log on to the network.
2. The policy should be explicit as to what activities are permitted and forbidden.
3. The policy should clearly set out what information is logged and who in the organization has rights to access the logs and content of staff e-mail and browsing activities.
4. The policy should refer to the organization's computer security policy. Improper use of e-mail may pose a threat to system security, the privacy of staff and others and the legal liability of the organization.
5. The policy should outline, in plain English, how the organization intends to monitor or audit staff compliance with its rules relating to acceptable usage of e-mail and web browsing.

Website Privacy Management

Organizations collecting information via their Websites have to comply with the Privacy Act aand NPPs. Following are the ongoing measures to be undertaken by an organization:

- Preparation of privacy statement and publishing it on the websites to comply with openness guidelines (NPP5). The statement should be easy to find (on the Home page and links from most pages), indicate type of click stream data collected if any, advise the use of cookies if used by the site, identify type of personal information collected and its use.
- Wherever it is lawful and practicable, individuals must have the option of not identifying themselves when entering transactions with an organization (NPP8).
- Every page collecting personal information has adequate NPP2 statement or a direct link to the privacy statement. The 'NPP2 statement' must advise the individual of the purpose for collection, the legal authority or requirement for collection and any usual disclosures of the information. Where an online form is used to collect personal information the statement should be on the same page as the form or prominently linked to it.
- The site warns users of the risks of transmitting data across the Internet to comply with security requirements or provide secure transmission of personal information by way of using encryption methods to comply with NPP 4. If online purchasing is offered, site should provide secure facilities for transmission of payment data (Secure Socket Layer (SSL), digital certificates as a proof of security available etc).
- If the site contains personal information, organization must ensure that it complies with the disclosure guidelines

Data Security Management

National Privacy Principle (NPP) 4.1 provides that an organization must take reasonable steps to protect the personal information it holds from misuse and loss and from unauthorized access, modification or disclosure. Data security is an important way of ensuring that personal information is only used for permissible purposes. In general, personal information should be treated as confidential and sensitive information as highly confidential. To promote an organization culture that respects privacy would be to develop a security policy. A security policy would cover all organizational systems used for processing, storing or transmitting personal information. The security risks faced by the organization could be assessed in the development of the policy, and then cost-effective measures devised to reduce the risks to acceptable levels. To be effective, a security policy would need to be monitored and periodically reviewed. The range of security measures to consider covers physical security, computer and network security, communications security and personnel security. (Guidelines to the National Privacy Principles, 2001)

Data Integrity Management

Based on the guidelines on NPPs published by the Office of the Federal Privacy Commissioner (OFPC) in September 2001, following are the steps to be undertaken by the organisations collecting the personal information:

- Take reasonable steps to ensure the personal information collected, used or disclosed is accurate, complete and up-to-date. This may require correcting the information- NPP 3, 6
- Take reasonable steps to destroy or permanently de-identify personal information if no longer needed for any purpose for which the information may be used or disclosed -NPP 8

- If an individual asks, you must give access to the personal information you hold about them unless particular circumstances apply that allow you to limit the extent to which you give access – these include emergency situations, specified business imperatives and law enforcement or other public interests. (NPP 6)
- Only adopt, use or disclose a Commonwealth Government identifier if particular circumstances apply that would allow you to do so. A Commonwealth government identifier is a unique combination of letters and numbers, such as a Medicare number, Tax file Number (TFN) which Commonwealth government agencies or contracted service providers allot to an individual. (NPP 7)
- Only transfer personal information overseas if the requirements of NPP 9 are met.
- Health Care providers need to take special measures to comply with sensitive personal information privacy principle NPP 10.

Commercial Products Available

- The majority of the commercially available products provide a Privacy Management plan which includes publishing Privacy Statement on the website. Privacy management software is offered by Tivoli Systems Inc, e-Privacy Management Systems Inc., Invertix Corporation, IBM and PriceWaterhouse & Watchfire. An example of typical product functionality as indicated by the supplier is as follows: "WebCPO uses Watchfire's proven Web Experience Management technology to provide automated, ongoing monitoring, analysis and reporting of potential privacy compliance issues across Internet, intranet and extranet websites. Designed for large, multi-user environments, the reporting functionality of WebCPO allows organizations to better understand their data collection, use and potential data sharing practices. WebCPO also sends real-time alerts to key privacy officials within the organization via wireless devices, e-mail and network broadcasts, informing them when changes are made to privacy-sensitive areas of the website."

- A number of organizations have developed Web seals designed to let their participants publicize that they adhere to certain privacy policies and practices. An effective online seal program has three key components namely a) sufficient privacy principles to which participating Web sites must adhere; b) a sound method for resolving disputes between consumers and Web sites; and c) a robust mechanism for ensuring that "sealed" Web sites complied with the seal's standards. Seals are only in their early stages of development and will likely evolve and improve over time. They could come into their own as a powerful facilitator of globalization of consumer transactions if they are able to provide acceptable and enforceable privacy protection across multiple jurisdictions. Objective assessments of the extent to which seals provide true privacy protection, dispute resolution and enforcement, may be a crucial factor in determining the degree and speed with which they become more accepted by consumers. The Recently announced Safe Harbor Agreement reached between the European Union and the United States has further heightened the profile and potential importance of Web seals. The agreement identifies privacy self-regulatory organizations (such as Web seals) as acceptable mechanisms for determining compliance with its privacy principles. Three leading privacy seal programs are BBBOnLine, TRUSTe, and WebTrust. (Cavoukian A and Crompton M, 2000)

P3P Technology – Concept And Application

Opinion surveys consistently show that privacy concerns are a leading impediment to the further growth of Web-based commerce. Initial efforts by Web sites to publicly disclose their privacy policies have had some impact. But these policies are often difficult for users to locate and understand, too lengthy to read, and change frequently without notice. To overcome these difficulties and automate the privacy related communication between websites and user agents, World Wide web Consortium (W3C) developed a technical specification "Platform for Privacy Preferences Project (P3P)" in collaboration with its industry member associations and EU communities. Following P3P related discussion is based on the information published on W3C website.

What is P3P

P3P 1.0, developed by the W3C, is emerging as an industry standard providing a simple, automated way for users to gain more control over the use of personal information on Web sites they visit. P3P enhances user control by putting privacy policies where users can find them, in a form users can understand, and, most importantly, enables users to act on what they see. The goal of P3P is to increase user trust and confidence in the Web.

P3P does not set minimum standards for privacy, nor can it monitor whether sites adhere to their own stated procedures. P3P enables Web sites to translate their privacy practices into a standardized, machine-readable format (Extensible Markup Language XML) that can be retrieved automatically and easily interpreted by a user's browser. Translation can be performed manually or with automated tools. Once completed, simple server configurations enable the Web site to automatically inform visitors that it supports P3P. P3P is intended to be complementary to both legislative and self-regulatory programs that can help enforce web site policies. In addition, while P3P does not include mechanisms for transferring or securing personal data, it can be built into tools designed to facilitate data transfer. Future versions of P3P could support automatic negotiation of individual privacy agreements and digital signature-based authentication.

P3P 1.0 uses the normal HTTP 1.1 protocol for the exchange of policies, and the matching of policies to user preferences takes place on the client-side. Web sites can implement P3P 1.0 on their HTTP servers by translating their human-readable privacy policies into P3P syntax and configuring their servers to identify the location of the P3P policy. On the user side, P3P clients automatically fetch and read P3P privacy policies on Web sites. A user's browser equipped for P3P can check a Web site's privacy policy and inform the user of that site's information practices. A P3P user agent can detect when different policies apply to different objects on a page (embedded content), and can fetch and review each of these policies. The browser could then automatically compare the statement to the privacy preferences of the user, self-regulatory guidelines, or a variety of legal standards from around the world. P3P client software can be built into a Web browser, plug-ins, or proxy servers. They can also be implemented as Java applets or JavaScript; or built into electronic wallets, automatic form-fillers, or other user data management tools.

P3P Technology Implementation

Even before the P3P specification was completely finalized, a number of implementations were already under development. P3P compliant user agent tools are developed by Idcide (Privacy Companion), ENC, GMD, and YOUPowered (Orby Privacy Plus), while server-side policy generators are available from IBM (P3P Policy Editor), YOUPowered (SmartSense Consumer Trust), and PrivacyBot.com. P3P is complementary to cookie blocking software and anonymity tools. In fact, some of these tool vendors are building P3P into their products e.g. Internet Explorer 6 gives you more control over cookies and more information on a Web site's privacy policy.

The main criticism of P3P 1.0 specification is that the final specification is watered down from the original objective of developing a scheme to achieve 'informed consent through user choice.' In the words of Dr Roger Clarke, the visiting fellow at the Australian National University, Canberra,

"the specification contains no minimum requirements of web-browsers. This had to be omitted in order to avoid constraining competition among browser-providers. The original promise of P3P has been neutered. P3P is nothing more than a 'privacy policy declaration' standard. That's a mere fraction of what is was meant to be, and of what the situation demands. The key proponents of the P3P protocol have laboured long and hard in an endeavour to deliver a PET, but the interests of W3C's members have resulted in it being watered down to a mere pseudo-protection."

However, this author believes that this specification is not the end but just the beginning of a long road ahead for all those involved in e-commerce and participating in privacy protection.

Conclusion

In this information age, governments and private organizations collect, use and disclose personal information using Internet and modern technologies. To protect the privacy of this personal information and thereby individual's fundamental rights, many countries have adopted Privacy laws. In Australia with the Private Sector Privacy Act passed in 2000, all organizational entities in public and private sector dealing with personal information are being brought under common regulated environment. Getting ready for the Act when it becomes effective on 21/12/2001 is a big task for the Australian businesses (Small business have reprieve of another 12 months). However, with the guidance from the Federal Privacy commissioner in their efforts, they will need to meet the challenge successfully by making appropriate changes in the organizational culture and their IT systems. Changes in the IT systems and business practices can be made with the help of external experts, in-house development adhering to industry standards, implementation of off-the-shelf products or a combination of both. Implementation of Privacy laws may involve revamping old systems especially to make them compliant with NPPs related to access disclosure and security issues. Following Australian or International standards and carrying out periodical privacy audits would provide the organization's senior management assurance of organization's ongoing Privacy Act compliance.

References

Crompton M (October 2001) "The Internet Stripped Naked", Privacy Commissioner's speech at WA Internet Association http://www.privacy.gov.au/news/speeches
Fraser H. (2001), ready, set, privacy", *elaw Practice*, Issue 06 September 2001, ISBN 2962E0601, www.elawpractice.com.au

About Australia's privacy laws (2001), www.privacy.gov.au

Guidelines to the National Privacy Principles (September 2001), www.privacy.gov.au

Guidelines on Workplace E-mail, Web Browsing and Privacy (30/3/2000)
http://www.privacy.gov.au/issues/p7_4.html

Kirk G (September 2001), Payroll Specialists" speech by Director Promotion and Education, Office of the Federal privacy Commissioner, www.privacy.gov.au/news/speeches.html

Information Sheet 1 (2001) "Overview of the Private Sector Provisions " www.privacy.gov.au

Information Sheet 2 (2001) "Preparing for 21 December 2001" www.privacy.gov.au

Information Sheet 4 (2001) " Access and correction" www.privacy.gov.au

Information Sheet 6 (2001) "Security and Personal Information" www.privacy.gov.au

Informati on Sheet 12 (2001) "Coverage of and exemptions from the private sector provisions" www.privacy.gov.au

Guidelines for Federal and ACT Government World Wide Websites(2000),
http://www.privacy.gov.au/issues/p7_2.htm

Privacy and P3P, www.w3c.org/p3p

Cavoukian A and Crompton M (2000), "Web Seals: A Review of Online Privacy Programs", A Joint Project of The Office of the Information and Privacy Commissioner/Ontario and The Office of the Federal Privacy Commissioner of Australia, 22nd International Conference on Privacy and Personal Data Protection, *Venice*, September 2000

Privacy Policy-Amendments to February 1999 Version-New Legislation,
http://www.dhs.vic.gov.au/privacy/ipp/amend.htm

Roger Clarke (March 2001), " P3P Re-visited" http://www.anu.edu.au/people/Roger.Clarke/DV/P3PRev.html

The Utilisation of Internet Anonymity by Cyber Criminals

H.L. Armstrong[1] and P.J. Forde[2]

[1] School of Information Systems, Curtin University of Technology, Western Australia
email: H.Armstrong@curtin.edu.au
[2] CBS – Research Fellow, Curtin University of Technology, Western Australia
email: P.Forde@curtin.edu.au

Abstract

Criminals are attracted to the Internet. In addition to useful software tools and valuable knowledge, criminals utilise the Internet's global communications system and they participate in virtual communities of disguised people. The Internet proffers opportunities for people with criminal intent to associate and exchange intelligence with reduced risk to their personal identification. Money laundering, drug dealing, terrorism, hacking, fraud and the distribution of objectionable material are crimes that are perpetrated on the Internet. Using the example of paedophile and hacker Internet practice, this paper proposes an association between criminal Internet activity and Internet anonymity. A relationship is described that indicates a propensity to use anonymity techniques when perpetrating cyber crime. Consequently, as society attempts to counter the endeavours of cyber criminals, pressure will develop to erode some of the individual freedoms that all members of society enjoy.

Keywords

Anonymity, Cyber crime, Free speech, Hacker, Internet, Paedophile.

1. Introduction

The popularity of the Internet illustrates its ability to provide millions of people with easy access to useful and important services. This massive assembly of people is, in effect, a huge vibrant market that is open 24 hours a day and 7 days a week. This market is not bound by national boundaries and participants are representative of all strata of societies. The regulation of market conduct is patchy and pseudo identities abound. It is therefore not surprising that this environment attracts the attention of criminals.

This paper aims to raise the awareness of criminal uses of the Internet. By focussing upon the Internet facilities and practices used by both the paedophile and hacker communities, it is obvious to see how organised crime groups can use global communications facilities to aid anonymity in their activities. The paper concludes with a realisation that individual rights to privacy may have to be subdued in an effort to reduce cyber crime and use of the Internet for criminal activities.

2. Criminals Utilise the Internet

The Swedish National Criminal Investigation Department stated that "as the number of Internet users increases, so does the criminal usage of the Internet", indeed there were "clear indications that the Internet and other IT structures are to an increasing extent being used in criminal contexts" (SNCID, 1998). The FBI recently declared that cyber crime (crimes perpetrated with the assistance of Internet services) "represented the most fundamental challenge for law enforcement in the 21st Century. By its very nature, the cyber environment is borderless, affords easy anonymity and methods of concealment and provides new tools to engage in criminal activity" (Vatis, 2000). The Chief Constable of Fife Constabulary (in Scotland) commented on the difficulties investigators face as they tackle criminal exploitation of the Internet. He pointed out that (Hamilton, 2000):

- continents may separate crimes with offenders and victims at different locations
- offences could be measured in seconds yet they occur in different time zones
- political (national) boundaries were usually ignored
- new crimes were emerging (i.e., on-line harassment, cyber stalking and hacking), and
- encryption techniques enabled offenders to securely communicate worldwide.

In May 2001, the United Nations Commission on Crime Prevention and Criminal Justice discussed international cooperation to combat transnational crime. The use of technologies that supported criminal activities were described. "Dedicated security products such as firewalls and encryption software shield criminal communications from interception or intrusion just as effectively as they protect legitimate communications" (CCP, 2001). The commission recognised that Internet technologies were enabling new forms of criminal organisation and cited paedophile offenders (with their ability to locate another and exchange materials anonymously) as an example of a new form of cooperation not covered by existing definitions of organised crime. "Sophisticated criminals can readily use the easy anonymity that the Internet provides to hide their crimes" (Holder, 2001).

For example, in an effort to hinder a police investigation of drug organisations in Holland, criminals from an information warfare division established to support organised crime collected information via eavesdropping and decrypting communications of attorneys, police officers and government officials. By analysing the data collected, the criminals were able to determine which law enforcement and justice units were collaborating on the investigation (Denning 1999). The information warfare division was reported to work in loosely-coupled cell structures that were illusive and difficult to capture - a common trait of organised criminal groups.

An individual's right to privacy provides an ongoing obstruction to law enforcement. The FBI stipulated that "respect for privacy was a fundamental guidepost in all of our activities" and that FBI conduct was "strictly limited by the Fourth Amendment, statues such as Title III and ECPA, and the Attorney General Guidelines" (Vatis, 2000). In November 2001, the preamble to the European Convention on Cybercrime alerted members states to the impact that efforts to control cyber crime can have on individual rights and called for an awareness to:

> ensure a proper balance between the interests of law enforcement and respect for fundamental human rights as enshrined in the 1950 Council of Europe Convention for the Protection of Human rights and Fundamentals, the 1966 United Nations International Covenant on Civil and Political Rights and other applicable international human rights treaties, which reaffirm the rights of everyone to hold opinions without interference, as well as the right to freedom of expression, including the freedom to seek, receive, and impart information and ideas of all kinds, regardless of frontiers, and the rights concerning the respect for privacy (COE, 2001).

Even though criminal utilisation of the Internet is widely recognised the implications of anonymous Internet practices have not received similar attention.

3. Paedophile Internet Community

Activists argue for a paedophile's right to free speech (Jay_h, 1997). They argue for a lifestyle that contradicts fundamental cultural practices and violates specific laws. Paedophiles maintained that free speech was not available to them and anonymity was necessary to avoid persecution (Spike, 1997). Most societies have considered paedophilia and have concluded that it was not an acceptable lifestyle. In fact, this behaviour is normally viewed with such alarm that most societies consider paedophiles to be criminals (and convicted criminals were expected to forfeit their personal rights).

Reducing opportunities for paedophiles to communicate and organise has been the major incentive behind a number of national investigations. For example, the 1995 Australian report on Organised Criminal Paedophile Activity reported that there was little evidence of organised paedophile groups and included the following findings (PJC & NCA, 1995):

- while very small paedophile-support groups operated openly in Australia in the 1980s there is no evidence they currently do so
- there is no evidence to suggest that organised paedophile groups have ever resembled what are traditionally thought of as organised crime groups in size, aims, structures, methods, longevity and so forth (to the extent that two or more paedophiles groups together to commit offences, the numbers involved have almost invariably been very small and the groupings very much ad hoc and on a peer-to-peer basis), and
- more commonly, where there are contacts between paedophile offenders, they consist of loose informal networks of peer-to-peer contacts.

However, a study that observed the Internet activities of paedophiles suggested that these findings were no longer accurate (Forde and Patterson, 1998). In contrast to the 1995 findings paedophiles were shown to be developing their own community and that the Internet was providing the forum for organised informal networks and peer-to-peer contacts on a global scale. The study concluded that paedophiles used the Internet to create communications structures, distribute objectionable materials and to archive their collections. A paedophile Internet community was observed that mentored its members with instruction on anonymity. In particular, it was noted that (Forde & Patterson 1998):

- Paedophiles were very concerned to conceal their identity.
  This was not unexpected given society's attitude to paedophilia. Many Internet links described anonymity and privacy techniques. Authors of e-mail sent their messages to newsgroups anonymously. WWW pages displayed disguised e-mail addresses while newsgroup discussions exchanged information about 'safe' locations and masking techniques. IRC chat sessions were conducted on private channels using direct one-to-one secure communication.

- Paedophiles needed to demonstrate their prowess to their peers.
  WWW pages were used to make coming-out presentations (although most presenters hid behind masked identities). These pages appeared to provide peer group status.

They also acted as a vehicle for soliciting communications from other paedophiles. Background profiles and descriptions of individual interests were often detailed on the presentation pages together with samples of images from private collections. The need to demonstrate the extensiveness of individual picture collections was vividly manifested within certain newsgroups. Sending pictures to newsgroups obviously enabled picture distribution however they were distributions to no one in particular. Newsgroup postings appeared to be most concerned with advertising the extent of personal collections.

These particular characteristics have also been noticed within the hacking fraternity.

4. Hacker Internet Community

The tools and techniques utilised by the hacking community have been widely discussed in both printed and electronic forums. Software tools for hacking all types of computer and communications systems are readily available on the Internet and most can be downloaded at no, or little, cost. Our concern in this discussion is not with the tools per se, but with the elements of the hacking community that are similar to those used in other organised crime groups (i.e., paedophiles).

The hacker community is using the Internet to communicate and attack systems on a global scale (Boni & Kovacich, 2000). The Computer Security Institute report 90% of respondents detected computer security breaches in the past twelve months and independent hackers are reported to form the likely source of attack in 80% of cases (CSI/FBI, 2002). Lack of security on the Internet and its protocols aids the hacker's quest by providing vulnerabilities and unrestricted access. By its nature (i.e., sheer size and open connectivity) the Internet provides a facility to encompass the hacker community and its sub-culture. The Internet is an open, interconnected communications infrastructure that is unregulated and largely unpoliced, and also unpoliceable (Ford & Baum, 2001).

Hackers comprise an "interesting subculture, technically astute and talented even if socially and morally depraved" (Nichols, Ryan & Ryan, 2000). The hacker's philosophy is well documented - information should be free and access to computers and information should be unlimited. They work in groups, some groups being limited to only the elite of their trade, others willing to take on inexperienced members and train them. Many hackers will mentor other hackers, particularly those who show promise, enthusiasm, or who have similar values. Hackers share and barter their tools and information including methods of avoiding detection. Many tutoring sites have been established on the web and hackers, other criminals and security specialists use these sites.

Hackers are motivated by a variety of factors, including the thrill and excitement of doing something illegal, challenge, pleasure, knowledge, recognition, power and friendship (Chantler, 1995; Denning, 1999). Other reasons noted by Chantler (1995) in his study of the hacker culture included self-gratification, addiction, espionage, theft, profit, vengeance, sabotage and freedom. Many hackers admit they are addicted to the thrill of doing something prohibited; they enjoy the associated 'high' and rush of adrenaline.

Hackers use Internet facilities extensively, including web sites, e-mail, chat rooms, FTP sites, Usenet newsgroups and discussion boards. Hacker software tools are stored on private and public web sites and protected systems. Hacker web sites are highly secured and access is given only to those who are trusted. Like other organised criminal groups hackers secure their communications using sophisticated encryption tools.

Hackers retain their anonymity by using handles (pseudo names), remailers, anonymous servers, email and IP spoofing (changing their IP address so that transmissions appear to come from another source). Hackers like to advertise their exploits but at the same time remain anonymous. Stephenson (2000) claims that vanity is a hacker trait. Hackers cannot keep quiet about their exploits and bragging rights are one of their chief motivations for cracking systems. The majority of hackers are loners who share their information in public and semi-public forums, however their desire to be recognised for their wares and expertise results in many leaving a mark of their trade on hacked sites and embedded in some tools. Many hackers can be identified by techniques and patterns unique to their work.

Whilst many hackers claim their intentions are noble, their actions remain criminal. The hacker community provides a training ground for those who wish to master computer networks and the Internet whilst remaining undetected and anonymous. Where else would organised crime go to train their operatives?

5. Internet Anonymity Practice

Hackers are viewed as criminals in most countries, however they claim their values and morals differ from other criminal groups (i.e., paedophiles). In fact, some hackers claim they trace the identity of paedophiles, attack their computers, and remove the images paedophiles post on the Internet (Denning, 1999). The hacking community is decades old and a high standard of technical expertise is normally a pre-requisite to membership (particularly of elite groups). They utilise covert channels and steganography to hide data in transmission (Skoudis, 2002) and their skills in sharing information and tools anonymously are honed and proficient. It is not unreasonable to project that hackers will sell information and expertise to organised crime and/or terrorist groups. The hacker community may be sheltering and training perpetrators to occupy the shadows of cyberspace in organised crime groups.

Paedophiles sought acceptance amongst their peers but they trusted the protection of Internet anonymity. While they do not have the technical expertise of the hacker community, paedophiles are obviously skilled in the use of encryption and remailers as well as the practice of Internet anonymity. Individual notoriety and personal anonymity are characteristics that have been observed in both communities and it is reasonable to expect that other criminal communities would also desire these outcomes. There appears to be an association between particular Internet activities and user identification. Internet practices that provide the strongest anonymity were used to camouflage extreme criminal behaviour (Forde & Patterson 1998). Therefore, a model of Internet anonymity practice can be proposed that illustrates the relationship between Internet activity and user identification. To assist the derivation of this model it is useful to think of individuals initiating activities as instigators and individuals that participate and readers.

Internet	Instigator			Reader		
service	Intension	Technique	Identification	Intension	Technique	Identification
World Wide Web	Low-level information distribution. Advertise contact details.	Use proxies to mask ownership. Use international ISP's. Plan to re-locate regularly.	**Weak anonymity** Relies on ISP's not to analyse logs or make them available to authorities.	Locate information and contacts.	Use anonymous proxies to hide identity.	**Weak anonymity** Relies on ISP's not to analyse logs or make them available to authorities.
Email	Confidential communication s. Material distribution.	Encrypted email. Free email a/c obtained using false ID. Post using anonymous remailers.	**Very Strong anonymity** Difficult to trace.	Confidential communication s. Material distribution.	Encrypted email. Free email a/c obtained using false ID. Reply using anonymous remailers.	**Very Strong anonymity** Difficult to trace.
File Transfer Program	Public and private distribution of electronic files.	Run and set-up own FTP server.	**Medium anonymity** Relies on regular change to avoid ISP attention.	Risky download of files.	Anonymous access.	**Weak anonymity** Relies on FTP owner's tolerance.
News groups	Broadcasting illegal or objectionable messages.	Anonymous email posting.	**Very Strong anonymity** Difficult to trace.	Downloading illegal or objectionable messages.	Proxy masked www to news. Use open news servers. Regularly change to avoid attention of news server administrators.	**Medium anonymity** Depends on tolerance of new server administrator.
Internet Relay Chat	Private real-time chat. Exchanging electronic files.	False identity. Private channels. Personal contacts.	**Strong anonymity:** Relies on regular identity changes. Skipping across channels to avoid the attention of moderators.	Private real-time chat. Exchanging electronic files.	False identity. Private channels. Personal contacts.	**Strong anonymity:** Relies on regular identity changes. Skipping across channels to avoid the attention of moderators.

Table 1: Internet Anonymity Practices

The model presented in Table 1 supports the proposition that an association exists between the intent of criminal Internet activity and Internet anonymity. When the intended activity is considered benign then low strength anonymity will be acceptable. However, when criminal activities are to be perpetrated then the use of strong anonymity techniques are to be expected.

While encryption techniques are readily available, an awareness of the penalties associated with transactional security has to be taken into account by perpetrators. For example, securing a SSL (secure socket layer) requires a hand-shaking process that identifies the parties at each end of the connection. This facility makes it difficult for external parties to read the communication, however it requires communicators to declare their virtual identities. Therefore, even though perpetrators can create 'secure' networks they must address the issue of member identification and the attendant risk of membership exposure. Consequently, virtual private networks (VPN's) are a dual edged sword. Their technological construction provides excellent protection against external attack; nevertheless members could be compromised by an individual member's inappropriate action. As a result, if very high levels of trust exist between group members then they can be expected to use VPN's. Otherwise they can be expected to use Internet services offering (or allowing) anonymity.

A recent inspection of paedophile Internet communications confirmed the continuing adoption of anonymous practices and the distribution of knowledge about those practices. Apart from a well-known portal that provides a vast array of 'benign' information to paedophiles, one current technique of distributing 'offensive' information uses a combination of discussion boards (e-Boards) and virtual groups (e-Groups). These boards and groups are the Internet's replacement of the old bulletin board systems (BBS). Usually e-Boards do not have passwords and are open to anyone using the Internet. As the ISP (Internet Service Provider) hosting e-Boards or the owner of an e-Board could log transactions, visitors usually mask their IP numbers using proxies. Anonymous remailers are often used to post messages to these boards. Apart from benign (possibly coded) discussion, messages distribute links to e-Groups that archive offensive material. Even though e-Board users try not to attract outside attention these boards have a short life expectancy as ISPs attempt to eradicate abuse of their services. Therefore, many messages point to replacement e-Boards. e-Groups provide more services than e-Boards (i.e., picture galleries, bookmarks, chat and message boards) and they have membership structures that require identification information. Requiring membership of hacker and paedophile e-Groups means that outsiders are less likely to visit these groups. However, in order to attract Internet users to their web sites ISPs make it easy for new members to join. Easy membership enables paedophiles and hackers to utilise virtual identities and anonymous email addresses when creating e-Groups. Despite the membership risk, paedophiles in particular are currently participating in e-Boards and e-Groups because they seem to think that their anonymity practice protects them against the danger of identification.

6. Conclusion

The Internet provides an unmanageable infrastructure, protocols and facilities that support anonymity. Both paedophiles and hackers have established organised communities via the Internet to support communications and dissemination of information, tools and techniques via web sites, e-mail, chat rooms, FTP sites, Usenet newsgroups, encryption tools, remailers and anonymous server facilities. These two organised criminal groups use anonymity to protect their members. While the Internet remains unregulated and unpoliced organised crime groups such as paedophiles and other sexual abusers, hackers, money launders, drug dealers, terrorists and fraudsters will continue to use its infrastructure and facilities to communicate and distribute materials.

An individual's right to privacy granted by numerous international covenants and treaties shelters not only innocent parties but also organised crime. What constitutes an acceptable balance between law enforcement, individual privacy and human rights? The new European Convention on Cybercrime discloses that member states have agreed to adopt legislation and other measures that will empower competent authorities to collect or record (and compel a service provider to collect, record or cooperate) real-time traffic data and the interception of content data. Societies are apparently prepared to tolerate an erosion of personal freedoms in an effort to support the community's core values.

7. References

Boni W. & Kovacich G.L. (2000), *Netspionage: The Global Threat to Information*, Butterwoth Heinemann.

COE (2001), *Convention on Cybercrime*, Council of Europe, European Treaty Series No: 185, November 23, http://conventions.coe.int/Treaty/EN/CadreListeTraites.htm (14/12/2001).

CCP (2001), *Conclusions of the study on effective measures to prevent and control high-technology and computer-related crime*, Report of the Secretary -General, Commission on Crime prevention and Criminal Justice, United Nations Economic and Social Council, March 30, Http://www.odccp.org/adhoc/crime/10_commission/4e.pdt (14/12/2001).

Chantler A.N. (1995), *Risk: The Profile of a Computer Hacker*, PhD Thesis, Curtin University, Perth, Western Australia.

CSI/FBI (2002), 2002 CSI/FBI Computer Crime and Security Survey, *Computer Security Issues & Trends*, Vol VIII, No. 1, Spring 2002, Computer Security Institute

Denning D.E. (1999), *Information Warfare and Security*, Addison-Wesley, Reading Massachusetts.

Ford W. & Baum M.S. (2001), *Secure Electronic Commerce*, Prentice Hall PTR.

Forde P.J & Patterson A. (1998), *Paedophile Internet Activity*, Trends and Issues in crime and criminal justice, Australian Institute of Criminology, No: 97, November, http://www.aic.gov.au/publications/tandi/tandi97.html (14/12/2001).

Hamilton J.P. (2000), Speech by Chief constable of Fife Constabulary, UK, on 23rd March 2000 at the Microsoft *'Combating cross border crime 2000'* conference, Cape Town, South Africa, http://www.microsoft.com/europe/public_sector/Gov_Agencies/125.htm (14/12/2001).

Holder E. (2001), *Testimony before Deputy Attorney General*, Department of Justice, Washington, D.C. http://www.senate.gov/~judiciary/229200eh.htm (14/12/2001).

Jay_h (1997), *The Boylove Manifesto*, http://www.stream.ru/homes/bla/e-manifest.html (November 1998).

Nichols, R.K., Ryan, D.J. & Ryan J.C.H. (2000), *Defending your Digital Assets against Hackers, Crackers, Spies and Thieves*, McGraw-Hill, New York.

PJC & NCA (1995), *Organised Criminal Paedophile Activity*: A report by the Parliamentary Joint Committee on the National Crime Authority, November, http://www.aph.gov.au/senate/committee/nca_ctte/ncapedo/ncapedo1.htm (14/12/2001).

Skoudis, E., (2002), *Counter Hack*, Prentice Hall PTR, New Jersey, USA

SNCID (1998), *Organised Crime in Sweden 1998*, Swedish National Criminal Investigation Department, http://www.police.se/gemensam/rps/rkp/orgcrime.htm (14/12/2001).

Spike (1997), *Anonymity Made Easy*: A necessity for most newcomers to the BL community, http://www.demon.nl/freespirit/fpc/pages/spike/anon.htm (November 1998).

Stephenson P. (2000), *Investigating Computer-Related Crime*, CRC Press, Washington DC, USA.

Vatis (2000), Statement of the Director, National Infrastructure Protection Center, Federal Bureau of Investigation on Cybercrime before the Senate Judiciary Committee, Criminal Justice Oversight Subcommittee and House Judiciary Committee, Crime Subcommittee, Washington, D.C. February 29, 2000 http://www.usdoj.gov/criminal/cybercrime/vatis.htm (14/12/2001).

The Misuse of the Internet at Work

Craig Valli

School of Computing and Information Science, Edith Cowan University, Mount Lawley, Western Australia
e-mail: c.valli@ecu.edu.au

Abstract

Employees undertake a wide range of activities when they use the Internet in the work place. Some of these activities may leave the modern Internet connected organisation vulnerable to undue or unknown risk, potential productivity losses and expense as a result of misuse or abuse of the organisationally provided Internet access. Much of the existing literature on this subject matter points to a purported epidemic of misuse in the workplace.

Keywords

Internet, World Wide Web, misuse, abuse.

1. Introduction

There is much hype currently in the media and industry press with respect to non-business or abusive use of the Internet in the workplace. The claims made in these reports are most disturbing and alarming when taken within the context of loss, risk and liability to most modern Internet connected businesses:

- "Almost 25 percent of employees' online time is given over to surfing the Internet for recreational purposes." (Ohlson, 1998)
- "Nearly two-thirds of companies report that employees access sexually explicit Web sites at work" (Hickins, 1999)
- "...online trading during working hours is costing corporate America $11 billion annually" (Ballard, 2000)
- "According to Nielsen/Netratings, 21.1 percent of adult sites are accessed at work. Viewing time is an average of four minutes per person" (Anonymous, 2001)
- "Xerox Corp. said it has fired about 40 employees this year in the U.S. for "excessive misuse of the Internet." The main problem was among employees who, while at work, viewed pornographic Web sites" (Anonymous, 1999)
- "Last September, a survey by the career Website *vault.com* found that 90% of employees surf non-work-related Websites at the office. Only 4% admitted to looking at pornography, but the other numbers are hardly reassuring to employers: 37% have looked for jobs; 34% check stocks; 26% send non-business instant messages." (Cohen, 2001)

For the purposes of this paper the term misuse will be adapted from (Straub & Nance, 1990) to be the unauthorised, deliberate, and internally recognisable misuses of assets of the local organisational information system to access materials on the world wide web. This would include materials that the user accesses that are against the established organisational policy or law for example, accessing copyrighted MP3 files. Non-business use for this paper will mean any activity on the Internet that is not directly related to fulfilment of a persons job description or is not done in the course of processing a work-flow related to their job.

The possible abusive activities that employees or users undertake may leave the organisation open to undue risk or liability for example – the accessing of pornography creating a hostile workplace or the activity being simply illegal. In addition, there is the actual cost associated with the provision Internet for the purposes of misuse or non-business usage. A tangible productivity loss does occur when users are accessing material that is not directly related to processing a workflow. The silent, intangible loss of a missed business opportunity that can occur when people using the connection for non-business related activities unduly compromise the Internet connection's performance. However, it is important (as stated later) not to understate some of the beneficial side effects such as the relief of boredom and stress, and the efficient use of time on personal activities that otherwise might detract from work time.

Take something like the now famous *John West Salmon Video* that is touted as a master-stroke of 'viral marketing'. This file is size is about 1.5MB or around 25c Australian to deliver to a desktop personal computer. If the number of people in the organisation who might have received it a least once, is multiplied by the actual time off assigned tasks to access and view it then the some of the wider problem starts to become more apparent.

2. Internet Misuse – Mis-defined and Mis-represented?

The widespread use of the Internet and in particular the World Wide Web and email have introduced a wide range issues that relate directly to employee productivity (Wen & Lin, 1998). The non-business use of the Internet in a 1000 seat organisation is estimated to cost that as much as $35 million in lost revenues and wages (Holtz, 2001). Recent surveys have figures between 60-80% of employees accessing pornographic material in the workplace (Hickins, 1999) and as well most staff are sending private e-mails (Holtz, 2001). A January 2000 study by the Saratoga Institute found that nearly two-thirds of U.S. firms have disciplined employees for Internet abuse. Fifty-six percent admitted they knew employees use the Internet to gamble, look at pornography, and engage in other activities that are not work-related (Institute, 2000). A 1999 study by the American Management Association found that more than 50 percent of all Internet activity taking place within companies is not business-related (Greengard, 2000).

These above statistics and commentaries beg the question as to why organisations are letting employees supposedly spend 50% of their Internet time doing something other than work related tasks. Notwithstanding that these activities are potentially something that may see the individual or the organisation in a court of law. Why would an organisation in these times of increased competitiveness and globalisation allow such as gross waste of resource to occur?

Herein lies one of the big problems with most of the existing literature relating to the level of Internet misuse and abuse. A vast majority of it is based on limited survey and often blatantly commercial bias (Holtz, 2001). The current literature and information on Internet abuse also suffers from similar problems identified by (George, 1996): "The advocacy literature devoted to computer-based monitoring is marked by three criteria: (1) its foundation on small (and usually biased) sample sizes; (2) the monolithic character of its findings; and (3) the consistency of its conclusions."

There is also often no real attempt to measure or rate the level of misuse that does actually occur within an organisation across all stakeholder groups. Most of the readily available statistics provided are founded on the basis of limited survey of one stakeholder group normally management.

Whether this non-business use is deemed appropriate or a misuse often depends upon the type of non-business use and the organisational context within which it is done. When interviewing a supplier of Internet monitoring software (Cohen, 2001) got this response from a market leader "Some customers are draconian, shutting everything down; others are much more progressive, saying they're going to block pornography, but everything else is fair game." There is of course material that is strictly forbidden by law, human rights and industrial relations acts such as viewing of pornographic materials, racist, sexist or hate based materials.

2.1 Productivity - Lost or Found?

Excepting the instances where an organisation may be held liable to damages from such accesses, the responses from organisations and research conducted in the literature also varies as to whether non-business use actually results in lost productivity or has a detrimental effect at all on employees performances.

There is an argument that as the working week has increased and increased communication has become more invasive for employees extending into their personal lives so should organisations be more understanding of non-business use. Many people who work these extended hours now have to legitimately conduct errands, pay bills and arrange other non-business-related activities as a result of these extended business hours.

Not all non-business access is also construed as a bad event or threat and can provide often-intangible benefits to an organisation:

> "Complicating things further is the fact that personal use of the Internet might actually provide a positive benefit. An August study conducted by Xylo, Inc., a work/life programs provider based in Bellevue, Washington, found that 56 percent of employees who use the Internet for personal reasons report that it helps them do their jobs better or simply makes them happier or less stressed-out employees. About 43 percent claim that the Internet has no real impact -- positive or negative -- on their performance." (Greengard, 2000 p.22)

Some organisations also see it as a means of educating the user base to help increase information technology skills or help in the adoption of the Internet as a technology itself. So apart from the quantifiable loss of "off-task" wages there are potentially other intangible benefits countering these purported losses.

2.2 Filter Folly

Organisations are increasingly employing policies and filtering systems to counteract some of the threats and risks that the use of the Internet poses to the organisation. The difference in 2 surveys conducted in 1999 and 2000 conducted by Vault.com there was an increase from 31% to 42% of employers who said they restricted or monitored Internet use (Cohen, 2001).

However, the effectiveness of filtering systems alone is proving ineffectual in some cases to preventing this sort of abuse (Hunter, 2000; Neumann & Weinstein, 1999; Nunberg, 2001).

Content filtering systems typically work by denying access based upon a list of keywords. This is problematic as often words may be used in a different semantic context, which entirely changes the meaning of those words from offensive to non-offensive, business to non-business. For example, the word 'sex' could be used to search for 'Essex', 'Middlesex', or 'sexes' all of which would be a legitimate use of the word 'sex' for various organisations.

In a study of popular commercial Internet filtering software as to how under-inclusive - (failing to block the worst pornography) and over-inclusive (blocking non-sexual, non-violent content) they were (Hunter, 2000) found alarming varying rates. "Overall, filters failed to block objectionable content 25% of the time; on the other hand, they improperly blocked 21% of benign content. This finding is alarming when vendors of this software claim to block 90-95% of undesirable content.

There is concern also that overt, oppressive regimes of monitoring do in fact reduce employee productivity and previous studies in the general area of electronic monitoring of employees would concur with this (George, 1996; Phipps, 1996). In some of the more severe cases in the literature employee health suffered greatly as a result of the stress caused by this monitoring of activity.

2.3 Time versus Bandwidth

Of course, it is not just the time an employee spends on the Internet that matter but the bandwidth that is being used. In a recent study by the OECD (Paltridge, 2000) high speed Internet access on cable and DSL saw charges ranging from 3 cents to as high as 36 cents per extra megabyte downloaded that went above the included megabyte limit for the services offered. For example, if an organisation incurs a charge for 2GB of traffic, which when spread across 50 users is only 40Mb a month or 2 megabytes extra per working day per user. If we take the lowest price as per the OECD study this is an additional $60 charge not much but take the highest and this is $720 or $8640 per annum. To illustrate what 2 megabytes per person could some examples follow:

- Viewing a funny video clip for instance of the John West Salmon video
- An e-mail broadcast to 20 friends that has a 100K graphic embedded in it
- 10 checks of stock prices per day.

The author has personally seen costs that went from around $300 per month in total charges based on a 17 cent per megabyte charge to almost $2400 per month as result of one person accessing streaming video from the Internet. The other unseen cost here is the fact that the Internet pipe will, in many instances, be choked with extraneous materials and hence reduces the performance of the organisations e-business systems. In the above case the use caused a 4Mbit link to be at 100% utilisation for 6 hours per working day which rendered the transactional web site ineffective during this time. This misuse of the Internet is problematic in that the equation for loss to the organisation is not just *Time Lost* for a traditional parallel analogy employee smoking a cigarette. Organisations now have *Lost Time* + *Cost of Network Bandwidth* + *Lost Opportunity* or to take the cigarette analogy – you have an employee smoking a cigarette, provided free of charge by the organisation, near the front door of the organisation that makes certain customers go to the competition to transact their business.

2.4 Policy – The Panacea and Paragon of Reason & Right?
Policy is touted one of the keystone blocks of building a system that has low non-business use. Access policy implementation has been slow to catch on and most estimates indicate that only 50-60 percent of organisations have developed acceptable usage or access policies. This means that as many as one out of two organisations does not have access policies to the stage of being documented let alone enforced. An acceptable usage policy often only attains organisational legitimacy once the organisational management enforces it.

The policies implemented are simplistic and lack the specificity needed to get the message across to the users of the system. "The policies themselves can typically be boiled down to one key point: Web access is a company resource that should not be used in any way that would embarrass or otherwise cause grief for the company.'(Cohen, 2001)

In a study on the use of computer ethics codes (Harrington, 1996) which could be easily parallelled to be effectively policy documents it was noted that they had some effect on user behaviour. The positive effect upon user behaviour was greatly increased if management actively enforced the policy which is further substantiated by other studies in this area (Straub, Carlson, & Jones, 1993). Furthermore, if there is overt and deliberate publicising of the fact that the policy has been broken and what action was taken this added again to the effectiveness of the policy.

3. Conclusion

There is a definite need for further objective, inclusive studies in the area of Internet misuse that involves all stakeholder groups within an organisation. In particular the inclusion of end users in studies, examination of policy documents and critical examination of traffic usage would help better inform us what misuse of the Internet by people within organisations is being perpetrated. Much of the data that can provide objective measures for an analysis of Internet misuse such as quantitative examination of Internet traffic usage logfiles patterns appears to be largely ignored in many studies. Further data such as *sextracker.com* providing statistics that 72% of all accesses to pornographic sites they monitor occurs during business hours is possible further indication that there is something not quite correct in how organisations are monitoring and deploying their Internet connectivity.

Much of the evidence in existence for the touted malaise of Internet misuse is from limited survey of management groups. Furthermore some of the surveys are based only what management thinks is occurring not the actual true reality at the router. If we were to believe some vendors claims there is a cesspool of iniquity occurring in the workplace and they have the 'silver algorithmic panacea', organisations have all been waiting for. Current countermeasures that are being deployed by organisations are often in isolation and appear to be largely ineffective in reducing much of the misuse. Given that many organisations do still not have acceptable usage policies in place how can users be reliably expected to even grasp what is appropriate or inappropriate use of the Internet. But, it is clear from the literature that effective deployment and diligence of countermeasures can have some positive effects on user behaviours.

The often-touted issue of productivity seems to be also largely still vexed. How much non-business use of the Internet by individuals does it take to become a productivity problem or be detrimental to the organisations Internet connection such it is no longer within an optimal range. Some other issues that need consideration are that of copyright and intellectual property particularly when i comes to MP3 and other streaming media formats. There are also the various human and industrial resource issues that confront Internet connected organisations that like the productivity issue are problematic for organisations.

The issue of misuse of the Internet in the workplace is not a simplistic problem and cannot be solved with the silver bullet application. Internet misuse with organisations will need further extensive research from a wide variety of perspectives before we can begin to understand the phenomenon. This understanding will then hopefully then allow use to take appropriate steps to lessen the impact of Internet misuse on the modern Internet connected organisation.

4. References

Anonymous. (2001). *Human Resources Management - the Missing Link in Controlling Internet Access*. Strategic HR Services. Retrieved 20th Jan 2001, 2001, from the World Wide Web: http://www.strategichr.com/shrsweb2/InternetAccess.shtml

Ballard, K. (2000, 22 November 2000). *Online trading and entertainment sites to impact workplace productivity*. ITWeb Limited. Retrieved Jan 8th, 2001, 2001, from the World Wide Web: http://www.itweb.co.za/sections/internet/2000/0011220831.asp

Cohen, A. (2001). Worker watchers. *Fortune, 143*, 70-80.

George, J. F. (1996). Computer-based monitoring: common perceptions and empirical results. *MIS Quarterly, 20*(4), 459-481.

Greengard, S. (2000, December 2000). The High Cost of Cyberslacking. *Workforce, 79*, 22-24.

Harrington, S. J. (1996). The Effect of Codes of Ethics and Personal Denial of Responsibility on Computer Abuse Judgments and Intentions. *MIS Quarterly, 20*(3 (September)), 257-258.

Hickins, M. (1999). Fighting surf abuse. *Management Review, 88*(6), 8.

Holtz, S. (2001). Employees online: The productivity issue. *Communication World, 18*(2), 17-23.

Hunter, C. D. (2000). Social impacts: Internet filter effectiveness--testing over-and underinclusive blocking decisions of four popular Web filters. *Social Science Computer Review, 18*(2), 214-222.

Institute, S. (2000). *Websense Survey on Internet Use in the Workplace*. St.Clara, California: Saratoga Institute.

Neumann, P. G., & Weinstein, L. (1999). Risks of content filtering. *Association for Computing Machinery. Communications of the ACM, 42*(11), 152.

Nunberg, G. (2001, Jan 15). The Internet filter farce: why blocking software doesn't--and can't--work as promised. *American Prospect [H.W. Wilson - SSA], 12*, 28-33.

Ohlson, K. (1998). *Recreational Web Surfing at Work Is on the Rise*. PC World Online. Retrieved 21st February, 2001, 2001, from the World Wide Web:

Paltridge, D. S. (2000). *LOCAL ACCESS PRICING AND E-COMMERCE* (94030). Paris, France: OECD - Committee for Information, Computer and Communication Policy (ICCP).

Phipps, P. A. (1996). Electronic monitoring in the workplace. *Monthly Labor Review, 119*(3), 33-35.

Straub, D. W., Carlson, P. J., & Jones, E. H. (1993). Deterring Cheating by Student Programmers: A Field Experiment in Computer Security. *Journal of Management Systems, 5*(1), 33-48.

Straub, D. W., & Nance, W. D. (1990). Discovering and Disciplining Computer Abuse in Organizations: A Field Study. *MIS Quarterly, 14*(1 (March)), 45-62.

Wen, H. J., & Lin, B. (1998). Internet and employee productivity. *Management Decision, 36*(6), 395-398.

Towards An Adaptive Multimedia Learning Environment: An Australian Solution to Cross-Cultural And Offshore Delivery Issues

F.Kurzel[1] and J.Slay[2]

[1]School of Communication, Information and the New Media, University of South Australia
MAGILL, S.A. 5072, Australia
[2] School of Computer and Information Science, University of South Australia, MAWSON
LAKES, SA5095, Australia
email:[Frank.Kurzel][Jill.Slay]@unisa.edu.au

Abstract

The move to online learning environment for the delivery of Australian computing programs in remote parts of Asia has heightened the need for adaptive interactive learning environments. This paper examines the implementation of Adaptive Multimedia Learning Environment, (AMLE), a networked multimedia learning environment which attempts to provide the functionality of a traditional intelligent tutoring system. AMLE also deals with student preferences and some of the cultural learning issues which tend to impede deep learning.

Keywords

Adaptive, multimedia, online learning, cross-cultural

1. Introduction

Australian universities, motivated by their need to compensate for the reduced amount of government funding, and their prime location on the edge of education-hungry Asia, has moved quickly into the online learning market. With the problems imposed by large classes in Australia over the last few years, and the large range of individual approaches needed to deal with some of student learning issues raised at home, computing academics have been some of the first to develop and use web-mediated networked learning environments for enhancing student learning, while maintaining a large proportion of traditional face-to-face tutorial and practical content within their subjects. As has been pointed out (Slay, 1998a; Slay, 1998b) the Web provides a vehicle for the development of the learning environment and teaching can be structured to develop lifelong learning skills and to cater for the expectations and learning styles of students from different cultures and backgrounds.

Early Australian examples of the use of the WWW in IT education abound. Boalch (1996) provides an examination of the use of the WWW as a support medium for the delivery of a first year unit in Information Systems at Curtin University. He provides an evaluation of site utilisation and user feedback in the case where subject information and course details were provided on the WWW for students. The Eklunds (1996) examine the use of the WWW to supplement traditional IT teaching. They provide case studies of two examples of the restructuring of traditional forms of IT course for Web-delivery. Jones (1996) of Central Queensland University gives details of case study involving the design, presentation and evaluation of an undergraduate unit in Systems Administration taught completely via the WWW to on-campus and distance students.

However these and many newer systems that have been developed rely on the low-level concept of interactivity (derived from a distance education paradigm) as the relationship between an individual student and text, and fail to use the technological interactivity which is available. Common online learning environments often fail to maximise the potential of current multimedia research. While the value of HTML pages and threaded discussions is acknowledged, especially for those who do not have English as a first language, they do not display the ability to adapt teaching material for the needs of individual students.

Moves to offshore and wholly-online environments have forced academics to consider other methods to increase adaptivity of content and interactivity, especially now as their students who may be studying in the far North of China or in rural East Malaysia, may be totally dependent on the online material for their learning (although this is sometimes supported by local tutors who may be in the same physical location as the student). This means that distinct measures need to be taken to get an accurate profile of students pre-existing skills and concepts before learning of the specific subject commences

2. Adaptive Teaching on the WWW

Various researchers who have experimented with adaptive teaching on the WWW have used techniques and principles derived from Intelligent Tutoring Systems (ITS) and particularly Anderson's rule based cognitive modelling (Anderson, 1983). Others have used Adaptive Navigation Support to provide adaptive navigation through hypertext pages and thus developed adaptive textbooks for the tutoring, particularly, of software applications (Brusilovsky, 1996).

An ITS is traditionally formed of two parts, an expert system and a communication module. Within the expert system, there are three modules, the student module, the pedagogical module and the domain knowledge module. The student module gives the student history; the pedagogical model is provides information about the teaching process and the domain knowledge module provides the material that is being taught. ITS have been shown to enhance student motivation and learning (Anderson, 1983). While proving useful, adaptive teaching on the WWW has not yet been able to supply the full functionality of traditional ITS.

This paper presents techniques that have been used to provide adaptivity within Multimedia Concepts, an introductory course within the multimedia studies stream offered at the University of South Australia[1]. The aim of this course is to provide the foundational knowledge and skills required to create and utilise a range of media items within multimedia presentations. With the movement of courses to an on-line mode, there was a need to develop and enhance the learning environment's web with a range of features that stimulate the complete learning experience. We have developed a prototype for a multimedia learning environment for the presentation of this course that displays adaptive characteristics and has become an Adaptive Multimedia Learning Environment. (AMLE). The aim is to develop the full functionality of a traditional ITS

---

[1] http://www.unisa.edu.au

3. Implementation of the Adaptive Multimedia Learning Environment (AMLE).

The advantages of this delivery format of learning materials include firstly, the greater flexibility for the student in pursuing the course; the materials is available on-line and at the students' convenience. Furthermore, staff have convenient on-line access to all materials within the course. Accommodating new students with a range of backgrounds is often a problem for both the learner and the teacher in standard teaching situations. An adaptive system that makes available specific content (adaptive presentation) (da Silva *et al*, 1998) provides students with only new knowledge and skills, allowing them to progress at a faster rate through the content.

The technology supporting hypertext and hypermedia systems have been with us for some time. The use of a range of interactive multimedia materials to support the learning is seen as a major motivation; these media rich systems have the potential to enhance the student learning in very positive ways. In providing the students with a range of media forms and tasks to satisfy, we are accommodating different learning styles. An adaptive system has the potential to monitor student usage of different modules and respond accordingly. This episodic adaptivity will provide real time modification to any survey generated preferences gathered at the beginning of the course.

We have developed this generic multimedia learning system using Macromedia Director, Flash, ColdFusion, HTML and CGI Perl script that allows rapid prototyping and use of various teaching strategies as alternate paths through the presented material.

3.1 Interface details

The main interface provided for students to access the learning materials can be classified as a hybrid browser. It takes advantage of the multimedia development environment and enables a range of concepts players used. These range from a concept being displayed as text formatted with HTML tags, to a concept displaying an acrobat postscript file, containing both textual and graphical information.

Video and audio formats can be utilised, along with appropriate animations. A programming player exists to display the result of an execution, with the appropriate programming feature described and displayed. A range of other appropriate tools is provided in the interface to enhance the learning environment. For example, on-line tutorial groups can be established with the ability to discuss particular content-based issues. Content experts can address any problems that are not accounted for by peer group interactions.

The main interface is a windows environment that initially provides authenticated logging on/off facilities. Once registered, the user is provided with the current session, or the pre-test for that session if this is the first time in. From there, individual concepts can be accessed. The default player is one that displays the content in pdf format. This was chosen so that the format of the content (images and text) could be guaranteed while still providing web facilities for hypertext links in the documents.

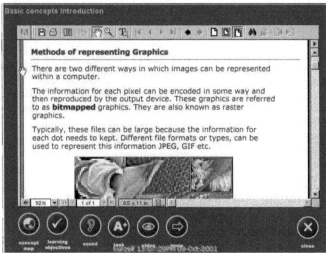

The Default Concept Viewer

3.2 Domain knowledge

Our course model is organised hierarchically into courses, sessions, concepts and documents. Sessions have been defined from concepts; sessions can have any number of concepts but one concept appears once within any session of a course. A concept consists of many documents; a document can be the content of a concept, its objective, any pre-requisites, and assessment criteria; alternately, it might be a problem to be solved. There is a player associated with each document; the player displays the information in an appropriate manner. These players are generally located with the client.

We have treated our documents as child-pages similar to hanging-pages in (Murray*et al*, 1998). Each document can exist in multiple media formats that include text, video, audio, HTML files, Director movies and Acrobat pdf files. The list of documents needed for a concept is stored in AMLE Microsoft Access database and is stored on a remote server. We have an 'Authoring Tool' for lecturers to maintain the course model. This tool consists of html files with embedded server-side ColdFusion tags. It accesses the AMLE database via an OBDC driver on an NT server.

The generic implementation is supportive of other possible domains of knowledge; the delivery system then is content independent. Tools for both the generation and subsequent use of the system have been investigated and an on-line database supporting both the student and course models, have been established. The placement of content into well defined modules, provides a mechanism for the flexible reuse. The course metadata is stored on a remote server along with the student profile information. Existing management tools allow for the easy creation of course structures, course lists, and the registering of assessment results.

The content is organised as a number of concepts and/or skills that need to be satisfied. Currently we organise this content into sessions that correspond to associated groups of concepts (a week's worth of work). To accommodate a range of students at various levels in their programs, we want to pre-test at the session level. We are suggesting this because if we pre-test at the beginning of the course, and multiple-choice questions form the basis of this testing mechanism, a lot of questions will need to be asked. For the practical components, students might be able to demonstrate the possession of some particular skills; this then needs to be handled manually and/or electronically.

The concepts/skills that we discern the student to have competence in, are highlighted by the system but still available to the student if they wish to access the materials for revision purposes. The assessment of concepts is still an area of investigation; topics which are being investigated further include identifying how many multiple choice questions need to be completed correctly before it can be said that a concept is understood, determination of other methods of assessing the acquisition of these concepts/skills and other summative tasks that might cover a range of concepts.

The content of the delivery system is relatively static; that is, the teaching components that are delivered through a range of players accommodating text, pdf modules, video, audio, animations, etc. and any other media format that might become available in the future, are stored at the client side. The dynamic components of the delivery system involving the course structure and assessment pieces, student profiles and assessment results, episodic data mapping student usage, and data of those on-line, is stored at the server side.

This 'dynamic' data allows the system to indicate to the users, information about the concepts/tasks that they have covered. It also provides them with a current 'report' of results of assessment pieces. The registration of students and tutors online, coupled with profiling information, enables the establishment of online groups that reflect the stored data; these groups may be assigned at the expertise level or by any other criterion considered educationally worthwhile.

A number of 'hanging pages' in the concept player provide information about the learning outcomes of the concept and alternate presentation mechanisms eg video, audio. Assessment tasks are specified at this level, as are pages of further explanation. The system utilises the student profile information, greying out options that are not required. Other tools that are used that might be used in the learning process eg email, chat facilities, submission mechanisms, glossary, search engine etc. along with more general facilities like audio players, web television, CD player, notepad etc are provided.

3.3 Student administration

Similarly an on-line instructional management system has been constructed generically to establish courses based on concepts and sessions. We have an 'Administration Tool', which enables lecturers and tutors access to our student model. Lectures can add/delete a tutorial group, add a new student, search for existing student, and update student's detail such as tutorial scores, assignment scores and exam scores. Tutors have access to update and search facilities of students' tutorial and assignment details. AMLE uses and maintains student profiles that contain a summary of the student's past experiences and other preference information. The course model and student profile allows students to proceed at their own rate through the learning environment with this access being influenced by a student's competencies and preferences (i.e. the student history of the traditional ITS).

The management system enables tutors to enter marks electronically and subsequently manage the assessment components of the course. Reporting mechanisms then cope with student, tutor and course co-ordinator requirements.

4. Current and Future Work

Our major concern is to provide adaptivity and interactivity for our students since we recognise that our students backgrounds and cultures have given us a wide range of of learning styles and expectations among our students. Currently, we have created a range of hybrid browsers with varying interfaces to access the course model; a number of players have been created to display the content. These players are dynamically activated, depending on the page type. The student's history and preferences will be fully developed in future implementations. A range of tools including tutorial chat facilities, notebooks and email, are also provided in the interface for the users to take advantage of. Further work will involve the pre-testing of students and the full utilisation of student preference data collected.

Currently, the materials or concepts have been grouped into sessions that correspond to a multimedia topic that could be covered in a week.The content for each concept can be accessed sequentially; a range of tests and tasks have been generated to ensure that the student understands the concept, or is able to complete an associated task. The monitoring of these competencies is conducted by the delivery system with the student competency profile being updated as the student accesses each task. For tasks that require demonstration, the tutor can record these competencies within the student compentency profile via a web interface. To allow for prior knowledge, students are pre-tested at the session level. A range a questions and question types are randomly presented and marked by the system; these results then form the basis of the student's compentency model. Tutors are able to enter marks directly into the student compentency profile for tasks where the compentency for a concept can be demonstrated. The student's compentency profile is further enhanced by an assessment profile that includes summative ctivities that could extend over a number of sessions. Both profiles are available to the students through a web browser interface that displays their current competency and assessment states. The pre-test results manifest themselves at the session level with the links to concepts 'known to the student' being highlighted in a different colour. These are still available if required. The concept structure of the course materials does not then necessitate that students access materials in this sequential manner. A number of instructional methodolgies could be employed on a weekly (session) basis, or alternately at the assignment level. Weekly tasks might be assigned that require the student to create some multimedia object. For example, we might be introducing the topic of Sound in Multimedia with the practical task being to create an MP3 player. Areas to be addressed would include:

- the possible application of sound in multimedia applications;
- theory of sound - representation, capturing characteristics etc;
- sound formats - compression, filetypes, size etc.
- sound capture;
- sound control within multimedia applications;
- ethical considerations re: copyright etc.

The extension of this is to use the materials based on larger assignments that also address similar areas and could include summative tasks incorporating prior knowledge eg. incorporating images and textual information within the player.

We are establishing student/student and tutor/student interactions via online discussion groups. Students can opt to be assigned to a tutorial discussion group with a number of their peers currently logged on. The number participating in these discussion groups is 4 by default; however, this is a system parameter and can be changed. Students are initially allocated on a first in, first allocated basis but any part of the student profile could be used for this purpose. For example, students could have their own preference list, or might be assigned using academic or cultural
information. There also exists an online helpdesk that simulates a tutorial helpdesk situation where students pose questions to tutors who are currently on line. A range on tools will be implemented to facilitate these dicussions including an electronic blackboard which will allow tutors to broadcast solutions, graphics, scripts etc to help with any explanation.

5. References

Anderson, J. 1983. *The architecture of cognition.* Cambridge, MA.

Boalch, G.. 1996. *WWW as an Educational Support Medium: An Australian Case Study.* AusWeb96, Gold Coast, Australia, July 1996.

Brusilovsky, P. 1996 *Integrating Hypermedia and Intelligent Tutoring Systems: From Systems to Authoring Tools. AIED* 1996

Ecklund, J. & Ecklund, P. 1996.   *Integrating the Web and the teaching of technology: Cases across two universities.* AusWeb96, Gold Coast, Australia, July 1996.
Jones, D. 1996. *Solving some problems of University Education: A Case Study.* AusWeb96, Gold Coast, Australia, July 1996.

Pilar da Silva, D., Van Durm R, Duval, E, Olivie H. 1998, *Concepts and documents for adaptive educational hypermedia: a model and a prototype,* proceedings of the 2nd Workshop on Adaptive hypertext and hypermedia HYPERTEXT98. Pittsburgh, USA, June 20-24, 1998.

Slay, J., 1998a.   *Using the World Wide Web to Create Foundations for Lifelong Learning - An Australian Perspective.* Teleteaching, IFIP World Computer Congress98, Vienna, Sept 2nd 1998.

Slay, J., 1998b. *Using the WWW to Create an Effective Cross-Cultural Learning Environment.* Hong Kong Web Symposium 98, Hong Kong University, April 9th-12th, 1998.

Murray,T., Condit, C., & Haugsjaa,E. 1998, *A Preliminary Framework for Concept-Based Adaptive Hypermedia',* ITS-98 workshop on WWW-Based Tutoring.

An Online Course Material Copyright Protection Scheme

Joe C.K. Yau[1], Lucas C.K. Hui[1], Bruce Cheung[2], S.M. Yiu[1]

[1] The Department of Computer Science and Information Systems
The University of Hong Kong, Pokfulam Road
e-mail: {jckyau, hui, smyiu}@csis.hku.hk

[2] School of Professional and Continuing Education
The University of Hong Kong, Pokfulam Road
e-mail: bruce@hkuspace.hku.hk

Abstract

Online education has emerged as one of the major channels for dissemination of learning materials. As more and more organizations offer online distance learning courses, with and without formal qualifications, the security concerns of these online education systems become more and more critical, especially when the organizations rely on the registration fees of students to maintain the smooth running of the courses. Most of the security studies in this domain have been concentrated on the user authentication and access control. The problem of copyright protection of the learning materials has only been raised recently. In this paper, we provide a mechanism, the *Secure e-Course exchange (eCX)*, to protect the learning material from unauthorized dissemination and show how this mechanism can be integrated in the operation model of online learning course providers. The design of eCX is general enough to fit two operating models, namely the *Institutional Server Model* and the *Corporate Server Model*. As a remark, the design has been implemented in the online learning system (SOUL) of the School of Professional and Continuing Education of the University of Hong Kong, one of the leading adult education providers in Hong Kong.

Keywords
E-Learning, Security, Copyright

1. Introduction

Online education becomes one of the most important channels for students to acquire knowledge and learning material. Currently, there are about three types of courses provided through this education medium: 1) Short courses without formal qualifications; 2) Diploma or Degree or even Higher Degree courses with formal qualifications; and 3) Courses which *help* students to take public examinations or to get a formal degree such as an External London University degree. Although many projects and researches have been conducted on online distance learning, the issues of security have only been studied recently (Cheung et al, 1999a, Cheung et al, 1999b, Furnell et al, 1998, Furnell et al, 1999).

In fact, there are quite a number of security concerns in this type of education system, for example, user authentication and access control. For more information on what security issues an online learning system may consider, one can refer to the security framework given by Furnell et al (Furnell et al, 1998). For more information on the problem of user authentication and access control, one can refer to (Cheung et al, 1999a, Cheung et al, 1999b). In particular, (Cheung et al, 1999a) provides a security model such that a legitimately registered student cannot easily share the account with a non-registered student.

Depending on the types of courses offered by an organization, the security concerns may differ slightly. There is one security problem, *the copyright protection problem*, which is important to courses of types (1) and (3). Typical scenarios include the following. A registered student passes the teaching materials to a non-registered student. Usually, the organization, which provides the teaching materials, will count on the registration fee to maintain the running of the company. This jeopardizes the benefit of the organization. This security issue is not addressed in details in (Furnell et al, 1998) and has been only considered recently (Furnell et al, 1999).

However, the authors of (Furnell et al, 1999) do not provide an effective approach for copyright protection and copyright detection in the domain of online education. In this paper, we give a design, the *Secure e-Course exchange (eCX)*, on how to make the process of copying "extremely difficult" for users so as to protect the copyright of the learning materials disseminated through an online course. More importantly, we also demonstrate how this design can be incorporated in the operation model of online learning course providers. And the design can be shown to fit two operating models, namely the *Institutional Server Model* and the *Corporate Server Model*.

This study was conducted by the SPACE Online Universal Learning (SOUL) Project Group of the School of Professional and Continuing Education (SPACE)[1] and has been implemented in the SOUL system. For more information about the SOUL system, please refer to (SOUL, 2002). The rest of the paper is organized as follows. Section 2 briefly describes the copyright protection problem. The core technologies used in eCX will be given in Section 3. Section 4 will discuss the operations of eCX. Finally, how to incorporate eCX in an e-Institute will be shown in Section 5 and Section 6 concludes the paper.

2. Background

Although digital copyright protection in the domain of online learning system is a rather new subject, there have been studies on this problem in other domains, for example, see (Brin et al, 1995, Dittmann and Nack, 2000, Memon and Wong, 1998). The security concerning copyright is basically divided into two major topics: copyright detection and copyright protection. Interested readers can refer to (Wayner, 1997) for more information.

Copyright detection makes it easier to discover the activities of unauthorized copying or dissemination of the copyrighted materials. Copyright detection techniques can be used to assure the ownership of the copyrighted material and/or the identity of the customer who bought the materials so as to proof the ownership and track down the unauthorized use of the materials. One major technique used for copyright detection on multimedia data is watermarking. While watermarking is quite useful in imaging data, the applicability of the technique in text-based materials is not straightforward. Moreover, in the domain of online distance learning, copyright detection seems not an effective approach to stop this illegal activity.

---

[1]**Background of SPACE and the SOUL Project:** SPACE, being one of the leading adult education providers in Hong Kong, provides life-long learning for the public. The number of students registered with SPACE programs is more than 70,000 and the figure is expected to go up in a tremendous rate. In order to provide effective support for online distance learning, the SPACE Online Universal Learning (SOUL) Project Group was established in 1998. The aim of the project is to provide online support for educational purposes; to develop SPACE online support courses in both Hong Kong and the Mainland China; and to carry out researches related to online learning. The SOUL platform is the major product of the Project Group. Currently, more than 10,000 students and teachers are using the platform.

On the other hand, copyright protection tries to make unauthorized copying of materials difficult or "impossible". Existing techniques (Furnell et al, 1999, Wayner, 1997) include the followings. The customers cannot obtain a permanent copy of the materials and must access the materials using a "secure" and proprietary browser. In other words, the users have to stay online while using the materials. This approach creates some inconvenience to the users. Another approach is to encrypt the materials using the *hardware* key, the key includes some information about the configuration of the machine used to access the materials. In this case, even if the materials have been passed to another user, the unauthorized user may not be able to open the materials. These approaches of copyright protection have been used in some e-book systems and software such as the product activation technique used in Microsoft Windows XP (Microsoft, 2002).

In this paper, we will show how these techniques can be used in the domain of an online education system and how the whole methodology can be incorporated in the operation model of an e-Institute. In the design, we will allow students store a local copy of the materials while make the unauthorized sharing of material difficult for them. As a remark, due to the nature of the digital data, none of the existing approaches can provide perfect security regarding these copyright problems. And it is very unlikely that such methods exist. However, as long as it is difficult for students to pass the materials to a non-registered student, most of the students will register for the courses in order to get the learning materials.

3. The Secure e-Course eXchange (eCX)

In this section, we will give a brief description on the *PowerEdBuilder* (the architecture for the SOUL platform) and the core technologies used in eCX. The Secure e-Course eXchange (eCX) is a set of software modules designed to work together to protect the copyright of the online course material. It is composed of a number of modules shattered among and integrated into the PowerEdBuilder. The following diagram shows the components of the PowerEdBuilder.

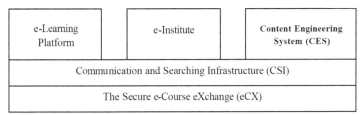

Figure 1: An Overview of PowerEdBuilder

The Secure e-Course exchange (eCX) provides a secure layer for protecting the copyrighted materials. The *Communication and Searching Infrastructure (CSI)* provides efficient communication channels among administrators, teachers, and students. The *Content Engineering System (CES)* is mainly used by instructors to create online course materials and launch online courses. The *e-Institute* is the administration center of the platform. Finally, the *e-Learning platform* is where students will interact for studying and downloading relevant learning materials. Inside the e-Learning platform, there is an intelligent software, called *SmartTutor* , which provides guidance to students like a human tutor. For details of these components, please refer to the documentations and publications of the SOUL project. In this paper, we will only focus on the eCX related modules.

There are two core technologies in the eCX that form the foundation of eCX. They are the *Offline-Online Course* and the *Computer License*.

3.1 The Offline-Online Course

The *Offline-Online Course* is a proprietary technology designed to protect the copyright of the online course material. Ordinary online course implementation requires students to view the course material online. The material is stored in the server hosting the course. On the contrary, the Offline-Online Course permits the students to download the course material to their computer and view the material offline while makes it difficult to perform unauthorized copying.

Basically, an instructor will compose online course materials in the Content Engineering System. When the preparation is done, the instructor can make use of the *Course Launcher*, one of the eCX modules situated at the CES, to launch a new online course to an affiliated e-Institute server (see Section 4.1 for more details on course launching). The launching process will create two objects based on the online course material. They are the *Course Package* and the *Course Voucher*. The Course Package contains the online material, and is encrypted by some symmetrical encryption algorithm. The Course Voucher contains various information about the course, including the encryption key for viewing the course material. After the online course is successfully launched, the Course Package will be distributed over network and could be downloaded by students either through the Peer-to-Peer network or the World Wide Web.

To take an available online course, students have to register for it (see section 4.2 for details). Students can download the Course Package. And they must also obtain the Course Voucher from the e-Institute server in order to view the course material. Please note that students are charged for obtaining the Course Voucher, but *not* for downloading the Course Package. The Course Voucher will then be encrypted and stored securely on the student's computer which can only be accessed by the e-Learning Platform. When the student possesses both the Course Package and the Course Voucher, he/she can view the online course material offline. The next subsection will show why the offline material obtained cannot be easily transferred to others.

3.2 Computer License

The *Computer License* is a special object that resides in the student's computer. It is unique to each computer, and it contains many information, including the student's personal information and credit card information, the computer's public encryption key, and a hardware profile of the student's computer. It is created when the e-Learning Platform is installed to the student's computer. It is created, issued and digitally signed by the Computer Licensing Server which is a module in the e-Institute. It has an expiry date upon which the student has to renew this Computer License.

The encryption key contained in the Computer License is the public encryption key of a *PKI* key pair which is also created during the installation of the e-Learning Platform. The private encryption key to this key pair is stored in some special location on the computer's hard disk.

Upon the invocation of the e-Learning Platform, the hardware configuration of the student's computer is examined. A hardware profile reflecting the current hardware configuration of the student's computer is created. This hardware profile is compared with the hardware profile stored in the Computer License. The e-Learning Platform is permitted to continue with its invocation if the two hardware profiles matches and the Computer License has not expired. When a student has registered for an online course, both the Course Package and the Course Voucher will be under the student's possession. As mentioned above, the Course Package is protected by some symmetric encryption. Since the encryption key to the Course Package is contained in the Course Voucher, the Course Voucher must also be protected on the student's computer. When the Course Voucher is received from the e-Institute, it will be encrypted with the computer's public encryption key using some asymmetric encryption algorithm. This public encryption key is stored in the Computer License. After this encrypted Course Voucher is received from the e-Institute, it will be stored in the student's computer in this encrypted form. Since it is asymmetrically encrypted, it can only be decrypted by using the computer's private encryption key. The only time that it is not encrypted is when the student is viewing the online course. Please refer to Section 4.3 for details about course viewing.

The Computer License is vital to the design of eCX. It can prohibit users from using illegal copies of the material, not by file copying or by disk copying, because the Computer License guarantees that the e-Learning Platform can only be invoked on the computer where it was originally issued to, and the material can only be viewed on this same computer. However, there is one disadvantage of using this approach. If the hardware configuration of the system is changed substantially, the License may be made invalid and the student needs to contact the institute for appropriate action.

4. Operations of eCX

In this section, we will describe the details of the key operations, such as Course Launching, Course Registration, and Course Viewing, of eCX.

4.1 Course Launching

As mentioned above, when an online course is launched by the Course Launcher, two objects, the Course Package and the Course Voucher, will be created from the online course material. The Course Launcher will send these two objects through a secure channel (e.g. SSL) to the Voucher Administrator, which is integrated into the e-Institute (see Figure 2). Under the Voucher Administrator, the objects are stored in a database and made available for students to download.

4.2 Course Registration

To register for an online course, the student has to invoke the *Course Downloader* (see Figure 2), which is integrated into the e-Learning Platform. The Course Downloader will establish a SSL connection with the Voucher Administrator to get the Course Voucher. Students are not charged for downloading the Course Package, but are charged electronically and automatically (only once) for obtaining the Course Voucher. The Voucher Administrator will validate the student's Computer License sent by the Course Downloader and encrypt the voucher with the student computer's public encryption key. The encrypted Course Voucher will be sent to student's Course Downloader, then stored in the Voucher Store of the student's machine in its encrypted form.

4.3 Course Viewing

After registering for an online course, the student can use the *Personal Classroom* module of the e-Learning Platform to view the course material. The Personal Classroom will obtain the Course Voucher from the Voucher Store for decrypting the Course Package. Note that both the Personal Classroom and the *Voucher Store* are processes executing on the student's computer. However, to guarantee the security of the system, and to ensure the online course material is well protected, these two processes will go through a special authentication process to authenticate each other.

When this authentication process is done, the Voucher Store will use the computer's private encryption key to decrypt the Course Voucher which was previously encrypted using computer's public encryption key (see Section 4.2). Afterwards, the Voucher Store will release the decrypted Course Voucher to the Personal Classroom where it will be used for decrypting the Course Package. Note that for security reasons and performance reasons, the Personal Classroom will decrypt the course material from the Course Package in a *material-on-demand* fashion.

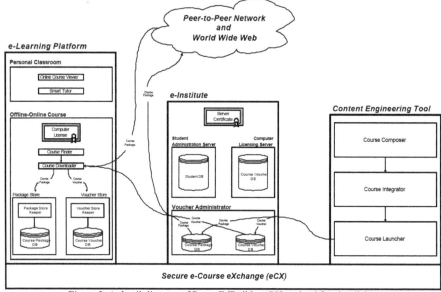

Figure 2: A detail diagram of PowerEdBuilder (CSI omitted for simplicity)

5. Trusting Hierarchy and Operating Models of e-Institutes

5.1 The Trusting Hierarchy

The PowerEdBuilder is designed so that there can be many e-Institute servers exist on the network. These servers together with the student computers form a trusting hierarchy (see Figure 3). The lowest level of the hierarchy are the student computers, which have the least privilege and are authenticated by checking their Computer Licenses. The only authority they have is to digitally signing payment confirmations for registering online course. The middle level of the hierarchy are the e-Institute servers. These servers are the *Certificate Authorities (CA)* for issuing Computer Licenses to student computers. Each of these servers possesses a *Server Certificate* which is used for proving its own identity to others. The top level of the hierarchy is the *Root Certificate Authority*. It possesses the *Root Key* to the whole PowerEdBuilder trusting hierarchy, and is the Root of the hierarchy. It signs the Server Certificate of all of the servers in the middle level.

5.2 The Two Server Models

The eCX is designed to suit the needs of two different operating models. They are the *Institutional Server Model* and the *Corporate Server Model*.

The Institutional Server Model is a server model that is tailored to be used by educational organizations. All Institutional Servers are equipped with a Server Certificate signed by the Root Certificate Authority. They have the authority of signing and issuing Computer License for students registered under them. As there can be many servers operating under this model, and each server is authorized to issue Computer Licenses, they can be configured to honor or not to honor Computer Licenses issued by other Institutional Servers. However, they will never honor Computer Licenses issued by any Corporate Servers.

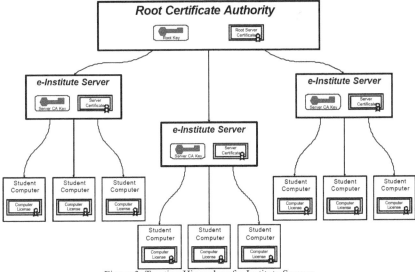

Figure 3: Trusting Hierarchy of e-Institute Servers

Institutional Server has no limitation as to the number of "copies" of an online course that it can issue to students. The revenue generated from the course will be split with the course instructor according to the payment agreement.

The Corporate Server Model is a server model that is tailored to be used by business olrganizations for corporate training. All Corporate Servers are equipped with a Server Certificate signed by the Root Certificate Authority. They have the authority of signing and issuing Computer Licenses for students registered under them (ie, their own staff).

Servers operating under the Corporate Server Model function are very much like those under the Institutional Server Model except in three ways. The first difference is that a Corporate Server only honor Computer Licenses issued by itself. It will not honor any Computer Licenses from any other servers, regardless if the license is issued by another Institutional Server or another Corporate Server. The second difference is that since a Corporate Server is operated within the same corporation, it can have a different mechanism for the payment system. The course registration may be free for all of its staff members, or charging according to cost centers, etc. The third difference is that a Corporate Server pays the instructor (ie, the online course provider) at a bulk rate. The corporate pays the instructor certain amount of money for a fixed number of copies of the online course, and the server will be limited to issue that many copies of the online course. In other words, the server can only send limited number of copies of Course Voucher to its staff members.

6. Conclusion

In this paper, we consider the problem of copyright protection of online learning material in the domain of online learning courses. We propose a mechanism, called the Secure e-Course eXchange (eCX) which allows students to store a local copy of the material while makes the sharing of the material with a non-registered student difficult. The design of eCX is flexible to fit two operating models, namely the Institutional Server Model and the Corporate Server Model. The eCX has been implemented in an actual online learning system, the SOUL platform for the School of Professional and Continuing Education of the University of Hong Kong. Evaluation on the eCX will be performed shortly and results of the evaluation will be reported once available. In fact, there are many other security issues regarding online learning systems, such as online submission of assignments (Luck and Joy, 1999), which are not addressed in this paper. Please refer to other publications of the SOUL project on how the PowerEdBuilder tackles these security problems.

7. References

Brin, Sergey, Davis, James, and Garcia-Molina, Hector (1995), "Copy Detection Mechanisms for Digital Documents", *SIGMOD 95*, pp398-409.

Cheung, Bruce, Hui, L.C.K., Yim, T., and Yung, V.W.L. (1999a), "Security Design in an Online-Education Project", In *e-Education: Challenges and Opportunities. Proceedings of the Fifth Hong Kong Web Symposium*, pp1-14.

Cheung, Bruce and Hui, L.C.K. (1999b), "Student Authentication for a Web-based Distance Learning System", *Proceedings of the Fifth International Conference on Information Systems Analysis and Synthesis*, pp441-446.

Dittmann, Jana and Nack, Frank (2000), "Copyright – Copywrong", *IEEE Multimedia*, Vol. 7, No. 4, pp14-17.

Furnell, Steven et al (1998), "A Security Framework for Online Distance Learning and Training", *Internet Research: Electronic Networking Applications and Policy*, Vol. 8, No. 3, pp236-242.

Furnell, Steven et al (1999), "Security Considerations in Online Distance Learning", *Proceedings of Euromedia 99*, pp131-135.

Harasim, Linda (1999), "A Framework for Online Learning: The Virtual-U", *IEEE Computer*, pp44-49.

Luck, Michael and Joy, Mike (1999), "A Secure On-line Submission System", *Software-Practice and Experience*, Vol. 29, No. 8, pp721-740.

Memon, Nasir and Wong, Ping Wah (1998), "Protecting Digital Media Content", *Communications of the ACM*, Vol. 41, No. 7, pp35-43.

Wayner, Peter (1997), *Digital Copyright Protection*, AP Professional.

Web site of Microsoft Corporation (2002), http://www.microsoft.com

Web site of SOUL project (2002), http://soul.hkuspace.org

A Virtual University using Mobile Agent Technology

Ingo Stengel[1,2], Udo Bleimann[2], Jeanne Stynes[1]

[1] Cork Institute of Technology, Ireland
[2] University of Applied Sciences Darmstadt, Germany
e-mail: ingo@stengel.com

Abstract

To view Virtual Universities as an extension of real Universities and of Distant Learning Institutes, new concepts in the area of distributed systems and virtual universities are needed. Mobile Agents satisfy many requirements of such a highly dynamic system. The integration of a dynamic workflow, which has been implemented using a mobile agent system, with an updated virtual university concept results in a new virtual university concept. This paper presents the first results of a joint research project and gives an overview of the problems that confront us.

Keywords

Mobile Agents, Education, Virtual University, Distant Learning

1. Introduction

This paper presents preliminary results in the development of a Virtual University (VU) Architecture using different workflows, which have been implemented using mobile agent technology. The project is funded by the University Research Program ATG-99 of the County of Hessen, Germany.

Life-Long-Learning (LLL) is the main motivation behind Virtual Universities, i.e., people should be able to integrate various learning phases during their life time (Fischer 2001). It is essential to keep up-to-date with current trends and technologies as well as learn new skills and knowledge throughout one's working life. This assists their professional development, ensuring lifetime employment prospects. In addition, Virtual Universities enable less mobile members of the community, e.g., employed people, handicapped people, etc., to gain access to the same learning facilities as the ordinary student attending a traditional university.

The main teaching methods (Friedrich 2000) available in a University are:
- *Presentation oriented learning*, where the teacher is active and the students are passive.
- *Self organizing learning*, where students work on topics/content that can be found on a local machine or on the network, e.g. Computer Based Training (CBT).
- *Cooperative oriented learning*, where the teaching staff supports the students and students work together in communities in a networked environment, e.g. Computer Supported Cooperative Learning (CSCL).

Since learning derived from a community of practice, social interaction is of major significance on the constructive cognitive development of individuals (Vygotski 1978). A few years ago computers took a mediating role in learning groups (Newmann 1996). Now the network has become the mediator. We therefore see a high potential in applying *cooperative oriented learning* in Virtual Universities.

2. Our Concept of a Virtual University

A Virtual University is a virtual place of higher learning, providing wide spread access, regardless of location, to higher education. During the last years different models of Virtual Universities have been developed. They can be classified as follows:

- **The Stand-Alone Virtual Universities** are not based on any traditional university. They have own infrastructure and staff. The Global Virtual University is an example that follows this stand-alone principle of a virtual university.
- **Virtual Universities based on a Traditional University** are built as an extension to the traditional university, allowing students to earn credits from the traditional university without having to physically attend classes there. Stanford Online University is the perfect example of this type of university.
- **The Virtual Campus:** This is the most common form of a virtual university. It consists of a group of colleges and universities from a geographical area that come together to offer their pooled knowledge and experience to the students. For example, the 'Virtuelle Hochschule Oberrhein' is a group of traditional universities from Freiburg, Heidelberg, Karlsruhe and Mannheim that are working together to offer multimedia lectures.

There are some successful Virtual Universities, e.g., New Jersey Virtual University, Canadian Virtual University. Virtual Universities that failed (Pollock 2000) tend to fail because

- the university setup process is too slow,
- the resource requirements are too high,
- the implementation is not robust,
- there are not enough students to support its existence.

To be successful, VUs need at least to fulfill the following conditions:

- the VU model must be positioned close to the real university model,
- processes that have traditionally been kept away from Virtual Universities, e.g., enrollment, must be integrated in the new model,
- the complexity of a Virtual University must be reduced, e.g. complex workflows and process flows must be mapped.
- there is a critical mass of students,
- passive students must become active users.

The model we chose is a traditional University that, in addition, offers services for a Virtual University because: traditional Universities have obvious know-how in academic teaching, including course contents and administration, there are didactic reasons why an alternation between presence and network phases makes sense, the work involved in setting up a new Virtual University from scratch is considerable and finally, Virtual Universities still rely on traditional institutes of education to provide important services such as examinations.

Our Virtual University consists of :

- The Traditional University
- The Network University
- The Mentorship Concept
- Personal Agents for every Student
- The Evaluation Service
- Additional services for assisting the teaching staff & students, e.g. examination/assignment pre-correction service, tutoring service, student services.

The Traditional University offers the normal well known facilities and resources of an institution providing education for undergraduate and postgraduate students in various fields of study.

The Network University is the virtual part of the University that provides access to higher education using online as well as offline facilities. While online facilities allow the student to benefit from the cooperative oriented learning approach while accessing the VU, offline facilities, e.g. CD-ROM/DVD, allow only self organizing learning, e.g. computer based training (CBT).

The Mentorship Concept, where every student is assigned a *Mentor* to guide and advise the student throughout his program of studies, should be implemented in a VU. The mentor will automatically receive the examination results of the student he is mentoring to enable him to assist the student if necessary. The Mentor will be recruited from the teaching staff, which can include postgraduate students.

Every student is guided by **a Personal Agent**, which will help the student to survive in the VU. This Agent will guide him through tasks like:
- administrative tasks, e.g., a student might want to find the procedure for enrolling in the next academic year or he might want to know how much he must pay for a particular course
- academic tasks, e.g., he might have to find the first Computer Science-lecture, or how to submit his first assignment etc.

The Evaluation Service can be used by every student to evaluate lectures, assignments and tests. This system has been included to monitor and control the teaching quality . A statistical evaluation is also available. A detailed solution will be described in the next section.

If students wish to send enhancement proposals the message can be rendered anonymous. The same process takes place when students submit assignments or tests. Student names are deleted from the assignment/test and replaced with a Unique Identifier (UID).

Additional services for assisting the teaching staff and students include:

- **A Pre-correction Service,** that automatically mark multiple-choice questions, has been defined to decrease the staff workload. The professor gets the results of the pre-correction. He will still have to correct the free text questions. The results will be sent to the database where the UID is exchanged with the real names. Comments relevant to the correction can be sent back to the student in a similar manner.

- **A Tutoring Service:** A tutoring hierarchy corresponding to the complexity of the questions, that students may have, can be established. This looks like a pyramid, at the bottom of which lies the ordinary student, who has questions to ask. He will ask an advanced student (tutor), positioned in the next layer. Tutors will get points for every successfully served student. The number of points ranges between 1-10 and is awarded by the student.

If tutors from the first level can not answer the question they pass the question to the tutors at the second level, who are more skilled students (postgraduate students). Here the range of the possible points awarded is from 1-20. If the question remains unresolved, it will be forwarded to the teacher/professor, who is positioned at the top of the pyramid. His possible points range from 1-40. The amount of points earned will be calculated and used to determine the pay of the tutoring staff.

- **Student Community Services:** Student Services allow students that are interested in the same topics and/or lectures to form groups and communities. This is especially important for a distant learning environment, because the student could feel very much alone without them. Furthermore it would support the ideas of the CSCL.

3. The Technical Implementation of our Virtual University

This paper does not cover the organizational part of the real university, but addresses the following aspects: mentoring, the delivery of assignments and evaluation. To solve the needs of the virtual university we employ the mobile agent technology.

3.1 Mobile Agents

Agents are autonomous software components, which can communicate. Mobile agents are agents that additionally have at least the following properties: mobility, i.e. moving code and data through the network, and the ability to live in a world of agents. This world is a network of mobile agent platform instances.

These attributes of mobile agents, namely,
- *Autonomy* – Mobile Agents can act on their own. They are able to control their own status and to take decisions,
- *Mobility* – Mobile Agents are able to travel all over the net (where a mobile agent platform is available),
- *Sociable* – Mobile Agents are able to exchange information and to communicate using a communication language,
are crucial for the implementation of a highly dynamic distributed system.

69 Mobile Agent Systems (MAS) have been evaluated and tested using the following main criteria:
- Java based MAS that must be Java 1.2 compliant
- an extension of the system should be possible
- the system should have good security mechanisms implemented
- source code and documentation must be available
After the second evaluation phase, four mobile agent systems appear to comply with our needs. These Systems were Aglets (IBM 2001), D'Agents (Kotz 1999), SeMoA (Roth 2002)

and Nomads (Suri 2001). The next selection criterion used was the way in which different security problems have been addressed in each system (Table 1).

Systems\ Sec. \ Probl.	Agent vs. Host	Host vs. Agent	Agent vs. Agent	Host vs. Host
SeMoA	Very good	good	good	Good
Aglets	not available	sufficient	good	insufficient
D'Agents	not available	sufficient	good	sufficient
Nomads	not available	very good	Very good	Not available

Table 1: Evaluation of the addressed security problems

Because it addresses most of the known security problems, the Secure Mobile Agents (SeMoA) System (Roth 2002) from the Fraunhofer Gesellschaft Darmstadt has been selected as the right system for our project.

3.2 Data Management

All data used in this Virtual University must be kept in different databases stored in Extensible Markup Language (XML) format. Therefore the Tamino-Database has been used. We have chosen XML because most of the different Metadata Standards that deal with teaching rely on XML or at least XML can be used as an exchange format. The most important Metadata are:
- The Dublin Core,
- IEEE Learning Object Metadata (LOM),
- Instructional Management System Metadata (IMS),
- Resource Description Framework (RDF).

Additionally TeachML adapted XML for use in teaching. The use of these new standards for producing better and more useful educational documentation can be recommended. The 2MN Project (Modules for higher education using multimedia and the network) in Darmstadt is at present evaluating these different approaches.

3.3 The Infrastructure

The most important departments involved in our Virtual University (AIDA 2002) are (see Figure 1):
- The Network Department handles all the servers which handle Web-technology and email in the VU.
- The Mail Department is needed for mail communication, which will periodically increase. The main cause lies in the personalized lecture CDs that will be sent out after the students have registered for certain courses.
- The Film Department is the department in which videos of lectures will be produced. At the same time this department is responsible for archiving the old videos.
- The Student Administration Department handles all the administrative student requests, e.g. enrollment.

The functionality of the Virtual University Administration will be performed by the Administration of the real University.

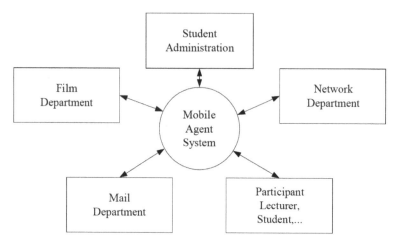

Figure 1: Mobile Agents as a communication basis between different departments

Mobile Agents are used to implement the different workflows in the Virtual University. Here Mobile Agents work as a container. They carry out different requests or information depending on the downloaded rules. These rules are downloaded from workflow servers. If a Mobile Agent gets stuck somewhere, after a certain amount of time, it redirects itself. Therefore it uses alternative routes stored at the first contact with a workflow server.

Other projects dealing with similar problems, e.g. the ABITS Project (Capuano 2000), rely on Intelligent Agents and the use of a Multi Agent Platform. This does not apply in our case as we do not need different types of agents to fulfill different requests. Every instance of an agent works task oriented and therefore gets the right rules from the server. To increase reliability the workflow server might be implemented as an Object Request Broker - Service.

The above scenario gives an idea of the implemented system. Security is not considered at the moment. To simplify the scenario the different databases have been positioned in one small box (see Figure 2). In reality these databases (DB) are distributed.

First the student sends his personal agent to the Virtual University with a request for the assignment. The mobile agent contacts the workflow server (1) and receives a set of rules (2) (a description of the workflow). The mobile agent identifies the user and gives him the requested assignment (3). Additionally the user will be provided with questions concerning the evaluation of the assignment.

The agent forwards the student's answers (4) to the Result-Database where the two kinds of information are separated. To make the process anonymous, the student's name is replaced with a UID and the answers to the assignment, after being processed by the pre-correction service, are sent to the teacher for correction (5). The evaluation information, excluding personal information, will be submitted to the evaluation database (Teachers will periodically get an automated report of their evaluations).

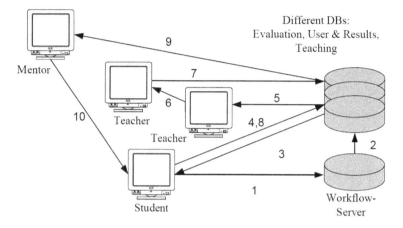

Figure 2: Student sending homework in, evaluating and mentoring

After the agent arrives at the first teacher it might happen that there is nobody available or the agent gets stuck in the queue. In this case the agent will move to the next possible teacher (6). The necessary information will be available from the workflow server. If this next teacher is also not available, the agent will ask for update information from the workflow server.

After the assignment has been corrected by one of the teachers, it will be returned to the Result-Database (7), together with his comments. The student will get the credit points and the comments of the teacher from the Result-Database (8).

After every new result the mentor automatically receives the results of the student (9) he is supervising. If the student obtains poor results more than once, the mentor might give the student a phone call or send him an email to discover the reasons for failure (10), if any exists.

The main problems we faced during the development were mainly limitations of the mobile agent system, e.g. the amount of data that could be transported with the SeMoA mobile agent system is around 64 KBytes. After some modifications we are now able to transport 8 MBytes with an agent.

4. Conclusions & Outlook

Mobile Agent Systems bring a significant contribution to the support of teaching staff and students, e.g. evaluation. They are able to handle problems of high complexity using asynchronous communication.

Our main goal is to propagate cooperative oriented learning, with an active integration of the students in a Virtual University. Therefore the mobile agent system must be extended to include the following features:
- The system must be able to localize mobile agents.
- It must allow inter-agent communication.
- It must support the concurrent processes, including agent cloning.
- A new security concept that supports a highly dynamical system must be developed.

5. References

AIDA Institute of Applied Informatics Darmstadt, *Aida Website - Projekte*,
Available from: http://www.aida.fh-darmstadt.de [Accessed 8 April 2002]

Capuano, N., De Santo, M., Marsella, M., Molinara, M., Salerno, S. (2000). "A Multi-Agent Architecture for Intelligent Tutoring". In: *Proceedings of the International Conference on Advances in Infrastructure for Electronic Business, Science, and Education on the Internet*. CRMPA, Salerno, University di Salerno, Italy
Available from: http://www.ssgrr.it/en/ssgrr2000/papers/capuano.pdf [Accessed 8 April 2002].

Fischer, G. (2001). "Lifelong Learning and its Support with new media". In: N.J.Smezer and P.B.Baltes (eds.) *International Encyclopedia of Social and Behavior Sciences*, Elsevier.
Available from: http://www.cs.colorado.edu/~gerhard/papers/isfst2001.pdf [Accessed 8 April 2002].

Friedrich, S., Lippmann, J., Meissner, K., Wehner, F. (2000). "Kommunikation und Kooperation in komponentenbasierten Lehr-Lehr-Systemen" In: *Proceedings of ICL99*, Villach, Austria, ISBN: 3-7068-0755-6.

IBM Tokyo Research Laboratory. (2001). *About Aglets* [online].
Available from: http://www.trl.ibm.com/aglets/about_e.htm/ [Accessed 8 April 2002].

Kotz, D., Gray, S.R., (1999). "Mobile Agents and the Future of the Internet" [online]. In: *ACM Operating Systems Review*, 33(3), August 1999, pages 7-13.
Available from: http://www.cs.dartmouth.edu/~dfk/papers/kotz:future2/ [Accessed 8 April 2002].

Newmann, D.R. (1996). "How can WWW-based groupware better support critical thinking in CSCL ?"
In: Busbach, U., Kerr, D., Sikkel, K. (Eds.) *CSCW and the Web – Proceedings of the 5th ERCIM/W4G*, GMD, Sankt Augustin.

Pollock N., Cornford, J. (2000). "Report on UK universities use of new technologie - Theory and Practice of the Virtual University". *Ariadne* Issue 24 ,June 2000, ISBN: 1361-3200.

Roth V., (2002). *Documentation on Secure Mobile Agents*[online] , Fraunhofer Gesellschaft Darmstadt.
Available from: http://www.semoa.org [Accessed 8 April 2002].

Suri, N., Bradshaw, J., Breedy, M., Groth, P., Hill, G., Jeffers, R., Mitrovich, T.(2001). *An Overview of the NOMADS Mobile Agent System* [online]. University of West Florida.
Available from: http://nomads.coginst.uwf.edu/ECOOP2000.pdf [Accessed 8 April 2002].

Vygotski, L. and Cole, M. (1978). *Mind in Society. The development of higher psychological processes.*
Cambridge: Harvard University Press.

Author Index

www.ingramcontent.com/pod-product-compliance
Lightning Source LLC
Chambersburg PA
CBHW051043050326

40690CB00006B/581